A Companion to Modern British and Irish Drama
1880–2005

Blackwell Companions to Literature and Culture

This series offers comprehensive, newly written surveys of key periods and movements and certain major authors, in English literary culture and history. Extensive volumes provide new perspectives and positions on contexts and on canonical and post-canonical texts, orientating the beginning student in new fields of study and providing the experienced undergraduate and new graduate with current and new directions, as pioneered and developed by leading scholars in the field.

Published

1.	*A Companion to Romanticism*	Edited by Duncan Wu
2.	*A Companion to Victorian Literature and Culture*	Edited by Herbert F. Tucker
3.	*A Companion to Shakespeare*	Edited by David Scott Kastan
4.	*A Companion to the Gothic*	Edited by David Punter
5.	*A Feminist Companion to Shakespeare*	Edited by Dympna Callaghan
6.	*A Companion to Chaucer*	Edited by Peter Brown
7.	*A Companion to Literature from Milton to Blake*	Edited by David Womersley
8.	*A Companion to English Renaissance Literature and Culture*	Edited by Michael Hattaway
9.	*A Companion to Milton*	Edited by Thomas N. Corns
10.	*A Companion to Twentieth-Century Poetry*	Edited by Neil Roberts
11.	*A Companion to Anglo-Saxon Literature and Culture*	Edited by Phillip Pulsiano and Elaine Treharne
12.	*A Companion to Restoration Drama*	Edited by Susan J. Owen
13.	*A Companion to Early Modern Women's Writing*	Edited by Anita Pacheco
14.	*A Companion to Renaissance Drama*	Edited by Arthur F. Kinney
15.	*A Companion to Victorian Poetry*	Edited by Richard Cronin, Alison Chapman, and Antony H. Harrison
16.	*A Companion to the Victorian Novel*	Edited by Patrick Brantlinger and William B. Thesing
17–20.	*A Companion to Shakespeare's Works: Volumes I–IV*	Edited by Richard Dutton and Jean E. Howard
21.	*A Companion to the Regional Literatures of America*	Edited by Charles L. Crow
22.	*A Companion to Rhetoric and Rhetorical Criticism*	Edited by Walter Jost and Wendy Olmsted
23.	*A Companion to the Literature and Culture of the American South*	Edited by Richard Gray and Owen Robinson
24.	*A Companion to American Fiction 1780–1865*	Edited by Shirley Samuels
25.	*A Companion to American Fiction 1865–1914*	Edited by Robert Paul Lamb and G. R. Thompson
26.	*A Companion to Digital Humanities*	Edited by Susan Schreibman, Ray Siemens, and John Unsworth
27.	*A Companion to Romance*	Edited by Corinne Saunders
28.	*A Companion to the British and Irish Novel 1945–2000*	Edited by Brian W. Shaffer
29.	*A Companion to Twentieth-Century American Drama*	Edited by David Krasner
30.	*A Companion to the Eighteenth-Century English Novel and Culture*	Edited by Paula R. Backscheider and Catherine Ingrassia
31.	*A Companion to Old Norse-Icelandic Literature and Culture*	Edited by Rory McTurk
32.	*A Companion to Tragedy*	Edited by Rebecca Bushnell
33.	*A Companion to Narrative Theory*	Edited by James Phelan and Peter J. Rabinowitz
34.	*A Companion to Science Fiction*	Edited by David Seed
35.	*A Companion to the Literatures of Colonial America*	Edited by Susan Castillo and Ivy Schweitzer
36.	*A Companion to Shakespeare and Performance*	Edited by Barbara Hodgdon and W. B. Worthen
37.	*A Companion to Mark Twain*	Edited by Peter Messent and Louis J. Budd
38.	*A Companion to European Romanticism*	Edited by Michael K. Ferber
39.	*A Companion to Modernist Literature and Culture*	Edited by David Bradshaw and Kevin J. H. Dettmar
40.	*A Companion to Walt Whitman*	Edited by Donald D. Kummings
41.	*A Companion to Herman Melville*	Edited by Wyn Kelley
42.	*A Companion to Medieval English Literature and Culture c.1350–c.1500*	Edited by Peter Brown
43.	*A Companion to Modern British and Irish Drama: 1880–2005*	Edited by Mary Luckhurst

A COMPANION TO

MODERN BRITISH AND IRISH DRAMA

1880–2005

EDITED BY MARY LUCKHURST

Blackwell
Publishing

BLACKWELL PUBLISHING
350 Main Street, Malden, MA 02148-5020, USA
9600 Garsington Road, Oxford OX4 2DQ, UK
550 Swanston Street, Carlton, Victoria 3053, Australia

First published 2006 by Blackwell Publishing Ltd

1 2006

Library of Congress Cataloging-in-Publication Data

A companion to modern British and Irish drama, 1880–2005 / edited by Mary Luckhurst.
    p. cm.—(Blackwell companions to literature and culture ; 43)
  Includes bibliographical references and index.
  ISBN-13: 978-1-4051-2228-3 (alk. paper)
  ISBN-10: 1-4051-2228-5 (alk. paper)
  1. English drama—20th century—History and criticism—Handbooks, manuals, etc. 2. English
drama—Irish authors—History and criticism—Handbooks, manuals, etc. 3. Ireland—Intellectual
life—20th century—Handbooks, manuals, etc. 4. England—Intellectual life—20th century—
Handbooks, manuals, etc. I. Luckhurst, Mary. II. Series.

  PR736.C575 2006
  822′.9109—dc22   2006010966

A catalogue record for this title is available from the British Library.

Set in 11 on 13pt Garamond
by SPi Publisher Services, Pondicherry, India
Printed and bound in Singapore
by Markono Print Media Pte Ltd

For further information on
Blackwell Publishing, visit our website:
www.blackwellpublishing.com

for Mike Cordner

theatrical genius
inspirational visionary
professor extraordinaire
family man and dog-lover

Katharine Hepburn enthusiast
(nobody's perfect)

Contents

Acknowledgements   xi
List of Illustrations   xii
Notes on Contributors   xiii

Introduction   1
Mary Luckhurst

Part I   Contexts   5

1   Domestic and Imperial Politics in Britain and Ireland:
     The Testimony of Irish Theatre   7
     Victor Merriman
2   Reinventing England   22
     Declan Kiberd
3   Ibsen in the English Theatre in the *Fin de Siècle*   35
     Katherine Newey
4   New Woman Drama   48
     Sally Ledger

Part II   Mapping New Ground, 1900–1939   61

5   Shaw among the Artists   63
     Jan McDonald
6   Granville Barker and the Court Dramatists   75
     Cary M. Mazer
7   Gregory, Yeats and Ireland's Abbey Theatre   87
     Mary Trotter

8   Suffrage Theatre: Community Activism and Political Commitment   99
     Susan Carlson

9   Unlocking Synge Today   110
     Christopher Murray

10   Sean O'Casey's Powerful Fireworks   125
     Jean Chothia

11   Auden and Eliot: Theatres of the Thirties   138
     Robin Grove

Part III   England, Class and Empire, 1939–1990   151

12   Empire and Class in the Theatre of John Arden
     and Margaretta D'Arcy   153
     Mary Brewer

13   When Was the Golden Age? Narratives of Loss and Decline:
     John Osborne, Arnold Wesker and Rodney Ackland   164
     Stephen Lacey

14   A Commercial Success: Women Playwrights in the 1950s   175
     Susan Bennett

15   Home Thoughts from Abroad: Mustapha Matura   188
     D. Keith Peacock

16   The Remains of the British Empire: The Plays of Winsome Pinnock   198
     Gabriele Griffin

Part IV   Comedy   211

17   Wilde's Comedies   213
     Richard Allen Cave

18   Always Acting: Noël Coward and the Performing Self   225
     Frances Gray

19   Beckett's Divine Comedy   237
     Katharine Worth

20   Form and Ethics in the Comedies of Brendan Behan   247
     John Brannigan

21   Joe Orton: Anger, Artifice and Absurdity   258
     David Higgins

22   Alan Ayckbourn: Experiments in Comedy   269
     Alexander Leggatt

23   'They Both Add up to Me': The Logic of Tom Stoppard's
     Dialogic Comedy   279
     Paul Delaney

24   Stewart Parker's Comedy of Terrors   289
      Anthony Roche

Part V   War and Terror   299

25   A Wounded Stage: Drama and World War I   301
      Mary Luckhurst

26   Staging 'the Holocaust' in England   316
      John Lennard

27   Troubling Perspectives: Northern Ireland, the 'Troubles' and Drama   329
      Helen Lojek

28   On War: Charles Wood's Military Conscience   341
      Dawn Fowler and John Lennard

29   Torture in the Plays of Harold Pinter   358
      Mary Luckhurst

30   Sarah Kane: From Terror to Trauma   371
      Steve Waters

Part VI   Theatre since 1968   383

31   Theatre since 1968   385
      David Pattie

32   Lesbian and Gay Theatre: All Queer on the West End Front   398
      John Deeney

33   Edward Bond: Maker of Myths   409
      Michael Patterson

34   John McGrath and Popular Political Theatre   419
      Maria DiCenzo

35   David Hare and Political Playwriting: Between the Third
      Way and the Permanent Way   429
      John Deeney

36   Left in Front: David Edgar's Political Theatre   441
      John Bull

37   Liz Lochhead: Writer and Re-Writer: Stories, Ancient and Modern   454
      Jan McDonald

38   'Spirits that Have Become Mean and Broken':
      Tom Murphy and the 'Famine' of Modern Ireland   466
      Shaun Richards

39   Caryl Churchill: Feeling Global   476
      Elin Diamond

40   Howard Barker and the Theatre of Catastrophe   488
     Chris Megson

41   Reading History in the Plays of Brian Friel   499
     Lionel Pilkington

42   Marina Carr: Violence and Destruction: Language, Space and Landscape   509
     Cathy Leeney

43   Scrubbing up Nice? Tony Harrison's Stagings of the Past   519
     Richard Rowland

44   The Question of Multiculturalism: The Plays of Roy Williams   530
     D. Keith Peacock

45   Ed Thomas: Jazz Pictures in the Gaps of Language   541
     David Ian Rabey

46   Theatre and Technology   551
     Andy Lavender

Index   563

Acknowledgements

This volume was peculiarly beset with catastrophic events, the first and worst of which was the very sad death of Clive Barker. Clive would have written the essay on drama and World War I; instead readers got me. Following Clive's last exit contributors suffered mysterious palsies, hospitalization, the death of close relatives, the hospitalization of close relatives, chronic administration syndrome, deadline phobia, cricket addiction, and domestic flooding. That this volume was completed at all says much about the extraordinary dedication of its essayists and to all I extend my warmest gratitude. I would like, in particular, to thank John Brannigan, John Bull, John Deeney, Gabriele Griffin, Declan Kiberd, Lionel Pilkington, David Ian Rabey, Anthony Roche and Katharine Worth for very helpful conversations and correspondence. Andy Lavender, Jan McDonald, and Victor Merriman came on board late in the project and delivered superb chapters. Christy Adair, Maggie Gale, Dan Rebellato and Simon Mills all gave useful feedback. John Lennard was, as ever, a generous and enlightening discussion partner. My work on this Companion was greatly helped by financial support from the Department of English's F. R. Leavis Fund at the University of York. My colleagues were supportive and enthusiastic: Laura Chrisman and Victoria Coulson were excellent readers, Lawrence Rainey commiserated heartily, Derek Attridge gave sound advice, and Ben Harker was an astute conversationalist. Mike Cordner and Richard Rowland are beyond compare as colleagues and friends. Emilie Pine's proof-reading was a godsend. Thanks go to Duncan Wu, who spoke words of wisdom at critical points. Dawn Fowler and Kate Holeywell gave invaluable help with administration and research. During the summer when I was editing most intently Kai Low's company and cooking made me almost light-headed with happiness. There are no words for Vike Plock's steadfast and careful editorial assistance: she is superhuman and you heard it here first. Lastly, I would like to thank Emma Bennett for commissioning me to do this fantastic project; Astrid Wind for her unfailing and good-humoured efficiency; Fiona Sewell for her meticulous copyediting; Greg Callus for indexing with a conscience; and Tom Hunt for laconic support.

Mary Luckhurst

List of Illustrations

Rejane rehearsing for a Paris production of *A Doll's House* by Henrik Ibsen   39

A poster advertising *The New Woman* by Sidney Grundy   55

George Alexander, Mrs Patrick Campbell and Helena Rous in *The Importance of Being Earnest* by Oscar Wilde   215

Mrs Beere and Herbert Beerbohm Tree in *A Woman of No Importance* by Oscar Wilde   216

Tim Preece, Alfred Lynch and Norman Rossington in *Prisoner and Escort* by Charles Wood   344

Ben Tyler-Wray in *Far Away* by Caryl Churchill   486

Jim Stevenson, Kai Low, Alex Crampton, Fran Trewin, Fiona Cooper and Lewis Charlesworth in *Far Away* by Caryl Churchill   486

Meredith MacNeill and Paul Rhys in Theatre de Complicite's *Measure for Measure*   557

Olaf Reinelke, Tom Hanslmaier and Konstantin Mishin in *Vivisector*   557

Notes on Contributors

Mary Luckhurst is senior lecturer in modern drama at the University of York. She is the author of *Dramaturgy: A Revolution in Theatre* (2006) and co-author of *The Drama Handbook* (2002). She is co-editor of *Theatre and Celebrity in Britain, 1660–2000* (2005), *On Acting* (2001), *The Creative Writing Handbook* (2000) and *On Directing* (1999). She is also a playwright and director and most recently directed Caryl Churchill's *Far Away* at the York Theatre Royal.

Susan Bennett is university professor in the Department of English at the University of Calgary, Canada. She is the author of *Theatre Audiences* (1990), *Performing Nostalgia* (1996) and *Feminist Theatre* (2006), as well as very many essays on a wide range of theatre and performance topics.

John Brannigan is senior lecturer in English at University College Dublin. He is the author of *Pat Barker* (2006), *New Historicism and Cultural Materialism* (1998), *Brendan Behan: Cultural Nationalism and the Revisionist Writer* (2002), *Literature, Culture and Society in England, 1945–1965* (2002) and *Orwell to the Present: Literature in England, 1945–2000* (2003).

Mary Brewer is a lecturer in the Department of Theatre, Film and Television at the University of Wales, Aberystwyth. She is author of *Race, Sex and Gender in Contemporary Women's Theatre: The Construction of 'Woman'* (1999) and *Staging Whiteness* (2005), and has edited *Exclusions in Feminist Thought: Challenging the Boundaries of Womanhood* (2002).

John Bull is professor of film and drama at the University of Reading. He is author of *New British Political Dramatists* (1984), *Stage Right: Crisis and Recovery in British Contemporary Mainstream Theatre* (1994) and *Vanbrugh and Farquhar* (1998).

Susan Carlson is associate provost and professor of English at Iowa State University. She has published two books on women and comedy and, in addition to her work on suffrage theatre, has published recent essays on Aphra Behn, Timberlake Wertenbaker and Shakespearean production.

Richard Allen Cave is professor of drama and theatre arts at Royal Holloway, University of London. He has published extensively on aspects of Irish theatre (particularly on Yeats, Wilde, Beckett, Friel and McGuinness); on Renaissance, nineteenth-century and recent

English drama; on stage design and theatre history; and on physical theatre and the body. He has edited the plays of W. B. Yeats (1997), Oscar Wilde (2000) and T. C. Murray (1998), and the manuscripts of Yeats's *The King of the Great Clock Tower* and *A Full Moon in March*.

Jean Chothia is reader in drama and theatre at the University of Cambridge. She is the author of *Forging a Language: A Study of the Plays of Eugene O'Neill* (1979), *Directors in Perspective: André Antoine* (1991) and *English Drama of the Early Modern Period, 1890–1940* (1996), and editor of *'The New Woman' and Other Emancipated Woman Plays* (1998).

John Deeney is a theatre director and senior lecturer in drama at Manchester Metropolitan University. He has contributed to the volumes *British Theatre Between the Wars* (2000) and *Women, Theatre and Performance: New Histories, New Historiographies* (2000). His current projects include a monograph on Mark Ravenhill.

Paul Delaney is a lecturer at Westmont College in Santa Barbara, California. He is the author of *Tom Stoppard: The Moral Vision of the Major Plays* (1990) and editor of *Tom Stoppard in Conversation* (1994).

Elin Diamond is professor of English at Rutgers University. She is the author of *Unmaking Mimesis: Essays on Feminism and Theatre* (1997) and *Pinter's Comic Play* (1985), and editor of *Performance and Cultural Politics* (1996). Her essays on performance and feminist theory have appeared in *Theatre Journal*, *Elh*, *Discourse*, *TDR*, *Modern Drama*, *Kenyon Review*, *Cahiers Renaud-Barrault*, *Art and Cinema* and *Maska*, and in anthologies in the USA, Europe and India.

Maria DiCenzo is associate professor in the Department of English and Film Studies, Wilfrid Laurier University, Canada. She is the author of *The Politics of Alternative Theatre in Britain, 1968–1990: The Case of 7:84 (Scotland)* published in 1996, and has authored essays on feminist theatre, Italian Canadian theatre and cultural funding.

Dawn Fowler is a researcher at the University of York working on the Charles Wood manuscripts.

Frances Gray is a reader in drama at the University of Sheffield. Her books include *John Arden* (1982), *Noël Coward* (1987), *Women and Laughter* (1994) and *Women, Crime and Language* (2003). She is also a playwright for stage and radio – and her most recent play featured Noël Coward as one of the characters.

Gabriele Griffin is professor of gender studies and deputy dean for research and enterprise at the University of Hull. Her recent publications include *Research Methods for English Studies* (2005) and *Contemporary Black and Asian Women Playwrights in Britain* (2003). She is co-editor of *Thinking Differently: European Women's Studies* (2002) and of the academic journal *Feminist Theory*.

Robin Grove is honorary senior fellow in English and cultural studies at the University of Melbourne. He has published on literature from Chaucer to Beckett, and worked for many years as a dance critic. His most recent book is *Thinking in Four Dimensions: Creativity and Cognition in Contemporary Dance* (2005). From 1962 to 1974 he was one of the board of directors of Ballet Victoria, for which he choreographed six works.

David Higgins is lecturer in English at the University of Chester. He is the author of *Romantic Genius and the Literary Magazine: Biography, Celebrity and Politics* (2005), and has published articles on Wordsworth, Hazlitt and nineteenth-century constructions of race.

Declan Kiberd is chair of Anglo-Irish literature and drama at University College Dublin, and a member of the Royal Irish Academy. His books include *Men and Feminism in Modern Literature* (1985), *Inventing Ireland: The Literature of the Modern Nation* (1995) and *Irish Classics* (2000). He is a regular essayist and reviewer for the *Irish Times*, the *TLS*, the *London Review of Books* and the *New York Times*.

Stephen Lacey is professor of drama, film and television in the Department of Arts and Media at the University of Glamorgan. He has published widely on postwar British theatre and television drama, is the author of *British Realist Theatre: The New Wave in its Context 1956–65* (1995), and is co-editor of *Popular Television Drama: Critical Perspectives* (2005). He is a founding editor of *Critical Studies in Television*.

Andy Lavender is head of postgraduate studies at Central School of Speech and Drama, University of London. He is the artistic director of the theatre/performance company Lightwork and has directed devised, multimedia and physical theatre productions. He is the author of *Hamlet in Pieces: Shakespeare Reworked by Peter Brook, Robert Lepage and Robert Wilson* (2001) and has written a number of essays on contemporary theatre and performance.

Sally Ledger is professor of English at Birkbeck, University of London. She is the author of *The New Woman: Fiction and Feminism at the Fin de Siecle* (1997) and of *Henrik Ibsen* (1999). She is currently working on Dickens and popular radical imagination.

Cathy Leeney is subject leader in drama studies at University College Dublin. She is co-editor of *The Theatre of Marina Carr: 'Before Rules Was Made'* (2003). She is currently completing a book on Irish women playwrights in the early twentieth century.

Alexander Leggatt is professor of English at University College, University of Toronto, and is a fellow of the Royal Society of Canada. His books include *English Stage Comedy 1490–1990: Five Centuries of a Genre* (1998) and *Shakespeare's Tragedies: Violation and Identity* (2005). He is editor of *The Cambridge Companion to Shakespearean Comedy* (2002).

John Lennard is professor of British and American literature at the University of the West Indies, Mona, in Jamaica. His published work includes *But I Digress* (1991) and *The Poetry Handbook* (1996 and 2005), and he is co-author of *The Drama Handbook* (2002).

Helen Lojek is professor of English at Boise State University in Idaho. She is author of *The Theatre of Frank McGuinness* (2002) and *Contexts for Frank McGuinness's Drama* (2004). She has also written widely on Charabanc Theatre Company and Brian Friel.

Cary M. Mazer is associate professor of theatre arts and English at the University of Pennsylvania. He is author of *Shakespeare Refashioned: Elizabethan Plays on Edwardian Stages*, and articles and review essays on Shaw, Granville Barker, Edwardian theatre, Shakespeare and performance, and dramaturgy.

Jan McDonald is emerita professor of drama at the University of Glasgow and vice-president of the Royal Society of Edinburgh and of the Citizens' Theatre, Glasgow. She has published on Shaw and the 'New Drama', on women in nineteenth-century theatre, and on contemporary Scottish women dramatists.

Chris Megson is a lecturer in drama and theatre at Royal Holloway, University of London. He has published essays on Howard Barker, Howard Brenton, David Edgar and David Hare, contemporary documentary/verbatim theatre, and British playwriting during the Cold War.

Victor Merriman is head of creative and performing arts at Waterford Institute of Technology. He publishes regularly on contemporary Irish theatre, postcolonialism, drama pedagogy, public policy and critical practice. He was a member of the Arts Council of Ireland (1993–8) and chaired the council's review of theatre in Ireland (1995–6).

Christopher Murray is associate professor of drama and theatre history in the School of English and Drama, University College Dublin. He is author of *Twentieth-Century Irish Drama: Mirror up to Nation* (1997) *and Sean O'Casey, Writer at Work: A Biography* (2004), and has edited *Brian Friel: Essays, Diaries, Interviews 1964–1999* (1999). He is currently editing the selected plays of George Shiels and a collection of Thomas Davis's lectures on Beckett.

Katherine Newey is professor and head of department of drama and theatre arts at the University of Birmingham. She is author of *Women's Theatre Writing in Victorian Britain* (2005) and co-editor of the journal *Nineteenth Century Theatre and Film*. She is currently engaged on a study of John Ruskin and the popular theatre.

Michael Patterson is emeritus professor of theatre at De Montfort University, Leicester. He has published a number of books on German drama; his most recent books include *Strategies of Political Theatre* (2003) and *The Oxford Dictionary of Plays* (2005).

David Pattie is reader in drama and theatre studies at the University of Chester. He is the author of *The Complete Critical Guide to Samuel Beckett* (2001), and has published widely on Beckett, contemporary British theatre and performance in popular culture.

D. Keith Peacock is a senior lecturer in the Department of Drama and Music at the University of Hull. His books include *Harold Pinter and the New British Theatre* (1997) and *Thatcher's Theatre* (1999). He has recently completed *The Aesthetics of Performance in Postwar British Theatre* (2006).

Lionel Pilkington is a senior lecturer in English at the National University of Ireland, Galway. He is the author of *Theatre and the State in Twentieth-Century Ireland: Cultivating the People* (2001) and of numerous essays on Irish theatre and cultural history.

David Ian Rabey is professor of drama and theatre studies at the University of Wales, Aberystwyth, and a director, dramatist and performer. His publications include *English Drama since 1940* (2003), *David Rudkin: Sacred Disobedience* (1997) and *Howard Barker: Politics and Desire* (1989). He is artistic director of Lurking Truth/Gwir sy'n Llechu Theatre Company, for whom he has written various plays, and an associate of The Wrestling School theatre company.

Shaun Richards is professor of Irish studies at Staffordshire University. He is the co-author of *Writing Ireland: Colonialism, Nationalism and Culture* (1988) and editor of *The Cambridge Companion to Twentieth-Century Irish Drama* (2004), and has published widely on Irish drama in major journals and edited collections.

Anthony Roche is senior lecturer in the School of English and Drama at University College Dublin and the director of the Synge Summer School. His books include *Contemporary Irish Drama: From Beckett to McGuinness* (1994) and *The Cambridge Companion to Brian Friel* (2006). He contributed the chapter on 'Contemporary Irish Drama: 1940–2000' to the two-volume *Cambridge History of Irish Literature* (2005).

Richard Rowland is lecturer in drama and English at the University of York. He has specialized in the editing of early modern dramatic texts, including plays by Chapman,

Jonson, Marlowe and, most recently, Thomas Heywood, upon whom he is currently writing a monograph.

Mary Trotter is an assistant professor in theatre and drama at the University of Wisconsin at Madison. She is the author of *Ireland's National Theatres: Political Performance and the Origins of the Irish Dramatic Movement* (2001), and has written numerous articles on Irish theatre. She is currently working on a cultural studies history of the modern Irish stage.

Steve Waters is a playwright, whose plays include *After the Gods* (2002), *World Music* (2003) and *The Unthinkable* (2004). He teaches drama in the Faculty of Education at the University of Cambridge.

Katharine Worth is emerita professor of drama and theatre studies and honorary fellow of Royal Holloway, University of London. Her award-winning adaptation of Beckett's *Company*, performed by Julian Curry and directed by Tim Pigott-Smith, was produced in London, Ireland, New York and elsewhere in 1987. She is editor of *Beckett the Shape Changer: A Symposium* (1975) and author of *Samuel Beckett's Theatre: Life Journeys* (1999). She has also written books on modern English drama, Irish drama, Sheridan and Goldsmith, Wilde, and Maeterlinck.

Introduction

Mary Luckhurst

'Modern British drama' is a tricky label and a contested notion. The idea that certain playwrights and certain plays might be representative of various cultures and various communities is troubling. If the English were later than most to acquire a national theatre, it was in many ways because it was not seen to be needed: there was Shakespeare, there was the English language and there was imperial self-regard. The fact that the National Theatre came into existence during the postimperial crisis is no surprise. But recognizing the power of that seismic crisis and acknowledging the continuing quakes is another matter entirely for the English. Only very slowly indeed is that happening, and as Declan Kiberd points out in chapter 2, it has been at the prompting of plays by modern Irish dramatists, which the English have imported to view themselves at a safe remove. 'The project of inventing Ireland', Kiberd says, 'presupposed the task of helping the neighbouring people to reinvent the idea of England' and the 'shaping of the modern democratic *polis* has been rehearsed in the dramas of England over the past half-century'. A major difficulty for the idea of English drama is that it has been consumed by the notion of British drama, just as 'England' has been consumed by the idea of 'Britain'. Englishness needs redefining just as English drama needs re-viewing and reassessing with postcoloniality in mind. Irish drama, Scottish drama and Welsh drama can all be seen to be engaged in the political project of interrogating histories and identities, and reimagining past and present. Drama in England is generally not thought about in this sense, and the academy lags behind the inventive endeavours of many playwrights and theatre companies. The postcolonial agenda, then, is strong in this *Companion to Modern British and Irish Drama*, and because of recent history the forum for much reflection, as Victor Merriman elucidates in chapter 1, is the dramatic traffic that has flowed from Ireland to England and vice versa.

If imperial history is a significant and passionately discussed narrative in this volume then so is the feminist agenda – and in the case of Winsome Pinnock they, of course, overlap, as Gabriele Griffin discusses in chapter 16. 'Postfeminism' is an invidious ideological construct and there is no credence given to it on these pages. Too many retrospectives of twentieth-century British and Irish drama have paid shockingly tokenistic attention to plays by female authors despite the important advances made in theatre criticism. As Sally Ledger makes clear in chapter 4, there is still a huge amount of work to be done in evaluating the extraordinary contribution of women dramatists in their outstandingly effective political campaign. The post-Ibsen realist project has overwhelmingly been written up as a male enterprise, and unhappy as the term 'women playwrights' is, it will be used as long as the academy treats them inequitably. Periodicity comes into the equation here. The negative constructions of the New Woman still tend to be feted more in conservative plays than in the extraordinary and radical plays by women such as Elizabeth Robins. Suffrage plays still tend to be treated as something apart from the canon. John Osborne has been privileged over an infinitely more progressive Shelagh Delaney. Sarah Kane and Marina Carr are privileged apparently because they write violent plays, and stray into a territory that prejudice has reserved for the masculine. The theatre industry itself has problems: the Royal Shakespeare Company (RSC), the Royal Court and the National Theatre (NT) have never employed a female artistic director, and women directors find the profession notoriously difficult to navigate. Certain voices, it seems, are still too dangerous to be heard, as Gurpreet Bhatti discovered when her play *Behzti* was closed down because of riots at the Birmingham Rep in 2004 and she had to go into hiding. Without doubt, there are other voices in Britain and Ireland that go unheard – one of the last taboos certainly appears to reside in being an openly lesbian playwright, and lesbian theatre, unlike gay theatre, really struggles with visibility. There are chapters in this volume that look penetratingly at these issues and insist on wholesale re-examination.

If feminist and postcolonial agendas dominate this volume, it is not at the expense of many other vitally important questions. Why the history of modern British theatre, for example, is predominantly refracted through the lenses of three institutions – the Royal Court, the NT and the RSC – is quite baffling. Similarly, the Abbey Theatre with its particular literary and performative traditions has dominated the history of modern Irish drama for good and bad.

The question of the metropolis versus the regions is also raised. Without doubt the histories of regional theatres and performance events in Britain and Ireland have been marginalized, and urgent work is needed to chase away some of the myths about conservatism and the supposed lack of modernist experimentation. Kate Newey reflects on this in chapter 3, wondering at the adoption and naturalization of Ibsenite realism by the English, and what that whole project may have steam-rollered and erased.

This Companion is divided into six parts. The first sets out broad historical and political frames; the second examines modern playwrights and theatrical events that had a profound influence on the mid- to late twentieth century. The third considers specific aspects of class and empire. Part IV celebrates the different comic modes that have been famously deployed by many British and Irish dramatists. Chapters in 'War and Terror' explore the representation of conflict, atrocity and trauma on stage – subjects which have not received enough critical attention from theatre historians. In chapter 26, for example, John Lennard reflects on Holocaust drama in Britain, and in chapter 28 Charles Wood is rightly identified as the most significant living dramatist of war. Part VI traces significant developments in theatre since 1968 and looks at a plethora of very diverse playwrights engaging with a variety of agendas. Many questions are posed, many dialogues conducted. This Companion is polemical and provocative and, hopefully, far from representative.

PART I
Contexts

1

Domestic and Imperial Politics in Britain and Ireland: The Testimony of Irish Theatre

Victor Merriman

I wish I could find a country to live in where the facts were not brutal and the dreams not unreal.

Shaw (1984: 88)

The whole Irish-British cat's cradle...a subject for drama which is comprised of multiplying dualities.

Parker (2000: xiii)

The relationship of Ireland and Irish people to modernity has come about, primarily, as a function of the country's colonial status.[1] British colonialism produced in Ireland a mediated experience of modernity, manifested, for most of the twentieth century, both as material disadvantage and as critical opportunity. While exclusion from the mainstream had baneful economic consequences, it seemed to confer advantages at the level of critical consciousness and cultural vitality. Yeats's poetic characterization, 'We Irish... thrown upon this filthy modern tide', apprehends succinctly this ambiguous position (Yeats 2000: 122): the experience of psychic and material buffeting inspires a search for positions other than those dictated by modernity. For Irish nationalist movements of the late nineteenth century, alternative locations – in which one could act on history as more than a mere 'other' to a colonial reality – were to be found by cultural means. Domination generates psychic experiences of being other than oneself: 'to be is to be like; to be like is to be like the oppressor' (Freire 1985: 25). In consequence, throughout the colonial period, and, in the mid-nineteenth century, intensely so, Ireland witnessed a series of attempts by anti-colonialists 'to speak a true word' (ibid.: 60). The question of 'authenticity' became a key one in dramatizing the Irish race and the Irish nation, either in the theatres of the English-speaking world (Grene and Morash 2005: xv), or in public sites of armed insurrection.[2] To enunciate one's Irishness was to affirm for local audiences one's sense of being other than the empire decrees one to be – a crucial step in the formation of anti-colonial consciousness.[3] It was also to claim space among a broader *polis* for the proposition that colonial practices are fundamentally destructive of the humanity of those subject to them.[4] The latter argument requires, in the first instance, that such persons' humanity be acknowledged, and is useful in grounding anti-colonial movements for national self-determination. It applies also, as Freire argues, to the 'dehumanized' oppressors produced in the metropole by the practices of empire (Freire 1985: 32).

In contemporary Irish Studies, Ireland and Britain are, first and foremost, ideas (see Kiberd 1996; Kirby et al. 2002). Irish Studies interrogates constructs of Ireland and of Britain, as functions of utopian desires and dystopian terrors, exposing relationships in which they antagonize and complement each other. Such constructs are negotiated in practices of representation and interpretation, public and private, metropolitan and peripheral. Irish perceptions and experiences of the drama of Ireland in – and after – the British Empire testify to tensions common among colonized peoples between insurrectionist and quietist versions of postimperial desires (Amkpa 2004: 1–18). The insurrectionist notion of Britain as interloper is encoded in the phrase, 'the British presence in Ireland'. The quietist account of Britain as (problematic) neighbour gives rise to discussions of 'British–Irish' or 'Irish–British' relations. As he contemplates his execution in Belfast, following the failed rebellion of 1798, Stewart Parker's Henry Joy McCracken poses a key question for insurrectionists: 'So what if the English do bequeath us to one another some day? What then? When there's nobody else to blame except ourselves?' (Parker 2000: 81). In his final moments, Parker's McCracken suggests that independence conceived of simply, or mainly, as the absence of the colonizer will bring problems of its own (Merriman 1999: 305–17). Irish experience shows that statehood is all too easily, and all too often, separated out from anti-colonial aspirations to universal liberation, once the state has been achieved. New institutions command popular allegiance for their 'national' character, even as they reinscribe the social relations which characterized the colonial apparatus they claim to have transformed.[5]

In the penultimate decades of direct imperial rule in Ireland (1880–1910), the battle for the right to narrate the nation was joined on many fronts, with the idea of national culture a crucial site of struggle (see Matthews 2002: 22–37). For generations raised in Independent Ireland, the sense of gradual amelioration of the imperial perspective on Irish independence, prior to the rebellion of 1916 and the War of Independence (1919–21), has been difficult to appreciate. Nationalism's ideological appropriation of the insurrection of 1916 as an inevitable manifestation of the historical will of the people distorts the reality that it came as a huge shock to the general population. To elites, both Gaelic and Anglo-Irish, who had been in the vanguard of a relatively sedate progress towards national autonomy within the United Kingdom, it was a cataclysm. Yeats's phrase in 'Easter 1916', 'a terrible beauty is born' (Yeats 2000: 60–2), registers its impact on those of his class and political outlook. It is a pointed historical irony that, post-independence, the phrase itself became a commonplace of nationalist rhetoric deployed to erase the complexity of pre-1916 Ireland, and recruit, *ex post facto*, a huge majority engaged with the quietist project of Home Rule to a historically inevitable movement towards popular insurrection.[6] The quietist approach – in which 'constructive unionism' finds common cause with 'constitutional nationalism' – privileges contiguity over conflict, stresses 'what we have in common' over 'issues that continue to divide us', and finds its fullest expression in the Good Friday Agreement (1998).

As contemporary Independent Ireland wrestles to transform itself from colonial province to EU member-state, a sense of the radical unreliability of received accounts of Ireland's historical formation in relation to empire begins to emerge, drawing attention to the politics of critical valorizations of culture. Lionel Pilkington argues for 'a cultural history of Ireland that accounts for Irish theatre's complex relationship to colonialism and modernity',[7] and this chapter attempts to enable reflection on insights which drama's 'masterful images' may make available. As a broad schematic structure, I suggest that where history purports to deal in the ordering of 'facts', and political movements in the realization of collective dreams, cultural artefacts are wrought from utopian desires. My critical wager is that performance texts make available unique and often unusual insights into the social, political and cultural circumstances of the moments in which they are produced and reproduced. Read in this light, they enable the critical interpreter to locate, and to exceed, both the brutality of reductive facts and the unreality of elitist dreams. Critical concentration on artefact and consciousness, sharpened by sensitivity to what Pilkington calls 'the libidinous physicality of performance' (Pilkington 2001: 5), enables acts of theatre to yield up vital insights in radically unstable, even unforeseeable ways. Intellectually useful schemas such as 'insurrectionist' and 'quietist', and positions such as 'cultural elitist' and 'Fabian socialist', simply collapse in the face of the passionate performance of utopian desire:

> The extraordinary kinetic impact of [Yeats and Gregory's *Cathleen ni Houlihan*] could work surprisingly even with those of very unnationalist convictions. Gregory recorded the reaction of Shaw watching a London performance in 1909: 'When I see that play I feel it might lead a man to do something foolish.' She was, she said, 'as much surprised as if I had seen one of the Nelson lions scratch himself.' (Grene 1999: 69–70)

In the late nineteenth and early twentieth centuries, Yeats, Gregory and others saw a national theatre as a contribution to cultural revival which would drive the transformative dynamics of Ireland under Home Rule (Pilkington 2001: 6–34). Home Rule for Ireland would usher in a spiritual renaissance, in which a noble, submerged culture would proclaim itself as radical other to urban, industrial modernity. *Cathleen ni Houlihan* (1902) makes use of the insurrection of 1798 – mythologized in countrywide commemorations during 1898 – in order, allegorically, to assert the native heroism of the Irish, in keeping with a utopian formulation of nation-as-culture (Yeats 1991: 2–13). Shaw, a rational socialist thinker, saw Ireland modernizing when joined in radical complementarity with Britain. Confronted with *Cathleen ni Houlihan*, he was moved, not to detached appreciation of allegory, but by the visceral shock of the performance of a young man's rejection of homestead and marriage bed for battlefield and grave, in the name of the captive nation. When utopian allegory and rational consciousness met, the encounter was mediated in and through performance, producing the kind of remarkable effects witnessed by Gregory. Thus, performance practice intervenes to create unpredictable excesses of meaning, fundamentally affecting the significance of the artefact and its potential impact on individual and public consciousness.

Imperialism produces lived experiences which are psychically injurious (Moane 2002: 109–23), and gives rise to needs for recuperative strategies in the consciousness of *both* dominated and subordinated. In the metropole, such strategies emerge as a *mythos* (Kearney 2002: 3–14) in which the dominated other is stripped of its humanity, and becomes a complex focus of anger, contempt, fear and pity.[8] The ethical collapse involved in colonialism's oppressive practices is accommodated by culpable habits of moral occlusion: 'That blessed old head of yours with all its ideas in watertight compartments, and all the compartments warranted impervious to anything it doesn't suit you to understand' (Shaw 1984: 83). In the colony, the imperial *mythos* emerges in barbaric practices of domination, and is countered by collective narratives of resistance, grounded in demands for respect, justice and liberation: 'Empire: a name that every man who has ever felt the sacredness of his own native soil to him, and thus learnt to regard that feeling in other men as something holy and inviolable, spits out of his mouth with enormous contempt' (Shaw, 'Preface to the Home Rule Edition', ibid.: 59). The coercive realities of domination require that counter-narratives remain, as their usual designation, 'subversive', suggests, below the surface. Over time, utopian desires, produced by prolonged experience of oppression, become powerful historical actors in their own right, as Yeats acknowledges in 'The Man and the Echo' in relation to *Cathleen ni Houlihan*:

> Did that play of mine send out
> Certain men the British shot?
> (Yeats 2000: 130)

It would seem that 'facts', brutal or otherwise, are at best partial perspectives on human experiences formed among historical encounters, between and within Britain and Ireland (Flannery 2005: 454–5). Cultural work, and especially the testimony of theatre, enables us to take account of 'dreams', no less significant for their manifest unreality. Plays in performance are complex artefacts in time, producing excesses of meaning from the flux of competing material conditions and *mythos* in play at any given moment. Critical sensitivity to theatre's characteristic complexity, and the critical courage to hazard interpretations alive to the pressing circumstances of the day, vindicate theatre's public role. Fully engaged in dialogue with its society, theatre enables radical public questioning, essential to social regeneration and the common good.

George Bernard Shaw (1856–1950) remains Ireland's outstanding public intellectual, a status vindicated by his *John Bull's Other Island* (1904), which deals directly with Ireland's relationship with imperial Britain. In this work, which Patrick Mason asserts is *'the* Irish play',[9] Shaw stages historically rooted contradictions arising from relationships between persons mandated by their Britishness, and people mediated by their Irishness. As such, it is an exemplary artefact of Irish–British relations, and, with its accompanying prefaces and related essays, a robust intervention in a politics at once incorrigibly domestic and definitively imperial. Crucially for this chapter, *John Bull's Other Island* functions both as a play and as a kind of critical metatext, which provides a means of interrogating the radical credentials of subsequent artefacts of Irish theatre, and of strategies deployed to critique them. In re-engaging with sites, persons and dilemmas produced among the contests of an imperial past, Shaw makes cultural material itself available as a generative public resource (Grene 1999: 18–34). As the twentieth century progresses, Irish drama returns again and again to the dramatic material of *John Bull's Other Island*, reworking what Shaw's dramaturgy positions as primal scenes. Those reworkings seek, on the one hand, to endorse the pristine credentials of the national state (Pilkington 2001: 86–165), and, on the other, to expose and critique the continuities of oppression visited on the people of Independent Ireland, as decolonization is indefinitely postponed, and colonialism mutates into neo-colonialism (see Merriman 1999).

John Bull's Other Island opens in the 'Office of Broadbent and Doyle, Civil Engineers, Great George Street, Westminster. Summer 1904, 4.40pm' (Shaw 1984: 68). In this room in metropolitan London, plans for Ireland's future in Imperial Modernity have been made. Tom Broadbent is about to depart for Ireland to advance a scheme to set up a 'Garden City' in Rosscullen, the townland in the west of Ireland from which his partner in business and in this scheme, Larry Doyle, is in self-imposed exile. On the walls of the office 'hang a large map of South America, [and] a pictorial advertisement of a steamship company' (ibid.: 69) – icons of the empire in which Ireland is to be fully integrated. Empire's engineers are men of the modern world, grounded in unassailable epistemologies, expressed in stern binaries of progress and stagnation. Larry's professional 'enlightenment' is a function of his formation at the centre of empire: 'It is by living with you and working in double harness with you that I have learned to live in a real world and not an imaginary one. I owe more to you than to any Irishman' (ibid.: 83). Harnessed to the imperial project, he is locked in a historical contest with Irish 'benightedness': 'The dullness! The hopelessness! The ignorance! The bigotry!' (ibid.: 80). His father, Cornelius, is 'a Nationalist and a Separatist', but a civil engineer undertakes to 'join countries, not separate them' (ibid.: 84), placing 'Galway within 3 hours of Colchester and 24 of New York'. This office, dedicated to precision and efficiency, houses an 'Anglicized Irishman' (ibid.: 161) countenancing, not the development of actually existing Ireland, but an imperialist's dream of a modernist utopia. Compounding the dramatic irony, Broadbent, a 'Gladstonized Englishman' (ibid.: 161), and begetter of Larry's 'reality', is wholly taken in by a grotesquely sentimental idea of Ireland – embodied in Glaswegian Tim Haffigan's 'stage Irishman':

BROADBENT: But he spoke – he behaved just like an Irishman.

DOYLE: Like an Irishman!! Man alive, don't you know that all this top-o-the-morning and broth-of-a-boy and more-power-to-your-elbow business is got up in England to fool you . . . He picks up . . . the antics that take you in . . . in the theatre or the music hall.

(ibid.: 78)

Broadbent's falling for an Irish grotesque, simultaneously endearing and degraded, illustrates Bhabha's account of the double effect of racial stereotype. The desire/terror dynamic is underscored by Broadbent's instruction to his servant to pack a revolver and ammunition for his 'delightful' trip to Ireland (ibid.: 70). Performativity is central to imperial relations, and in its multiplying confusions around power, identity, nation and empire, *John Bull's Other Island* enacts the contradictions embedded in ideas of Britain and Ireland, and aspirations arising from them, as Ireland anticipated the achievement of national autonomy within the empire.

Act II moves the action to a '*desolate . . . lonely*' landscape near Rosscullen (ibid.: s.d. 90). Defrocked cleric and self-styled madman Peter Keegan, conversing pleasantly with a grasshopper, offers a contrast with the London office that could hardly be more extreme. Change is afoot in the west of Ireland, now that Wyndham's Land Act has transformed tenant-farmers into owners of smallholdings. Rosscullen's social organization turns on grotesque mimicry of metropolitan order, in the performance of which the right to narrate the debased Other is appropriated, and exercised, by petty local elites. In Act III a meeting of the expanded local worthies consider the qualities required of a new MP for Rosscullen. The sitting MP has been found unsuited to changed circumstances:

MATTHEW [*breaking out with surly bitterness*]:   Weve had enough of his foolish talk agen landlords. Hwat call has he to talk about the lan, that never was outside of a city office in his life?

CORNELIUS: Were tired of him. He doesn't know hwere to stop. Every man cant own land; and some men must own it to employ them. It was all very well when solid men like Doran an Matt were kep from ownin land. But hwat man in his senses ever wanted to give land to Patsy Farrll an dhe like o him?

(ibid.: 115–16)

Cornelius articulates precisely the rationalization of effortless passage from colonial to neo-colonial social organization, from which significant numbers of persons remain socially and economically disqualified. Shaw anticipates with chilling accuracy the nature of the social order which emerges in Independent Ireland from 1922 on:

AUNT JUDY: Theres harly any landlords left; and therll soon be none at all.

LARRY: On the contrary, therll soon be nothing else; and the Lord help Ireland then!

(ibid.: 112)

The curriculum vitae of the desired 'new class of man in parliament' (ibid.: 117) includes attitudes pro-farmer, anti-labour and pro-church, and means sufficient to live in London.

With the possible exception of the last-mentioned qualification, all of these 'attributes' characterize what Joe Lee refers to as 'the official mind' of Independent Ireland.[10]

Legislated into solid economic roles, the chosen of Rosscullen have no wish to disrupt imperial governance in Ireland, and locate their heart's desire, in the shape of a new master. What is required is one who will mediate between them and metropolitan legislators, in order to protect their recently acquired economic status. Those who will fund their aspirations still languish at the bottom of imperialism's social pyramid – persons such as Patsy Farrell.

MATTHEW: Was Patsy Farrll ever ill used as I was ill used? Tell me dhat?
LARRY: He will be, if ever he gets into your power as you were in the power of your old landlord . . . you, who are only one step above him, would die sooner than let him come up that step; and well you know it.

(ibid.: 118–19)

Farrell, possessed of '*a cunning developed by his constant dread of a hostile dominance*' (ibid.: s.d. 92), repeats the dramatic functions of such as Danny Mann, in Dion Boucicault's *The Colleen Bawn* (1860), and, as a beast of burden for the members of Father Dempsey's ad hoc committee, anticipates Lucky in Samuel Beckett's *Waiting for Godot* (1953). Patsy functions, then, as a kind of fulcrum in the dramatic world of the play, and among dramas of Ireland, from the desolate aftermath of the Famine to the enervating disappointments of independence.

Like Danny Mann and Lucky, Patsy's terror is of 'hostile dominance', and not of domination itself, which he accepts as his lot. His life is a struggle to ameliorate dominance by subterfuge: 'he habitually tries to disarm [hostile dominance] by pretending to be a much greater fool than he is. Englishmen think him half-witted, which is exactly what he intends them to think' (Shaw 1984: s.d. 92). In other words, Patsy deploys the same performative tactics as Tim Haffigan, to similar ends. Obediently accompanying Broadbent on a ludicrous errand – 'It will be quite delightful to drive with a pig in the car: I shall feel quite like an Irishman' (ibid.: 127) – Patsy is injured when the pig bolts. Addressing a crowd in the bar afterwards, Broadbent, unconscious of the fact that he is the butt of a huge joke among the general population, eulogizes Patsy:

I greatly regret the damage to Mr Patrick Farrell's fingers; and I have of course taken care that he shall not suffer pecuniarily by his mishap. [*Murmurs of admiration at his magnanimity, and A Voice* 'Youre a gentleman, sir']. I am glad to say that Patsy took it like an Irishman, and, far from expressing any vindictive feeling, declared his willingness to break all his fingers and toes for me on the same terms. (ibid.: 136)

The link between Patsy and Danny Mann is explicit:

HARDRESS: Ten years ago he was a fine boy – we were foster-brothers and playmates – in a moment of passion, while we were struggling, I flung him from the gap rock into the reeks below, and thus he was maimed for life.

DANNY: Arrah! Whist aroon! Wouldn't I die for yez? Didn't the same mother foster us? Why wouldn't ye brake my back if it plazed ye, and welkim!

(Boucicault 1987: 193–4)

Larry's grim predictions of Patsy's aggravated servility under a native master are anticipated in dramatic action, in Act II. Broadbent has broached with Father Dempsey the historical significance of Rosscullen's Round Tower, which frames the setting when the dramatic action moves from England to Ireland:

FATHER DEMPSEY: They are the forefingers of the early Church, pointing us all to God. *Patsy, intolerably overburdened, loses his balance, and sits down involuntarily. His burdens are scattered over the hillside. Cornelius and Father Dempsey are furiously on him, leaving Broadbent beaming at the stone and the tower with fatuous interest.*
CORNELIUS: Oh, be the hokey, the sammin's broke in two! You schoopid ass, what d'ye mean?
FATHER DEMPSEY: Are you drunk, Patsy Farrell? Did I tell you to carry that hamper carefully or did I not?
PATSY [*rubbing the back of his head, which has almost dinted a slab of granite*]: Sure me fut slipt. Howkn I carry three men's luggage at wanst?

(Shaw 1984: 98)

This physical action itself prefigures the entrance of Lucky and Pozzo in Act I of *Waiting for Godot*:

Lucky carries a heavy bag, a folding stool, a picnic basket and a greatcoat. Pozzo a whip . . . Noise of Lucky falling with all his baggage . . .
POZZO: Be careful! He's wicked. (*Vladimir and Estragon turn towards Pozzo.*) With strangers.

(Beckett 1975: 22)

Lucky is spoken of as a domestic animal, content in his own way with his habitual master. The relationships of domination staged in the persons of Danny Mann, Patsy Farrell and Lucky are demonstrably related, and specifically different. Danny draws meaning and fulfilment from proximity to Hardress Cregan; Patsy's relationship with Broadbent, and his ability to accommodate personal injury, turn on hard cash. The point here is not simply to expose the currency of a key dramatic type in Irish theatre. The significance of the body of the oppressed, burdened and broken, alters with the material circumstances of the actual world critically interrogated by dramatic imagery and action. Thus, Danny Mann is so grateful for a benign Irish master, when the option is an English one tolerant of death by mass starvation, that the breaking of his body itself may be accommodated in a grotesque quietism. Patsy Farrell has come to understand that, though the Englishman may have a revolver in his pocket, his liberal sensibilities make him amenable as a business proposition, should he cause harm to those in his employ. In Act I of *Waiting for Godot*, the Pozzo/Lucky pairing plays out the stark dynamics of colonial oppressor and oppressed. In Act II, Pozzo, no longer a power in the land, is blind. Lucky remains trapped in an abusive existence from which there is no escape. His grinding neo-colonial reality reprises colonial coercion without any prospect of mitigation, and so crushes him that he is reduced to alternating acts of silence and babbling, compliance and collapse.

John Bull's Other Island stages other points of fulcrum, reinterpreting past episodes in Irish dramatic worlds, and pointing to future reinterpretations of those episodes as potent strategies for critical cultural interventions. There is the figure of the English/Irish heterosexual couple, which enables the play to be read, as Grene points out, as a version of the Irish National Romance (Grene 1999: 28–9). Quietist anti-colonial critique acknowledges the power of the gendered trope, while arguing that it is insufficient to the task of representing what has been described as 'the totality of relationships'. The ludicrous encounter between an intoxicated Broadbent and a bemused Nora Reilly (Shaw 1984: 101–6) ironically prefigures Friel's appropriation of the same trope in scenes involving George Yolland and Máire Chatach (Friel 1989: 47–9, 49–53). The ironic quietism of Shaw's version enables, perhaps, a more searching reading of Friel's approach to this primal figuration of the colonial encounter. Similarly, Larry Doyle's ambiguous position between modernity and Ireland[11] might be set against Owen in *Translations* (1980), and against the highly complex border-crosser, Sanbatch Daly, in *The Wood of the Whispering* (see Merriman 2004). Reading Sanbatch and Sadie as an ironic restaging of the English/Irish heterosexual couple has considerable potential as a challenge to critical perspectives on other reworkings of this primal figuration.

Performances are circumscribed as much as liberated by the dynamics of the theatrical encounter, elegantly schematized by Susan Bennett (Bennett 1992: 183). For critical projects to realize transformative potential, they must take account not only of the fertile indeterminacies of performance moments, but also of their limitations. All too often, critical perspectives accept the world as an unproblematic given, of which the stage world is a skewed version. In performance, dramatic action exists in dialogue with the world in which it is staged, and may function mimetically, allegorically or analogically as a representation of that world. From the very beginning, *John Bull's Other Island* was regarded in Ireland as a 'difficult' play,[12] that it might be wiser to stage seldom, if at all, and – ironically – elsewhere. This view persists among those 'interpretative communities' who assemble prior to the theatrical moment to determine repertory choices. Plays whose fictional worlds stage realities and figures that pose sharp challenges, moral, political or intellectual, to the actual worlds inhabited by comfortable audiences are even more likely, as cultural production moves 'steadily toward easy, globally digestible narratives', to be excluded from the repertoire.[13]

The great play of 1960s Ireland, Tom Murphy's *Famine* (1984), is such a work, and has much in common with *John Bull's Other Island* as a cultural intervention and a theatrical challenge. *Famine* is a drama from the abyss, rich in examples of the doubleness of experience and desire. It was produced first at the Peacock Theatre in 1968, revived in Galway by Druid Theatre Company in 1984, and by Garry Hynes at the Abbey in 1993. In terms of Irish dramaturgy, *Famine* is formally innovative, and the dramatic content takes in multiple locations and extremes of human experience.[14] The play's episodic structure enables the juxtaposition of human intimacy ('Scene 4: The Love Scene' and 'Scene 12: The Springtime') with public affairs and the mechanics of colonial rule and resistance efforts ('Scene 2: The Moral Force' and 'Scene 5: The Relief Committee'). 'The Relief Committee' is a stark reworking of Shaw's primal scene of elite deliberations on the fate of an abject people. The Irish potato famine, or the Great Hunger (1845–7), devastated the population of Ireland by starvation and forced emigration. It is the dystopian touchstone in the narrative of British imperialism in Ireland, and has been imagined more than once by Irish artists as a metaphor for the national condition since independence.[15] Bread is central to life, but bread alone will not sustain humanity, as O'Casey's praise for James Larkin makes clear: 'A man who would place a rose as well as a loaf of bread on every table.'[16] *Famine* is true to the practicalities of this utopian dialectic, in that its dramatic world, and the range of meaning of its dramatic actions, are wrought not only of social reality but of existing dramatic strategies. In 'Scene 4: The Love Scene' Liam Dougan has a secret hoard of nuts and apples. Even though the fruit is sour, it transforms Maeve Connor's demeanour from that of a bitter old hag to that of a 16-year-old girl. What transforms Maeve is not food only, but the type of food, to which J. M. Synge compared the ideal language of drama: 'In a good play every speech should be as fully flavoured as a nut or apple, and such speeches cannot be written by anyone who works among people who have shut their lips on poetry' (Synge 1995: 96–7). Indeed, after eating the apple Maeve joins in singing an eighteenth-century ballad, *The Colleen Rua*, in which the language is excessive and mellifluous (Murphy 1984: 47). Metaphorically, it is food specifically linked to 'the imagination of the people . . . rich and living' that rejuvenates Maeve, and occasions the only moment of desire for life fulfilled in the entire play (Synge 1995: 96).

As in the case of *John Bull's Other Island*, there is a lot at stake in *Famine*, for playwright, actors and directors. The play's cultural significance is generated by its dual identity as an apparently historical play that is also always a refusal of the ideological consensus at the core of contemporary Independent Ireland. The burning critical question concerns the extent to which the play's intervention is of such an order that its audience can begin to lay down its own stake as it enters the theatre. David Lloyd locates the challenge to audiences in the content of cultural artefacts, in the decisions made by artists as they work and rework material. Cultural workers must 'begin to trace alternative histories, histories which may not spell success in terms of the dominant paradigm, and may even . . . spell a certain kind of failure' (Lloyd 1999: 105). Lloyd sees in such histories 'a repertoire for what I would call the history of possibilities, thinking, once again, of the ways in which even the defeated struggles and gestures of the oppressed remain in memory to re-emerge as the impulse to new forms of solidarity' (ibid.). *Famine* demonstrates that, in engaging with 'many, less well-documented memories of other decisions and other affiliations' (ibid.), drama finds a present resource from which to draw critical content.

The infrequency with which *Famine* has been staged may have more than a little to do with its mobilization of the dynamics of colonial oppression in order to critique the inequities of contemporary Ireland. This much it shares with *John Bull's Other Island*. There is also the problem that neither *Famine* nor *John Bull's Other Island* sits easily with popular interpretative positions. Lloyd's exhortation explicitly rejects the 'Great Man' approach to historical narration, and it is salutary to extend that refusal to habits of mind which seek the grand design of a play in the actions and dilemmas of its protagonists. To construct *Famine* as a narrative of John Connor's dilemmas is about as useful as approaching Brecht's *Galileo* as the struggle of a troubled genius against a cruel world. It is a commonplace of criticism that Murphy is an angry navigator of the great binary of 'individual versus society'. Richard Kearney accurately presents Murphy as an iconoclast of 'the consumerist Irish bourgeoisie who resent any deviant flight of creativity, force many of their artists into exile, and . . . try to destroy those who remain'.[17] However, Kearney queries the radical potential of what he reads as an 'angry, at times apocalyptic attitude to contemporary Irish society' in Murphy's work (Kearney 1988: 170). He locates the problem in the playwright, detecting in him a tendency to the position of the *poète maudit*, and finds 'Murphy's heroes' responding to 'the threat of the irrational collective' with a 'fierce individualism' (ibid.: 170). Such critical practice centres the 'tragedy' of John Connor as the dramatic focus of *Famine*, even though epic form inaugurates spatial and temporal conventions which critique and position tragedy itself as an ideological construct. This suppresses the actual cultural significance of *Famine*, which dramatizes individuals and collectivities as socially produced relations in dynamic dialogue with each other.

Even if *Famine* is fruitfully regarded as a tragedy – and its material is such as to risk exhausting the concept – it would be wise to approach it with Wole Soyinka's observation in mind:

> The persistent search for the meaning of tragedy, for a re-definition in terms of culture or private experience is, at the least, man's recognition of certain areas of depth-experience which are not satisfactorily explained by general aesthetic theories . . . There, illusively, hovers the key to the human paradox, to man's experience of being and non-being, his dubiousness as essence and matter, intimations of transience and eternity, and the harrowing drives between uniqueness and Oneness. (Soyinka 1995: 140)

The tragedy of *Famine*, worked out in scenes from the imperial encounter, is the tragedy of all the persons in the dramatic world: 'If Murphy's theatre is anything, it is a theatre of "several things happening at once", with the stage full of oppositions and collisions, presenting both a world of actuality and a world of metaphor.'[18] Connor's 'human paradox' is a part of the fabric of *Famine*, and not the privileged point of engagement for critical interpretations of the play. Murphy's dramaturgy is crucially that of human interdependency, of several *people* 'happening at once', as it were, and no one is 'isolated' as a natural state. When, in the final scene of the play, John Connor stands *in his isolation* with a loaf of bread in his hand, he undergoes an epiphany. He is staged, not in a typical, but in a liminal moment. The Irish Romance is reworked in *Famine* in scenes of thwarted fecundity which ironize notions of natural order and romantic aspiration in a struggling social unit.[19] Collective living is the goal here, writ small in narratives of human intimacy, and large in the dramas of public events which occur in the same dramatic space as parallel dramatic worlds interact. The real contest, as the vicious argument between Mickeleen O'Leary and Fr Horan demonstrates (Murphy 1984: 28–30), is not between an isolated individual and a malevolent collective, but between competing social models, between opposing visions of collective living. Where John Connor is the focus of critical attention, the dramatic importance of Maeve's emergence from awful years of hunger to contemplate the possibility of a future is read as a commitment to 'redemption', cited as characteristic of Murphy's work. Maeve's moment of personal refusal, of bread, and of the notion of ending, is a bold gesture. In the final moment of the play (ibid.: 87), her clear apprehension is that what is now before her is not the possibility of a future, but a finite range of available future possibilities. In its final moments, *John Bull's Other Island* confronts the limited possibilities for those living in a twentieth-century Ireland which has become a neo-imperial dystopia:

> KEEGAN: [*low and bitter*] When at last this poor desolate countryside becomes a busy mint in which we all slave to make money for you, with our Polytechnic to teach us how to do it efficiently, and our library to fuddle the few imaginations your distilleries will spare, and our repaired Round Tower with admission sixpence, and refreshments and penny-in-the-slot mutoscopes to make it interesting, then no doubt your English and American shareholders will spend all the money we make for them very efficiently in shooting and hunting, in operations for cancer and appendicitis, in gluttony and gambling; and you will devote what they save to fresh land development schemes. For four wicked centuries the world has dreamed this foolish dream of efficiency; and the end is not yet. But the end will come.
>
> (Shaw 1984: 160)

In many respects, Keegan's excoriation of 'the foolish dream of efficiency' retains currency. Acts of theatre are themselves compromised by precisely the same 'efficiencies' as those which now confine all other-focused practices in contemporary social organization: disinterested public provision in areas of shared human need. In the current phase of Keegan's nightmare vision, strategies of representation and interpretation which go beyond the 'limit situations' (Freire 1985: 74–5) imposed by systems of domination are urgently required. Gerry Smyth charges a 'radical' Irish studies with 'the production of cognitive maps which enable Irish people to locate themselves in relation to both their own local environments and to the series of increasingly larger networks of power which bear upon those environments' (Smyth 2001: 19). What mediates Irish – and British – experience of contemporary reality is the prevalent, and quite probably dangerous, fantasy of a new imperium: a transnational 'Anglosphere'. David Lloyd's argument that 'the integration of Ireland and the Irish into Western modernity is not only not the only story, but not the only possibility' (Lloyd 1999: 105) is an urgent reminder of the ethical imperative to think critically and otherwise about history. If Britain and Ireland are ideas, they are contesting ideas with histories of fact, counter-narratives of desire, and futures in human capacities to dream. If what remains is indeed a 'cat's cradle', then, in a world shrunk by technology, and with imagination confined within a nexus of fear and coercion, it stands as a reminder that social and political arrangements are accommodations with the chaos produced by domination and resistance. What Maeve Connor embodies is a way of mitigating the unreality of dreams, in resolutely living through the violent contradictions of contemporary states, formed among coercive imperial practices. Independent Ireland may well be irretrievably implicated in a new imperium, but Irish cultural production, marked by centuries of colonial and imperial experience, testifies to lessons learned, utopian desires too strong to suppress, and the capacity of critical cultural practices to perform a generative, public, role.

NOTES

1 Debates around Ireland's colonial status are summarized in Eóin Flannery (2005). 'External Association: Ireland, Empire and Postcolonial Theory' in Lucy Cotter (ed.). *Third Text* 19:5. London: Routledge, 449–59.

2 Young Ireland Rebellion (1848); Fenian Rebellion (1867).

3 'Postcolonial writing ... is initiated at that very moment when a native writer formulates a text committed to cultural resistance' (Kiberd 1996: 6).

4 Note the prevalence of metaphors of destruction, ruin and loss, of body and of mind, throughout plays from Synge to O'Casey to Beckett.

5 Lee records a dissenting contribution to the report of the Commission of Inquiry into the Civil Service (1932–5), 'sounded by a Labour figure, Luke Duffy: "I entertained the hope that the present Commission ... would sketch the outlines of an organisation ... which harmonises with the traditions and responds to the aspirations of the Irish people ... and regret that they should have based their conclusions on the existence of an organisation designed to serve other purposes"' (Lee 1990: 197).

6 See my discussion of the film *Mise Éire* (1959) in Merriman (2004).

7 See Lionel Pilkington (2005). 'Historicizing is Not Enough: Recent Developments in Irish Theatre History', *Modern Drama* 47:4, 729.

8 'This conflict of pleasure/unpleasure, mastery/defence, knowledge/disavowal, absence/presence, has a fundamental significance for colonial discourse' (Homi K. Bhabha (1983). 'The Other Question: The Stereotype and Colonial Discourse', *Screen* 24:6, 27).

9 Patrick Mason, artistic director, Abbey and Peacock Theatres (1992–8), unpublished conversation with the author, October 2005.

10 Lee argues that, from 1927, the 'official mind ... clung to existing economic orthodoxy ... nurtured ... an aversion to the working class in general, and to organised labour in particular' (Lee 1990: 108).

11 'But sure Larry's as good as English: arnt you Larry?' (Shaw 1984: 117).

12 *John Bull's Other Island* is 'astonishingly demanding as a play, demanding significant resources, not least a cast of bravura actors' (Mason, in conversation with the author, 2005).

13 Debbie Ging (2002). 'Screening the Green: Cinema Under the Celtic Tiger' in Kirby et al. (2002: 185).

14 *'Famine* is clearly Brechtian in its use of projected (usually ironic) titles above each scene,
its episodic structure, and, as Fintan O'Toole
has argued, in its insistence on the link between material and economic conditions on
the one hand, and the intimate life of the
mind' (Morash 2002: 229).
15 Éibhlís ní Dhuibhne, 'Milseog an tSamhraidh', in (1997). *Milseog an tSamhraidh
agus Dún na mBan trí thine*. Dublin: Cois Life,
1–67; Tom McIntyre and Patrick Mason, *The
Great Hunger*, Peacock Theatre 1983 and 1986;
Tom McIntyre (1991). *The Great Hunger: Poem
into Play*. Dublin: Lilliput.
16 'Larkin . . . was insistent that workers should
demand flowers as well as bread on the table.

O'Casey was in complete agreement' (Murray
1997: 109).
17 'Tom Murphy's Long Night's Journey into
Night' in Kearney (1988: 169).
18 Fintan O'Toole (1987). *The Politics of Magic:
The Works and Times of Tom Murphy*. Dublin:
Raven Arts, 55–6. Note the persistence of an
opposition between the actual and the metaphorical. In a semiotic reading of theatre, of
which O'Toole is elsewhere a subtle exponent,
all stage action is both actual to the dramatic
world(s) depicted, and metaphorical in relation to the experience/desire dynamic of the
world(s) into which it plays.
19 For Brecht, the smallest social unit is not one
person, but two people.

Primary reading

Beckett, Samuel (1975). *Waiting for Godot*. London
and New York: Faber.
Boucicault, Dion (1987). *The Colleen Bawn* in
Andrew Parkin (ed.). *Selected Plays: Dion Bouci-
cault*. Gerrards Cross and Washington, DC:
Colin Smythe/Catholic University of America
Press, 191–256.
Friel, Brian (1989). *Translations*. London: Faber.
Molloy, M. J. (1998). *The Wood of the Whispering* in
Robert O'Driscoll (ed.). *Selected Plays of M.
J. Molloy*. Gerrards Cross and Washington,
DC: Colin Smythe/Catholic University of
America Press, 113–77.
Murphy, Tom (1984). *Famine*. Dublin: Gallery
Press.

Parker, Stewart (2000). 'Foreword' in *Northern
Star*. London: Methuen, xii–xiv.
Shaw, George Bernard (1984). *John Bull's Other
Island*. London and New York: Penguin.
Synge, J. M. (1995). 'Preface to *The Playboy of the
Western World*' in Anne Saddlemyer (ed.). *The
Playboy of the Western World and Other Plays*.
Oxford: Oxford University Press, 96–7.
Yeats, W. B. (1991). *Cathleen ni Houlihan* in A.
Norman Jeffares (ed.). *W. B. Yeats: Selected Plays*.
Dublin: Gill and Macmillan, 2–13.
Yeats, W. B. (2000). 'Easter 1916', 'The Statues'
and 'The Man and the Echo' in Seamus Heaney
(ed.). *W. B. Yeats: Poems Selected by Seamus Hea-
ney*. London: Faber, 60–2, 122, 130.

Further reading

Amkpa, Awam (2004). *Theatre and Postcolonial
Desires*. London and New York: Routledge.
Bennett, Susan (1992). *Theatre Audiences: A Theory
of Production and Reception*. London and New
York: Routledge.
Flannery, Eóin (2005). 'External Association: Ire-
land, Empire and Postcolonial Theory' in Lucy
Cotter (ed.). *Third Text: Ireland Special Issue*
19:5, 49–59.
Freire, Paulo (1985). *The Pedagogy of the Oppressed*.
London: Penguin.

Grene, Nicholas (1999). *The Politics of Irish
Drama: Plays in Context from Boucicault to Friel*.
Cambridge: Cambridge University Press.
Grene, Nicholas and Morash, Christopher (eds.)
(2005). *Irish Theatre on Tour*. Dublin: Carysfort
Press.
Kearney, Richard (1988). *Transitions: Narratives in
Irish Culture*. Manchester: Manchester University
Press.
Kearney, Richard (2002). *On Stories*. London and
New York: Routledge.

Kiberd, Declan (1996). *Inventing Ireland: The Literature of the Modern Nation*. London: Vintage.

Kirby, Peadar, Cronin, Michael and Gibbons, Luke (eds.) (2002). *Reinventing Ireland*. London: Pluto.

Lee, J. J. (1990). *Ireland 1912–1985*. Cambridge: Cambridge University Press.

Lloyd, David (1999). *Ireland After History*. Cork: Cork University Press.

Matthews, P. J. (2002). 'A Battle of Two Civilizations?: D. P. Moran and William Rooney', *Irish Review* 29, 22–37.

Merriman, Victor (1999). 'Decolonisation Postponed: The Theatre of Tiger Trash', *Irish University Review* 29:2, 305–17.

Merriman, Victor (2004). 'Staging Contemporary Ireland: Heartsickness and Hopes Deferred' in Shaun Richards (ed.). *The Cambridge Companion to Twentieth-Century Irish Drama*. Cambridge: Cambridge University Press, 244–5.

Moane, Geraldine (2002). 'Colonialism and the Celtic Tiger' in Peadar Kirby, Michael Cronin and Luke Gibbons (eds.). *Reinventing Ireland*. London: Pluto, 109–23.

Morash, Christopher (2002). *A History of Irish Theatre 1601–2000*. Cambridge: Cambridge University Press.

Murray, Christopher (1997). *Twentieth-Century Irish Drama: Mirror up to Nation*. Manchester: Manchester University Press.

Pilkington, Lionel (2001). *Theatre and the State in Twentieth-Century Ireland: Cultivating the People*. London and New York: Routledge.

Smyth, Gerry (2001). *Space and the Irish Cultural Imagination*. Basingstoke and New York: Palgrave.

Soyinka, Wole (1995). *Myth, Literature and the African World*. London and New York: Canto.

2

Reinventing England

Declan Kiberd

If the idea of England was invented by Shakespeare in his Tudor historical cycle, it may well have been reinvented through the twentieth century in a variety of plays. Although versions of Shakespeare in cinematic form did much to establish components of the national culture during World War II, thereafter intellectuals became more and more suspicious of attempts to project a 'national theme'. To a sceptical and cosmopolitan intelligentsia, virtues began to be seen as individual, vices as national, for fascism had left people uneasy at all definitions of a national essence. By the 1980s the very notion of international solidarity had changed its meaning, having ceased to denote the pooling of national resources and become instead an *alternative* to nationalism, a style of compulsory internationalism. Much of the talk in that decade was of 'world novels' and 'world music' in a global economy. Yet these were also the years in which sports fans began to fly the Cross of St George at rugby and cricket internationals, rather than the Union Jack. After the fall of the Iron Curtain in 1989, cultural nationalism began to enjoy a new vogue among exponents of critical theory. In 1997 John Rutherford's socialist analysis *Forever England* concluded with a lament that England remained as yet unmade and undefined (Rutherford 1997: *passim*).

Rutherford was unusual in seeking to blend left-wing ideas and a theory of nationhood. Only rare thinkers, such as Tom Nairn, had by then registered the fact that, far from being just a backward-looking philosophy, nationalism might also be the sign and shape of the future (Nairn 1996: *passim*). The collapse of communism in 1989 simply speeded up a process which had marked the growth from about fifty recognized nation-states in 1945 to something like two hundred at the century's end. Paradoxically, one of the major functions of the United Nations has been to give formal ratification to an ever-increasing number of nation-states. Political analysts are now becoming open to the suggestion that many international arrangements from the European Union to the Organization of African States have been little more than mechanisms for reinforcing the hegemony of one strong nation over its neighbours. It is by no means clear that such strong states invariably prosper while enjoying such influence; Germany, whose economy dominated the European Union in the later decades of the twentieth century, entered the new millennium in a fragile state. And 'Great Britain' also seemed to be fraying at the edges, as English thinkers sought to repossess a national idea. As yet, however, these intellectuals have not managed to explain what psychological developments challenge the people-nation which allegedly enjoys such a controlling power within the larger arrangement. If the strain of running an empire has driven many decent people mad over the centuries, the stress of maintaining a United Kingdom or a European Union may also be damaging to the national verve. In *The Satanic Verses* Salman Rushdie mischievously marvels at the willingness of so many young people in 1980s London to abandon the idea of England – and one of his characters explains this with the remark that the British don't really know who they are because so much of their history has happened overseas (Rushdie 1988: 343). The same might be said of many other peoples.

If social class has not become the basis of international solidarity, as radicals once hoped it would, perhaps a new liberal nationalism can, permitting peoples to pursue legitimate interests as a brake upon the global economy. Tom Nairn has complained that events since 1989 have prompted no new theories to explain the resurgence of nations (Nairn 1996: 59ff.). Instead, commentators have resurrected all the old left-liberal warnings against chauvinism and fascism, using the tools of yesterday to analyse the challenges of tomorrow. But perhaps some of the even older analyses, forgotten in some quarters but still a part of the cultural record, could be of help to us now.

To explain this, I will begin with the situation I know best – and then work outward. Postcolonial theory has talked itself into a profound depression on the subject of nationalism, which it routinely accuses of inscribing into its own actions and texts all the major tyrannies of the imperial system which it promised to extirpate. So, in Irish terms, the old colonial capital of Dublin was seen as having continued to swell, even after independence, at the expense of the provinces; a compulsory version of standard Irish was beaten into schoolchildren as once a compulsory version of standard English had been imposed upon them; and British guns which had been used to suppress the 1916 Rebellion were called back by Michael Collins to quell dissident republicans.

But if the postcolony carries the after-image of empire on its retina, might not the process be more complicated? Perhaps the colony before independence might be found to have borne a proleptic image of a liberated home country. The post boxes in Dublin whose 'Victoria Regina' insignia were spray-painted green by nationalists too poor or too exhausted to imagine an alternative are often cited as an instance of postcolonial torpor. They may, however, tell a different story, for Ireland in the 1830s and 1840s had a streamlined postal system well before England. The 'laboratory theory' of history reminds us that the rulers of Westminster saw nineteenth-century Ireland as a sounding-board, a place in which intrepid experiments could be tried, a land that existed in a parabolic relation to England.[1] Some of the more successful experiments were so radical that even more than a century later they have not been fully implemented in England: the de-linking of the official connection between the Anglican church and the state, the dismantling of a feudal aristocracy, and so on. The colony was, in short, not only a site of nightmarish fears but also an anticipatory illumination of real potential, an image of a future England. George Bernard Shaw liked to joke that all Englishmen should be sent for a spell to Ireland in order to learn flexibility of mind.[2] Shaw was, of course, a reader of Marx, who had argued that Ireland was the key to revolution in Britain, since overthrow of the old paternalist aristocracy was more likely to occur in the land of the Fenians first. Far from being saved by British radicals, the Irish saw themselves as saving them. The project of inventing Ireland presupposed the task of helping the neighbouring people to reinvent the idea of England. Hence the involvement of a Land League leader like Michael Davitt in the Labour interest during the general elections in Britain. That process was reciprocal, however, indicating that it was not only among left-wing activists that the dialectic was at work. Many traditional Englanders, sensing that a pristine version of their cultural heritage (Elizabethan English and all) was still to be encountered on the other island, came over to savour its ruralist ethos and its Shakespearean speech. Some, like Wilfrid Scawen Blunt, found themselves also supporting the Land League. Ireland just might turn out to be, as Shaw liked to joke, the last spot on earth still producing the ideal Englishman of history, the freedom-loving defender of rural life (Shaw 1988: 18). Blunt saw no contradiction between his support for the Land League, which sought to expropriate landlords, and his own continuing prosperity as a landholding aristocrat in the south of England. He has been accused of misreading the political message of the Land League – but did he? After all, what followed the League's campaigns was not the communitarianism of Davitt's dream but a much more English kind of property-owning democracy. Anyway, whether Blunt's interpretation was right or wrong is scarcely important now. He is significant, rather, as an example of the emerging sort of intellectual who tried to undo the deforming effects of the British Empire (with all its energy-sapping demands for service and self-extinction) on the English folk-mind. Some of these emergent intellectuals, from William Blake to William Morris, were social radicals, while others were highly conservative Little Englanders. Nowadays, after Enoch Powell, sponsors of English nationalism tend to get a bad press, but their ideological range was broad enough to comprehend such figures as H. G. Wells, George Orwell and (in the current period) Tony Benn.

Oscar Wilde and Bernard Shaw were early exponents of this viewpoint. They considered that the strain of running an empire had left Britain a deeply distorted society. Whatever the material benefits (and they were questionable), the psychic costs were just too high. In order to harden themselves for the task of colonial administration and military coercion, the British had devalued in themselves many of those qualities of poetry, sensitivity and imagination once celebrated by a Shakespeare or a Blake (Nandy 1983: 7ff.). And the projection of despised, soft, 'feminine qualities' onto Celts or Indians had led inexorably to a diminishment of womanhood at home.

The colonial adventure had not just led to suffering overseas, but had corrupted domestic British society to the core. Worse than that, it had left the *English* with their own unresolved national question, for the motive of imperialism might not have been, after all, economic gain so much as the attempt to escape from some terrible emptiness within. In the end, the role of boredom may have been at least as important as that of wealth in setting up the imperial adventure. In that very act of escaping, some hoped to find the 'England' which had eluded them at home: but apart from the caricatures available in the writings of Noël Coward and in the operettas of Gilbert and Sullivan, few people had any clear idea as to what 'England' might mean.

Wilde and Shaw concurred that England was simply the last and most completely penetrated of all the British colonies. Their espousal of androgynous heroes and heroines may be seen as a critique of the prevailing macho-imperial styles. 'I would give Manchester back to the shepherds and Leeds to the stock-farmers', proclaimed the youthful Wilde (see Kingsmill-Moore 1930: 45), already as worried as any BBC 2 presenter about the disappearing of the English countryside. 'Home Rule for England' became Shaw's favourite slogan; and whenever he was asked by bemused Londoners for the meaning of the terrible words Sinn Féin, he told them 'It is the Irish for John Bull' (Shaw 1962: 149).

That programme of English self-recovery had a set of cultural corollaries, best outlined by W. B. Yeats. His re-reading of Shakespeare at the start of the twentieth century was based on the attempt to restore 'English' in place of a 'British' Shakespeare, one who loved the doomed Celtic complexity of Richard II and scorned the usurper Bolingbroke's merely administrative guile. If Edward Dowden had praised Shakespeare for mastering 'the logic of facts' in pursuit of the imperial theme, Yeats saw him rather as one who would never deny his own imagination for the sake of mere power. Like so many usurpers, Bolingbroke was in flight from his own emptiness 'and saw all that could be seen from very emptiness' (Yeats 1955b: 108). In his own drama, Yeats sought to recover the earlier verbal energies of the English language and the poetry of the carnivalesque. His resolve to tour London, Oxford and Cambridge with his plays was based less on a forelock-tugging desire for ratification in the great cultural centres of Britain (as nationalist detractors back in Dublin alleged) than on a thoroughly admirable ambition to unfreeze the drama of post-Victorian Britain from its torpor, by restoring to it some of the authentic energies of the English poetic drama. For he too was anxious, in inventing Ireland, to reinvent England.

This manoeuvre, initiated with Yeats's visit to Stratford-upon-Avon at the start of the twentieth century, was replicated at the century's end by A. S. Byatt, when she attempted to define an English canon of shorter narrative fiction in *The Oxford Book of English Short Stories*. By 1998 this was no longer seen as a laughable thing to want to do and most reviews of her volume were supportive, suggesting that hers was a difficult but worthwhile task (*Sunday Times* 26 April 1998, 31). The problem posed for it was that over the two preceding centuries the ideas of Englishness had been evacuated of content to provide stuffing for the notion of Britishness. Britain had become in effect a flag of convenience for English interests, but the price was that many specifically English traditions, such as the frock coat, had been accepted first as British and then, by a national expansion, as imperial-international style. Even as it puffed Englanders up, the British scheme sucked from them much of what cultural identity they achieved. English people consequently often seemed unsure of who they were or of what they represented; and that jeopardized identity, then confronted by more assured peoples, often became shrill and over-assertive. Hence the notorious violence of football fans and holiday-makers in overseas cities.

One thing that the British scheme did not dispossess England of was its cult success. As W. B. Yeats wrote in an essay after visiting Stratford-upon-Avon, 'the popular poetry of England celebrates her victories; but the popular poetry of Ireland remembers only defeats and defeated persons' (Yeats 1900: 101). By the late 1990s, and despite the shapes being thrown in the name of Cool Britannia, even that seemed to be disappearing, as devolution came to Scotland, Wales and Northern Ireland. Unnerved by all this, Ferdinand Mount, a former editor of the *Times Literary Supplement*, predicted that the Scottish National Party would in time engineer a bust-up with London, but he took some comfort in the thought that the loyalty of diverse peoples to the United Kingdom would win through in the end. Asking just how far Prime Minister Tony Blair wanted to go in Balkanizing Britain, Mount pointed somewhat persuasively to the endless interactions of Welsh, Scots, Irish and English: 'as intermarriage and work further mongrelize us, it seems an odd time to split off into separate nations after three centuries together' (*Sunday Times* 26 April 1998, 15).

But just how 'together' did these people ever manage to be? Linda Colley's *Britons: Forging the Nation 1707–1837* suggests an answer implicit in the double entendre of the word 'forge'. 'It was an invention forged above all by war' she says downrightly at the outset (Colley 1992: 5) — war against the Other that was Catholic Europe. But nowadays both the empire and the Protestant faith which gave that war-making some meaning have all but disappeared, and so the question of separate nationalism re-emerges, just as it re-emerged among the nationalities of Eastern Europe which were held formerly as part of the Soviet Union scheme. Any Irish person who marvels at the immense 'militaria' sections in British bookshops (presumably supported by people who none the less subscribe to the myth of the 'fighting Irish') can only endorse Colley's view that 'this is a culture that is used to fighting and has largely defined itself through fighting' (ibid.: 9).

Those writers of English Romanticism who objected to the imperial agenda, such as William Blake, insisted that it would be better to build a New Jerusalem 'in England's green and pleasant land'; and after the late 1780s the rebirth of England as England became a major theme of these poets (Lucas 1991: 75ff.). Many sensed that the strain of running a far-flung empire could bring down the home country. Edmund Burke suggested as much in his impeachment of Warren Hastings, and Edward Gibbon openly toyed with the analogy in his *Decline and Fall of the Roman Empire*. But fighting a common set of external enemies helped to forge a unity at home and to head off energies which might in peace-time have led to internal conflict. Perhaps

Tony Blair's devolutionary policies were an attempt to find a peace-time way of saving the union by making it more fuzzy and less abrasive at the edges. However, once let out of the bottle, the genie of devolution might, as Mount feared, have taken many people much further than they intended to go.

That was certainly the interpretation which Sinn Féin and – in all likelihood – the Irish government was banking on. There was a telling phrase in the Belfast Agreement of April 1998 which, though it went unnoticed in the British press publication, was full of implications for the future. Strand Three, Article Two, said, *inter alia*, that membership of a British-Irish Council would comprise representatives of British and Irish governments, devolved institutions in Northern Ireland, Scotland and Wales, when established, and if appropriate, elsewhere in the United Kingdom, together with representatives of the Isle of Man and the Channel Islands. The phrase 'if appropriate, elsewhere in the United Kingdom' could only have betokened some sort of home-rule government in England. Perhaps in the fullness of time Bernard Shaw and Oscar Wilde will have their wish after all.

There are signs that the British Council has already read the runes. Once fabled for its willingness to underwrite trips by visiting Irish or reggae authors under the wide umbrella of an inclusive Britishness, it has in recent years shown signs of a return to events featuring the great English tradition of Shakespeare, Milton, Blake and Shelley, safe in the knowledge that Irish or West Indian writers, or the promotion of 'cultural studies', can be safely entrusted to the literature departments of the nearest local university. Ever since 1989 the right and left have been making pitches to reclaim and redefine an idea of Englishness. Prime Minister John Major's much-documented 'lift' in 1994 of a passage from an essay by George Orwell on the theme was one kind of manifesto for a Protestant, cricket-playing village culture. Tony Benn's invocation of the Levellers and Diggers in speeches throughout the 1980s was another. Even the developing republican undertone may ultimately be connected back to the monarchy, which was apparently so secure in the later 1780s that people felt free to engage in all kinds of subversive debate. One consequence was that the Americans in the late eighteenth century came to believe that under the skin of monarchy England was a republic in all but name (Wood 1991: *passim*).

'In the theatre', said Victor Hugo, 'the mob becomes a people' (see Yeats 1955a: 461). Such a shaping of the modern democratic *polis* has been rehearsed in the dramas of England over the past half-century. If the logic of Yeats's re-reading of Shakespeare were to be carried forward and applied to some of the keynote players of modern Britain, then it might be possible to read John Osborne's *Look Back in Anger*, no less than *The Hostage* by Brendan Behan, as a postcolonial text. One could, for example, analyse that year-of-Suez drama of 1956 in the light of some of the themes adumbrated in this chapter. Jimmy Porter's late speech could then be read as climaxing in that long-postponed confrontation of the British male with his repressed feminine aspect:

> There aren't any good, brave causes left. If the big bang does come, and we all get killed off, it won't be in aid of the old-fashioned, grand design. It'll just be for the Brave New Nothing-very-much-thank-you. About as pointless and inglorious as stepping in front of a bus. No, there's nothing left for it, me boy, but to let yourself be butchered by the women. (Osborne 1966: 51)

Porter's indictment is not that the upper class is repressive, but rather that it has no remaining code of belief at all. Though seeming a dissident, he is really a frustrated traditionalist. To himself, of course, he appears as an effeminate half-man. Brave enough to admit the feminine as none of his military forebears could have done, he is none the less unnerved by that very freedom, and he seeks to ratify his jeopardized sense of his own virility in talk and acts of downright misogyny.

The diagnosis offered by Osborne is astoundingly similar to that made by D. H. Lawrence after World War I. When the attempt by soldiers at blood-brotherhood fails, one is left only (said Lawrence) with 'cocksure women and hensure men', leading to that moment when 'men lose their hold on the life-flow'. Lawrence's remedy was to flee the country on the grounds that 'England's done for... in England you can't let go.'[3] Jimmy Porter cannot leave but, in remaining, he becomes a study of what Lawrence might have become – a powerless witness of the decline of romantic England from a dynamic, open society to a packaged heritage industry. Porter's wife and her friends will stay in old cottages and visit ancient churches not because they retain any belief in traditional codes, but simply as a style option, a matter of external form. Jimmy Porter is appalled: 'Reason and progress... the old firm is selling out... all those stocks in the old free enquiry' (Osborne 1966: 38).

For all his faults, Porter sees the English past as something to learn *from*. For his wife's friends, it is something to learn *about*, something now museumized but scarcely the basis for a national future. Porter's analysis of upper-class paternalism and pusillanimity is sound enough. The problem is that he has not worked the dialectic through, and so his revolt is in the end less against the imperialism of the aristocracy than against the timidity with which its members gave the empire up. The rebel is a conservative at heart, and there are moments in the play when he voices a very personal resentment against those seductive British forces which dispossessed his generation of the idea of England:

> I think I can understand how her Daddy must have felt when he came back from India, after all those years away. The old Edwardian brigade do make their brief little world look pretty tempting. All home-made cakes and croquet, bright ideas, brighter uniforms. Still, even I regret it somehow, phoney or not. If you've no world of your own, it's rather pleasant to regret the passing of someone else's. (ibid.: 49)

The clashes between Jimmy Porter and his wife might be taken as a version of the class war disfiguring British society, after the safety valve of empire has been removed

— with the Welsh lodger Cliff cast in the role of a reluctant Celtic witness who is constantly tempted to opt out of the entire arrangement. Too young to have fought in World War II, too old to forget, Osborne's generation could never subscribe to the warlike Old Britannia described by Linda Colley. So it had no option but to look back in a kind of muffled anger on the rhetoric of a diminished empire.

One of the major themes of John Osborne's autobiography, *A Better Class of Person*, is in fact the sheer impossibility of recovering a personal or national past. England, allegedly underwritten by centuries of tradition, is depicted as a geriatric in the grip of a terminal amnesia. The famous challenge posed by E. M. Forster in an essay on racial purity is repeated: 'Can you give the names of your eight great-grandparents?' Forster had suggested that the betting would be 8–1 against and, true enough, the young Osborne never could find out who his ancestors were or what they did. All he ever got were vague anecdotes from family members who never asked the boy about himself. The autobiography (a far finer work than the plays) becomes a long protest against the conditions of its own impossibility, and against a family which, having no sense of its own nation or tradition, substituted for them a tissue of platitudes about class and empire (Osborne 1981: *passim*).

Look Back in Anger is a protest against a society in which the age of heroes has been replaced by that of the instalment plan, and in which the writing of tragedy has had to make way for farce. The struggle of a protagonist against an immovable object has given way to a struggle against a ridiculous object. What is presented is not the old revolt of the proletarian against a tyrannical aristocracy, but rather the complaint of a frustrated lower-middle class against the failure of its overlords to define any code at all, around which the community could conduct a debate about who should inherit England. Porter seeks to goad and prod his 'betters' in the hope of eliciting a response. In that sense he is a counterpart to the adolescent rebels of the pop culture of the United States in the 1950s, those rebels without a cause in open revolt against the complacency of tolerant postwar parents who had read Dr Benjamin Spock and had indulged their children after the privations of the previous decade. The style and attitude of these fifties rebels seemed radical, but the content of their ideas was deeply conservative – from James Dean to Elvis Presley they were in the great frontier tradition of Tom Sawyer, that seeming rebel who turned out upon inspection to be a super-straight.

Although beatnik males could make the breakthrough of admitting a feminine element in their personalities, whether in Jimmy Porter's long hair or in Elvis Presley's intermittent falsetto, no sooner had they done this than they were unnerved by the very freedoms they had taken; and so the woman within each of them cried out for proof that they were still, despite everything, macho and masculine. One way of asserting a jeopardized virility was to engage in acts of occasional cruelty, something found not only in Porter's behaviour but also in that of the many gangs which flourished in Anglo-American culture through the period. These acts of violence were often attempts to compel the ruling class to abandon its pusillanimity by making a clear statement of what in fact it believed. Porter, with all his references to Wordsworth, Eliot and so on, is more of a traditionalist than the aristocrats, who so easily surrender their traditions to the forces of the market. He is, in short, a conservative revolutionary. Most of Osborne's generation of 'angry young men' re-emerged in the 1980s as apologists for Margaret Thatcher (as he did himself). Nor was this a betrayal of youthful ideals: Mrs Thatcher, in fact, stood for their implementation. She represented the coming to power of an insurrectionary lower-middle class within the Tory tradition, a group deeply resentful of the paternalistic old guard who liked to fudge all issues as they kept a firm hold of their gilt-edged bonds. If Osborne's play had really been as revolutionary as people pretended, it would probably never have been staged: but he, like Mrs Thatcher three decades later, came to conclude that there no such thing as society. The nihilism at the close of *Look Back in Anger*, as the central couple regress into an infantile game of bears and squirrels, robbed the play of much of its power: yet in that refusal to believe or assert anything lay a desperate kind of hope, captured by Kenneth Tynan when he wrote: 'One cannot imagine Jimmy Porter listening with a straight face to speeches about our inalienable right to flog Cypriot schoolboys' (Tynan 1961: 57).

The commercial success of Osborne's play had one important effect: it encouraged writers who might have thought of a career in film or television to try their hand at drama. Yet the underlying lesson in *Look Back in Anger* proved true: the more things seemed to change, the more they remained the same. The very success of writers from the 'lower' classes afforded them places in an English establishment which had long enjoyed a reputation for assimilating clever scholarship boys and girls. So the upper-middle class found it relatively easy to tame most of the Angry Young Men and to transform their bitterest attacks into pleasing entertainments.

There was one exception to all this, however, in the next generation: *The Romans in Britain* (1980) by Howard Brenton seemed to resist all attempts at domestication. This drama set out to empty the word 'Britain' of its residual content. It implied an equation between the Roman rape of ancient Britain and the contemporary conduct of the British army in Northern Ireland. That such a critique of British policy should have been enacted on the boards of the National Theatre in London added insult to injury. It was as if in the year 1920 a play extolling the Black-and-Tans had been staged on the boards of the Abbey Theatre in Dublin.

Brenton clearly exposed the paradox of all empires. Their sponsors, supposed to represent the higher home types, are more often the dregs of the ruling country, or else the wily careerists in search of a promotion. So even the class system of the home country serves as a potent weapon in recruiting the more affluent imperialists. There is one difference between Rome and Britain in the play, however. Caesar ostensibly defers to an incompetent upper-class legate, while privately arranging to have him bumped off, whereas the British army permits the deranged but aristocratic Major Thomas Chichester to pursue a disastrous private war in South Armagh. The Romans, it turns out, were less hobbled by an idiotic class system than the British. That ancient Britain invaded by the Romans seems to be a patchwork quilt of warring fiefdoms, to which the outsiders bring the notion of a single administration – precisely the benefit which the English have claimed to bring to Ireland. Thus, the very nationalist notion of a united Ireland turns out to have been a British rather than an Irish invention, just as the notion of a British imperialism was itself derived from that Roman empire-building which first worked to unite the British in opposition to it.

There is a large-scale irony underlying Brenton's play: the parallel between Romans and Britons is not of his making but had been implicit for decades in a public-school system of education which emphasized the study of Latin as character-forming. The stock justification for this was that Latin provided the basis for the systems of many modern languages: but there was often a deeper agenda. This was the desire to implant in schoolboys an administrative-imperial mentality, developed through the study of Caesar's writings of the Gallic War; and so on. The use of Roman numerals to describe a school XI or XV; the nomenclature of Smith minor or Smith major; the SPQR mentality of the Roman legionary was all-pervasive. Here is an extract from L. A. Wilding's introduction to *A Latin Course for Schools: Part One*:

> By a knowledge of Latin we are introduced to a great people, the Romans. The Romans led the world as men of action; they built good roads, made good laws, and organized what was in their time almost world-wide government and citizenship. At their best, too, they set the highest standards of honour, loyalty and self-sacrifice. (Wilding 1949: vi)

What was elided in such texts was the barbarism which Brenton chose to centralize. However, exercise 65 in Wilding's textbook almost gives the game away, via Tacitus, as Agricola moves towards Scotland: 'at first he wastes the land; then he displays to the natives his moderation' (ibid.: 63).

The unspoken assumption of L. A. Wilding was that in the 1800 years between the Roman and British empires, nothing of commensurate value had befallen western civilization. The constant references in Brenton's play to pretty arses on men provides a context for that scene of homosexual rape which led to a prosecution by Mrs Mary Whitehouse on grounds of 'gross indecency'; but the link implied with the public schools was obvious to all. The main implied equation is, however, with Ireland – stone-throwing British children in Act I become Northern Irish attackers of the British army in Act II; both groups of soldiers build water closets everywhere they go; the Celtic villagers who have never set eyes on a Roman become the Irish farmers who have yet to meet a British soldier; and so on.

Brenton's thesis is deeply troubling: that beneath this thin Roman overlay the British are more fundamentally Celtic in their origins – just like their current enemies in the Irish Republican Army. If imperialism succeeds in turning former enemies into current doubles, then it may also happen that current enemies were former doubles. Such a point is made repeatedly by Thomas Chichester to his comrades: 'It's Celts we're fighting in Ireland. We won't get anywhere till we know what that means. King Arthur was a Celtic warlord! Who fought twelve great battles against the Saxons. That is, us.' And then the clincher: 'If King Arthur walked out of those traces, now – know what he'd look like to us? One more fucking mick' (Brenton 1980: 75).

True enough: but an Irish playwright might have suggested that the converse could also be true. Sinn Féin leaders with names like Adams and Morrison had genealogies which in all likelihood evoked not a Celtic past but Cromwell's invading soldiery. Yet Brenton chose not to make that point, preferring to stress the steady course of the Celtic past through all subsequent British and Irish presents. It didn't require much imagination to find in a figure such as Brac, dyeing his hair three different colours, a precursor of contemporary British street punks; or to equate the relish with which Brac pulverizes and kills an enemy before a night of heavy drinking with the behaviour of the lager louts of the 1980s. If traits thought peculiar to one race can be found on inspection among their enemies, then Brenton must face the possibility that nationalism itself is a sham. The English and Irish elements in Thomas Chichester cancel one another out, leaving him a madman, devoid of any culture. The Irishman at the play's end may contest the right of the English to be on Irish soil; but that play itself opened with two Irishmen cheerfully offering 'Greek wine from Ireland' as they made their murderous trek across England. No wonder that Brenton might ask his audience to consider the possibility that the very source of British identity was a king who never was.

Not that Brenton can leave it at that. As a radical, he rejects the idea of the native's irretrievable 'otherness', insisting instead that the natives are 'us', the audience of Britons at the National Theatre. So the ancient Britons in the play are repeatedly called 'wogs', 'niggers' and 'nig-nogs' – all terms of abuse resorted to by members of the British National Party. What will the audience at a national theatre do when it learns that the Irish, far from being the barbarians at the gate, may be England's alter ego? Those neurotics who once defined the Irish as the opposite of all things English will have to rethink.

Some accused Brenton of being over-anxious to dismantle a British nationalism but unwilling to subject Irish nationalism to an equally stringent critique. In fact, Brenton portrayed the Irish (especially women) as no less bloodthirsty than their enemies. Nevertheless, he did allow a sort of glamour to the Irish side. In the play they have a cultural code in which they steadfastly believe, one that gives their lives coherence, whereas the members of the British army do not. Brenton may have been setting his face less against national essences than against imperial ideas. It was the *British* scheme which he wished to drain of meaning, the better to make way for an English nation sufficiently at ease with itself not to want to run other people's affairs. The lesson was that already taught by Claude Lévi-Strauss: our own system is the only one we can reform without destroying.

The increasing vogue for Irish plays, as well as Irish subjects, in the London theatre after Brenton's controversial drama was due in part to a remarkable theatrical revival among Irish authors. But the premiering of many of these plays in the English capital

– such as Frank McGuinness's *Mutabilitie* in 1988 – allowed audiences to approach their own deferred national question from a safe remove. Once again, Irish culture existed in a kind of parabolic relation to England's; once again, the Irish in renovating their own consciousness were also helping, wittingly or unwittingly, to reanimate England's.

Englishness surely needs redefining. It is a mark of how sunk beneath the level of consciousness it now is that in large tracts of the world people entirely miss the element of parody in a comic-opera song like 'He is an Englishman' or the drawing-room plays of Oscar Wilde. Those works which are known to be parodic, such as the lyrics of Noël Coward, have been esteemed among formerly colonized peoples for what are at best dubious reasons: they allow people to laugh gently at Englishness, while also reassuring them that as an act it is hilariously easy to mimic. But what is mimicked is not Englishness so much as an unconvincing, unconvinced imitation of those higher home types who never really existed. The postcolonial diagnosis which Douglas Hyde reported from Ireland and Homi Bhabha from India may now be found to trouble the citizens of London and Manchester themselves, for they are now making the painful discovery that to be anglicized is not at all the same thing as to be English (see Hyde 1894: 87ff.; Bhabha 1994: *passim*).

The inner history of England will be found eventually elsewhere – not in a people given to play-acting (was it really *Englishmen* who went out in the midday sun?) but in a community who were, and remain, rather suspicious of play-actors. These are the people of whom E. P. Thompson and Christopher Hill, A. S. Byatt and E. M. Forster have written so well, the ones who (in Thompson's telling phrase) need saving from the enormous condescension of posterity (Thompson 1968: 13). Whether they also need saving from the enormous condescension of those Irish who tried to help them to help themselves is another matter. But it should be said that the project sketched by Shaw and Wilde in no way militates against a multicultural society. Since all identity is dialogic, 'England' is more likely to achieve a satisfying definition in endless acts of negotiation with those of other identities, not just Irish and Welsh, but Indian and Trinidadian too. In that way, England might once again become truly interesting to the English.

Notes

1 For an exemplary application of the parabolic interpretation, see the writings of Gearóid Ó Tuathaigh, especially (1972) *Ireland Before the Famine 1798–1848*. Dublin: Gill and Macmillan.

2 Quoted by Michael Holroyd (1976). 'GBS and Ireland', *Sewanee Review* LXXXIV, 41.

3 See for the first quotation D. H. Lawrence (1979). *Selection from Phoenix*, ed. A. A. H. Inglis. Harmondsworth: Penguin, 373–4; and for the second D. H. Lawrence (1969). *Women in Love*. Harmondsworth: Penguin, 341.

Primary reading

Brenton, Howard (1980). *The Romans in Britain*. London: Methuen. (The first major revival of this play occurred at the Crucible, Sheffield, in February 2006.)

Osborne, John (1966). *Look Back in Anger*. London: Faber and Faber.

Osborne, John (1981). *A Better Class of Person*. London: Methuen.

Rushdie, Salman (1988). *The Satanic Verses*. London: Viking.

Shaw, George Bernard (1962) in David H. Green and Dan H. Laurence (eds.). *The Matter with Ireland*. London: Hart-David, 33–42.

Shaw, George Bernard (1988). *John Bull's Other Island*. Harmondsworth: Penguin.

Yeats, W. B. (1900). 'The Literary Movement in Ireland' in Lady Gregory (ed.). *Ideals in Ireland*. London: Batsford, 85–90.

Yeats, W. B. (1955a). *Autobiographies*. London: Macmillan.

Yeats, W. B. (1955b). *Essays and Introductions*. London: Macmillan.

Further reading

Bhabha, Homi K. (1994). *The Location of Culture*. London: Routledge.

Colley, Linda (1992). *Britons: Forging the Nation 1707–1837*. New Haven: Yale University Press.

Hyde, Douglas (1894). 'The Necessity for Deanglicizing Ireland' in Charles Gavan Duffy (ed.). *The Revival of Irish Literature*. London: A. P. Warr, 89–128.

Kiberd, Declan (1995). *Inventing Ireland*. London: Jonathan Cape.

Kingsmill-Moore, T. C. (1930). *Reminiscences and Reflections*. London: Methuen.

Lucas, John (1991). *England and Englishness*. London: Jonathan Cape.

Nairn, Tom (1996). *Faces of Nationalism*. London: Verso.

Nandy, Ashis (1983). *The Intimate Enemy; Loss and Recovery of Self Under Colonialism*. Bombay: Oxford University Press.

Rutherford, John (1997). *Forever England*. London: Lawrence and Wishart.

Thompson, E. P. (1968). *The Making of the English Working Class*. Harmondsworth: Penguin.

Tynan, Kenneth (1961). *Curtains*. London: Longman.

Wilding, L. A. (1949). *A Latin Course for Schools: Part One*. London: Methuen.

Wood, Gordon S. (1991). *The Radicalism of the American Revolution*. New York: Vintage.

3

Ibsen in the English Theatre in the *Fin de Siècle*

Katherine Newey

Henrik Ibsen (1828–1906) is an equivocal figure in the history of the English theatre of the twentieth and twenty-first centuries.[1] On the one hand, his work was championed by a select group of English and Irish critics and theatre practitioners at the vanguard of the 'New Drama' from the 1880s. On the other hand, he became an accepted and even canonical playwright in the English repertoire quickly, and with this acceptance came a concomitant diminution of awareness of Ibsen's aesthetic and social theatrical innovation. In the English theatre, Ibsen's work has come to stand for a certain type of dramaturgical, aesthetic and political approach to the theatre and theatricality; to stand, too easily perhaps, as a metonymic reference to that most complex of theatrical phenomena, the representation of 'the real' on the stage. And in tracing the adoption of Ibsen's work on the London stage it is possible to see how the radical potential of his work, recognized by his early advocates, was lost in the absorption of his naturalist dramaturgy into the English theatrical vocabulary. So uncontentious did Ibsen's works become in the English theatre that by 1930, Harley Granville Barker could look back on the Ibsen controversies of the 1880s and 1890s and comment that 'The theatre that would have none of him soon found itself setting out to emulate him' (Postlewait 1986: 131). Put simply, against all the early signs of his first shocking impact in England in the late nineteenth century, Ibsen became a canonical figure, considered by the subsequent generations of avant-garde artists to be 'a fuddy-duddy old realist who never truly became modern'.[2] This transformation of the reputation and treatment of Ibsen tells us much about English theatre history and the ways in which it has been constructed.

The process of Ibsen's reception, adaptation, and acceptance into the mainstream of the English theatre, and his subsequent reputation – shuttled between the avant-garde and the mainstream of English theatre – is significant, not only for the influence of the plays themselves, but also for what it reveals about some underlying assumptions in mainstream English theatre practice. The introduction of Ibsen's work to the English theatre emphasizes the central place of realism and naturalism on the English stage and in native English theatrical conventions and traditions, but also points to the varieties of realism embraced by that term. In looking at the transformation of Ibsen from the creator of *Ghosts* (London premiere 1891) – famously described by Clement Scott as 'a wretched, deplorable, loathsome history'[3] – into the playwright whose work underpins the English 'well-made' play (from the French *pièce bien faite*) of the twentieth century, what is striking is the endurance of a particular approach to the representation of the 'real world' on the stage. Raymond Williams identifies the emergence of English realism with the bourgeois drama of the eighteenth century, arguing that by the late nineteenth century, marked by the arrival of Ibsen's plays in English, 'a new major form' is established by the convergence of the secular, the contemporary and the 'socially extended' – that is, the view that serious action was not limited to people of rank.[4] Ibsen's plays were absorbed into the theatrical mainstream so readily because his dramaturgy speaks to this sense of the 'native' or 'ethnic' English concern with dramatizations of the contemporary, the bourgeois (and increasingly the - domestic), and the feeling individual of bourgeois social status, set against a background of recognizable social realism. This ethnic dramaturgy is intertwined with English theatre history and historiography – that is, by what we deem worthy of recording as history, and how we process and construct that history. So this chapter is as much a discussion of the cultural politics of the introduction of Ibsen to the English stage as it is a performance history or literary analysis of his plays.

The standard narrative of English theatre is of a theatre profession, a set of theatrical practices and aesthetic doctrines which are held to be inevitably inclined towards naturalism, or more broadly, towards literal and material stage representations of the world off-stage. This narrative was relatively fixed in English theatre practice and commentary in the 1820s, and by the time of Ibsen's death in 1906 was accepted as orthodoxy.[5] It is a teleological narrative of dramaturgy, performance style, and production and industrial practices which focuses on the development of English theatre towards realist staging, naturalistic performance styles through internalized and psychological representations of dramatic character, and play texts that embodied high-cultural 'literary' qualities, rather than visual spectacle. It is class-based and class-bound, and it leaves out more of English (and British) theatrical culture than it includes. And yet, it was a narrative powerful enough to appropriate one of the most shocking and radical European writers of the 1870s and 1880s, writing in the minority language of Norwegian, probing bourgeois social values and behaviours, into the English ethnic tradition. Concomitantly, the emphasis on Ibsen's social dramas in English has obscured other areas of his work – his poetry, and his visionary and mythical dramas.

Early Versions of Ibsen in England

Almost uniquely for a European playwright at this time, Ibsen's plays were caught up in a series of cultural and aesthetic campaigns in their first translations into English.

In Britain in the 1870s and 1880s, Ibsen's plays were variously enlisted in the theatrical, literary and political campaigns of the avant-garde. Edmund Gosse's early translations of Ibsen's poetry, and his critical writing on Ibsen from 1872, proclaimed Ibsen as a satirical writer, in protest against the 'cowardly egotism' and 'exalted sentiment' of his 'too-sensitive nation'.[6] The first translators of Ibsen's plays into English, Catherine Ray and Henrietta Frances Lord, were more or less motivated by what they interpreted as Ibsen's feminism. Eleanor Marx (daughter of Karl Marx) and her partner, Edward Aveling, claimed his work for the socialist-feminist cause. Havelock Ellis's interest in Ibsen as a critic of 'the conventional lies which are regarded as the foundations of social domestic life' (Egan 1972: 73) is of a piece with Ellis's other work as a progressive social critic and controversialist in matters of sexuality. William Archer, the theatre critic and activist most clearly identified with Ibsen and the 'Ibsen campaign' in England in the 1880s and 1890s, incorporated his support of Ibsen into his overall campaign for the reform and renovation of the English stage. George Bernard Shaw, with Archer the other prominent 'Ibsenite' in Britain, promoted Ibsen's plays as part of his wide-ranging critical and dramatic onslaughts against late Victorian conventionalities. While Archer's published critical judgements of translations, productions and play scripts were carefully measured and placed within his overriding concern for the reform of English drama and theatre, the energy of Shaw's advocacy in the 1890s swept Ibsen's plays into more general debates, tending to focus contemporary response on the shocking ideas Ibsen apparently advocated, rather than his dramaturgy.

Many of these 'Ibsenites' had little else in common than their championing of Ibsen's work, but this use of Ibsen's plays to promote other interests and campaigns in the late nineteenth and early twentieth centuries was typical of the way his plays were first introduced into the English theatre of the *fin de siècle*. And this tendency for Ibsen's plays to be picked up by British cultural and literary radical elites, to be used for political and aesthetic causes which may indeed have been ones Ibsen himself was not committed to (as was the case with his ambivalence over women's suffrage), is one of the intriguing features of Ibsen's place in any account of 'Modern British and Irish Drama'.[7] That it was Ibsen, not his near-contemporaries Gerhart Hauptmann or August Strindberg, or slightly later writers such as Anton Chekhov, Frank Wedekind or early Bertolt Brecht, whose work was taken up in this way is again to do with what English theatre practitioners and cultural activists (and only much later, theatre audiences) found in his work. As I argue below, what they found in Ibsen was a questioning and radical social thinker, grounding his social critiques in the drawing rooms, behaviour and language of the *fin de siècle* middle class, with all its anxieties about money, status and sex.

Edmund Gosse was the first English critic to comment on Ibsen's work, introducing him as the foremost contemporary Norwegian writer in both poetry and drama. Gosse's critical essays on Ibsen's poetry and *Peer Gynt* in the early 1870s (Egan 1972: 41–50) were part of his general interest in modern literature from continental Europe, particularly literature which answered to the new mood for the combination of poetry and acute social observation. Although Gosse was Ibsen's earliest proselytiser, he did not offer translations of Ibsen's writing. It is Gosse, Archer and Shaw who are now credited with the introduction of Ibsen into English, but it was largely women writers who were active in making early English translations of Ibsen's plays, and doggedly promoting Ibsen as a playwright of great importance for contemporary English theatre. Catherine Ray, Henrietta Lord (signing herself Frances Lord) and Eleanor Marx all made significant early translations of Ibsen's plays, and circulated Ibsen's work in London's intellectual and artistic circles. What is notable here is that the adoption of Ibsen's work started slowly and took some time. The first translation of Ibsen's drama into English was Ray's translation of *Emperor and Galilean* in 1876. This was followed four years later by Archer's adaptation of *The Pillars of Society* as *Quicksands*, which was produced as a matinée in December 1880 at the Gaiety Theatre. In Archer's own words, the perform- ance 'fell perfectly flat' (Woodfield 1984: 37), although an unsigned review in the *Theatre* records that the play was 'tentatively produced and fairly successful' (Egan 1972: 55–6), and Egan notes that a Copenhagen newspaper reported that the author was called for by an enthusiastic audience. William Archer took that curtain call as Ibsen's English translator (Egan 1972: 55–6). In 1884, Henry Arthur Jones's and Henry Herman's very loose adaptation of *A Doll's House* as *Breaking a Butterfly* failed,[8] and it was not until 1889 that Janet Achurch's and Charles Carrington's production of *A Doll's House* combined comparative commercial success with artistic integrity of translation and production.

Although, as Postlewait documents in *Prophet of the New Drama*, Archer became the central mover in the 'Ibsen campaign', Marx, Ray and Lord served Ibsen well. Their persistence introduced his work to an influential group of London intellectuals who began to see the potential of the theatre for circulating ideas for social change (Stokes 1972: 3).[9] Their early translations of Ibsen's plays into English carried particularly heavy weight in anxious debates about the relationship between the sexes in the 1870s and 1880s. Of a number of continental European writers whose new techniques or subject matter made an impact in Britain, Ibsen's work was rapidly appropriated into specifically English debates over gender which bubbled up into the 'New Woman' movement in the 1880s and 1890s, and as a preface to the renewed campaign for female suffrage in the early decades of the twentieth century. As Shepherd-Barr argues, the English identification of Ibsen's playwriting with New Woman literature was unique in Europe (Shepherd-Barr 1997: 29), and the engagement of women – and activist feminist women at that – is a significant part of the Ibsen story in England, and important for his subsequent reputation. Arguably, it was the connections Ibsen's plays drew between money, status, men and women – and more particularly the position of women in modernity – which first attracted English translators and producers of Ibsen.

A brief public debate between Frances Lord and William Archer over Lord's trans- lation of *A Doll's House* is an example of women's active interventions in the 'Ibsen campaign'. Lord's translation, titled *Nora,* first appeared in the avant-garde journal *To-Day* in 1882, and was then published independently with a long preface which included her analysis of the play as a contemporary essay about marriage. As soon as 'a great and popular poet' writes about marriage, she writes, 'we see how little woman's own voice has been heard in other poetry'.[10] Lord's approach in her analysis of the play is feminist and theoretical, looking chiefly at the play's arguments about the inadequacies of late nineteenth-century bourgeois marriage. However, her time spent living in Scandinavia gave her a clear sense of the controversy caused by the play on its first performance, and she later defended her principles of translating as formed by what actors might find playable on the stage. Lord's translation was the subject of some decidedly territorial sparring with Archer; in a review of Lord's translation in the *Academy* (1883), Archer accuses 'the lady who has attempted an English version of *Et Dukkehjem*' of having neither good enough Norwegian nor good enough English to 'reproduce the crispness and spontaneity of the dialogue', going on to 'suspect' that the translation was made from a Swedish translation of the original Norwegian (Egan 1972: 61–2). Lord replied briefly the following week, insisting that she had worked from the Norwegian original, and her dramaturgical practices were undertaken 'for the practical convenience of actors' (Egan 1972: 63). Over the quality of Lord's dialogue, Archer may well have had a point: unlike Archer, whose connections in the theatre profession gave him access to knowledgeable actors and producers for the staging of his translations, Lord wrote into a vacuum, although her work was instrumental in starting to create the knowledgeable audience of spectators and readers of Ibsen.

Rejane rehearsing for a Paris production of Ibsen's *A Doll's House*, *Tidende* 4 June 1894. Courtesy of Mary Evans Picture Library.

My aim here is not to weigh the merits of the various translations of Ibsen for their accuracy or dramatic quality, but rather to identify the cultural work done by the feminist-sponsored appearance of Ibsen's plays in London in the mid-1880s. What I find interesting about Archer's critique of Lord is the difference in each writer's assumptions about the end and purpose of their translations. Lord's emphasis is on the play as a script for performance (however remote she was from the theatre profession), and on performance as a direct intervention in the current state of relations between middle-class men and women. Archer is more concerned with introducing Ibsen as a 'prophet of the New Drama' (to use Postlewait's phrase), and protecting a literary approach to Ibsen founded on the principles of textual and aesthetic fidelity. His protectionism is of a piece with other campaigns for the advancement of the English drama which, as Simon Shepherd and Peter Womack argue, constituted a push to professionalize playwriting in the 1880s in order to exclude certain types of writers and plays (Shepherd and Womack 1996: *passim*).[11] Archer's enthusiasm for Ibsen is put to work as a prescriptive model for an improved English (literary) drama and (realist) staging practice, as opposed to Marx and Lord's broader interest in Ibsen's plays as vehicles for social change, and as vehicles for female performers. In the hands of the reformers of the drama and advocates of Ibsen such as Archer and Shaw, the work of these first female translators and promoters of Ibsen was set aside, and subsequent histories have continued this invisibility. The effect of Archer's promotion of Ibsen, in particular, was to establish a version of Ibsen in Britain mediated through Archer's preference for the well-made play, and as Errol Durbach argues, Archer's attraction to Ibsen was mainly as 'the champion of a fundamentally well-made form of Realism' (McFarlane 1994: 235). Ibsen's poetic and epic dramas, such as *Peer Gynt* (Christiana/Oslo, 1876; Edinburgh, 1908) or *John Gabriel Borkmann* (Berlin, 1897; London, 1897), have always figured less significantly in British Ibsenism.

Eleanor Marx and Ibsen

There has recently been an upsurge of interest in Eleanor Marx as a key figure in several intersecting circles of late nineteenth-century British intellectual life.[12] Her role as a champion of Ibsen was an active expression of her feminist theories and practices and her general belief in the importance of art at the centre of political activity, and in the political meanings to be found in contemporary art. Inviting Havelock Ellis to a reading of Lord's translation of *A Doll's House* in her Bloomsbury home, Marx wrote that 'I feel I *must* do something to make people understand our Ibsen a little more than they do, and I know by experience that a play read to them often affects people more than when read by themselves.'[13] Marx's letter to Ellis in 1886 is typical of the appropriation and adaptation of Ibsen into contemporary English campaigns for social and political change. But it is also an explicit acknowledgement of the power of live performance to promote ideas through powerfully emotional and affective art, a feature of English realist drama throughout the nineteenth century. Marx staged the play literally in her drawing room, with a cast of socialist luminaries. Marx played Nora to her husband's Torvald, May Morris (William Morris's daughter) played Kristine Linde, and George Bernard Shaw was cast as Krogstad. This cast list alone highlights the personal connections upon which political and intellectual networks in London were founded, and the interconnections between radical politics and avant-garde art in the late nineteenth century.

If this drawing-room production of a play about the necessity of leaving such claustrophobic spaces had an impact on a small circle of bohemian intellectuals, then several later events in which Marx was the driving force put the plays of Ibsen in front of a much wider audience. The first, in 1888, was Havelock Ellis's 1888 edition of three Ibsen plays: *The Pillars of Society* (translated by Archer), *Ghosts* (Archer's translation adapted from Lord's translation) and *An Enemy of Society* (Eleanor Marx's version, better known now as *An Enemy of the People*). This volume was seen by Ibsenites then, and historians now, as marking the arrival of Ibsen's work in the English literary consciousness; not least because, as Tracy Davis points out, the availability of Ibsen in a good and affordable reading edition made his work accessible to many – an observation based on sales of over 14,000 in the first years of the volume's publication (Davis 1985: 21). In a preface which extends well beyond the three plays he presents, Havelock Ellis divides Ibsen's work into three categories: his 'Historical and Legendary Dramas', his 'Dramatic Poems' and his 'Social Dramas';[14] but Ellis explains that he has selected the plays for this first volume of 'adequately presented' translations because they are 'the most remarkable of his social dramas' (ix). Ellis argues that in these plays, Ibsen applies the powerful imaginative drive evident in his poetic plays such as *Peer Gynt* to issues of contemporary significance: 'an eager insistence that the social environment shall not cramp the reasonable freedom of the individual, together with a passionate hatred of all those conventional lies which are commonly regarded as "the pillars of society" ' (xviii). This is clearly an Ibsen who resonates with the urgent desire for the reorganization of personal and public lives to free them from convention advocated by Ellis, Marx and other radical intellectuals of the *fin de siècle*.

The lasting impression of Ibsen's work in performance in Britain was created by the first public season of one of his plays in London: Charles Carrington's and Janet Achurch's production of *A Doll's House* in 1889. Again, Marx was instrumental in getting this play in front of an audience – she and Achurch approached Henry Irving for a subsidy of £100 to stage a comedy, *Clever Alice*. Instead, Marx and Achurch staged the first professional production of *A Doll's House*, at the Novelty Theatre. Irving saw the production, and according to his grandson, commented that 'If that's the sort of thing she wants to play she'd better play it somewhere else.'[15] With the help of Irving's hundred pounds, the production was a critical success, attracting what Sally Ledger calls 'a dazzling array of bohemians and intellectuals [. . .] an "alternative" and highly politicized audience' and a 'roll-call of New Women', and its short season lost 'only' £70.[16] The production would have run longer if Achurch and Carrington had not had a

commitment to tour Australasia, where they continued performing *A Doll's House*.
Marx, following pioneers Ray and Lord, was joined by Marion Lea, Janet Achurch and
Elizabeth Robins, who between them developed a series of strong and commercially
viable productions of Ibsen's plays – principally *Hedda Gabler* (Munich, 1891; London,
1891), *Ghosts* (Chicago, 1882; London, 1891) and *Little Eyolf* (Berlin, 1895; London,
1896) – around central and charismatic female performers.[17] While Ibsen's plays moved
into the mainstream of commercial production by the early twentieth century, assimilated into the English traditions of the 'well-made play', focus on this early translation
and production history by feminist women usefully reminds us of the radical and
oppositional potential of the English realist tradition.

Ibsen and Realism in the History of the English Theatre

Perhaps the high point for the 'Ibsen campaign' was 1891, when four new produc-
tions of Ibsen's plays were presented in London in the first half of the year.[18] In
January, there was a revival of *A Doll's House*, followed by productions of *Rosmersholm*
(Vaudeville Theatre, London), *Ghosts* (Royalty Theatre, London), *Hedda Gabler*
(Vaudeville Theatre, London) and *The Lady from the Sea* (Terry's Theatre, London)
(Shepherd-Barr 1997: 29). The potentially problematic content of *Ghosts* for the censors
– particularly its references to venereal disease, however veiled – was avoided in this first
season by J. T. Grein's organization of his Independent Theatre as a private club.
However, by 1896, when Lea's and Robins's production of *Little Eyolf*, starring Mrs
Patrick Campbell as the Rat Wife, attracted good audiences, the production of Ibsen no
longer caused the acerbic public commentaries triggered by *Ghosts* five years earlier;
indeed, in 1897, Shaw speculated on what Queen Victoria's thoughts might have been
had she seen the revival of *Ghosts* at the Independent Theatre during her Jubilee
celebrations (Egan 1972: 378–83). By the time of Ibsen's death in 1906 it seemed that
his plays had ceased to outrage audiences, or offer theatre practitioners quite the same
sense of new discovery as twenty years earlier. In the first decades of the twentieth
century, those practitioners whom Frederick Marker and Lise-Lone Marker call the 'new
Modernists', such as Edward Gordon Craig, Max Reinhardt and Vsevolod Meyerhold,
'shared [an] anti-naturalistic determination to present a heightened conceptual image
of the inner thematic [. . .] spirit of the work at hand, rather than a photographic
reduplication of its surface reality'.[19] The Markers go on to discuss a number of
key 'new modernist' productions of Ibsen in continental Europe staged by Craig and
others, but critical and historiographical narratives of English drama move elsewhere,
away from the emphasis on 'surface reality' of Ibsen's dramaturgy which had been
so shocking a half-generation earlier. Notwithstanding the introduction of Ibsen
onto the English stage through a feminist and socially engaged frame, the radical
potential of late nineteenth-century naturalist and realist approaches to theatrical
representation were quickly superseded by the modernist avant-garde. Although the

early twentieth-century avant-garde answered Ezra Pound's admonition to 'Make it new!' in many different ways,[20] they shared a common practice in the rejection of previous bourgeois art practices. The dominant unifying principle of an otherwise heterogeneous movement was, so Huyssen argues, its construction as 'a reaction formation'.[21] Ibsen had become an 'old' modernist – or perhaps reconsidered as never really a modernist at all, as Moi protests has been his fate since, in what she identifies as the profoundly anti-theatrical nature of modernist aesthetics and criticism (Moi 2004: 249).

Perhaps Ibsen's plays were so readily set aside from the main tradition of the aesthetic and political avant-garde in the twentieth century because so much of his work is able to be interpreted within the frames of nineteenth-century theatrical practices and aesthetics. As I mentioned earlier, Raymond Williams has identified a substantial tradition of bourgeois drama in English theatre. Once the controversial content of his plays, with their frank introduction of the consequences of adultery, syphilis, fraud, divorce and separation, are set aside, it is clear to see how comfortably Ibsen sits within the English traditions of bourgeois drama and melodrama, and the well-made play. Eric Bentley argues passionately that Ibsen needed 'the highly theatrical, and yes, highly artificial dramaturgy of the French well-made play'.[22] Indeed, Étienne Sardou and Eugène Scribe used much the same sort of material as Ibsen (adultery, disease, fraud, infidelity) in plays which were widely translated, adapted and produced throughout Britain. The 'New Drama' of Arthur Wing Pinero and the later plays of Henry Arthur Jones drew heavily on the technical and formulaic structure of the well-made play, with its plot generally centred on a secret known to the audience but hidden from most of the characters, causing misunderstandings which are obvious to the audience. In the well-made play, stage business is organized around deliberately timed exits and entrances, and the plot is built up through carefully calibrated suspense and the deliberately complex intertwining of characters' stories and sub-plots, which are all mechanically unpicked in the play's denouement. Of course, Ibsen does not always tell the audience the 'secret' at the heart of the play – is Hedda pregnant? – but a thinking audience could guess at the scandal of inherited venereal disease in *Ghosts*, or the subtle blend of coercive sensuality and ignorance at the centre of the Helmers' marriage which causes Nora to leave.

Ibsen's concern with contemporary issues, explored through the staging of ordinary life (two of the three key features of Williams's definition of English realism), was not new to the English stage. Concern with contemporary social issues combined with heightened theatricality in visual staging, plotting, characterization, and the playing of extremes of emotion could well be a quick summary of the defining characteristics of melodrama, particularly the native 'domestic drama' so popular across Britain from the 1820s. There is a discernible trajectory to be traced in the popular theatre from the domestic melodramas of Douglas Jerrold or John Baldwin Buckstone in the 1820s and 1830s, to the sensation melodramas of Dion Boucicault, C. H. Hazlewood, and the many adaptations of the sensation novels of Wilkie Collins, Mary Braddon and Mrs Wood in the 1850s and 1860s, to the fashion for Sardou at the end of the century, lampooned by Shaw as 'Sardoodledom'. In this context, Ibsen's plays, with their complex plots, drawing spectators into an intense engagement with the morality of his characters' behaviour, and their interactions within the enclosures of the bourgeois home, ending with a simple but deliberate and shocking action – the slamming of a door, the suicidal shot of a pistol – sit well within the English tradition of melodrama. The fact that Ibsen's plays are distinct from run-of-the-mill melodramas because he was never content with denouements according to conventional morality has tended to overshadow just what his dramaturgy shared with the mainstream of English popular theatre; but it his common ground with this vernacular tradition which has enabled Ibsen's scripts to have been adapted and translated so that they seem literally to have been absorbed into the English ethnic tradition, as if Ibsen were an *English* Victorian writer, writing in the imperializing English language, and not the little-known Norwegian tongue, for the bourgeois theatres of the West End and regional repertories of Britain, rather than the cosmopolitan theatres of Europe.

Ibsen as a Canonical Writer in English-Language Theatre

As I write this, I'm remembering the productions of Ibsen's plays I've seen over the years, and the variety of ways his plays are now produced and adapted. I've seen *Peer Gynt* in English, in French, and as a ballet in Germany. I remember a Festival of Sydney production of *Hedda Gabler* in 1991 set in the New Zealand of the 1950s, which used disquieting and disjunctive staging techniques to suggest the parallels between women's experiences of social incarceration in late nineteenth-century Norway and mid-twentieth-century New Zealand.[23] I missed seeing Cate Blanchett as Hedda in Sydney in 2004 (just as I will probably miss this same production in New York, planned for 2006). However, I did manage to see Judy Davis in the same role in the same theatre in 1986, and Amanda Donohue playing Hedda in a bird-cage of a set in the round at the Royal Exchange Theatre, Manchester. And as I write, Eve Best is playing in Richard Eyre's production in London's West End. This litany of casting suggests that *Hedda Gabler* and *A Doll's House* are still prime vehicles for powerful female stars in the international English-speaking theatre market, just as when Achurch and Carrington first toured Ibsen in Britain and Australasia, and Elizabeth Robins reshaped her career by playing Ibsen's heroines in London and New York. Recently, the West Yorkshire Playhouse production of *A Doll's House* (March, 2005) featured black British actor Tanya Moodie as Nora, in a production which combined twenty-first-century minimalist staging with the detailed replication of late nineteenth-century dress, albeit in the same monochrome palette as the set. The colour-blind casting, although generally not commented upon by critics, offered interesting connections between late nineteenth-century anxieties about gender roles and early twenty-first-century concerns about racial identity. Ibsen's harnessing of the power of theatre to *embody* ideas about the way we live – in this case the performance of the outsider or the 'Other' – was here played out in ethnic as well as gendered terms.

Even this individual record of fairly casual Ibsenite theatre-going demonstrates the frequency of performance of two of the best-known plays in the English-language Ibsen repertoire, and the adaptability of these plays. This flexibility, and the repeated desire of directors and actors to adapt some of Ibsen's scripts to contemporary political and aesthetic concerns, suggest a continuing paradox in English readings of Ibsen. Ibsen – in so many ways, the quintessential Victorian as persistent questioner of the social and emotional certainties of his own time – is also a playwright who speaks to theatre artists and audiences generations later; the radical of his time is now the classic of our time.

NOTES

1 I use the term 'English theatre' throughout deliberately. My focus is on the theatre industry in London from 1880. London's position as a metropolitan centre of the hegemonic culture of Britain (that is, English culture) at the time suggests that it is more accurate to refer to 'English theatre' than to assume that London was representative of the theatrical culture of all of Great Britain. As various postcolonial theorists observe, we must start to see 'Englishness' as a specific ethnic identity, rather than as normative.

2 Moi (2004: 247). It should be noted, however, that Moi in no way endorses this view of Ibsen.

3 See Egan (1972: 187). A further review of *Ghosts* by Scott for the *Illustrated London News* (21 March 1891) is reprinted in George Rowell (ed.) (1971). *Victorian Dramatic Criticism*. London: Methuen, 291–3.

4 Raymond Williams (1977). 'A Lecture on Realism', *Screen* 18:1, 63–5.

5 For a more extended argument about the establishment and ideological underpinnings of this grand narrative, see Jacky Bratton (2003). *New Readings in Theatre History*. Cambridge: Cambridge University Press, 10–14, and *passim*; Thomas Postlewait explores the same territory in American theatre in 'From Melodrama to Realism: The Suspect History of American Drama' in Michael Hays and Anastasia Nikolopoulou (eds.) (1996). *Melodrama: The Cultural Emergence of a Genre*. Basingstoke: Macmillan, 39–60. For a brief account of the fading of the 'Ibsen campaign', and certainly his controversial status at the

time of his death, see Shepherd-Barr (1997: 167–8).

6 Edmund Gosse (1872). 'A Norwegian Drama', *Spectator* 45, reprinted in Egan (1972: 48).

7 See Ian Britain's comments on Fabian socialists' use of cultural media to extend their political arguments into the community, in (1982). *Fabianism and Culture: A Study in British Socialism and the Arts, c.1884–1918*. Cambridge: Cambridge University Press.

8 For a plot summary and description of the substantial changes to *A Doll's House* made by Jones and Herman (including four new characters introduced, and two of Ibsen's removed) see Thomas Postlewait (1986). *Prophet of the New Drama: William Archer and the Ibsen Campaign*. Westport, CT, and London: Greenwood Press, 37–8.

9 Britain (1982), *Fabianism and Culture*.

10 Henrietta F. Lord (1907). 'Preface' in Henrik Ibsen, *The Doll's House*, trans. Henrietta F. Lord. New York: D. Appelton, 4–5.

11 See also J. S. Bratton (1996). 'Miss Scott and Miss Macaulay: "Genius Cometh in All Disguises" ', *Theatre Survey* 37:1, 59, and *New Readings in Theatre History* for parallels with the 1820s and 1830s.

12 See the essays collected in John Stokes (ed.) (2000). *Eleanor Marx (1855–1898): Life, Work, Contacts*. Aldershot: Ashgate; and Sally Ledger's discussion of Marx's role in the Ibsen cause (1999) *Henrik Ibsen*. Plymouth: Northcote House, 1–3.

13 Cited in Yvonne Knapp (1979). *Eleanor Marx*, vol. 2: *The Crowded Years: 1884–1898*. London: Virago, 103.

14 Havelock Ellis [1888]. 'Preface' in *The Pillars of Society, Ghosts, and An Enemy of Society*. London: Walter Scott, xiii–xiv.

15 Lawrence Irving (1989; 1951). *Henry Irving: The Actor and his World*. London: Columbus Books, 535.

16 Sally Ledger (2000). 'Eleanor Marx and Henrik Ibsen' in Stokes (2000: 54); Ruth Brandon (2000; 1990). *The New Women and the Old Men: Love, Sex and the Woman Question*. London: Papermac, 96.

17 For audience figures and profits in Robins's and Lea's Ibsen productions, see Davis (1985: 33–5). For detailed discussions of Elizabeth Robins's engagement with Ibsen's plays, see Angela V. John (1995). 'Ibsen and the Actress' in *Elizabeth Robins: Staging a Life, 1862–1952*. London and New York: Routledge, 89–100; Kerry Powell (1997). 'Elizabeth Robins, Oscar Wilde, and the "Theatre of the Future"' in *Women and the Victorian Theatre*. Cambridge: Cambridge University Press, 99–101; and Penny Farfan (2004). *Women, Modernism, and Performance*. Cambridge: Cambridge University Press, ch. 1, esp. 14 and 29–33.

18 Simon Williams calls 1891 the *annus mirabilis* for Ibsen in England: 'Ibsen and the Theatre, 1877–1900' in McFarlane (1994: 167).

19 Frederick J. Marker and Lise-Lone Marker, 'Ibsen and the Twentieth-Century Stage' in McFarlane (1994: 183).

20 In 1934, Pound published a collection of essays under the title *Make It New* (London: Faber and Faber), but he had used this exhortation, translated from Confucius, as his catchphrase throughout the composition of the *Cantos* (which he began in 1915, although they were published in fragments and parts throughout the first half of the twentieth century), and in his editorial work with T. S. Eliot on *The Waste Land*.

21 Andreas Huyssen (1986). *After the Great Divide: Modernism, Mass Culture, Postmodernism*. Bloomington and Indianapolis: Indiana University Press, 53.

22 Eric Bentley (2003). 'What Ibsen Meant', *Southwest Review* 88:4, 534.

23 For an account of this production and its use of various translations, see May-Brit Akerholt (1995). '"I Had Better Not Return You to the Croft then, Nils, Had I?" The Text, The Whole Text, and Nothing but the Text in Translation' in Gay McAuley (ed.). *About Performance: Translation and Performance, Working Papers, Vol. 1*. Sydney: Centre for Performance Studies, University of Sydney, 1–13.

PRIMARY READING

There are numerous translations of Ibsen's plays into English, as well as some translations of his non-dramatic work. The most accessible – in that they are published and widely distributed in paperback – are by Michael Meyer, published by Methuen. The other standard edition in English is the *Oxford Ibsen*, translated by James McFarlane.

A complete list of Ibsen's work, including his non-dramatic writing, can be found in Michael Meyer's 3-volume biography (1967–71), *Henrik*

Ibsen. London: Hart-Davis, 1967–71, or his one-volume abridgement (1985). *Ibsen: a Biography*. Harmondsworth: Penguin. A chronology of Ibsen's life and work is given in James McFarlane (ed.) (1994). *The Cambridge Companion to Ibsen*. Cambridge: Cambridge University Press.

Two anthologies of critical responses to Ibsen are useful: Michael Egan (ed.) (1972). *Ibsen: The Critical Heritage*. London and Boston: Routledge and Kegan Paul; and Michael Meyer (1985). *Ibsen on File*. London: Methuen.

FURTHER READING

Davis, Tracy (1985). 'Ibsen's Victorian Audiences', *Essays in Theatre* 4:1, 21–38.

Johnston, Brian (1989). *Text and Supertext in Ibsen's Drama*. Westport, CT, and London: Greenwood Press.

Ledger, Sally (1999). *Henrik Ibsen*. Plymouth: Northcote House for the British Council.

McFarlane, James (ed.) (1994) *The Cambridge Companion to Ibsen*. Cambridge: Cambridge University Press.

Moi, Toril (2004). 'Ibsen, Theatre, and the Ideology of Modernism', *Theatre Survey* 45:2, 247–52.

Postlewait, Thomas (1986). *Prophet of the New Drama: William Archer and the Ibsen Campaign*. Westport, CT, and London: Greenwood Press.

Shepherd, Simon and Womack, Peter (1996). *English Drama: A Cultural History*. Oxford: Blackwell.

Shepherd-Barr, Kirsten (1997). *Ibsen and Early Modernist Theatre, 1890–1900*. Westport, CT, and London: Greenwood Press.

Stokes, John (1972). *Resistible Theatres: Enterprise and Experiment in the Late Nineteenth Century*. London: Paul Elek Books.

Woodfield, James (1984). *English Theatre in Transition, 1881–1914*. London: Croom Helm.

4

New Woman Drama

Sally Ledger

No dramatist has ever meant so much to the women of the stage as Henrik Ibsen.

Elizabeth Robins (1928: 31)

Ibsen's knowledge of humanity is nowhere more obvious than in his portrayal of women. He amazes me by his painful introspection; he seems to know them better than they know themselves.

James Joyce (1900; in Egan 1972: 388)

The plays of Henrik Ibsen were an inspiration to a generation of actresses and women dramatists in the 1890s. Elizabeth Robins, the great American actress who lived in London at this period, later reflected on 'the joy of having in our hands [. . .] such glorious actable stuff' (Robins 1928: 31–2). Robins both produced and took the lead role in *Hedda Gabler* and *A Doll's House* in 1891, and *The Master Builder* in 1893 (Powell 1998: 79). In 1889 Janet Achurch played Nora in the first unbowdlerized production of *A Doll's House*: she and her actor husband Charles Carrington approached William Archer, the highly influential drama critic and translator of Ibsen, for assistance in staging the play at London's Novelty Theatre (Marsh 2005: 24). This was a seminal event that importantly influenced the subsequent direction that British theatre would take in the late nineteenth century and beyond.

Actress-producers such as Janet Achurch and Elizabeth Robins were not, though, content simply to promote Ibsen's middle-period realist plays in London, significant though their role was in that respect. They also harboured ambitions as playwrights, and produced in *Alan's Wife* (1893, which Robins co-wrote with Florence Bell) and *Mrs Daintree's Daughter* (1894, written by Achurch) two of the most representative New Woman plays of the *fin de siècle*. Neither would have concurred with James Joyce, in 1900, that Ibsen 'seems to know [women] better than they know themselves' (in Egan 1972: 388): by shifting from the acting and production of woman-centred plays in the

1890s to actually writing them, Achurch and Robins became pioneering figures in the canon of modern feminist drama. Never recognized in their role as playwrights during the rise of Ibsenite New Woman drama in the 1890s, they none the less occupy an historically significant – if until recently an occluded – position in theatre history.

George Bernard Shaw was intensely aware of the challenges that women posed to the London theatre of the 1890s. In his preface to William Archer's *Theatrical 'World' of 1894* he reflected that: 'We cannot but see that the time is ripe for the advent of the actress-manageress, and that we are on the verge of something like a struggle between the sexes for the dominion of the London theatres' (Archer 1895: xxix). Shaw – a great admirer of Robins – acknowledged that her productions of Ibsen in the 1890s were harbingers of a gender revolution in the theatre industry (Powell 1998: 79). The growing role of the actress-manageress and women's increasing incursions into the production and directing of plays were aspects of this revolution that Shaw could contemplate with something approaching equanimity. What he could not countenance, though, was the idea that the new drama of the *fin de siècle* might not only be acted and produced by women, but also written by them. Ibsen's uncompromisingly naturalistic new drama made a major impact not only on the London stage, but also on a number of female playwrights who wished to follow his example. Whilst Shaw and Arthur Wing Pinero blended their social realism with the theatrical mode of the society comedies that a middle-class London audience would have been familiar and comfortable with, some of the female playwrights of the *fin de siècle* were uncompromising in their adherence to the theatrical naturalism that had been announced by the arrival of Ibsen's plays in London in the 1890s.

Eminent amongst such naturalistic plays is Elizabeth Robins's and Florence Bell's *Alan's Wife*, first conceived of in 1892 and performed in 1893.[1] Robins and Bell disguised their authorship of the play from Herbert Beerbohm Tree, whom they hoped would put it on at the prestigious Haymarket Theatre. Their anonymity was well advised given Beerbohm Tree's known view that 'women can't write' (Carlson and Powell 2004: 238). More specifically he had told Robins that he had 'never [. . .] read a good play from a woman's hand' when she described her playwriting ambitions to him (Powell 1998: 83). Beerbohm Tree was not alone in his opinion; it was shared by a majority of the more eminent literary men of the 1890s. When Robins told Henry James of her desire to write plays he had reacted 'with a start, and a look of horror' (Robins 1932: 144–5). Even Archer, who had worked behind the scenes to help Robins stage her 1891 production of *Hedda Gabler*, doubted her ability to write a play: 'To tell you the truth,' he wrote to her in 1892, 'I don't think you have the power of concentration required for playwriting. Certainly you could find a novel far easier than a play' (Powell 1998: 83). Archer later confirmed his opinion of the several female playwrights whom he had known at the *fin de siècle* by airbrushing them from his canon-forming study of modern drama from 1923, *The Old Drama and the New*.

Alan's Wife was first staged on 2 May 1893 at Terry's Theatre, London, by J. T. Grein's Independent Theatre Company, an avant-garde ensemble that welcomed women playwrights: 'six of the twenty-seven playwrights produced by the company from its inception in 1891 to its dissolution in 1898 were women' (Marsh 2005: 17).

Robins herself played Jean Creyke, a role that gave her – as did Ibsen's plays – a chance to dramatize the psychological and sexual subjectivity of a woman of emotional substance. Robins's and Bell's dramatic naturalism differs from Ibsen's in that their sharply focused snapshot of northern provincial life takes as its central dramatic subject a working-class woman. Ibsen's own critical dissection of provincial morality always took the middle classes as its subject matter. The influence of Florence Bell is pertinent in this respect: she is best known for her book *At The Works: A Study of a Manufacturing Town* (1907), and it is 'likely that she provided some of the contextual detail of *Alan's Wife* from her first-hand observations of working-class domestic life in Middlesborough' (Fitzsimmons and Gardner 1991: 3)

The working-class setting of *Alan's Wife* allies it in some respects more nearly with Zola's and Gissing's fictional naturalism than with Ibsen's dramatic naturalism. The exploration of maternal love and sexual desire that is at the play's centre is, though, straight out of Ibsen. The play revolves around Jean Creyke's marriage to the manly, eugenically superior Alan Creyke, a factory worker whom she chooses in preference to the scholarly but physically inferior local minister of religion, Jamie Warren. Alan dies in a factory accident, and his posthumously born son is a weak, crippled infant, whom Jean kills out of pity for the physically disabled life that awaits him. She fears for him a future of suffering in which he may lack the maternal care he needs should she die before him. She weeps as she smothers the baby, and is hanged for it: the play ends with her calmly awaiting death.

The play caused a furore. As Robins herself put it: 'controversy raged round the authorship of the play, and ink continued to be spilt on the dreadfulness of the theme' (Robins 1932: 118). Archer wrote a lengthy introduction to the play that defended its testing of the frontiers of dramatic realism, 'the question whether art has limitations of subject' (Fitzsimmons and Gardner 1991: 4). The *Athenaeum* failed to identify the modernity of the play's realist aesthetic, judging it instead by the conventions of the old-fashioned 'well-made play' and finding it wanting: it 'does not pretend to be a play. It consists of three disconnected scenes, the links between which are easily supplied by the audience' (Fitzsimmons and Gardner 1991: 5). Much the most perceptive of the reviews was J. T. Grein's, in the *Westminster Review*. He noted the play's strengths as a:

> psychological and physical study of a woman's character. [...] What we admire so greatly in *Alan's Wife* is the utter simplicity [...] If ever tragedy has been written by a modern Englishman, *Alan's Wife* has a right to claim that title. We know but one more powerful, modern play, equally sad, equally simple: Ibsen's *Ghosts* – that is all. (Fitzsimmons and Gardner 1991: 4)

Grein's identification of *Ghosts* (1881, first performed in London 1891) as one of the play's theatrical antecedents is observant, for *Alan's Wife*, like Ibsen's play, has at its heart a mother's moral struggle, and an emotionally searing examination of the nature of maternal love. Towards the end of the second, central scene in the play, Jean Creyke reflects on her son's possible future, and imagines how he, like Osvald Alving, may come to prefer death to the sufferings of a diseased life:

JEAN: [. . .] Oh, I see you in some far-off time, your face distorted like your body, but
with bitterness and loathing, saying, 'Mother, how *could* you be so cruel as to let me
live and suffer? You could have eased my pain; you could have saved me this long
martyrdom.'
(Robins and Bell 1893: sc. 2; in Fitzsimmons and Gardner 1991: 21)

The eugenic discourse that pervades the play is characteristic of a great deal of *fin de
siècle* literature and drama, deriving as it does from theories of heredity and fears of
racial decline that had a strong currency in the period.

The New Woman drama also shared with the more widely disseminated New
Woman fiction of the *fin de siècle* a preoccupation with female sexuality and desire.
Jean Creyke's strong physical attraction to her husband is fulsomely expressed in
Robins's and Bell's play:

JEAN: I want a husband who is brave and strong, a man who [. . .] loves to feel [. . .]
the blood rushing through his veins! Ah! to be happy! to be alive!
(Robins and Bell 1893: sc. 1; in Fitzsimmons and Gardner 1991: 12)

George Egerton's short story collections from 1893 and 1894, *Keynotes* and *Discords*,
similarly give expression to female desire, particularly in stories such as 'A Cross Line'
and 'The Regeneration of Two'. There was considerable interplay between the New
Woman fiction and drama of the period: some of the popular New Woman novelists
turned to playwriting later in their careers (Netta Syrett, George Egerton, Sarah Grand
and Victoria Cross all wrote plays, albeit to little critical acclaim); and Robins developed
her play *Votes for Women!* (1907) into a novel, thereby increasing its public exposure.

Alan's Wife closes with a powerful expression of maternal anguish: an interrogation
of the experience of motherhood is another feature common to New Woman drama
and New Woman fiction at the end of the nineteenth century.[2] Jean Creyke's mother,
Mrs Holroyd, is a poignant, bereft figure as her daughter is led away to imminent
execution, unable to rescue her child from the harsh mechanisms of the law. It is a
harrowing final scene that provides an arresting secondary female role in the play:

MRS HOLROYD: . . . No, no! You can't take her from me like that! Your worship, she's
the only child I've ever had – the only thing I have in the world! Eh, but you'll let me
bide with her the day, till tonight, only till tonight! Just these few hours longer!
Think, your worship – I must do without her for the rest of my life!
(Robins and Bell 1893: sc. 3; in Fitzsimmons and Gardner 1991: 24)

Alan's Wife is undoubtedly an emotionally powerful, disturbing play that bravely
articulates a subject position that infuriated large parts of the theatrical press. Shaw,
although a self-announced radical, was characteristically unimpressed by anything that
emanated from the pen of a female playwright. He regretted the moments of intense
emotion in the play, writing them off as a debased form of melodrama; and in a letter to
William Archer, he described how he would have written the play himself:

> I should represent Jean as a rational being in society as it exists at present; and I should
> shew [*sic*] her killing the child with cool and successful precautions against being found
> out. . . . When I think of that wasted opportunity, I feel more than ever contemptuous of
> this skulking author who writes like a female apprentice of [Robert] Buchanan.
> (Laurence 1965: 393–5)

In seeking to empty Robins's and Bell's play of its most intensely affective moments,
and of its exploration of the suffering endemic to motherhood, Shaw misunderstands
almost completely the impetus of the New Woman drama, which perhaps partly
explains his persistent derision of it. For he was equally dismissive of Janet Achurch's
play *Mrs Daintree's Daughter* (1894).

Achurch, whose performance of Nora Helmer in 1889 Shaw had so much admired,
discussed with him the possibility of dramatizing *Yvette*, a short story by Guy de
Maupassant. In the event she herself adapted the story for the stage, and Shaw later
acknowledged that the eponymous Mrs Daintree was the original for the lead role in his
own play from 1894, *Mrs Warren's Profession* (Laurence 1965: 409). The plays have great
similarities of plot: both female leads are highly successful brothel keepers (although
Mrs Daintree is rather more circumspect about the nefarious nature of her business than
the more brazen Mrs Warren, openly disclosing only her gambling and money-lending
activities); both have a daughter whom they have had educated in the countryside and
protected from the moral contamination of their respective businesses; and both are
rejected by their daughters. But whereas Shaw's play is driven by an economic
argument, Achurch's focuses more single-mindedly on gender issues concerning sexual
morality and the mother–daughter relationship. And whereas Shaw's Vivie Warren has
grown into a briskly independent, puritanical New-Womanish figure, Achurch's
Violet Daintree (known as Violet Meredith) has a taste for decadent novels and, despite
her sanitized upbringing, longs for the sexual excitement of the metropolis.

Achurch's play has nothing of the language of society comedy that Shaw's drama
retained, aiming instead for sustained and intense emotional effects. Leila Daintree is
dismayed that her careful nurturing of her daughter from a distance, and the sacrifices
she has made, have failed to produce the 'daughter of Arcadia' she had hoped for
(Achurch 1894: 7). In a dramatic final scene she declares to her daughter, who has
dismissed her mother as 'selfish and cruel': 'Violet, you'll kill me!' (Achurch 1894: 87,
96). In a denouement full of dramatic irony, Violet does unintentionally kill her mother
with a morphia overdose, the young woman repenting in her dying mother's arms:

VIOLET: . . . I'll do anything you tell me, mother, always – always, only, don't – ah!
                                                                                    (Achurch 1894: 98).

The emotional close of Achurch's play seems to owe something to Arthur Wing Pinero's
The Second Mrs Tanqueray, written in the previous year. Pinero's play also concerns a
'woman with a past' whose daughter (in this instance her stepdaughter) rejects her and
then repents at the play's close. Achurch's, Pinero's and Shaw's plays have clearly
discernible similarities of plot, and yet received a remarkably unequal critical response.

Pinero, like Shaw, was to become one of the most successful playwrights of the period; Achurch's play did not survive the first critical onslaught. Although Shaw's play was banned by the censors, and initially not even Grein's Independent Theatre Company would stage it, it got its first performance in 1902 and went on to receive great critical acclaim. Shaw was shockingly ungenerous to the woman whose play he had borrowed from for his own more successful drama, savagely attacking it as soon as he knew that Achurch was trying to persuade Lewis Waller, the actor manager of the Haymarket Theatre, to stage it: '[T]he ending is not the sort of thing for his [upmarket] audience' he wrote in 1895, sneeringly adding that 'I told you that you hadn't written your play' (Powell 1998: 85). Refusing to recognize *Mrs Daintree's Daughter* as fit for the 1890s theatre, Shaw declared it to be not so much a modern play as something 'for a Bernhardt to star in' (Laurence 1965: 478–9), once more objecting to the intense emotions of New Woman drama. Shaw's aversion to the New Woman drama's combining of Ibsenite naturalism with the emotional affects of melodrama is quite striking given the considerable residual investment in the melodramatic aesthetic that is a feature of Ibsen's middle plays, whose naturalism Shaw was to champion. Shaw seems to have been blind to Ibsen's own debt to melodrama in such moments as Nora's frenzied tarantella dance and her frantic attempts to hide Krogstad's letter from her husband; and in Hedda Gabler's and Rebecca West's dramatic suicides. Both Martha Vicinus and E. Ann Kaplan have commented on the way that melodrama in the theatre – maligned as it was by high culture – had considerable proto-feminist potential in its foregrounding of issues of gender and power, and in its highlighting of the role of the central women characters, however much suffering they may have to endure (Vicinus 1981, Kaplan 1988). It was this, I think, that appealed to the New Woman playwrights of the *fin de siècle*, whatever Shaw's disparagement.

Negotiating the social status of the sexually experienced woman who has defied social mores concerning the marriage vow is a central preoccupation of a great deal of New Woman drama in the Lord Chamberlain's Collection in the British Library. There is a cluster of such plays around 1894, the year that Lyn Pykett has described as the '*annus mirabilis* of the new woman' (Pykett 1995: 137). Pykett is referring to the numerous New Woman novels written by women that enjoyed popular success in 1894; but an equally rich vein of new drama was written by women in the same year. The New Woman playwrights of 1894 – Janet Achurch, Constance Fletcher and Dorothy Leighton – did not enjoy the popular success of the female New Woman novelists, but their plays dramatically stage the very same issues concerning gender and sexuality that the novelists of the period sought to address.[3] The only one of these plays written by women in 1894 to enjoy theatrical success was Constance Fletcher's *Mrs Lessingham*, which she wrote using the pen name 'George Fleming'. Licensed by the lord chamberlain in April 1894, Fletcher's play survived 33 London performances, to considerable critical acclaim (Marsh 2005: 28). Always seeking to promote strong plays by and about women, it was Elizabeth Robins who persuaded John Hare to put on *Mrs Lessingham* at the Garrick, and she was cast in the lead role (Powell 1998: 83). The play has a harrowing plotline. Gladys Lessingham, like Nora Helmer some twenty-five years before her, walks out of an unhappy marriage. But whilst Nora's future remains unclear, Constance Fletcher's play details in agonising detail the future course of Gladys's life. She lives in an illicit relationship with Walter Forbes for five years in Algiers; but tiring of the expatriate life, he leaves her, and without her knowledge engages himself to a young woman without 'a past'. When Gladys's husband dies, she returns to London to seek Forbes, not knowing that he is about to marry. His fiancée insists that he should marry the woman he had lived with as husband and wife; he complies, but the marriage is very unhappy. A social pariah, Gladys commits suicide.

Like *Mrs Daintree's Daughter*, the plot of *Mrs Lessingham* resonates remarkably with some aspects of *The Second Mrs Tanqueray*: Gladys Forbes, like Paula Tanqueray, is not forgiven her sexual past, brings social opprobrium upon her husband, and kills herself. It seems, though, that Fletcher's play influenced Pinero's rather than the other way around. Archer reflected in 1895 that 'several critics have assumed that *Mrs Lessingham* must have been in some way inspired by *The Second Mrs Tanqueray*; I may mention that I read "George Fleming's" play three or four months before the production, and that it had then as I understood, been in existence for at least a year' (Archer 1895: 102).

Mrs Lessingham's power partly derives from the emotional anguish of its main female protagonist, Gladys Lessingham, an anguish that isn't tempered by the angry defiance of Pinero's Paula Tanqueray:

> GLADYS (*slowly*):   If I don't make him happy, – if he cares for Anne still – what do you think it would cost me to put an end to a life which is the burden and the curse of the two people in this world who have been kind to me? . . . I wish I had had a child! . . . I hope it won't hurt – much? – Yes, she can be happy now, with Walter.
>
> ('Fleming' 1894: 48–9, 70–1)

Unlike Pinero's play, *Mrs Lessingham* focuses intently on female solidarity. Whilst society at large condemns Gladys Forbes, Anne Beaton, the ostensible rival for her husband, demonstrates great sympathy. Hardy, a close friend of Forbes, advises Anne against visiting Gladys Lessingham (as she then is), condemned as she is by the sexual 'double standard' of late nineteenth-century English society. Anne, though, is quick to spot the hypocrisy, and instead of condemning Gladys firmly supports her cause:

> ANNE: Ah, – I know what you would say! I ought not to be here. I ought not to be in the same house with – her. I ought not to mention her name; to breathe the air of the room she lives in. But, naturally, you can see no sort of objection to my marrying Walter! . . . Do you think I cannot understand – her? She loved him too – when I did not know him, before I had a chance. I have promised to marry him, and, for five years she – she was his *wife*. (*A silence*). Do you know I – I am very sorry for Mrs Lessingham?
>
> ('Fleming' 1894: 36)

The female solidarity expressed here contrasts sharply with Pinero's *The Second Mrs Tanqueray*, in which the young Ellean Tanqueray is willing to forgive Hugh Ardale his

A poster advertising Sidney Grundy's *The New Woman*, from *Les Affiches Etrangères* 1896. Courtesy of Mary Evans Picture Library.

sexual past but harshly condemns Paula Tanqueray for the same. She repents her harshness at the play's close, in a scene that resonates with the end of *Mrs Daintree's Daughter*, in which another mother–daughter relationship is restored during a death-bed scene.

Mrs Lessingham's clinical dissection of middle-class marriage and sexual morality closely allies it to Ibsen's project in his middle plays; like Ibsen, Constance Fletcher was writing naturalistic tragedy concerned not with the lives of historic figures from a mythical past but with unheroic, unexceptional middle-class people who speak in plain, idiomatic prose. Ibsen's naturalism is characteristically blended with melodramatic affects: the painful, accidental initial encounter between Gladys, Forbes and Anne is full of heightened emotion, whilst the suicide scene is brave in its full delineation of Gladys's anguish. The *Athenaeum* acknowledged the play's emotional power, reflecting that its 'almost sepulchral gloom . . . is harrowing' (Anon. 1894: 92; quoted in Marsh 2005: 171).

The denouement of *Thyrza Fleming*, another of the New Woman plays from 1894, is more ambiguous in tone. This is the only one of the female-authored New Woman plays of that year that explores cultural stereotypes of the New Woman that were widespread in the period and that would also be satirically staged in Sidney Grundy's play from the same year, *The New Woman*. Theophila Falkland, a secondary character in the drama, is a man-hating but mannish figure of fun, who cows her husband and hires detectives to check out the sexual purity of any men who court the attentions of young women of her acquaintance. Theophila is described in the stage directions as 'a woman of about 30, close-cropped hair, manly attire, divided skirt. Bustles in a swinging, breezy fashion; slaps John Heron on the back' (Leighton 1894: 42). In a comic vignette at the centre of the play, Theophila and her husband Bobby act out a gender reversal that was replicated in many a *Punch* cartoon from 1894 and 1895:

> THEOPHILA: . . . (*Nods to Bobby, walks to fireplace and begins opening letters which she has in her hand*). Breakfast ready, Bobby?
> BOBBY: (*advancing timidly*) Yes, Theophila.
>
> (Leighton 1894: 42)

Much less two-dimensional, and taken much more seriously by the play text, is Thyrza Fleming, the play's eponymous lead. Picking up on Ibsen's and Achurch's theme, Thyrza Fleming walks out of an unhappy marriage, leaving behind her a baby daughter. She tells the play's central male actor, Hugh Rivers, that she left her husband:

> THYRZA: . . . to be free. He had hideous ideas of woman's duty, and he thought because he owned my person he possessed my soul. He wanted to restrict my every action, my books, my friends, my pursuits. He thought Art wrong and all beauty and Joy immoral. I left him to *live*.
>
> (Leighton 1894: 33)

At the start of the play's action Thyrza is a hugely successful actress returned to London from North America. Her style of New Womanhood – bookish, confident and independent – is clearly affirmed in the play, and contrasted with the stereotyped anti-male hysteria of Theophila Falkland. Her husband still alive, Thyrza has been unable to formalize her long-standing but sporadic relationship with Hugh Rivers, with whom she is deeply in love. This is one of the most radical of the New Woman plays of the period in its exploration of the possibility of a new kind of relationship between man and woman, based on friendship and trust as well as sexual love. Moving beyond the usual parameters of the plot that interrogates the sexual double standard, Leighton presents in Thyrza Fleming a woman who has been to Hugh Rivers 'my best friend', with whom he has shared 'sympathy, friendship, council, *comprehension*'. As Thyrza puts it: 'I have been his friend, his best and most loving friend, all these years' (Leighton 1894: 33, 35, 59). Clearly it has been a sexual relationship too, and one can see in the play script the lexical contortions Leighton wrestled with in trying to express this without offending the censor. When Pamela Rivers, whom Hugh has precipitately fallen in love with and married, demands of Thyrza whether she had been Hugh's mistress, the dialogue circles awkwardly around the issue:

> THYRZA: A man's mistress is a woman he keeps for his own pleasure; his toy, his plaything, his caprice. She is a woman who has forfeited his respect in losing her own self-respect, and one of whom any wife would have a right to be jealous. If I had been such a woman to your husband, should I come hear and implore you to go back to him?
>
> (Leighton 1894: 51)

In a melodramatic twist to the plot, it transpires that Pamela is Thyrza's daughter. The knowledge of this plunges Thyrza into despair, regretting, finally, that she had deserted her infant daughter years before. Like so much New Woman drama, *Thyrza Fleming* focuses on motherhood as a defining experience in a woman's life, without ever straightforwardly affirming it. Thyrza's self-recrimination is intense and the play text quite explicitly reprises Nora's closing speech in *A Doll's House* at this point: 'I deserted her... when she was a baby... I wanted freedom; I thought I owed a higher duty to myself than to my child' (Leighton 1894: 63). Like Hedda Gabler before her, Thyrza puts a gun to her head. But Leighton revises the melodramatic close to Ibsen's play: just as Thyrza is about to end her life, her daughter hurls her arms around her mother, to stop her.

This is in many respects the most Ibsenite of all the female-authored New Woman plays of the period: its detailed stage descriptions of a bourgeois milieu; its sequence of intensely personal dialogues between two people in a domestic setting; its close scrutiny of the nature of relationships – including sexual relations – between men and women; and its dissection of the meanings of motherhood – all these closely ally it to the project of Ibsen's middle-period drama.

The most affirmative – and in terms of critical reception the least successful – of the female-authored New Woman plays of the *fin de siècle* is *The Finding of Nancy* by Netta Syrett. Syrett was an established author of New Woman fiction when she turned to playwriting in 1902; the best-known of her novels is *Nobody's Fault* from 1896. She turned to the drama as a consequence of a playwriting competition set up by the Playgoers' Club and organized by Beerbohm Tree and George Alexander (Carlson and Powell 2004: 240; Marsh 2005: 22). The purpose of the competition was to breathe new life into the theatre by uncovering fresh talent, and the prize was a performance of the winning play at St James's Theatre, Piccadilly.

Like each of *Mrs Lessingham, The Second Mrs Tanqueray* and *Thyrza Fleming*, Syrett's play considers the social standing of a 'woman with a past'; but unlike the previous three plays, the plotline of *The Finding of Nancy* asserts the right of such a woman to an emotionally fulfilled future without recrimination. Nancy Thistleton, a typewriter girl who dresses as a New Woman in a 'plain serge gown with tie, collar and cuffs' (Syrett 1902: 2), rebels against the penury of an economically independent female office worker in the city. She accepts the love of Will Fielding, a man separated from his alcoholic wife, and goes to live with him. Like *Thyrza Fleming*, the play asserts the value of an equal relationship between the sexes, where man and woman can be friend and confidant as well as lover. At various points in the play Nancy enthuses about the fullness of her unmarried relationship to Fielding:

> NANCY: Oh, Isabel, we were so happy – so quietly happy you know . . . our talks over the
>   fire – our trust in one another – our dependence on one another . . . all the little things.
>   (Syrett 1902: 45)

In a melodramatic twist, Fielding is feared dead, believing Nancy to love another man. Nancy despairs at the apparent loss of 'my friend, my child, my *lover* . . .' (Syrett 1902: 55). Alone of the New Woman plays, the denouement of *The Finding of Nancy* is positive: Fielding is discovered alive and well, his wife has died, and he and Nancy – unheeding and uncaring of the whispers of 'society' – formalize their relationship through marriage.

This play too, with its emphasis on the staging of intensely personal dialogue between two people, its interrogation of the marriage tie and of sexual relationships between men and women, owes a debt to Ibsen. It also, though, counterpoints Ibsenite social and sexual realism with a more conventional social comedy of middle-class match-making on the continent, with an attendant Wildean repartee.

The single performance of the play at St James's Theatre, with Elizabeth Robins in the lead role, was a success. But a number of influential critics were outraged by a play that celebrates and defends a sexual relationship that exists beyond the marriage tie, and that allows a 'woman with a past' an emotionally and socially fulfilled future. *The Times* complained that:

> The play is written not only by a lady . . . but for ladies . . . that is to say, it assumes . . . that the great interest for all of us in life, the thing we want most to hear about and that we go to the play to see, is the career of a woman. (9 May 1902, quoted in Marsh 2005: 23)

More damningly, Clement Scott, the lead reviewer for the *Daily Telegraph*, suggested that the play's action was based on Syrett's own experiences of life (Marsh 2005: 23). There were a few positive critical responses, with the *Saturday Review* giving it high praise: 'I do not hesitate to say that in my time there has been nothing on the stage so interesting, so impressive, so poignant, as the first act of Miss Syrett's play' (17 May 1902, quoted in Marsh 2005: 23). The play did not survive its first performance, cancelled because of the weight of critical hostility it provoked. Syrett wrote two further plays but, like Janet Achurch, Constance Fletcher and Dorothy Leighton before her, she failed as a playwright. The gender revolution in the theatre that Bernard Shaw had predicted would be a feature of the *fin de siècle* was insufficiently complete to be able to embrace female-authored New Woman plays. Often striking in their modernity and in their willingness to challenge contemporary social and sexual mores, it is remarkable that this rich vein of drama should continue to languish unperformed in the Lord Chamberlain's Collection in the British Library.

NOTES

1 Other notable naturalistic plays of the *fin de siècle* written by women include the slightly later *Chains* by Elizabeth Baker (1909), and *In The Workhouse* by Margaret Nevinson (1911).
2 New Woman novels that centrally concern themselves with motherhood and maternity include Olive Schreiner's *The Story of an African Farm* (1883) and Mona Caird's *The Daughters of Danaus* (1894).
3 New Woman fiction from 1894 includes Edith Arnold's *Platonics*, Mona Caird's *The Daughters of Danaus*, George Egerton's *Discords*, and Ella Hepworth Dixon's *The Story of a Modern Woman*.

PRIMARY READING

Achurch, Janet (1894). *Mrs Daintree's Daughter.* British Library: Lord Chamberlain's Collection 53542.

Anon. (1894). '*Mrs Lessingham*', *Athenaeum* 14 April, 92.

Archer, William (1895). *Theatrical 'World' of 1894.* London: Scott.

Archer, William (1923). *The Old Drama and the New.* London: William Heinemann.

Arnold, Edith (1894; repr. 1995). *Platonics: A Study.* Bristol: Thoemmes Press.

Baker, Elizabeth (1909; repr. 1991). *Chains* in Linda Fitzsimmons and Viv Gardner (eds.). *New Woman Plays.* London: Methuen, 43–101.

Bell, Florence (1907). *At the Works: A Study of a Manufacturing Town.* London: Edward Arnold.

Caird, Mona (1894). *The Daughters of Danaus.* London: Bliss, Sands and Foster.

Egerton, George (1893 and 1894; repr. 2003). *Keynotes* and *Discords.* Birmingham: Birmingham University Press.

'Fleming, Guy' [Constance Fletcher] (1894). *Mrs Lessingham*. British Library: Lord Chamberlain's Collection 53546A.

Grundy, Sidney (1895; repr. 1998). *The New Woman* in Jean Chothia (ed.). *The New Woman*

and Other Emancipated Woman Plays. Oxford: Oxford University Press, 1–59.

Hepworth Dixon, Ella (1894; repr. 1990). *The Story of a Modern Woman.* London: Merlin.

Ibsen, Henrik (1879; repr. 1990). *A Doll's House*, trans. Michael Meyer. London: Methuen.

Ibsen, Henrik (1881; repr. 1992). *Ghosts*, trans. Michael Meyer. London: Methuen.

Ibsen, Henrik (1886; repr. 1992). *Rosmersholm*, trans. Michael Meyer. London: Methuen.

Ibsen, Henrik (1890; repr. 1990). *Hedda Gabler*, trans. Michael Meyer. London: Methuen.

Ibsen, Henrik (1892; repr. 1992). *The Master Builder*, trans. Michael Meyer. London: Methuen.

Ibsen, Henrik (1894; repr. 1996). *Little Eyolf*, trans. Michael Meyer. London: Methuen.

Leighton, Dorothy (1894). *Thyrza Fleming*. British Library Lord Chamberlain's Collection 53565.

Nevinson, Margaret (1911). *In the Workhouse*. London: International Suffrage Shop.

Pinero, Arthur Wing (1893; repr. 2003). *The Second Mrs Tanqueray.* London and New York: Samuel French.

Robins, Elizabeth (1907; repr. 1998). *Votes for Women!* in Jean Chothia (ed.). *The New Woman and Other Emancipated Woman Plays*. Oxford: Oxford University Press, 135–210.

Robins, Elizabeth (1928). *Ibsen and the Actress*. London: Hogarth Press.

Robins, Elizabeth (1932). *Theatre and Friendship*. London: Jonathan Cape.

Robins, Elizabeth and Bell, Florence (1893; repr. 1991). *Alan's Wife* in Linda Fitzsimmons and Viv Gardner (eds.). *New Woman Plays*. London: Methuen, 1–42.

Shaw, George Bernard (1894; repr. 1946). *Mrs Warren's Profession* in Dan Laurence (ed.). *Bernard Shaw: Plays Unpleasant*. London: Penguin, 178–286.

Schreiner, Olive (1883; repr. 1992). *The Story of an African Farm*. Oxford: Oxford University Press.

Syrett, Netta (1896). *Nobody's Fault*. London: John Lane.

Syrett, Netta (1902). *The Finding of Nancy*. British Library: Lord Chamberlain's Collection Vol. 14.

FURTHER READING

Carlson, Susan and Powell, Kerry (2004). 'Reimagining the Theatre: Women Playwrights of the Victorian and Edwardian Period' in Kerry Powell (ed.). *Cambridge Companion to Victorian and Edwardian Theatre*. Cambridge: Cambridge University Press, 237–56.

Egan, Michael (1972). *Ibsen: The Critical Heritage*. London: Routledge and Kegan Paul.

Fitzsimmons, Linda and Gardner, Viv (eds.) (1991). 'Introduction' in Linda Fitzsimmons and Viv Gardner (eds.). *New Woman Plays*. London: Methuen, 1–7.

Joyce, James (1900). 'Ibsen's New Drama', *Fortnightly Review*, 1 April: 575–90 (repr. in Egan 1972: 387–9).

Kaplan, E. Anne (1988). 'The Political Unconscious in the Maternal Melodrama: Ellen Wood's *East Lynne*' in Derek Longhurst (ed.). *Gender, Genre and Narrative Pleasure*. Hemel Hempstead: Unwin Hyman, 31–50.

Laurence, Dan (1965). *Bernard Shaw: Collected Letters*. Vol. 1. New York: Dodd, Mead.

Marsh, Jacqueline (2005). 'New Woman and Suffrage Drama 1880–1928'. University of London, unfinished PhD thesis.

Powell, Kerry (1997). *Women and Victorian Theatre*. Cambridge: Cambridge University Press.

Powell, Kerry (1998). 'New Women, New Plays, and Shaw in the 1890s' in Christopher Innes (ed.). *Cambridge Companion to George Bernard Shaw*. Cambridge: Cambridge University Press, 76–102.

Pykett, Lyn (1995). *Engendering Fictions: The English Novel in the Early Twentieth Century*. London: Edward Arnold.

Vicinus, Martha (1981). ' "Helpless and Unfriended": Nineteenth-Century Domestic Melodrama', *New Literary History* 13, 127–43.

PART II
Mapping New Ground, 1900–1939

5

Shaw among the Artists

Jan McDonald

For art's sake alone I would not face the toil of writing a single sentence.

Shaw (1976: 35)

I have, I think, always been a Puritan in my attitude towards Art.

Shaw (1946c: xii)

George Bernard Shaw (1856–1950) was a committed socialist, a successful, if controversial, dramatist, an inspired theatre director of his own work and an influential commentator on contemporary music, drama and fine art. In all his endeavours he demonstrated an indefatigable zeal to reform existing social conditions, sterile theatrical conventions and outworn artistic orthodoxies.

In this chapter I shall focus on Shaw's views on art and artists, examining some of his many critical and theoretical writings, but concentrating on how his opinions were expressed in dramatic form in plays which particularly engage with such issues, namely, *Candida* (1895), *Caesar and Cleopatra* (1899), *Mrs Warren's Profession* (1902), *Man and Superman* (1905), *The Doctor's Dilemma* (1906), *Pygmalion* (Berlin: 1913; London: 1914) and *Back to Methuselah* (New York: 1922; London: 1923).

Towards a Shavian Aesthetic?

Shaw's opinions on art and artists are scattered throughout his work, in his critical and journalistic writing, in letters and notebooks, as well as in his plays and the prefaces to them. These observations, spanning many years, are not consistent and can seem almost wilfully contradictory. His comment that 'Wagner can be quoted against himself almost without limit' (Shaw 1930: 265) is at least as applicable to Shaw. As Sidney P. Albert among others has pointed out Shaw was much influenced by his reading of Hegelian dialectics, a methodology well suited to his inclination to play with conflicting ideologies, particularly in his dramas (Albert 1956: 423–4). In addition, his taste for polemics, his mischievous flying of multi-coloured kites and his sense of irony – which he engaged on occasion to subvert ideas that he had previously endorsed – all militate against the expression of a structured aesthetic philosophy.

Finally, and most importantly, for much of his life Shaw was politically engaged, both theoretically and practically, as a socialist, and his writings demonstrate his attempt to balance a utilitarian ethic of improving social conditions with a deep attachment to the creative and performing arts. 'I am an artist, and, it is inevitable, a public moralist', he announced in a letter to Robert W. Welch in September 1905 (Laurence 1972: 560).

Judith B. Spink believes that Shaw failed to achieve the desired equilibrium and that his aesthetics were seriously compromised by his politics: 'Shaw's complete commitment to the socialist cause led him eventually to such contorted views on art as are perhaps more familiar from more uncompromisingly Marxist critics and artists' (Spink 1963: 83). It is certainly true that Shaw passionately eschewed the notion of 'Art for Art's sake', as the first epigraph above makes clear, and he repeatedly asserted that his prime motive for engaging in aesthetic pursuits was to promote political ideas. The preface to his first play, *Widowers' Houses* (1892), is unequivocal: 'It is not my fault, reader, that my art is the expression of my sense of moral and individual perversity rather than my sense of beauty' (West 1950: 115). In a letter to Henry Arthur Jones (8 January 1899), he went further, asserting not only that a work of art should have a social function, but that a sense of purpose and social responsibility was essential, a *sine qua non* of excellence: 'The best established truth in the world is that no man produces a work of art of the very first order except under the pressure of strong conviction and definite meaning as to the constitution of the world' (Laurence 1972: 71). In this, as in many other respects, Shaw was a true Platonist. Plato, as Albert has noted, 'praised art only when it is allied with philosophy in the pursuit of the Form of Beauty which is also intellectually viewed, Truth, and morally considered, the Good' (Albert 1956: 430). The artist-philosopher was the only artist Shaw took seriously. On occasion he implied that art was *only* of value as a means of making radical ideas pleasing. He wrote in the preface to *Mrs Warren's Profession*: 'I am convinced that fine art is the subtlest, the most seductive, the most effective instrument of moral propaganda in the world' (Shaw 1946b: 7).

In practice, in Shaw's best work, the 'art' is not merely the handmaiden of his favoured philosophy, whether he is promoting Fabian socialism, the Schopenhaurian Life Force, the Nietzschean Superman or the theories of Lamarck, Bergson et al. on Creative Evolution. Nevertheless, it is, paradoxically, in two passages in which the art of the dramatist is least effective that Shaw expounds his aesthetic theory at some length, the 'Don Juan in Hell' episode in *Man and Superman* and Part V of *Back to Methuselah*, 'As far as thought can reach'. A brief comparison of these non-dramatic sections – 'non-dramatic' because the two-dimensional characters are merely mouthpieces for opposing ideologies – is useful, bearing in mind the twenty years between the two plays, years which encompassed World War I. The latter is rarely performed in whole or in part, and Shaw himself gave permission to the directors of *Man and Superman* to omit the 'hell' scene.

Both passages have as their subject Creative Evolution; in the first the instrument of humankind's ascent is the Nietzschean 'Superman': in the second, it is time and abstract thought. Shaw believed that in *Man and Superman* as a whole the 'message' had been obscured in order to fit the drama to the tastes of his contemporary audience; that is, one might say, to engage with the 'art' of playwriting. The later development of the 'religion' of Creative Evolution makes no such concessions.

In 'Don Juan in Hell' the artist-philosopher, Don Juan/John Tanner, rails against the aesthetic hedonism of the Devil, comparing his religion of love and beauty to 'sitting for all eternity at the first act of a fashionable play' (Shaw 1976: 139). 'Hell is the home of the unreal and the seekers of the happiness'; the 'masters of reality' inhabit Heaven (139) – artists such as Rembrandt, 'a fellow who would paint a hag of seventy with as much enjoyment as a Venus of twenty' (171) and Mozart, and by implication from the preface, Bunyan, Hogarth, Ibsen and Tolstoy among others, artists who committed to a struggle for reform, artist-philosophers like Shaw himself.

In Part V of *Back to Methuselah* the 'artist-philosopher' becomes the 'artist-prophet' while retaining much of his earlier Platonism. Believing that great art of the past was 'great' because of the religious conviction that inspired its creation, Shaw seeks to be 'an iconographer of the religion of my time [i.e. Creative Evolution] and thus fulfil my natural function as an artist' (Shaw 1945: lxxxv).

In a futuristic pastoral nightmare, beautiful children play at love and art; they abandon both pursuits by the age of four. At the 'Festival of the Arts', the sculptor Arjillax shocks his spectators by producing busts of the Ancients; that is, he seeks to represent the reality of the world around him rather than an idealized prettiness. Martellus goes further for, in collaboration with the scientist Pygmalion, he creates two 'living' creatures. 'Anything alive is better than anything pretending to be alive', he asserts (ibid.: 240). But they have made mere automata, and Pygmalion dies at the bite of his female 'monster'. The She-Ancient, a true Platonist, rebukes the artists and aesthetes: 'Art is the magic mirror you make to reflect your invisible dreams in visible pictures' (ibid.: 268). 'You can create nothing but yourself' (ibid.: 267). As art and artists dissolve into an abstract world of thought, however, the future seems bleak and cold, a *reductio ad absurdum* of [Shaw's] puritanic distrust of the senses' (Woodbridge 1963: 111).

If 'As far as thought can reach' is the piece by Shaw that is most 'anti-art', his great defence of art and artists is his response to Max Nordau's celebrated treatise on *Degeneracy* (1895). This first appeared as 'A Degenerate's view of Nordau – an Open Letter to Bernard Tucker in NY Weekly, LIBERTY, 27 July 1895', and was reprinted in 1908 as *The Sanity of Art*. The kernel of Nordau's thesis was thus summarized by Shaw: 'Nordau's message to the world is that all our characteristically modern works of art are symptoms of disease in the artists, and that these diseased artists are themselves symptoms of the nervous exhaustion of the race by overwork' (Shaw 1930: 328). Many of the works which Nordau characterized as 'degenerate' were by artists whom Shaw regarded as outstanding contributors to contemporary culture: Ibsen, Wagner and Tolstoy, for example. The fact that Nordau identified such geniuses with 'the refuse of our prisons and lunatic asylums' (ibid.: 339) only confirmed to Shaw that Nordau was 'the dupe' of a fashionable theory, namely psychiatry. He dismissed the theories of the German writer as 'nothing but the familiar delusion of the used-up man that the world is going to the dogs' (ibid.: 326–7). While admitting that when a new movement in art, literature or music is initiated a great deal of imitative rubbish can be accepted temporarily by critics seeking to embrace new forms, Shaw remains adamant (and eloquent) about the intrinsic possibilities of the creative and performing arts improving the human condition. His spirited defence was much appreciated in the United States, where his response was first published. The *Kansas City Journal* was only one paper to review it enthusiastically: 'Probably never before has there appeared such a wonderful defence of modern art and music as Mr Shaw has given us in his criticism' (see Edwards). But – and there is always a but with Shaw – in his Lecture on Art at Bedford (10 December 1885) he wrote: 'The arts contain methods of seeking happiness: and they are mischievous or beneficial, moral or immoral, just as other methods of seeking happiness are' (Weintraub 1989: 59). There is no special pleading for art as a 'palliative for social gangrene', and all artists are not equally worthy either in their pursuit of their vocation or as members of the community. In seeking to examine further Shaw's complementary or contradictory views, I shall turn to his dramas for illumination.

Shaw's Portraits of the Artists

Spink commented that Shaw attributed to his fictional artists 'less of heroic stature and more of biting satire that one has any reason to expect in so inveterate an artist' (Spink 1963: 82). There are clear parodic elements in his approach at times, but rather than describe the overall approach as 'satiric', I would suggest that he is attempting a comprehensive and objective appraisal of representative samples of a genus of which he is a member.

The artists (and the art lovers) will be investigated, first through their physical appearance, secondly by testing the quality of their creative production, and thirdly by assessing the manner in which they relate to the other characters, in order to extrapolate, if possible, their place in society.

With the important exception of Eugene Marchbanks in *Candida*, the artists in Shaw's plays are explicitly endowed with a handsome appearance, tastefully dressed, perfectly groomed, amiable, engaging and socially at ease. There is more than a hint in the descriptions that the characters have self-consciously created themselves according to some preconceived image of the artist or aesthete. In *Man and Superman* even Octavius's mourning dress is a carefully contrived costume to enable him better to undertake the role of the bereaved, one in which he takes some pleasure. The artists present themselves with a studied attention to their appearance, more commonly associated with women than with men. In this gallery of charming matinée idols, Eugene Marchbanks is an alien creature, *'so uncommon as to be almost unearthly'*, described variously as *'a strange shy youth of eighteen'* – he is younger than the others

– '*slight effeminate with a delicate childish voice and a hundred tormented expressions*'. His clothes are '*anarchic*' and '*there is no evidence of his ever having brushed them*' (Shaw 1946a: 120). He is nervous and socially inept. His youth, unkempt appearance and vulnerability naturally appeal to Candida's indefatigable maternalism. The description of Eugene as '*effeminate*' – Dubedat is specifically labelled '*not effeminate*' – requires some investigation. A review in the *Manchester Guardian* (15 March 1898) described him as a 'childlike creature...a boy of eighteen got up to look like Shelley, not a man, femininely hectic and timid and fierce' (see Evans 1976: 71). The association of Eugene with effeminacy has led critics such as Sally Peters in *The Ascent of the Superman* first to associate the Shavian artist with homosexuality, and secondly, by viewing the character of Eugene as a self-portrait of the young Shaw, to deduce that he himself had veiled homosexual sympathies. Her carefully documented argument concludes: 'Shaw created a vaguely allusive atmosphere that bathed Marchbanks in a coded homosexuality – a character with autobiographical parallels to the playwright' (Peters 1996: 165). 'Coded' messages are always seductive, but the final deduction is not proven. Nevertheless, leaving aside Shaw's personal gender preferences, which are irrelevant here, it is useful in the context of examining his representation of the artist to probe further. Praed, 'hardly past middle-age' (Shaw 1946b: 211), is unmarried, and is the only one of the older generation in *Mrs Warren's Profession* who has not taken advantage of the services she offers. In *Man and Superman,* Ann Whitefield observes, 'Tavy will never marry'; 'The poetic temperament's a very nice temperament, very amiable, very harmless and poetic, I daresay; but it's an old maid's temperament' (Shaw 1976: 204). Shaw may have been influenced in the representations of some of his fictional artists by the *fin de siècle* fascination with homosexuality – popularly but by no means solely associated with Oscar Wilde – and the sexologists' investigations into the 'Uranian' or 'Urning', the intermediate sex, that was, as some would have it, superior to the male and the female. Edward Carpenter, for example, himself a homosexual, associated this gender type specifically with the artist's nature and the artist's sensibility and perception (Carpenter 1908). Was Shaw rendering some of his artists and aesthetes 'barren' because he was influenced by Carpenter and others, or because he was intent on effecting a meaningful opposition between the artist and the procreative dynamic of the Life Force? Or, in Eugene's case, was he simply showing the first immature heterosexual impulses of an adolescent boy?

How Talented are Shaw's Artists?

In the plays under examination, Shaw portrays two poets, an easel painter, an artist-craftsman, an architect and two sculptors. One might add the two 'Pygmalions', creators of living things, Henry Higgins in *Pygmalion* and the Martellus/Pygmalion partnership in Part V of *Back to Methuselah*. There is no musician and no actor, surprising perhaps if one considers that Shaw focused on the portrayal of such artists in his novels. And there are no women artists. In the Epistle Dedicatory to *Man and*

Superman, Shaw wrote: 'I am sorry to say that it is a common practice with romancers to announce their hero as a man of extraordinary genius, and then leave his works entirely to the reader's imagination' (Shaw 1976: 26). Hence the inclusion of 'The Revolutionist's Handbook' in the appendix to the printed play text. This prompts the question: what is the perceived quality of the work of the artists represented in Shaw's drama, and how does he convey that quality to an audience?

The quality of Octavius's literary endeavours (perhaps they do not exist) remains unknown. A review in the *Times Literary Supplement* referred to him as an 'alleged' poet: 'So far as the play is concerned the "poet" might just as well have been a dry-salter' (Crompton 1971: 113). A. M. Gibbs astutely remarked that 'In the larger allegory of the play, Octavius is associated with sentimentality, debased romanticism and the poetic idealization of women . . . the qualities he is associated with . . . are seen forming part of the condition of hell' (Gibbs 1983: 124). The quality of the work of Eugene, Louis Dubedat, Apollodoru, and the Martellus and Pygmalion partnership is more germane to the theme of the play in which each appears. Charles Berst asserts that, in Eugene's case, 'his spirit is more poetic than his talents' (Berst 1973: 57). Eugene's passages of poetic prose, notably the speech about his dream of taking Candida away to 'where the marble floors are washed by the rain and dried by the sun; where the south wind dusts the beautiful green and purple carpets' (Shaw 1946a: 142), are meretricious, no doubt deliberately so. This example, together with the description of Candida as the Madonna (ibid.: 161), might be designed as parody, assigning Eugene to the category of poets described by Shaw in *The Sanity of Art*, 'who have nothing to versify but the commonplaces of amorous infatuation' (Weintraub 1989: 383). The truth of Eugene's poetic genius remains suspect, and Shaw does not provide the audience with any of his original work – probably because the dramatist himself was no poet.

One is left in no doubt as to the genius of Louis Dubedat in *The Doctor's Dilemma*. It is an integral feature of his character and of the 'dilemma' explored in the play. The doctors are agreed about his brilliance as a painter, but this is difficult for the audience or the reader to judge. Shaw, however, evolved a clever device for actualizing Dubedat's talent. The painting on which he is working in Act III is of his wife, and Jennifer is seen modelling for it on the throne, beautiful, caring and draped in brocade. We can have a clear impression of what the picture will be – Louis, having 'Pygmalion-like' transformed a naïve young Cornishwoman into the splendid creature she now is, will continue posthumously to create beautiful Jennifers according to his preordained instructions. But Louis's art is not only two-dimensional. Today, he would be credited with a talent for 'installations' or 'live art', as witnessed by his staging of his own death-scene before an invited audience. In his invalid's chair, flanked by Jennifer and Sir Ralph, he occupies the position in which his easel was previously placed, the embodied 'picture' replacing the painted one. Louis is *'making the most of his condition, finding voluptuousness in languor and drama in his death'* (Shaw 1987: 169). Urging his wife to remarry and always to remain beautiful, and assuring her that he will live on in her, he utters his artist's creed: 'I believe in Michael Angelo,

Velasquez, and Rembrandt; in the might of design, the mystery of colour, the redemption of all things by Beauty everlasting, and the message of Art that made these hands blessed. Amen. Amen' (ibid.: 174). His final posthumous work of art is the appearance of Jennifer created according to his directions, '*wonderfully and beautifully dressed and radiant, carrying a great piece of purple silk, handsomely embroidered, over her arm*' (ibid.: 179). With this cloth she covers his dead body: another triumph for the artist.

Dubedat's paintings are on exhibition in the gallery which is the setting for Act V, but are hardly sufficiently visible for an audience to make any serious judgement. On the occasion of the first production at the Royal Court, however, Shaw borrowed paintings from the Carfax Gallery to dress the stage. As Weintraub describes, these were the works of 'Beardsley, Rothenstein, Augustus John, Charles Ricketts and Charles Shannon' (Weintraub 1989: 28). This evinced a scathing notice from Max Beerbohm in the *Saturday Review* (24 November 1906): 'Dubedat seems to have caught, in his brief lifetime, the various styles of all the young lions of the Carfax Gallery... Masterpieces of painting must be kept to an audience's imagination. [...] only by suggestion can these masterpieces be made real to us.' The solecism was, however, committed by Shaw the director, not Shaw the dramatist.

In *Caesar and Cleopatra* Apollodorus's exquisite taste in craftsmanship, very much in the style of William Morris, Shaw's mentor and friend who promoted the art of the beautifully useful, is evident in his sword: 'designed as carefully as a medieval cross [which] has a blued blade shewing through an openwork of purple leather and filigree' (Shaw 1946c: 184). This, 'the only weapon fit for an artist' (ibid.: 189), is put to use by its owner, who is an accomplished duellist, Cleopatra's 'perfect knight' (ibid.: 188), and a not inconsiderable soldier besides.

The work of those who 'create' or 'transform' human creatures is also available for judgement as to its quality. In *Pygmalion* Henry Higgins does 'make' a beautiful duchess from the apparently unpromising material of Eliza Doolittle (with help from Pickering and his mother), but his creation takes control of herself, and surpasses the imagination of her creator. Martellus and Pygmalion in *Back to Methuselah* (Part V) are less fortunate in their collaborative project and produce only primitive monsters, who are finally exterminated. Except in the last two examples, it is difficult to convey on stage the genius of the artist. It is much easier, as in the case of Octavius (*Man and Superman*) and Eugene (*Candida*), to indicate the absence of it, but using the devices with which he engages in *The Doctor's Dilemma*, Shaw makes a most convincing attempt.

The Artist in Society or Who Changes the World?

In all of Shaw's dramas which feature an artist or an aesthete, that character is brought into direct confrontation with one who holds a contrasting view of life – variously, soldiers, scientists, rationalists and social reformers. This section will examine how, or if, the conflicts are resolved.

Three of the plays, *Candida, Man and Superman* and *The Doctor's Dilemma*, have a triangular pattern of characterization, with a woman at the apex, and the artist and the other with whom he is in opposition or competition at the base. The woman is given an additional symbolic dimension: Candida 'is' the Virgin Mother, Ann 'is' Everywoman, and Jennifer 'is' the Muse. In competing for her, the men are, therefore, not merely sexual rivals but philosophical adversaries. Eugene is matched with James Morell, a Christian socialist; Octavius with Jack Tanner, a revolutionary and philosopher; Louis Dubedat with Ridgeon, a physician/scientist. Shaw thus 'tests' his artists in the boxing ring of contemporary social preoccupations.

In *Candida*, Morell, the charismatic preacher, and Eugene, the embryonic poet, are both equally engaged with words. Neither, however, has any sympathy with the manner in which the other chooses to deploy them. Candida is impressed by neither; she trivializes the effects of Morell's oratory, attributing his rhetorical effectiveness to his sex appeal, and Eugene's verses bore her. She would rather he reverted to his usual conversational 'moonshine'. The men's accomplishments are directly juxtaposed in Act III. The exhilaration of the returning Lexy and Prossy, in Dionysian high spirits, intoxicated not only by Burgess's champagne but by the excitement of Morell's revolutionary socialism, is set in sharp contrast to Candida's strictures on temperance and her failure to engage with Eugene's poetic endeavours. The 'artist' emerges as the 'stronger' man in terms of his self-sufficiency and capacity for coping with an independent existence, but Morell's successful commitment to social reform, in which Eugene has absolutely no interest, renders him the more effectual member of society.

Octavius Robinson in *Man and Superman*, would-be poet and playwright, is a highly conventional young man, firmly embedded in the manners and mores of English upper-middle-class society. His role as a poet is largely constructed by Jack Tanner. As Berst has pointed out: 'To prop his metaphysics [Tanner] gives Octavius a role which is entirely disproportionate to the ineffectual, untalented, romantic stripling' (Berst 1973: 114). Tanner has to create his generic adversary for the hand of Ann; Shaw does not provide one. Tanner's 'true artist' who 'will let his wife starve, his children go barefoot, his mother drudge for his living at seventy, sooner than work at anything but his art' (Shaw 1976: 61) is a million miles from Octavius Robinson. Just as Candida decides that Morell will better serve her maternal purposes, Ann selects and pursues Tanner because she needs a father for the Superman, and the barrenness of the so-called 'poetic temperament' is of no use to her. Jack Tanner's revolutionary fervour, his endless quest to improve society, as well as his sexual energy, select him as the chosen partner of 'Everywoman'. In each play, the 'poet' is defeated by the social reformer.

The Doctor's Dilemma, while broadly adhering to a similar triangular structure and maintaining the confrontational trope of the other plays, engages with these dramaturgical strategies to develop a somewhat different issue. True, in this last instance, the artist wins the woman who does not even notice the existence of his rival, but Shaw's purpose is to show the similarities between the artist and the man of science rather than their differences. The 'dilemma', as Sir Patrick expresses it, is 'a plain choice between a man and a lot of pictures', but 'the most tragic thing in the world', ironically articulated by Ridgeon, is 'a man of genius who is not a man of honour' (Shaw 1987: 176). Neither Dubedat or Ridgeon is an honourable man, although each is a highly gifted one. Ultimately the artist is the victor, for he achieves immortality for Jennifer, his Muse, and for his art. Ridgeon saves lives for this world alone.

The 'dilemma', or to be more explicit, the contest between the artist's output and his contribution to society, is further explored in two other plays by Shaw that do not adhere to the 'triangle' formula described above. In *Mrs Warren's Profession*, described by Berst as 'A moral allegory – the Battle for the Soul of Vivie Warren' (Berst 1973: 29), Praed is the most attractive tempter whom she encounters. Crofts, Frank and even her mother (finally) are more easily dismissed. But Praed is not tainted like the rest. He represents a cultured and civilized world, demonstrating to Vivie, and to the audience, that the capitals of Europe may be the sites of a chain of capitalist whorehouses but they are also centres of great art. Vivie's crude dismissal of the Gospel of Art which Praed preaches diminishes her and renders her final appearance alone in the putative seat of 'honour', the actuary's office, a bleak picture.

In *Caesar and Cleopatra*, Apollodorus, the Sicilian patrician, whose universal password 'Art for Art's sake' should render him among the damned, is not so much in an adversarial position in relation to Caesar as a complementary one. Caesar is represented as a great soldier and a wise and judicious ruler. He is a successful 'man of the world' in the best sense of the phrase. Although he jestingly dismisses Apollodorus as a 'popinjay' (Shaw 1946c: 216), he immediately acknowledges the wit and imagination of his conversation. On Caesar's departure from Egypt, he leaves Apollodorus in charge of the art of the 'colony' with the words (surely ironic and referring to the British as well as the Roman Empire):

CAESAR: Remember: Rome loves art and will encourage it ungrudgingly.
APOLLODORUS: I understand, Caesar. Rome will produce no art itself; but it will buy up and take away whatever the other nations produce.
CAESAR: What! Rome produce no art! Is peace not an art? Is war not an art? Is government not an art? Is civilization not an art? All these we give you in exchange for a few ornaments.

(Shaw 1946c: 239)

Caesar and Cleopatra reaches a nice balance in endorsing aesthetic sensibility as having a rightful place in the ideal state and in extending the concept and function of creativity to permeate all aspects of government. Thus, in the plays, as in his theoretical writings, Shaw questions the nature of art, the function of art, the engagement of art with political and social concerns – with the same ambiguities and the same dialectic.

Pictures in the Plays and on Stage

The printed texts of Shaw's dramas abound in references, explicit and implicit, to works of art, and his directorial notes to actors and scenic artists frequently offer advice on costume and setting. A key visual property in *Candida,* described as a 'modern Pre-Raphaelite play' (Shaw 1946a: vi), is the *'large autotype of the chief figure in Titian's Assumption of the Virgin'* (ibid.: 104) which hangs above the mantelpiece in Morell's study. One learns much about the characters and the meaning of the play from this picture (Adams 1966). Shaw notes in the stage directions that: *'A wise-hearted observer ... would not suspect either {Candida's} husband or herself of ... any concern with the art of Titian'* (ibid.: 104). Candida and Morell belong to the practical everyday world, of domestic chores in her case, and of social work in his. Shaw later was to comment that the picture has been 'boiled down to a cockney Candida' (Weintraub 1989: 20). It was a gift from Eugene, chosen because of the resemblance he perceived between Candida and the depiction of the Madonna. Eugene is the aesthete, the Pre-Raphaelite whose adoration of Candida is, as Margery Morgan aptly observes, 'a blend of erotic with religious emotion' (Morgan 1972: 76), expressed in his idealized description of her: 'Her shawl, her wings, the wreath of stars on her head, the lilies in her hand, the crescent moon beneath her feet' (Shaw 1946a: 161). The choice of Titian's painting over Shaw's earlier selection of Raphael's 'Sistine Madonna' was made because the former did not include the Christ child. There are no distracting children in *Candida* either. Conveniently the 'real' ones are still recuperating in the country where their mother has left them, and she makes virtually no reference to them throughout the play. It is first Eugene, and then Morell, who sits in the child's chair. Of the two adults whom Candida reduces to childhood, paradoxically but not surprisingly, it is the artist who leaves, taking with him the much-debated 'secret' in his heart. The man, poet or not, who saw the Madonna (Raphael's or Titian's) in a commonplace and predatory suburban housewife – 'a sentimental prostitute', according to Beatrice Webb (Morgan 1972: 72) – having the scales lifted from his eyes, must effect his escape. As for the mysterious 'secret', there is no reason to doubt Shaw's own explanation:

> The poet then rises up and says 'Out, then into the night with me' – Tristan's holy night. If this greasy fool's paradise is happiness, then I give it to you with both hands: 'life is nobler than that'. That is 'the poet's secret'. (Letter to James Huneker, 6 April 1904; Laurence 1972: 415)

Weintraub also draws attention to pictorial references in stage settings which give the spectator or reader important insights into character, for example the interior decoration of Roebuck Ramsden's study in Act 1 of *Man and Superman* and Mrs Higgins's drawing room in *Pygmalion.* The former contains *'autotypes of allegories by GF Watts'* (Shaw 1976: 25), a fashionable Victorian painter, first husband of the actress Ellen Terry. (Is this a Shavian quip, one wonders, considering his amorous correspondence with the lady?) Watts's allegories fit well with Ramsden's inherent conservatism and conventional moral attitudes. The collection of busts of John Bright and Herbert Spencer again attests to Ramsden's erstwhile radicalism, and the impression of the whole room gives physical corroboration to the description of him in the stage directions, namely that he '*believes in the fine arts with all the earnestness of a man who does not understand them*' (ibid.: 42). Similarly, in *Pygmalion* the decor of Professor Higgins's laboratory, with its arid engravings of architectural perspective drawings, is sharply contrasted with the elegance of his mother's Chelsea drawing room, with its Morris wallpaper and soft furnishings, and a selection of paintings in the Burne-Jones manner.

It is difficult to determine the extent to which an audience, certainly a twenty-first-century audience, would be qualified to read such visual references. But it is likely that at a time when women's fashions and home decoration were dictated by 'society drama' on the West End Stage, Shaw's contemporaries would be visually sophisticated. Even if specific references proved elusive, the overall effect of Shaw's artistic choices in terms of setting could not fail to illuminate an understanding of character and theme.

Conclusion: Platonist, Philosopher, Puritan and Playwright

It is easy to become enmeshed in the complex web of Shaw's opinions on art and artists. A few constants do, however, emerge: a work of art must be grounded in the society from which it grows and must contribute to the progress of that society, spiritually, morally or practically. Romance, prettiness and superficial sentiment will not serve. Great artists, be they poets, painters, craftsmen or dramatists, must be philosophers, moralists or prophets of their own 'religion', from which their art will draw its power. Shaw's own work is testimony to his aesthetics.

PRIMARY READING

Shaw, George Bernard (1930). *Major Critical Essays*. London: Constable.

Shaw, George Bernard (1931). *Our Theatre in the Nineties*. 3 vols. London: Constable.

Shaw, George Bernard (1945). *Back to Methuselah*. Oxford: Oxford University Press.

Shaw, George Bernard (1946a). *Plays Pleasant*. London: Penguin. (Includes *Candida*.)

Shaw, George Bernard (1946b). *Plays Unpleasant*. London: Penguin. (Includes *Mrs Warren's Profession*.)

Shaw, George Bernard (1946c). *Three Plays for Puritans*. London: Penguin. (Includes *Caesar and Cleopatra*.)

Shaw, George Bernard (1976). *Man and Superman*. London: Penguin.

Shaw, George Bernard (1987). *The Doctor's Dilemma*. London: Penguin.

FURTHER READING

Adams, Elsie B. (1966). 'Bernard Shaw's Pre-Raphaelite Drama', *PMLA* 81:5, 428–38.

Albert, Sidney P. (1956). 'Bernard Shaw: The Artist as Philosopher', *Journal of Aesthetics and Art Criticism* XIV:4, 419–38.

Berst, Charles A. (1973). *Bernard Shaw and the Art of Drama*. Urbana, IL, and London: University of Illinois Press.

Carpenter, Edward (1908). *The Intermediate Sex: A Study of Some Transitional Men and Women*. London: Allen and Unwin.

Crompton, Louis (1971). *Shaw the Dramatist*. London: Allen and Unwin.

Doan, William J. (2001). 'The Doctor's Dilemma: Adulterating a Muse', *Annual Conference of Bernard Shaw Studies* 21, 151–61.

Edwards, Sashona 'The Worthy Adversaries: Benjamin R. Tucker and G. Bernard Shaw'. www.uncletaz.com/liberty/shaw.html.

Evans, T. F. (ed.) (1976). *Shaw: The Critical Heritage*. London: Routledge and Kegan Paul.

Gibbs, A. M. (1983). *The Art and Mind of Shaw*. London: Macmillan.

Laurence, Dan H. (ed.) (1972). *Bernard Shaw: Collected Letters: 1898–1919*. London, Sydney and Toronto: Max Reinhardt.

Meisel, Martin (1984). *Shaw and the Nineteenth-Century Theatre*. New York: Limelight Editions.

Morgan, Margery M. (1972). *The Shavian Playground*. London: Methuen.

Peters, Sally (1996). *The Ascent of the Superman*. New Haven, CT, and London: Yale University Press.

Spink, Judith B. (1963). 'The Image of the Artist in the Plays of Bernard Shaw', *Shaw Review* 6, 82–8.

Weintraub, Stanley (1989). *Bernard Shaw on the London Art Scene*. University Park and London: Pennsylvania University Press.

West, Alick (1950). *A Good Man Fallen Among Fabians*. London: Laurence and Wishart.

Woodbridge, Homer (1963). *Bernard Shaw: Creative Artist*. Carbondale, IL: South Illinois University Press.

6

Granville Barker and the Court Dramatists

Cary M. Mazer

'Well, my dear Tommy, what are the two most important things in a man's character? His attitude towards money and his attitude towards women' (5), says Philip Madras to his friend Major Hippisley-Thomas at the very beginning of *The Madras House* (1910) by H. Granville Barker (1877–1946) – dramatist, actor, progressive theatre manager, pioneering stage director, national theatre advocate, theorist and scholar.[1] Unpack the word 'money' to include what the Victorians and Edwardians called 'political economy', and the word 'women' to include courtship, marriage and sex, from both a male and a female perspective, and you have not only a summation of Granville Barker's chief dramatic and theatrical concerns, but also one of the boldest statements of its kind in British theatre until one of the characters in Caryl Churchill's 1979 *Cloud Nine* opines that 'you can't separate fucking and economics' (Churchill 1985: 309).

The intersection of gender and political economy is not self-evident in Barker's plays. Many critics want it one way or the other: the first book-length study of Barker as a dramatist, titled *A Drama of Political Man* (Morgan 1961), emphasizes the political; and a more recent biography (Salmon 1983), taking its title from a later Barker play unproduced in its day, *The Secret Life* (published in 1923), emphasizes the inwardly psychological. And yet clearly Barker's plays deal with the interplay of both. Four of Barker's six solo-authored full-length plays – *The Marrying of Anne Leete* (1902), *Waste* (1907), *The Secret Life* (1923) and his last play, also unproduced in his lifetime, *His Majesty* (published in 1928) – deal explicitly with intricate parliamentary manoeuvres, party affiliation, reform initiatives and (often fictional) public policy, to so great an extent that the plays run the risk of sinking beneath near-impenetrable expositions and plot complications. And yet the final sequences of all of these plays, as well as Barker's two non-parliamentary plays – *The Voysey Inheritance* (1905) and *The Madras House* – involve a man and a woman, whether husband and wife, fiancé and fiancée or brother and sister, sitting down and talking, negotiating or renegotiating their partnership and their attitudes towards romance and sexuality. No plot – political, economic, legal or financial – resolves itself independently of the relation between a man and a woman, or between men and women at large. Although *The Madras House* clearly deals with the fashion industry, the marriage market, 'surplus' women, the morality of the 'live-in' system of industrial labour, and the commodification of women (Kaplan and Stowell 1994: 121–40), I am not arguing that Barker's plays are *about* sex any more than they are *about* politics or social policy. Barker's ostensible topics (legislation, finance, fashion) are stand-ins for more complex issues: the life of the mind, the soul and the imagination, as it is manifest in the most basic of human relationships and the shape, structure and spirit of the larger community. In Barker's dramatic universe, the personal and the political are en-meshed and inseparable.

In *Waste*, for example, his play most centrally concerned with politics, the premise, while mirroring contemporary events, is ostentatiously fictitious: the Conservative party is about to form a government, and is trying to strengthen its power base and disarm a Liberal party issue by crafting a comprehensive bill to disestablish the Church of England. Henry Trebell, nearing 50 and at the height of his energies, is an independent MP, until recently aligned with the Liberals, who is being courted by the Conservatives with the promise of a Cabinet position. He is using his promised new power to craft a visionary version of the disestablishment bill that will radically restructure the nation's education system, and potentially the class system – the very fabric of society. Trebell is also an amoralist. On the eve of the election, he seduces Amy O'Connell, a Catholic, childless and neglected married woman. A few months later, as the government is forming, she comes to him revealing that she is pregnant, and tells Trebell that she is seeking an abortion, which he opposes.[2]

A political scandal looms after she dies at the hands of the abortionist and her estranged Irish husband threatens to go public. The soon-to-be prime minister and his party cronies meet to try and avert a political disaster, and though the husband agrees to keep quiet at the inquest, the politicians decide, over the course of a long, excruciatingly intricate and theatrically fascinating discussion, to jettison Trebell and to drop virtually everything visionary from his bill. Trebell waits to hear the outcome of their deliberations through the long night back in his study. He hears late that night that the scandal has been avoided, but learns early the next morning by private post that he and his bill have been dropped. He goes off to his room, and as we learn in the next scene, puts a bullet through his head.

Why does Trebell kill himself? We learn all there is to learn during the play's final scenes. Early in the morning, Trebell sits with his sister Frances, an unmarried schoolmistress now devoting her life to assisting Trebell's political career, and explains his state of mind. The reasons he gives for his despair are multiple. Certainly there is the politics: the evisceration of his bill, and the prospect that his great political opportunity has passed him, that even if he were to return to being an independent or join the opposition, he is, with regards to his ability to transform society, now useless – a wasted man as the result of a wasted opportunity. Certainly there is Amy's abortion: though he had no desire actively to father her child, his eyes were opened, from hearing her renounce motherhood, to the new life he was bringing into the world: a life that, like Amy's own, is now wasted. And certainly he becomes aware of the waste of human vitality represented by the limited opportunities open to women of the ruling classes, which he (and we) witness: the spectacle of the political wives and mistresses orbiting around the party polls; Amy's social uselessness, adrift as an estranged wife; and the devotion of Frances, whose intellect he values but exploits in his service.

Writing about John Barton's 1985 production for the Royal Shakespeare Company at the Pit (which drew its script from both the 1909 published text and Barker's radical revision of 1926), theatre critic Michael Billington praised Daniel Massey for conveying 'the sense of a public idealist suddenly awakening to the flatness and vacancy of his private life'.[3] But *is* this what Trebell discovers? *Is* his private life – even without the ability to procreate – flat and vacant? And even if so, is *that* the problem? No: what is going on in the final tragic movement of *Waste* cannot be summed up so simply; to select any one of the reasons that Trebell identifies is to neglect the others.

As Barker returned to his Edwardian plays to revise them later in his career, these final duologues received the most attention. In the 1926 version of *Waste* (Barker called it not a revision but a re-write), the scene between Trebell and Frances is streamlined, but by no means simplified. 'This one piece of work,' Frances asks her brother, 'had it come to mean everything to you?' 'I'd never given myself away before', he replies: 'It's a dreadful joy to do that … to become part of a purpose bigger than your own. Another strength is added to your own … it's a mystery. But it follows, you see, that having lost myself in the thing … the loss of it leaves me a dead man' (105). That 'one piece of work' is clearly the bill; but it is also, if only symbolically, the baby. The truth of Trebell's motivation, upon which the tragedy hinges, lies between (or rather among) reverberant multiple causes. What Barker has created in Trebell is a psychological complexity, which exceeds virtually all of his theatrical contemporaries writing in English.

Barker aspired to complexity of character in every facet of his work in the theatre. As a stage director, he was famous for asking his actors to create back-stories for their characters (McDonald 1984; Mazer 1984). In his work as an actor he played not only eloquent Shavian mouthpieces such as John Tanner and poetic cads such as Shaw's Frank Gardner and Dubedat, and Pierrot in his own Maeterlinckian fairy-tale play *Prunella* (1904, and co-authored with Laurence Housman), but also troubled, neurasthenic visionaries such as Shaw's Marchbanks, Cusins and Father Keegan. In his published scripts, Barker often used elaborate instructions. One critic has observed that 'it is as if Stanislavski had written stage directions for Chekhov's plays' to pin down the social stratum, breeding, education and consequent values of his characters with precision (McDonald 1986: 89). But as Trebell reveals, Barker creates characters who can't be fully pinned down; and often they cannot even pin themselves down. In many ways Barker was writing dramatic characters for an acting approach that had

not yet been articulated in Britain. It is no surprise then that Barker was impressed by
Stanislavski and his work at the Moscow Art Theatre, which Barker visited in 1914.
Barker's obsession with the psychological in his two postwar plays, and the oblique-
ness of much of his dialogue, led some of his friends to wonder whether his plays
could be acted at all. Barker disagreed. As he wrote to William Archer in 1923, 'I
never have – I *cannot* – write an unactable play. . . . But there is no English company
of actors so trained to interpret thought and less crude emotions, nor, as a consequence, any select audience interested in watching and listening to such things'
(Salmon 1986: 96). As Barker often complained (increasingly so after World War I,
when he was no longer involved in theatre management), he was writing for a theatre
that did not yet exist.

But though he worked tirelessly to bring that theatre into being, he was also
prepared to work within the structures and material conditions of his time. In all
things – acting, management, playwriting and politics – Barker was always both
visionary and realist.

By 1904, still only in his twenties, Barker was a seasoned theatre professional and
also a theatrical revolutionary. On stage since his childhood, first as a platform
recitalist, then with various regional repertory companies, Barker had already co-
authored several plays (with fellow actor Berte Thomas).[4] He had acted Richard II
(1899) and Edward II (1903) for the Elizabethan revivalist director William Poel;
performed numerous parts for the Stage Society;[5] created the roles of Frank in Shaw's
censored *Mrs Warren's Profession* (1902) and Marchbanks in *Candida* (1900); and his
first solo-authored play, *The Marrying of Anne Leete*, had just been presented by the
Stage Society. The Stage Society had deputized Barker and the progressive theatre
critic William Archer (Shaw's friend, and champion and translator of Ibsen) to draw
up a detailed prospectus for a national theatre, a version of institutional theatres such
as the Comédie Française and the Burg- and Staatstheaters of Central Europe. British
advocates envisioned an officially recognized theatre that would perform old and new
plays in repertoire, and would be subsidized by an endowment, freeing it from the
pressures of commercial viability. 'It is not an "Advanced" theatre that we are
designing', Barker and Archer lied, excluding from the sample repertoire 'all plays
of the class which may be called disputable [. . .] For this reason the names of Tolstoy,
Gorky, Ibsen, Björnson, Hauptmann, D'Annunzio, and Bernard Shaw do not figure in
our list of authors' (Archer and Granville Barker 1907: 44).

But an 'advanced' theatre for the 'advanced' drama was precisely what Barker and
Archer really wanted. At the very time that the privately printed edition of their 'blue
book', *Schemes and Estimates for a National Theatre*, appeared – with endorsements from
leading actor-managers, managers and playwrights (several of whom would have been
scared off by Ibsen and Shaw) – Barker was taking on the management of the Court
Theatre in London's Sloane Square, which he ran from 1904 to 1907. 'It seems to me
that we may wait a very long time for our National Theatre,' Barker wrote to Archer,
shortly before launching the first of three Court seasons, 'and that when it comes we
may have no modern national Drama to put in it' (Salmon 1986: 42). New plays and

productions were introduced in a limited series of matinées to evade censorship, and some of these plays then moved into extended runs in the evening. By the end of Barker's third and last Court season, the theatre had produced 21 plays – 13 by British and Irish authors, five by modern European dramatists and three by Euripides (in Gilbert Murray's translations). With 701 performances of 11 plays by Bernard Shaw (out of 988 performances overall), the Court was perceived to be the House of Shaw (Euripides ran a distant second, with 48 performances, tied with Barker's and Housman's *Prunella*). But Barker's principal goal was to provide a home to and serve as an incubator for less prolific and less logorrhoeac 'New Dramatists'. In his subsequent seasons at other more centrally located theatres – the Savoy, St James's, the Kingsway and the Duke of York's (in a commercial venture with the American impresario Charles Frohman) – Barker was involved with eight more Shaw productions. He also produced and directed more plays by Arnold Bennett, George Meredith, Thomas Hardy, John Galsworthy, St John Hankin and John Masefield, whose earlier works he had first produced at the Court. If Barker's goal, as expressed in a letter to Archer, was to nurture a 'modern national Drama', he had arguably succeeded by World War I. He had produced Shaw and numerous other promising playwrights; he had brought to the stage the plays of Elizabeth Robins and Elizabeth Baker, which were then taken up by women-led theatre societies and managements (see chapters 4 and 8 of this volume). He had also inspired his protégés to found new repertory theatres in Manchester, Liverpool, Birmingham and Glasgow – all modelled on the Court Theatre.[6]

Barker's lifelong quest for a new theatre, and his willingness to compromise and work within existing structures, are consistent with the socialist politics of the Fabian Society, which Barker joined on Shaw's urging in 1901. The Fabian Society, founded by Shaw and Beatrice and Sidney Webb in 1884, called for the complete restructuring of political and economic institutions into an egalitarian socialist state. It also proposed that these new institutions could be built up gradually by the incremental transformation of existing structures. The plays by Barker and the other playwrights of the New Drama – most of which premiered under Barker's management and/or under his direction – demonstrably borrowed many Fabian strategies.

John Galsworthy (1867–1933) foregrounds social problems: class inequity in *The Silver Box* (1906); labour unrest in *Strife* (1909); and the criminal justice system in *Justice* (1910). He creates materially detailed portraits of parallel social and economic worlds, above stairs and below. The political-economic dramas are always seen through the lens of the human agents forced to act within them, often at the expense of political analysis. In *Strife*, for example, the stand-off between the corporate board of directors and the tin factory's wild-cat strikers is as much the product of the stubbornness of Anthony, the company's chairman, and Roberts, the hot-headed leader of the wild-cat strikers, as it is of the inherent conflict of capital and labour. A major focus of Galsworthy's plays seems to be the failure of liberalism to combat systemic inequities. In *The Silver Box*, the liberal MP realizes that his chambermaid's unemployed alcoholic husband, on trial for theft, is no more nor less responsible than his own ne'er-do-well son, who, drunk after a night out, has stolen his lady-friend's purse to 'score off her' (Galsworthy 1929: 3). Yet he cannot summon the courage to speak in the thief's defence. Anthony's daughter (who is married to the tin-factory manager) in *Strife* finds that the basket of jelly that she brings to Roberts's starving wife is unwelcome. And in *Justice*, the junior partner fails to stand up to his father, who chooses to press charges against Falder, a clerk caught altering a cheque and pocketing the difference. Falder's lawyer is unable to persuade the judge to be lenient; and Cokeson, the managing clerk who continues to pity Falder during his three years' hard labour, fails to persuade the warden to move him out of solitary confinement. Galsworthy's emphasis is, admirably, always on the human cost of social injustice – to Falder above all – but it is also on the incidental victims: the chambermaid accused of her husband's crime in *The Silver Box*; Mrs Roberts in *Strife*, whose death from starvation and exposure precipitates the fall from power of both Roberts and Anthony; and Falder's lover, an abused wife on whose behalf he has embezzled from his employer. Even in *Justice*, his most explicitly agitational play, Galsworthy's politics are Dickensian: seeking reform through exposing social ills, rather than contemplating, let alone proposing, systemic change.

The satiric comedies of St John Hankin (1869–1909) – anti-romantic retellings of Victorian and Edwardian cup-and-saucer comedies and 'problem' plays – are political in the same way as Galsworthy's. Detailed group portraits of conflicting strata of society demonstrate how the morality and ethics of one class function in differing ways in another. The social criticism, if any, lies in the characters who traverse class boundaries, who are cynically able to manipulate these contradictions for their own purposes. The titular ne'er-do-well in *The Return of the Prodigal* (1905) returns to extort money from his industrialist father and striving brother, and in doing so explicitly draws a parallel (much as Galsworthy does in *The Silver Box*) between the leisured lives of the upper middle classes and the forced idleness and alcoholism of the chronically unemployed labouring classes. And the mother in *The Cassilis Engagement* (1907), Hankin's cynical retelling of T. W. Robertson's 1867 *Caste*, entraps her son's lower-class fiancée and her disreputable mother in an extended country-house visit so that they will ultimately call off the engagement themselves. Like Galsworthy's condemnation of failed liberalism, Hankin's satire is often directed at the upper classes; but it is levelled as mercilessly at the lower- and lower-middle-class characters as well: witness the fiancée and her mother in *The Cassilis Engagement* and the middle-class social outcasts in *The Charity that Began at Home* (1906), who are ridiculed with even greater cruelty than are the upper-middle-class mother and daughter who misguidedly bestow their hospitality on them.

In many ways, John Masefield (1878–1967) is the obverse of Hankin, with early-nineteenth-century labourers' rustic cottages in Gloucestershire replacing the contemporary country houses, and with events leading not to acid comedy but to heightened tragedy. There are no villains in Galsworthy's and Hankin's plays, only well-meaning but impotent do-gooders, con-men and stooges, stuffed shirts and fools. But in Masefield's plays, a single argument is enough to motivate a ne'er-do-well son to send his mother and brother and himself to the gallows for a murder that never took place in *The Campden Wonder* (1907). And one spiteful foster-mother can turn the Cinderella-like title character of *The Tragedy of Nan* (1908) into a righteous, vengeful murderess out of a Greek tragedy. Though Masefield's dramatic voice is closer to those of his friends W. B. Yeats and J. M. Synge, and his sense of fate closer to Thomas Hardy's than to that of his Court-Theatre contemporaries, one can understand Barker's advocacy of the plays (over the objections of his business partner, J. E. Vedrenne). As in Galsworthy's and Hankin's plays, a trivial incident or a small physical object (a soiled coat, a broken Toby jug) can reveal the personal and material values of the characters, and can unleash the inexorably collective values of the community. And above all, Barker as stage director and nurturer of New Drama is interested in community (he was famous for crowd scenes, such as the union meeting in *Strife* and the suffrage rally in Trafalgar Square in *Votes for Women!*).

Granville Barker shares with his fellow New Dramatists an attention to telling detail, and an ability to peg his characters not only in their essential behavioural traits but in their precise position in the social and economic order. He is a master of seemingly throwaway details that offer a glimpse into a world just beyond the confines of the play's main action. For example, the youngest Voysey sister, Ethel, who is promised an engagement present by her father in Act II and misses his funeral in Act III because of her pregnancy, disappears from the play with a sighing reference to 'Poor little Ethel' in Act V (152). Barker also shares Hankin's flair for comedy: witness the raucous portrait of the interclass wedding party in Act IV of *The Marrying of Ann Leete*, the scathing satire of the extended Voysey family around the dinner table in *The Voysey Inheritance*, and the gentle comedy of the antiphonal 'how d'you do's' of the six spinster daughters in the Huxtable household in Denmark Hill throughout the first act of *The Madras House*.

At first glance, Barker's central characters seem to be more passive than those of his contemporaries. Shaw called them 'worms' (letter to Barker, 19 January 1908, in Shaw 1957: 115), and observed that Barker's style was as different to his own as 'Debussy's to Verdi's'.[7] Always suspicious of grand theatrical effects (what the Victorians called 'strong curtains'), Barker tried to dissuade Galsworthy from having Falder jump out of the window at the end of *Justice* as he is about to be rearrested for violating his parole. Yet the apparent passivity of Barker's protagonists is, paradoxically, what makes them seem more three-dimensional and more complex than Galsworthy's, Hankin's, Masefield's and even Shaw's. Until those signature final duologues, the central characters spend more time listening than speaking, more time reacting than acting, all the while thinking and brooding until the moments they are forced to decide their future and reformulate their relation to the larger world. Even Trebell, Barker's most vital and active protagonist, spends most of Act II – when not trying to persuade his new Cabinet colleagues to support his bill – listening to others: to his physician, his sister, the distraught Amy and the young fiancée of his private secretary, who is grooming herself as a political wife. Trebell's final actions are ultimately based as much on what he hears from others as on what he is and does.

Barker employed a protagonist both passive and reactive as early as his first solo play, *The Marrying of Ann Leete*. A *fin de siècle* piece set one hundred years earlier at the previous *fin de siècle*, the play depicts Ann's realization that love, marriage and sex are subordinated to issues of party politics, money and class. The play opens at the dead of night, when she is kissed by a young aristocrat in what turns out to be her father's elaborate manipulations to switch parties and return to Parliament. Even if we consider her an Edwardian 'New Woman' a century before her time ('I could become all that you are and more,' Ann says to her sister, 'but I don't choose'; Barker 1987: 68), her sudden decision to propose to John Abud, the family gardener, seems to come out of nowhere, until we track what she experiences and learns from her older sister's political marriage from a decade earlier, and from her brother's sudden joy at his *déclassé* wife's off-stage childbirth. That she barely knows Abud, and has not articulated what love and sex might mean to her, make the final dialogue between the newlyweds, illuminated by a single candle in his cottage, less a resolution than an unsolved proposition, the beginning of the next chapter in an ongoing drama rather than the conclusion of this one.

The Voysey Inheritance is less elliptical than *The Marrying of Ann Leete*, more linear, and more Galsworthy-like in its subject. Voysey is a family solicitor who has systematically embezzled the low-interest earnings from his clients' trust funds to put towards his own higher-risk speculations. On his death, his son and junior partner Edward, who has only recently learned the true nature of his 'inheritance', must decide what to do next. The play's topicality, its relatively clear exposition, and its freedom from the Cabinet-room intrigues of *The Marrying of Ann Leete*, *Waste* and *The Secret Life* have made it the most revived of Barker's plays (both during Barker's lifetime and in recent decades). But the play's ostensible topic is really a synecdoche for the capitalist system as a whole. Immediately after the funeral, Edward Voysey tells his siblings about their father's extra-legal activities. He is surprised to learn that they would rather he continue working within the morally (and literally) near-bankrupt system than let it all go bust and go to jail. Old Voysey may have been a thief but, as Edward comes to learn, all capital accumulation, investment and living off unearned income is theft. Edward's series of choices is a tidy analogue for the choices available to the progressive intellectual working in a capitalist world: should one – indeed, *can* one – work within an inherently inequitable system to try to protect the weakest victims of that system? Can one remodel, let alone bring down, the master's house using the master's tools?

Here again, the seeming passivity of the protagonist is a key both to his character and to the complexities of the moral and ethical choices facing him over the course of the play. While Edward grapples with his decisions about whether, and how, to continue working within a business and the larger political system that have become increasingly abhorrent to him, he witnesses the posturings of his siblings and family friends around the family dinner table (which dominates three of the play's five acts).

As is characteristic for a Barker play, Edward's final decision is intertwined with his decision to enter into a romantic partnership with his long-time intended, Alice Maitland, an orphaned family ward with her own income. Alice gives him the vocabulary to describe what he is already sensing about the capitalist system. More significantly, she offers to share his new-found vocation. At the end of the play, Alice offers Edward a choice: 'to refuse me my work and happiness in life and to cripple your own nature ... or to take my hand' (Granville Barker 1987: 158). '*She puts out her hand frankly, as a friend should*', the stage directions read; '*With only a second's thought he, happy too now, takes it as frankly.*' And with that handshake (which disappears in Barker's 1934 revision), the political and the personal, the sociological and the sexual, are once again intertwined. 'The world', Alice concludes, 'must be put tidy' (159).

The Madras House is structured entirely around Philip's reactions to the events unfolding before his eyes. There is nothing immediately at stake: before the play begins, he has already decided to sell off the family couturier house to an American investor, and to run for the London County Council (LCC). All we see in the play itself is a series of encounters that Philip experiences, a parade of scenes and vignettes about the political economy of marriage: the household of his unmarried Huxtable cousins; a case of a secret marriage, an extra-marital affair and a secret pregnancy among the workers in the Huxtable ready-to-wear factory and showrooms; and Philip's best friend's confession that he is on the verge of an affair with Jessica, Philip's neglected high-society wife. The play's brilliant third act is all show: a fashion show for the benefit of the American investor; an eloquent Shavian-style discussion of femininity, beauty, sex and marriage between Philip's abashed uncle, the bloviating American (who both idolizes women and sees them as consumers of his retail products), and Philip's long-absent father Constantine, who has converted to Islam and become a polygamist. But it is not until the final discussion in Act IV that Philip, whom we have observed watching the parade of women and listening to the debates about gender, finally gets to renegotiate his romantic, sexual and intellectual relationship with his wife. And, as in the final scenes of *The Marrying of Ann Leete*, *The Voysey Inheritance* and *Waste*, he attempts to negotiate between the personal and the political, the individual life of the spirit and what is no less than the future of modern civilization. If civilization is measured by women's fashions and the marriage market, Philip explains to Jessica, then maybe their daughter Mildred, in boarding school, should be taught instead to appreciate what is ugly rather than what is beautiful but merely ornamental. The ending is ambiguous. We have reason to doubt the degree of satisfaction Philip will derive from his work on the LCC, dealing with the material conditions of his community while important matters go unresolved. He is none too confident that he and Jessica can escape the 'farmyard world of sex' (Granville Barker 1977: 136). But, just as Edward and Alice join hands at the end of *The Voysey Inheritance*, Philip and Jessica literally meet one another halfway and kiss,[8] then stand before the hearth together contemplating their future. 'Male and female created He them ... and left us to do rest. Men and women are a long time in the making', he tells Jessica. 'I grant it's not easy', he adds, 'But it's got to be done' (137).

Barker's postwar plays end with the principal characters withdrawing from an engagement with the political world: Evan Stroud, the politician making a comeback in *The Secret Life*, throws over his parliamentary race to catch a liner bound for America to be with his one-time lover, who he knows will have died by the time he arrives. King Henry, in the Ruritanian political melodrama *His Majesty* (premiered 1992), who has returned to his civil-war-ravaged country to mediate between rival factions, is ultimately forced to abdicate and go into permanent exile. Those dramas, along with a 1915 one-act play tellingly titled *Farewell to the Theatre*, have led many of Barker's critics and biographers to relate his work to his own postwar withdrawal from theatre management and political activism, for a life as a country squire with his second wife. Barker spent most of his time writing Shakespeare criticism (the *Prefaces to Shakespeare*, still in print, for which he is now perhaps best known), translating plays from Spanish and French, occasionally directing, writing book-length schemes for theatre education and his beloved national theatre, developing his pioneering ideas on dramaturgy and literary management[9] and revising his early plays into versions of greater obliquity, deeper psychologizing, and less and less conclusiveness.

It is tempting to read Barker's almost mythic withdrawal backwards into his pre-war plays: Ann Leete, sitting with her new husband in his gardener's cottage, has dropped out from the political and social world; Trebell has put a bullet through his head; and though Edward and Philip choose to continue to engage in the world, they both end their plays, holding their partners' hands, uncertain of their ability to effect the Herculean transformation of the world of which Shaw's protagonists seem so sublimely confident. But to condemn Barker and his characters for withdrawing from the world is to view the personal and the political as a binary, something that Barker, even in his postwar plays and revisions, refuses to do. 'Our fireside problem is the world's in a sense', Philip Madras reminds his wife Jessica, in the final moments of the 1925 revision of *The Madras House*. Jessica has the last word in this version, bringing the cosmic issues of the play back into the scale of the interpersonal:

> JESSICA: I suppose we've still to set ourselves free. *(Then, lest life should seem too tremendous, and too dull, she turns to him with her pretty smile.)* So don't talk too much about things you don't understand.
> PHILIP: *(humorously meek)* I'll try not
> JESSICA: Poor Phil!   (Granville Barker 1977: 160)

Yes, Evan Stroud withdraws from politics and King Henry abdicates. But when Barker returns to his Edwardian plays to re-write them, it isn't to make his characters conform to a postwar pattern of withdrawal and abdication. Philip and Jessica, like Ann and Abud, Edward and Alice, and the despairing Trebell, even in their 1920s and 1930s incarnations, are still grappling with their relationships while, with as much energy and even greater sense of purpose, they struggle, in Trebell's words, 'to become part of a purpose bigger than [their] own'(105).

NOTES

1 Barker didn't start hyphenating his name as Granville-Barker, or using his full first name, Harley, in his published work until after World War I.

2 The abortion was the reason given by the Examiner of Plays for refusing the play a license, though Elizabeth Robins's *Votes for Women!* from the same year, which also featured an abortion, was approved.

3 Quoted in *Royal Shakespeare Company* 1984/5 (Stratford: RSC Publications, 1985), 101.

4 *The Family of the Oldroyds* (unproduced, 1895–6), *The Weather-Hen* (1899) and *Our Visitor to 'Work-a-Day'* (unproduced, 1898–9).

5 A members'-only society dedicated to presenting advanced European and British drama, often ones that could not pass the lord chamberlain's censorship. Established by Parliament in the Licensing Act of 1737, the requirement that new plays and translations be submitted to the lord chamberlain (specifically to the 'examiner of plays' in the lord chamberlain's office) to receive a licence for public performance persisted even after most of the provisions of the Act were abolished in the Theatre Reform Act of 1843, until a separate act of Parliament in 1967. Advanced plays of the 'New Drama', including Ibsen's *Ghosts*, Maeterlincks's *Mona Vanna*, Shaw's *Mrs Warren's Profession* and Barker's *Waste*, were denied licences. Private societies were able to evade censorship by charging membership fees and making the performances free to members. Barker, Shaw, Galsworthy and other playwrights testified against censorship to a Parliamentary Joint Committee in 1909.

6 Barker's legacy as a fosterer of new dramatic writing can still be seen, if only indirectly, at the Royal Court Theatre, which, since 1956, has been home to the English Stage Company, and has served as incubator to several generations of new writers.

7 'Granville-Barker: Some Particulars' (1946), *Drama* n.s. 3, repr. in West (1958: 266).

8 In the 1925 version, they offer to kiss, but when they come together hold hands instead.

9 Granville Barker is Britain's major theorist of dramaturgy; see Luckhurst (2006).

PRIMARY READING

Archer, William and Granville Barker, H. (1907). *A National Theatre: Schemes and Estimates*. London: Duckworth.

Galsworthy, John (1929). *The Plays of John Galsworthy*. London: Duckworth.

Granville Barker, H. (1919). *Waste* [revised version]. London: Sidgwick and Jackson.

Granville Barker, H. (1923). *The Secret Life*. London: Sidgwick and Jackson.

Granville Barker, H. (1928). *His Majesty*. London: Sidgwick and Jackson.

Granville Barker, H. (1938). *The Voysey Inheritance* [revised version]. London: Sidgwick and Jackson.

Granville Barker, H. (1977). *The Madras House* [1909 version, with an appendix of the 1925 revisions], ed. Margery M. Morgan. London: Methuen.

Granville Barker, H. (1987). *Plays by Granville Barker* [*The Marrying of Ann Leete*, *The Voysey Inheritance* (1913 version), *Waste* (1907 version)], ed. Dennis Kennedy. Cambridge: Cambridge University Press.

Hankin, St John (1912). *The Dramatic Works of St. John Hankin*. London: Martin Secker (repr. Great Neck: Core Collection Books, 1977).

Masefield, John (1925). *Prose Plays*. New York: Macmillan.

FURTHER READING

Churchill, Caryl (1985). *Plays: 1*. London: Methuen.

Clarke, Ian (1989). *Edwardian Drama*. London: Faber and Faber.

Johnston, Denis (ed.) (2002). *Granville Barker at the Shaw Festival*. Niagara-on-the-Lake: Academy of the Shaw Festival.

Kaplan, Joel and Stowell, Sheila (1994). *Theatre and Fashion: Oscar Wilde to the Suffragettes*. Cambridge: Cambridge University Press.

Kennedy, Dennis (1985). *Granville Barker and the Dream of Theatre*. Cambridge: Cambridge University Press.

Luckhurst, Mary (2006). *Dramaturgy: A Revolution in Theatre*. Cambridge: Cambridge University Press.

Mazer, Cary M. (1984). 'Actors or Gramophones: The Paradoxes of Granville Barker', *Theatre Journal* 36, 5–23.

McDonald, Jan (1984). 'New Actors for the New Drama' in James Redmond (ed.). *Drama and the Actor (Themes in Drama 6)*. Cambridge: Cambridge University Press, 121–39.

McDonald, Jan (1986). *The 'New Drama' 1900–1914*. New York: Grove Press.

McDonald, Jan and Hill, Leslie (eds.) (1993). *Harley Granville Barker: An Edinburgh Retrospective 1992*. Glasgow: Theatre Studies.

Morgan, Margery M. (1961). *A Drama of Political Man*. London: Sidgwick and Jackson.

Purdom, C. B. (1955). *Harley Granville Barker: Man of the Theatre, Dramatist and Scholar*. London: Rockliff.

Salenius, Elmer W. (1982). *Harley Granville Barker*. Boston: Twayne.

Salmon, Eric (1983). *Granville Barker: A Secret Life*. Rutherford: Fairleigh Dickinson University Press.

Salmon, Eric (ed.) (1986). *Granville Barker and his Correspondents*. Detroit: Wayne State University Press.

Shaw, George Bernard (1957). *Letters to Granville Barker*, ed. C. B. Purdom. New York: Theatre Arts Books.

West, E. J. (1958). *Shaw on Theatre*. New York: Hill and Wang.

7

Gregory, Yeats and Ireland's Abbey Theatre

Mary Trotter

On 27 December 1904, the Irish National Theatre Society, or the Abbey Theatre, opened its doors for the first time to an audience of Irish nationalists and literati. The Abbey actors performed a series of one-act plays by two of the leaders of the organization, William Butler Yeats (1865–1939) and Lady Augusta Gregory (1852–1932). The audience warmly received the theatre's debut and praised its mission to establish a distinctive Irish theatre aesthetic. But, even during this first evening, the tensions between some of the artists of the theatre and the nationalist community they claimed to serve were foreshadowed in Yeats's curtain speech. 'Authors', he said, 'must be free to choose their own way; but in their pilgrimage towards beauty and truth they require companions by the way' (Hogan and Kilroy 1976: 129). Yeats and Gregory, with the help of many others, had established the Abbey Theatre as a space for imagining and reinventing Irish culture, politics and drama; and went so far as to declare themselves the 'national theatre' of a nation yet to be recognized by the world. But they were still learning the craft of integrating their vision with the necessary 'companions by the way': actors, designers, other playwrights and an Irish audience deeply sensitive to how their culture would be represented before the world on this new, 'national' stage.

This chapter explores the critical, cultural and political negotiations surrounding the founding of Ireland's Abbey Theatre. It traces that history through the work of the two individuals who stayed with the Abbey project the longest of all its original members: Gregory and Yeats. It is easy to oversimplify their work in the theatre, either revering them as the sole founders of the movement, or caricaturing Yeats as a pontificating elitist, and Gregory as his faithful right hand. In truth, both artists brought different and important gifts to the Abbey, and both grew in very different ways politically and artistically thanks to their involvement in it. The ultimate success of the Abbey Theatre, and the dramatic movement of which it was a part, was largely generated out of the dynamic interactions between politics and art, playwrights and patrons, plays and players, individuals and groups, in its formative years. In working for the transformation of Irish culture through theatre, both Yeats and Gregory, like others who engaged in the Irish dramatic movement, were themselves transformed in both their art and their political ideals.

The Irish Literary Renaissance and the Politics of Cultural Performance

The Irish dramatic movement, like all modern drama movements, emerged out of a larger cultural revolution. Events like the inclusion of Ireland into the United Kingdom in 1800 (Act of Union), the death of almost a million in the Famine of 1845–9, and the emigration of one and a half million in the following decade (see Kiberd 1995: 21) created a cultural crisis; for now Irish nationalists had to fight not only the negative images of Ireland in the British media, but also what Douglas Hyde termed an increasing 'Anglicization' of the Irish people.[1] By the 1890s, cultural nationalist activities had sprung up at both high-art and grassroots levels. Through 'self-help' organizations like the Gaelic League and the Gaelic Athletic Association, Irish nationalists began taking Irish language courses, playing Irish games and consuming art that offered positive images of Irish culture. At the same time, artists and scholars supplied translations of ancient Irish myths and sagas, tracked down and published folk tales and created new work based on Irish themes and motifs, proving that ancient and modern Irish culture were worth serious intellectual inquiry.

Performances at Irish festivals and concerts became a natural community outlet for celebrating national identity, and such events nurtured a generation of amateur artists, actors and playwrights (Mathews 2003). During this period, three general types of nationalist plays emerged: the play based on an ancient Irish legend, usually written in verse and elaborately staged; the folk play celebrating an idealized image of Irish rural life; and the less popular but still present urban drama examining contemporary political pressures on Irish persons. At the same time, commercial stages like the Queen's Royal Theatre in Dublin saw their opportunity to attract nationalist audiences with melodramas on patriotic Irish themes (Herr 1991).

But the images of both ancient Ireland and contemporary rural Irish culture that emerged from these nationalist performances were in large part invented, designed to create an idealized image of Irish life that reflected the mores and desires of the contemporary movement more than those of heroes of ancient Irish sagas or modern fishermen on the Aran Islands. In other words, Irish cultural nationalism strove to produce what Eric Hobsbawm terms an 'invented tradition', one that could lift up the people while glossing over the internal class, religious and cultural rifts within the movement itself (see Hobsbawm and Ranger 1983). Of course, those rifts never disappeared and deeply affected the history of the movement. But regardless of their identity positions within the contemporary Irish scene, all artists involved in the cultural nationalist movement – and in the Irish dramatic movement that emerged from it – collaborated in the act of imagining and inventing an Ireland which moved away from political, economic and cultural domination and dependence on England. How an artist went about that task, therefore, was observed very carefully by other participants in the nationalist movement. And it was in this milieu that Yeats and Gregory offered their theatrical imaginings of Ireland.

Cultivating Playwrights: The Irish Literary Theatre

Yeats's and Gregory's interest in an Irish national theatre emerged from their work with cultural and political groups in Ireland, England and continental Europe. In the early 1890s, Yeats lived in London, rubbing shoulders with symbolists like Arthur Symons, pursuing an interest in mysticism and the occult with theosophists like Madame Blavatsky, and discussing Irish literary and political life through groups like the Irish National Literary Society. Yeats did participate in activist politics during this period, including heading the Wolfe Tone Memorial Committee and protesting against Queen Victoria's jubilee visit to Dublin. Along with the influence of nationalist revolutionary and writer John O'Leary, much of Yeats's political activism was inspired by his friendship with the beautiful, fervently anti-imperialist Maud Gonne – the subject of many of Yeats's most famous poems, and the inspiration for his most famous dramatic character, Cathleen ni Houlihan. But instead of devoting most of his time to public political activism like Gonne, Yeats wished to devote his energies to developing a modernist Irish idiom through his poetry, articulating a fascination with Celtic folklore and mysticism through the style of the European literary avant-garde.

Yeats's ideas about the theatre found stylistic inspiration from a range of writers in the symbolist movement of Europe, including Arthur Symons and André Antoine. But for the subject matter for his own drama, the myths and legends of his homeland, he came to rely heavily on the collaboration, support and expertise of his friend and patron, Lady Augusta Gregory. Augusta Persse Gregory was one of eight children in a politically conservative ascendancy family. Gregory escaped the philistinism of her family at 23 when she married Lord William Gregory, a former governor of Ceylon 39 years her senior. Her marriage enabled Gregory to travel throughout Europe, to meet influential people in government and the arts (Alfred, Lord Tennyson, was a friend of the family and she even had a brief affair with Wilfred Scawen Blount), and to begin to discover her gifts as a writer. After William's death in 1892, Gregory continued to pursue her career as an author, furthered her studies in the Irish language and gathered and translated folk stories from the Irish-speaking peasants in the west of Ireland. Her house at Coole Park, County Galway, soon turned into a centre for Irish literary and cultural activity. She supported and promoted the development and modernization of local industries in her community (McDiarmid and Waters 1995: xvi), and Irish artists and thinkers found themselves welcome guests in Gregory's home. While never abandoning completely her ascendancy sensibilities, Gregory's involvement in such a range of Irish cultural and political activities led to an increasing sympathy with – and involvement in – the move towards Irish independence. And it was Yeats who helped Gregory find the vehicle in which she could best combine her talents for the cause of Irish culture – the theatre. Gregory and Yeats met at a party in London in 1894, and by 1897 they had become fast enough friends, and sufficiently aware of the artistic influence they could gain from one another, for Yeats to spend much of the summer at Lady Gregory's estate. Yeats would consider Coole Park a second home and sanctuary for many summers to come. But they weren't the only theatre enthusiasts in the neighbourhood. That summer, Yeats and Gregory, along with Gregory's neighbour Edward Martyn and his cousin George Moore, decided that it was time to bring modernist theatre aesthetics to Irish stages in the service of cultural nationalism, and they resolved to establish an Irish literary theatre.

The project was an optimistic one. Yeats's only foray into professional theatre before this time had been the 1894 production of his play *The Land of Heart's Desire* at the Avenue Theatre in London. Gregory had no theatre experience and Edward Martyn had written only a few minor plays. George Moore was the only one of the four with any significant professional experience in the theatre: in fact, the notion of a high-art Irish theatre for an elect audience was first conceived by Moore in the early 1890s (Frazier 2000: 264–5). But what they did not have in experience, they made up in talent, connections and wealth. The theatre they imagined, while ultimately nationalist, was also an elite theatre, designed in the mode of the Independent Theatre Clubs in London or the Théâtre Libre in Paris, for the enjoyment of an intellectually discerning audience, in which the authors would have the freedom to experiment without the pressures of box office receipts. Yeats remarked that their ideal audience members were persons 'who read books and have ceased to go to the theatre' (Jeffares and Knowland 1975: 140). Such a theatre was pointedly counter to the democratic, community performances promoted by other Irish nationalist groups.

The Irish Literary Theatre's first public document was a letter to solicit funds for the project, which also served as a manifesto:

> We propose to have performed in Dublin, in the spring of every year certain Celtic and Irish plays, which whatever be their degree of excellence will be written with a high ambition, and so to build up a Celtic and Irish school of dramatic literature. We hope to find in Ireland an uncorrupted and imaginative audience trained to listen by its passion for oratory, and believe that our desire to bring upon the stage the deeper thoughts and emotions of Ireland will ensure for us a tolerant welcome and that freedom to experiment which is found in theatre of England, and without which no movement in art or literature can succeed. We will show that Ireland is not the home of buffoonery and of easy sentiment, as it has been represented, but the home of an ancient idealism. We are confident in the support of all Irish people, who are weary of misrepresentation, in carrying out a work that is outside all the political questions that divide us. (Gregory 1913: 8–9)

This statement exposes both the ideals of the company and their blind spots to the then Irish theatre scene. To the potential subscriber, regardless of his or her opinions about Home Rule (several of the original subscribers were against it), there was the excitement of supporting the establishment of an indigenous Irish dramatic avant-garde, led by internationally noted personages, that would create images of the Irish and their culture to counter the Irish stereotypes prolific on the British stage. However, the idea that the theatre would build up a Celtic and Irish school of dramatic literature highlights the theatre's focus on texts over performance, as well as their erasure of two hundred years of Irish theatre history. Furthermore, as Christopher Morash has pointed out, the group's reference to the Irish as an 'uncorrupted . . . audience' fails to take into account the number of sophisticated play-goers to be found in Ireland during this period – play-goers who had been exposed to a wide range of theatrical forms from Ireland and abroad (Morash 2002: 117).

Like other cultural nationalist projects of the day, the Irish Literary Theatre founders alluded to an 'ancient idealism' found in an imagined, pre-Christian Celtic past. Such a turn to an ancient past 'outside all the political questions that divide us' offered the naïve, or perhaps disingenuous, promise that the drama would somehow exist outside the centuries of racial, religious and economic segregation, prejudice and violence that continued to cause fissures within the Irish nationalist community. For the Anglo-Irish Yeats and Gregory, this was a history that they especially wanted overlooked by Ireland's Catholic majority.

Despite the implicit elitism of the project, most members of the cultural nationalist movement met the news of the Irish Literary Theatre with great excitement. Although only in his thirties, Yeats was regarded as one of Ireland's great poets, and Lady Gregory's Irish translations and writings were attracting interest. The Irish Moore was returning to Dublin as a kind of prodigal son after years living in London. And Martyn, a recognized minor playwright, added to the credibility (and the coffers) of the project. Thanks to general enthusiasm, the deep pockets of some of Lady Gregory's friends, and Martyn's promise to cover any losses, the theatre was funded and, in 1899 was ready to perform its first play.

While the Irish Literary Theatre was one of many companies that contributed to what would become the Abbey Theatre, its three-season life taught Yeats and Gregory a great deal about both their own work and the audiences to whom their work was directed. In the first season, Yeats's drama *The Countess Cathleen* (1899) drew fury from a number of Catholic organizations, critical of what they saw as an elitist and anti-Catholic portrayal of one of the greatest tragedies in Irish history, the Great Famine of the 1840s. In the play, the title character offers to sell her soul to the devil to earn money for her starving tenants. The argument against the play was not about Cathleen's altruism, but about the implication that a landed Anglo-Irish aristocrat's soul was worth more to the devils than those of her Catholic tenants. The other drama, Edward Martyn's *The Heather Field* (1899), fared better with its public, and was praised for its Ibsenesque portrayal of a man who is destroyed by his choice to sacrifice his pursuit of writing to farm an estate, at the urging of his materialistic family. The second season's production of Alice Milligan's *The Last Feast of the Fianna* (1900), a verse drama portraying a legend from Irish mythology, was also well received. Milligan, a Belfast poet and playwright and editor of the nationalist journal the *Shan Van Vocht*, helped to attract a more democratic audience to the Irish Literary Theatre. George Moore's *The Bending of the Bough* (1900) rounded out the second season.

In the third season, the missing link in the Irish Literary Theatre's work became clearer: they staged a retelling of an Irish myth, *Diarmuid and Grania* (1901), written by Moore and Yeats, and acted by Frank Benson's prestigious Shakespearean Company. The problem with the production, however, was not that the actors were not skilled, but that they were English, and could not pronounce appropriately – or even consistently – the Irish names in the drama. In one review, J. C. Trewin remarked that the name Caoilte in the play was pronounced as 'Wheelchair', 'Cold Tea' and 'Quilty' (Hogan and Kilroy 1975: 96). The great success of that season was Douglas Hyde's *Casadh an Tsúgáin* (translated by Lady Gregory as *The Twisting of the Rope*, 1901), a one-act Irish-language drama recounting a legendary story about Raftery, a famous, wandering Irish poet. Performed in Irish by members of the Gaelic League, this production captured the imagination and hearts of its Irish audience more than any of the other productions.

As Yeats and Gregory drew the Irish Literary Theatre experiment to a close, while Moore and Martyn moved on to other projects besides the theatre, it was clear that forming a more authentic Irish theatrical aesthetic required collaboration with Irish actors.

Cultivating Players: The Irish National Dramatic Company

While Yeats, Gregory, Martyn and Moore were pursuing a revolution in Irish theatre with English actors, hundreds of Irish persons participating in cultural nationalist groups were staging amateur theatre events as part of their work for Irish cultural independence. The Gaelic League regularly held playwriting contests or performed plays as part of their cultural campaign, and out of these amateur productions a body of players and playwrights, and a uniquely Irish performance aesthetic, began to emerge. Alice Milligan's verse dramas based on ancient Irish myths were performed by several groups, including the Irish Literary Theatre. Patrick Colum, a working-class Dubliner, got his start in playwriting after winning a Gaelic League contest. And many acting stars of the early Irish theatre, like Maire Nic Shiubhliagh, Dudley Digges and Sarah Allgood, began their acting careers in amateur theatricals produced as part of larger cultural nationalist events. But the individual who most clearly linked the Irish Literary Theatre's work with that of other Irish nationalist theatre groups was William G. Fay.

W. G. Fay was a professional electrician in the late 1890s, but his heart belonged to the theatre. As a teenager, he worked briefly as a scene painter at the Gaiety Theatre,

Dublin, and later as an actor and advance man[2] for popular theatrical entertainments in Ireland and England (Hunt 1979: 33). With such an extensive background in performance, it is not surprising that Fay found himself deeply involved in the amateur theatre scene around Dublin. His brother, Frank Fay, also earned a theatrical name as an actor, elocution teacher, and review writer for the nationalist newspaper the *United Irishman*.

In 1900, the Daughters of Erin (*Inghinidhe na hEireann*), a very active nationalist group that used tableaux and theatre as a regular part of their activism, hired W. G. Fay to coach and direct their theatrical events. Fay committed himself to the company and, through them and his own theatre group, the Ormonde Dramatic Society, formed W. G. Fay's Irish National Dramatic Company. The Fay brothers opposed the flagrant histrionics that accompanied melodramatic Irish stage-fare (a style which amateur actors can fall into to this day) in favour of a style inspired by the French actor Constant Coquelin, marked by clear speaking and physical self-control. This acting style later became a signature of the Abbey Theatre.

Watching the Irish National Dramatic Company perform in 1901, Yeats knew that these were the actors necessary to make his vision for an Irish theatre a physical reality. As he said in his autobiography, 'I came away with my head on fire. I wanted to hear my own unfinished *Baile's Strand*, to hear Greek tragedy spoken with a Dublin accent' (Yeats 1936: 72). Shortly after this meeting, the Daughters of Erin agreed to sponsor a production of Yeats's and Gregory's new drama, *Cathleen ni Houlihan* (1903), and George Russell's *Deirdre* (1902), with the Irish National Dramatic Company performing the works. The production was a tremendous success. Russell's play, with its valorizing of a heroic mythic Irish past, lush, symbolist-influenced sets, and strong acting, was well received. The true hit of the night, however, was *Cathleen ni Houlihan*.

Although attributed exclusively to Yeats until very recently, *Cathleen ni Houlihan* was actually a joint effort between Yeats and Lady Gregory, which partly accounts for its sharp stylistic difference from other Yeats dramas. The project gave Gregory one of her first tastes of playwriting, and led to her own, prolific drama career. Yeats and Gregory based this play on the Irish folk legend of the *Shan Van Vocht*, or poor old woman, who calls the men of Ireland to avenge the loss of her four green fields (representing the four provinces of Ireland), which have been stolen by strangers – that is, the English. The Irish man's blood sacrifice for Ireland revives the old woman so that she once again becomes a young beauty. Set in a cottage in Kilalla on the eve of the battle there during the Irish rebellion of 1798, the play shows a family preparing for the marriage of their son, Michael Gillane, when a mythic character enters the cottage and calls on Michael to renew his nation by sacrificing himself in the upcoming battle.

The curtain rises on a scene one might find in a play by Hauptmann or Ibsen. Mr Gillane sits by the fire, while his wife lays out her son's wedding clothes and counts the dowry money on the kitchen table. The family is rejoicing in their economic prosperity when an old woman knocks on the door, asking shelter of the family.

Obeying their society's rules of hospitality, the family admits her and asks her to sit by the fire. The play then slips into the supernatural, as the old woman reveals through the questions she is asked that she is, in fact, Cathleen ni Houlihan, the poor old woman calling on the young men of Ireland to win back her four green fields. Despite the attempts of his mother and fiancée to hold him back, Michael is mesmerized and follows the old woman when she leaves. After his exit, his little brother, Patrick, enters the house. His father asks him if he saw an old woman on the road. Patrick answers, 'I did not, but I saw a young girl and she had the walk of a queen' (Yeats 1966: 231). With these words, the audience knows that Michael's sacrifice for his nation has renewed the land.

Several factors led to the success of this play. First, *Cathleen ni Houlihan* is the most straightforwardly patriotic drama of all Yeats's works (Gregory would write some equally incendiary pieces) and, despite the anti-bourgeois undertones of the piece, its rallying cry for Irishmen and women to come to the aid of their nation made it an immediate success with its nationalist audience. But the audience in that first performance was also deeply moved because they recognized the actors in the drama as off-stage activists in the nationalist movement. The title role, for example, was written for and played by Maud Gonne, a woman whose startling beauty and active role in nationalist politics caused many audience members to identify her personally with the mythic figure she portrayed on stage. In later decades, when Yeats found his drama alienated from the popular sentiment of his Irish audiences, he would call on the memory of this performance to attest to his importance to the movement and faithfulness to the cause. But in 1902, the Irish National Dramatic Company would ride the tide of this evening's success to form a permanent company, which would lead to the establishment of the Abbey Theatre.

The Abbey Theatre: Collaboration, Conflict and Regeneration

The Irish National Theatre Society, which was partially the result of *Cathleen ni Houlihan*'s popular success, was composed of actors from W. G. Fay's Irish National Dramatic Company, dramatists like Yeats and Gregory and nationalist leaders like Arthur Griffith. It was built on democratic principles, with all members having an equal vote in administrative decisions. Yeats, as the elected president of the organization, soon used his authority to procure control over artistic and administrative decisions. In 1904 the company secured a subsidy to purchase and establish a permanent theatre company in the heart of Dublin from an English patron of the arts and deep admirer of Yeats, Annie Horniman. It was a terrific opportunity for Yeats to establish an internationally famous house for Irish drama, and to gain more artistic control over his work in the process; but the deal contained some difficult stipulations that would lead to the dissolution of the organization as originally conceived. For instance, Horniman insisted on high ticket prices to keep 'cheap entertainments' out of the theatre, thus limiting the audience to those who could pay twice the ticket price at other commercial theatres in town. The most controversial of her stipulations, however, was her insistence on 'no politics' in the theatre – a requirement the directors planned to define loosely or ignore, but one which would create a great deal of tension between Yeats, Gregory and Horniman in the years to come (see Frazier 1990; Saddlemyer 1982).

About six months after the company moved into the Abbey, they re-wrote their charter and became a limited liability company. Many of the actors were infuriated by this shift in power, which put almost all artistic and administrative authority in the hands of the directors – Yeats, Gregory and a relative newcomer, the playwright J. M. Synge – while the actors became mere employees. Within months, many of the original actors left the company to form their own company, the Theatre of Ireland, or *Cluithcheoiri na hEireann*.

From 1904 Gregory and Yeats had administrative control of the Abbey Theatre; but, at least for Yeats, they had won the battle and lost the war. The theatre would cultivate many new Irish playwrights and valiantly defend controversial work. But the aesthetic of the Abbey increasingly turned to realism, and while Yeats's poetic works still appeared on the Abbey stage, he grew away from the Abbey's dominant repertoire. In the first years of the Abbey, when Yeats was most involved with the theatre on-stage as well as off, he wrote plays like *On Baile's Strand* (1904) and *The Green Helmet* (1910), adaptations of Irish mythic stories designed to make ancient Irish heroes models of nationalist action and sacrifice for contemporary Ireland. These plays were written in verse, and heavily influenced by symbolism and Yeats's interest in mysticism. His non-realistic sets, some designed by Gordon Craig, created a sense of simplicity and unity on stage. In many ways, these plays reflect Yeats's own conflict between what Joep Leerssen calls 'his mystical-elitist worldview and his sense of responsibility to engage in public affairs' (Leerssen 2004: 50), as mythic heroes spoke of duty and action amid smoking bowls of incense or among archetypal figures like the fool and the blind man. From 1910, when Horniman revoked her subsidy to the Abbey (leading to a greater commercialization of the theatre), to the end of the Irish civil war in 1923, Yeats moved away from the daily affairs of the Abbey and pursued a more aristocratic theatre, influenced largely by his work with Ezra Pound and his exposure to Noh theatre practice. Yeats began to incorporate dance into his dramas and to develop his ideas on the importance of scenography, music and gesture in the staging of plays. In works like *At the Hawk's Well* (1916) and *The Only Jealousy of Emer* (1922), Yeats wrote for an elite audience, 'like a secret society where admission is by favour and never to many' (Yeats 1962: 254). Many of these plays were performed in non-traditional spaces like drawing rooms or at small, independent theatre clubs. Although Yeats claimed in the introduction to his 1921 play collection *Four Plays for Dancers* that he 'rejoiced in my freedom from the stupidity of an ordinary audience' (Jeffares and Knowland 1975: 107), in fact he continued to concern himself with the 'ordinary audiences' at the Abbey, and his plays were still performed for them, as well as for Europe's intellectual elite. By the mid-1920s, as the Abbey officially became the National Theatre of the Irish Free State and Yeats became a senator, his work shifted again. Christopher Murray notes that, at this point in Yeats's career, he 'assumed the mantle of national bard', and 'the difficulty for him now as playwright was to make some sort of truce between the aristocratic Noh form and the unashamedly democratic Abbey form' (Murray 1997: 28). The great poet abandoned verse plays for prose, and adapted an ironic tone, reflecting his negative opinions about the Catholic middle-class mentality of the Free State government, which had overtaken the spiritual vision of Irish nationalism earlier in the century. The tragic irony of works from this period, like *The Words Upon the Window Pane* (1930), *The Herne's Egg* (published 1938, first produced at the Abbey 1950) and *Purgatory* (1938), is the triumph of the everyday over the heroic, the material over the spiritual. Thus, as Katharine Worth and others have remarked, they point towards the absurdist visions of another Irish playwright, Samuel Beckett (Worth 1978: 241–67).

While Yeats's career in the theatre led him across a wide geographic and aesthetic terrain, Lady Gregory's work stayed closer to home; and her work on- and off-stage at the Abbey profoundly affected the future of modern Irish drama. The image of Gregory as a matronly lady, whose contributions to the Abbey consisted of Barmbrack cakes in the green room on opening nights and quaint folk plays, is disappearing in favour of a more accurate portrayal of her important work for the modern Irish stage. As a theatre director, Gregory worked tirelessly from 1904 to 1929, and continued to support the theatre until her death in 1932. Archives are full of her thoughtful letters and advice to aspiring playwrights, and she often served as the pacifier in internal debates. She fought valiantly for the freedom of the theatre during the riots at the Abbey at the premiere of Synge's *The Playboy of the Western World* (1907), managed to produce Bernard Shaw's *The Shewing-Up of Blanco Posnet* (1909) even though it was banned in England, and defended Sean O'Casey and his work during the riots over *The Plough and the Stars* (1926). And, while leading the Abbey's controversial tour of *The Playboy of the Western World* in the United States in 1911, she withstood riots against the production, and even a death threat against herself, to ensure the success of the tour, and of the theatre's project, outside Ireland. Her tactics for placating American audiences included enlisting the help of Theodore Roosevelt, who accompanied Lady Gregory at an Abbey Theatre performance in New York.

As a playwright, Gregory was equally energetic, writing dozens of Irish plays. She wrote moving tragic plays, such as her one-act drama *The Gaol Gate* (1906), which portrays two women seeking an imprisoned revolutionary at a prison gate, paralleling the medieval English liturgical drama *Quem Quaeritis* (965). And her own adaptation of the Diarmuid and Grania legend, *Grania*, offers a rich characterization of one of the most famous women in Irish myth. But her greatest gift was for folk comedy and farce. These comedies, the most prevalent in her oeuvre, may seem on the surface like quaint pictures of peasant life, but in fact these plays show a keen awareness of the power of language to subvert authority, and both to assert and to transform identity. In *The Rising of the Moon* (1907), for example, an Irish police sergeant seeks a revolutionary fugitive along a dock. The fugitive appears in disguise, and the two men begin to pass the time talking. While the sergeant has the authority of the state, the fugitive is in control of the situation, as he teases out through stories and songs the policeman's memories of the past, and his feeling of loyalty to Ireland. His stories reveal a love of Ireland, but also the sense that the revolution is inevitable, that 'the small rise up and the big fall down ... when we all change places at the Rising of the Moon' (Gregory 1995: 372). The fugitive reveals himself, and shows that he has a gun and is willing to escape by force. Still, he uses language to convince the policeman to let him escape quietly in a waiting boat. The play ends with the sergeant breaking the fourth wall, as he asks the audience, 'A hundred pounds reward! A hundred pounds! I wonder, now, am I as great a fool as I think I am?' (ibid.: 372). In a brief comic drama, Gregory remarks on both the need to overturn Ireland's imperial plutocracy and the surety of its overthrow; yet in the spirit of the Victorian panto (or perhaps foreshadowing the Brechtian *Lehrstück*, a didactic political theatre form that urged the audience to engage critically with the issues of social injustice expressed in the production, and to inspire political action), she gives her audience the last word.

In 1897, Yeats and Gregory imagined building up 'a school of Celtic and Irish dramatic literature'. Three decades later, their work in the theatre was profoundly different from what they had originally imagined. Rather than settling into an international literary life in London as his contemporaries Wilde and Shaw had done, Yeats chose to involve himself in the active invention of an Irish national identity at home (Kiberd 1995: 115–32). His experience of Irish cultural and political controversies, concomitant with his theatre work, led to a series of self-conscious reinventions of himself and his art throughout his life. Gregory defied the expectations of her family and the prejudices of her class, transforming herself according to her belief in both the rightness and the inevitability of Irish independence. In working towards that political goal, she found her talent as a translator, theatre director and playwright. By engaging in the business of production and the art of performance, as well as the craft of writing, Yeats and Gregory helped establish one of the most influential theatres of the twentieth century. But just as Gregory and Yeats helped change the face of Irish theatre, the Irish theatre and the playwrights, actors and audiences with whom they collaborated profoundly changed them. The Abbey Theatre in its formative years was not just a site of imagination, but also of action.

NOTES

1 'The Necessity for De-Anglicising Ireland' in *The Revival of Irish Literature: Addresses by Sir Charles Gavan Duffy, K.C.M.G., Dr George Sigerson and Dr. Douglas Hyde*. London: T. F. Unwin, 1894: 117–61.

2 The advance man drummed up business by putting up posters and stirring up interest in the community before the show came to town.

PRIMARY READING

Gregory, Lady Augusta (1913). *Our Irish Theatre*. New York: G. P. Putnam's Sons.

Gregory, Lady Augusta (1971). *The Collected Plays of Lady Gregory*, ed. Anne Saddlemyer. Gerrards Cross: Colin Smythe.

Gregory, Lady Augusta (1995). *Lady Gregory: Selected Writings*, eds. Lucy McDiarmid and Maureen Waters. New York: Penguin.

Hogan, Robert and Kilroy, James (1975). *The Irish Literary Theatre: 1898–1901*. Atlantic Highlands, NJ, and Monmouth: Dolmen.

Hogan, Robert and Kilroy, James (1976). *Laying the Foundations: 1902–1904*. Atlantic Highlands, NJ, and Monmouth: Dolmen.

Jeffares, A. Norman and Knowland, A. S. (eds.) (1975). *A Commentary on the Collected Plays of W. B. Yeats*. Stanford: Stanford University Press.

McDiarmid, Lucy and Waters, Maureen (1995). 'Introduction' in Lucy McDiarmid and Maureen Waters (eds.). *Lady Gregory: Selected Writings*. New York: Penguin.

Saddlemyer, Anne (1982). *Theatre Business: The Correspondence of the First Abbey Directors: William Butler Yeats, Lady Augusta Gregory, and J. M. Synge*. Gerrards Cross: Colin Smythe.

Yeats, W. B. (1936). *Dramatis Personae*. New York: Macmillan.

Yeats, W. B. (1962). *Explorations*. New York: Macmillan.

Yeats, W. B. (1966). *The Variorum Edition of the Plays of W. B. Yeats*, ed. Russell K. Alspach. London: Macmillan.

FURTHER READING

Castle, Gregory (2001). *Modernism and the Celtic Revival*. Cambridge: Cambridge University Press.

Foster, R. F. (1997). *W. B. Yeats: A Life: I: The Apprentice Mage, 1865–1919*. Oxford: Oxford University Press.

Frazier, Adrian (1990). *Behind the Scenes: Yeats, Horniman and the Struggle for the Abbey Theatre*. Berkeley: University of California Press.

Frazier, Adrian (2000). *George Moore 1852–1933*. New Haven, CT: Yale University Press.

Herr, Cheryl (1991). *For the Land they Loved: Irish Political Melodrama, 1890–1925*. Syracuse, NY: Syracuse University Press.

Hobsbawm, Eric and Ranger, Terence (eds.) (1983). *The Invention of Tradition*. New York and Cambridge: Cambridge University Press.

Hunt, Hugh (1979). *The Abbey: Ireland's National Theatre, 1904–1978*. New York: Columbia University Press.

Kiberd, Declan (1995). *Inventing Ireland*. London: Jonathan Cape.

Leerssen, Joep (2004). "The Theatre of William Butler Yeats" in Shaun Richards (ed.). *The Cambridge Companion to Twentieth-Century Irish Drama*. Cambridge: Cambridge University Press, 47–61.

Levitas, Ben (2003). *The Theatre of Nation: Irish Drama and Cultural Nationalism 1890–1916*. Oxford: Oxford University Press.

Mathews, P. J. (2003). *Revival: The Abbey Theatre, Sinn Fein, the Gaelic League and the Co-operative Movement*. Notre Dame, IN: Notre Dame University Press.

Morash, Christopher (2002). *A History of Irish Theatre, 1601–2000*. Cambridge: Cambridge University Press.

Murray, Christopher (1997). *Twentieth Century Irish Drama: Mirror Up to Nation*. Syracuse, NY: Syracuse University Press.

Nic Shuibhliagh, Maire (1955). *The Splendid Years*. Dublin: James Duffy.

Pilkington, Lionel (2001). *Theatre and the State in Twentieth-Century Ireland: Cultivating the People*. London: Routledge.

Toibin, Colm (2002). *Lady Gregory's Toothbrush*. Madison: University of Wisconsin Press.

Trotter, Mary (2001). *Ireland's National Theatres: Political Performance and the Origins of the Irish Dramatic Movement*. Syracuse, NY: Syracuse University Press.

Worth, Katharine (1978). *The Irish Theatre of Europe from Yeats to Beckett*. London: Athlone.

8

Suffrage Theatre: Community Activism and Political Commitment

Susan Carlson

The theatre associated with the early-twentieth-century suffrage movement in England is a bundle of contradictions. The suffragists were mostly middle-class women, women bred for the interiors of the home who became strategists of public space and massive public events. Their theatre, which ranged from public-hall skits to full-length plays in West End theatres, was at once conservative and radical. The suffragists dressed in harmony for public events, wearing the identifiable, co-ordinated colours of their organizations; at the same time they destroyed public art, torched golf courses and chained themselves to fences. In sum, the women (and men) involved with suffrage theatre drew from theatrical conventions which they knew and modified them for the commotion of the public square, the public hall and the streets as well as for the theatres. Memorable plays were not necessarily the main product of suffrage drama, but rather a concept of theatre which involved the streets as well as the stage and an expanded sense of women's roles in both places. Suffrage theatre had a duration of less than a decade, but it foreshadowed the now familiar conventions of subsequent community-based political theatre.

The Suffrage Community and its Affinity with Theatre

Most historians of the British suffrage movement date its beginnings to the advocacy of Mary Wollstonecraft or John Stuart Mill, but decades of nineteenth-century strategizing and commitment are overshadowed by the best-known and most intense years of the campaign, those in the decade preceding World War I, stretching roughly from 1905 to 1914. While the primary goal of the suffrage movement was obtaining the vote for women, the drive for enfranchisement was entwined with a variety of debates on related issues such as women's position in law, white slavery, the economic conditions of marriage, education, birth control and family roles, and taxation. The radical tactics of the Women's Social and Political Union (WSPU, founded in 1903), who preached 'deeds not words', were well known; they engaged in prison hunger strikes, breaking windows in public buildings and disrupting public events. Yet each of the major suffrage organizations, from the most radical to the most conservative, made use of public space and theatrically inspired events to promote the cause of the vote for women. Suffragists performed everything from monologues to tableaux, pageants to parodies, one-act to full-length plays in West End theatres, Hyde Park, labour halls, garden parties, and city streets and squares. The entity of 'suffrage theatre' was as much influenced by the political organizations and arguments of its day as it was by the aesthetics and practices of the theatre – and the fact that the two realms came together is a significant moment in theatre history.

The WSPU, the NUWSS (National Union of Women's Suffrage Societies), the WFL (Women's Freedom League) and other suffrage organizations provided the backbone of suffrage campaigning in the early twentieth century, but they were bolstered by groups of more specific affiliation such as the Actresses' Franchise League (AFL) and the Women Writers' Suffrage League, two groups central to suffrage theatre. Founded in 1908, the AFL had a membership of practising actresses, and the group was the gravitational centre of the explosive phenomenon of suffrage theatre. These actresses banded together, pledging to use their professional skills to advance the cause of women's suffrage: they trained activists in public speaking and presentational skills and, in extreme circumstances, helped costume suffragists on the run from government officials. With a literary department run by Australian-born Inez Bensusan, the AFL was responsible for the creation and production of a large share of the plays which directly staged the issue of suffrage. Working with branches of the suffrage societies to schedule performances of the plays, Bensusan and the AFL enlisted established writers like Beatrice Harraden, Cicely Hamilton, Laurence Housman and Bernard Shaw along with little-known and first-time playwrights. Motivated by the AFL's efforts, many women whose prior role in theatre had solely been acting became leaders, activists and, most importantly, writers. With some overlap in personnel, the Women Writers' Suffrage League operated in a parallel fashion as a location for women writers to pool their talents in support of women's suffrage. Cicely Hamilton and Elizabeth Robins, two writers who played key parts in the theatre of the day, were joined in this second group by Sarah Grand, Olive Schreiner, Ivy Compton Burnett and others. The plays that resulted were lively, sometimes raw, sometimes refined, but always provocative and engaged, and they were performed variously to a scattering or to thousands. As Julie Holledge has documented, the AFL played the more significant role, and while not solely responsible for suffrage theatre, this organization ensured that theatre and performance were a staple in the politics of the suffrage cause.

Of course, the context for suffrage theatre goes far beyond such organizations, and its activism must also be contextualized in terms of the other major political issues of the time: imperialism, nationalism and liberalism (Mayhall et al. 2000: xv). The suffrage theatre rarely addressed issues of race and nation which Britain's early-century global reach might have raised. In general, the suffragists writing plays and producing theatrical events tended to rely on conventional dramatic forms and concentrated on one political issue – the vote; their plays did not interrogate other social and cultural assumptions. In the main, suffrage theatre supported the politics of a variety of pro-suffrage groups, but there are moments when the critique also stretches to the power stratifications of marriage and class.

Theatre on Demand: Portable and Provocative

In the end, it is very difficult to separate the intensity of the politics between 1905 and 1914 from the innovations of suffrage theatre, and it is hard to imagine the campaign for the vote without its highly visible performative aspects. Hilary Frances describes some of the WFL's interventions as fun-filled and highly symbolic, strategies she refers to as 'non-violent militancy' (Frances 2000: 189). The campaign for suffrage was configured in terms which were celebratory, transgressive and civil, and elsewhere I have used the words 'comic militancy' to convey the same idea (Carlson 2000: 198). As the mostly middle-class women involved moved the suffrage campaign into more public spaces in the years just before the war, they deployed a variety of performance venues and outlets, from social gatherings to newspapers, from political rallies to theatre stages.

Perhaps the most comfortable theatrical moments were those that took place as a part of the at-homes (neighbourhood suffrage meetings) and festivals put on to bring together those who were members of suffrage organizations and to persuade others to join them. Such meetings conducted business, featured speakers and often included performances of plays to rally those in attendance. Some of the one-act suffrage plays that were most popular included Cicely Hamilton and Christopher St John's *How the Vote was Won* (1909), Evelyn Glover's *A Chat with Mrs Chicky* (1912) and Hamilton and St John's *The Pot and the Kettle* (1909). The 'Garden Fete', put on by the Croydon branch of the WFL in the summer of 1912, serves as a representative example of the oftentimes elaborate but domestically rooted suffrage 'events'. It welcomed women, children and men; offered food and embroidered items for sale; included a children's chorus and a political speech by WFL president C. Despard; and boasted as a capstone event performances of Glover's *A Chat with Mrs Chicky* and Graham Moffat's *The Maid and the Magistrate*.

Even larger events, like the Yuletide Festival held in the Albert Hall in December 1909, followed similar patterns of using theatrical performance as a climax to a programme of speeches, participatory events, networking and socializing. The programme included many of the plays which were most successful at buoying the suffragists: *The Pot and the Kettle*, *How the Vote was Won*, and Cicely Hamilton's *A Pageant of Great Women* (staged by Edith (Edy) Craig). As reported in the *Vote*, the climactic *Pageant* was memorable: 'There has never been anything like this Pageant, which brought the day to a fitting close. It sang in one's blood with its colour harmonies and the sonorous sound of its message' (*Vote*, 16 December 1909, 89). The suffrage newspapers of the day document constant performances of suffrage plays in meetings of the London suffrage societies as well as in society meetings around the country (see Carlson 2001: 339–40).

The four London suffrage newspapers contributed to suffrage theatre by publishing plays regularly;[1] some of these plays saw performance, but many are a curiously unstageable mixture of dialogue and politics. Unlike the plays which saw heavy use at suffrage society meetings and which were generally upbeat and comic in form, plays in this second group were often more probing in their politics and tended to be unwieldy as theatre. The *Vote*, the organ of the WFL, published the largest number of such plays, including Alice Chapin's *At the Gates* (slated for performance at the Yuletide Festival in 1909 but dropped from the programme due to time-pressure), a play in which a suffragist sits through the night at the gates to Parliament, handing out petitions to all who pass by. From those who walk by, she accumulates responses which range from abuse to sympathy. The play is reflective and hopeful, but promises no political victory. Winifred St Clair's *The Science of Forgiveness* (*Vote*, 21 November 1913, 51, and 28 November 1913, 71–2; no known performance) places the argument for the vote in the context of sexual infidelity and a double standard for men and women involved in extra-marital affairs. While the play ends with key parties agreeing to equal treatment for men and women, it is not clear that this equitable agreement will lead to happiness for anyone. Perhaps the most common suffrage narrative in these newspapers is the 'conversion' play, in which the main event is the conversion of a non-believer to the cause of women's suffrage. Good examples are 'A. N.'s *Mr Peppercorn's Awakening* (pub. 1912), Edith M. Baker's *Our Happy Home* (pub. 1911) and A. L. Little's *The Shadow of the Sofa* (pub. 1913).

One of the most interesting developments in the newspapers was a collection of plays about selling suffrage newspapers, the most striking of which is Gladys Mendl's brief piece *Su'L'Pavé*, subtitled 'Half an hour in the life of a paper-seller' (*Votes for Women*, 9 January 1914, 224; no known performance). From the many people who walk by as she hawks her copies on the street, the paper-seller receives verbal batterings as well as unexpected support. The play's attention to women in new public spaces was one of many dramatic reflections on the ways in which the suffrage campaign was redefining public space as well as women's use of it.

From 1907 on, London itself also became a stage for the suffragists, who planned marches, meetings, and processions drawing hundreds of thousands at a time. In 1908, the WSPU arranged for 30,000 suffragists to take seven different processional routes through London to Hyde Park, where they were joined by up to half a million supporters. The Women's Coronation Procession of 1911, the 1913 funeral procession for suffrage martyr Emily Wilding Davison (who died after running in front of horses on the Derby race course), as well as the massive protest marches, like that in 1908, were often planned by women of the theatre and were in essence performances designed to drum up political support.

The conventional stages of London's early-twentieth-century theatre were also conscripted for the suffrage cause, beginning with the performance of Elizabeth Robins's three-act play *Votes for Women!*; the play was staged under Harley Granville Barker's direction at the Royal Court in 1907. It set a high standard of writing for the suffrage plays to follow, but also opened a floodgate through which flowed the hundreds of suffrage plays written in the next seven years. Robins's play, like many other suffrage plays, was given a matinée performance, and many of London's key West End theatres, as well as its well-known actors and actresses, followed suit with the staging of plays directly about the vote as well as plays focused on issues of gender equity and gender roles. More notable efforts include Cicely Hamilton's *Diana of Dobson's* (1908), George Bernard Shaw's *Press Cuttings* (1910) and Charlotte Gilman's *Three Women* (1912). Matinée performances remained a constant, in part a reflection of the availability of the largely female audience they appealed to and in part a result of an explicitly political content. As was the case for many small theatre societies, censorship was a constant threat.

Women began to take on more prominent theatrical roles, perhaps as a result of such suffrage activism. Most importantly, women had key responsibilities in theatrical management in London and other cities: Annie Horniman did ground-breaking work at the Gaiety Theatre in Manchester, as did Edy Craig, Lena Ashwell, Gertrude Kingston, Lillah McCarthy and Lilian Bayliss in London. In addition, a simple cross-check of suffrage events with theatre events reveals that many of the most prominent actors played roles in suffrage plays or politics. Those active in the cause included Ellen Terry (whose daughter Edy Craig was one of the most important suffrage strategists), Laurence Housman, Johnston Forbes-Robertson, Gertrude Elliott, Henry Ainsley, Dorothy Minto, Ben Webster, Nigel Playfair, May Whitty and Harcourt Williams.

Suffrage Plays

Sheila Stowell has defined the term 'suffrage drama' as referring to the 'auspices under which these plays were produced, not their specific content' (Stowell 1992: 42); and indeed, while the vast majority of plays staged by suffrage organizations made direct references to the vote, not all did, some preferring a more general focus on social issues. The plays reviewed below will, in general, offer at least some direct attention to the vote or will have been used in some major way by those campaigning for the vote.

Robins's *Votes for Women!* offered an auspicious start to suffrage drama. Drawing both from comedy of manners and from agit-prop pageantry, the play is simultaneously predictable and subversive, and exemplifies the contradictory theatre practices of the time. Act I offers recognizable drawing-room comedy in which a group of country-house weekend guests mix social flirtations with politics. Vida Levering, a politically active campaigner whose presence raises questions about her past, stands shoulder to shoulder with Jean Dunbarton, a politically naïve heiress. Both are inextricably linked to MP Geoffrey Stonor, as becomes clear in Act II, in the Trafalgar Square suffrage rally. The play is a curious mix of suffrage rhetoric and melodramatic revelations about Geoffrey's and Vida's shared past. Harley Granville Barker's innovative staging of the rally was praised for its authenticity, and its melding of theatre and suffrage protest set a standard for theatrically effective political speech which other suffrage plays aspired to during the next decade. The depiction of women in political action is stunning and has a rawness that still challenges audiences. Act III returns to the drawing room, where Jean, Vida and Geoffrey sort out their complex personal relationships through a rhetoric of suffrage politics. Jean and Geoffrey move towards marriage, but also join Vida in support of the women's vote. Vida's unwavering commitment to the vote inspires others and she stands as a complex portrait of the suffragist.

Of all suffrage drama, Robins's play has received the greatest critical attention. Although rarely staged, the play is on a par with the work of Harley Granville Barker, Henry James and others who deal with the nuances of Edwardian women's social and political options. Robins's conversion narrative and her radical Act II, which broke free of the drawing room, became a model for much of the suffrage drama to follow.

Not surprisingly, very few suffrage plays assume the three-act structure of Robins's play, since time-constraints made a full-length play generally unworkable for rallies and meetings – and it was primarily at such events that most performances took place. Thus the one-act, the monologue and the duologue became the mainstays of suffrage theatre, and many of them take from Robins the comic form as well as the selling of the vote through an examination of personal relationships. Cicely Hamilton and Christopher St John's *How the Vote was Won* is perhaps the best of these politically expedient plays. When, in the cause of the vote, a general strike is called for women, all women are directed to return to their 'nearest male relative' for support; the goal is to demonstrate to men how much they have come to rely on women's independence. The play reveals what this clever strategy means for one Horace Cole, a 30-year-old clerk living with his wife in Brixton. Through the course of the play's events, he realizes the ridiculousness of thinking 'today's' women need men, and he converts to the cause, concluding the play with a litany of reasons for women's vote: 'You may depend on me – all of you – to see justice done. When you want a thing done, get a man to do it! Votes for Women!'(Spender and Hayman 1985: 33). Such conversion is central to many of the suffrage plays published in newspapers (*Mr Peppercorn's Awakening, The Shadow of the Sofa, Our Happy Home*) as well as to those frequently performed at local rallies (for example, Evelyn Glover's *A Chat with Mrs Chicky* and her *Miss Appleyard's Awakening* (1913b)).

Edy Craig, Cicely Hamilton and others argued that such plays worked by promoting a change of heart among ideologically uncertain men and women while also reassuring others already committed to the cause. As Craig put it in a 1910 newspaper interview: 'I do think plays have done such a lot for the Suffrage. They get hold of nice frivolous people who would die sooner than go in cold blood to meetings. But they see the plays, and get interested, and then we can rope them in for meetings' (Carlson

2000: 201). The political expediency of such an approach also relies on comedy; what Craig's subversive strategy does *not* acknowledge is that the comic form, while allowing for rebellion in its topsy-turvy world, also has a companion structural reliance on the status quo. Thus in the celebratory endings of these conversion plays, there is often a tension between the affirmation of the vote and the affirmation of a relationship (often a marriage or engagement) which reifies social convention. While some of the plays did critique social institutions like marriage, many more made explicit that the vote would not threaten marriage, motherhood or social codes.

Many of the conversion plays have a processional element, as multiple people join a conversation or repeat an argument, swelling the scene until a whole community unites in agreement over the need for women's vote. Actual pageants were among the most influential suffrage plays, and may be among the most notable contributions of suffrage theatre. Perhaps the centrality of pageants is predictable, since suffrage activism of this era was marked by a reliance on demonstrations and large-scale meetings. The best and most influential of these pageants was *A Pageant of Great Women*, a collaboration of Cicely Hamilton's writing and Edy Craig's directing. With a cast ranging between 50 and 90 players, productions usually needed large spaces to amplify the play's grand scheme, and Craig was primarily responsible for its performance both in London and around the country, beginning in 1909 at London's Scala Theatre (Cockin 1998a: 94–107).

Hamilton provides a frame for the play in the three characters of Justice, Prejudice and Woman, who initiate the action with a debate about the possibility of women leading lives beyond the confines of their relationships to men. To prove the point that women have always functioned independently, there follows a procession of famous women in six groups: The Learned Women, The Artists, The Saintly Women, The Heroic Women, The Rulers and The Warriors. While each of the processing women has a very small speaking part, the cumulative effect of their stately presence and potent proclamations about women's abilities is to shame Prejudice into silence and retreat. Justice then tells the Woman that the 'world is thine', and the Woman concludes the play by letting men know they are not forgotten, but that women are now laughing as they feel 'the riot and rush of crowning hopes, / Dreams, longings, and vehement powers' (Nelson 2004: 229). This pageant was a powerful theatrical and political tool, not just because of its long and impressive line of influential women, but because in production key suffrage supporters could adopt the roles of the 'great' women. While some London productions boasted the most successful actresses of the day, many local productions used the opportunity to dress high-profile political supporters in the garb of such glorious figures as Jane Austen, Sappho, Florence Nightingale, Elizabeth I and Joan of Arc.

Christopher St John's *The First Actress* (1911) puts the processional in the narrower sphere of British theatrical history, and shows how the processional quality of suffrage campaigning seemed to influence the imagining of theatrical space. St John, a woman whose chosen male name confronts gender issues, creates a pageant of 11 famous actresses who line up to give encouragement to Margaret Hughes, assumed by St John

to be the first actress on the English stage in 1661, performing the part of Desde-
mona. Hughes's performance is belittled by her male colleagues and she is about to
conclude that women's acting is a failed experiment, but then the pageant begins.
Coming from the future (post-1661), the 11 actresses reassure Hughes of the historic
importance of her role. Performed initially by Edy Craig's Pioneer Players in 1911 and
later for suffrage events, the play made easy connections between theatre and suffrage
politics. This piece of theatre about theatre, in other words, made an effective
argument for women's long-standing independence. In essence, such pageant plays
use the procession of characters to visualize political progress.

While St John's play is not anthologized in any of the existing collections of suffrage
drama (see Fitzsimmons and Gardner 1991; Holledge 1981; Nelson 2004; Spender and
Hayman 1985), her well-crafted writing most clearly shows how the suffrage drama
born in the initial efforts of Robins matured in the compressed political agitation of the
next seven years. St John's 1914 play *Her Will* returns to the domestic interiors of
Robins's world to bring suffrage politics squarely into the drawing room again; this
time the drawing room has been transformed into a space controlled by independent
and powerful women. As the play opens, suffragist Helen Wilton has just died, and the
disposition of her estate brings her heirs into political contortions as they attempt to
satisfy the demands of her will. A victim of a Holloway Prison stay (and its forced
feedings), Wilton names as her first heir the suffrage cause itself, specifying that her
money be used to support suffragists until the vote is awarded to women. Her second set
of heirs (her family) are forced into a quick recognition of the several ways in which
expanded suffrage will serve them, and they become objects of comedy as they
begrudgingly move towards conversion. In this play, the drawing room is owned by a
woman and becomes the space for political conversation, conversion and, most importantly, female autonomy (Carlson 2001: 344–5).

While the majority of suffrage plays deploy the comic form, using a feel-good
factor to reinforce the rewards of political support for the suffrage cause, a sizeable
number turn to both one-act and full-length dramas with darker endings. Stowell
(1992) rightly names Hamilton's *Diana of Dobson's*, staged by Lena Ashwell at the
Kingsway Theatre in 1908, as one of the key plays of the suffrage era, not because it
deals with the issue of the vote, but because it forces questions about happiness and a
woman's life choices. Act I, set in the dormitory of the shop girls employed at
Dobson's, captures the bleak life of the women who work endless days for minimal
wages. The promise of romance powers the next two acts, but the conclusion leaves
the question of happiness unanswered. Many in the suffrage campaign were not
willing to discuss the prejudicial legal situation in relation to marriage, since they
felt it would jeopardize the possibility of the vote. Hamilton's play does, however,
allow for the issue to be raised.

Margaret Wynne Nevinson's *In the Workhouse* (1911) is a protest against the laws of
coverture, which denied most married women legal standing, and as Nevinson says in
her preface, 'married women are still in captivity at the will of some worthless
husband' (Nevison in Nelson 2004: 247). The play takes place in a workhouse

where seven women share experiences and beliefs, most focused on how marriage laws have compounded difficult lives. One character, Lily, begins the play by saying that she is eager to marry the father of her new baby, and ends – after listening to the life stories of the other women – by telling her baby that maybe she won't get married after all. In sharp contrast to most suffrage plays, this one clearly separates marriage from happiness. Most plays enlisted in the suffrage cause did not make such foundational critiques, though several skirt the issue, such as St Claire's *The Science of Forgiveness*.

Most studies of suffrage theatre focus on the plays and events created in the cause of women's vote, yet this review of suffrage theatre would not be complete without a note on the anti-suffrage plays which attempted to turn such pro-suffrage theatre in on itself. Many of these 'anti' plays used comic strategies which were conservative rather than subversive. Typically, the suffragist characters themselves were devoid of social skills and their politics inept; such qualities were meant to expose the suffragists' dangerous political goals. The women become comic targets when they give up their politics for love or when they are shown to be underhanded, illogical and promiscuous; Inglis Allen's *The Suffragettes' Redemption* (1909) and George Dance's *The Suffragettes* (1907) are good examples of such plays which undercut the suffrage cause (Carlson 2000: 207). One notable attempt to discredit women's arguments for the vote has a play full of children claiming that they too deserve the vote; Ernest Hutchinson's *Votes for Children* (1913) equates suffragists with a group of children who don't even know what a 'vote' is. The way in which anti-suffragists turned to theatre to counter the pro-suffrage plays is perhaps a back-handed compliment, an admission that the theatre was indeed a powerful political tool. But the anti-suffrage plays also suggest that the suffragists' frequent use of comedy might have been vulnerable to parody.

Conclusion

English suffrage theatre is a potent, brief example of a politically inspired theatre which leaves us with a legacy: it made new assumptions about theatrical space, domestic space and public space simultaneously; it catapulted women into the full range of roles in theatre; and it played a key role in women writers' conscriptions of dramatic form. World War I brought the suffrage theatre to a virtual halt, along with the suffrage campaign itself. Many of the women who had directed its militant efforts continued with theatre, but the concentrated urgency of the moment evaporated into other projects and concerns. Since the vote was not actually granted women until after the war (and even then in stages), it is not possible to make definitive claims about the political effectiveness of this theatre. These suffrage plays do, however, show a remarkable political energy, and more importantly, are a showcase for the political reach of the art form.

NOTE

1 The four papers were *Votes for Women*, the *Suffragette*, the *Vote* and *Common Cause*.

PRIMARY READING

A. N. (1912). *Mr Peppercorn's Awakening*, Vote, 1 August, 229 (no known performance).

Allen, Inglis (1909). *The Suffragette's Redemption*. Lord Chamberlain's Plays, British Library (first performance 1909).

Baker, Edith M. (1911). *Our Happy Home*, Vote, 30 December, 115–17 (no known performance).

Chapin, Alice (1909). *At the Gates*, Vote, 16 December, 94 (performance licensed 1909).

Dance, George (1907). *The Suffragettes*. Lord Chamberlain's Plays, British Library (first performance 1907).

Fitzsimmons, Linda and Gardner, Viv (eds.) (1991). *New Woman Plays*. London: Methuen.

Gardner, Viv (ed.) (1985). *Sketches from the Actresses' Franchise League*. Nottingham: Nottingham Drama Texts.

Glover, Evelyn (1913a). *A Chat with Mrs Chicky: A Duologue* in Dale Spender and Carole Hayman (eds.). (1985). *How the Vote was Won and Other Suffragette Plays*. London: Methuen; and in Carolyn Christensen Nelson (ed.). (2004). *Literature of the Women's Suffrage Campaign in England*. Peterborough, Ontario: Broadview Press (first performance 1912).

Glover, Evelyn (1913b). *Miss Appleyard's Awakening: A Play in One Act* in Carolyn Christensen Nelson (ed.). (2004). *Literature of the Women's Suffrage Campaign in England*. Peterborough, Ontario: Broadview Press (first performance 1911).

Hamilton, Cicely (1908). *Diana of Dobson's* in Linda Fitzsimmons and Viv Gardner (eds.). (1991). *New Woman Plays*. London: Methuen, 27–77 (first performance 1908).

Hamilton, Cicely (1948; 1909). *A Pageant of Great Women* in Carolyn Christensen Nelson (ed.). (2004). *Literature of the Women's Suffrage Campaign in England*. Peterborough, Ontario: Broadview Press (first performance 1909).

Hamilton, Cicely and St John, Christopher (1909a). *How the Vote was Won* in Dale Spender and Carole Hayman (eds.). (1985). *How the Vote was Won and Other Suffragette Plays*. London: Methuen; and in Carolyn Christensen Nelson (ed.). (2004). *Literature of the Women's Suffrage Campaign in England*. Peterborough, Ontario: Broadview Press (first performance 1909).

Hamilton, Cicely and St John, Christopher (1909b). *The Pot and the Kettle*. Lord Chamberlain's Plays, British Library (first performance 1909).

Hutchinson, Ernest (1913). *Votes for Children*. Lord Chamberlain's Plays, British Library (first performance 1913).

Little, A. L. (1913). *The Shadow of the Sofa*, Vote, 24 December, 139–41 (no known performance).

Moffat, Graham (1912). *The Maid and the Magistrate: A Duologue in One Act* in Carolyn Christensen Nelson (ed.). (2004). *Literature of the Women's Suffrage Campaign in England*. Peterborough, Ontario: Broadview Press (first performance 1912).

Nelson, Carolyn Christensen (ed.) (2004). *Literature of the Women's Suffrage Campaign in England*. Peterborough, Ontario: Broadview Press.

Nevinson, Margaret Wynne (1911). *In the Workhouse: A Play in One Act* in Carolyn Christensen Nelson (ed.). (2004). *Literature of the Women's Suffrage Campaign in England*. Peterborough, Ontario: Broadview Press (first performance 1911).

Robins, Elizabeth (1907). *Votes for Women* in Dale Spender and Carole Hayman (eds.). (1985). *How the Vote was Won and Other Suffragette Plays*. London: Methuen (first performance 1907).

St John, Christopher (1911). *The First Actress*. Lord Chamberlain's Plays, British Library (first performance 1911).

St John, Christopher (1914). *Her Will*. Lord Chamberlain's Plays, British Library (performance licensed 1914).

Spender, Dale and Hayman, Carole (eds.) (1985). *How the Vote was Won and Other Suffragette Plays*. London: Methuen.

FURTHER READING

Carlson, Susan. (2000). 'Comic Militancy: The Politics of Suffrage Drama' in Maggie B. Gale and Viv Gardner (eds.). *Women, Theatre and Performance: New Histories, New Historiographies*. Manchester: Manchester University Press, 198–215.

Carlson, Susan (2001). 'Portable Politics: Creating New Space for Suffrage-ing Women', *New Theatre Quarterly* 17:4, 334–46.

Cockin, Katharine (1998a). *Edith Craig (1869–1947): Dramatic Lives*. London: Cassell.

Cockin, Katharine (1998b). 'Women's Suffrage Drama' in Maroula Joannou and June Purvis (eds.). *The Women's Suffrage Movement: New Feminist Perspectives*. Manchester: Manchester University Press, 127–39.

Cockin, Katharine (2001). *Women and Theatre in the Age of Suffrage: The Pioneer Players, 1911–1925*. Basingstoke: Palgrave.

Frances, Hilary (2000). ' "Dare to Be Free!": The Women's Freedom League and its Legacy' in June Purvis and Sandra Stanley Holton (eds.). *Votes for Women*. New York and London: Routledge, 181–202.

Green, Barbara (1997). *Spectacular Confessions: Autobiography, Performative Activism, and the Sites of Suffrage 1905–1938*. New York: St Martin's Press.

Hirschfield, Claire (1985). 'The AFL and the Campaign for Women's Suffrage 1908–1914', *Theatre Research International* 10:2, 129–53.

Hirschfield, Claire (1991). 'The Suffrage Play in England 1907–1913', *Cahiers Victoriens and Edouardiens* 33, 73–85.

Holledge, Julie (1981). *Innocent Flowers: Women in the Edwardian Theatre*. London: Virago.

Mayhall, Laura E. Nym, Levine, Philippa and Fletcher, Ian Christopher (2000). 'Introduction' in *Women's Suffrage in the British Empire: Citizenship, Nation, and Race*. London and New York: Routledge, xiii–xxii.

Stowell, Sheila (1992). *A Stage of their Own: Feminist Playwrights of the Suffrage Era*. Ann Arbor: University of Michigan Press.

Tickner, Lisa (1987). *The Spectacle of Women: Imagery of the Suffrage Campaign 1907–1914*. London: Chatto and Windus.

9

Unlocking Synge Today

Christopher Murray

Like any other major author whose centenary has come and gone, in his reception John Millington Synge (1871–1909) has endured several phases of interpretation and reinterpretation. The first turbulent years, between the staging of *The Shadow of the Glen* (1903) and of *The Playboy of the Western World* (1907), found Synge under attack from oversensitive nationalist critics in Dublin. If it hadn't been for W. B. Yeats, who stubbornly defended Synge in print and from the Abbey stage, it is unlikely that Synge's reputation would have survived the 1907 riots. Yeats saw Synge as a cause, a writer who represented in an acute form the necessity to uphold the claims of art over the pressure of politics within a national theatre. Yeats stood firm on principle: 'We have claimed for our writers the freedom to find in their own land every expression of good and evil necessary to their art', where the echo of Nietzsche in the inclusion of 'evil' as a 'necessary' component of art was freshly provocative. As Yeats saw the matter in 1907: 'The quarrel of our theatre today is the quarrel of the theatre in many lands; for the old Puritanism, the old dislike of power and reality have not changed' (Yeats 1962: 225). His championing of Synge was magnificent, inflexible and fundamentally creative. The Synge the world came to know – the solitary, brooding artist totally dedicated to his art, 'that rooted man' – was largely Yeats's invention, for, wanting a hero as example, he suppressed Synge's early work revealing the weaker, morbid side of Synge.[1] In line with Yeats's agenda the Abbey Theatre, of which Synge was one of the three founding directors, was to be a 'free' and independent theatre in precisely the sense in which its European and even its English counterparts were: André Antoine's Théâtre Libre, Otto Brahms's Die Freie Bühne and J. T. Grein's Independent Theatre. They were all in some measure experimental. In addition, Yeats, a true Celticist, opposed Anglophone modernism. So far as his defence of Synge's *Playboy* was concerned, however, Yeats's was a pyrrhic victory, since the failure of the first audiences to understand and appreciate Synge as artist was also the Abbey's failure. Synge created a split. Nationalists within and without the Abbey withdrew their support and the Gaelic League told its members to stay away. After Synge's death in 1909 Yeats's mythologizing of Synge (in his essays as well as in certain poems) constructed an Anglo-Irish writer who for a long time stood in for the real Synge, whom biographies and his *Collected Letters* were to reveal. The reception of Synge's *Playboy* in the USA, meanwhile, in 1911–12, reinforced nationalist bias and served to condemn Synge, for all that Yeats could say, to enemy status.

Whereas Synge's plays continued to be performed at the Abbey, where the one-act plays in particular, *Riders to the Sea* (1904) and *The Shadow of the Glen*, proved reliable companions for longer plays, new and old, in the days when it was usual to have a double or triple bill in the theatre, there was a division of opinion between literary and theatre people. Theatre people, those not bothered by the political implications of the row over the *Playboy*, recognized Synge's genius and supported the Abbey accordingly. Not all of the six plays in the canon found their way into the repertory: *Deirdre of the Sorrows*, premiered in 1910 after his death, was not shown again until the centenary year of 1971; *The Tinker's Wedding* (London, 1909) was regarded as 'too immoral' to be staged;[2] *The Well of the Saints* (1905) was performed regularly while Yeats was alive and seldom afterwards.[3] Literary people, heartened by Maurice Bourgeois's biography in 1913 and Ernest Boyd's positive view in his histories of Irish literature and drama, probably accepted Synge's genius on Yeats's terms. That is, until Daniel Corkery first published his influential study *Synge and Anglo-Irish Literature* (1931). It might be too strong to describe this work as sectarian but it nudged in that direction. By Corkery's criteria – that Irish writing is properly concerned with three themes: the land, Irish nationalism, and the religious consciousness of the people (1966: 19) – Synge did not qualify as Irish, rather as Anglo-Irish in the colonialist sense. This became the received view. *The Playboy* seemed to transcend such criteria, though Corkery frowned at the profusion of oaths and blasphemies uttered in the play in forms he refused to believe were true to the Irish way. Synge had never been at a Munster hurling final. Thus if to Irish-Americans Synge was at least one leaf short of a shamrock, to the good Catholic population of Ireland Synge was a 'black Protestant' who could not altogether be trusted as one of our own. Although an excerpt from Synge's *Aran Islands* (1907) was included in the primary-school text *Our National Progress*, in use until the 1960s, it was a safe piece on the difficulties of harvesting and the jolly attitude of the natives rather than anything on the desolation and loneliness of the place or Synge's affinity with its residual pagan beliefs.

Not much of Synge was getting unlocked in the years between Yeats's death in 1939 and Synge's centenary in 1971. It is 1971 that is the turning point. As part of the centenary, there was a major Synge conference in Trinity College Dublin; productions of all six canonical plays at the Abbey; a one-man show at the Theatre Festival (Maurice Good in *John Synge Comes Next*); a television documentary scripted by Denis Johnston; productions and revivals on Radio Telefís Éireann (RTE) radio; an exhibition; a postage stamp. It wasn't just the centenary, however, that made 1971 a turning point – often these can be dutiful and rather meaningless occasions – but the social and cultural changes that coincided around this time. After decades of stagnation the Irish economy was on the move. The arrival of an Irish television service at the end of 1961 made a huge difference to the reception and dissemination of ideas. Politically the commemoration of the jubilee of the 1916 Rising in 1966 gave rise to revisionism of all kinds, in the writing of history, in the challenging of old authorities, especially church authority in the age of the Ecumenical Council. And in 1969 the outbreak of what are fondly termed the Troubles in Northern Ireland threw all stable views and categories into confusion in the south. Looking afresh at Synge was perhaps a minor matter in the face of all that was being revolutionized but was significant nevertheless.

The context for this fresh look had begun to be created by an important critical biography published by David Greene and Synge's nephew Edward Stephens in 1959. This enabling study drew for the first time on Synge's papers and notebooks and showed sides to him opaque to Yeats, not to mention Lady Gregory (to whom Synge was something of a weakling), including his musical training, his wide reading, his family history and difficult struggle to escape his mother's evangelical influence, and how his love affair with actress Molly Allgood helped create the roles of Pegeen, Mike and Deirdre. Stephens's own manuscript on Synge's life, edited by Andrew Carpenter (1974), also helped expand the biography. Robin Skelton's major editorial undertaking, Synge's *Collected Works*, appeared from Oxford in 1968, containing a volume each on the poems and the prose with two volumes of the plays, all meticulously edited. Once the definitive texts were established, and the early autobiographical work in prose and drama was included for the first time, fresh critical studies could follow, from Gerstenberger (1964) through the anthologies of centenary papers (Harmon, Bushrui), to Skelton, Grene and Kiberd in the 1970s. From here on Synge was being unlocked to reveal more and more riches. In 1990 Nicholas Grene initiated the Synge Summer School in Rathdrum, County Wicklow, and it could be said that Synge the major writer had come intellectually, socially and culturally home at last. In 2000 McCormack's biography reintegrated Synge into Irish social history.

In theatre what Jonathan Miller calls 'subsequent performances', or new productions of established plays (or operas), call for a clean slate. Indebtedness to earlier productions, unless by way of *hommage*, or postmodernist referencing, is not the issue; rather it is the animating of a text anew. At such times tradition is reinvestigated and reimagined. Accordingly, when historically someone like Hugh Hunt arrives on the Dublin scene and reintroduces Synge's *The Well of the Saints* at the Abbey in 1969–70 after a 25-year gap, we are not to imagine that many people today are going to remember this event as significant. But in so far as the production reinterpreted the original for the 1960s, it altered the tradition within which a classic may be read. Indeed, I would argue that Hunt's arrival as artistic director of the new Abbey (opened 1966) was just as important for Synge as a new edition or even a new biography (although that may be stretching the point). The theatre has its own way of enabling us to reread texts. My purpose in this chapter is to explore how.

DruidSynge, the extraordinary production of all six canonical plays by the Druid Theatre Company in July–August 2005, works to that end. One means of establishing that case is via the pioneering ideas of Hugh Hunt.

Hunt had been a young director at the old Abbey in the 1930s, invited there by none other than Yeats himself. During his time there Hunt got into hot water over his production of *The Playboy* because it lacked what was then called Peasant Quality or traditional style; the play was redone by another native director in a 'porthery' style to appease the ghost of Synge (Hunt 1979: 155). Hunt also directed *The Well of the Saints* in the 1930s, and when he returned to it in 1969 he was struck by the different way in which the Abbey cast now played up the violence in Act III of the text. In the 1930s, he reflected, even the more obvious violence in Act III of *The Playboy* was 'treated as lightly as possible' so that the 'dragging of Christy to the peelers at the end of a rope was treated as high comedy'. Now in the comparable scene in *The Well of the Saints* 'the violence and cruelty of the people in stoning the blind Martin and Mary broke out so spontaneously from the actors themselves that they dislocated the machinery of one of the stage lifts' (Harmon 1972: 73). To Hunt, the change represented a cultural shift in the Irish (for as professor of drama at Manchester Hunt had been absent from Ireland for thirty years). He put the change down to the northern situation and an awareness (through television, obviously) of violence over the American civil rights movement and the Vietnam war. Suddenly it became clear to the outsider, which Hunt basically was, that Synge's plays contained a lot of violence waiting to be unleashed. This insight, related to the cultural changes in Ireland in the 1960s, was to bring to an end the era of the romantic Synge, most recently seen in the film version (1961) starring Siobhán McKenna as Pegeen.[4]

The Druid Theatre Company, established in Galway in 1975, came to fame through the rugged, anti-romantic style of its *Playboy* productions. We are talking here about a whole shift in perspective. As capital of the west, Galway lies at the gateway to the hidden Ireland Synge as traveller visited and to some extent exposed three-quarters of a century before Druid. The Aran Islands, which 'were the making of Synge as a writer' (Tracy 1998: 139), and gave him plot details for four of his plays, lie within Galway Bay; Connemara and West Mayo, which he toured with Jack Yeats in 1905 and which gave him not only plot material but atmosphere for *The Playboy*, lie in the hinterland to the north-west. This area, as much as Wicklow in the east, can be regarded as Synge country. By reclaiming Synge Druid removed him from the sophistication of Dublin interpretation and reinserted his plays into the landscape from which, arguably, they had been carved. What has emerged as a result is on the one hand a new realism, a dirty realism if you will, and on the other a somewhat unfortunate inference that west is best and that the Abbey never truly understood Synge. Part of this argument, which has not yet been fully debated, is the language question.

It is undeniable that whereas Synge knew Irish and was able to profit from that knowledge by translating and transforming its richnesses into English (Harmon 1972: 35–62), the Abbey – as founded by Yeats, Lady Gregory, Synge and, let us not forget, the redoubtable Annie Horniman, English merchant and patron – was Anglophone. There were other Irish writers, notably Patrick Pearse and Thomas MacDonagh, who believed in the possibilities of a Gaelic theatre. MacDonagh, for instance, believed that if the Gaelic League sent four or five one-act plays in Irish on tour through Irish-speaking districts the problem would be solved (MacDonagh 1996: 113–14). MacDonagh's dream did not come to pass, and he himself had an appointment elsewhere, in the GPO, as it happened. In 1928, to be sure, a national Gaelic theatre was established in Galway, but as time passed this Taibhdhearc did not deliver the goods. Druid has availed itself of the vacuum and has stepped into the Irish-drama space with Synge and, in addition, Martin McDonagh, the illegitimate heir of Synge's west, and no relation to the patriot.

The Druid Theatre Company is, should it choose to exercise the option, bilingual. Its founding members, Garry Hynes, Marie Mullen, Maeliosa Stafford, Mick Lally and such prominent associates as Seán McGinley and Ray McBride, would all be capable Irish speakers. To them, accordingly, Synge's language would come naturally. They have the *blas* or appropriate accent. It is a matter of the kind of English Synge wrote, a dialect which was an 'inspired compromise', as Kiberd (Kiberd 1979: 202) puts it, between Irish and English. Because of its roots in Gaelic this dialect is still amenable to westerners. In contrast, when the Abbey undertook the *Playboy* in 2004 they had to make use of a voice director.

So far as Synge's work is concerned, Druid's concern has been to unlock the sense of reality which decades of romantic productions had suppressed. By 1982 *The Playboy* was restored to the western world. 'Setting her face against the quaint and the picturesque', as Nicholas Grene has put it, Hynes gave to the play 'a new grotesquerie and a new violence' (Frazier 2004: 82). This production was taken on tour to the Aran Islands not only as a gesture towards its roots there but also, surely, as a proud manifestation of its authenticity. It was then taken to Dublin, with no doubt a different purpose in mind. There it was received as it was meant, an in-your-face representation of the squalor, ignorance, cruelty and at the same time the passion and beauty of a culture viewed ambivalently by Synge himself. It was a ground-breaking production, which travelled the world. And there were no riots this time.

In 2004 Hynes began to consider tackling Synge's whole dramatic canon, that is, the six plays but not the early and academically interesting *When the Moon Has Set* (RTE Radio, 6 November 1984).[5] Druid staged *The Playboy* and *The Well of the Saints* and then set about planning the full cycle. The 2004 *Playboy* cast the film star Cillian Murphy as Christy and the inexperienced Anne-Marie Duff as Pegeen. Thirty-year-old Aisling O'Sullivan played a very strong Widow Quin. This casting did not work. In other respects Hynes directed an alienating production, making Shawn Keogh 'like an engravature illustrating an 1890s *Punch* cartoon about Ireland' (Frazier 2004: 116), and deliberately exaggerating the drunkenness of Michael James, Philly Cullen and Jimmy Farrell in the manner of the caricatures or stage Irishry which 'the national theatre movement had [originally] pledged itself to banish, drunks and dunderheads, clods and clowns'.[6] This was clearly not the production to be the centrepiece of a Synge cycle. As Adrian Frazier describes it in his indispensable *Playboys*, it was 'Postmodern Paddywhackery' (Frazier 2004: 115–24).

For the DruidSynge cycle *The Playboy* was freshly cast, and Hynes was pleased she 'could put a company of actors together and have the one creative team working across all the plays'.[7] On the other hand, as may appear in the next section of this chapter, the abandonment of the in-your-face approach ensured a conservative approach for the cycle as a whole. But if unity is to be achieved no one play can be allowed to stand out awkwardly, even if provocatively. In short, *The Playboy,* necessarily the linchpin of any Synge festival, had to be in some sense tamed again in order to take its place in an unfolding exploration of tradition. The purpose of the project, according to a programme note, was 'to re-evaluate and re-engage with one of Ireland's greatest and most influential playwrights'.[8] That is a more serious affair than shocking the intelligentsia. For, as Nicholas Grene put it, 'If the Abbey audience rioted at the original production in 1907, they might have torn the theatre apart if they had seen this 2004 version.'[9]

The main programme note for DruidSynge was a brief biography of Synge by Tim Robinson, well known for his archaeological *Stones of Aran*. But there was no essay on or interpretation of Synge the dramatist. This is significant, given that in most theatres nowadays there is an anxiety to make a bridge between the academic and the theatrical interpretations of plays. The inference here is anti-intellectual, that is, that the plays must speak for themselves. Of course, this is never really the case. As Jan Kott memorably said about *Hamlet*: 'There are many subjects in *Hamlet*. [. . .] There is everything you want, including deep psychological analysis [. . .]. One can select at will. But one must know what one selects, and why.'[10] As for *Hamlet,* so for *The Playboy* and the rest of Synge.

The way the DruidSynge plays were paired, however, and how they were designed for the stage allow us to form a basis for interpretation. *Riders to the Sea* was paired with *Deirdre of the Sorrows* for one evening's programme, *The Tinker's Wedding* and *The Well of the Saints* for another, and *The Shadow of the Glen* with *The Playboy* for a third. It could be said that notions of genre were being explored: tragedy in the first grouping, farce and comedy in the second, tragicomedy in the third. But on the days when all six plays were presented (from 2.00 to 10.30 p.m.) the order was altered to arrange for *Riders* to start and *Deirdre* to finish the set. The suggestion here is that the tragic vision unifies Synge's work, and this is a legitimate and a challenging way of looking at the six plays. It is supportable by reference to Synge's prose, the seminal secondary text *Aran Islands*, and several essays from *In Wicklow and West Kerry* in particular. One item in the design served to reinforce the tragic idea as the controlling one. Two white boards, called for in the text of *Riders to the Sea* to make a coffin for the drowned son Michael, remained on-stage for all six plays as a memento mori. The overall design (by Francis O'Connor) was naturalistic. Yet the high walls, reaching up beyond the usual peasant cottage, strained against realism, as did the lack of a chimney for the open fire. The space designed allowed for a dignity in the lives of the people inhabiting it, however impoverished. *Riders,* for all its brevity (Joyce called it a 'dwarf tragedy' as he set about translating it into Italian in 1909), has in its foreboding and inevitability the air of Greek tragedy. The world it conjures up is remote, ancient, primitive in the positive cultural sense. It dramatizes the struggle for survival in its most Darwinian and elemental form. It denies the consolations of religious belief. In the play Maurya refuses to accept what the young priest (kept off-stage because, as in *The Playboy*, Synge had no regard for the pronouncements of the clergy) promised Cathleen, that God would not leave this family destitute: 'It's little the like of him knows of the sea' (Synge 1995: 9). What kind of knowledge, then, can help? Maurya's knowledge comes from beyond the grave. Once she sees the dead Michael on horseback she *knows* that Bartley will be drowned also: the dead need companionship. So strong is Synge's empathy with the kind of people he met and lived among on Aran that superstition is not a factor in the play. These people live so close to death that it is always around the next corner. The power of *Riders to the Sea* resides in the calmness with which Maurya reads the signs and accepts the inevitable. 'No man at all can be living for ever and we must be satisfied' (12). As Marie Mullen played the old woman, with complete naturalness, she was far from senile: a beautiful, ageing woman fighting impossible odds and losing with supreme dignity.

Liberation is the strangely unexpected theme sounded at the end of *Riders to the Sea*. It was the keynote for all five plays which followed. *The Tinker's Wedding*, a farce in the medieval style, while offering a sharp contrast to the tragic mood of *Riders*, is fundamentally centred on a woman's yearning for a better life. Here Synge presents two worlds, that of the tinkers or nomads and that of the settled community, always seen by Synge as hypocritical. Vivian Mercier is partly correct in regarding *The Tinker's Wedding* as 'mock-pastoral' in form (Bushrui 1972: 75–89). Bearing in mind William Empson's *Some Versions of Pastoral* (1935), I would argue that Synge makes use of pastoral all through his work, but in quite radical ways. Although his art is, in effect, 'proletarian' it is not dialectic in the way Empson understands pastoral and even mock-pastoral to be. Synge went for a unified style, a unified social experience. Giffard argues that there are two kinds of pastoral, one sentimental and the other critical (Gifford 1999: 10). A pastoral deals Wordsworth-fashion with human affairs within a rural landscape (even if Wordsworth complicated the matter by insisting on 'the language really used by men'; see Wordsworth and Coleridge 1992: 57) so Synge was unquestionably a Wordsworthian. But the general problem with pastoral is whether there is a hero. Empson says that 'there is a natural connection between heroic and pastoral before they are parodied' (Empson 1935: 196), but this is not true of Synge. Paul Aspers rightly says pastoral is concerned with 'herdsmen and their lives' (Aspers 1996: x). After that it all depends on how these herdsmen are represented. Wordsworth, again, idealized them. Synge, being a drama-tist, looks at them empathetically without sentimentalizing their plight but without parodying either. In his preface to *The Tinker's Wedding* the phrase he uses is 'being laughed at without malice'. This has nothing to do with manners in Empson's very British sense. So there are not two levels of style as in Empson's model, *The Beggar's Opera* (1728). In judging, Synge simply satirized some figures, but always the bourgeois types and always with robust rather than courtly humour. His purpose is liberation, both of his anti-social characters and of his urbanized audience.

Druid's *The Tinker's Wedding* beautifully balanced the gaiety and sombreness which make up the two moods of the play. No matter how hilarious the action and characters are in a Synge play the darkness is never far away. Here, when a priest sits down among tinkers to have a drink and some talk, it is not long before he begins to sigh and feel miserable at what he sees as the contrast between their easy lives on the road and his put-upon life as servant of the people and his bishop. At the same time, although the younger tinkers are not lonely the mother, Mary Casey, is, and left alone she fears the dark and the onset of age in terms not much different from the priest's. Her son's partner Sarah wants to break into the ways of the settled community by getting married, a whim which appals her partner Michael as much as his mother: they both see it as irrational and unnecessary. But there is a reason, and it has to do with Sarah's wish to belong and her illusion that the settled life will bring comforts she lacks at present, such as freedom from pain in childbirth. So she perseveres. To do so she has to promise the priest a hefty sum to marry herself and Michael. Synge shows how unnatural the idea is from the point of view of the tinkers' world and culture. Mary drinks the money, the priest is cheated and turns nasty; they stuff him into a sack to get their own back, Sarah by this time having seen through her dream. She sees the dichotomy in society and is freed of her longing to cross over. The violent and Molière-influenced scene[11] in which the priest is put into a sack proved too much for the Abbey directors to accept. But it shows clearly where Synge stood.

The Well of the Saints deals with the same social opposition but makes use of the pastoral mode in more complex terms. The fact that Marie Mullen, who played Mary Casey with wild abandon, also played the blind Mary Doul in this play served to make the link obvious. Eamon Morrissey, who played the priest, now played her husband Martin Doul. This was Synge's first full-length play, and he took the opportunity to develop it schematically act by act to show how the blind couple are at first content as imaginative beggars, then disillusioned when a visiting holy man cures them, and finally rebellious when he tries to cure them again in spite of their preferring now to be blind again. The point Synge makes is that society seeks to coerce into conformity whereas true emancipation lies in the choice, even if wilful, to be non-conformist, as Martin's exit speech indicates:

> We're going surely, for if it's [a] right some of you have to be working and sweating the like of Timmy the smith, and a right some of you have to be fasting and praying and talking holy talk the like of yourself [the Saint], I'm thinking it's a good right ourselves have to be sitting blind hearing a soft wind turning round the little leaves of the spring and feeling the sun, and we not tormenting our souls with the sight of the grey days, and the holy men, and the dirty feet is trampling the world. (93)

Of course, this is romantic revolt, and some would say Synge is ideologically an escapist in his plays. But he does not disguise in these exits that the rebel figures go forth into a Darwinian world where drowning is the likely outcome. Synge is no sentimentalist.

Druid paired *The Shadow of the Glen* with *The Playboy*, even though four years separated them in composition and first staging. It was a wise decision, since the conjunction makes the continuity with *The Well of the Saints* all the clearer. All three plays are meditations on *possibility*, on the discrepancy between the given life, with all its compromises, and the dream life, beautiful, complete, sanctioned by nature itself. This 'other' life is one worth fighting for, in Synge's opinion, and may miraculously be achieved, as Christy Mahon shows in *The Playboy* and Martin Doul before him in *The Well of the Saints*, if the individual first has a vision of the beautiful and secondly has the self-belief to reject authority. This is why I am inclined to call Synge an 'ironic revolutionary': he is no Shaw calling for social change but he can nevertheless imagine revolt as positive. At the centre of *The Shadow of the Glen*, absent yet dominating the atmosphere and meaning, is Patch Darcy, the dead shepherd, a type of artist as hero, expert and at the same time overwhelmed by the conditions nature has provided. He ran mad one night, it seems, up into the back hills and was found days later dead in a ditch. Here is the pastoral as re-written by Synge, who knew of such a herdsman in Wicklow (McCormack 2000: 232–4; Grene 2000: 36–7; cf. Synge 1968: 2, 209–10). As she mourns Patch Darcy in the play, Nora officially mourns her old husband Dan, who is in fact feigning death in order to catch her out with her latest love, a would-be farmer, Michael Dara. That is the situation the Tramp finds when he knocks on her door for shelter one wild, wet night.

Synge based the play on a story he heard in Aran of a jealous husband who pretended to be dead in order to entrap his 'bad' wife with her lover. Synge's narrator told the story as participant, the traveller who took part by helping the resurrected man to kill wife and lover in bed. Synge completely overturned the morality of the tale by changing the Tramp's agency. At the crucial moment, the Tramp stands up and takes Nora's side: 'It's a hard thing you're saying, for an old man, master of the house, and what would the like of her do if you put her out on the roads?' (24). The Tramp steps out of his role as spectator/audience, intervenes in the action, and goes off with the woman. Nothing could be more theatrical, and Synge provokes his audience to be likewise transformed by the Tramp's action. His first audiences, in 1903 and even more so in 1905, led by Arthur Griffith and Maud Gonne (without whom no nationalistic protest could be conducted at the time), were outraged by what they saw as the immorality of Synge's story. As editor of the *United Irishman* and founder of Sinn Féin, Griffith denounced Synge as a decadent Parisian artist bent on slandering the Irish people. This is where Yeats came in and began the defence of Synge which was to last through the *Playboy* riots and beyond. All that needs saying here is that Synge had early shown how pastoral can be subversive without being parodic. The Druid production superbly realized the play's potential: the playing of Catherine Walsh as Nora and Mick Lally as the Tramp firmly maintained the moral high ground against Eamon Morrissey's righteous Dan.[12]

The Playboy came next. As said earlier, citing Jan Kott, a choice has to be made of what to focus on for a coherent production of a complex play. Hynes abandoned her postcolonialist reading of 2004 for an interpretation which allowed the *Playboy* as pastoral to flow from *The Shadow of the Glen*. Synge himself said there are 'several sides' to the *Playboy* just as there are many ways of reading Shylock and Molière's Alceste. He added that the reviewer who had called the play 'more a psychological revelation than a dramatic process, but it is both' was on the right lines.[13] Arguing that there are really two plays at odds here, Edward Hirsch says this fact allows two basic but conflicting interpretations, 'the modernist and the representational' (Bloom 1988: 102). It was the representational or realistic production in 1907 that enraged the first audience: 'By the third act, the subversion of characters was interpreted as a frontal attack on the audience's ideology. This reaction led in turn to the breakdown of the play's rhetorical conventions, the necessary cooperative relationship between the actors and the spectators' (Bloom 1988: 107). Hynes's interest is normally in the representational. Responses to the 2004 *Playboy* she directed, cited above (see Frazier's 2004 collection, *Playboys*), support this view. Hynes's direction of Martin McDonagh's and Marina Carr's plays also suggests that this is her preferred theatrical style. But in DruidSynge she pulled back. Hirsch explains what is involved:

> the strategy of reading the play as a modernist text is designed to undermine and attack the claims to *The Playboy*'s representational nature, in essence denying the middle-class code of the play. Yeats first established this tradition by claiming that the play's fantastic mode placed it not in a tradition of realism, but within the aristocratic literary tradition of Irish fantasy. The key to the modernist *Playboy* is the play's exuberant language. (Bloom 1988: 113)

It is the choice between the 'gallous story' elaborated every which way and the 'dirty deed' graphically enacted. In the 2005 Druid production, riskily played without interval, the poetry, the fantasy, and the *possibility* of transcendence were always latent and gradually in Act III dominant, before being ground down by the harsh realism of Christy's punishment. A balance was struck and maintained by fine performances. Liberation in this play is confined to one character, who becomes a hero accordingly, while Pegeen is plunged back into a diminished world. It is still difficult for the audience today to accept Synge's unconventional ending. The pastoral world reclaims only Christy, transmogrified into a genuine rogue. I see little of the 'carnival' spirit here, as Grene does (Grene 1999: 103). Pegeen's 'I've lost him surely' sounds a tragic note at final curtain.

Yet this note left no easy bridge to *Deirdre of the Sorrows*. This is a problem play in many respects. Had Synge lived to re-write it, Yeats claimed in a preface, it 'would have been his masterwork, so much beauty is there in its course, and such wild nobleness in its end, and so poignant is [*sic*] an emotion and wisdom that were his own preparation for death'.[14] As it stands now the play has its admirers but nobody calls it a masterpiece. Hynes did what she could with it, keeping the same set as for the realistic plays and trying to make Conchubar credible by dressing Mick Lally in a modern lounge suit and lending him two sticks in Act III to give an impression of psychosomatic characterization. Although *Deirdre* ought to fit in with the other five plays, being more purely pastoral than any other of Synge's, and enacting a tragic attempt at liberation under those auspices, it does not. Perhaps with *Riders* it may have worked better. But it seems too contrived. Is it that, as Heaney says, 'pastoral cannot actually function as a mode without writer and audience being completely alert to the ill fit that prevails between the beautifully tinted literary map and the uglier shape that reality has taken in the world'?[15] Though Hynes worked hard in the operatic Act III to create a *mise en scène* of war and destruction at Emain, even risking explosions and tentative expressionism, Synge let her down. The union of peasant play and mythology fell apart.[16] The play remains unconvincing. In 2005 the Abbey staged a new version of the Deirdre legend, Vincent Woods's *A Cry from Heaven*. What it offered, apart from a clarity of motivation indebted, I suggest, to Thomas Kinsella's 1969 translation of the *Táin*, was what Synge had copiously in his other plays: a disturbing sense that life and not artifice was dominating the stage.

DruidSynge has put Synge's oeuvre squarely before postmillennial audiences. If the productions were essentially conservative, they showed the beauty and vibrancy of all but one of the canonical plays. Side by side they shone like stars in a brilliant constellation, even *Deirdre*'s literary beauties emanating their own fitful light. Seen as a continuing cycle or at any rate an assemblage of plays with themes in common, DruidSynge was more than the sum of its parts and more, too, than mere *hommage* to an elusive playwright. It was a theatrical tour de force.

But in the context of the title and theme of this chapter DruidSynge raises major questions. First, how valid is the exercise, this conjoining of all the canonical plays as one complete entity? A more important point is the nature of the challenge offered to the Abbey Theatre. Put crudely, who now 'owns' the plays of Synge? A recent letter to the *Irish Times* indicated that this question is already in the public domain. Having seen and enjoyed DruidSynge in Dublin, the correspondent claimed 'it may be time we reconsidered who should lay claim to being the real national theatre'. He concluded that the question regarding the new location of the national theatre is now not a choice between north or south of the Liffey 'but east or west of the Shannon'.[17] This notion might be thought irrelevant did the same paper not report Garry Hynes's plans to tour DruidSynge to Inis Meáin in the Aran Islands following its stint at the Edinburgh Festival. The venue was to be outdoors in an old walled fort, so that audiences could hear Synge's words 'echoing out around the stone walls *where he created them*'.[18] But of course Synge did not actually write any of his plays on the Aran Islands.

As indicated above, the Druid Theatre Company abolished the older romantic vision of Synge through its realistic staging of *The Playboy* in 1982. It was superbly equipped to do so. But Edward Hirsch is right: there are two *Playboys* within the one play, and both the representational and the modernist views of the play are valid. Yet one must choose. At present the Abbey has chosen the modernist. In 2004 the Abbey mounted an experimental *Playboy* as part of its centenary celebrations. Director Ben Barnes removed the play from its west-of-Ireland setting and held it up for theatrical exploration, introducing a new character, The Bellman, to recite parts of Synge's preface as prologue and thereafter to be present as illusionist on stage. The Abbey had already presented an experimental interpretation in its annex, the Peacock, in 2001; Barnes's production was aimed at no less than 'a re-invention of the play' (Drury 2004: 62). It is ironic, perhaps, that the Abbey, so often accused of traditionalism, should in this instance stand in contrast to the Druid, often hailed as at the cutting edge of contemporary Irish theatre. It is equally ironic, perhaps, that Barnes's stylish and stylized production of the *Playboy* should have been dismissed in New York when on tour, not because it offended Irish-Americans any more but because it was 'self-conscious, wayward and dispiritingly grim'.[19]

On the other hand, Fintan O'Toole, the *Irish Times* drama critic, called DruidSynge 'one of the greatest achievements in the history of Irish theatre'. Not even *Deirdre of the Sorrows* dampened his enthusiasm, his fear that it would prove anti-climactic being dispelled by 'a magnificent third act' in which 'the resonances generated throughout the earlier plays and the overarching rituals of life and death are folded back in with a devastating and thrilling effect'. Even if this is too vague to be useful as theatrical analysis, and 'overarching rituals' something of a bridge too far in criticism, for O'Toole, here 'the seal [was] placed on greatness'.[20]

It comes to this then: unlocking Synge today is a matter of contextualizing the history of reception and reformulating the arguments for assessing the canon. The obvious link here is between Hugh Hunt and Garry Hynes; but is it a link or a baton passed in a race for authenticity? In the re-establishment of tradition in theatre production is there not an element of appropriation of the original(s)? The main issue seems to me to be emblematized just now in the opposition between Ben Barnes's approach to the *Playboy* at the Abbey and Garry Hynes's at Druid. There are ideological and aesthetic bases to the differences between them, which may yet serve as grounds for fruitful redefinitions of Synge. In that regard the DruidSynge is a mighty challenge. And yet it is noteworthy that in all of this discussion the emphasis has remained on Synge and Ireland, when one would have thought a more cosmopolitan dimension exists. Is Ireland so globalized now that provincialism is invisible? Or is it still possible to have a debate on Synge's universal qualities? There may be other ways to unlock Synge: in the context of multiculturalism, for example, or in relation to histories other than the familiar ones dealt with here. With the centenary of Synge's death due in 2009 perhaps we can look forward to a whole new stage – pun definitely intended – in re-reading and reinterpreting this remarkable writer.

NOTES

1 See W. B. Yeats's poem 'The Municipal Gallery Revisited' in Yeats (1950: 369).

2 Denis Donoghue (1955). '"Too Immoral for Dublin": Synge's *The Tinker's Wedding'*, *Irish Writing* 30, 56–62.

3 Apart from tours to Britain and the USA, *The Well of the Saints* was revived 11 times before 1939 and after that only once (in 1945) before 1969–70. It was revived again in 1979, 1994 and 1996.

4 In an otherwise very useful piece on the film of *The Playboy*, Adrian Frazier (2004: 59–74) misses the point clear to Hunt, namely that a major change overtook audience sensibilities at the end of the 1960s. The film of *The Playboy* was of its time, halfway between *The Quiet Man* (1950) and *Ryan's Daughter* (1970).

5 *When the Moon Has Set* has not been produced on stage. For a good analysis of the play see King (1985) and Richards (2004: 79–92).

6 Nicholas Grene, 'Redesigning *The Playboy*', in Frazier (2004: 127).

7 Garry Hynes in interview, 'Synge When You're Winning', *Sunday Tribune* 24 July 2005, 'Arts', 7.

8 Unsigned, 'About Druid', in programme for DruidSynge: The Plays of John Millington Synge, July–August 2005, 105.

9 In Frazier (2004: 127). In her review of this *Playboy*, Helen Meany regarded the provocation in a more positive light. See 'Reviews: *The Playboy of the Western World*: Town Hall Theatre, Galway', *Irish Times* 12 February 2004, 31.

10 Jan Kott (1967). *Shakespeare Our Contemporary*, trans. Boleslaw Taborski, 2nd edn. rev. London: Methuen, 48.

11 There is a similar scene in Molière's *Les Fourbières de Scapin*, which Synge directed in Lady Gregory's translation (*The Rogueries of Scapin*) at the Abbey.

12 Anthony Roche offers a fine reading of the play in relation to Synge's affair with Molly Allgood (Grene 2000: 163–76).

13 Synge to the *Irish Times*, 30 January 1907, in Synge (1983–4, 1: 286–7 and n. 3).

14 W. B. Yeats, 'Preface to *Deirdre of the Sorrows*', in Synge (1995: n.p. [148]).

15 Seamus Heaney (2003). 'Eclogues *In Extremis*: On the Staying Power of Pastoral', *Proceedings of the Royal Irish Academy* 103C:1, 6.

16 Although most readings of *Deirdre* are literary, they usually use the unfinished state of the play as an excuse to praise its fragments. I know of no defence of the play as theatre. In a rave review of DruidSynge at Edinburgh, Susannah Clapp called *Deirdre* 'the only disappointment [. . .] no one could make it interesting'. 'Playwright of the Western World', *Observer* 4 September 2005, 'Review', 11.

17 Paul Thornton, 'Real National Theatre?', *Irish Times* 13 August 2005.

18 Garry Hynes, quoted in 'Druid Turns Aran Tropical', *Irish Times* 20 August 2005, 'Review', 8, emphasis added. See also Judy Murphy, 'Druid Works its Magic on Synge in Inis Meáin', *Irish Times* 12 September 2005, 5.

19 Charles Isherwood, 'A Seductive Fellow Returns, but in a Darker Mood', *New York Times* 28 October 2004.

20 Fintan O'Toole, 'Bringing Death to Vivid Life', *Irish Times* 19 July 2005, 10.

Primary reading

Synge, J. M. (1968). *The Complete Works of J. M. Synge*, 4 vols., gen. ed. Robin Skelton. Vol. 1: *Poems*, ed. Robin Skelton; Vol. 2: *Prose*, ed. Alan Price; Vol. 3: *Plays 1*, ed. Ann Saddlemyer; Vol. 4: *Plays 2*, ed. Ann Saddlemyer. Oxford: Oxford University Press (repr. Gerrards Cross: Colin Smythe, 1982).

Synge, J. M. (1971). *Letters to Molly*, ed. Ann Saddlemyer. Cambridge, MA: Harvard University Press.

Synge, J. M. (1983–4). *The Collected Letters of John Millington Synge*, 2 vols, ed. Ann Saddlemyer. *Vol. 1: 1871–1907; Vol. 2: 1907–1909*. Oxford: Clarendon.

Synge, J. M. (1995). *J. M. Synge: Riders to the Sea, The Shadow of the Glen, The Tinker's Wedding, The Well of the Saints, The Playboy of the Western World, Deirdre of the Sorrows*, ed. Ann Saddlemyer. Oxford and New York: Oxford University Press.

Secondary reading

Aspers, Paul (1996). *What is Pastoral?* Chicago and London: University of Chicago Press.

Bloom, Harold (ed.) (1988). *Modern Critical Interpretations: John Millington Synge's 'The Playboy of the Western World'*. New York: Chelsea House.

Boyd, Ernest A. (1918). *The Contemporary Drama of Ireland*. Dublin: Talbot Press.

Boyd, Ernest A. (1922). *Ireland's Literary Renaissance*, rev. edn. New York: Knopf.

Bourgeois, Maurice (1913). *John Millington Synge and the Irish Theatre*. London: Constable.

Bushrui, S. B. (ed.) (1972) *Sunshine and the Moon's Delight: A Centenary Tribute to John Millington Synge 1871–1909*. Gerrards Cross: Colin Smythe and the University of Beirut.

Carpenter, Andrew (1974). *My Uncle John: Edward Stephens's Life of J. M. Synge*. Oxford: Oxford University Press.

Casey, Daniel J. (ed.) (1994). *Critical Essays on John Millington Synge*. New York: G. K. Hall.

Corkery, Daniel (1966). *Synge and Anglo-Irish Literature*. Cork: Mercier (1st edn. Cork: Cork University Press, 1931).

Deane, Seamus (1985). *Celtic Revivals: Essays in Modern Irish Literature 1880–1980*. London and Boston: Faber and Faber.

Drury, Martin (ed.) (2004). *The Page and the Stage: The Playboy of the Western World*. Dublin: Abbey Theatre.

Empson, William (1935). *Some Versions of Pastoral*. London: Chatto and Windus.

Frazier, Adrian (ed.) (2004). *Playboys of the Western World: Production Histories*. Dublin: Carysfort.

Giffard, Terry (1999). *Pastoral*. London and New York: Routledge.

Gerstenberger, Donna (1964). *John Millington Synge*. New York: Twayne (rev. edn. 1990).

Greene, David H. and Stephens, Edward M. (1959). *J. M. Synge: 1871–1909*. New York: Macmillan.

Gregory, Lady Augusta (1913). *Our Irish Theatre: A Chapter of Autobiography*. London: Putnam (3rd edn. Gerrards Cross: Colin Smythe, 1972).

Grene, Nicholas (1975). *Synge: A Critical Study of the Plays*. London: Macmillan.

Grene, Nicholas (1999). *The Politics of Irish Drama: Plays in Context from Boucicault to Friel*. Cambridge: Cambridge University Press.

Grene, Nicholas (ed.) (2000). *Interpreting Synge: Essays from the Synge Summer School 1991–2000*. Dublin: Lilliput.

Harmon, Maurice (ed.) (1972). *J. M. Synge Centenary Papers 1971*. Dublin: Dolmen.

Hogan, Robert and Kilroy, James (1978). *The Abbey Theatre: The Years of Synge 1905–1909*. Vol. 3: *The Modern Irish Drama: A Documentary History*. Dublin and Atlantic Highlands, NJ: Dolmen and Humanities.

Hunt, Hugh (1979). *The Abbey: Ireland's National Theatre 1904–1979*. Dublin: Gill and Macmillan.

Kiberd, Declan (1979). *Synge and the Irish Language* (2nd edn. Basingstoke: Macmillan, 1993).

Kiberd, Declan (1995). *Inventing Ireland*. London: Cape.

Kilroy, James (1971). *The 'Playboy' Riots*. Dublin: Dolmen.

King, Mary C. (1985). The Drama of *J. M. Synge*. Syracuse, NY: Syracuse University Press.

Kopper, Edward A. Jr. (ed.) (1988). *A J. M. Synge Literary Companion*. Westport, CT: Greenwood.

Krause, David (1982). *The Profane Book of Irish Comedy*. Ithaca, NY: Cornell University Press.

Krause, David (2001). *The Regeneration of Ireland: Essays*. Bethseda: Academica Press.

MacDonagh, Thomas (1916). *Literature in Ireland: Studies Irish and Anglo-Irish*. Dublin: Talbot (repr. Nenagh: Relay, 1996).

Maxwell, D. E. S. (1984). *A Critical History of Modern Irish Drama 1891–1980*. Cambridge: Cambridge University Press.

McCormack, W. J. (2000). *Fool of the Family: A Life of J. M. Synge*. London: Weidenfeld and Nicolson.

Mercier, Vivian (1962). *The Irish Comic Tradition*. London and New York: Oxford University Press.

Miller, Jonathan (1986). *Subsequent Performances*. New York: Viking Penguin.

Morash, Christopher (2000). *A History of Irish Theatre 1601–2000*. Cambridge: Cambridge University Press.

Murray, Christopher (1997). *Twentieth-Century Irish Drama: Mirror Up to Nation*. Manchester: Manchester University Press (repr. Syracuse, NY: Syracuse University Press, 2000).

Nic Shiubhlaigh, Maire (1955). *The Splendid Years: Recollections of Maire Nic Shiubhlaigh, as Told to Edward Kenny*. Dublin: Duffy.

Richards, Shaun (ed.) (2004). *The Cambridge Companion to Twentieth-Century Irish Drama*. Cambridge: Cambridge University Press.

Saddlemyer, Ann (1965). *J. M. Synge and Modern Comedy*. Dublin: Dolmen.

Saddlemyer, Ann (1987). *Theatre Business: The Correspondence of the First Abbey Directors: William Butler Yeats, Lady Gregory and J. M. Synge*. Gerrards Cross: Colin Smythe.

Skelton, Robin (1971). *The Writings of J. M. Synge*. London: Thames and Hudson.

Tracy, Robert (1998). *The Unappeasable Host: Studies in Irish Identities*. Dublin: University College Dublin Press.

Welch, Robert (1999). *The Abbey Theatre 1899–1999*. Oxford: Oxford University Press.

Wordsworth, William and Coleridge, Samuel Taylor (1992). *Lyrical Ballads*, ed. Michael Mason. London: Longman.

Yeats, W. B. (1950) *Collected Poems*. London: Macmillan.

Yeats, W. B. (1961). *Essays and Introductions*. London and New York: Macmillan.

Yeats, W. B. (1962). *Explorations*. London and New York: Macmillan.

10

Sean O'Casey's Powerful Fireworks

Jean Chothia

Recalling his youth in Dublin in the early 1920s, the theatre director Tyrone Guthrie wrote that '*Juno and the Paycock* and *The Plough and the Stars* were two powerful fireworks to shoot from a small and lowly endowed organization in a small, remote island' (Guthrie 1961: 258). The image registers the unexpected brilliance as well as the theatrically explosive nature of these two Sean O'Casey plays, which, along with his first-performed piece *The Shadow of a Gunman* (1923), are his most highly regarded and frequently discussed works. These 'Dublin plays' – written and set in the city – gave new life to the Abbey Theatre. The success of *Juno and the Paycock* (1924) probably saved the Abbey from bankruptcy (Gregory 1946: 75; Murray 1997: 104) and *The Plough and the Stars* (1926) became its most frequent and successfully performed play. But the reception of O'Casey's plays was marked by contention from the outset, and they continue to provoke more controversy than is usual for works so thoroughly accepted into the international repertoire.

O'Casey's relationship with Ireland has been thoroughly recorded (Grene 1999; Lowery 1984; Moran 2005). That it was embattled is not disputed. If, as Ronald Ayling puts it, O'Casey's intention was to 'startle, shock, even scandalize Irish audiences into questioning inherited political and religious beliefs and, indeed, reverential national attitudes on all levels of public life' (Ayling in Kilroy 1975: 84), he evidently succeeded. Scattered objections to his treatment of Irish nationalism in the Dublin plays culminated in the notorious riot against *The Plough and the Stars*, led by the mothers and widows of the 1916 Easter Rising, who believed the play traduced this totemic event of Ireland's independence struggle. W. B. Yeats's angry upbraiding of the audience, 'you have disgraced yourselves again. Is this to be an ever-recurring celebration of the arrival of Irish genius?' (Lowery 1984: 31), did not prevent him from rejecting O'Casey's next play, *The Silver Tassie* in 1928. Moreover, the outrage stirred by *The Plough* reflected back onto earlier plays. Noting the burning of two reels of Alfred Hitchcock's film of *Juno and the Paycock* (1930) in Limerick, O'Casey asked 'if they do that with Juno, what will they do with *The Plough*?' (O'Casey 1975: 551). When, in

1935, *The Silver Tassie* was finally produced in Dublin, the outcry against its perceived mockery of religion cut short its run (Murray 1997: 35).

For his part, although settled in England since the *Plough* riots, O'Casey continued to set his plays in Ireland. His teasingly satirical representation of religious and social restrictions intensified in his post-World War II plays. In 1955, sectarian fighting between the students of Trinity and University Colleges greeted the premiere of *The Bishop's Bonfire* (Guthrie 1961: 265–8) and, in 1958, the archbishop of Dublin's machinations against *The Drums of Father Ned* led to the collapse of that year's Theatre Festival when other dramatists, including Beckett, withdrew their work in sympathy. The ban on further productions of his plays in Ireland that O'Casey then imposed, and maintained for five years, evinces something of his bitterness at the successive rejections, a bitterness also registered in his *Autobiographies* (1963) and his often vituperative theatre criticism.

O'Casey's location of his Dublin plays among the city's tenement dwellers in the context of actual and very recent political events, the independence war, the civil war and then the Rising, broke new ground, even in a period notable for plays engaged with historical reality. It created a different immediacy from the reconfiguring of a distant past, as in George Bernard Shaw's *Saint Joan* (1924); reflection on the present by way of a recreated past, as in Gerhart Hauptmann's staging of the Silesian strikes of 1844 in *The Weavers* (1892), or fictional shadowing of recognizable *kinds* of social disruption as in John Galsworthy's *Strife* (1909). Moreover, O'Casey's specific frame of reference – to Irish history and legend; to religious controversy and questions of allegiance; to demotic political slogans, quotations and sentimental ballads; to occupying British forces, gunmen on the run and punishment killings – was shared by his Dublin audience. He could be sure that the significance of Seumas having 'taught Irish six nights a week' (*Gunman* in O'Casey 1925: 126) or the heroic moments in the struggle for Irish independence, reeled off by Boyle (*Juno* in O'Casey 1925: 48), would be immediately recognized.

While such references contribute to the impression of realism of these plays, the kind of recognition they invite is important to the tenor and the positive reception of O'Casey's comedy. The presumption of a shared joke is flattering to the audience who respond to such seemingly inconsequential statements as Mrs Grogan's 'the Foresters is a gorgeous dhress. I don't think I've seen nicer, mind you, in a pantomime' (O'Casey 1926: 53), or Mary's comment on Boyle's attempt at pious Irish, 'Oh father, that's not Rest in Peace; that's God Save Ireland' (*Juno* in O'Casey 1925: 43). References to cultural and political nationalism are ubiquitous in the plays, but the most scurrilous characters are the most ready to cite Celtic myth or republican history to endorse their self-serving claims. Seumas's 'the land of Saints and Scholars 'ill shortly be a land of bloody poets' (*Gunman* in O'Casey 1925: 121) and 'O Kathleen Ni Houlihan, your way's a thorny way' (122), or Boyle's ''tisn't Juno should be her pet name at all, but Deirdre of the Sorras, for she's always grousin' (*Juno* in O'Casey 1925: 13), are representative; while Seumas's boasting that the braces he peddles would 'do Cuchullian' (*Gunman* in O'Casey 1925: 124) or

Boyle's that 'today, Joxer, there's goin' to be issued a proclamation be me, establishin' an independent Republic, an' Juno'll have to take an oath of allegiance' (*Juno* in O'Casey 1925: 35) have fun at the expense of nationalist rhetoric, but also reflect back diminishingly on the characters when – a much-used comic convention – they immediately prove hollow. Darker suggestion can reside in such light statements as Seumas's protest at being woken early: 'I'm beginning to believe the Irish People are still in the stone age. If they could they'd throw a bomb at you' (*Gunman* in O'Casey 1925: 120). The potentially challenging quality of such references, fun to most, seemed grossly insulting to others. It is hardly surprising that riot ensued when O'Casey not only brought the flags of the Citizen Army and Irish Volunteers into the public-house setting of Act II of *The Plough and the Stars*, but introduced into the scene a common Dublin prostitute and recognizable extracts from the speeches of the revered republican leader Padraic Pearse.

There has been a tendency among those of what Ronan McDonald, in an incisive analysis, labels 'the humanist tendency' (McDonald 2002: 36–9) to admire what they see as O'Casey's promotion of the family, represented by the female characters, over political action and male aspiration. Recent revisionist readings reiterate such Manichaean claims to argue that O'Casey's failure to be even-handed and give proper attention to the politics of the independence struggle cripples his work (Deane 1985: 108–23; Kiberd 1995: 218–38). In Seamus Deane's words, O'Casey pits 'the humanizing effects of being involved in people rather than in ideas and ideologies' against 'the dehumanizing effects of visionary dreaming' so that, for example, Pearse's 'ferocious political rhetoric' is 'juxtaposed with Rosie's humanity, much to Pearse's dramatic discomfiture' (Deane in Kilroy 1975: 153). But the response the plays demand is more complex than this. Pearse's 1915 claim of the Great War, that 'the last sixteen months have been the most glorious in the history of Europe. Heroism has come back to earth' (O'Casey 1926: 57), couldn't but carry an overlay of irony in 1926, when O'Casey appropriated it, but the rhetoric *is* still potent. It was powerful enough in performance for Augusta Gregory to feel that 'those who heard it were forced to obey its call' (Gregory 1946: 97) as, indeed, within the play, is Rosie herself, before she subordinates her intuitive response to her need to curry favour with prospective clients. The 'discomfiting' is most likely to be with the observing audience.

It is true that political arguments are not much rehearsed by O'Casey. The hard men who appear do so briefly. What they say is precise and emotionless; what they do, hard-headed. Maguire, foisting his bombs on the unsuspecting Seumas, speaks just eight lines of urgent, coded language (*Gunman* in O'Casey 1925: 124–5); Johnny's doom is pronounced tersely by the Irregulars who come for him (*Juno* in O'Casey 1925: 106–7), and in *The Plough* Jack Clitheroe's reluctance to shoot at Irish men and women engaged in looting is dismissed abruptly by Captain Brennan:

> Irish be damned! Attackin' an' mobbin' th' men that are riskin' their lives for them. If these slum lice gather at our heels again, plug one o' them, or I'll soon shock them with a shot or two meself! (O'Casey 1926: 97)

Characters who have previously participated in political activity are in retreat: Seumas before the reality of guns; Johnny, having served his time, now spiritually as well as physically crippled. Those who do engage, like Clitheroe, or like Harry and Ted in *The Silver Tassie*, will be killed or damaged. Audiences are likely to share the need of characters affected by collateral damage to find meaning in and identify positive results from private loss, and to want works of art to help them do so. O'Casey's plays offer no such consolation. Hopes founder on random mischance; death and injury are haphazard. Historical forces are demonstrably oblivious to the private and individual. But if O'Casey is offering a simple argument for the family and against public action, he goes strangely about it.

In so far as the family is staged, it is a notably dysfunctional structure. The tenement settings allow loose configurations of constantly intruding neighbours, many of whom live alone. The central grouping of *The Plough and the Stars* consists of husband and wife, wife's uncle and husband's nephew. The Boyles in *Juno and the Paycock* are the only centrally figured nuclear family in the Dublin plays, and their relationships, fraught with bickering and misunderstanding from the beginning, have broken down by the end of the play. Whatever refuge the family offers, it is full of discord, opposing interests and misunderstandings. These might be trivial, as with the Covey's deliberate needling of Uncle Peter:

> NORA: Willie has only assed you if you wanted th' sugar.
> PETER: He doesn't care a damn whether I want th' sugar or no. He's only thryin' to
>   twart me!
>
> (O'Casey 1926: 27–8)

Or they may be more thoroughly destructive. But mutual 'thwarting' is a feature of all the relationships, particularly the marital ones. There is hardly trust between Jack and Nora in *The Plough* before his summons by the Citizen Army. Wanting adoration, she delights in his sentimental love song but rejects his sexual advance, saying 'I thought you were tired of that sort of thing long ago' (O'Casey 1926: 32). She swings between hysterical possessiveness, expressed in resentment of his absences and interception and destruction of his mail (ibid.: 33), and wheedling performances as 'your own little Nora' (ibid.: 36), reminiscent of Ibsen's Nora Helmer before she understands the need to leave the doll's house. Mrs Foran, in *The Silver Tassie,* sings her joyful anticipation of her husband's departure for the war, and Mrs Heegan's hurrying her son on his way is fuelled by her anxiety to retain his blood money.

Despite claims that 'women are elected to heroic status while men stand condemned of various forms of folly' (Murray 1997: 99), men, such as Fluther in *The Plough and the Stars*, have their moments of courage and female characters are as likely as male to be grotesques, to have idiosyncratic speech and behaviour. Mr Gallogher and Mrs Henderson mirror each other in their opinionated malapropisms and Mr and Mrs Grigson match each other in their traditionally farcical sparring *(Gunman* in O'Casey 1925); in *The Plough* Mrs Gogan's relish of all things funereal is as ghoulish as it is absurd; and, in the wild Act II, she not only takes her baby into the pub and wets its lips with whiskey, but dumps it on Peter to free herself to fight, then leaves, forgetting the infant entirely (O'Casey 1926: 56–62). The 'tragic women' – Minnie, Juno, Nora or Bessie – are sentimentalized and their variousness sold short by critics who overlook O'Casey's presentation of their naïvety, venality or callous response to the sufferings or deaths of other characters, as in Nora's 'what do I care for th' others. I can think only of me own self' (O'Casey 1926: 82); Bessie's gloating over an injured republican, or Juno's narrow-spirited mocking of her daughter's support for a sacked fellow worker, and her harsh response to the grieving Mrs Tancred: 'in wan way, she deserves all she got; for lately, she let th' Die-hards make an open house of th' place' (*Juno* in O'Casey 1925: 72). Yeats registered the force of O'Casey's refusal of simple heroizing when, defending the vituperation from the dying Bessie in *The Plough and the Stars,* he wrote:

> We are inclined to think the word 'bitch' in Act IV is necessary. It occurs when Bessie, receiving her mortal wound, turns furiously upon the woman whose delirium has brought it on her. The scene is magnificent and we are loath to alter a word of it. (Gregory 1946: 90)

The ferocity driving O'Casey's writing incorporates words demonstrably at odds with what the audience witnesses, as in Brennan's statement 'Mrs Clitheroe's grief will be a joy when she realizes that she has a hero for a husband' (O'Casey 1926: 114), and it denies any character more than a brief transcendence. Already in *The Shadow of a Gunman,* Donal Davoren, like Christie Mahon in J. M. Synge's *Playboy of the Western World,* accepts the role that local gossip thrusts on him: in his case the role of republican gunman on the run. Glamour *does* attach to shadowy presences coming and going, to willingness to sacrifice self-interest for a cause, so Davoren's enjoyment of such borrowed glamour is understandable, his encouraging it as enjoyable as Christie's, except that the specific political context gives the audience a more ominous insight into the dirty deed behind the 'gallous story'. Davoren and Seumas, the pedlar whose tenement room he shares, through their fears and fantasies bring about the death of Minnie, a naïve romantic. Far from Minnie's death making 'Davoren see himself with terrifying clarity' (Krause 1960: 67), this would-be poet immediately, like the similarly self-deluded Hjalmar Ekdal at the close of Henrik Ibsen's *The Wild Duck,* begins to adjust the innocent death to his own self-aggrandizing, signalled in his recourse to his habitual Shelleyan sigh: 'Ah me, alas! Pain, pain, pain ever, for ever!' (*Gunman* in O'Casey 1925: 199).

Not for nothing are Shakespeare and Shaw the dramatists to whom O'Casey owed most allegiance. Characters who share O'Casey's known views are as susceptible to mockery as those who do not. Extraneous information might suggest that the Covey voices O'Casey's own opinion when he declares of the Citizen Army flag, whose plough and stars give the play its title, 'it's a flag that should only be used when we're buildin' th' barricades to fight for a Workers' Republic!' (O'Casey 1926: 29), but he and his dogmatic communism are as derided as any. Moreover, sound insights can be voiced even by the most disreputable, although they are soon dissipated, as when, to Boyle's 'I'm goin' to tell you somethin', Joxer, that I wouldn't tell to anyone else – the clergy always had too much power over the people in this unfortunate country', Joxer responds, 'You could sing that if you had an air to it!' (*Juno* in O'Casey 1925: 31), or Fluther modifies his objections to being imprisoned by British troops in the Protestant church with a gratified, 'I don't think we'd be doin' anything derogatory be playin' cards in a Protestan' Church' (O'Casey 1926: 127). This is in marked contrast to the post-*Silver Tassie* plays, where, since the positive ideas and sound opinions come invariably from the politically radical and free-thinking characters, the mean-spirited and repressive ones from the representatives of conservative forces, the author's political position is evident.

The bewildering power of the closing sequences of O'Casey's plays up to and including *The Silver Tassie* lies in his refusal to allow the audience easy emotional satisfaction. In *Juno and the Paycock*, Juno's echo of Mrs Tancred in her 'take away these hearts o' stone' lament might indeed seem a figure of all bereaved mothers (Kilroy 1975: 41). The contrast with the surrounding disintegration and the cadences of the speech usually make this a moving human cry in performance, but the echo gives astringency to a speech that could seem merely histrionic. The *Irish Statesman's* judgement that Boyle and Joxer's drunken re-entrance after this was 'artistically indefensible . . . a painful mistake' (*Irish Statesman* 15 March 1924) has been echoed by critics who felt it dissipated the force of Juno's lament (Kilroy 1975: 42). But the ironic echoes struck between the drama of love and loss and the anarchic comedy, moving through to Boyle's slurred repetition of his catch-phrase, 'I'm telling you . . . Joxer . . . th' whole worl's . . . in a terr . . . ible state o' chassis' as the final line, are crucial to the experience of a play that has teased, provoked and stimulated the audience to a perception of a chaos deeper and more disturbing than anything imaginable by Boyle.

Samuel Beckett, in a 1934 review for the *Bookman,* identified in O'Casey's writing 'the principle of disintegration in even the most complacent solidities', and claimed *Juno and the Paycock* as O'Casey's best work 'because it communicates most fully this dramatic dehiscence, mind and world come asunder in irreparable dissociation – "chassis" ' (Beckett in Kilroy 1975: 167). Beckett's word 'dehiscence' is characteristically apt: its mainly botanical usage is defined in the *OED* as 'the bursting open of capsules, fruits, anthers etc. in order to discharge their mature contents'. Like Guthrie's 'fireworks' metaphor, the suggestion of a dynamic, not a passive coming asunder helps explain why – despite the underlying pessimism about human activity and relationship – the plays are such compelling theatre.

Despite the supposed realism of the Dublin plays, the comic routines and exaggerations quickly begin to alert the audience to 'chassis'. Based in traditional farce and the comic duos of music hall, they present what D. E. S. Maxwell describes as 'a world of pratfalls that collect into an image of a disintegrating society, a world whose nature is to fall apart' (Maxwell 1984: 100). As Peter Brook has claimed, 'it is always the popular theatre that saves the day' and, surely, it was that 'roughness, salt, sweat, noise, smell' (Brook 1968: 73) that O'Casey offered to the Abbey. His comic pairs, beginning with Seumas and Donal and continuing through to Simon and Sylvester in *The Silver Tassie*, are both engaging and despicable. At their most achieved and most appalling in Boyle and Joxer, the one vain and self-centred, the other an unashamed parasite, they share cowardice, sloth and insouciance and fill the stage with words. The humour and vitality of the comedy of avoidance and bombast encourage audiences to take the scurrility and self-serving lightly, if with a frisson of appalled recognition. This makes more shocking the falls from grace when the comedy is brought up short: Seumas's cold-hearted reception of the death of Maguire; his and Donal's craven cowardice in letting the naïve Minnie take Maguire's incriminating cache of bombs (*Gunman* in O'Casey 1925); Boyle's carelessness of family needs and angry rejection of his pregnant daughter; Joxer's self-demeaning flattery and quick acts of malice towards his sworn comrade (*Juno* in O'Casey 1925). It is to Shakespeare's anarchic creations that commentators turn most convincingly in attempting to grasp the essence of O'Casey's. Ayling finds something of the moral ambiguity of Falstaff (Ayling in O'Casey 1985: 173); Beckett suggests Toby Belch and Andrew Aguecheek (Kilroy 1975: 167). Raymond Williams's parallel, if more jaundiced, perception is that surface warmth for these characters is underpinned by 'a deeply resigned contempt – a contempt which then allows amusement – for these deprived, fantasy-ridden talkers' (Williams 1968: 56).

The introduction of comic pairs, sparring married couples and melodramatic plot-devices into ostensibly realistic portrayals of tenement life are demonstrative of the mixed mode of O'Casey's plays; his particular kind of dialectic. The texture of his dialogue is significant here. The impression of everyday Dublin talk, established through the inclusion of specific speech markers – relaxed syntax, dialect words ('chiselurs' for 'children'; 'a make' for a 'halfpenny'), political terminology ('a Stateser'; a 'Die-hard'), and local place names (O'Connell Street; bog o' Allen) – give an appearance of realism to a dialogue that is notably artificial and often exaggeratedly garrulous. Comic effects are achieved through hyperbole, malapropism and specific verbal idiosyncrasies. Joxer's tendency to ingratiating repetition and sententious couplets is a case in point, as is the widespread use of catch-phrases: Fluther's 'derogatory'; Mrs Gogan's prevaricating 'they do and they don't... there is and there isn't'. Characters refer to themselves in the third person, particularly when expounding their notably idiosyncratic attitudes; they burst into song and engage in alliterative riffs, all of which vary the verbal surface of the dialogue.

Identification of O'Casey's dialogue as 'Shakespearean' or 'Elizabethan' (O'Riordan 1984: 175), while it acknowledges the artifice, is facile. Certainly, there are echoes and, indeed, direct quotation of Shakespeare as well as Shaw, the King James Bible, popular song and ballad, but the texture is less metaphoric than alliterative, more showy than poetic. Revising his earlier dismissal of O'Casey's language as authorial self-display, Williams suggests that, in the Dublin plays, excess derives from characters who speak 'the inflated engaging language of men avoiding experience' (Williams 1968: 56). The fantastical verbal elements, inventive or gaseous, which can get out of hand when they occur promiscuously in such later plays as *Red Roses for Me* (published 1942), are, indeed, usually linked to character in the Dublin plays. The audience is invited to notice the excess and relish its gusto and fluency. Idiosyncrasy and self-deception as well as sheer absurdity are on display when, for instance, Boyle interrupts his rhapsodically extended fiction of life at sea –

> Ofen, an' ofen, when I was fixed to the wheel with a marlinspike, an' the wins blowin' fierce an' the waves lashin', till you'd think every minute was goin' to be your last, an' it blowed, an' blowed –

with his carefully pedantic explanation, 'blew is the right word, Joxer, but blowed is what the sailors use' (*Juno* in O'Casey 1925: 33).

As with the speech texture, the tenement activity offers a recognizably naturalist representation of the financial scrimping and gossip of the urban poor. A young man lying late in bed; a landlord demanding rent; a complaint about subletting; neighbours borrowing milk, taking in another's parcel, minding another's child and learning one another's business; passing hawkers of coal-blocks or sewing machines: all contribute to the impression of closely observed mimesis. But the frequent coming and going enabled by the tenement or the public-house setting also chimes with the traditional comic pattern of successive entrances and accompanying misunderstanding, deception and mounting confusion of, for example, Ben Jonson's *Volpone* and *The Alchemist* or, more recently, Synge's *Playboy of the Western World*. In its simplest form, in *The Shadow of a Gunman*, where tenement dwellers enter, one after another, to pay respects to and promise to keep secret the supposed gunman, each new addition compounds the confusion and contributes to the eventual disaster. Such through-movement facilitates the play's marked shifts in tone, as when, immediately following the intense scene of Nora's failed effort to hold back her husband, Fluther enters roaring drunk, staggering under the weight of a half-gallon jar of whiskey and wearing the brightly coloured woman's hat he has looted (O'Casey 1926: 104). Such farce elements – drunken spats, bickering over who has rights to the pram each needs for looting, Joxer's escape through a window – are ubiquitous.

The set, similarly, may seem to present the characteristic enclosed space of the realist domestic stage, but closer examination reveals a sure and inventive scenic imagination. To follow a potent example: windows, always required in O'Casey's stage directions, figure as thin membranes through which the off-stage noise of the outside world sounds realistically; the public world penetrates the private. Already in *The Shadow of a Gunman*, the opening directions prescribe *'two large windows'* that *'occupy practically the whole of the back wall space'*. Although moonlight, apostrophized in Donal's poem, streams through to light the second act, the signals here are mainly aural: the cries of a passing newsboy announce the ambush of Maguire; shouts and shots from the street register Minnie's arrest and death. A more complex development comes in *Juno* when, the Boyles' raucous party having been interrupted by Tancred's funeral, they first watch through the window then exeunt to view it, leaving a cowering Johnny alone. This is the signal for the Mobilizer to enter with the summons which reveals that Johnny is compromised by his betrayal of Tancred and draws from him the cry, 'I've lost me arm, an' me hip's desthroyed so that I'll never be able to walk right agen! Good God, haven't I done enough for Ireland?' The Mobilizer's response, 'Boyle, no man can do enough for Ireland', ends the act, while through the window come the murmured 'Hail Mary's' of the crowd, mourning the slaughtered Tancred (*Juno* in O'Casey 1925: 77). A seemingly mundane element of the set has become a significant enabling device of moral complexity.

Such simultaneity of perception, demanding audience attention, is extended in *The Plough and the Stars*. In Act I, Mrs Gogan, at the window, gives a running commentary on the assembling and marching away of the Citizen Army, while Peter, moving angrily between back room, fender at front right and mirror at front left, accumulates his ostentatious costume, and the Covey and Fluther, at the front of the stage, wage an absurd argument about the origin of the universe. The technique gathers force in Act II, where *'three fourths of the back is occupied by a tall, wide, two-paned window'* (O'Casey 1926: 43), and the brief appearance of a woman at the window in *The Shadow of a Gunman* (*Gunman* in O'Casey 1925: 119) is reworked now in the shadow of a real gunman: the attention of audience and characters is transfixed by the orator's silhouette. In another of O'Casey's complex endings, the fragile barrier between inside and outside world is penetrated literally when Bessie, like Old Hilse in Hauptmann's *The Weavers*, supposedly safe from the fighting outside, is killed by the mischance of a bullet through the window. The ironies and implications are registered by the audience, not the characters, when the intruding British soldiers sit for their cup of tea amid the chaos and catastrophe and casually comment, 'there gows the general attack on the Powst Office'. The decisive moment in the collapse of the Rising is registered in the deepening red flares, visible through the window, while the home-sick soldiers sing 'Keep the Home Fires Burning' (O'Casey 1926: 137).

The introduction of Ivor Novello's popular wartime song into the ending of the play varies the verbal texture but is also the culminating reminder of the other massive conflict of 1916, and the thousands of Irish as well as English killed and crippled in it. Consciousness of World War I is a minor but recurrent strain in the play. Not only is Pearse's speech hailing its bloodshed included, but Act I also ends with the sound of the Dublin Fusiliers on their way to the Front, singing 'It's a Long Way to Tipperary' (O'Casey 1926: 41), and loyalist Bessie mourns her absent soldier son and derides Irish Catholics who 'won't lift a finger to help poor little Catholic Belgium' (O'Casey 1926: 55). O'Casey's concern with the terrible Europe-wide conflict was evident well before his writing of *The Silver Tassie*.

It is a critical commonplace that O'Casey's break with the Abbey following the rejection of *The Silver Tassie,* in 1928, damaged his writing (Maxwell 1984: 107) but the Abbey itself, lacking the vitality O'Casey brought, went into evident decline after the break. Shaw's perception that *Tassie* was 'literally a hell of a play', which would 'clearly force its way on to the stage' and to which Yeats should have submitted 'as a calamity', was sharp, as was his observation that in rejecting the play Yeats had treated

O'Casey 'as a baby' (Lowery 1984: 128, 131). While the situation of Shakespeare or Molière writing for and from within a company might be the ideal, the rejection made it all too clear that the Abbey was in no way available for O'Casey's explorations as, for example, Granville Barker's Court seasons were for Shaw, or the Provincetown Players for another admired near-contemporary, Eugene O'Neill. The Abbey directors' trammelling expectations made the dramatist's breaking away inevitable.

The Silver Tassie is a pivotal work. Intended for the Abbey like the earlier plays, but written in England like the subsequent ones, three of its four acts share the earlier ostensibly realist setting and include a comic pair, colloquial language, individual idiosyncrasies of speech and behaviour, and identifying catch-phrases, demotic songs and quotation. The agit-prop methods of O'Casey's subsequent plays are already evident in Act II, which, set in a generic 'war zone', introduces expressionist methods of anonymized characters, chanting, rhythmic movement, symbolic set and two-dimensional, satirized authority figures. Even here, while the figures on stage are depersonalized, flashes of individuality within the mass are glancingly present for the audience, in the elegantly varied abusive epithets and the first soldier's cockney pronunciation in this sequence, for example:

2ND SOLDIER:	Lifting shells
3RD SOLDIER:	Carrying shells.
4TH SOLDIER:	Piling shells.
1ST SOLDIER:	In the falling, pissing rine and whistling wind.
2ND SOLDIER:	The whistling wind and falling, drenching rain.
3RD SOLDIER:	The God-dam rain and blasted whistling wind.
1ST SOLDIER:	And the shirkers sife at home coil'd up at ease.
2ND SOLDIER:	Shells for us and pianos for them.
3RD SOLDIER:	Fur coats for them and winding-sheets for us.

(O'Casey 1928: 45)

The sardonic humour, evident in the contrast between 'fur coat' and 'winding sheet', marks the difference between life and death but also between class expectations.

Location among working-class characters, common to all O'Casey's plays, is foregrounded by the expressionist method of *Tassie*: the hostility of the men to the officer class is registered in their mockery of every authority figure who crosses their path, as well as in O'Casey's parodic presentation of such figures. The centring on common soldiers rather than officers differentiates O'Casey's from such contemporary war plays as J. R. Ackerley's *Prisoners of War* (1925) or R. C. Sherriff's *Journey's End* (1928), as does the resistance of a cataclysmic final explosion. O'Casey's pursuit of his damaged soldiers back to the savage and complex emotion of the scrap-heap that is their civilian life is what makes this such 'a hell of a play'. With economic depression and the rise of European fascism in the 1930s, a newly urgent need to engage directly with social and economic injustice motivates and energizes O'Casey's fantasies of social transformation; post-World War II, he satirizes social and religious oppression with renewed savagery and anarchic gusto.

Few commentators make more than passing and dismissive reference to the post-*Tassie* plays. Maxwell suggests they 'flounder – in restless, fascinating experiment' but 'eventually, die in a programmed didacticism' (Maxwell 1984: 109). Although, with distance, the partisan allegorizing of *Within the Gates* (1934), *The Star Turns Red* (1940) or *Red Roses for Me* (produced 1943) can seem crude, and the anarchic satire of the post-World War II *Cock-a-Doodle Dandy* (1949), *The Bishop's Bonfire* (1955) or *The Drums of Father Ned* (1959) are hectic rather than dehiscent, they share a restless theatrical inventiveness that gives credence to Christopher Murray's claim that, 'undeservedly neglected', these plays are 'so full of theatrical energy and daring that they cry out for new directors to take them in hand' (Murray 1997: 91, 112).

For all their differences, there is more continuity between the earlier and later plays than is usually allowed. The progressive theatricality of the first three Dublin plays demonstrably stretched the boundaries of realist presentation. Undisguised expressionism was already evident in the reiterated off-stage chant: 'Red Cro . . . ss, Red Cro . . . ss Ambula . . . lance, Ambulance!' that punctuates the nightmarish last act of *The Plough and the Stars* (O'Casey 1926: 110, 122, 127, 130, 136). Post-*Tassie* characters may be generic worker, priestly or bourgeois figures but vernacular speech, domestic bickering and fleeting idiosyncrasy still offset flights of rhetoric. As well as ringing political oratory, the worker's leader, Jim, in *The Star Turns Red*, engages in straight talk:

JIM: Don't raise your voice here. There's no maternity money due to you.
BRANNIGAN: And who the hell is it due to then?
JIM: To your wife. She has the only right to it. She's got it, and I sent word that you
     weren't to get a penny of it.
BRANNIGAN: That's hitting below the belt Jim.

(O'Casey 1940: 101)

Continuity is manifest, too, in O'Casey's capacity to create potent scenic images which, bringing word, figure and set into telling relationship, demand audience response.

Vital elements of O'Casey's theatrical vocabulary, such as my earlier example of windows, re-emerge with newly compelling presence. Act II of *The Silver Tassie* not only features a stained glass window which places a vividly lit Virgin Mary in ironic juxtaposition with existence in the war zone, but:

> *At back a lost wall and window are indicated by an arched piece of broken coping pointing from the left to the right, and a similar piece of masonry pointing from the right to the left. Between these two lacerated fingers of stone can be seen the country.* (O'Casey 1928: 41)

Broken, the membrane can no longer provide separation. The ending of *The Star Turns Red* introduces a more positive use, appropriate to its fantasy of messianic socialist strikers triumphing over fascist storm troopers. As the defiant central characters declare allegiance to the cause, their clenched fists signalling workers' unity, off-stage voices are heard singing 'The Internationale' and, through the full-length double windows at the back of the stage, a great crowd of workers, soldiers and sailors appears, fists raised in support while the star that has shone throughout the play turns red, as promised in the title.

Perhaps these plays don't survive their period any more than other immediately powerful agit-prop, politically committed or directly satirical plays do, but when staged they evidently fulfilled the significant dramatic function of speaking potently to their own time. Their imaginative ferocity drew from experienced contemporary theatre critics images of 'sweeping along', of 'a withered theatre redeemed', of 'poetic fire and prosaic fun' (Chothia 1996: 97–8) and led John Arden, a major inheritor, to claim that 'O'Casey's exile caused him to write like a European rather than an Irishman' (Arden 1977: 23). The method and energy as well as the projection of striking scenic images, apparent in the published texts and in the archive of contemporary responses, at the very least endorse Murray's challenge to latter-day directors to investigate their theatrical energy, dialectic and fundamental seriousness.

O'Casey lashed out bitterly in his theatre criticism against plays he thought trivial, but he showed a capacity for vividly accurate assessment of work he admired. Of one of his prime mentors, he declared: 'Shaw never wrote a tragedy, yet his comedy and his wit were a rushing mighty wind that swept through the theatre, tearing a mantle of false grandeur from the thousand trivialities that strutted on its stage' (O'Casey 1957: 65). O'Casey's words are at least as appropriate to his own explosive and dehiscent work.

PRIMARY READING

O'Casey, Sean (1925). *Two Plays: Juno and The Paycock; The Shadow of a Gunman*. London: Macmillan.

O'Casey, Sean (1926). *The Plough and the Stars*. London: Macmillan.

O'Casey, Sean (1928). *The Silver Tassie*. London: Macmillan.

O'Casey, Sean (1940). *The Star Turns Red*. London: Macmillan.

O'Casey, Sean (1942). *Red Roses for Me*. London: Macmillan.

O'Casey, Sean (1957). *The Green Crow*. London: W. H. Allen.

O'Casey, Sean (1963). *Autobiographies*, 2 vols. London: Macmillan.

O'Casey, Sean (1975). *Letters. Vol 1: 1910–41*, ed. David Krause. London: Macmillan.

O'Casey, Sean (1985). *Seven Plays: A Student's Edition*, ed. Ronald Ayling. London: Macmillan.

FURTHER READING

Arden, John (1977). *To Present the Pretence*. London: Methuen.

Brook, Peter (1968). *The Empty Space*. London: Faber and Faber.

Chambers, Colin (1989). *The Story of Unity Theatre*. London: Lawrence and Wishart.

Chothia, Jean (1996). *English Drama of the Early Modern Period: 1890–1940*. London: Longman.

Deane, Seamus (1985). *Celtic Revivals: Essays in Modern Irish Literature*. London: Faber and Faber.

Gregory, Augusta (1946). *Journals, 1916–1930*, ed. Lennox Robinson. London: Puttnam.

Grene, Nicholas (1999). *The Politics of Irish Drama: Plays in Context from Boucicault to Friel*. Cambridge: Cambridge University Press.

Guthrie, Tyrone (1961). *A Life in the Theatre*. London: Hamish Hamilton.

Kiberd, Declan (1995). *Inventing Ireland*. London: Cape.

Kilroy, Thomas (ed.) (1975). *Sean O'Casey: A Collection of Critical Essays*. Englewood Cliffs, NJ: Prentice-Hall.

Krause, David. (1960). *Sean O'Casey: The Man and his Work*. London: MacGibbon and Kee.

Krause, David and Lowery, Robert G. (1980). *Sean O'Casey: Centenary Essays*. Gerrards Cross: Colin Smythe.

Lowery, Robert G. (ed.) (1984). *A Whirlwind in Dublin: The Plough and the Stars Riots*. Westport, CT: Greenwood Press.

Maxwell, D. E. S. (1984). *A Critical History of Irish Drama 1891–1980*. Cambridge: Cambridge University Press.

McDonald, Ronan (2002). *Tragedy and Irish Literature*. London: Palgrave.

Moran, James (2005). *Staging the Easter Rising: 1916 as Theatre*. Cork: Cork University Press.

Murray, Christopher (1997). *Twentieth-Century Irish Drama: Mirror Up to Nation*. Manchester: Manchester University Press.

O'Connor, Garry (1988). *Sean O'Casey: A Life*. London: Hodder.

O'Riordan, John (1984). *A Guide to O'Casey's Plays*. London: Macmillan.

Watt, Stephen (1991). *Joyce, O'Casey and the Irish Popular Theater*. Syracuse, NY: Syracuse University Press.

Williams, Raymond (1968). *Drama from Ibsen to Brecht*. London: Chatto.

11

Auden and Eliot: Theatres of the Thirties

Robin Grove

By 1930, among poetry-readers, Thomas Stearns Eliot (b. 1888, St Louis, Missouri) and Wystan Hugh Auden (b. 1907, York) were the modern names. Yet for the writers themselves the printed page was not enough. During the 1930s, the two were responsible for at least a dozen stage works – a lot of theatre for poets to have shaped; which perhaps is why each was wary of calling his pieces 'plays'. That term might have suggested something more solidly made or, contrariwise, something lighter than they were prepared to offer. So Auden's *Paid on Both Sides* (1930) is described as a 'Charade', while Eliot's *Sweeney Agonistes* (1933) calls itself 'Fragments of an Aristo-phanic Melodrama'. The subtitles, unassuming in one instance, portentous in the other, point to an inter-war theatre of evacuation or displacement of settled modes. In the age of George Bernard Shaw's and John Galsworthy's plays, who would have expected music-hall, pantomime and country-house dress-ups to be singled out as the 'most living drama of today' (Auden 1935: 1)? Yet such hyper-English forms as these helped to produce work that from the start was teasing, reckless and often violent – as in the opening of *Paid on Both Sides*, an enacted blood-feud.

> W. How did they get him?
> T. In Kettledale above Colefangs road passes where high banks overhang dangerous from ambush. To Colefangs had to go, would speak with Layard, Jerry and Hunter with him only.
>
> (Auden 1988: 15)

The violent ambush not only takes off the assassinated chief of the Nower family, but is inflicted on the body of language itself. The speech sounds as if it has been translated, with difficulty, word by word. But are its distortions – ludicrous, yet striking – a parody of saga, or a straight-faced homage to northern epic's power? We are hardly allowed to weigh the possibilities before the murdered man's son is born. (The shock of the killing brought on a premature birth.) *Tableau*: 'A Child of the Feud': the mother is shown with her husband's corpse beside her and her new-born infant at her breast. She utters three rhymed quatrains, then the curtains round her child-bed close. Three more verses, this time from the Chorus, and the baby, now a young man, steps onto stage.

We are just minutes into the drama, but each development takes us further from naturalism. Character, which might have meant personality shaped by period and place, is swept aside by Function and Destiny, while language is skewed until spy-story argot ('Number Six wishes to see you, sir'; 17) jostles against lyric, while 'real-life' figures with names like John share the stage with Father Xmas, Bo and Po. If it sounds bewildering, that's what it was. Dada hadn't been forgotten, nor did Auden mind baffling his audience. How artificial, how un-lifelike to expect to understand everything! As if on short-wave radio, voices are picked up in snatches, to signal deep meanings perhaps, while haphazardly spoofing them at the same time.

Charades, however, are allowed to be silly, at least in part. To fulfil their task, they must use what is at hand by way of costumes, players, props – and in consequence are liable to appear improvisatory even when carefully planned. This suited Auden, whose habits of revision make his writing a game-in-progress anyway.[1] He hesitates over finality; often, what he achieves is no solo at all, but something shared in the making (he was a frequent collaborator) and in the reception (his audiences are to be participants, not consumers, and their role is to decipher what is hidden or obscure).

Suppose for a moment then, that, watching this Charade, we must in the traditional manner identify a word whose syllables individually make sense, but when combined are able to produce a further meaning. Such a word, for example, might begin as *dead*, acted by the slain head of the Nower clan, then paralleled by the enemy chieftain, as the past repeats itself, and will repeat again, 'no news but the new death' (Auden 1988: 19). Different scenes, however, half-promise a new world:

> The Spring unsettles sleeping partnerships,
> Foundries improve their casting process, shops
> Open a further wing on credit till
> The winter. In summer boys grow tall
> With running races on the froth-wet sand,
>
> (21)

suggesting through glimpses of rejuvenation a further syllable: the hope of disasters, like seasons, coming to an *end*. Yet, put together, *dead-end* tells the grimmer truth about the feud and the poisoned Europe it represents. Equating honour with revenge, both sides are remorselessly paid back, thereby doubling destruction.

So, while a resolution may, via the Father Xmas scenes, hover like a ridiculous dream, the wedding that should unite the two houses becomes the occasion for yet more murder. First, the Man-Woman is shot for being and speaking something too 'un-natural' to face (23–4); then even the joining of the protagonist's two parts,

Accuser and Accused, John and The Spy, gives way to further death, since these 'sharers of the same house' (26) – the warring clans of self itself – cannot live together, at least not here, not yet.

Is the tragedy personal, then, or society's own neurosis? As the closing sequence unfolds, the scope widens, from individual, to family, nation, continent. Yet the larger the claims, the vaguer they become. 'Though he believe it, no man is strong', begins the final threnody (33): that is, no one is to blame, but equally no one is called upon to act. 'This fellow is very ill', says Xmas of the heir to the feud, 'but he will get well' (23). Perhaps in the days of Hitler's ascendancy, mass unemployment, ruined banks, strikes and marches, that unlikely prognosis was not optimistic enough for the country-house gathering where the Charade was originally to be staged. At any rate, 'The village won't stand it', Auden was told, and the proposed performance had to wait.[2]

By the later Thirties, however, Londoners might pride themselves on being able to stand almost anything offered by the theatre of their day. The extraordinary, even the outrageous, was readily available, 'highbrow' content mingling with 'popular' forms like revue and cabaret. Modernism's disregard for divisions of class and genre particularly appealed to Auden, who liked the friction of one idiom against another, and in *Paid* had gathered Anglo-Saxon heroics, school slang, psychology and satire, all under the heading of 'A parable of English Middle Class (professional) family life 1907–1929'.[3] It was but a short step to avant-garde ventures like the Group Theatre, a leftish, marginal, but not inconspicuous ensemble founded in 1932 by Auden's school-mate, Robert Medley, and Medley's partner, Rupert Doone.

What fired the enterprise was Doone's dedication to 'total theatre': the co-operative exploration of the resources of poetry, music, drama and dance, where technicians would work with artists, and audiences become part of the action. 'Because you are not moving and speaking, you are not a passenger. If you are seeing and hearing you are co-operating', says a Group manifesto (Medley 1983: 147; Auden 1988: appendices 1 and 3). Doone himself, a dancer, actor, choreographer and director, did not hesitate to strike whatever operatic pose the moment called for. But perhaps because of this, his productions, for all their sophistication, kept the look of school plays where the troupe, inwardly unconvinced by the spectacle it is making of itself, piles emphasis on overemphasis, giving it all they've got. To judge from production photos, Doone's high style strove mightily to rise above 'commercialism' (see illustrations in Sidnell 1984). Classes were prescribed in improvisation and choral speaking; postulants learnt tableau formation and mime; rhythmic gesture half-concealed individual shortcomings, and performances deployed masks and music to heighten what the director called 'realistic fantasy' (Doone 1951: 5). In almost all plays, a drama of voice, gesture, *mise en scène*, facial movement, pause and silence extends what the script declares; but Doone went further. The commonplace had to be exaggerated until, seemingly of its own accord, a lipsticked mouth or gloved hand might indicate the frightening worlds conventionality labours to conceal.

Something of the sort was already a feature of Auden's verse, with its nursery-rhyme zest for nightmarish transformations, 'Where daisies claw and pebbles shriek' (Auden 1966: 273–4).

> 'O where are you going?' said reader to rider,
> 'That valley is fatal when furnaces burn,
> Yonder's the midden whose odours will madden,
> That gap is the grave where the tall return.'
> (Auden 1950: 253)

Throughout the Thirties he and Eliot contributed substantially to Group Theatre repertoire, so that by the time the former's *Dance of Death* and the latter's *Sweeney Agonistes* appeared as a double bill at the Westminster (October 1935), critics treated the season as a significant event. Twenty reviews fastened on the performances in their opening week.

Paid on Both Sides had thrust us into a version of 'this country of ours where nobody is well' (Auden 1932: para. 2). *The Dance of Death* offers to present 'the decline of a class, and how its members dream of a new life, but secretly desire the old, for there is death inside them. We show you that death as a dancer' (Auden 1988: 83). Actually, what is provided is even wilder and more flippant. For all its ostensible politics, the promiscuous spectacle makes life flit by as in some *Goldwyn Follies* with silk dressing-gowns, sunbathing, fitness, speed. Soon, though, the fine feathers of the pleasure-seekers are plucked away; charleston rhythms leave the Chorus upheld by nothing but their own skittish moves, till ultimately the puppets reclothe themselves in military gear to plunge after the Dancer in spasms of patriotism and power-worship. The audience is called to action – to that extent the flavour is Brechtian – but the propaganda is so uncomplicated that even if we left our seats to help unfurl the giant red flag, or urge Death's dance to go faster, we would hardly be compromised, for the end of this *danse macabre* was inevitable, says godlike Mr Marx – admitting Death has been 'liquidated', but simultaneously absolving us of responsibility, since the star of the show was moribund anyway and tonight's production has simply worn him out: 'The instruments of production have been too much for him' (Auden 1988: 107). Thus, Death dies. Victory in highest heaven? Or just another giggly joke? Even as we weigh up the evening's entertainment, Mendelssohn's *Wedding March* blares out, letting the *Dance* enjoy the benefit of its doggerel-cantata style (verve, wit, liberty), but leaving us uncertain whether the satire is as shrewd as it thinks it is, or not savage enough to achieve a cartoon's unforgiving accuracy of line.

Death's partial success, however, served to usher in the bolder comedy and more complex emotional landscape of Auden's next stage-piece, a collaboration with Christopher Isherwood, *The Dog Beneath the Skin* – or *Dogskin*, as it soon got called (1934–6).[4] In contrast to titles of earlier works, such as *Enemies of a Bishop: A Morality in Four Acts* (try omitting the first space in the subtitle), *Dogskin* is happy to be known simply as 'A Play'. Appropriately, its hero is a norm-man, mild Alan Norman. And he exists only in whichever imaginary village 'your heart directs you most longingly to look' (Auden 1988: 191). So construct *what you want*, says the Prologue in effect, making the fantasy ours as much as the authors'. The paradoxes and dilemmas of free will in this make-believe place seem ready to become the most interesting feature of the piece.

How can they be, though, when the figures patrolling the stage are so expertly deprived of self? Auden's cut-outs proudly lack all inwardness.[5] Thus, with Gilbert-and-Sullivan élan, they promenade the footlights, introducing themselves in due order: 'Here come I, the Vicar good / Of Pressan Ambo, it's understood.' The Cloth is followed by the Empire ('I rule my house like a brigade / With discipline of iron'), then by the General's Wife:

> Woman, though weak, must do her part
> And I who keep the General's heart
>   Know well our island story
> And do my utmost to advance
> In India, Russia, Finland, France,
>   The just and English glory.

At which the chorus immediately shines rather a different colour on feminine self-effacement:

> With subtle wile and female smile,
> With speech and vote she will promote
>   The just and English glory.
>   (Auden 1988: 195)

The reprise-line at the end of every stanza completes the figure's self-definition. And if this seems a caricaturist's trick, we see that, from title onwards, *The Dog Beneath the Skin* has lampooned the idea of interiority. Where would Hamlet's 'that within which passeth show' be found in the play's Journalists, Lunatics, Prostitutes, its lovers in Paradise Park, or Ninevah Girls waiting to be eaten in the hotel cabaret (263)? Add 'Grabstein: a Financier', Madam Bubbi, Sorbo Lamb and Chimp Eagle: virtually all the parts are Humours rather than portrayals of that human race 'to which', as Swift hoped, 'so many of my readers belong'. Innerness? True self? Even the dog in *Dogskin* turns out not to be canine.

Dogskin, however, has an alternative title, Where is Francis?, and Francis is the play's most poignant and telling figure. Without him, despite some scornful hits – like the chief lunatic's paean to 'grand old Westland Mania', which lets you go mad in 'the time-honoured Westland way' (1988: 231), or the Journalists' proof that facts are non-existent until materialized into newsprint (238) – the would-be satiric edge of the drama cuts through nothing much (emptiness is the essence of its presented world, except in Francis's case). Yet somewhere inside the self-indulgent length and undergraduate clutter is the play-that-might-have-been: one where formal poetry, thoughtful, lyrical, joined powers with musical comedy. A play that really engaged with the beneficent rituals of folk tale (vanished heir, quest-hero, mythic journey), and psychological drama was made from the clash of understandings, as when Francis learns to see life 'from underneath', or when the Guardians' duet – 'You are the town and we are the clock' – dramatizes the mind's self-policing and self-damage:

> We've been watching you over the garden wall
> For hours.
>   The sky is darkening like a stain,
>   Something is going to fall like rain
>   And it won't be flowers.
>
>   (194)

Onto the idea of autonomy each stanza topples a gravestone ('I shouldn't dance'), matching the poetry's volatility of invention with a series of sinister extinctions. That is *Dogskin*'s most memorable achievement.

Power drawn from self-defeat: some such electric charge is similarly stored in the 1936 Auden–Isherwood collaboration, *The Ascent of F6*, with its sense of gathering disaster, and of the self's watching itself as destruction grows. It was the authors' most-admired play – perhaps because in a world of burgeoning military bombast, it reversed the myth of the hero as the Truly Strong Man who dares all. As the drama sees it, he who must challenge himself to prove his strength is not Strong but secretly driven by neurotic fear of being (what in fact he is) Truly Weak.[6] Such a man is the peak-scaling, portentously named Ransom who believes himself called to save his paltry admirers. The Thirties were not short of such figures, but to F. R. Leavis, reviewing the script on its first publication, 'we are unmistakeably expected to feel towards this school hero . . . the respect and awe felt by his school-fellow followers' (Leavis 1936: 326). Actually, it is Leavis who is taken in by Ransom's high speeches; Auden–Isherwood style is too camp and wayward to manage 'respect'; and as for 'awe', while the Abbot of the mountain monastery is greeting the visitor with puffery ('to the complicated and sensitive like yourself, Mr. Ransom'; Auden 1988: 326), the monks are chanting their Tibetan chorus (ibid.: 323),

> Ming ting ishta sokloskaya
> No rum ga ga, no rum ga ya,

and voices from the world beyond add their own intercessions: 'Give me a car', 'Make me a star' (325). No one could call this subtle, but it is hardly deferential either. Starting with Ransom's first soliloquy, the writing exposes the central figure to as much scepticism as his self-importance needs.

He remains a painful figure, though, and his burden of destiny gives the play its weight. Instead of the smug sarcasms that would nail Mr and Mrs A in their box – 'Shall we be like this when we are dead?' (298) – Ransom's struggles with his Demon have a dignity that survives the glibly Oedipal end (353–4). He is responsible for destruction, and admits it, neither lessening nor spreading the blame. To refuse at the end to be Truly Strong accomplishes his life.

Compared to previous Auden and Isherwood plays, *F6* has a decisive momentum. And if it is not as surprising as the earlier drama, or so restless, mixed and funny, neither is it so liable merely to titter. The play that appeared shortly before World War II, *On the Frontier: A Melodrama in Three Acts* (1938), is even more restrained. Admittedly, it prolongs and repeats effects; its staging of political life is altogether sketchy; but the private struggle between individual and state is strongly drawn. A few years earlier, and the play might have been more adventurous, utilizing the experimentalisms of *The Dance of Death*. Now, much of its verve depends on items like the Journalists' Quartet:

> We fly to a cabinet crisis
> We motor out to the wars
> Where the general's temperature rises
> Or the little orator roars,
> Where over the tyrannous waters
> The flag of revolt is unfurled
> You will find us, the ace reporters
> *{Unison}* Presenting the world to the world.
> (Auden 1988: 414)

Mostly, though, the speakers must pedal away for minutes in order to work up the urgency they need. Yet the idea of a room invisibly divided between Ostnia and Westland, each side retaining its own customs and paranoias, is an effective piece of stage-thought, and creates a metaphoric space within which the action will ferment and swell, so while there is nothing so surreal as *Dogskin*'s portrait of the Leader whose face is a loud-speaker,[7] the *Frontier* sequence in which a raving demagogue works himself into a thousand-year commitment to peace, only to ricochet next instant into a frenzied declaration of war, is among the period's most memorable scenes in theatre (396–7; see also Martin 1938).

Three months later, in January 1939, Auden and Isherwood arrived in New York, two of the decade's best-known and most denounced exit-seekers. The Group Theatre's day was virtually over – so, indeed, was the moment of *l'entre deux guerres*. Auden's interest in performance had already diversified. He wrote for radio, for documentary films, opera, cabaret. His own poetry, colloquial/mandarin, became increasingly performative, so close the reader can almost smell its breath. He gave lectures and readings. He wore himself like a crumpled dressing-gown. That story can be left unfinished, because it concludes itself; and of Eliot, I have written elsewhere (Grove in Moody 1994: 158–75).

I go therefore to London in March 1939: on the brink of the inevitable killings of the war, *The Family Reunion* has just been performed and published. A man comes home, having killed his wife, whether in actuality or in the deeps of his will. Around him gathers the generation of his crime – the lovelessness, fatuity, rejected self-knowledge, embodied in his 'relations'. Comforts are offered, but none alleviates his revulsion from the infected world. Finally, he understands, expiation – not cure or escape – is what he must seek, and he disappears to find it. It is not immediately evident that this is *Murder in the Cathedral* folded inside out. Thanks to school and church performances, the latter was much the best-known of Eliot's plays. Yet this hardly explains why *The Family Reunion* revisits it. Despite four years and much else separating the plays, the psychic map stays eerily unchanged: maybe because it meant more to Eliot than he allowed himself to know.

'A man comes home foreseeing that he will be killed, and he is', he wrote of Becket (Eliot 1955: 80). Harry's death reflects and reverses Becket's. Death has already happened in him, and his new existence centres on this fact as Becket's centres on *his* coming martyrdom. The one drama occupies the country estate, House of the Mother, the other the cathedral city, House of the Father. So, matching Wishwood's matriarch, aunts and retainers is the Archbishop with his family of priests and Women of Canterbury. They, like the other household, would bend the hero this way and that. Temptations assail both men, but both step beyond mere surcease into a 'higher' death. First, though, each play sets its protagonist in a world diseased and filthied as if by some sexual taint.

> I have tasted
> The savour of putrid flesh in the spoon. I have felt
> The heaving of earth at nightfall [. . .]
> The whelk and the prawn live and spawn in my bowels.
> Corruption in the dish, incense in the latrine.
> (269–70)

We are soiled by a filth that we cannot clean, united to supernatural vermin [. . .] a world that is wholly foul. (Eliot 1969: 276)

> I can clean my skin,
> Purify my life, void my mind,
> But always the filthiness that lies a little deeper.
> (327)

> Weaving with contagion of putrescent embraces
> On dissolving bone. In and out, the movement . . .
> Until the chain breaks [. . .]
> And the desert is cleared, under the judicial sun
> Of the final eye, and the awful evacuation
> Cleanses.
> (335)

Pressing, heaving, ingesting, giving birth, copulating, voiding: the metaphors (embedded in some of the most striking verse of either play) portray spiritual states in terms of almost involuntary physicalities. Even Harry's imagined purification is not

his doing. 'The chain breaks': such images hide causality until we cannot know what
is going on in that inward theatre, the soul. As the Archbishop gives himself to the
slaughter, it may be that he has indeed conformed his will to God, but how could
anyone tell? We hear his words, but God alone can see his heart and judge whether the
chosen martyrdom is selfless or vainglorious. And just as Becket's spiritual decision
has disappeared from view, so the murder in *Reunion* (if 'murder' is the name for it) is
invisible, 'a momentary rest on the burning wheel' (294), a hiatus, followed by two
days of 'contented drowsiness' (295). When Harry's wife goes overboard on that
cloudless mid-Atlantic night, the agent is virtually absent from the deed. Evil is
hardly any longer what someone *does*; smelt, ingurgitated, spewed, evacuated, soiling,
breeding, entering, it has taken on a life of its own, like a haunting or a possession.
And this replacement of actor by undergoer is intensified by verse that often sounds as
if the speakers existed for the sake of the pentameters, rather than the poetry for the
sake of the drama.

But if these are difficulties, it is harder still to see how a 'Classical' *agon* of the
cursed House, the doomed protagonist, and the Eumenides as agents of retributive
justice could ever fit a 'Christian' drama of sin, purgation and grace. The Oresteian
pattern implies a fixed universe, the Christian perspective a universe where astonishing transformations of divine order have already begun (Miles 1985 and 2001).
Neither in the *Murder* nor in the *Reunion* are the characters equipped with the
power to be autonomous agents in so revolutionary a world.

In *The Rock* (1934), individual presence is almost obliterated in the pageant's
oratorio-like Choruses, stage-Cockney turns and semi-sermons. All is impersonal,
collectivist, exhortatory:

> Let the work not delay, time and the arm not waste;
> Let the clay be dug from the pit, let the saw cut the stone,
> Let the fire not be quenched in the forge.
>
> (Eliot 1969: 153)

'The work', 'the arm', 'the saw' leave us without individuals, and therefore without
community either. At best, the Choruses are speaking for their author, as he himself
admitted (Eliot 1955: 91); but words and silences speak for him in a very different
way in *Sweeney Agonistes*.[8] Parts may have been drafted as early as 1923, between *The
Waste Land* and 'Doris's Dream Songs' (Moody 1979: 64–5). The 'Prologue', at any
rate, appeared in *Criterion* IV, 1926. From the start, however, it was presented as a
'Fragment'. But what has fragmented this material? Not Eliot's inability to finish the
play, or the passage of time that disintegrates a statue, but twentieth-century
imagination itself, aware of an antiquity co-existing with the present: stichomythia
inside the walls of a twenties walk-up,[9] St John of the Cross contemporaneous with
pagan myth and with flappers. The effect is at once classical and vaudevillian, comic,
nervy and frightening. The piece occupies page-space as calculatedly as a production
might occupy the stage.

```
DUSTY:     How about Pereira?
DORIS:     What about Pereira?
           I don't care.
DUSTY:     You don't care!
           Who pays the rent?
DORIS:     Yes, he pays the rent
DUSTY:     Well some men don't and some men do
           Some men don't and you know who
DORIS:     You can have Pereira
DUSTY:     What about Pereira?
```
(Eliot 1969: 115)

Already the voices are coloured by tunes, rhymes, rhythms, a music whose melo-drama makes Dusty and Doris jerky marionettes controlled by something beyond themselves. The only sentence securely closed by punctuation is Doris's 'I don't care.': all the rest are suspended in question-marks and exclamations, or project into empty space. 'You can have Pereira' – answered (if a question *is* an answer) by words that have already been uttered into exhausted air: 'What about Pereira?' The speakers caught in this to-and-fro enclose the emptiness between them, moving neither back nor forward in time.

Both 'Prologue' and 'Agon' thus circle around obsessions, the participants trapped by each other, none able to break free.

```
SWEENEY:   I'll carry you off
           To a cannibal isle.
DORIS:     You'll be the cannibal!
SWEENEY:   You'll be the missionary!
           You'll be my little seven-stone missionary!
           I'll gobble you up. I'll be the cannibal.
DORIS:     You'll carry me off? To a cannibal isle?
SWEENEY:   I'll be the cannibal.
DORIS:     I'll be the missionary.
           I'll convert you!
SWEENEY:   I'll convert *you*!
           Into a stew.
           A nice little, white little, missionary stew.
```
(Eliot 1969: 121)

For the self to be 'converted' from what it was to what it might be is too terrible to contemplate. Yet how much worse again is one's fate when change is everywhere disallowed?

Earlier, it was *absence* of punctuation that conveyed the inability to reach conclusion. Now, the lines are so overpunctuated that each phrase seems isolated from its neighbour in a damnation of conjoined separateness. Dreadful violence is retold:

```
           I knew a man once did a girl in.
           Any man might do a girl in
```

Any man has to, needs to, wants to,
Once in a lifetime, do a girl in.
Well he kept her there in a bath
With a gallon of lysol in a bath.
(Eliot 1969: 124)

The casualness with which that ordinary 'Well' is interjected is perhaps the most terrible moment. But where, in *Paid on Both Sides*, the propelling force was the circular motion of the blood-feud, here the horror is that the dead will not *be* dead. No full stop finishes the bath; the body preserved in lysol mimics life; Mrs Porter has been killed and returns and will be killed again (Sidnell 1984: 91–2).[10] Always the injunction is 'Let Mr. Sweeney continue his story', for in this circular nightmare 'Death is life and life is death.' Sooner or later each becomes the other, and if you want to ask questions, 'Talk to live men about what they do' (Eliot 1969: 124–5), for 'doing' is not what this drama does. In its annulment of humanist assumptions, and in its shrivelling up of what would commonly be regarded as Christian too, *Sweeney* is the most shockingly successful of all its author's writings for the stage.

There is nothing adventitious about the stance being taken here. Eliot, like Auden, wanted theatre to play out something other than the drama of personality. So, singers, dancers, orators or chorus displaced the actor in a succession of shows whose inner world was political, psychological, religious. Each time (it's suggested), the reality we are to look towards is greater than that of mere people. But *Sweeney* convinces us otherwise. Not even exorcism would shift Dusty, Doris and their visitors out of the place they inhabit. They are tougher than ideas, more frightening than categories or ideologies; they persist in a squalid changelessness, like the body unforgettably lying in the bath.

NOTES

1 'A poem is never finished, it is only abandoned': (Valéry in Auden 1966: 16). *Paid on Both Sides* had two completed versions, 1928 and 1929. I use the second one here. *The Reformatory* (1929) fed into *The Enemies of a Bishop* (1929), ultimately contributing, together with *The Chase* (1934) and *The Fronny* (1930), to *The Dog Beneath the Skin* (1935). *The Fronny* also

influenced *The Dance of Death* (1933). Shape-shifting is almost the hall-mark of these plays.
2 As reported in Carpenter (1981: 82), but see also Auden (1988: xv), where the Big House, not the village, vetoed the play.
3 Auden's description of *Paid on Both Sides* is quoted in Carpenter (1981: 93). The first date (1907) is that of Auden's birth, the second

(1929) marks the completed revision of the work.

4 Isherwood's part in the writing of *Dogskin* is usefully outlined in Osborne (1980: 114). More detail about likely authorship of specific passages in plays is given in Auden (1988: 526).

5 'The drama is not suited to the analysis of character, which is the province of the novel. Dramatic characters are simplified; easily recognizable and over-life size' (Auden 1935: 2).

6 Edward Mendelson (ed.). (1998). *The English Auden* (London: Faber and Faber) reprints (320–1) a very relevant review by Auden of Liddell Hart's book on T. E. Lawrence.

7 In a milieu like that which produced the Diaghilev–Picasso *Parade* (1917), not just the portrait on the wall but the performer's own body would have become part of the construction, as with *Parade*'s American Manager whose body is a living skyscraper.

8 *Sweeney Agonistes* came late to its present form of two linked 'melodramas'. Begun about 1923, it was imagined as part of a considerably longer work, but remained unpublished until it appeared in the *Criterion*, 1926–7. It seems not to have been performed in England until the Group Theatre's staging of 1934, which was hailed by several critics as a real advance in dramaturgy, and given strong publicity by two striking photos by Humphrey Spender and a review by Desmond McCarthy in the *Listener* (9 January 1935). Thereafter, interest was accelerated even in those who thoroughly disliked the work.

9 'Walk-ups' is an Americanism for flats without lifts.

10 Sidnell (1984: 91–2) prints evidence from early sketches of the drama. Eliot meditates on the central fact of *Sweeney* and *The Family Reunion* in 'Eeldrop and Appleplex', 1917: 'In Gopsum Street a man murders his mistress. The important fact is that for the man the act is eternal, and that for the brief space he has to live, he is already dead. He is already in a different world from ours.'

Primary reading

Auden, W. H. (1932). *The Orators*. London: Faber and Faber.

Auden, W. H. (1935). 'I Want the Theatre to Be', London, Group Theatre Manifesto.

Auden, W. H. (1950). *Collected Shorter Poems: 1930–1944*. London: Faber and Faber.

Auden, W. H. (1966). *Collected Shorter Poems: 1927–1957*. London: Faber and Faber.

Auden, W. H. (1988). *Plays and Other Dramatic Writings by W. H. Auden and Christopher Isherwood*, ed. Edward Mendelson. Princeton, NJ: Princeton University Press.

Eliot, T. S. (1955). *On Poetry and Poets*. London: Faber and Faber.

Eliot, T. S. (1969). *The Complete Poems and Plays of T. S. Eliot*. London: Faber and Faber.

Further reading

Carpenter, Humphrey (1981). *W. H. Auden: A Biography*. London: Allen and Unwin.

Cunningham, Valentine (1988). *British Writers of the 'Thirties*. Oxford: Oxford University Press.

Doone, Rupert (1951). 'The Theatre of Ideas', *Theatre News Letter* VI, 4.

Leavis, F. R. (1936). 'Irresponsible Immaturity: Mr. Auden's Talent', *Scrutiny* V: 3, 323–37.

Martin, Kingsley (1938). 'Outspoken Topicality', *New Statesman and Nation* 19 November, 826–7.

Medley, Robert (1983). *Drawn from the Life: A Memoir*. London: Faber and Faber.

Miles, Jack (1985). *God: A Biography*. New York: Schuster and Schuster.

Miles, Jack (2001). *Christ: A Crisis in the Life of God*. New York: Knopf.

Moody, A. D. (1979). *Thomas Stearns Eliot: Poet*. Cambridge: Cambridge University Press.

Moody, A. D. (ed.) (1994). *The Cambridge Companion to T. S. Eliot*. Cambridge: Cambridge University Press.

Muggeridge, Malcolm (1940). *The Thirties: 1930–1940 in Great Britain*. London: Collins.

Osborne, Charles (1980). *W. H. Auden: The Life of a Poet*. London: Eyre Methuen.

Page, Norman (1990). *The Thirties in Britain*. London: Macmillan.

Sidnell, Michael (1984). *Dances of Death: The Group Theatre of London in the 'Thirties*. London: Faber and Faber.

Woolf, Virginia (1982). *The Diary of Virginia Woolf, IV, 1931–35*, ed. Anne Olivier Bell. London: Hogarth Press.

PART III
England, Class and Empire, 1939–1990

12

Empire and Class in the Theatre of John Arden and Margaretta D'Arcy

Mary Brewer

The Quest for a Secular Eucharistic Theatre

John Arden's and Margaretta D'Arcy's 1972 decision to withdraw from the 'meaningless foam rubber of the jumbo-jet culture' and the 'international art hypermarket' (Arden and D'Arcy 1988: 4) of British theatre poses a critical challenge. While their work can be located within British and Irish institutional and aesthetic contexts, it also resists the values and boundaries of both. Criticism that reads their plays within paradigms rejected by the playwrights themselves has often produced misunderstandings concerning the meaning of individual texts and the overall significance of their work in the theatre.

Born in Yorkshire in 1930, Arden came to prominence as part of the new generation of British writers fostered by George Devine at London's Royal Court in the 1950s. His early plays, *The Waters of Babylon* (1957), *Live Like Pigs* (1958), *Sergeant Musgrave's Dance* (1959) and *Soldier, Soldier* (1960), contain many of the oppositional concerns that preoccupied the so-called 'angry young men'. However, Arden always exceeded the limits of 'kitchen-sink' drama. His quest for a popular theatre led him to experiment with a variety of dramatic structures and styles, and he drew a great deal upon Brecht for inspiration. In particular, he is noted for his inventive use of the English ballad form and his exploitation of British and Irish histories to narrate stories about contemporary society.

As early as 1959, Arden lamented British theatre's lack of a collective social purpose. He derided the institutional focus on producing renewable commodities to increase box office receipts rather than works of art. Instead of the 'dreary platefuls of warm water' offered up, Arden called for a theatre that would bring people together for a secular Eucharist so that they left the building feeling they were a united society, not just a collection of 'odds and sods' (Arden 1959: 42).

Until his self-imposed exile, Arden remained a leading playwright in the opinion of most critics. Not only was *Sergeant Musgrave's Dance* considered one of the most important plays of the modern era, but others such as *The Workhouse Donkey* (1963) and *Armstrong's Last Goodnight* (1964) were taken as evidence that Arden had the potential to become one of the 'great' writers of British theatre. Indeed, the famous literary agent Peggy Ramsay, who worked with him during his dispute with the Royal Shakespeare Company (RSC) in 1972, considered him 'the finest talent writing in England and possibly the English-speaking-world' (Chambers 1998: 29).

None the less, Arden has failed to live up to his potential in establishment eyes. Although a few of his early plays remain popular in revival, those written after he dissociated himself from mainstream theatre are seen rarely, if at all, and generally his work written in collaboration with D'Arcy is not accorded much critical kudos. Michael Counts dismisses the majority of their collaborations as 'minor efforts' with only two exceptions, *The Little Grey Home in the West* (1972), aka *The Ballygombeen Bequest*, and the *Non-Stop Connolly Show*, premiered in 1975 (Counts 1996: 4).

Criticism has reflected sometimes as much on the playwrights' personalities or production issues as upon dramatic content, and D'Arcy's contributions to plays have always been treated as contentious. Born in Ireland in 1934, D'Arcy was an actor when she met Arden in 1955. They married in 1957 and began writing together in 1960. Their first professional project, *The Happy Haven* (1960), received mixed reviews, and was considered less significant than Arden's solo work. When Arden began writing plays exclusively with her in the 1970s, critics blamed D'Arcy for a perceived decline in his artistic powers. In Arden's words, they cast her as 'the serpent in my garden' (Arden and D'Arcy 1988: 57).

D'Arcy has frequently been stereotyped as a virago, who has bullied her husband into sacrificing his art to her misguided politics – a strain of misogyny and/or anti-Irish feeling all too evident, especially during the infamous dispute with David Jones, the director of the RSC's production of *The Island of the Mighty* (1972). In the playwrights' view, the RSC failed to represent the progressive elements of the work. Jones's emphasis on characters' inner motivations, as in realist theatre, clashed with their intentions for an anti-realistic, ironic presentation of character. Furthermore, Arden and D'Arcy were dissatisfied with the stage and costume design, and the style of music and song, all of which they felt worked against the audience adopting the necessary critical distance for understanding the play's political message. The playwrights requested a meeting with the company to negotiate these issues; when this did not happen, they complained to their union. Arden has explained that, in his view, they were hired to attend rehearsals and make necessary changes to the script, the completion of which was hindered by the RSC's failure to provide satisfactory working conditions, that is, a meeting with the full company (Arden 1977: 159). Arden and D'Arcy resigned and the RSC accepted their notice, but the company refused to admit a contractual violation or that the disagreement amounted to an industrial dispute; neither would the executive consider changes to the production. As a result, Arden and D'Arcy picketed the theatre, and during one of the public dress rehearsals, Arden took to the stage in an attempt at an impromptu general meeting. When he asked the audience if they wanted him to speak, however, a majority responded negatively, thereby ending the playwrights' protest.

Although Arden was just as active during the dispute itself, it was D'Arcy who was held to be responsible for the breakdown in relations with Jones. Christopher Innes sees the events not as an argument over dramatic meaning and an author's right to control his or her work, but as a Byzantine political manoeuvre on D'Arcy's part to protest against British activity in Northern Ireland. Innes appears to accept without question, or indeed much evidence, the opinion of the RSC's literary adviser at the time, Ron Bryden, who blamed D'Arcy for engineering the dispute. Accordingly, Innes claims that D'Arcy was angered by the recent arrest of a member of the IRA, and used the dispute with the RSC to create a convenient establishment whipping-post on which to take out her frustrations (Innes 2002: 149).

D'Arcy is not the first woman artist to suffer for challenging patriarchal assumptions and practices through the content of her work and in her working relationships. Pam Gems has related that she was warned to see Arden alone for an interview because '*she* usually does the talking' (Gems 1973: 16, italics mine). And despite D'Arcy's presence at the same interview and her co-authorship of the play under discussion, Gems titled her piece 'The Island of the Ardens: Pam Gems talks to John Arden'. As Tish Dace has made clear, there has been a tendency to ignore D'Arcy's contributions to modern theatre. Either critics obscure her input by referring to the Ardens (she does not use his name professionally), or they mention only Arden, even when discussing plays credited as D'Arcy/Arden (see Dace 2001: 1–16).

Such experiences led Arden and D'Arcy to boycott the professional mainstream theatre. They stopped viewing their work as part of British theatre. Arden contended that they were 'classified as British because the British fail to see Ireland as separate – a symptom of British imperialism' (Itzin 1980: 36). However, as the discussion of their Irish plays will show, they often transgress the comfortable institutional confines of modern Irish theatre as well.

Radical Reformer to Theatre Revolutionary

Arden's career is usually described as having three writing phases. From 1980 to the present he has been devoted to writing fiction and radio drama, forms which he prefers because there are fewer mediators between the playwright's imagination and the audience and because he is more in control of working conditions (Arden and D'Arcy 1988: 41). From the production in 1955 of his first play *All That Fall* to 1972 Arden wrote alone for the stage. From 1972 to 1978 Arden wrote with D'Arcy; their last major stage-work was *Vandaleur's Folly*. D'Arcy has traditionally been demonized as the destroyer of Arden's career, but in contrast to the usual pre- versus post-D'Arcy divide Arden himself provides a political differentiation for the first two phases, which he refers to sardonically as the 'genuine' versus 'non-genuine' Arden periods.

The first coincides with widespread critical acceptance because it contains plays that are read as offering no firm political conclusion; whereas the 'non-genuine' phase, more often dismissed by critics, presents plays that affirm 'from his own hard experience the need for revolution and a Socialistic society' (Arden 1977: 158).

Arden has always been a political radical, wary of authority and overarching social institutions. Asked in 1966 whether he considered himself a political or sociological writer, he responded that it was not possible *not* to be a political playwright because any play that deals with people in a society must necessarily be a political one (Wager 1966: 45).

There is no denying, though, that Arden was a different type of radical at the start of his career, before his conversion to radical Marxism in 1970. The trajectory of his political development and its impact on his drama is complicated and difficult to trace. Firstly, Arden has moved a considerable distance from his own early analyses of his plays, and, secondly, critics have ascribed to his early drama a variety of leftist ideologies. In fact, Arden's and D'Arcy's political positions have grown organically out of an eclectic array of philosophies and social movements. Michael Cohen chooses 'anarchistic pacifism' to summarize Arden's early political viewpoint, but also identifies shades of Marxism (Cohen 1985: 198–9). Redmond O'Hanlon opts for 'a vague Left-wing quasi-liberalism' as opposed to a later 'affirmative neo-Marxism (O'Hanlon 1980: 218), and D. Keith Peacock links Arden's ideological shift to the New Left movement after 1968 (Peacock 1991: 55). The best guide to the influences on their political thinking and theatre-making are the playwrights' two collections of essays, *To Present the Pretence: Essays on the Theatre and its Public* (Arden 1977) and *Awkward Corners: Essays, Papers, Fragments* (Arden and D'Arcy 1988). D'Arcy's account of her stay in Armagh prison (where she was interned under the Prevention of Terrorism Act), *Tell Them Everything* (1981), is also important. Together these books chronicle the development of their political and dramatic theory. They provide explanations of individual plays and refreshingly honest meditations upon the difficulties encountered in their careers, and offer a rich vein of literary biographical information.

Tell Them Everything highlights the breadth of theoretical material that has influenced them, referring to philosophers as diverse as G. W. F. Hegel and Paulo Freire. It charts the couple's involvement with the anarchistic-pacifistic Committee of One Hundred (a sub-group of CND) in the late 1950s and early 1960s, and the impact of the alternative political thinking of the Black Panther movement. In *To Present the Pretence*, Arden recounts a trip to India with D'Arcy in 1970, where they met members of the Gandhian non-violence movement as well as Maoist revolutionaries (Arden 1977: 101–2). Elsewhere Arden expands on how this experience transformed his political and artistic visions. In India he witnessed the war between the haves and have-nots waged with great ferocity. This led him to recognize 'as the enemy the fed man, the clothed man, the sheltered man, whose food, clothes, and house are obtained at the expense of the hunger, the nakedness, and the exposure of so many millions of others' (Arden 1971: 17). In *Awkward Corners*, both writers discuss the impact of the Irish 'Troubles'. Based in Ireland since 1962 (and now resident in Galway), Arden and

D'Arcy noticed parallels between the Indian guerrilla movement and Irish resistance to British occupation. Ultimately, the India experience, combined with the outbreak of violence in Northern Ireland, especially British army activity against Irish republicans, encouraged Arden to shift his view of the playwright's role in society. During his Royal Court years, Arden claimed that the playwright's job was to set up conflict and to dramatize clashes of temperament (Arden 1960b, 1961). After India, as he embraced a Marxist revolutionary doctrine, he could no longer accept the artist as a detached commentator, but argued that he should take on the role of revolutionary intellectual activist.

'Foreign Despots and Self-Generated Capitalist Maggots'[1]

I argue here against dominant critical opinion, which holds that there is a vast difference, sometimes thematic, often qualitative, between Arden's dramatic outputs prior to and after his collaboration with D'Arcy (see, for example, Anderson 1976; Innes 2002; Schvey 1981). The politics of Arden's solo plays show distinct similarities to his later collaborative plays. The problems identified as blighting the social lives of individuals, and their roots in imperialism and capitalism, remain the same. The aims Arden seeks to achieve via writing for the theatre, whether alone or with D'Arcy, again are similar. In 1964, Arden calls for the theatre to serve the spectator's mental and sensual satisfaction by presenting an image of common humanity and the potentialities of the human spirit and intellect (1964d: 30), which he links to society's socialist transformation. Anthony Hozier, interviewing Arden and D'Arcy in 1985, finds the same issues still motivating them. They seek to work within communities for whom the expression of cultural life, the 'total development of the human being in relation to his/her society', is part of a process of social and political liberation (Hozier 1985: 13). D'Arcy explains this as reclaiming the ancient function of theatre as an act of communal celebration and mourning, the goal being to erase the divide between 'artistic activators and a passive recipient audience' so characteristic of modern theatre practice (Arden and D'Arcy 1988: 137).

None of these statements differs much from Arden's desire for a secular Eucharistic theatre. What changes is his opinion about the most efficacious political means to resolve the fundamental inequalities separating people. Consequently, with the premiere of *The Ballygombeen Bequest* in 1972 the plays become more explicitly Marxist in their analysis of what lies at the heart of social conflict and how to bridge social divides. Political theory must accord with the choice of dramatic form and space, and as Javid Malick has argued, Arden and D'Arcy prefer approaches that reinforce a collectivist ethos among 'new and truly popular audiences', 'those larger plebian sections of society that the bourgeois theatre has systematically banished' (Malick 1995: 14, 35).

After 1972, Arden and D'Arcy increasingly sought to address their plays to audiences of socialists and republicans. *The Non-Stop Connolly Show*, staged at Liberty

Hall, the headquarters of the Irish Transport and General Workers Union in Dublin, took place over 24 hours at Easter weekend in 1975. It recounts the life of Irish revolutionary leader James Connolly, executed after the failed Easter Rising in Dublin in 1916. The six plays comprising the cycle represent a dramatic form of political life-writing. Connolly's life reveals and challenges certain repressive forces in British and Irish history that D'Arcy and Arden suggest remain active in contemporary life. The intent is not only to celebrate the achievements of one extraordinary Irishman, but more importantly, to record and analyse events in his life in a way that frames his personal experiences within a communal 'I'. The production was advertised almost exclusively in leftist newspapers and trade union publications, providing an audience for whom the plays' politics were important in daily life. This does not equate to an audience of the already converted, for Irish opinion remained divided concerning the value of socialism versus republicanism.

As well as foregrounding the difficulty of balancing nationalist and socialist aims, *Connolly* interrogates the complicity of the British left in Irish colonialism, to the detriment of both sides. D'Arcy and Arden wrote six plays rather than one after noticing a pattern in Connolly's history that showed that every time the revolutionist cause gained ground the capitalist lost ground and vice versa (Arden and D'Arcy 1988: 99). Thus, the action revolves around two complementary binaries: capital versus labour and reform versus revolution.

Connolly's story validates the idea that one can be an Irish patriot *and* a socialist; and his history presupposes that Irish republicanism will remain under stress until the movement couples with that of world socialism. The belief that these issues remain of vital import to working-class people, especially those caught up in the Northern Ireland conflict, is illustrated by Connolly's final words, which interrupt the cycle (the plays refusing conventional closure). Tied to a chair and about to be shot by the British, Connolly refers to the Irish revolution as a founding moment in Marxist revolutionary struggle, which, though unsuccessful in his day, necessarily continues:

> We were the first to show the dark deep hole within
> Could be thrown open to the living sun.
> We were the first to feel their loaded gun
> That would prevent us doing it any more –
> Or so they hoped. We were the first. We shall not be the last.
> This was not history. It has not passed.
>
> (ibid.: 106)

The Connolly cycle, therefore, attempted to intervene in the Irish 'Troubles' by resisting, among other things, historical revisionism. D'Arcy and Arden wanted to counter the idea that the Easter uprising was unnecessary, or futile, or that Irish independence would have come about just as soon through parliamentary action.

The cycle highlights the often well-meaning but mistaken view among the British left that the government would honour its commitment to liberate Ireland. Home rule leading to independence is seen as a means of defusing working-class anger, of limiting socialist activity in Ireland, and of driving a wedge between Irish and British socialism. Connolly's dispute with the British labour activist and liberal MP Keir Hardie highlights the connections between imperialism and class oppression.

Referring to the Boer war, Connolly argues that 'England's difficulty should be Ireland's opportunity' (ibid.: 3: 43). Hardie accuses him of threatening the welfare of all working-class people through political opportunism. He insists that exploiting British weakness in wartime damages their cause because the British army is a working-class institution, not an imperial tool for Irish oppression (47–9). Hardie sees Irish and British workers firstly as proletariats with identical interests. Connolly, in contrast, reiterates the impossibility of improving the rights and living conditions of either without an end to British imperialism in Ireland and elsewhere.

The plays demonstrate the similarities between British governance of its colonies and of its working class to serve ruling-class interests. The savagery and duplicity of British imperialism in its quests for raw commodities and trading markets accompanies the increasing degradation of British and Irish workers, afforded no real protection by trade unions. At times, D'Arcy and Arden highlight the naïveté of labour bureaucracy, but more often portray union officials as corrupt in their negotiations.

The labour movement's transformation into an instrument of capitalist production, colluding with the efforts of the upper class and bourgeoisie to control the means of production, becomes clear when British union leaders refuse to call a sympathetic strike with Irish workers. They rely on spurious excuses to postpone action because, if they violate the contracts and agreements they made with the employers, they lose their hold on power, which relies on the ability to speak for and manipulate the workers (ibid.: 5: 72).

This is emphasized further when workers across Europe are dissuaded from pursuing the creation of a broad-based socialist order when war erupts between the imperial powers (64–5). Here, we see Irish leaders again bought off with the promise of home rule after the war, while British trade union officials fall for the false promise of state ownership of the means of production *if* they pledge their workers to the war effort.

If the plays present a Marxist worldview, they do not lack ideological complexity. While they help orientate the spectator to socialist principles, differing socialist views always get full weight, as Cohen recognizes (Cohen 1990: 87). Of all Arden's and D'Arcy's work, *Connolly* gives the most comprehensive and sophisticated account of the motives for antagonism between social classes and how class differences can be exploited to serve imperialism. The playwrights explore the political tensions that exist within and between working-class communities and the ever-present tension between desires for reform and revolution. Perhaps most importantly, they demonstrate the difference between the promise of socialism, the small gestures towards social justice contained in welfare capitalism, and the actual potentials of a socialist state.

The trilogy that serves as the transition between Arden's radical and revolutionary perspectives, *The Island of the Mighty*, addresses the Marxist link between the history of oppression and that of language or literature, offering a subversive account of Arthurian legends to highlight their legacy of class-based imperialist oppression. The plays draw parallels between the breakdown of society after the exodus of Roman troops from Britain in the fifth century and contemporary postcolonial societies. In his preface, Arden describes how he became aware that the decline of British imperialism post-Suez had much in common with its Roman predecessor (Arden and D'Arcy 1974: 12). The plays represent Arthur against type in order to foreground the real, communal hero behind the myths – the peasants who endure despite all efforts to destroy their indigenous culture. Albert Hunt (1974) notes that Arthur and his followers perform chivalry against a background of widespread peasant suffering and poverty. Thus, Arthur is located 'firmly inside the framework of an oppressive [class based] social system' (Hunt 1974: 158).

Like *Connolly*, the trilogy illustrates how the wealthy and powerful have more in common with each other than with the poor of their own nation-states. We see represented again colonialism's destabilizing and splintering effects. The story of Balan and Balin, recounted in part 1: 'Two Wild Young Noblemen', demonstrates the breakdown of familial or clan bonds. This is reinforced in part II: 'Oh, The Cruel Winter', the battle between the Romanized Arthur and his son Medraut, which illustrates the divide between those who assimilate the conqueror's values and those who maintain native beliefs. The postimperial elite is shown capitalizing upon class and ethnic difference to impose a form of interior colonialism.

Part III, 'A Handful of Watercress', is particularly interesting for the way it reflects the playwrights' theory of the artist as political agent in revolutionary struggle. The three poets featured show different roles that the artist may play in relation to the organization of power. Taliesin supports the status quo, providing patriotic verse glorifying Arthur and the Christian church. Merlin, official court poet, is neither reactionary nor revolutionary, but swings diplomatically between these poles. His indecisiveness renders him ineffectual in any cause. Aneurin represents the progressive artistic voice. His writing champions the cause of the people, suggesting that there are available alternatives to the system of government that dominates their lives. He is the only member of the trio to survive, which lends a note of optimism to a work otherwise filled with violence and despair. The legend of Lazarus that he narrates at the end serves as a metaphor for the Marxist dialectic of history, as a force moving towards the inevitable triumph of oppressed over oppressor. The final promise that the people 'are going to take hold / So hideous and bloody greedy / We take hold of the whole world!' (ibid.: 235) promotes the genuine possibility of socialist revolution.

Echoes of this idea, so seminal to *Connolly* as well, appear even in Arden's early classic *Musgrave*. Though less concerned to advocate that the spectator take up a revolutionary stance, *Musgrave* shares the optimistic view that the communal human spirit will find a way to resist the despots and capitalist maggots who wish to consume it. The play explores what might happen if colonial practices came home to the colonizers. Its plot involves the activities of four soldiers, ostensibly on a recruiting mission but who, in reality, have deserted after taking part in the massacre of 25 civilians in reprisal for a soldier's death. One of Arden's sources was an incident that took place in Cyprus in 1958, when terrorists shot a soldier's wife and the military responded with indiscriminate killings. Thus, one can understand his description of the play as realistic, while not naturalistic, for it is firmly rooted in the excesses and regrettable legacy of British imperial history.

Sergeant Musgrave and three of his men flee what he describes as a 'war of sin and unjust blood' (Arden 1960a: 33). However, arriving in town during an industrial dispute between miners, they find themselves in the midst of another kind of unjust warfare. Musgrave explicitly links imperial wars and class warfare when he speaks of the strikers' riots and the war he has fled as 'the same one corruption' (36). Hence, the play offers much more than a window on an isolated experiment, and asks how colonialism might affect a typical northern English town.

The main thrust of the play is not a study of the particular experience of one man or the subjective effects of colonialism on a group of soldiers (although Arden does not entirely ignore the men's psychology). The objective is to demonstrate how colonialism functions as an instrument for control that serves the ruling class at home as much as abroad. By presenting the connection between the material conditions of the working class and their relationship to colonial ideology, Arden's critique attempts to intervene in and modify the controlling discourse of imperialism by enabling the spectator to recognize at least, if not resist, its processes at home and abroad.

How imperialism operates in the contest between the miners and bosses comes through in exchanges between characters that represent social institutions: the Mayor symbolizes the state; the Parson voices the church's interests; and the Constable signifies the repressive arm of the state apparatus. The Mayor wants to use Musgrave in order to rid the town of the most militant workers, telling the Parson: 'The Queen's got wars, she's got rebellions. Over the sea. Get rid o' the troublemakers' (ibid.: 22). The soldiers communicate their sense of being fodder in a system geared to maintaining the power, wealth and prestige of the upper orders. Hurst complains about being 'treated like dirt, out there, and for to do the dirty work' (ibid.: 30).

Musgrave has journeyed to the town intent upon payback, in particular, for the death of Private Billy Hicks, a local boy whose murder precipitated the bloody repercussion in the colony. Hicks acts as a figurehead for all the casualties of colonial wars, those who live with the guilt of their dirty work and its literal casualties. Revealing Hicks's skeletal remains, Musgrave invites the townspeople to join his 'madness': 'I brought it back to England, but I've brought the cure too – to turn it on to them that sent it out of this country' (ibid.: 92). The miners and their families, however, have internalized the master discourse of class to such a degree that they are as horrified by his suggestion that they turn on their 'betters' as are the Parson and the Mayor. They do not take up the dance Musgrave performs beneath Billy's skeleton, what Douglas Bruster calls his 'ritualized expression of ideological rage' (Bruster 1995: 46). Instead, the play ends with the re-establishment of the status quo: a contingent of dragoons enter the town, surround Musgrave and Attercliffe, his surviving accomplice, and without resistance from the crowd lead them off to prison and to their eventual execution.

Despite this, the play does not end without the hope that change may come, indeed, it could be taken as pointing towards the inevitability of it. Mrs Hitchcock observes that when hungry, men think only of the immediate need to fill their stomachs and that of their families: 'One day, they'll be full, though, and the Dragoons'll be gone, and then they'll remember' (Arden 1960s: 102). In this way, the play leaves the audience with the thought that the struggle goes on. As in the other plays discussed, the question is how much time must pass before we not only remember, but also take up Musgrave's challenge to rectify the social injustices that Arden puts under the spotlight.

Note

1 From *The Non-Stop Connolly Show* (Arden and D'Arcy 1977: Part III, 77).

Primary reading

Arden, John (1959). 'Correspondence', *Encore* 6: 3, 41–2.

Arden, John (1960a). *Sergeant Musgrave's Dance*. London: Methuen.

Arden, John (1960b). 'Telling a True Tale' in Charles Marowitz, Tom Milne and Owen Hale (eds.) (1965). *The Encore Reader*. London: Methuen, 125–9.

Arden, John (1961). 'Some Thoughts upon Left-Wing Drama', *International Theatre Annual* V, 187–203.

Arden, John (1964a). *Armstrong's Last Goodnight*. New York: Grove.

Arden, John (1964b). *The Happy Haven in Three Plays*. Harmondsworth: Penguin.

Arden, John (1964c). *Live Like Pigs*. New York: Grove.

Arden, John (1964d). 'Theatre and Leisure', *Socialist Commentary*, August, 29–31.

Arden, John (1964e). *The Waters of Babylon* in *Three Plays*. Harmondsworth: Penguin.

Arden, John (1964f). *The Workhouse Donkey*. London: Methuen.

Arden, John (1967). *Soldier, Soldier and Other Plays*. London: Methuen.

Arden, John (1971). 'Preface' in *Two Autobiographical Plays*. London: Methuen, 9–17.

Arden, John (1977). *To Present the Pretence: Essays on the Theatre and its Public*. London: Methuen.

Arden, John and D'Arcy, Margaretta (1974). *The Island of the Mighty*. London: Methuen.

Arden, John and D'Arcy, Margaretta (1977). *The Non-Stop Connolly Show: Parts 1–6*. London: Pluto.

Arden, John and D'Arcy, Margaretta (1982). *The Little Grey Home in the West*. London: Pluto.

Arden, John and D'Arcy, Margaretta (1988). *Awkward Corners: Essays, Papers, Fragments*. London: Methuen.

D'Arcy, Margaretta (1981). *Tell Them Everything: A Sojourn in the Prison of Her Majesty Queen Elizabeth II at Ard Macha*. London: Pluto.

FURTHER READING

Anderson, Michael (1976). *Anger and Detachment: A Study of Arden, Osborne and Pinter.* London: Pitman.

Bruster, Douglas (1995). 'Why Read Arden?' in Jonathan Wike (ed.). *John Arden and Margaretta D'Arcy: A Casebook.* New York: Garland, 41–50.

Chambers, Colin (1998). *Peggy: The Life of Margaret Ramsay, Play Agent.* London: Methuen.

Cohen, Michael (1985). 'The Politics of the Earlier Arden', *Modern Drama* 28:2, 198–210.

Cohen, Michael (1990). 'A Defence of D'Arcy's and Arden's Non-Stop Connolly Show', *Theatre Research International* 15:1, 78–88.

Counts, Michael L. (1996). 'John Arden' in William W. Demastes (ed.). *British Playwrights, 1965–1995.* Westport, CT: Greenwood Press, 3–14.

Dace, Tish (2001). 'Who Wrote John Arden's Plays?' in Kimball King (ed.). *Modern Dramatists: A Casebook of Major British, Irish, and American Playwrights.* New York: Routledge, 1–16.

Gaston, Georg (1991). 'An Interview with John Arden', *Contemporary Literature* 32:2, 140–7.

Gems, Pam (1973). 'The Island of the Ardens: Pam Gems Talks to John Arden', *Plays and Players* 20:4, 16–19.

Hozier, Anthony (1985). 'From Galway to Managua, From Kissinger to Constantine', *Red Letters: A Journal of Cultural Politics* 17, 11–26.

Hunt, Albert (1974). *Arden: A Study of his Plays.* London: Methuen.

Innes, Christopher (2002). *Modern British Drama: The Twentieth Century.* Cambridge: Cambridge University Press.

Itzin, Catherine (1980). *Stages in the Revolution: Political Theatre in Britain since 1968.* London: Methuen.

Malick, Javid (1995). *Toward a Theatre of the Oppressed: The Dramaturgy of John Arden.* Ann Arbor: University of Michigan Press.

O'Hanlon, Redmond (1980). 'The Theatrical Values of John Arden', *Theatre Research International* 5:3, 218–36.

Peacock, D. Keith (1991). *Radical Stages: Alternative History in Modern British Drama.* Westport, CT: Greenwood Press.

Schvey, Henry I. (1981). 'From Paradox to Propaganda: The Plays of John Arden' in Hedwig Bock and Albert Wertheim (eds.). *Essays on Contemporary British Drama.* Munich: Hueber, 40–7.

Wager, Walter (1966). 'Who's For A Revolution? Two Interviews with John Arden', *Drama Review* 11:2, 41–8.

13

When Was the Golden Age?
Narratives of Loss and Decline:
John Osborne, Arnold Wesker
and Rodney Ackland

Stephen Lacey

The moment of John Osborne's *Look Back in Anger* (Royal Court, 1956) was undoubt-edly a symbolic one in the history of postwar British theatre and of postwar culture generally. This may seem surprising to readers and audiences encountering the play some fifty years later, but it is still possible to acknowledge it, even though the rhetoric of revolution that greeted the play now seems overblown and simplistic. There have been much-needed correctives to some of the wilder claims made about the play, and both Rebellato (1999) and Shellard (1999) have argued persuasively for different views of the drama of the 1950s, seeing radicalism and theatrical innovation elsewhere. Certainly, the play was helped by its connection to the emerging and critically successful English Stage Company at the Royal Court Theatre, and in turn helped to establish the Court as the cradle for new writing (with implications for the way that the history of British drama in the 1960s and 1970s has been written). *Look Back in Anger* does not seem to be obviously a political play, and was certainly not radical in a formal sense. There were other plays emerging at about the same time, performed by companies other than the English Stage Company, which show a greater spirit of innovation: Shelagh Delaney's *A Taste of Honey* (Theatre Workshop, 1958) and Brendan Behan's *The Hostage* (Theatre Workshop, 1958), for example, both produced by the legendary director and theatrical innovator Joan Littlewood, played with naturalist theatre form – and challenged contemporary assumptions about race, class and gender – in a far more adventurous way than Osborne's play had. The significance of *Look Back in Anger* lay more in its impact on the realignment of culture and politics in the mid-point of the decade than in its direct contribution to the development of British[1] drama and theatre (although one should remember that some playwrights of a later generation, notably David Edgar, would still argue that it contributed here as well – see Edgar 1988). The purpose of my chapter, however, is not to rehearse these arguments but to pursue them in a different direction, exploring contradictions between narrative form and political stance in theatre of the mid- to late 1950s. I will do so by examining certain key texts of the period ('key' meaning much-discussed) and, as a kind of antidote, one play by a writer from earlier in the decade.

Look Back in Anger was successful – and significant – largely because it seemed to represent a social and historical experience that was distinctively of the mid-fifties; it was undisputedly *contemporary*, marking the separation of 'then' (the domination of the pre-war symbolism of church and monarchy, the austerity of the postwar years) from 'now' (the sensibility of a newly engaged mid-fifties Britain). It also occurred in a year that delivered a series of shocks to British self-confidence and complacency, both at home and abroad, notably the Suez fiasco, in which British imperial hubris was exposed by the reality of US power, and the Soviet invasion of Hungary. Almost immediately the play was rapidly co-opted for the political and cultural left. Tynan's influential review of the first production in the left-leaning *Observer* constructed Jimmy Porter as a liberal hero, exhibiting 'qualities one had despaired of ever seeing on the stage – the drift towards anarchy, the instinctive leftishness, the automatic rejection of "official" attitudes' (Tynan 1984: 178). Clearly, responses to *Look Back in Anger* were shaped by attitudes to its protagonist, Jimmy Porter. Porter was a symbolic figure in public and political discourse in the decade, ripped out of the play and paraded across the newspaper headlines, often collapsed into a composite figure with his creator, 'Osborne/Porter' or into the ubiquitous yet ill-defined 'Angry Young Man'. *Look Back in Anger* and its author can lay claim to being at the centre of the first theatrical celebrity event in postwar media history, circulated and discussed in ways that have become familiar in more recent times.[2] However, this view of the play masks other more problematic characteristics, especially a complex relationship to British (or rather, English) history that reaches back beyond 1945. This is not to deny the play's undoubted importance for postwar culture and theatre (despite *Look Back in Anger*'s diminished stock it seems pointless to pretend that its significance to its contemporaries was simply a delusion). However, it is these connections to the past, and the political dilemmas that result, that are of the most concern here.

Osborne's next play, *The Entertainer* (Royal Court, 1957), had more obvious political relevance than *Look Back in Anger* (being set at the time of the Suez crisis), but in fact neither has a narrative that follows the expected trajectory of drama of the left – that is, they neither offer a diagnosis of a political situation nor pose questions that reach forward beyond the life of the play and ask for answers from the audience. If there is an ideal to which drama of this kind aspires, it is available only in the future; the narratives of both *Look Back in Anger* and *The Entertainer* constantly pull the spectator towards the past. This is partly because they are essentially negative, looking at contemporary Britain and finding little that could be admired or salvaged; and the vacuum that is left is filled by a reverence for the past – not the past in general, but a specific historical moment, from which subsequent history is a sad and remorseless decline. It is the past, not the present, that is the site of authentic action and values ('authentic' is a term much used in the decade). Both plays exhibit what might be termed 'Golden Age-ism' in this respect, looking back (as the title of Osborne's play prompts us to recognize) with anger at what has been lost. What is surprising, however, is that the Golden Age to which these plays are symbolically linked is the moment of crisis in the postimperial project, the moment that epitomizes the empire, Edwardian England.

The Suez crisis disturbed one of the central delusions of postwar British history: Britain, it was claimed, had managed to divest itself of its empire in an orderly manner, whilst maintaining a moral leadership of the western world (see Cannadine 2001; Ward 2001). This is a narrative of a rueful and well-managed retreat (with the brutal suppression of the Mau-Mau forces in Kenya and the nationalists in Cyprus relegated to a footnote). It carried particular resonance in a country struggling to avoid the lengthening shadow of American power and the uncomfortable realities of the Cold War. There is no escaping the fact, however, that after Suez it is a narrative of *loss* – loss of British influence in the world, with a consequent, and inevitable, decline in prestige. This historical narrative finds a direct correlation in the narratives of both *Look Back in Anger* and *The Entertainer*, and, as a recurrent pattern, in other plays of the 1950s as well. The Golden Ages under discussion may differ, but the political effect is the same – looking back is always a sign of impotence, of an inability to engage politically with the present.

It seems at times as though Jimmy Porter's anger is directed against the whole world, but at others it crystallizes around his wife Alison's family. If the play were as straightforwardly left-wing as its reputation suggested then this would be a simple matter, since Alison's family is resolutely upper-middle class, connected to the empire via military service (her father, Colonel Redfern, served in India). The Redferns are set up to be the symbolic enemy, representing the values of that part of society that retained power yet were embedded in pre-war social and political values. For much of the early part of the play this is the case, and a great deal of Jimmy's venom is directed towards Alison's mother and brother ('The Platitude from Outer Space'; Osborne 1960: 20). However, as several critics have pointed out, Osborne shows an unexpected sympathy for Alison's father, Colonel Redfern, and a surprising nostalgia for the age of empire (see Rebellato 1999: 140–1). The play is careful to present him as supportive of Alison's predicament and understanding of both her feelings and Jimmy's anger. Jimmy has prepared us for this earlier in the play:

> I hate to admit it, but I think I can understand how her Daddy must have felt when he came back from India, after all those years away. The old Edwardian brigade do make their brief little world look pretty tempting ... Phoney too, of course. It must have rained sometimes. Still, even I regret it somehow, phoney or not. If you've no world of your own, it's rather pleasant to regret the passing of someone else's. (Osborne 1960: 17)

Colonel Redfern confirms Jimmy's view of the centrality of the experience of empire in a speech that articulates his (the Colonel's) longing for India and sense of loss and dislocation when he was forced to return home.

> The England I remembered was the one I left in 1914, and I was happy to go on remembering it that way ... When I think of it now, it seems like a dream. If only it could have gone on forever ... I think the last day the sun shone was when that dirty little train steamed out of that crowded, suffocating Indian station, and the battalion band playing for all it was worth. I knew in my heart it was all over then. Everything. (ibid.: 68)

This speech conflates a sense of a 'timeless' pre-World War I Britain with his experience of service in the army in India. Alison's rejoinder to her father is that 'You're hurt because everything is changed. Jimmy is hurt because everything is the same' (ibid.: 68). This is often taken as a statement of where the political balance of the play lies, placing Jimmy on the left, his anger rooted in a frustration caused by the inability of British society to alter. However, Jimmy is actually on the same side as Colonel Redfern, mourning the loss of the Edwardian Golden Age, which was for them both a moment when it was possible to feel in tune with society, one's personal identity resonating with the national one (even though only the Colonel could know this at first hand). It is a conservative, not a radical, view of British history, and one that equates the end of empire with a loss of nerve and the passing of an essential idea of Englishness. Osborne's lingering nostalgia for empire is sharpened by a knowledge that it cannot return. It is not that Osborne, or even the most ardent empire royalist, wanted to see the British army marching back into India, but rather that the loss of authenticity, of the sense that personal fulfilment and historical mission are as one, is mourned. As is so often the case, the imagery of empire cloaks an anxiety about Britain itself.

The nostalgic heart of the play becomes even more apparent when it is compared with the 1959 film version (directed by Tony Richardson). The film, which stars Richard Burton as Jimmy Porter, took the action out of the single room and into the wider social world, representing locations only referred to in the play: we see the street market where Jimmy and Cliff run a sweet stall, for example, and the hospital where Ma Tanner is dying. Burton was, as Alexander Walker has pointed out, much more like a liberal-left hero of a kind that would be more familiar to the international (especially American) target audience for the film (Walker 1974: 62). Indeed, Richard Burton's Jimmy Porter is much more the kind of instinctively leftish figure that Tynan created in his review of the play than was Kenneth Haigh's interpretation on the stage in 1956. The targets of Jimmy's anger had also begun to change by 1959, and the film recognizes a changing political and social climate, connecting to postimperial Britain in new ways. The most obvious example is the introduction of racism as an issue. Richardson introduced a sub-plot involving an Indian market-trader, Kapur, who is the victim of both the institutional racism of the market inspector and the casual, instinctive racism of other stall-holders. Jimmy and Cliff defend Kapur, but to no purpose, as he is forced off the market. The film was made in the aftermath of the first postwar 'race riots' (a misnomer for a series of unprovoked attacks on West Indians by white racists) in Notting Hill in 1958. It might also be seen as a response to a decade of immigration from the ex-colonies, especially those in the Indian subcontinent, as Britain sucked in a ready supply of labour for its burgeoning consumer economy. There is, then, much less emphasis in the film on the heyday of empire, and much more on the beginnings of postwar, multicultural Britain. Nostalgia for the Edwardian Golden Age is evident in Osborne's second play for the Royal Court, *The Entertainer*. The play concerns Archie Rice, a comic and impresario who has lost faith in both his art and himself, and his family in the aftermath of Suez. *Look Back in Anger* was written before the events of 1956, but *The Entertainer* makes direct reference to the Suez debacle, and Archie's son, Frank, is killed whilst fighting in the Canal zone. Indeed, the play was seen as one of the first postwar 'state of the nation' plays, representing a national malaise. As Tynan opined, once again interpreting the play in terms of a liberal-left agenda, 'Osborne has had the big and brilliant notion of putting the whole of contemporary England on to one and the same stage. *The Entertainer* is his diagnosis of the sickness that is currently afflicting our slap-happy breed' (Tynan 1984: 201). The main way in which Osborne achieves this is by framing the family scenes with interludes comprised of Archie's variety turns. With songs such as 'Why Should I Care' (Osborne 1961: 24), Archie expresses a personal despair that is also a comment on the national mood of corrosive self-interest induced by consumerism, with the theatre building operating as a metaphor for the British nation on the point of collapse. Once again, however, the narrative looks backwards to the Edwardian era in search of a Golden Age. Some of the same structural motifs are evident here as in the earlier play, and in many ways the historical process of decline is clearer. There is, for example, the same juxtaposition between the 'authentic', located in the past, and the 'false' or inauthentic, rooted in the present. In *The Entertainer*, the Edwardian era is celebrated for another reason, as the moment when the English music-hall was at its zenith. Osborne explicitly recognizes this in a note at the beginning of the published text: 'The music hall is dying, and, with it, a significant part of England. Some of the heart of England has gone; something that once belonged to everyone, for this was truly a folk art' (Osborne 1961: n.p.). This indicates another version of historical and cultural decline, one which centres on popular culture and captures a very 1950s unease about the effects of consumerism and the mass media on popular entertainment.

This era of the halls is represented in the play in the person of Archie's father, Billy Rice. Billy is clearly of another age, and is frequently juxtaposed with his son, both as a man and as a representative of his time. Archie's rock'n'roll revue is explicitly contrasted with the heyday of the halls. In the play, the reader/spectator has to infer that this is the case, since we do not see Billy perform, but in the 1960 film version (once again directed by Tony Richardson) he is allowed to do so. In one telling sequence the film narrative cuts between Billy, who is asked to sing spontaneously in a pub, and Archie, who performs a song 'Thank God I'm Normal' in his theatre. Archie's audience is sparse and unresponsive, whilst Billy's is warm and enthusiastic. It is an indication of the film/play's lingering affection for the empire that Billy's song is 'Don't let Them Scrap the British Navy', which, as Rebellato has pointed out, is a pastiche of well-known jingoistic Edwardian songs (Rebellato 1999: 140). The corollary of this opposition between past and present is that the true villain is rock'n'roll. Osborne is not alone in using contemporary popular music, and popular culture generally, as a symbol for affluent Britain, which has gained prosperity and lost its soul.

There are few plays of the New Wave that betray this unexpected affection for Edwardian England, but motifs of loss and decline can be found elsewhere, albeit mapped onto different historical narratives. The trilogy of plays by Arnold Wesker, for example, offers a very different view of contemporary history to that of Osborne's plays, one that is connected to the history of European socialism in the twentieth century. The trilogy, *Chicken Soup with Barley* (1958), *Roots* (1959) and *I'm Talking About Jerusalem* (1960), was performed initially at the Belgrade Theatre, Coventry, and then transferred to the Royal Court Theatre, London, where it was widely discussed. Like many plays of the late 1950s, the trilogy was set amongst the British working classes, but in this case amongst a subset. The main focus of all three is the Kahns, a family of communist Jews in London's East End (a family much like Wesker's own), especially the matriarch, Sarah, and her son Ronnie, who provide the thematic and political heart of the trilogy, even when they are not on-stage. It is the first play, *Chicken Soup*, that is of particular concern here, since, in tracing the family history from 1936 to 1959, it provides both the historical and familial logic that drives all three plays.

The key historical event in the trilogy is the moment in the summer of 1936 when British fascists (the blackshirts), under the direction of Sir Oswald Mosley, were driven from the streets of London's East End by the organized resistance of London's radical Jewish community and its many supporters on the political left. As an undoubted victory for the left in a decade that witnessed many defeats, the battle of Cable Street, as it came to be known (after the street that saw the most direct confrontations), had immense symbolic as well as actual significance in the domestic resistance to fascism. In *Chicken Soup with Barley*, this victorious moment is seen as a high point of left-wing idealism, in which political action unifies personal integrity and identification with class. Moreover, the play links the battle against British fascism with the wider anti-fascist struggle. The year 1936 was also when the Spanish Civil War commenced, and one of the key figures in the play, Dave Simmonds, announces that he is off to fight for the republican cause. The republican government of Spain, the first to be elected democratically, was threatened by the ultra-conservative and traditionalist forces led by the fascist General Franco. Left-wing idealists from across the world went to Spain to join the International Brigades to fight for the republican cause. By 1939, the government was defeated, many members of the Brigades were dead or disillusioned and Franco was installed as dictator. In

1936, however, Spain was a powerful rallying cry, a defining moment for a generation. Dave states this very clearly: expressing his unease and doubt about the act of killing, he says 'I'm not even sure that I want to go, only I know that if I don't then – then – well, what sense can a man make of his life?' (Wesker 1973: 23).

The trilogy is at one level a response to both victory and defeat. As the narrative moves into the postwar era (which it does from Act II of *Chicken Soup* onwards), it mirrors a particular view of postwar change from the political left. The post-1945 era may have brought the welfare state and a Labour government (and, in 1945, two communist MPs), but it has been at the cost of political and personal idealism and community responsibility. The Kahns move into a new council flat, but, as Cissie, Sarah's sister-in-law, observes 'You live a whole lifetime here and not know your next-door-neighbour' (ibid.: 68). It is, once again, a narrative of loss and decline from a moment of 'authentic' personal behaviour and political idealism, and this is made tangible in the figure of Harry, Sarah's husband. Harry, it is clear from the start, is a weak man, who hides at his mother's during the battle against the blackshirts. He suffers a stroke that makes him physically as well as morally crippled, and his progressive deterioration is a metaphor for the decline of idealism and radical politics that other characters discuss.

Ultimately, these rich and complex plays are concerned with the necessity of hope and courage against the grain of history. This is embodied in the women who lie at the trilogy's heart, Sarah Kahn and Beattie Bryant (Ronnie's girlfriend, who is the protagonist of *Roots*). Beattie struggles and finds her own voice at the conclusion of the play, speaking not as a surrogate for Ronnie, as she has done throughout, but as herself. And Sarah, in the last lines of *Chicken Soup*, chastises Ronnie with words that capture the passion that the play offers as a counter to political disillusion: 'Ronnie, if you don't care you'll die' (ibid.: 76). But, within a narrative that locates authentic political action twenty years in the past, there is little that the present can offer by way of a model of political engagement. The logic of the trilogy, then, is a retreat from a 'public' politics of political action into a 'personal' politics of integrity, and this is both its emotional attraction and the source of its political weakness.

It is worth noting that World War II rarely surfaces as a point of reference in the plays of the New Wave (a notable exception being Willis Hall's *The Long the Short and the Tall* (Royal Court, 1959) which is set in the Malaysian jungle at the close of World War II). This is not treated as a moment of lost opportunity, or of political certainty and personal authenticity, which could be compared to 1936. One might expect this to be the case in a drama of the left, since World War II was a major victory against the arch-enemy of European fascism, and it is seen in terms similar to this two decades later by writers of the left such as David Hare (see *Plenty*, National Theatre, 1978) and Trevor Griffiths (see *Country*, BBC 1, 1981). The absence of the war from much stage drama was due partly to the sense that it had been appropriated for the right by a conservative imagery of masculinity and nationhood. Traditional versions of masculinity were particularly strong in the 1950s, with World War II as a point of reference (see Segal 1990). This was also fuelled by the experience of compulsory National Service (the term given to military conscription in Britain, which existed from 1945 to 1963). The experience of service life promoted a masculinity that was identified with 'the near obligatory smoking, swearing, drinking, aggressive sexual boasting and phallic symbolism of military equipment' (Segal 1990: 19). It was also propelled by popular fiction and cinema. As Worpole has noted, in the fifties 'the most widely read books in Britain were books that dealt with the experiences of male combatants in World War II' (Worpole 1983: 50) – and the readership for this fiction was almost exclusively male.

A very different engagement with the experience of war and its immediate aftermath can be found in Rodney Ackland's *The Pink Room* (Lyric Theatre, Hammersmith, 1952). It was reworked in 1988 as *Absolute Hell*, as part of a renewed interest in Ackland's work generally, and first performed at the Orange Tree Theatre, Richmond.[3] It is analysed here because it offers a counterpoint to narratives of loss and decline, and is a more complex engagement with history than many of the more famous plays that followed it. This ambitious and, in the fifties, much-reviled play was set amongst the denizens of a faded night club, La Vie en Rose, in the summer of 1945. Although the play had its supporters (Terence Rattigan helped to promote it and was a great admirer of Ackland's work), the critical consensus was very hostile, with the influential impresario Binkie Beaumont describing it as 'a libel on the British people' (cited in Dromgoole 1995: 9). *The Pink Room* was a disaster, and remained unpublished in its original version. *Absolute Hell*, following on from its success at the Orange Tree Theatre, was adapted by Michael Hastings for the BBC in 1991, and directed by Anthony Page, who went on to stage the play for the National Theatre in 1995.

It is not hard to see why the original production should have created such a furore. Staged just one year after the Festival of Britain, which provided a triumphalist version of a Britain emerging from the vicissitudes of war, its institutions and values intact, the play offers an array of characters, many of whom are homosexual, alcoholic, bohemian and otherwise socially marginal. *Absolute Hell* offers an alternative view of World War II, in which the key experiences are not of stoicism and sacrifice but of sexual freedom, the dissolving of social and sexual boundaries, and survival (a view that Hare also adopts in *Plenty* and elsewhere). It is this unblinking and revisionist view of Britain at war that links the play to the political drama of the 1970s, rather than the post-Osborne drama of the late 1950s.

Absolute Hell has a large and diverse cast and is conceived as an ensemble piece, its many different narrative lines flowing in and out of each other. Ackland's most obvious point of reference is Chekhov, and the play has a strong structural resemblance to *The Cherry Orchard*, though it is bleaker in mood. La Vie en Rose functions both as a metonym of postwar London and as a metaphor for Britain, faded and crumbling, and its demise, like that of the Ranyevskaya estate, is symbolic of the end of an era. The last act, again as in *The Cherry Orchard*, is a prolonged goodbye, the night-club's owner, Christine, forced to close as the building visibly collapses. The characters are viewed sympathetically, though not without criticism. There is no hint of nostalgia in the play, and no looking back to an imagined Golden Age. The play looks forward, and characters talk incessantly about what they must do now; salvation lies in the future, not the past.

Absolute Hell makes clear reference to the political world that lies beyond the stage. Through a window at the back of the space can be seen the Labour Committee Rooms, always in view and a constant reminder of a very different future and a challenge. On the eve of the 1945 general election, which returned a Labour government, this peripheral space threatens to spill onto the forestage, metaphorically if not literally; as La Vie en Rose collapses, the Committee Rooms burst with activity. The central challenge for realist drama is to link public and private worlds, and in *Absolute Hell* this is done by a discourse around notions of 'reality', which shapes the theme of how to live now, personally and socially. Most characters, by their own admission, avoid reality, through drink, sex or both. Most can't even be bothered to vote, although their instincts are pro-Labour. References to reality/unreality saturate the play. The consequences of avoiding reality are, subjectively, summarized in admiring comments made by a young Canadian serviceman to Hugh, a fading writer:

> But, you know, it's the way you kinda get into people's minds in some of your stories ... that one where the young guy catches sight of himself in the mirror and kinda realizes he can't prove that anybody's real except himself and he doesn't know who the hell he is anyway – or why. (Ackland 1995: 48)

The difficulty of knowing who you are and why is central to the play. It is partly a result of the elaborate strategies used to mask feeling and avoid disclosure. Characters constantly 'perform' to each other, and the play is full of fits of self-consciously hysterical laughter, elaborate asides and put-downs. Clothing is described as if it were costume for its wearer and there are several acts of mischievous impersonation. The performative nature of this largely homosexual subculture (shared by many of the heterosexual characters), which would be seen much more positively were it in a play of the early 2000s, is presented here as a strategy of evasion. It masks pain and uncertainty, and will be rendered redundant by the events symbolized by the Labour Committee Rooms. It is also not a pain that is felt by a gay sensibility alone. As Hugh remarks to his lover, Nigel, who is about to leave him for a woman, it doesn't in the end matter what your sexual proclivities are: 'What *is* the difference? What *is* it? The emotion's the same – the unhappiness, the misery, the *hurt's* the same' (ibid.: 91).

A different kind of pain is also represented in *Absolute Hell* – the historical obscenity of the concentration camps. Douglas, a soldier who participated in the liberation of Ravensbruck, arrives at La Vie en Rose to deliver a message to one of its regular inhabitants, Elizabeth, from an old friend who died in the camp shortly after the troops arrived. Douglas has photographs of the friend and other inmates, which temporarily silence everyone, their brute documentary presence contrasting with the unreality of the club. To live with such reality is not granted to most characters in this play. Some – Nigel, for example, and the two outsiders Sam and Douglas – find reality in social action: Sam announces he is going to India, and Nigel goes to work for an organization that helps refugees. But the central symbolic figure, the owner of La Vie en Rose, is allowed no such relief. The play ends with Christine, who has become both Madame Ranyevskaya and Firs, drunk and ill, sobbing in the dark.

Absolute Hell was well received when it was revived in the 1980s and 1990s, partly because its view of World War II has now become more acceptable, but also because its characters are clearly connected to the historical context in which they exist. Though not a political play in the accepted sense, it is about the processes of history and the legacy of the war. There is no Golden Age on this stage, not even one to come; and Ackland's characters are freer to face the reality of their situation than either Jimmy Porter or Archie Rice is to confront his.

NOTES

1 This chapter will continue the practice of referring to the theatre of this time as 'British', but it should be noted that it is with English plays performed by English companies (in reality London-based) that I am concerned. Whether this is a defensible practice or not is another matter, and should be the subject of an essay in itself.

2 For the only sustained study of theatrical celebrity see Mary Luckhurst and Jane Moody (eds.). (2005). *Theatre and Celebrity in Britain, 1660–2000*. Basingstoke: Palgrave.

3 This newer version of the text is the one that is now in circulation. *The Pink Room* was heavily censored, and its successor should be regarded as being closer to the play Ackland wanted to write and will be used here.

PRIMARY READING

Ackland, Rodney (1995). *Absolute Hell*. London: Oberon Books.

Osborne, John (1960). *Look Back in Anger*. London: Faber and Faber.

Osborne, John (1961). *The Entertainer*. London: Faber and Faber.

Wesker, Arnold (1973). *The Trilogy*. London: Penguin.

FURTHER READING

Buse, Peter (2001). *Drama and Theory: Critical Approaches to Modern British Drama*. Manchester: Manchester University Press.

Cannadine, David (2001). *Ornamentalism: How the British Saw Their Empire*. London: Allen Lane.

Dromgoole, Nicholas (1995). 'Introduction' in Rodney Ackland. *Absolute Hell*. London: Oberon Books, 1–7.

Edgar, David (1988). *Second Time as Farce*. London: Lawrence and Wishart.

Hall, C. (ed.) (2000). *Cultures of Empire: A Reader*. Manchester: Manchester University Press.

Hare, David (1978). *Plenty*. London: Faber and Faber.

Hare, David (1991). 'Now Think This Time: An Introduction to the History Plays' in *Writing Left-Handed*. London: Faber and Faber, 73–84.

Innes, Christopher (1992). *Modern British Drama: 1890–1990*. Cambridge: Cambridge University Press.

Patterson, Michael (2003). *Strategies of Political Theatre: Post-War British Playwrights*. Cambridge: Cambridge University Press.

Rebellato, Dan (1999). *1956 and All That: The Making of Modern British Drama*. London: Routledge.

Rebellato, Dan (2001). 'Looking Back at Empire: British Theatre and Imperial Decline' in S. Ward (ed.). *British Culture and the End of Empire*. Manchester: Manchester University Press, 73–90.

Segal, Lynne (1990). *Slow Motion: Changing Masculinities, Changing Men*. London: Virago.

Shellard, Dominic (1999). *British Theatre Since the War*. New Haven, CT, and London: Yale University Press.

Tynan, Kenneth (1984). *A View of the English Stage*. London: Methuen.

Walker, A. (1974). *Hollywood England: The British Film Industry in the Sixties*. London: Michael Joseph.

Ward, S. (ed.) (2001). *British Culture and the End of Empire*. Manchester: Manchester University Press. (See esp. the introduction.)

Worpole, Ken (1983). *Dockers and Detectives*. London: Verso.

14

A Commercial Success: Women Playwrights in the 1950s

Susan Bennett

At least two words in this chapter's title might appear unusual in terms of other accounts of British theatre in the 1950s: 'commercial' and 'women'. After all, theatre history has generally insisted that it was the woeful state of postwar commercial theatre that explains both the rising popularity of cinema-going and the success of Angry Young Men writing for the Royal Court Theatre stage so spectacularly launched, of course, on 8 May 1956 by John Osborne's *Look Back in Anger*. As Shellard has pointed out, 'much of the polemic that was to sustain the new realist theatre after the advent of *Look Back in Anger* was predicated on an impassioned rejection' of the commercial West End theatre and its values – 'an obsession with glamour, a refusal to stage works that glanced at contemporary life or political concerns, a blind adherence to favoured house dramatists, such as Terence Rattigan and a continual representation of upper-middle class (and for realists, irrelevant) milieus' (Shellard 2000: 31). Thus, Taylor was to write in his foundational critical work for the period *Anger and After* (first published in 1962): 'The whole picture of writing in this country has undergone a transformation in the last six years or so, and the event which marks "then" off decisively from "now" is the first performance of *Look Back in Anger*' (Taylor 1962: 9). More recently, however, the centrality of both this year and this play in conventional narratives of twentieth-century British theatre and drama has been challenged by revisionist historians who argue for a new evaluation of what Shellard calls 'an enduring fallacy' (Shellard 2000: 28).

The first new decade of the postwar period in Britain was one characterized both by optimism – inspired by the coronation in 1953 of the young queen ('the new Elizabethan age') – and by crisis – the Anglo-French invasion of the Suez canal that Stephen Lacey notes 'had considerable effects on Britain's international standing' (Lacey 1995: 16). At home, however, this was a period of new-found economic prosperity and, with that, an unprecedented access to education and wealth for the nation's youth. But if superficially everything seemed to bespeak a revised social order, not everyone rejoiced in the kinds of opportunities and expectations now available. Thanks in large part to Osborne's Jimmy Porter, the epitome of a new wave of attention given to this younger generation and their prospects, the 1950s were (as championed by critic Kenneth Tynan and as subsequent theatre histories have told us) definitively the era of the Angry Young Men. As Lacey puts it, 'The ease with which the Angry Young Men could be identified with youth resided partly in the fact that they were signified as a "new generation," distinct from – and opposed to – the cultural and political establishment as teenagers were from their parent cultures and social values' (Lacey 1995: 27). In other words, the hero of Osborne's play has been seen as representative of a new cultural reality that characterized the immediate postwar period, and the play itself as the engine that changed both the style and content of British playwriting in the late twentieth century.

As Rebellato rightly concludes 'The story of British theatre in 1956 has been so often retold that its shape, its force, its power and meaning have been lost in the familiarity of the telling. If nothing else, there is a need to make the familiar unfamiliar' (Rebellato 1999: 225–6). Revisionist histories, then, have studiously re-evaluated the significance of *Look Back in Anger*: among them, Shellard suggests the play only entered the popular imagination through the film version, starring Richard Burton (Shellard 2000: 13); Nandi Bhatia argues that it reveals 'Osborne's complicity in the act of consolidating the practice of empire by naturalizing the social relations in the play in ways that construct the other as subordinate' (Bhatia 1999: 392). Other critics have turned away from the paradigmatic *Look Back in Anger* and expanded the range of playwrights taken to exemplify the decade, often suggesting that writers such as Samuel Beckett, Terence Rattigan and Christopher Fry have been undervalued in traditional histories of the period. My own scholarship adds to this retelling of the story through an insistence on the inclusion of women dramatists who wrote prolifically and successfully for the commercial stage of the period.

In *Modern British Drama: The Twentieth Century* Christopher Innes opens a chapter on 'the feminist alternative' with the following comment: 'Apart from some minor exceptions, such as Elizabeth Robins' *Votes for Women* (1906), female playwrights have been conspicuous by their absence from British theatre up until the late 1950s. Even then, Anne [*sic*] Jellicoe found the commercial stage inappropriate to her feminist aims, while Shelagh Delaney's only success was a compromise with popular taste' (Innes 2002: 233). This brief synopsis of women dramatists' contributions to the first half of the twentieth century is just not true, yet Innes and more or less every other historian of the last century – and particularly of postwar British theatre – repeat, in one way or another, the assumption that women did not play any major role in writing for the stage. In fact, it has not yet even been part of revisionist theatre history to account comprehensively for the more than one hundred and thirty plays single- or co-authored by women produced on London stages during the 1950s. One or two may be familiar from their marginal status in histories of the Angry Young Men – Shelagh Delaney's *A Taste of Honey* (1958) and perhaps Ann Jellicoe's *The Sport of My Mad Mother* (1958) (the two women Innes mentions, albeit cursorily). Two imports to the West End have since become classics in the canon of twentieth-century American drama, although they are not generally discussed for their impact on the London stage: Lillian Hellman's *The Children's Hour* – an early, and rather depressing, representation of lesbian desire, originally banned in England by the lord chamberlain's office – ran for 47 performances at the Arts Theatre in September and October 1956; and Lorraine Hansberry's *A Raisin in the Sun* (78 performances at the Adelphi Theatre, August–October 1958) is now considered an important landmark for African-American drama on the New York stage. One of the decade's plays would become definitive for London's commercial theatre: Agatha Christie's *The Mousetrap* opened on 2 November 1952 at the Ambassadors Theatre and continues today at the St Martin's Theatre. It celebrated its twenty-thousandth performance in 2000. Some of the names are familiar for reasons other than playwriting: these include the extraordinary Joan Littlewood, who wrote, co-wrote or adapted five plays between 1953 and 1955 with Theatre Workshop in Stratford East; and Enid Blyton, who adapted her enormously popular *Famous Five* children's books for the stage, and whose shows ran for 26 performances at the Princes Theatre for the Christmas season 1955–6 and for 36 matinees at the Hippodrome over Christmas 1956–7.[1] Furthermore, as theatre historians have neglected to tell us, over the course of the 1950s there were more than thirty plays written by women that ran for more than one hundred performances, although I suspect few of us (even the few of us who would identify ourselves as feminist historiographers) would be able to name any of their titles.

The insistence by Innes on an absence of women playwrights until the end of the 1950s is, then, typical but entirely misleading, given the actual data on women-authored plays produced on the London stage through the whole decade – a reality that has the immediate effect of challenging the obligatory citation of *Look Back in Anger* as the high point of 1950s theatre and the single most important influence on everything that happened afterwards in the century. The tenacity of the claims made of and around 1956 has led Loren Kruger to ask: 'What is lost in the presumption that the postwar theatre begins only in 1956?'[2] Although they are neither an interest nor a concern to Kruger, her question might be answered quite straightforwardly: plays by women. Or, perhaps more emphatically, successful plays authored by women for West End stages, since the decade might be more accurately defined by a significant number of women playwrights who enjoyed tremendous success in commercial theatre, seeing their plays transferred regularly to or from Broadway and often rapidly adapted into feature films. Several of these women were also successful novelists. It is one such writer – perhaps better known for work outside the theatre – whom I take as my subject here. Enid Bagnold (1889–1971) remains best recognized for her 1935 novel *National Velvet*, the story of a teenage girl who wins a horse in a raffle and then rides it to an unlikely win in Britain's most famous horse race, the Grand National. The novel was later adapted for screen (1944), starring a young Elizabeth Taylor in the central role. But it is Bagnold's most successful play, *The Chalk Garden* – which had its London opening on 11 April 1956, just a few weeks before Osborne's play arrived to take over the period's theatre history – that I want to suggest is an important counterpoint to the resilient and still prevailing obsession with *Look Back in Anger*.

Bagnold's *The Chalk Garden* ran at the Haymarket Theatre for 658 performances (closing on 9 November 1957); by comparison, *Look Back in Anger* ran for 284 performances over 1956 and 1957. This numerical difference is noteworthy. While Osborne's play has come to exemplify this period in English stage history, it did not come close to generating the box office success of a *Chalk Garden*.[3] If, at first glance, the plot and setting of Bagnold's play seem to affirm the notion that 'the commercial theatre had been taken to be a typical institution of that society, recycling plays based on worn-out formulas, set in now-dead worlds' (Shepherd and Womack 1996: 275), both its production history and its account of 'upper-class snobbery and repressive proprieties' (ibid.) provide a significant challenge to those received – and dismissive – histories.

A first observation about *The Chalk Garden* is that its London opening at the Haymarket was not the play's premiere. In 1953 Bagnold had sent her playscript, via her agent Harold Freedman, to Hugh 'Binkie' Beaumont, head of the dominant H. M. Tennent theatrical empire, only to have it disappointingly rejected: 'I am sorry to be so discouraging,' Beaumont wrote, 'but I feel that in its present form no ordinary theatre audience could disentangle so many cross-sections of life' (cited in Sebba 1986: 180). With a London production now out of the equation, Freedman turned to American managements, where he found a champion for *The Chalk Garden*. In the Samuel French edition of Bagnold's play, published in 1956, the author provides this foreword:

> THE CHALK GARDEN owes its New York production (and therefore its outer life) to the devotion of IRENE MAYER SELZNICK.
>
> In America 'producer' is the word for the Management. In this case it is difficult to limit Mrs. Selznick's dynamic activity by a word. For two years she lived with one end – to put on this play. She flew, she cabled, she battled. She 'cast.' In casting she would have ransacked the Shades.
>
> More imperious than I on my behalf she was filled towards the play with an unfaltering magnificence of loyalty.
>
> These few lines are written with my deep thanks and affection.
> ENID BAGNOLD

It is surprising, perhaps even shocking, to realize that a well-established and popular author would struggle so obviously to get a London production of her latest play (she had written six novels, two plays and a stage adaptation of *National Velvet*, a children's book, and various works of non-fiction before *The Chalk Garden*). In fact both her autobiography and the biography by Anne Sebba detail the difficulties she experienced in getting productions for all of her plays. Without Selznick's backing it might have proven impossible, and even then, according to Lenemaja Friedman (the author of the only full-length critical study of Bagnold), this was a relationship not quite as magnificent as the foreword implies. Friedman writes: 'Irene came to England to work with the playwright, but even from the beginning there were differences, some as basic as to how much emphasis to place on theme. Irene insisted on a central theme evident throughout the play. For Bagnold, working in terms of several themes criss-crossing, appearing, and disappearing, this requirement was frustrating' (Friedman 1986: 85).

As well as these differences there were ongoing problems in the rehearsal process (the original director, George Cukor, had to be replaced by Albert Marre, whom Bagnold felt did not understand the play) and a far from enthusiastic reception of the pre-Broadway run. As Bagnold herself described it:

> Dilapidated, slowed-down by the 'approximating', scenes at every scene, divided by schisms, we stumbled into Boston, hobbled into Philadelphia, took less and less money, and it was said we'd never make New York. Gladys [Cooper, playing the main character, Mrs St Maugham] didn't learn the words. All the comedy – replies and couplets – woven-for-laughter failed to get a laugh. It was shame-making every night. (Bagnold 1969: 232)

With only the slightest hope of success, then, *The Chalk Garden* opened at the Ethel Barrymore Theatre on 26 October 1955. It turned out to be a hit with both critics and audiences, running for 181 performances before it closed at the end of March 1956. *New York Times* reviewer Brooks Atkinson summed up the play as 'an odd, unyielding comedy by a witty writer with a highly personal style. There's a keen mind behind it, and one that is not intimidated by either the theatre or the world.'[4] Sebba notes: 'Within hours of the New York reviews, Binkie cabled: he wanted *The Chalk Garden* on in London as soon as possible' (Sebba 1986: 192). As well as a six-month run on Broadway, the play garnered a Tony nomination (1956) for Best Play of the Year – an award that went to *The Diary of Anne Frank* by Frances Goodrich and Albert Hackett – but Bagnold was in good company with other unsuccessful nominees: Tennessee Williams for *Cat on a Hot Tin Roof*, William Inge for *Bus Stop*, and Christopher Fry for his adaptation of Jean Giraudoux's *Tiger at the Gates*. Moreover, Bagnold gained further recognition for her stage work in the United States, too, winning the Award of Merit Medal for Drama from the American Academy of Arts and Letters and the National Institute of Arts and Letters, presented in New York on 23 May 1956. In his presentation address, Maxwell Anderson, president of the Academy, commented:

> About once a decade the American public has been fortunate enough to hear from Enid Bagnold, and sometimes her cryptic and humorous messages have come by way of the American theatre. To my mind, *The Chalk Garden*, of this last season, is the most delightful of her writings. Everything she has sent out has been sensitive, merry, fugitive, oblique, unorthodox in form and style, unpredictable – and somehow im-mensely effective. *The Chalk Garden* is all these things and just a bit more – distraction,

irrelevance and enchantment suddenly by a stroke of genius taking on shape and pattern and breathing the breath of daily life. It is a pleasure and an honour to present her with the Award of Merit and all that goes with it in the way of admiration, affection and thanks.[5]

The medal also came with a substantial cash prize of $1,000. It is particularly interesting that Bagnold was deemed eligible for this American award because of her frequent visits there and that the Academy named her 'as a highly outstanding person in America' (cited in Bagnold 1956: 117).

Not surprisingly, then, Beaumont began working on a London production of *The Chalk Garden*, engaging the 'A' list of London's theatre professionals to work on the play: Sir John Gielgud agreed to direct and he convinced Dame Edith Evans and Dame Peggy Ashcroft to take on the lead roles of Mrs St Maugham and Miss Madrigal. This second production fared much better in its preview run than had the New York production, with Bagnold basking in 'glory over the thrilling reviews the play received in Birmingham and then Brighton' (cited in Sebba 1986: 195). *The Chalk Garden*, presented by H. M. Tennent Ltd., opened at the Haymarket Theatre on 11 April 1956 – an event that caused Kenneth Tynan to comment in his review for the *Observer*: 'On Wednesday night a wonder happened: The West End Theatre justified its existence' (cited in Bagnold 1956: 115). Although *The Chalk Garden* is, in some ways, exactly the drawing-room drama that critics would soon identify as too old-fashioned for the contemporary English theatre, it is by no means a typical example. Certainly it seems to be in its setting in the main reception room of a manor house in Sussex, with open French windows leading out to an English country garden. As the opening stage direction suggests:

> Beyond the open French window a bosky, be-lillied garden runs slightly uphill. A June gale blows. The room has a look of vigour and culture. The furniture is partly inherited, partly bought in Mrs. St. Maugham's young days. It is probably Regency, but the owner of this house does not tie herself to anything. She has lived through many moods, and is a jackdaw for the Curious and Strange. (Bagnold 1956: 10–11)

This is but a short extract from two full pages of description that constitute the playwright's instructions for setting the stage and shows a concern for a social realism that matches any of the 'new' drama of the 1950s. Bagnold's on-stage environment is, of course, not at all the working-class context that typified the work of the angry young men,[6] importantly providing a kind of alienation from the glamorous drawing rooms of, say, Noël Coward or other commercially successful playwrights of the first half of the twentieth century – remember that Beaumont had originally criticized the drama for its 'many cross-sections of life'.

The Chalk Garden, an unusual amalgam of comedic drama and detective story, does not easily lend itself to plot synopsis, but I will sketch a version here. Mrs St Maugham, described at her first entrance as 'an old, overpowering, once beautiful, ex-hostess of London society' (Bagnold 1956: 18), hires a governess for her 16-year-old granddaughter, Laurel, for whom she is primary caregiver; this comes after the girl's father committed suicide, and her mother remarried and moved overseas with her new husband, an army colonel. The only other occupants of the household are the manservant Maitland and, 'unseen and chained by a stroke upstairs, there broods the evil influence and faded grandeur of the butler [Mr Pinkbell] who has known all the magnificence of his employer's life in London' (ibid.: 18). Miss Madrigal, the successful applicant for the position of governess, is best described as enigmatic and aloof – attributes that are finally explained when an old friend of Mrs St Maugham, a judge, comes to lunch and it is revealed that Miss Madrigal is really Connie Dolly Wallis, who had only recently been released from prison after serving a 'life sentence' (15 years) for murder. Another plotline involves the return of Mrs St Maugham's daughter, pregnant with her new husband's baby and hoping to regain custody of her first child. But the strength of this play lies not so much in what happens; Brooks Atkinson insists 'the plot is the least interesting item in *The Chalk Garden*'. He continues: 'it is a sound rule not to pay much attention to Miss Bagnold when she is developing her story. But pay attention to the lines she throws away. A perverse writer, she squanders all her talent on the things that do not matter' (Brooks Atkinson 1955: 29).

Clearly audiences agreed with his positive assessment of the quirky attractions of *The Chalk Garden* and, for readers perhaps unfamiliar with this play, it is important to identify some features that make it differ significantly from the kind of formulaic plotting that tends to characterize stereotypical drawing-room dramas. The play opens with three applicants for the position of governess, waiting for their interviews and trying to extract family information from the servant Maitland. One asks him 'Is this a house where there are gentlemen?' (Bagnold 1956: 12). It is not a question that is answered but it signals, almost from the play's opening moment, that this is not the conventional family of the upper-class manor house, but rather a differently constructed social reality. The matrilinear organization of the household is soon confirmed by Laurel, the subject for whom a governess is sought, and who proceeds herself to interrogate the hopefuls.

The Chalk Garden is a play that is relentless in its interrogation of relationships between women, and between women and society. On the one hand, there is an onstage portrait of what happens to upper-class life in the absence of men – Mrs St Maugham is more concerned with her garden than with more human interactions. On the other, there is an always-present undercurrent of the effects of so-called deviant social relations – the off-stage and decrepit butler Pinkbell with his rude interventions; Maitland, who has spent five years in prison and, when asked by the judge if it was a deterrent, answers 'Yes and no. Yes and no' (ibid.: 65); and, of course, Miss Madrigal, the murderer, who claims 'For fifteen years, and alone, I have hammered out what I am' (ibid.: 79).

If 'the fifties was a period characterized by consensus that the family was *the* central unit in society',[7] then Mrs St Maugham's provides a very unconventional representation of that normative unit. In this context, it is especially interesting that Bagnold's play pursues the 'considerable body of Freudian writing on infancy and childcare in the fifties' with, as its governing principle, 'the status which it gives to women as mothers – their femininity carries with it special kinds of knowledge and love which are essential to the well-being of the child' (Birmingham Feminist History Group 1979: 56). The strange behaviours of the granddaughter (she is given to lighting fires and to hysterical screaming) are explained, at least in some sense, by the absent and unloving mother, and, even in her own summary of the play, Bagnold suggests that Laurel 'leads her grandmother by the nose and exploits her caprices and her leaning towards Freudian explanations' (Bagnold 1956: 7). Obviously this is inverse to expectations of family relationships.

In the interview scene between Miss Madrigal and Mrs St Maugham, set against the background of Laurel's screams emanating from the garden, the grandmother suggests: 'One must be tender with her. Alas, he [Laurel's father] died when she was three. Rich and a fine estate. Four Van Dykes and unique Sheraton furniture. (*Bitterly*) Her mother's one success—. (*Rises. To Left of table*) But why speak of it! She married again!' (ibid.: 22). The grandmother follows this with a tirade against her daughter which Miss Madrigal tries to divert by returning attention to her prospective charge: 'The child – is she fond of her stepfather?'

> MRS. ST. MAUGHAM (*Indifferent*): I never asked. His rank is Colonel. My grand-daughter has developed an interesting mother-hatred, which is clearly explained in Freud.
>
> (ibid.: 23)

This scene then provides one of the most startling revelations in the play, even though it is simply made and scarcely returned to, and this particular moment gives an important indication of what must have captured the imagination of theatre audiences at the time. In many ways, the play is a psychological thriller that spoke in terms that audiences of the 1950s would have found provocative and contemporary in the context of prevailing ideas of the family, mothering and Freudian interpretation. Miss Madrigal comments ('pursily' as the stage direction has it), 'The child is naturally alienated – that a sex-life has broken out again in her mother' (ibid.: 23), to which Mrs St Maugham replies 'You put it well. Exactly.' What follows is an extraordinary account of Laurel's reactions at her mother's wedding, something that is punctuated by the persistent ringing of the telephone and Mrs St Maugham's crossing the stage to answer it:

> When nothing would stop the wedding – she ran from the hotel into the dark –
>> (*Second* RING)
> MADRIGAL: There seems to be a bell ringing.
>> (PHONE *stop*.)
> MRS. ST. MAUGHAM (*getting up and talking as she crosses right to house telephone*):   – and by some extraordinary carelessness she was violated in hyde park at the age of twelve.

it has upset her nerves. we are waiting as it were for calmer weather. (*picking up house telephone*) you want me, pinkbell? one moment – (*hand over phone*) of course we put it less strongly to her mother.

(ibid.: 23–4)

And, apparently, it was put less strongly to English theatre audiences in 1956; the text notes: 'By the Lord Chamberlain's wish, and in all places within his jurisdiction, the word "violated" on page 24, Act One, must be played as "ravished," though it should remain "violated" on the printed page.'[8] As is evidenced in the dramaturgy for this particular scene, Bagnold is careful to build in her revelation about Laurel's traumatic past almost *en passant* as Mrs St Maugham is occupied with other stage business. The effect of this is to drop the bombshell, but to inhibit its development, particularly to stall the information's acting as an easy and singular explanation to Laurel's behaviours. This pattern of character development puts a great deal of emphasis on the audience's attentiveness and interpretative energies. In many ways, all the characters – and especially all the women – in *The Chalk Garden* function according to this strategy, something that Bagnold achieves effectively in the pace and wit of her drama.

The Chalk Garden was a popular play with the West End audience, certainly, but as Philip Hope-Wallace's review in the *Manchester Guardian* astutely notices, it may well have especially appealed to one demographic:

'The Chalk Garden' is an English rose of comedy – in high June. It has triumphed in America and in Birmingham, and it now wafts back to the Theatre Royal, Haymarket, our two leading actresses in a play which is an actress's paradise and a woman's play in the very best sense, being laconic, compassionate, and wonderfully gay-hearted.[9]

The production history of *The Chalk Garden* shows that it did not require Evans and Ashcroft for its sustained success – Gladys Cooper and Pamela Brown took over the roles at the Theatre Royal in August 1956. The play was re-reviewed in *The Times* on 9 August:

No one, whether he be colleague or admirer, can have envied Miss Gladys Cooper or Miss Pamela Brown their tasks of taking over the principal parts in *The Chalk Garden* from Dame Edith Evans and Miss Peggy Ashcroft.

Little short of perfection was required of them if they were to match the richness of the earlier portraits: that the play still remains a choice entertainment with its highly wrought lines glinting in some of their original brightness must be considered a tribute not only to the new performers, but also to the adaptability of the structure built by the author.

The first production in New York had won a Tony nomination, but the second in London gained equally high acclaim in year-end reviews. The theatre reviewer for the *Daily Sketch* noted 'My best evening since I wrote last has been "The Chalk Garden" at the Haymarket. I returned to the play – it was my third visit – when Gwen

Ffrangcon-Davies took over the part of Miss Madrigal from Pamela Brown, herself the successor to Peggy Ashcroft' (16 January 1957). A report in the *Illustrated London News* provided another multi-viewing endorsement:

> If I am asked to choose the best play of 1956 – and, with relish, I do hereby ask myself – my answer is 'The Chalk Garden.' Very few modern works can stand up to three visits. But I have met Enid Bagnold's play thrice, and hope to go on seeing it, and listening to some of the most civilized balanced, intricately-judged theatrical dialogue of our period . . . .
>
> It is a compliment . . . to the dramatist who has added these characters to the repertory of our English theatre. (19 January 1957)

Look Back in Anger, then, was not everyone's automatic first choice for the best play of 1956, and the enthusiasm of reviewers for *The Chalk Garden* suggests that it is a drama that might be expected to last, to join the repertory of English theatre. And it has, across the English-speaking world. Husband and wife Sir Lewis Casson and Dame Sybil Thorndike starred in a production that opened in Melbourne, Australia, on 31 August 1957 – although the notice in *The Times* announced with some disdain that Miss Madrigal was being played by an Australian actress! Other productions include very many little theatre and university productions in the United States, including the Spa Summer Theatre of Saratoga Springs (August 1956) – starring Lilian Gish as Miss Madrigal and Dorothy Gish as Mrs St Maugham – Macon Little Theatre (December 1956), Idaho State College (May 1957), Adelphi College, NY (August 1957), University of Denver (October 1957), State University of Iowa (August 1958) and Montana State University (July 1959).[10] And American productions have continued steadily over the years – New York's Circle in the Square (January 1966), New Orleans' Le Petit Theatre du Vieux Carre (October 1979), the American Conservatory Theatre and Roundabout Theatre (both in 1982), and the Berkshire Theatre Festival (1988) with Juliet Mills as Miss Madrigal. *The Chalk Garden* was released as a film in 1964 with Hayley Mills as Laurel, father John Mills as Maitland and Edith Evans once again playing Mrs St Maugham. In England, the play has also been regularly revived, notably in 1971, again at the Theatre Royal Haymarket, with Gladys Cooper at the age of 82 reprising her stage success as Mrs St Maugham. The play's 1992 revival inspired Charles Spencer to write in the *Daily Telegraph*:

> *The Chalk Garden* is an exotic bloom from the 1950s which miraculously retains its freshness more than 35 years after its première.
>
> When it opened . . . in 1956 Kenneth Tynan hailed it as perhaps 'the finest artificial comedy to have flowed from an English (as opposed to an Irish) pen since the death of Congreve.'
>
> But less than a month later, John Osborne's *Look Back in Anger* arrived at the Royal Court, and elegant, well-made drawing-room plays like this were supposedly consigned to the dustbin of theatrical history. Yet it is Osborne's drama which now seems strident, sentimental and old-fashioned.[11]

Against this background of an enduring stage presence, the history of *The Chalk Garden* prompts two important questions: why was it so hard for Enid Bagnold to get a first London production for her play and why, after all its success over a long period of time, has it been so ignored by theatre historians? These two questions might both be inflected by gender. In the first instance, in the social and economic push towards a new and productive youth in England, Bagnold was definitely not part of a cultural imperative. She had celebrated her sixty-sixth birthday the day after *The Chalk Garden* opened in New York. (Not that *The Chalk Garden* was her last work for the theatre; Bagnold's final play, *A Matter of Gravity* (Broadhurst Theatre, New York, 1977), was written when she was 86.) Moreover, the playwright was also part of the class establishment and this did not mesh with imaginations of more equitable and accessible English society (inspired by the 1944 Education Act); in 'real life' Enid Bagnold was Lady Jones, wife of Sir Roderick Jones, head of the Reuters News Agency. It is these same identity markers that make her awkward – and therefore absent – in theatre history. The success of a rich old woman is difficult to encompass in the predominant narrative of angry young men. Further, *The Chalk Garden*, so unlike *Look Back in Anger*, focused on the lives of women – a Freudian scene that prefigured the challenges to conventional gender roles that would become a mainstay of second-wave feminist drama little more than a decade later.

In the general preface to *The Cambridge History of British Theatre*, a three-volume set published in 2004, Peter Thomson writes that the 'aim has been to provide a comprehensive "history" that makes no vain pretence to all-inclusiveness. The character of the volumes is the character of their contributors, and those contributors have been more often asked to use a searchlight than a floodlight in order to illuminate the past' (Thomson in Kershaw 2004: xvi). I conclude with this quotation from a very recent theatre history (one where Bagnold does not appear at all) because I think Thomson frames his project in a most useful way. He is right that all-inclusiveness is a futile goal and would, in the end, tell us little about the range and relationships of dramas in the past. But what exactly is the distinction between comprehensive and all-inclusive that it so often occludes women's participation in this particular cultural enterprise, the theatre? Why is it that a searchlight cannot find their contributions (although perhaps a floodlight might)? With its extraordinary success both on Broadway and in the West End – and in all the many places it has been staged since 1956 – *The Chalk Garden* has surely more than earned its place in a comprehensive history of British drama in the twentieth century. Perhaps the searchlight that has had *Look Back in Anger* so long illuminated as the most important play of 1956, casting its long and influential shadow over the rest of English drama to appear in histories of the late twentieth century, need only be moved very slightly indeed to find in its beam a rather different candidate for the year's most important drama: Enid Bagnold's *The Chalk Garden*. If, at the least, Bagnold's play were seen as another significant node in postwar British drama, it might well be that the many women writing plays for the British stage over the last fifty or so years would less often find themselves consigned to 'the feminist alternative'.[12]

ACKNOWLEDGEMENT

The research for this chapter was conducted at the London Theatre Museum archives in October 2004 and the New York Public Library for the Performing Arts in December 2004.

NOTES

1 I am indebted to Maggie Gale's important book, *West End Women: Women and the London Stage 1918–1962* (1996), for its ground-breaking work on the plays of the 1950s as well as its invaluable appendix listing plays by women on the London stage from 1917 to 1959.

2 'History Plays (in) Britain: Dramas, Nations and Inventing the Present' in W. B. Worthen with Peter Holland (eds.). *Theorizing Practice: Redefining Theatre History* (Basingstoke: Palgrave Macmillan, 2003), 151–76, esp. 153. Kruger's chapter provides an important new perspective on the period, using 'history plays' as her focal point: 'history plays rather than immediate state of the nation, on stages outside London, and on the long 1950s rather than the moment of 1956 mythologized by Taylor and Tynan and confirmed in its centrality by Shellard's overview and even by more probing accounts by Lacey and Rebellato, this chapter will attempt to reform and reformulate the history of British theater at the turn of the half-century, at the moment when, as it were, the "contemporary" theater had its day' (154).

3 An earlier essay of mine discusses Lesley Storm's *Roar Like a Dove*, another example of a play with extraordinary commercial success. This play ran for some 1,007 performances between 1957 and 1960. See Bennett (2000: 38–52).

4 Brooks Atkinson (1955). 'The Theatre: Sparkling Cut Glass'. *New York Times* 27 October, L9.

5 A copy of this presentation address is held in the London Theatre Museum archives, consulted October 2004. This award was a prestigious honour, given to very accomplished artists in their respective arts field; for example, in the same year, Aaron Copland won the medal in music.

6 See, for instance, John Osborne, Arnold Wesker, Kingsley Amis, John Braine, Alan Sillitoe and John Wain.

7 Birmingham Feminist History Group (1979). 'Feminism as Femininity in the Nineteen-Fifties?', *Feminist Review* 3, 48. See also John Bowlby (1953). *Childcare and the Growth of Love.* Harmondsworth: Penguin; C. W. Valentine (1956). *The Normal Child and Some of its Abnormalities.* Harmondsworth: Penguin; D. W. Winnicott (1957). *The Child and his Family* and *The Child and his Outside World.* London: Tavistock.

8 This is given as a note in the unnumbered preliminary pages of the Samuel French edition of *The Chalk Garden* (Bagnold 1956).

9 All London reviews are taken from the clippings files for *The Chalk Garden* held in the archives at the London Theatre Museum, consulted October 2004. Hope-Wallace's review was originally published on 13 April 1956.

10 The American and other productions cited here represent a selection of the playbills held in the New York Public Library for the Performing Arts in a file for *The Chalk Garden.*

11 Available in *London Theatre Record*, 25 March–7 April 1992, 385.

12 The expression is taken from Innes's *Modern British Drama*, where 'the feminist alternative' forms the book's first section devoted to women dramatists, some 16 pages in a 572-page book. The only women playwrights to have their own sections are Caryl Churchill (15 pages) and Sarah Kane (8 pages). Thirty-five male playwrights (including John Osborne) appear in section titles.

Primary reading

Bagnold, Enid (1956). *The Chalk Garden*. New York: Samuel French.

Bagnold, Enid (1969). *Autobiography (from 1889)*. London: Heinemann.

Christie, Agatha (1995). *The Mousetrap and Selected Plays*. London: HarperCollins.

Delaney, Shelagh (1959). *A Taste of Honey*. New York: Grove Press.

Hansberry, Lorraine (1994). *A Raisin in the Sun*. New York: Vintage Books.

Hellman, Lillian (1953). *The Children's Hour*. New York: Dramatists Play Service.

Jellicoe, Ann (1964). *The Sport of My Mad Mother*. London: Faber and Faber.

Further reading

Bennett, Susan (2000). 'New Plays and Women's Voices in the 1950s' in Elaine Aston and Janelle Reinelt (eds.). *The Cambridge Companion to Modern British Women Playwrights*. Cambridge: Cambridge University Press, 38–52.

Bhatia, Nandi (1999). 'Anger, Nostalgia, and the End of Empire: John Osborne's Look Back in Anger', *Modern Drama* 42, 391–400.

Friedman, Lenemaja (1986). *Enid Bagnold*. Boston: Twayne.

Gale, Maggie B. (1996). *West End Women: Women and the London Stage 1918–1962*. London: Routledge.

Innes, Christopher (2002). *Modern British Drama: The Twentieth Century*. Cambridge: Cambridge University Press.

Kershaw, Baz (ed.) (2004). *The Cambridge History of British Theatre. Vol. 3: Since 1895*. Cambridge: Cambridge University Press.

Lacey, Stephen (1995). *British Realist Theatre: The New Wave in its Context, 1956–1965*. London: Routledge.

Rebellato, Dan (1999). *1956 and All That: The Making of Modern British Drama*. London: Routledge.

Sebba, Anne (1986). *Enid Bagnold: The Authorized Biography*. London: Weidenfeld and Nicolson.

Shellard, Dominic (2000). '1950–54: Was It a Cultural Wasteland?' in *British Theatre in the 1950s*. Sheffield: Sheffield Academic Press, 28–40.

Shepherd, Simon and Womack, Peter (1996). *English Drama: A Cultural History*. Oxford: Blackwell.

Taylor, John Russell (1962). *Anger and After: A Guide to the New British Drama*. London: Methuen.

15

Home Thoughts from Abroad: Mustapha Matura

D. Keith Peacock

Mustapha Matura was the first British dramatist to interrogate the effects of post-colonialism on national and individual identity and explore the immigrant experience of Britain. Matura challenged the stereotypical white representation of black people in the British theatre of the 1970s in narratives that repositioned black characters from the periphery to the centre and presented colonialism and its effects from the alternative perspective of the colonized rather than that of the colonizer. This repositioning reveals a more complex picture of colonization and immigration than previously conceived in Britain. In the plays by Matura set in Trinidad, the country's postindependence present is measured against its pre-independence past, represented by its traditional culture.

Noel Matura, born in 1939 in Trinidad of Indian parents, arrived in England in 1961. Having worked as a hospital porter, and spent time in Italy, he returned to England in 1963, where, inspired by the 1960s wave of black consciousness, he changed his first name to the less European 'Mustapha', and wrote four short plays. In 1970, Ed Berman of the Ambiance Theatre included these *Black Pieces* in his 'Black and White Power Season' of black American plays. In these short plays, which touch on racism and, in *Party*, on the politics of Black Power, Matura realistically portrays young, black immigrants. It was not only the representation of these characters that was innovatory, but also their use of the Trinidadian Creole that was subsequently to characterize his plays. In the 1970s, this was a political statement in that it challenged the standard English of white drama. Unfamiliar to white British audiences, the argot also identified the plays with the culture of a specific societal group. While the introduction of Trinidadian Creole is indeed a significant *dramatic* innovation, Matura's acute awareness of the visual semiotics of costume is a major feature of his *theatrical* aesthetic. Before taking up writing, Matura had initially intended to be a painter, and probably this, together with his experience of the powerful semiotics of costume exhibited in the Trinidadian carnival – to which he refers directly in *Play Mas* – are the major sources of his aesthetic.

Although Matura was resident in Britain and writing for British theatres and companies, his plays were predominantly set in Trinidad and concerned with the social and political changes that followed independence. Tobago had been a British colony since 1762 and Trinidad, officially, since 1802. The two were united in 1899 and became independent in 1962. Matura's view, as a first-generation immigrant to Britain, was that, 'it's more important where we're coming from. I think we've got to get that clear as a basis, and then we can go anywhere! There's no mental or creative challenge for us here.' For him, therefore, 'the challenge lies in the Caribbean' (Anon. 1981: 10) and 'the common starting point is colonialism' (ibid.: 10). Although his plays were not produced in Trinidad, probably because of their critique of its postindependence society, and it was Britain that nurtured Matura's career as a dramatist, it was his homeland that provided the subject matter and inspiration.

The tension the West Indian diaspora produced between 'where we're coming from' (ibid.: 10) and where we have arrived appears in his first full-length play, *As Time Goes By* (1971). The play, set in Britain, presents first-generation immigrants' attempts to find an identity for themselves at the interface between two cultures. In order to make a living and establish a social status, the Trinidadian-Asian, Ram, utilizes his racial difference to adopt a false identity while deceitfully reporting to his family at home in Trinidad that he is reading for a law degree. Ram, dressed all in white, poses as a swami who will be given 'the respect due to a holy man' (Matura 1992: 66). He is consulted by a number of black immigrants, who want him to find solutions to their problems arising from their emigration to Britain, and by an English couple, who use him to supply them with marijuana. In dramatic terms, besides providing an example of immigrant adaptation to a new culture, he acts as a vehicle for the portrayal of a range of individual experiences of the effects of immigration. The play is structured as a series of personal stories told to Ram and, in effect, the audience. Each of the black visitors who seeks help is in stereotypical immigrant employment, conveyed by his uniform – a black London Transport Underground guard, a London Transport bus conductor and a council dustman. This is the first example of Matura's employment of the visual semiotic of costume to reveal the individual behind the social role. The Underground guard wants to get back his wife, who he feels has abandoned Trinidadian cultural traditions. The bus conductor wants his partner to return to her husband, who is the Underground guard and his brother, by evoking her duty to respect his sick Trinidadian father's wishes. The dustman wants Ram to suggest how to deal with his skinhead son, who talks with a London accent and has thereby abandoned his race and culture. Ram's wife, Batee, who has hidden away in her kitchen for five years, conveys the immigrant's sense of dislocation and desire to return home. Her words, 'de only want we over here ter work fer dem an' ter make dem feel superior, don't mind dem, Trinidad en much but is we own is a heaven compared to dis', are contrasted with Ram's, 'Yer have ter get out an' meet people get ter know dem get ter understand dem' (63). Batee's opinion is substantiated by the two trendy young white characters in the play who use Ram to supply them with marijuana. The play draws no conclusions, it simply portrays in a humorous manner a variety of dilemmas faced by Afro-Caribbean and Indian immigrants from the West Indies. Its use of Trinidadian Creole offers authenticity, affinity and accessibility to an immigrant audience, while the exposure of individual character behind the external social role challenges white stereotyping of immigrants and explores their dilemmas.

Matura's visit to Trinidad in 1973, the first since his emigration to Britain, radically altered his dramatic perspective. After this he looked back, sometimes satirically, to his pre- and postindependence homeland. In these 'state of the nation' plays, Matura portrays Trinidad's various ethnic groups and explores the interracial tensions between Afro-Caribbeans and Asians and their desperate efforts to define themselves as true Trinidadians. He also dramatizes the social and political uncertainty, realignment and scramble for dominance created by independence from colonial subordination. This realignment is revealed to have produced financial corruption, social unrest and tension between commercial and traditional values, in an emergent consumerist society influenced by the United States and funded by petro-dollars. Finally, with implicit reference to attempted coups by Black Power activists in 1970, and Islamic extremists in 1990, Matura employs farce to comment on violent insurrection resulting from the scramble for political supremacy among the ethnic groups. Colonialism is shown to have robbed the country of its sense of history, leaving it searching for an identity in the modern world and prey to commercial and political exploitation from Marxist and capitalist countries. The plays are not, however, heavy political tracts but satirical comedies that focus on human fallibility, attack corruption in all its forms, and undercut pretentiousness and pomposity.

In the first of these plays, *Play Mas* (1974), the transition from pre- to postcolonial society is represented against the background of the traditional carnival, 'Play Mas', with its steel bands competition and spectacular costumes (Riggio 2004). As befits a play about *Mas* – meaning mask or masquerade – the visual semiotics of costume plays a significant role in the play not only in representing role and status but also in the action. The death of Miss Gookool, who owns a tailoring shop in Port-of-Spain, results from shock at the threatening incursion of her previous employee, Samuel, disguised in the 'Mas' of a US marine. The latter makes an oblique reference to the Black Power revolution of 1970, which actually began during the carnival with a Mas band, the Pinetoppers, portraying revolutionary heroes including Fidel Castro, Stokely Carmichael and Malcolm X.

Colonial Trinidad is portrayed as having a complex and rigid social structure divided along racial lines. Unskilled blacks, represented by Samuel, undertake menial tasks. Samuel, nevertheless, has his own sense of identity and refuses the appellation of 'African', which he considers to be a reference to the primitive. His description of Africans is also couched in visual terms – 'No, I do' live in a tree an wear no bush clothes an paint up my face, I is a Trinidadian' (Matura 1992: 119). As his native language is English, he also identifies with the colonial power and claims its nationality. Indians, like the matriarch Miss Gookool and her son Ramjohn, run small businesses, theirs being a simple tailoring shop. Ramjohn, however, also maintains a sense of individual identity and denies his Indian heritage, preferring to be recognized as a businessman and, like Samuel, as a Trinidadian. Miss Gookool considers herself to be superior to black Trinidadians, who she says 'en' human. Dey is dog, feed dem and they happy' (126). Such small businesses as theirs make little profit from poor black Trinidadians, represented by Frank. They are dependent for any significant income on the white employers, in this case Mr McKay, a British oilman who wears the colonial ruler's 'uniform' of short-sleeved white shirt, khaki shorts, knee socks and shoes. His order for factory overalls is so coveted that Miss Gookool is willing to bribe him with freshly baked roti.

The threat to this social hierarchy is posed by the call from the Afro-Caribbean-dominated People's National Movement (PNM) for independence. The call is supported by Frank, who considers that this will lead to more prosperity if the government reverses the split in oil profits from 75:25 in favour of the oil companies to 75:25 in favour of Trinidad. The social hierarchy, he contends, will also be altered so that the Afro-Caribbeans like himself will no longer be subservient, and will be given opportunities to advance equal to those enjoyed by the Indians, whose children become lawyers and doctors. When he is insulted and ordered out of the shop by Miss Gookool, his tone becomes more threatening, auguring the possibility of interracial conflict similar to that which emerged in Jamaica after independence: 'allyer Indian better watch out' (117). The threat appears to be realized in the following scene, in which the 'Mas' worn by Samuel and his Deparado Steel Band, who represent the American film *Sands of Iwo Jima*, is that of an American marine carrying a machine gun. The significance of Samuel's 'Mas' is reinforced by his assertion that Indians do not know how to play Mas and, implicitly, do not, therefore, share in Trinidadian culture and tradition. Samuel explains to Ramgool that he is now a member of the PNM and is in charge of an area. Like Frank he asserts black supremacy: 'wen we come ter power we go change dis whole island, upside down, we go make all dem people who was taking advantage a we, suffer, we go make dem bawl, yer go see' (132). Ramjohn's mother having died, the scene closes with him dancing out in a forlorn attempt to be seen as truly Trindadian, shouting 'Play Mas' and 'PNM, PNM' (138). By employing the semiotic connotations of the costume of an indigenous cultural event, the Mas, Matura conveys visually the postindependence reconfiguration of Trinidad's social hierarchy and its realignment from British colonialism to American economic imperialism.

In the second act, set after independence, Matura casts a satirical eye on the postcolonial administration's failings of authoritarianism, financial corruption, repression, self-aggrandizement, and political and economic incompetence. The setting of the first scene in an office with a barred window occupied by Samuel, who is now chief of police, immediately conveys the authoritarian nature of the new regime. The topic of corruption is introduced by the fact that Samuel does not wear a uniform but a flashy suit bought in New York. His suit signifies that he has rejected British colonialism in favour of the material benefits to be accrued from American imperialism. The corruption is made explicit by the arrival of Samuel's wife, who wants to share the financial advantages, in terms of clothes and having a chauffeur, enjoyed by the wives of other government officials.

As part of the government's repressive policy, Samuel wants to employ Ramjohn as a spy to discover if any potential unrest is fermenting in his neighbourhood that might threaten the government and discourage American corporate investment, represented by Chuck Reynolds, who has replaced the colonial employer, Mr McKay. As a result of earlier riots the administration has declared a state of emergency and banned public assembly. Now 'nobody car' give no public speech or criticise de Government' (155). A conflict between the old and the new arises when representatives of the church, the tourist industry and the undertakers petition Samuel to lift the state of emergency in order to permit the carnival, which, they argue, allows the people to vent their frustrations and promotes tourism. Samuel, however, considers the carnival to be a thing of the past, which must be eradicated if Trinidad is to be integrated into the modern global economy. 'We progressing, but Carnival en' progress, Carnival is long time colonial ting, ... what we want, we want buildings and engineers and investments' (158).

At the close of the play the Carnival Mas is again employed by Matura to reveal the characters' self-perceived roles and status. Samuel's wife bedecks herself as an aristocrat in a copy of Annigoni's portrait dress for Queen Elizabeth II. Reynolds's image is that of an American tourist, with his Hawaiian shirt and Bermuda shorts. The extent of Samuel's authoritarianism is signified by his South American general's uniform. The nature of his power is revealed by his police sergeant's full battle-dress and machine gun, while, off-stage, Samuel's police officers, dressed as German storm troopers, are arresting anyone they consider to be a potential terrorist. Using the distraction of the Carnival, which becomes a mask for his actions, Samuel orders his men to attack those on the hill whom he considers to be potential rebels, and who have promised to cease any rebellious activity in return for the rescinding of the state of emergency. The postcolonial governance of Trinidad is, therefore, satirized by Matura as a grotesque Carnival Mas, whose participants are corrupt, oppressive, and willing to abandon Trinidad's cultural heritage in return for personal wealth and status.

In *Independence* (1979), Matura muses, through the interplay of past and present, upon the effects of postcolonialism in Trinidad. The action takes place in 1978 in the overtly symbolic setting of the pool bar of the abandoned Imperial Hotel, signifying Trinidad's colonial past, which, in the new republic, is now a people's recreation area. The uniforms worn by the two waiters who work in the bar show that for them nothing has changed and that they are still 'servants', not now of the colonial rulers but of their own republican government. As the young waiter, Allen, describes it, 'dis place colonize we, it showed we something we never had an something we could never get' (Matura 1992: 230). The past is represented by the barman, Drakes, who is in his sixties and wears a correct waiter's uniform: 'I believe in de past. I could see de past, dat's why, look at dis hotel' (173). Hopes for the future are voiced by Allen, who is in his twenties and has been drafted by the government to work in the bar. He yearns to be a farmer and looks to the future: 'I have plenty of hope as long as dey have termorrow I have hope' (173). To convey the past Matura incorporates the Trinidadian oral tradition by having Drakes relate to Allen a history of the colonial past. Drakes is, however, unable to comprehend that history is evidence of colonial oppression. It is for Allen to recognize its iniquities and to suggest a plan for the future. Progress is to be made not through violence, represented by his reference to a Molotov cocktail, but by the development of an agrarian economy that will make the island self-sufficient. He realizes, however, that colonial history discourages this concept, for, in the black folk memory, slaves were chained to ploughs to work under the hot sun. For them the future lies not on the land but in an office or in driving a truck.

The present is represented by Howard, the bureaucrat from the 'Department' in his 'grade three suit' (189) with its 'Mao-type jacket' (193). He claims that things have changed:

> Surely you have heard of the Government's your Government I might add, efforts to eradicate all traces of class distinctions . . . . We are not ashamed of our colonial past, in fact they left us with some very sound institutions. The Civil Service for instance. But let us take the good an use it to our benefit, an the bad, like status and titles let them proceed to the dustbins. Let us be progressive an forward looking. (194)

Drakes points out that things are the same as they were under the colonial power – 'yer jump in de water like fish an carry on de same ting, power, power in yer mind' (226) – and that Allen 'is de only chance we have' (226) because he envisages a different way forward.

The bar has no customers and sells only beer, Coca-Cola and bottled rum-punch, making Drakes's bartending skills redundant. Howard threatens to close the bar, thereby abandoning the past, if, by the end of the day, there are no sales. Drakes will be unemployed but Allen will be released, government permitting, to become a farmer. The colonial past appears to come to Drakes's rescue when a former governor and his wife arrive in the hotel, the man to recall old times, his wife to exorcize past guilt. They represent the social and psychological legacy of colonialism, which again is conveyed by story-telling. 'We came here', says the wife, 'and caused things, we took things and left some, we made scars, deep scars, we can't pretend we didn't' (216). Allen adds colonialism's economic effects: 'Governed by greed, de English people drain dis colony dry an all de resources dey had' (231). The governor's wife caused a man's death. Having seduced a waiter, she was rushed from the island to avoid scandal, while he was left to stand trial for rape. In spite of being given a light sentence he hanged himself, knowing that he would not be able to prove his innocence. The truth about the cruelty and exploitation of colonization was, therefore, suppressed. In guilty recompense for her behaviour, while still not being prepared to reveal it, the governor's wife leaves Allen with a bundle of notes amounting to thousands of pounds. With this he can start a new life if he is permitted to resign, for the people's republic, like the oppressive colonial slave-system, commands the workforce.

The resolution of the debate concerning the future is portrayed in Act III, in which Allen and his girlfriend, Yvonne, return a year later to the now wrecked bar. Allen is a successful farmer who has come to town to celebrate Independence Day. During the short act Matura summarizes the symbolic implications of the play and the significance of independence.

> I needed this place ter show we where we come from an where we going yes, we need places like dis dat is one a de jokes about it, we need de horror ter show we or else we could never know, my eyes open in dis place, ter what we was, what we used ter be an I value if fer date ter push off, push off from it yes I need it, I need dis place ... .I saw tings clear here fer de first time in my life how der system operated how it killed people. (233)

The partial emergence of Drakes out of the darkness, his shoulders and face obscured, moves the play even further towards symbolism. Drakes's spectre claims to be the watchman who must not permit the hotel to be resurrected, and is slowly but purposefully trampling its crumbling remains. He challenges Allen to move forward, 'so go, do' look back, do' come back, it en go be here, you have notting ter look back here for dat's what I'm here for I is de watchman' (234). Although lessons may be learned from the past concerning individual freedom, history must be left behind in favour of the creation of more equitable social and economic structures. *Independence* is the most symbolic, most narratively focused and, although there is some humour, most serious of Matura's plays.

The future agrarian society envisaged by Allen in *Independence* is replaced in *Meetings* (1982) by an oil-rich, materialistic society in which the young are not farmers but 'Yuppies'. In place of the decaying hotel recalling the past, the setting is now a sparkling new, labour-saving, but clearly unused and therefore soulless kitchen in Trinidad. A young married couple, Hugh and Jean, have accrued material possessions ranging from a big house in the best neighbourhood with a swimming pool, to a Mercedes, golf clubs and a fur coat – for Jean's trips to New York.

In this location Matura illustrates the conflict between past traditions and modern global commerce. Although this is a domestic setting, its occupants are formally dressed in business suits and are not eating but merely drinking their morning coffee. This is a superficial world of capitalist spectacle, in which the minister of finance is made fun of by the couple because he is unaware of 'correct' external appearance, wears a grey suit and brown shoes, and has no experience in business. Because they are so busy with meetings, Hugh and Jean always eat in restaurants, and the play's action is generated by Hugh's yearning for traditional home-cooked Trinidadian fare.

The play develops as a moral fable in which Hugh meets a wise old woman who reconnects him with his culture and causes him to see the amorality of his position as a high-flying businessman, while Jean refuses to learn the lesson, which she considers as retrogressive. Matura satirizes the shallowness and greed of a society that puts money before people's welfare. Jean promotes imported American cigarettes geared particularly to the tropical market, the secret chemical ingredient of which is found to cause coughing fits and death. Tradition is represented by the old woman, Marie, selling mangos and other indigenous fruits at the roadside. Marie never appears on stage. Nevertheless, she profoundly influences Hugh's behaviour, as she provides him not only with food but also with a cook in the form of her granddaughter, Elsa. Hugh also turns to her for sage advice about the quality of his business colleagues. From Marie, Hugh learns about slave history, traditional medicine and Shango ritual. Somewhat romantically, Hugh rejects his material life and returns to his cultural roots, while Jean is dying from the effects of the dangerous commercial product she is trying to foist onto the community. *Meetings* is not, however, a political polemic, but simply a fable concerning loss of identity in postindependence Trinidad.

The Coup: A Play of Revolutionary Dreams was commissioned in 1991 by the National Theatre, by which time Matura was Britain's leading black playwright. A year after a short-lived Islamic coup in which Trinidad's president was held hostage, Matura portrays a fictional coup in which the president has been imprisoned and possibly executed. The play's surreal quality is established by the opening funeral oration for the president, Edward Francis Jones. It is delivered in a cathedral by an archbishop disconcertingly speaking in creole, in what turns out to be a dream sequence. The archbishop's Marxist historical approach, which links the man and the historical moment, is employed to point satirically to the Trinidadian national character.

> We made him, but a nation is a funny ting, yer know, it could make you or break you, especially, when it made up of every race, colour, creed, religion an sect with a lust an greed, to be bigger and better than their neighbours by any means possible, who could govern an make them live together, nobody, but for every moment there is the man, Edward Francis Jones, was that man. (Matura 1991: 2)

The president, the play reveals, indeed embodies the nation's moral fallibility. As trade minister he benefits from being provided with a whore in East Berlin as bribe to purchase much-needed flour. At the same time he has a mistress in Miami. In this, although operating in a wider international sphere, he claims proudly that beneath his public persona, in one aspect at least, he is a stereotypical 'Trinidadian man' (28). He is self-assured and calm during the crisis and exploits his captors' incompetence. These qualities, together with his humour, make him an attractive character despite his moral fallibility.

In this play Matura again casts the present against the past. In a dream sequence, Columbus arrives in Trinidad and, in claiming it for Spain and attempting to discover from the native Arawaks whether they have gold-mines and can fly, he unwittingly gives a prearranged signal for his ship lying off the coast to fire on the sandy hill on which they are standing.

The form of the play suggests that in Trinidad, history, as Marx asserted, is indeed repeated as farce. The coup descends swiftly into chaos, its leaders who have imprisoned the president fighting amongst themselves, unable to establish control, their actions becoming increasingly farcical. The rebels' command that television technicians broadcast a video-tape of their revolutionary aims and objectives is ignored in favour of an old *Wheel of Fortune* episode. A rebel leader, Major Ferret, attempts to shoot the president because his executioner, Black Lightning, who doesn't like hurting people, claims that he cannot break the president's neck because of a sore back. Instead Major Ferret shoots himself when the bullet ricochets off a wall during a sudden blackout, caused by one of the prison guards hanging his rifle on the fuse box handle. In another scene, after Lieutenant Chan has killed a rival rebel leader, he blames Black Lightning for the deed and inefficiently organizes a firing squad for his execution. After an absurd discussion concerning Black Lightning's claim that he is 'a tool in the hands of sociological, economic, genetic and more powerful forces', and that he is about to offer Chan 'the answer to man's search for total an complete control of the forces of nature', the lieutenant interrupts to ask for light, 'light as in fire, ye know wat dat means, fire, fire' (61), for the victim's final cigarette. In doing so, like Columbus, he orders the firing squad to shoot, in this case at Black Lightning, and thus never learns the answer. The rebellion ends in farce with Major Ferret and Lieutenant Chan blowing themselves up by lighting cigars as a sign of rapprochement in front of a leaking petrol tank. Ironically, they are killed by the substance that would provide the petro-dollars necessary to establish a new regime! The president's dream of his death and memorial provides a fittingly surreal conclusion to the play. The setting is again the cathedral, where two workman stand by the coffin:

WORKMAN 1:   A hear some reactionary elements, aided an abetted by South African
mercenaries tried to rescue him from de people's custody an a Uzi machine pistol fall
out if a sleeping sentry hand an start firing by itself an one of de bullets hit a nail on a
bean over he head an on de nail was a old iron anchor an dat fall on he head.

(67)

The explanation is farcical but it has a disturbing resemblance to justifications offered by tyrannical regimes throughout the world. Finally, two nuns discuss the gigantic size of the late president's penis, a priapic memorial he would have chosen to leave to the nation. In his dream, it is fought over by the Natural History Museum and the Agricultural Department as 'part of we history' (69). Although *The Coup* portrays Trinidadian politics as characterized by muddle and unsuccessful in establishing stable, equitable and moral governance, Matura also celebrates Trinidadian individualism in the form of the president, the stereotypical sexual 'Trinidadian man'.

Matura's emigration to Britain and his experience of Trinidad before and after independence gave him not only geographic but also cultural and critical distance from his homeland. 'Living in the UK and writing about Trinidad, that's the perfect distance and the safest way' (Lee 1999: 13), he told an interviewer in 1999. Through the rhythm of his characters' speech and his sometimes subversive humour and satire, together with his widespread employment of visual semiotics, Matura conveys a vibrant picture of multi-ethnic Trinidadian life and culture, whose sense of national and individual identity shifts between Afro-Caribbean, Indian and English. He also introduces into mainstream British theatre a serious critique of postindependence Trinidad from the point of view of the colonized, which, owing to continued immigration from its former colonies, still has relevance to Britain today.

PRIMARY READING

Matura, Mustapha (1972). *As Time Goes By and Black Pieces*. London: Calder and Boyars.

Matura, Mustapha (1991). *The Coup: A Play of Revolutionary Dreams*. London: Methuen.

Matura, Mustapha (1992). *Six Plays: As Time Goes By, Play Mas, Independence, Welcome Home Jacko, Nice, Meetings*. London: Methuen.

FURTHER READING

Anon. (1981). 'Finding a Name' in *Platform* 3. London: Calverts North Star Press, 7–14.

Childs, Peter and Williams, R. J. Patrick (1997). *An Introduction to Post-Colonial Theory*. Hemel Hempstead: Prentice Hall.

Fanon, Frantz (1965). *The Wretched of the Earth*. New York: Grove Press.

Fanon, Frantz (1968). *Black Skin, White Masks*. New York: Grove Press.

Gardner, Lyn (1985). 'Art and Soul', *Plays and Players*, May, 14–15.

Hall, Stuart (1992). 'New Ethnicities' in *James Donald and Ali Rattansi. 'Race', Culture and Difference*. London: Sage, 252–9.

Joseph, May (1995). 'Performing in the Postcolony: The Plays of Mustapha Matura' in Roman De la Campa, Michael Sprinker and Ann Kaplan (eds.). *Late Imperial Culture*. London and New York: Verso, 179–96.

Lee, Simon (1999). 'The Man in the Corner House', *Sunday Guardian* 19 December, 13.

McMillan, Michael (2000). 'Ter Speak in yer Mudder Tongue: An Interview with Playwright Mustapha Matura' in Kwesi Owusu (ed.). *Black British Culture and Society*. London and New York: Routledge, 255–64.

Meighoo, Kirk Peter (2003). *Politics and the Half-Made Society: Trinidad and Tobago 1925–2001*. Oxford: James Curry.

Nasta, Susheila (2004). 'Voyaging In: Colonialism and Migration' in Laura Marcus and Peter Nicholls (eds.). *The Cambridge History of Twentieth-Century English Literature*. Cambridge: Cambridge University Press, 563–82.

Riggio, Milla Cozart (2004). *Carnival: Culture in Action – The Trinidad Experience*. New York: Routledge.

Sivanandan, Ambalavaner (1982). *A Different Hunger: Writings on Black Resistance*. London: Pluto Press.

Williams, Patrick and Chrisman, Laura (eds.) (1994). *Colonial Discourse and Postcolonial Theory: A Reader*. Harlow: Longman.

16

The Remains of the British Empire: The Plays of Winsome Pinnock

Gabriele Griffin

It seems to me that when we look at plays and interpret them, we're not embracing what's actually happening in the world, that there is far more collision and clash and influence between different groups, and that things are breaking down much more than we acknowledge.

Pinnock (in Edgar 1999: 59)

Introduction

The gap[1] which Pinnock's pessimistic statement of 1999 identifies between seeing and reading plays, on the one hand, and what is 'actually happening in the world', on the other, points to the (perennial) question of the relationship between representation and material reality in agonistic contexts such as the current one. That context has, from the early 1990s – following on from the demise of the communist regimes in 1989 and the so-called Balkan wars of the 1990s, to various tragic events in Britain, such as the murder of Stephen Lawrence in 1993 and the Hatfield train crash in 2000, that have resulted in major public inquiries – fuelled a new wave of political theatre, nationally and internationally, which has closed the temporal gap between what is actually happening in the world and representation, through the immediacy with which writers have responded to those events in various cultural forms including performance.[2] The need to make sense of, and give meaning to, events that mark and shape public and personal histories becomes more acute at moments of crisis, but such crises do not necessarily occur unexpectedly or *ex nihilo*; they are the products of longer-term developments, histories, movements and interactions which cast their shadows on both the present and the future. And, as historiographies from the 1960s onwards, and in particular the work of working-class and feminist historians, have shown, 'what is actually happening in the world' may be measured in terms of the lives of 'ordinary' people, of the everyday, of the particular as expressive of the general (Summerfield 2005). Such is the case in relation to the British Empire and its transformation and demise in the course of the twentieth century, a history which informs the theatre work of Winsome Pinnock.

At the centre of this history is a series of key issues that one might describe as the remains or legacies of the British Empire – even as they are not exclusive to it.[3] Winsome Pinnock's plays explore and touch on many issues which now preoccupy postcolonial theorists:

- a history of colonization that involves migration to the colony by the colonizer, and a later migration of the colonized to the colonizer's country;
- an identification by those from the colonized countries with the colonizer's country as 'the motherland', which is not matched by an identification of the colonizers with the colonized, leading to disillusionment with 'the mother country' and sometimes attempts to reconnect to the homeland;
- a racialized power structure that maintains the inferiority of the colonized and the superiority of the colonizer;
- the impoverishment of the colonized countries through extraction of labour and goods;
- the colonized's dream of material improvement through migration to the centre;
- racism, sexism and persistent denigration of the colonized by the colonizer;
- the exploitation of women's sexual and non-sexual labour;
- the abandonment of women by men as part of the internalization of racism;
- cyclical experiences across female generations of exploitation, early pregnancy, lack of education, single motherhood, coupled with a persistent belief in the desirability of heteronormativity;
- a persistent search for identity, brought about by the experience of double alienation – from the 'homeland' and from the 'mother country'.

All these issues feature recurrently in Pinnock's work, which seeks to effect a negotiation between past and present, black and white, empiric histories and their legacies.

The Racial Politics of Theatre and Theatre-Going

One of the legacies of the British Empire in Britain is its multicultural society, a society whose members continue to have unequal access to resources, including cultural resources. Winsome Pinnock herself (b. 1961) is of Jamaican descent and grew up in London with three other siblings 'in a single-parent home', her mother a cleaner (interview with Dhingra 2005: n.p.). When asked by Dhingra 'Were you brought up with books in the house?' she replied: 'Well, "the book". I was brought up with "the book"in the house. In a West Indian household obviously the Bible is a very big thing. That was the main book.' Her interest in theatre stemmed from school trips: 'My family didn't, or didn't at the time, go to the theatre. But there were lots of school trips to the theatre and I just fell in love with the whole thing' (Dhingra 2005).

Pinnock's comments formed part of the programme notes for her play *One Under*, staged in February 2005 at the Tricycle Theatre in Kilburn, London, which previously premiered Winsome Pinnock's *Water* (2000) and which has a policy of promoting theatre work by black, Asian and Irish playwrights. Set in London and in part on the London underground, the play focuses on underground train driver Cyrus's experience of, and reactions to, someone throwing himself in front of his train and committing suicide. Cyrus embarks on a journey to try to understand why Sonny, the victim, killed himself.

The cast for the play was mixed, featuring three black men, three white women, and two black women. I sat through it, trying to decide what the racial politics of the play were, and whether or not the casting choices mattered. The remains of the British Empire? For Pinnock, according to the programme notes, they both did and did not matter. In her interview with Dolly Dhingra,[4] Pinnock responded to the question 'Have you felt that you need to write for black actors or that you need to tell black stories?' with an unambiguous 'Yes' and then explained that writing for black actors was part of her 'own personal belief in equality', and also that 'this play could actually be played by lots of different kinds of people, but I've stipulated that it's cast in various ways because I can do that as a writer' (Dhingra 2005). The published play text itself does not 'colour-code' the cast; other than in terms of the first names used (we may think that 'Cyrus', 'Sonny' and 'Aleysha' are names more likely to be given to black than to white people) and the intermittent use of patois, there is little to indicate any race-based casting. The play's narrative, too, is not one that articulates an obvious 'race issue'; Pinnock describes it as 'an exploration of life'. Yet on viewing it, I found myself dwelling on its potential racial politics, not least because Cyrus is a black underground train driver in London and one of his interlocutors is a black cleaner on the underground. This replays one particular employment history of the British Empire repeatedly presented in Pinnock's plays, such as *A Hero's Welcome* (1986), *Leave Taking* (1987), *A Rock in Water* (1989) and *Mules* (1996), namely the extraction of black labour from colonized countries to support the expansion of the post-World War II British economy in certain predominantly underpaid and menial employment sectors, such as public transport and the service sector, including cleaning and nursing. *One Under* thus starts from a specific post-empiric situation. Additionally, the performance I watched, and productions at the Tricycle Theatre in my experience in general, draw black as much as white audiences – when I went to see *One Under*, for example, at least 60 per cent of the audience was black and about a third of these were older black women, a group one rarely sees in theatres in Britain. Would that audience have come to the play if it had not been by a well-known black woman playwright and if the cast had not included black actors? I am not sure.

Pinnock herself is very aware of the racialized nature of theatre-going; in her interview with Heidi Stephenson and Natasha Langridge she pointed out that 'in a theatre like the Royal Court there isn't usually a single black face', and bemoaned the fact that although her plays attract 'new' audiences, 'they never stay, which is a real shame' (Stephenson and Langridge 1997: 53). She argued that the Theatre Royal, Stratford East, is 'the only theatre that's been successful in mixing its audiences' (ibid.). This, I presume, refers to London (where, in fact, the Tricycle and the Lyric Hammersmith have been equally effective in regularly securing mixed audiences), since theatres outside London such as the Birmingham Rep, the West Yorkshire Playhouse, the Leicester Haymarket, the Green Room in Manchester, the Square Chapel in Halifax and others have all been equally successful in regularly attracting mixed audiences, from Caribbean, Asian and other backgrounds, though, it also has to be said, such audiences tend to come to plays by playwrights and featuring actors from their communities. As playwright and director Paulette Randall put it in 2003: 'it's still a political act to put a black person on stage' (Kolawole 2003: 2).

That act is political because it talks of the history of empire and challenges the notion that those once colonized are not part of the cultural centre of the former empire. As such it both reminds of empire and attempts to transcend that legacy. This relates to issues of history, remembrance, identity and identification – all addressed in Paul Gilroy's *After Empire: Melancholia or Convivial Culture?* in which he, *inter alia*, analyses the impact of the 9/11 attacks on the United States on the production of contemporary history, and argues that those attacks have wrongly displaced our engagement with colonial pasts and empires in favour of the 'war on terror', seen as the latest agonistic structure overwhelming contemporary consciousness (Gilroy 2004: 11). Gilroy proposes continuities between 'racism and colonial history' and the political and ideological investments that have been spawned by the 9/11 attacks. Old world orders do not simply disappear but are transformed in the face of other disruptions, themselves not to be understood as something entirely new and unprecedented but an effect of those older world orders. It is in this spirit that I propose to discuss the plays of Winsome Pinnock, which in a number of ways grapple with the issue of historical and social dis/continuities as experienced by the Jamaican community whose members migrated to Britain.

Going Back to One's Roots

Pinnock herself has repeatedly discussed the importance of representing both her life as a black woman in Britain and that of her community in her work. To Stephenson and Langridge, for example, she said: 'I want to address certain subjects: the way that cultures collide and the way race and the whole issue of identity presents itself to me in my own life; the different stages I go through in my own life, the different developments I see in various communities that I am part of' (Stephenson and

Langridge 1997: 47). The agonistic struggle Pinnock refers to here is one embedded in and derived from the historical legacies of empire,[5] played out between post-World War II Britain and Jamaica, the two sites where the action of Pinnock's plays is predominantly located, frequently alternating between the two. *A Hero's Welcome*,[6] set in 1947, concerns the different views of England held by those who have been to Britain and those who have not. As in all of Pinnock's works, racialized and genderized/sexualized exploitation is at the centre of this play. Len, a man from Jamaica who joined the British forces during World War II, returns to Jamaica where he is treated like a war hero, not least because of the leg injury he has sustained. Unable to resist his community's pressure to be the hero, he maintains a narrative of battlefield experience, which is only shattered when he eventually reveals that he had an industrial accident in the munitions factory where he spent the war working because 'They wouldn't work beside us, they didn't want to pay us what we were worth, they even went on strike to get rid of us. We forgot where the real war was because we were fighting one right there' (Pinnock 1993: 54).[7] Len has learnt his lessons regarding the racism that pervades Britain and has no desire to return. Despite the poverty of Jamaica, there, at least, he can command respect and make a life for himself. Minda, the girl whom he marries, on the other hand, is determined to move beyond the poverty and limited material prospects which characterize her existence. Having already prostituted herself to the white local plantation owner in exchange for material goods, she dreams of a life in England that will be economically empowering and, in the end, is persuaded to run away with Stan, who succumbs to the call to provide labour for the 'mother country' ('All over the island them putting up posters: "Come to England", "Come find a job in England", "The motherland needs you"'; ibid.: 44) and does not understand the denigration and racial oppression that await him in England. Since neither Minda nor Stan knows what really happened to Len in England they have no way of understanding the problems they will face. They engage in a process of mutual exploitation: Stan wants Minda to join him because she has the pecuniary means to get them to England; Minda sees her own opportunities for her economic empowerment as tied to her choice of male and is thus repeatedly used – first by the plantation owner, who fobs her off with worthless trinkets in exchange for sex, and secondly by Stan, who benefits from her illicit earnings derived from stealing from the plantation owner.

The same gendered dynamic also underlies *Leave Taking* (1987),[8] which centres on the intergenerational differences and conflicts between first- and second-generation migrants in London.[9] Enid, a first-generation migrant, follows her husband from the West Indies to London, only to discover that he has deserted her for a white woman. She is left a single mother, to bring up her two daughters. Typically for first-generation migrants of her period, her main concern is to integrate into English society, and for her daughters to do the same. This includes a denial of one's background which comes to haunt the children of first-generation migrants as they try to find an identity of their own – between their parents' countries of origin (if such countries can be identified),[10] to which they may have little or no connection, and a Britain that rejects them in racist terms as inferior. Pinnock explains that denial of the past in terms of the discrepancy between expectation and reality, between aspiration and actual opportunity:

> That's based on when I was growing up. If you ask anybody my age they'll say, 'They never told us anything about where they came from, how they lived.' And in *Leave Taking*, in my own life, I suppose, the silence was to do with a sense of shame. The sort of poverty they came from was shameful, they thought. And there was a desire for their children to be British, and therefore to forget about the past. I remember being told off if I spoke with a West Indian accent. 'Don't. You're British. Speak English.'
> (Stephenson and Langridge 1997: 49)

The assumption that a denial of one's past might result in integration into British society proves erroneous since it also denies a key marker of racism, skin colour, which cannot be readily eradicated, and which immediately places those viewed as black – no matter what their 'actual' colour – in the position of other (Ahmed 1997). In Paul Gilroy's (1987) phrase, 'there ain't no black in the Union Jack'. Enid's exhortations to her daughters, often repeated in plays covering a similar period and phase of black migration to Britain,[11] to do everything to integrate themselves and in particular to 'speak properly', to avoid getting pregnant early, and to get an education, map her values and aspirations but do not coincide with her daughters' experiences and desires. Unmoored in their sense of identity by a lack of affinity with their mother's country of origin and unaccepted within British culture, Enid's daughters both do all the things she had wanted them to avoid, such as leaving school before finishing exams and getting pregnant early, and, importantly, seeking to reconnect to their mother's country against her wishes.

Pinnock's plays from the 1980s and 1990s in particular repeatedly highlight the importance of cyclicity, of connecting to one's roots, and indeed, the celebration of that connection to a female genealogy.[12] In *Leave Taking* Del, Enid's older daughter, feels empowered by her pregnancy and prospect of becoming a single mum to take control of her life and, with the help of Mai, an obeah or wise woman who plies her trade from a London bedsit, to become an obeah herself, thus setting herself up in a situation which enables her both to work from home and to look after her future child. Enid's other daughter, Viv, decides that she wants to go to the West Indies to reconnect to her mother's homeland, and Enid herself feels that she wants to return there. The final scene shows Enid and Viv in mutual embrace articulating their need to be mothered. If Enid's life suggests the impossibility of realizing one's dream and the dangers of cutting off from one's roots (in fact, it can also be argued that Enid has never done so), her daughters' experiences indicate the possibilities of recasting one's life through maintaining connection to one's ancestral cultures and lands.

This message is also vividly conveyed in *Talking in Tongues* (1991), in which Leela and Claudette, disappointed by their lives in London and the ways in which they are treated by the black men in their lives on the one hand, and by white people more generally on the other, decide to return to Jamaica for a holiday in order to regenerate themselves. In this play, too, Pinnock evokes a female genealogy through the narrative of Sugar, an island woman, who in the opening prologue describes observing adult women when she was a child, 'talking in tongues', having an epiphanic experience through physical release, through a coming to self via the body. Significantly, Sugar gives Leela a massage whilst telling her this story, and ends it by saying: 'But all that finish now, them women dead off long time. Me, I just go walk down by the beach, lift weight, jog, take aerobic exercise. No need now to go down the gully, eh?' (see prologue, Pinnock 1995: 174). This body-centred opening scene, which contrasts present-day body practices such as massage and exercising with 'talking in tongues', sets the agenda for the play in that it highlights women's need to (re)connect to themselves via their bodies.

Leela's alienation from British culture finds somatic expression in her difficulties with the embodied practice of speaking:

> I've always been really self-conscious about the way I speak . . . I mispronounce words . . . It's because this isn't my first language, you see. Not that I have a real first language, but sometimes I imagine that there must have been, at some time . . . If you don't feel you belong to a language then you're only half alive aren't you, because you haven't the words to bring yourself into existence. (ibid.: 195)

That linguistically manifested alienation lends expression to her sense of divorce from her own literal and metaphorical body, if the literal body is understood as the denigrated black female body (denigrated because it is black and female), and the metaphorical body is understood as a community of which one is part. Leela remembers the frightening sight of her mother 'surrendering to the spirit every Sunday afternoon' and its worrying somatic consequences: as 'she fell to the ground you'd pull back her eyelid and it was like looking into the eyes of the dead' (ibid.: 194). Irma, a hermaphroditic character, explains to Leela that 'our mothers had religion'[13] which was their way of 'releasing pain' and not allowing themselves to become victims (ibid.: 194). Whilst one may question the extent to which any religion can provide possibilities of transcending victim status for women, Pinnock's plays celebrate that possibility, not in terms of institutionalized religion but with respect to the recovery of the alienated body by women for themselves.

Pinnock also makes a very clear distinction in her work between the achievement of being reunited with the abjected body through a spiritual experience, and using the body for sexual purposes. Whilst Leela takes the opportunity in Jamaica to walk the island and get to know it through physically exploring it – thus undergoing a spiritually powered process of reunification with her alienated body – her friend Claudette spends her time acting like a conventional sex tourist, seeking to empower herself through the sexual desire she can create in those around her, with no regard to the feelings of the indigenous women whom she might hurt by her sexual exploitation of the local men. Claudette does unto those women as she feels is done unto her in Britain, where white women find it easy to usurp black men. Where Leela eventually regains her self ('I've got used to walking here...You've got to be in touch with your body'; ibid.: 225), Claudette has no such experience and remains embroiled in the disempowering interpersonal dynamics she has acquired through her experiences of racism and sexism in Britain. As Aston puts it: 'Carrying the trauma of racially marked relations does not, as Pinnock argues through her dramatization, constitute a progressive way forward' (Aston 2003: 132).

Refusing Victim Status

In *Mules* (1996), written for Clean Break Theatre Company, a company set up in 1979 by former women prisoners and commissioning plays that deal with women's experience of criminality, the legal system and prison, Pinnock picked up again the topic of female poverty in Jamaica, women's desire for material self-improvement and the ways in which women may be influenced by other, more experienced women or 'symbolic mothers', both for good and ill. In *Mules* sisters Lou and Lyla, who were abandoned by their mother, are persuaded by a sophisticated westernized black woman, Bridie, who later turns out to have been from the same slums as themselves, to act as mules or drugs carriers from Jamaica into Britain. Unbeknown to them, Bridie always overrecruits 'mules' in a deal with customs officers that some will be caught and others pass through. And, indeed, Lou, the sister who was more willing to take the risk, gets caught and ends up spending three years in prison. The play offers a powerful indictment of women's global exploitation under capitalism in that Lou's and Lyla's story in Jamaica is matched by a sub-plot in London also involving black girls who live criminalized lives as a way of making ends meet. *Mules* shows that even Bridie, who thinks of herself as middle management in terms of drugs dealing, is not exempt from the violence of the drugs barons who control the business; whilst the 'mules' carry the drugs and the can if anything goes wrong, the drugs barons are presented as living off the proceeds of their work in bourgeois comfort.

Pinnock has commented that 'One of my things in all the plays is examining the idea of the victim. To be black is always to be in the position of victim' (Stephenson and Langridge 1997: 51). Although, as she points out, none of her 'victim' characters wants to understand themselves as such and they all take action, Pinnock does not present an overly optimistic view of the possibilities of transcending victim status that can be achieved through such actions. In *Mules* Lou and Lyla, who had their own little business at the start of the play but longed for a less materially impoverished life, end up where they began – back in Jamaica, working on a ganja farm, owned, ironically and predictably, by the drugs baron to whom they owe the destruction of their previous life.

Such cyclicity, which speaks more to tragic than comic theatre traditions, and suggests the difficulty of achieving change, has been a recurrent feature of Pinnock's plays. In those from the 1980s and 1990s it usually involved strong central female characters seeking to improve their own and sometimes others' lives, but always facing a significant cost as a consequence of that aspiration. *A Rock in Water* (1989), one of Pinnock's earlier plays, for instance, centred on the life of Trinidad-born Claudia Jones, a black woman who was deported from the USA to Britain in December 1955[14] for her involvement in trade union and communist party activities, and who ran the *West Indian Gazette* and is credited with having founded the Nottinghill Carnival in London. Jones's deportation to Britain was possible because she held a British passport – the legacy of her birth country Trinidad's status as part of the British Empire. In Jones, Pinnock presents a woman full of ideals and longings for the transformation of black people's lives who ultimately finds herself isolated from the black London community in which she spends the final years of her life – not least because of her somewhat imperial behaviour – and dies alone. The opening scene of the play shows Claudia and her mother standing on a street corner in New York, hustling for work. The final scene takes place in a women's prison where Claudia confides how she enjoys being with her sisters and being able to be herself. Such all-female scenes, typical of Pinnock's plays until the turn of the century, show women constrained – by economic position, through imprisonment, through their identities as black and female.

This scenario changed, to some extent, with *Water* (2000), a 40-minute play which was put on at the Tricycle Theatre, London, together with Alice Childress's *Wine in the Wilderness* (1969), thus creating a dialogue between Childress's and Pinnock's inter-rogation of black identity in 1950s America and 1990s Britain respectively. Both plays ask how one can live as a black woman or black man in the period they portray. Importantly, *Water* features a London-based black woman and a black man who are seeking to make it in the middle-class worlds of the arts and the media rather than being working-class. Della, a black artist, and Ed, a black journalist, represent the second generation of migrants, taking on – and indeed taking in – a predominantly white establishment through exploiting stereotypes of black identity whilst denying (aspects of) their actual histories in order to succeed. As Lauren Booth put it: 'The play questions our own lust for the Tracey Emin school of "authenticity" and "autobiog-raphy" in modern art' (Booth 2001: 46). Della has become a successful Brit-Art artist by appropriating the stereotypical narrative of another woman's history of poverty and drug abuse, portraying it, supposedly autobiographically, as a story of deprivation transcended. Ed in the meantime is trying to dissociate himself from that kind of background, which his brother, it turns out, in fact, still inhabits. In the course of the play Ed and Della gradually reveal their stories to each other and to the audience, and arrive at a mutually empowering pact: Ed will tell Della's story in such a way as to indict the art establishment for both inciting and succumbing to certain types of transformative narratives which encourage artists in turn to produce such narratives irrespective of their 'truth'; at the same time, the telling of that story will provide him with the big break in journalism that he needs.

Water, just like *One Under* (2005), is about black people's strategies for living in urban Britain, a multicultural environment in which the legacies of empire are still all too present. But where Pinnock's previous plays were powerfully focused on black women's predicaments, *Water* and *One Under* give equal space to men and women, and present predicaments that might apply to non-black characters as much as black ones. Thus *One Under* centres on two (black) men's attempts to come to terms with the deaths they inadvertently caused, of a young man and a child respectively. In a complex, interwoven plot Pinnock deals with parental abandonment, loss and 'the kindness of strangers', as Aleks Sierz (2005) put it, centring – in contrast to previous plays by Pinnock such as *Leave Taking*, or *Talking in Tongues* – on men who care (and women who lose children). That focus on male vulnerability is new in Pinnock's plays from 2000 onwards – it shifts away from questions of overt economic exploitation and the struggle to make it, to a focus on the relationship between inside and outside, between appearance and what goes on inside.

That shift, which to some extent leaves behind the legacies of empire, has not been accompanied by a shift away from the stage naturalism that is typical for Pinnock's plays, which Aston (2003: 131) identifies as Eurocentric, and of which Reitz (2003: 47) wrote that 'in none of the plays is form central to the visualization of the intercultural and intracultural confrontations'. However, as I have argued elsewhere (2003b), such use of naturalism is partly about the insertion of second-generation migrants into English mainstream theatre, since their affinities, social, cultural and economic, often are with the country in which they were born and/or brought up, that is Britain, rather than with their parents' or grandparents' homeland and its cultural forms. And, as Aston, quoting Ponnuswami (2000), also suggests, 'realism . . . is transformed through the diasporic context of black experience' (Aston 2003: 131), through its permeation with 'questions of race, nation and capital', which moves realism beyond its traditional focus on the domestic and the familial. Simultaneously, plays such as *Mules* and *Water* suggest that the domestic and familial is not separate from questions of race, nation and capital – it is their interconnection, in fact, and the remains of the British Empire, its legacy of conquest, dislocation, abandonment, racism and sexism, which shape Pinnock's theatre.

Notes

1 This gap predates the post-2000 attacks on western cities such as New York, Madrid and, most recently, London, as well as the disastrous consequences of the war in Iraq.

2 The Tricycle Theatre in Kilburn, London, for instance, which has staged several of Pinnock's plays, also put on Richard Norton-Taylor's documentary plays *The Colour of Justice* (London: Oberon, 1999), 'based on the transcripts

of the Stephen Lawrence Inquiry' of 1998–9, and *Justifying War* (London: Oberon Books, 2003), 'scenes from the Hutton Inquiry'.

3 Reitz (2003) none the less argues that Pinnock's plays are written 'ostensibly for a British audience' and follows this with the rather curious comment: 'They shun exoticism of any sort, and they do not require any previous cultural or historical knowledge which an

average middle-class audience could not be expected to be acquainted with' (43). Why this should identify the plays as 'for a British audience' is unclear to me.

4   Dolly Dhingra is herself a playwright whose most recent play, *The Fortune Club*, premiered at the Tricycle Theatre on 10 March 2005.

5   For accounts of those legacies see Hall (2000); Wambu (1998); Solomos (1993); Ashcroft et al. (1989); Bryan et al. (1985); MacKenzie (1984); www.movinghere.org.uk.

6   *A Hero's Welcome* received its first rehearsed reading at the Royal Court Upstairs in 1986. It was subsequently performed there in 1989.

7   Andrea Levy's (2004) *Small Island* (London: London Review) offers an interesting fictional representation of the same issue. For a historicized account see Rose (2000).

8   *Leave Taking* was first performed at the Liverpool Playhouse Studio on 11 November 1987.

9   For an extended analysis of this play see Griffin (2003a: 36–63).

10 Since Pinnock's plays focus on migration from the West Indies to Britain, they usually present a clear migratory pattern. However, it has to be remembered that many migrant groups' histories are highly complex, involving mul-tiple countries and migratory paths which reduce the possibility of easy identification with particular countries and histories (see, for example, Brah 1996; Ang 2001). Plays which explore those complex histories include Gupta (2002); Wertenbaker (2001); Kay (1987).

11 See, for example, Miller (1999); Zindika (1993); Cooke (1990); Rudet (1986); Dayley (1985); Randall (n.d).

12 In an interview with the *New Statesman* (1995), she cited black women writers and their works such as Alice Walker, Toni Morrison, bell hooks, Maya Angelou and Jackie Kay as well as her mother and her sister as powerful influences on herself and her plays. When asked in the same interview which historical period she would like to visit Pinnock replied, 'Nineteenth-century Jamaica. I'd like to meet and talk to my ancestors, and record their memories. Oral history is the most useful' (*New Statesman*: 21).

13 The meaning of religion in the lives of black first-generation migrants is repeatedly explored in plays by black women playwrights (see Zindika 1989; Rudet 1985; Dayley 1985).

14 For further details see Buzz Johnson (1985). '*I Think of My Mother': Notes on the Life and Times of Claudia Jones*. London: Karia Press.

PRIMARY READING

Pinnock, Winsome (1989a). *Leave Taking* in Kate Harwood (ed.). *First Run: New Plays by New Writers*. London: Nick Hern Books, 139–89.

Pinnock, Winsome (1989b). *A Rock in Water* in Yvonne Brewster (ed.). *Black Plays: Two*. London: Methuen, 45–91.

Pinnock, Winsome (1993). *A Hero's Welcome* in Kadija George (ed.). *Six Plays by Black and Asian Women Writers*. London: Aurora Metro Press, 21–55.

Pinnock, Winsome (1995). *Talking in Tongues* in Yvonne Brewster (ed.). *Black Plays: Three*. London: Methuen, 171–228.

Pinnock, Winsome (1996). *Mules*. London: Faber and Faber.

Pinnock, Winsome (2000). *Water*. Playscript ms 9296, British Library, London.

Pinnock, Winsome (2005). *One Under*. World premiere: Tricycle Theatre, London, February.

FURTHER READING

Ahmed, Sara (1997). 'It's A Sun-Tan, Isn't It? – Auto-Biography as an Identificatory Practice' in Heidi Mirza (ed.). *Black British Feminism*. London: Routledge, 153–67.

Ang, Ien (2001). *On Not Speaking Chinese*. London: Routledge.

Ashcroft, Bill, Griffiths, Gareth and Tiffin, Helen (eds.) (1989). *The Empire Writes Back*. London: Routledge.

Aston, Elaine (2003). *Feminist Views on the English Stage*. Cambridge: Cambridge University Press.

Booth, Lauren (2001). 'Water and Wine', *New Statesman* 12, 44, 46.

Brah, Avtar (1996). *Cartographies of Diaspora: Contesting Identities*. London: Routledge.

Bryan, Beverley, Dadzie, Stella and Scafe, Suzanne (eds.)(1985). *The Heart of the Race*. London: Virago.

Cooke, Trish (1990). 'Back Street Mammy' in Kate Harwood (ed.). *First Run 2*. London: Nick Hern Books, 38–95.

Dayley, Grace (1985). 'Rose's Story' in Michelene Wandor (ed.). *Plays by Women 4*. London: Methuen, 55–80.

Dhingra, Dolly (2005). 'Interview with Winsome Pinnock', programme notes, *One Under*, Tricycle Theatre, London, February, n.p.

Edgar, David (1999). 'Winsome Pinnock' in David Edgar (ed.). *State of Play: Playwrights on Playwriting*. London: Faber and Faber, 56–61.

Gilroy, Paul (1987; repr. 1992). *There Ain't No Black in the Union Jack: The Cultural Politics of Race and Nation*. London: Routledge.

Gilroy, Paul (2004). *After Empire: Melancholia or Convivial Culture?* London: Routledge.

Griffin, Gabriele (2003a). *Contemporary Black and Asian Women Playwrights in Britain*. Cambridge: Cambridge University Press.

Griffin, Gabriele (2003b). 'Constitutive Subjectivities: Contemporary Black and Asian Women Playwrights in Britain', *European Journal of Women's Studies* 10: 4, 377–94.

Gupta, Tanika (2002). *Sanctuary*. London: Oberon Books.

Hall, Catherine (ed.) (2000). *Cultures of Empire: A Reader*. Manchester: Manchester University Press.

Kay, Jackie (1987). 'Chiaroscuro' in Jill Davis (ed.). *Lesbian Plays*. London: Methuen, 57–83.

Kolawole, Helen (2003). 'Beyond Bollywood', *Mail* and *Guardian Online*, ZA@Art, at server.mg.co.za/art/ 2003/2003aug/030801-bollywood.html, accessed 8 February 2005, 2–4.

MacKenzie, John M. (1984). *Propaganda and Empire*. Manchester: Manchester University Press.

Miller, Kara (1999). *Hyacinth Blue*, 4th draft. Playscript ms 8871. British Library, London.

New Statesman (1995). 'Interview with Winsome Pinnock'. *New Statesman and Society* 8: 337, 21.

Ponnuswami, Meenakshi (2000). 'Small Island People: Black British Women Playwrights' in Elaine Aston and Janelle Reinelt (eds.). *Modern British Women Playwrights*. Cambridge: Cambridge University Press, 217–34.

Randall, Paulette (n.d.) *24%*. Playscript no. 4974. British Library, London.

Reitz, Bernhard (2003). ' "Discovering an Identity which Has Been Squashed": Intercultural and Intracultural Confrontations in the Plays of Winsome Pinnock and Ayub Khan-Din', *European Journal of English Studies* 7:1, 39–54.

Rose, Sonya O. (2000). 'Sex, Citizenship, and the Nation in World War II Britain' in Catherine Hall (ed.). *Cultures of Empire: A Reader*. Manchester: Manchester University Press, 246–80.

Rudet, Jacqueline (1985). *God's Second in Command*, 2nd draft. Playscript no. 2824. British Library, London.

Rudet, Jacqueline (1986). 'Money to Live' in Mary Remnant (ed.). *Plays by Women 5*. London: Methuen, 145–81.

Sierz, Aleks (2005). 'One Under', *Stage Online – Reviews*, www.thestage.co.uk/reviews/ review. php/ 6638/one-under, accessed 19 July 2005.

Solomos, John (1993). *Race and Racism in Britain*, 2nd edn. Basingstoke: Macmillan.

Stephenson, Heidi and Langridge, Natasha (1997). 'Winsome Pinnock' in Heidi Stephenson and Natasha Langridge (eds.). *Rage and Reason: Women Playwrights on Playwriting*. London: Methuen, 45–53.

Summerfield, Penny (2005). 'Oral History as a Research Method' in Gabriele Griffin (ed.). *Research Methods for English Studies*. Edinburgh: Edinburgh University Press, 47–66.

Wambu, Onyekachi (ed.) (1998). *Empire Windrush*. London: Victor Gollancz.

Wertenbaker, Timberlake (2001). *Credible Witness*. London: Faber and Faber.

Zindika (1989). *Paper and Stone*. Unpublished ms, courtesy of author.

Zindika (1993). 'Leonora's Dance' in Kadija George (ed.). *Six Plays by Black and Asian Women Writers*. London: Aurora Metro Press, 76–110.

PART IV
Comedy

17

Wilde's Comedies

Richard Allen Cave

Recent queer theorists, most notably Neil Bartlett, Alan Sinfield and Joseph Bristow, have done much to re-evaluate Oscar Wilde (1854–1900), the man and the works, within the contexts of contemporary and subsequent gay culture. But the reclamations have often cast Wilde in the role of martyr to a cause, the flamboyant scapegoat who brought same-sex relations *out* into a society which responded punitively to any challenging of its mores and status quo. Terry Eagleton's play on the subject carries the significant but loaded title *Saint Oscar*. There is much value in this approach, but a casual glance at any surviving photographs of Wilde and Bosie Douglas, his partner, makes one ponder whether it is the whole truth of the matter. This is especially the case if that glance is informed by a reading of Wilde's *De Profundis* (wr. 1897). Bosie, despite the surface prettiness, has all the features of a spoilt brat, with pouting mouth, slouched posture and lifeless eyes; what is projected is a figure heavily obsessed with self. Glancing at photographs of the two of them together, one 'reads' Wilde as physically plump, but the eyes are ablaze with energy, for all their heavy lids. Beside the aristocrat in the making, he generally looks less well-dressed and there is the vaguest suggestion of coarseness. In making Bosie the object of his infatuation, Wilde (as events would show) would seem less the martyr than the architect of his own destruction. To be cruel, one could sum up the contrast as the neurasthenic English toff with the educated Irish social climber (and an Irishman who through his mother had inherited more than a rebellious streak). From a postcolonial perspective, one wonders what particular power games were played out in Oscar and Bosie's coupling. Who dominated whom? Who patronized whom? What forms did subservience take? The potential for intricate scenarios of sadomasochism was considerable. But who played which role and was there ever the possibility of reversals? 'Feasting with panthers?' 'Playing with fire?' Call it what you will, there was only one likely result, if the relationship were ever *outed*, which is precisely what Lord Douglas knew and relied on. Wilde's *An Ideal Husband* (1895) shows the English aristocracy closing ranks about a man whose career, for all its promise, suffers a moral lapse; they are quick to protect their own against an outsider. Wilde *knew* this to be the convention, and in continuing the relationship with Bosie structured his own inevitable demise. There is more of the masochist here than the martyr.

This may seem a curious introduction to a discussion of Wilde's comedies, but it places Wilde as a social misfit (and not just on sexual grounds) by interrogating the degree to which his Irish background impacts on his actions and thinking. It is also a way of accounting for the particular modes of performance and reception which became the norm for many decades after his social 'fall'. It is telling that George Alexander closed his production of *The Importance of Being Earnest* (premiered 1895) at the St James's Theatre once Wilde himself became the subject of a prosecution, then successfully restored it to his repertoire shortly after Wilde's imprisonment but with the dramatist's name expunged from the playbills and programmes. The upper classes had relished Wilde's wit; and they assimilated his comedies back into their culture sanitized of everything that might render them disturbing as the expression of an Irish critic and outsider. The history of Wilde's plays in performance is an object lesson in cultural (and colonial) appropriation (this was not so over the same period in the communist world, where the plays were regularly revived as powerful social satires). Generations of actors, extending to Margaret Lockwood and Wilfred Hyde-White in the postwar years, played the surface and ignored the more complex heart of the comedies, with a specially cultivated, mannered style of delivery designed to highlight the paradoxes and titillate audiences with anticipation of a well-known epigram. They became comedies of words: a view which even the queer poet W. H. Auden endorsed in describing *The Importance of Being Earnest* as 'the purest example in English literature' of a 'verbal opera' (Auden 1968: 92). Note how Auden added insult to injury by claiming Wilde as *English*. In one sense the process of what happened culturally and theatrically to Wilde's comedies in the theatre might be described as their systematic anglicizing, a subtle eliding of the wild, unpredictable, dangerous qualities in the plays which might be best defined as the Irish manifestation of Wilde's genius. It could, however, be argued that Wilde gave theatre practitioners and spectators the lead they wanted and that they were quick to put it to use. Open any of Wilde's critical essays and one finds him espousing the importance of surfaces (not depth) in art. 'The Critic As Artist', for example, takes for its theme how 'the art that is frankly decorative is the art to live with' (Wilde 1960: 990) and argues that, if an artist had something to say and said it, 'the result would be tedious. It is just because he has no new message that he can do beautiful work. He gains his inspiration from form [. . .] purely, as an artist should. A real passion would ruin him. [. . .] All bad poetry springs from genuine feeling' (ibid.: 991). Once again we find Wilde the architect of his own undoing, betraying his own best interests. Certainly his stance in his criticism is motivated by abhorrence of Victorian pietistic and moralistic writing, intense in its sense of purposefulness; but in the process of defining his antagonistic stance he could be misinterpreted as denying art any seriousness. His comedies set out seriously to expose the triviality and moral vacuity of a social class that rigidly polices its own continuance as a ruling elite. The problem with the performance technique that emasculates Wilde's plays by depriving them of this dimension is that it focuses on word play and supposes that the wit is a homogeneous entity, when in point of fact Wilde is master of a whole arsenal of comedic styles, verbal, visual and physical, and the wit is brilliant because multifaceted and multivalent.

The Lovers are Surprised by Lady Bracknell

Lady Bracknell: "Mr. Worthing, rise, sir, from this semi-recumbent position; it is most indecorous."

George Alexander as Jack Worthing, Mrs Patrick Campbell as Lady Gwendolen and Helena Rous as Lady Bracknell in Wilde's *The Importance of Being Earnest*, 1909. Courtesy of Mary Evans Picture Library.

An episode in *A Woman of No Importance* (1893) offers a good illustration of the issue. In Act II, the women have resorted to the drawing room at Hunstanton, leaving the men to their port; over coffee they prattle about husbands, the ideal man and what makes for boredom in relations between the sexes; Mrs Allonby pushes matters ever closer to the edge of what is permissible until Lady Hunstanton remembers that her young American visitor, Hester, is present in the room; she rather patronizingly if politely engages Hester in conversation in an effort to include her in the general discussion, telling her that she 'mustn't believe everything that was said' (Wilde 2000: 128). Hester seizes the opportunity to speak her mind about English society and castigate what she views as its moral inadequacy. Her fervour carries her away when the name of Lord Henry Weston is mentioned, dismissing him as 'a man with a hideous smile and a hideous past' (130). As she and we quickly learn, he is the brother of one of the other women present, Lady Caroline. Hester resorts in her passion to the rhetoric of the Bible, urging everyone to resist the temptation to dim their eyes to

THE PRODUCTION OF MR. OSCAR WILDE'S NEW PLAY, "A WOMAN OF NO IMPORTANCE," AT THE HAYMARKET THEATRE
Mrs. Arbuthnot (Mrs. Bernard Beere), in reply to the taunts of Lord Illingworth (Mr. Beerbohm-Tree), strikes him across the face with his gloves—Act IV.

Mrs Beere as Mrs Arbuthnot and Herbert Beerbohm Tree as Lord Illingworth in the original production of Wilde's *A Woman of No Importance* (1893), Haymarket Theatre, London. Courtesy Mary Evans Picture Library.

'Right, that pillar of fire, and Wrong, that pillar of cloud' (130). Her flow of oratory is at this moment punctured by Lady Caroline: 'Might I, dear Miss Worsley, as you are standing up, ask you for my cotton that is just behind you? Thank you' (130). Lady Caroline's lines invariably provoke sustained laughter, even applause.

But there are different ways of playing this moment, which incite different qualities of laughter. It could be seen as an insufferable puritan getting her deserved come-uppance, where vulgar evangelical rant meets its match in a cool, English civility. There is some truth in this interpretation but within the larger contexts of the scene and of the overall play, the incident is more complex. Juxtaposing the

rigours of Old Testament morality with upper-class nonchalance does expose the want
of real principle in Lady Hunstanton and her guests: the former almost immediately
defends Weston as 'such good company', and his sister, while admitting she finds him
'infamous', adds that 'he has one of the best cooks in London, and after a good dinner
one can forgive anybody'(131). It is because the moral tenor of the gathering is so lax
that the likes of Lord Weston can pursue their infamies unchecked. Weston is revealed
as an arch playboy, who has ruined the reputation of numerous women (they,
significantly, have not been allowed to pursue their lives in upper-class circles
unchecked). That Lady Caroline is prepared to be so indulgent towards him is ironic,
given her habit of intrusively policing her own elderly husband's life, cosseting him
partly in an exaggerated show of affection but partly through worry lest he show
philandering tendencies too, despite his advanced years. Wilde sustains a hilarious
running gag throughout the second and third acts, as Lady Caroline continually
appears and disappears, disrupting other characters' more urgent scenes together, in
quest of her Sir John in case he be sequestered alone somewhere with the unattached
Lady Stutfield. How much of her imperturbability in the episode with Hester is
merely a stance? Or is she to be played as so lacking in intelligence as not to perceive
the irony of her own inconsistent behaviour? Hester has the good grace later in the
play to see that her conduct deserved to be challenged: her morality was at that
moment inflexible for want of experience or understanding and she has the courage to
admit she was wrong and intemperate. She earns respect, where Lady Caroline
confirms her status as an absurd caricature.

\To play for the surface comedy of the moment when Lady Caroline disconcerts
Hester is to miss the constructional excellence of Wilde's dramaturgy, that subtle
preparing for effects, for sudden insights, where every detail carries resonances into
the larger organization of the play. More importantly it risks subverting Wilde's
moral scheme within the comedy: he continually holds up shallow moralizing as
risible but, while he does not preach an alternative morality, he does pose some
unsettling questions. Most of the characters that people the stage in this comedy are
titled nobility or hold a defined social status as politician, potential ambassador or
parson; their number is representative of the governing circle, the *best* society, of
which women are the cultural guardians. 'Best' is a qualitative and judgemental
adjective (one would hope morally and spiritually), but it is here seen allied only to
material values, matters of birth, income and (largely inherited) position and the
ability to live a good (in the sense of satisfyingly easy) life. In the circumstances of
Hester's discomfiture, Wilde holds up the pretensions of that social group for
analysis and shows them as empty mannerisms. The point is that he does this not
through statement but through the enacted devices of comedy, leaving the audience
to respond as they will: they must find the meaning experientially. It is in this
context that Wilde's Irish political background becomes important. Most of the
great analysers of English pretension have been Irish (Farquahar, Congreve, Sheridan,
Shaw) and the vehicle for their respective critiques has been the comedy of manners,
a style of comedy in which the values which a given society promotes are tested

against the way they inform the quality of life of that society in the more intimate aspects of its existence. The cultural endeavour that forms part of the colonizing process invariably engages in debasing all cultural expression of the colonized people: hence that centuries-long rhetoric about the 'wild' (untutored) Irish in need of superior English direction. Wilde had moved in upper-class circles from his Oxford days (the index to the volumes of his letters or the list of women sponsors and contributors to the magazine he edited, *Woman's World*, show the extent of his infiltration); but, as privileged outsider, the inevitable detachment attendant on his situation developed in him the scrutinizing eye of the comic satirist. What Wilde's comedies implicitly but relentlessly question are the grounds (social, moral, cultural) on which that English belief in superiority over its empire rests. If an audience's laughter is directed to side simply with Lady Caroline in the altercation with Hester, then they are expressing complicity with the moral vacuum in which she is repeatedly shown to exist; they are endorsing their own acceptance of the status quo, when the play invites spectators to be flexible and open to new possibilities of judging. Ideally the laughter should be altogether more complex in being directed against both women.

The potential for complexity of response is built into an episode in Act II of *The Importance of Being Earnest*, which it would be easy to play as merely a clever farcical device. Wilde could rely on the staging conventions of the theatre of his day to provide him with a central entrance to what is a garden setting at Jack Worthing's country home, and he devised a series of flamboyantly grand entrances throughout Act II, which are immediately punctured with audience laughter. The characters are all to be played as 'serious people', as the subtitle of the play insists, so they are not sufficiently self-aware to perceive their own absurdity (or 'triviality', as that same subtitle equally insists), which makes the laughter louder and longer. The fact that there are three such entrances creates audience expectation, which further heightens the amusement (repetition with variations is a hall-mark of good construction in comedy). The second involves the arrival of Jack in full mourning for the 'brother' that the audience know (but he does not) is at that moment establishing himself in a bedroom of the house before being given some light refreshment by Jack's ward, Cecily. The 'brother' is of course in reality Algernon engaged in a spot of bunburying; his arrival posing as Jack's wicked but hugely debonair 'brother' (or so Algernon conceives him in his role play) is framed by two observations from Cecily: before she sees him, she questions whether, despite his wicked reputation, 'he will look just like every one else'; the moment he stages his entrance she answers herself: 'He does!' (Wilde 2000: 320). Reality shatters her carefully constructed illusions, and a similar pattern is played out with Jack's entrance later, except Wilde trusts the audience to make the necessary connections so that just Jack's visual appearance stimulates their hilarity. All Jack's hopes of keeping the real reasons for his gadding up to London secret are blown asunder, chiefly because he overplays his hand, theatricalizing his entry by dressing in full mourning. Had he appeared in conventional attire he might well, with a spot of ingenuity, have got himself out of the fix he has landed himself in.

It's the costume that makes the retreat impossible and that reveals him for the actor, the player of multiple parts, he is.

Wilde appears to have supported Alexander in maintaining the laughter here for as long as possible. (Alexander directed the two actors playing Chasuble and Miss Prism to separate just before Jack's entrance as if in quest of Cecily and to come downstage on either side before turning to see him.) Why might Wilde have done this? He was already relying on the audience's intelligence to get the joke at Jack's expense; prolonged laughter would indicate that, having let their imaginations dwell on the situation, they had begun to perceive a range of implications in the bizarre figure that confronted them; the more the complexity of the moment impressed itself on spectators the longer they laughed; timing was of the essence in allowing that complexity to stand revealed. Laughter in farce always greets the unmasking of someone who has tried to humbug the other characters; but it is particularly welcome here, since Jack has consistently enforced a high moral tone in life at Woolton, even though he hardly lives up to his own standards, given his secret philandering in London. His vaunted rectitude is a pose like his mannered expression of grief. But would there not originally have been an element of shock to the laughter, given the particular impersonation Jack chooses to adopt? Mourning (with a queen who had luxuriated in her black-bedizened state for decades setting the pattern) had become ranked amongst the highest of Victorian pieties, with its required dress codes and sanctioned behavioural conventions; and here Wilde was setting it up as an object for fulsome derision. It's the measure of Jack's total want of responsible decorum that he is prepared to abuse such a piety in his efforts to protect his social image. The preservation of that image of himself as dedicated gentleman ultimately counts for more with him than playing with death. So much for the values that shape an English gentleman! The laugh is on Jack in many ways here; but the clothes, the agonized posturing, the vast black-bordered handkerchief that Alexander sported in the role, the whole theatrical charade carry a potent social critique. Farce is cruel in its exposure of duplicities and levels of self-deception, rarely more so than here, if one reads an anti-colonial edge into the satire. Yet it is that ideological *edge* which can so easily (or deliberately) be lost in the playing: Wilde, like Shaw after him, politicized the comedy of manners; indeed his dramaturgical genius was to deploy comedy (as in the two sequences under discussion) to anatomize manners and reveal the extent to which they are open to political definition.

What impresses in these two instances is how what are momentary experiences in the theatre are emblematic of the play overall. The detail, as in all fine drama, encapsulates the whole. This is true of the range of Wilde's dramaturgical excellences and especially of his command of stage space. *Lady Windermere's Fan* (1892) carries the provocative subtitle 'A Play about a Good Woman', which in the play's concluding line is firmly attached to Mrs Erlynne, even though before she actually appears in the action she has been castigated as a woman with a decidedly shady past. As in all of Wilde's comedies, the action will challenge conventional ways of judging morally and offer (Wilde never propounds or preaches) alternatives. It might be asked what this has to do with stage space; but it is Wilde's continual situating of Mrs Erlynne in dominant positions that accentuates precisely what she is doing and why within the narrative, and that causes spectators consistently to rethink their relation to her. She does not appear until Act II, though she has repeatedly been the subject of conversation in Act I, particularly of a heated exchange between the Windermeres. What Wilde does by delaying her entry is build up a particular set of expectations in the audience, all shaped by conventional attitudes to the 'fallen' woman and by her contemporary representation in fiction and drama. Lady Windermere speaks for the conventional mindset when she threatens to hit the woman with her fan, if Mrs Erlynne dares to attend her evening gathering. Her entrance is a veritable *coup de théâtre*: far from exhibiting brazen effrontery, Mrs Erlynne shows a calm self-possession, as on Windermere's arm she circles the entire stage space around its centre, speaking with effortless charm and civility to everyone she encounters. Lady Windermere by contrast is overwhelmed, drops her fan, and is soon quite marginalized within the stage picture. The intended battle of wills is quickly over, as Lady Windermere falters before the sheer force of Mrs Erlynne's command and magnificence; and the audience is left fascinated and perplexed, with its expectations wholly frustrated. The perplexity increases once spectators learn that she is in fact blackmailing Windermere, though the grounds on which she is doing so remain for a time unclear. Interestingly there is no voiced threat in their relations and he does not appear to be ashamed of some secret guilt that has been discovered. If one compares the tone of the seemingly comparable scene between Sir Robert Chiltern and Mrs Cheveley in *An Ideal Husband*, one detects immediate differences, since Sir Robert has a guilty past he prefers to have hidden and Mrs Cheveley, knowing of that past wrong, can manipulate him to her will by threats of exposure. What is very clear by the end of Act II is that Mrs Erlynne seems to have complete control over how husband and wife behave; and throughout, rather than appearing louche, loud or overbearing (as is Mrs Cheveley's manner, whether one is discussing her language, tone or dress sense), she is the epitome of graciousness. At an end-of-season party when everyone else is jaded (Wilde establishes that fact with some hilarious backchat amongst the guests) Mrs Erlynne exudes a consummate energy.

A controlling figure with boundless energy on-stage invariably engages audience sympathy with a positive immediacy, and with none of the superiority which would normally be the stance adopted with a recognized type such as the woman with a past. But, though Mrs Erlynne has a past, to Wilde importantly she is not a type but an individual with a distinct history, precision of motive, developed social acumen and a determination to succeed in re-establishing herself in society on her own terms. She refuses to play-act the contrite magdalen, since that is to *fix* herself permanently in a single role for which she possesses none of the required qualities: she would be casting herself against type, and rebels against every pressure to determine that role as her future. Her energy is momentarily dashed at the end of Act II when she discovers that Lady Windermere plans to elope with Lord Darlington, but it is only momentarily: within minutes her agile intelligence is planning ways to bring the situation back under her control, and with great skill she uses Lord Augustus to get Windermere out of the way while she puts her plan into action. Physical energy in the woman has its correlative in a prodigious mental energy. In Act III the space is Lord Darlington's drawing room and study, where Lady Windermere has established herself to await his return; Mrs Erlynne must use the full resources of her will power to manoeuvre her out of that space as quickly as possible. She all but succeeds again, when Darlington unexpectedly returns bringing a bevy of male friends, including Windermere, compelling the two women to hide independently. When Lady Windermere's fan is discovered, Mrs Erlynne again acts promptly: she appears (compromisingly from Darlington's bedroom) to attract the focus for the men's gaze, thereby marginalizing Lady Windermere, giving her the opportunity to escape unnoticed. By dressing Marion Terry as Mrs Erlynne in dazzling white satin in the original production of 1892, George Alexander ensured that amongst the black-evening-suited men she would provide a dominant point of attention, as they all turned to face her and the diagonal lines of the blocking met in her as apex. The problem for directors of the play is that Mrs Erlynne's entry is so powerful that it risks commandeering the gaze of the audience so completely that they may miss the all-important detail of the escape, because it is *too* marginalized. After watching the earlier demonstrations of Mrs Erlynne's nerve, energy and intelligence, spectators are left puzzling over the motivation for this entrance: is it as carefully calculated as all her previous actions have been or the product of a moment's reckless impulse? She is undeniably in control of everyone within the stage space, but at what personal cost? Energy and control are admirable attributes if used creatively, but they do not engage with the emotions. This has to be an astonishing moment that continues to resonate in the audience's imagination, since they have to believe in time that this is the proof that Mrs Erlynne has a heart and a mother's sensibility towards Lady Windermere, whom she previously abandoned when a child. Once again, what in the 1890s would be a decided challenge morally for an audience is posed through a brilliantly conceived use of stage space.

A mother's heart and sensibility put at the defence of an errant daughter teeter precariously on the edge of sentimentality and the conventionalized pieties that Wilde's critical writings continually satirize. If he were not to be found guilty of hypocrisy, he needed yet again to tutor his audience into new ways of viewing the circumstance his dramatic action had set up; and again an original use of stage space came to his aid. Wilde insisted in a letter to Alexander (Wilde 1987: 110) that a particular kind of divan sofa be used in the final act of *Lady Windermere's Fan* and that it should be placed at an angle from the centre, so that by seating Mrs Erlynne at its upper corner she would always relate to the audience *frontally*. Far from being abashed at the compromising situation she was found in at Lord Darlington's, Mrs Erlynne again adopts the commanding central position. Significantly the margins are not for her, even though the space is properly Lady Windermere's. If Wilde had wished to resolve his drama with the sentimental reconciliation of mother and daughter, here would be the place to do it. But it is such emotionalism that is meticulously marginalized. Not only does Mrs Erlynne work scrupulously hard to ensure her daughter never discovers their true relation from Windermere, and that he never learns from his wife her precise whereabouts the previous evening; but she also meticulously manoeuvres each of them off-stage when either excess gratitude in her daughter, or anger and disgust in her son-in-law, come sufficiently close to the surface for them to risk jeopardizing the coolly polite equanimity which she has determined will prevail. Comedies proverbially end in a marital resolution, but Mrs Erlynne knows that the Windermeres' marriage will only remain in a state of balanced affection if neither learns a particular truth from the other; that this is not the perfect accord generally celebrated at the close of the genre is ultimately the responsibility of a society that operates by a fixed and debilitating moral code. Despite her skilled control, Mrs Erlynne can effect only a partial restoration – and even that required a remarkable adjustment of their moral perspectives, if a contemporary audience were to accept it as a *resolution*. One has only to measure her achievement beside that of the equally worldly-wise and clear-sighted controlling figure of Rosalind in Wilde's favourite Shakespearean comedy to appreciate how limited Mrs Erlynne's resolution is. To effect even that degree of harmony Wilde had to bring a fallen woman from the margins, place her centre stage and, repeatedly from act to act, justify her *moral* right to occupy that position. It is her powerful centrality (in every sense of the word) that requires spectators to develop moral flexibility in relation to a stereotype, which they had previously been all-too-content to identify as *other*.

The zealous puritan (Hester), the English gentleman (Jack Worthing) and the fallen woman (Mrs Erlynne) are all type figures of comedy or melodrama that Wilde's dramaturgy freed from the confines of such categorization, making strange what was deemed the known and the familiar. The same is true of his treatment of Lord Goring in *An Ideal Husband*. It is fair to assume that the title applies to Sir Robert Chiltern; yet, as the action reaches its conclusion, it is rather to Goring that it most fittingly belongs; but by then 'ideal' has been shorn of its conventional meanings. Goring, like Mrs Erlynne, is an outsider, in his case in being a dandy, a man whose thoughts and behaviour seem centred on dress, witty repartee, aesthetic pleasures and an all-consuming leisure. His father, Lord Caversham, repeatedly chastises his son for lacking responsibility towards the serious matters of life, for not proving himself worthy of a private income by situating himself in the centre of things, where (to Caversham as to the Chilterns) the 'centre' means politics. *Worthiness*, one manifestation of the 'ideal', is the bane of Goring's existence, which he directs his wit at anatomizing continually. He happily chooses to situate himself on the periphery, seeing a danger in assuming the right to a place at the centre. When those like Chiltern, who are at the centre, are threatened by circumstance, it is surprisingly Goring who proves to have the coolest head, the shrewdest knowledge of the ways of the world, and the intelligence to reorganize matters to his own and his friends' advantage. The casually watchful outsider proves the most acute critic of society.

Act III of *An Ideal Husband*, in which Goring resolves the plot and saves Chiltern's reputation, is the most audacious dramaturgical display that Wilde attempted in terms of controlling dramatic tone. His opening stage direction describing the setting

(Wilde 2000: 232) is chiefly a list of doors; multiple doorways usually signify a farce and a farce is what an audience gets, as doors open continually to admit the last person that ought to be arriving at that given moment (Caversham and then Chiltern, both unexpectedly; then Mrs Cheveley instead of the expected Lady Chiltern). Goring is attempting throughout to salvage Chiltern's public reputation; it is the stuff of serious drama, yet the tone shifts wildly between the hilarious and the melodramatic. Through it all Goring comes unscathed, showing himself quite capable of dealing with any eventuality. The effect is to dramatize, in a highly entertaining fashion, how his apparent nonchalance masks nerves of steel and an intelligence that is ever-alert. Respect for him grows with every demonstration of his mastery of events. But at the same time the act shows the processes by which the upper crust closes ranks to protect one of its own against a predatory outsider (Mrs Cheveley). In a crisis, Goring's sympathies are with his own kind and not with the woman who to some degree shares his 'outsider' status. Which ultimately is his mask: his nonchalance or his class-consciousness? That the process of closing ranks is shown as material for a farce positions the audience in a problematized relation with the stage action. By what system of values do spectators *place* what is going on? Never did Wilde represent the relativity of judgement or of what constitutes identity more forcefully than here, where there is nothing firm to hold on to as solid or permanent. It is his most brilliant deployment of the devices of comedy for purposes of social satire. It was also his most dangerous take on the English ruling class, in which Goring as outsider is shown to be a figure neither to be dismissed lightly nor trusted for what he appears to be. As such, *An Ideal Husband* is a decidedly *Irish* take on the English comedy of manners.

PRIMARY READING

Wilde, Oscar (1960). *The Works of Oscar Wilde*, ed. G. F. Maine. London and Glasgow: Collins (1st edn. 1948).

Wilde, Oscar (1962). *The Letters of Oscar Wilde*, ed. Rupert Hart-Davis. London and New York: Hart-Davis and Harcourt Bruce.

Wilde, Oscar (1987). *More Letters of Oscar Wilde*, ed. Rupert Hart-Davis. Oxford: Oxford University Press.

Wilde, Oscar (2000). *The Importance of Being Earnest and Other Plays*, ed. Richard Allen Cave. London: Penguin.

FURTHER READING

Auden, W. H. (1968). *Secondary Worlds*. London: Faber and Faber.

Bartlett, Neil (1988). *Who Was That Man? A Present for Mr Oscar Wilde*. London: Serpent's Tail.

Bristow, Joseph (ed.) (1992). *Sexual Sameness*. London: Routledge.

Donohue, J. and Berggren, R. (eds.) (1995). *Oscar Wilde's 'The Importance of Being Earnest': The First Production*. Gerrards Cross: Colin Smythe.

Kaplan, J. and Stowell, S. (1994). *Theatre and Fashion: Oscar Wilde to the Suffragettes*. Cambridge: Cambridge University Press.

Kaplan, J. and Stowell, S. (1997). *Wilde on Stage: A Cultural and Performance History*. Cambridge: Cambridge University Press.

Powell, Kerry (1990). *Oscar Wilde and the Theatre of the 1890s*. Cambridge: Cambridge University Press.

Raby, Peter (ed.) (1997). *The Cambridge Companion to Oscar Wilde*. Cambridge: Cambridge University Press.

Sinfield, Alan (1994). *The Wilde Century*. London and New York: Cassell.

Worth, Katharine (1983). *Oscar Wilde*. London and Basingstoke: Macmillan.

18

Always Acting: Noël Coward and the Performing Self

Frances Gray

'All sorts of men suddenly wanted to look like Noël Coward – sleek and satiny, clipped and well groomed, with a cigarette, a telephone, or a cocktail at hand'. (Beaton 1954: 141). The sleek and satiny image from the 1920s is still potent. It pervades Coward's plays from *The Vortex* (1924) to *A Song at Twilight* (1966), it haunts his songs from early shellac recordings to *Twentieth Century Blues* released by the Pet Shop Boys in 1998. In the 1935 movie *The Scoundrel*, his best film performance, Coward maps it onto his own body for the camera, moving from nakedness to immaculate style in an apparently effortless opening sequence. From the outset, he gave his audience not just plays but a self-assembly kit, a way of speaking, moving and thinking that allowed them to become Noël Coward; the young of the 1920s were confident that they could not only adopt the kit but challenge their elders with it. It was witty, cynical, sexually adroit and casually elegant; it had a special language, employing terms like 'darling' and 'divine' for the most trivial things. It moved to a jazz-flavoured beat, the body more relaxed than the ramrod Victorians but charged with energy.

Coward (1899–1973) was the first playwright to understand that the entertainment of his era combined amateur and professional in a new way. It encompassed both the parlour piano and the gramophone, so *Poor Little Rich Girl* could be purchased on disc featuring Coward's distinctive voice but could also adapt to the taste and talents of a fan buying sheet music, and Coward's revue numbers played for patrons at the nightclubs mushrooming throughout the decade. The kit made it all look easy.

'Easy', however, does not mean 'natural'. Coward was born in comparative poverty and earned a significant part of the family income from the age of 11. He suffered from tuberculosis and more than one nervous breakdown. He travelled widely and during World War II sang to troops half a mile from the Japanese lines, with the smell of rotting bodies impeding breath control during his high-speed delivery of *Mad Dogs and Englishmen*. He radically reformed the Actors' Orphanage. He was homosexual at a time when friends and colleagues less lucky or discreet found themselves in the dock. Little of that lived experience, however, was addressed directly in his plays, and when it was, the results could be unconvincing. He preferred to construct himself as an effortlessly successful purveyor of ephemera; when he made money (this was not always the case) he was as unapologetic as his alter ego in *South Sea Bubble* (1956).

> CUCKOO [. . .]:   I've read all your books and, frankly, I didn't care for them.
> BOFFIN: Did you buy them or get them from the library?
> CUCKOO: I bought them of course . . .
> BOFFIN: Well, that's all right, then, isn't it?
>
> (Coward 1962: 159)

Admirers and critics alike were seduced by the image, sometimes resentfully. 'One can't read any of Noël Coward's plays now,' wrote Cyril Connolly in 1937, 'they are written in the most topical and perishable way imaginable, the cream in them turns sour overnight' (Hoare 1995: 277).

Coward was an adroit surfer of the Zeitgeist. In the 1920s he dramatized drug culture in *The Vortex* and explored changing sexual mores in *Fallen Angels* (1925), *Easy Virtue* (1926) and dozens of popular songs. He switched to operetta in the 1930s (*Bitter Sweet* in 1929 was the last hurrah of the British musical before it went down under the onslaught of American talent), and to patriotic spectacle with the best movie of 1942, *In Which We Serve*. When in the 1950s he found himself eclipsed by a new theatrical generation he tried out the role of reactionary but opted to make a success in cabaret instead. 'Dad's Renaissance', as he called his final decades, saw him directing *Hay Fever* at the National Theatre in 1964 and returning to the West End in 1966 with a triple bill including *A Song at Twilight*, starring as a homosexual novelist just as the Sexual Offences Act was passing through the House of Lords. On his seventieth birthday the queen offered him a knighthood. This flair for identifying how the public wanted to see him was perhaps responsible for the way he has been underestimated as a writer. As John Osborne observed, when Coward's reputation was at a low ebb: 'Mr Coward [. . .] is his own invention and contribution to this century. Anyone who cannot see that should keep well away from the theatre' (Morley 1974: 362) – praise which deftly sidestepped the question of Coward's abilities as a playwright.

However, public self-invention (and reinvention) in the era of Bowie and Madonna now receive critical investigation and respect as an important part of an artist's armoury. And nobody is under the illusion that it is easy. The editor of the *Sketch* who in 1925 captioned a front-page picture of a dressing-gowned Coward, after his smash success *The Vortex*, 'Noël the Fortunate' assumed that the relationship between Coward and his public was simple (*Sketch* 29 April 1925). In fact it was often painful and always volatile. The audience who copied the dressing-gowns and greeted jokes in his 1921 *succès d'estime The Young Idea* with 'Another Noëlism' made it clear that they were not offering unconditional adulation. In 1927 his comedy of (imaginary) adultery *Home Chat* prompted a shout from the gallery of 'We expected better', while the title of *Sirocco* (1927) became shorthand for theatrical disaster. People spat at Coward as he left the theatre. The following year, in 1928, his revue *This Year of Grace!* bounced back with skits on current playwrights; one entitled 'Any Noël Coward Play' consisted simply of a leading lady taking a curtain call to vigorous booing. *This Year of Grace!* played to packed houses and was praised by Virginia Woolf – though barely three years later she was remarking that Coward's gifts were 'out of the sixpenny box at Woolworth's' (Hoare 1995: 255). Such spats between Coward and his public were only partly about quality. Coward castigated the audience of *Home Chat* for bad manners but admitted that it was 'a little better than bad but not quite good enough' (Coward 1950: xiii); the same, he agreed, could be said of *Sirocco*. But *Sirocco* was also 'completely different in theme, atmosphere and characterization from anything that [he] had done hitherto' (ibid.: xi), and there was resentment on this score. It starred matinée idol Ivor Novello as an empty-headed and selfish seducer. The ending showed a dimwitted adulteress abandoned by husband and lover: rather than moralizing, she realizes that she is frightened but also, for the first time in her life, free. Such anti-romanticism was too strong and the audience could not forgive Coward's refusal to stick to the kit form of himself.

In later years Coward lectured the new generation of playwrights on consideration for the audience; however, he never equated consideration with dishing out what the public wanted. 'Above all, dear pioneers,' he warned, 'never, never, never bore the living hell out of it' (*Sunday Times* 15 January 1961). The volatile relationship between his image and his public became, ultimately, the root of his comedy; his best work, including the five comedies that he considered 'important' (Coward 1958: xxxii) – *Hay Fever* (1925), *Private Lives* (1930), *Design for Living* (1933), *Blithe Spirit* (1941) and *Present Laughter* (1943) – explore the creation, care and maintenance of the performing self and its relationship to the audience. He discussed performance in *Star Quality*, a short story about an actress (published in 1951). Superficially, it endorses Connolly's sour-cream verdict:

> Her whole life is passed in a sort of hermetically-sealed projection-room watching her own 'rushes'. She loves nobody and nobody loves her [. . .] she can be alluring, charming, very grand, utterly simple, kind, cruel, a good sort or a fiend [. . .] what really goes on, what is really happening deep down inside, no one will ever know – least of all herself. (Coward 1983: 483)

But what makes Coward's star a star is neither self-centredness nor the absence of an existential core. It is 'that extraordinary capacity for investing whatever she touches with her own truth' (ibid.: 429). Coward was to use his partnership with Gertrude Lawrence (thinly disguised in *Star Quality*) to proclaim his 'stubborn faith in the star system' (Coward 1954: xi) with *Tonight at 8.30* (1936), a series of one-act plays designed to show off their versatility – because for Coward 'truth' does not reside in what the performer articulates to the audience. It is not synonymous with social, political or religious convictions. Nor is it concerned with the performer's personality. 'Truth' inheres in the relationship between audience and star, in the giving and receiving of the self as constituted at any given moment. It demands emotional and intellectual investment on both sides of the footlights because its nature is constantly changing. The star, in Coward's sense, cannot rely for success on a formula, because the star gives the audience the right to see the process of self-creation and even participate in it. The audience, for their part, must strive to understand the new images on offer and reject them only on the grounds of quality, not novelty. The interaction, at its most profound, can offer epiphanies about what it means to be an individual in a world where the old structures are breaking up; at its shallowest, it can still offer some tips on personal style.

Coward's preoccupation with performance sprang from awareness of being a late Victorian. A character in his short story *This Time Tomorrow* distracts herself from a stressful air journey with *The Oxford Book of Victorian Verse*.

> How little they had to fear, those Victorians, compared with us today! Of course there were occasionally routine disasters like the Tay Bridge blowing down with a train on it [. . .]. many more people died of appendicitis than they did nowadays, and there were no anaesthetics [. . .] but taken by and large they had an easy time of it. They had leisure to think and plan and get their minds into a peaceful state of acceptance. The idea of death had so much more dignity and grace. Lovesick girls went into 'Declines' and had a little calves-foot jelly and expired: poets coughed their lives away in sanatoriums and died peacefully murmuring lovely things to their loved ones. There was hardly any banging and burning and being blown to bits and torn by jagged steel. (Coward 1983: 413)

This may be flippant, but it also expresses the mixed feelings about their heritage shared by a generation born, like Coward, at the time of the Boer War. They were conscious of being shaped by the jingoism and guilt of this last imperial adventure and by the optimism born of innovations like the cinema and the motor car. They were conscious of the transformation of values brought about by a world war in which people they knew and loved had been 'blown to bits and torn by jagged steel'. They were conscious of their grounding in Victorian traditions of sobriety and hard work. (Coward maintained all his life that 'work is more fun than fun' and was not disingenuous when he told the censor that *The Vortex* was a moral tract on the evils of drugs.) They experienced a need to give their times new shape and definition. As Eliot was to change the face of poetry and Joyce and Woolf the novel, Coward was to play a major role in making the theatre a very different place from that of the old century.

He did so by exploiting all the theatrical traditions in which he had worked as a boy. If these did not include those of the independent stage societies who introduced Ibsen and Chekhov to England, they embraced not only the end-of-the-pier concert party the Poppy Pierrots but German expressionism and the emerging cinema. In his teens he worked with Charles Hawtrey, Wilde's original Lord Goring; later he was Slightly in *Peter Pan* (and as Tynan famously remarked, Wholly in it ever since) where Gerald Du Maurier created the part of Hook. Hawtrey and Du Maurier pioneered a new comic style, deceptively relaxed, throwing away epigrams with studied carelessness rather than mugging their way to the punchlines, seducing with a mock-insult rather than a voice throbbing with passion. Coward regarded Hawtrey in particular as a role model, and when he wrote for himself he did not simply develop flip, colloquial dialogue but went further, constructing a world in which it could more convincingly be uttered. Coward, as Tynan pointed out, 'took the fat off English comic dialogue' (Tynan 1989: 221). The linguistic radicalism was a logical development of his plots – and these, in turn, sprang from a view of society that was distinctly modernist.

The comedy of Coward's early youth mocked social conventions – wittily, like Wilde, or unkindly, like Maugham – but left them intact, if threadbare. Marriage was still the logical conclusion of courtship and divorce meant ostracism; a writer might show the economic basis of these facts, but no real alternatives were considered. Shaw or Barrie might engage in acid dissection of sexual politics but their heroines did not rock the boat as Ibsen's Nora did, nor would the censor have permitted them to. The status quo was restored after complex plots which put the heart and conscience of the characters under every possible strain, plots which invariably involved secrets to be hidden and lies to be told exponentially until the resolution. The audience laughed *at* characters who found themselves trapped in the web of escalating deceit and *with* the more detached and cynical characters who commented on them.

Coward's characters sometimes make half-hearted attempts at concealment, but the real joke is that they are too lazy to sustain them. In *Private Lives* (1930) Amanda tries to persuade her new husband to leave before he discovers her former husband is honeymooning in the same hotel. Rather than milk the situation for concealment and chases, Coward throws it away with the utmost economy: Victor enters grumbling 'Why on earth didn't you think of your sister's tragedy before?' and lets Amanda improvise for less than a minute – 'I can see her now, lying dead with that dreadful expression on her face' – before she sulkily admits defeat (Coward 1934: 488).

This is funny because it deflates the sophisticated Amanda and renders her childlike; it does not perform the more usual comic function of increasing the tempo by showing us respectability at bay. Victorian comedy takes for granted that the discovery of a past love affair could be ruinous and that even unjustified suspicion must be avoided by lies and counterplots. In Coward's world – where Marie Stopes inserted discreet advertisements in the press, and changes in the divorce laws empowered women to an unprecedented degree – divorce did not necessarily mean social disgrace, and *everybody* had a past. Hence, Coward recognized, there was a need to reorganize the structure of light comedy. When characters no longer needed concealment, complexity was pointless. His plots became wafer thin. People meet, quarrel and pair off; these activities can be arranged in different orders, but in general that is all that actually happens. The endings can be deceptively conservative: in *The Young Idea* (1921) siblings engineer the reunion of their divorced parents; in *Private Lives* (1930) divorcees abandon their new partners and run away together; in *Present Laughter* (1942) the divorced actor returns to his wife; in *Hay Fever* (1925) the impossibly rude Blisses are abandoned in disgust by the people they have flirted with, and don't even notice because they are enjoying themselves as a family. But while these endings are, in Coward's words, 'clean as a whistle', they are only possible because the characters do not care about sexual conformity. In the modernist world divorce may no longer mean social ruin, but it concentrates the mind wonderfully and helps the characters reaffirm love. Previous sexual experience may lead to uncomfortable visions of the beloved 'bouncing about on divans with awful widows' but the happiest lovers are those who do not give in to jealousy (Coward 1934: 508). In 1933 *Design for Living* fulfilled Coward's long-held ambition to star with his friends Alfred Lunt and Lynne Fontanne. It is a response to what Coward called 'the whole bloody nine acts' of O'Neill's *Strange Interlude*, which featured Fontanne in 1928. Both plays show a woman torn between two men, but O'Neill's shows his trio destroyed by jealousy, which he takes for granted as the inevitable consequence of desire. Coward's threesome overcome jealousy (not to mention envy of artistic success) to settle down together.

Such apparent sensationalism made Coward a byword for sophistication, but his comic endings are grounded in something not more sophisticated than conventional marriage but more primitive: loyalty. Loyalty binds his quarrelling married couples, from the sybarites of *Private Lives* to the cheap music-hall act in *Red Peppers* (1936); it also binds families, like the Blisses in *Hay Fever*, and friends and colleagues, as in *Present Laughter*, where the whole group who look after Garry Essendine unite against the character who seeks to break them up; it can also create brand-new social units: Leo, Gilda and Otto in *Design for Living* can only meaningfully function as a trio, however often they try to pair off. Such loyalty is not a considered rejection of social norms but an animal instinct. When marriage – or remarriage – ends a Coward comedy it does not partake of the traditional symbolism of rebirth and fertility; it is evidence of survival to face another day.

Desire, in Coward's comedy, is not a life force that drives the characters to overcome a series of comic obstacles to fulfilment. Desire is a joke that fate plays on them. In Restoration comedy – which enjoyed a revival while Coward was dominating con-temporary theatre in the 1920s – 'wit' is the sign of moral health and the wittiest characters make love matches, while physical indignity is reserved for those who lack their verbal and moral awareness. Wit, however, does not save Coward's characters. Desire makes them ludicrous at all levels. 'We're figures of fun all right' says Elyot to Amanda (Coward 1934: 520); he is proved right by the second-act quarrels, which culminate in screaming insults and fighting on the floor just as they are surprised by the spouses before whom they have resolved to 'behave exquisitely' (ibid.: 519). Desire turns the quartet in *Private Lives* into a Bergsonian mechanism, popping on and off their Mediterranean balconies like figures in an art deco weatherhouse; it pushes the 'three sided erotic hotchpotch' in *Design for Living* (Coward 1934: 463) into a series of one-to-one encounters that mirror one another with ludicrous symmetry. Money, talent and intelligence are of no help; self-knowledge, the quality that for centuries separated witty observers like Wilde's Lord Goring from comic butts like Malvolio, saves nobody from what Peter Holland calls Coward's 'comic geometry' (1994: 267). The solution, according to Elyot, is to be aware of the self as performer and accept the geometrical indignities with grace because there is nothing beyond them:

> Let's be superficial and pity the poor philosophers. Let's blow trumpets and squeakers, and enjoy the party as much as we can, like very small, quite idiotic schoolchildren. Let's savour the delight of the moment. Come and kiss me darling, before your body rots, and worms pop in and out of your eyesockets. (Coward 1934: 521)

This sense of meaninglessness is articulated in Coward's more serious works, but with less clarity and style. In *Cavalcade* (1931) two families at different ends of the social spectrum live through the first 30 years of the twentieth century and experience the breakdown of old social structures and the futility of war; at times both sides seem locked in stale theatrical conventions; the lower-class Bridges family are seen as drunk and ignorant once they step out of the role of servants and attempt to work for themselves. It is when the play presents a series of expressionist images of social breakdown rather than trying to represent it naturalistically through its selected characters that it finds theatrical power. Fanny, the maid's daughter who, like Coward, has broken through the class system by her own talent, presides over the final tableau to sing *Twentieth Century Blues:*

> What is there to strive for
> Love, or keep alive for? Say –
> Hey hey hey, call it a day.
> (Coward 1934: 74)

She does not expect an answer, and does not get one; no character in Coward's explicitly political plays, from *Post Mortem* in 1930 to *Peace in Our Time* in 1946, finds a solution beyond personal loyalty or a patriotism that is that same loyalty writ large, an instinctive response to threat from without which finds its expression in unpretentious decency and courage.

But if the *experience* of the sybarites in Coward's light comedies looks insignificant alongside that of characters who have lived through war and recession, their response to the Twentieth Century Blues is valid within its limits. With the trumpets and squeakers Elyot begins to outline a survival strategy for the conscious performing self. When he cracks jokes to try and alleviate the tension between the irate spouses and their eloping partners and only Amanda laughs, we see the play's performing selves united in their understanding of style as a strategy of self-protection in a world where values are changing. This goes beyond a smooth coping mechanism at a particular narrative juncture. *Private Lives* was Coward's response to a mental picture of 'Gertie in a white Molyneux dress on a terrace in the South of France' (Coward 1999: 373). Elyot and Amanda have no apparent profession, but the musical interludes ensure their roots in the Coward–Lawrence double act are always on view. T. E. Lawrence watched them rehearse and found it impossible to decide when they were 'in character' or being themselves (Lesley 1976: 139). This foregrounding of the actor *as* actor invites the audience to share in the creative process, to endorse the elegant performance on the trumpets and squeakers as a way of dealing with a world where all are painfully aware that new relationships to love and desire must be forged to fit the times.

Such performance is carefully distinguished from affectation. *The Vortex* showed a world of posturing pseudo-intellectuals who bolster the illusion of their talent with drugs and sex. Coward borrowed from the expressionists to stylize its representation into a bleakly funny cartoon image. Never shy of pointing out his talent for theatrical innovation, he enshrined a challenge to those not familiar with new techniques of staging:

> There must be a feeling of hectic amusement and noise, the air black with cigarette smoke and superlatives. During the first part of the scene everyone must appear to be talking at once, but the actual lines spoken while dancing must be timed to reach the audience as the speakers pass near the footlights. *This scene will probably be exceedingly difficult to produce, but is absolutely indispensable.*

> HELEN: It's much too fast, Nicky
> TOM: Do slow down a bit.
> NICKY: It's the pace that's marked on the record.
> PAWNIE: I've never danced well since the War, I don't know why.
> FLORENCE: But your last act was so strong, when she came in half mad with fright and described everything minutely.
> BRUCE: I try to write as honestly as possible.

> (Coward 1934: 200)

One of the more innovative aspects of his drama is its erosion of the barrier between play and revue; while Maugham and Wilde kept to the three-act structure and solid prose, Coward was equally comfortable with the format of sketches and songs that had dominated the West End during World War I and trained the audience to expect relentless energy and speed, vigorous movement and constant shifts of pace and mood. Nicky, Pawnie and co. would fit seamlessly into the surreal masque *Dance Little Lady* or the acid sketch about debs slumming it on the Tube, both found in *This Year of Grace!*

> MILLICENT: Have you change for a pound?
> FRED: Mostly in pennies, mum.
> MILLICENT: How divine – we can buy things with them.
> FRED: I shouldn't do that, mum, if I was you. I should send them to the British Museum as curiosities.

> (Coward 1939: 6)

While these figures are so locked in their own absurd posturings that they attract only scornful laughter, Coward's comedy was more generous to those of the self-aware performer. The Blisses in *Hay Fever* are monsters, but also professionals, and they use the tools of their trade to negotiate personal relationships. Judith is ridiculous in her self-centred inability to master the language of another person's world; 'I must come to your first night', she absently assures the young boxer who fancies her (Coward 1934: 270). Nevertheless, the family creates an explosion of comic energy by their construction of a magnificent artifice out of the routine flirtatious insincerities of their guests. When the invited guest of each Bliss in turn selects an alternative family member to flatter, their response is the same: Victorian excesses of passion and sentiment, climaxing in a group improvisation around the second-act curtain of Judith's hit melodrama *Love's Whirlwind*. Sorel's diplomat boyfriend, who has been dallying with Judith, is knocked over as she emotes to Sorel 'Don't strike! He is your father!!!!' (ibid.: 321). While this wittily sends up Pinero, it also celebrates a spirit of conscious play triumphing over routine sexual game-playing that privileges promiscuity over real desire.

Coward explored the way the self develops performance as a survival tool only to find that the sheer mechanics of the 'trumpets and squeakers' are more challenging than they appear at first sight. In *Private Lives* Elyot and Amanda play and sing to enchant each other (and the audience), but both are frustrated by the gap between the romance evoked by their 'cheap music' and quotidian sex (Coward 1934: 19). Amanda pushes Elyot away because it is too soon after dinner to make love: he rages that she has 'no sense of glamour, no sense of glamour at all' (ibid.: 516).

The performer's stock in trade is sexuality. Coward once remarked that his audience 'must (not necessarily consciously) want to go to bed with me' (*Harpers Bazaar*, August 1960, interview with Robert Muller). But our comic pleasure in the roles he wrote for himself and his most valued acting partners does not lie exclusively – as it did in the work of Hawtrey or Du Maurier – in imagining oneself in the place of the object of desire. It lies equally in co-operating with them to subvert the role of the audience as voyeur. We are not hidden behind the fourth wall, and characters rarely spend much time in embraces and endearments that might give the sense of violating their privacy. Rather, the audience is acknowledged; they are sharing a game, a process of ironizing the erotic. In *Present Laughter* this becomes overt with a small in-joke: after the door-bell has signalled the entrance of three would-be lovers for Garry Essendine in succession, the fourth ring prompts him to say 'With any luck it'll be the Lord Chamberlain' (Coward 1954: 417).

Traditional gender roles are also refreshingly subverted. Elyot is scathing about Victor's 'highly traditional' insistence that they should come to blows (Coward 1934: 537). Otto in *Design for Living* goes off for maritime adventures on a freighter (as Coward did while writing the play), but rather than turning into a butch Hemingway hero merely gains a party piece – he can say 'How do you do?' in Norwegian (Coward 1934: 397). Larita in *Easy Virtue* (1924) knows that her image as a remarried divorcée is straight out of Pinero's *The Second Mrs Tanqueray*, and when her new in-laws are hostile she makes a show-stopping entrance covered in makeup and jewels.

Self-consciousness about role is inevitably self-consciousness about language. Du Maurier was a successful romantic comedian because he could make a witty insult sound sexier than a string of endearments. Coward pushed this relationship between words and emotions to new limits. *Shadow Play* (1935) uses movie conventions such as flashback with a casualness J. B. Priestley's 'time' plays never achieved. A character speaks of 'Small talk – a lot of small talk with quite different thoughts going on behind it' (Coward 1954: 179). This is not subtext in the Stanislavskian sense; while an older generation of dramatists might consider with Maugham that Coward 'exactly copied the average talk, with its hesitations, mumblings and repetitions, of average people' (*Sunday Chronicle* 26 April 1925), it is clear that Coward's characters are not linguistically 'average' but masters of using trivial discourse to express the emotions which underlie it. When they are polite, the more honest of them acknowledge, like Larita, that politeness is a 'refuge for our real feelings' (Coward 1939: 515). When they talk nonsense, it does not function as a disguise for desire but a strategy for performing it. This performance can be exuberantly irrelevant – Gilda and Otto begin their affair as he vaults over the sofa crying 'Hvordan staar der til?' (Coward 1934: 406). It can offer a way to say the unsayable: regret is inappropriate for Amanda and Elyot, honeymooning with new spouses, but to talk about sacred elephants as 'awfully sweet' imports a language of tenderness into the conversation. It can be playful deferral of the inevitable: in *Present Laughter* Coward spends almost half the play leading up to the moment when Garry Essendine lets himself be seduced by the wife of his manager; their kiss is then postponed for a discussion of London concert venues and the line which brings down the curtain on their entwined bodies: 'I won't hear a word against the Albert Hall' (Coward 1954: 376).

This level of accomplishment carries with it the risk that the self can be annihilated by its own glittering masks. Garry Essendine is Coward's wittiest exploration of this risk, because he has turned it into part of his seduction technique. Confronted by a dimwitted debutante who invites herself to spend the night, he makes himself even more fanciable by his admission that 'I'm always acting – watching myself go by – that's what's so horrible – I see myself all the time eating, drinking, loving, suffering – sometimes I think I'm going mad'(Coward 1954: 328). He plays a more sophisticated variation on the theme for the canny Joanna by commenting on her own performance, 'every word, every phrase, every change of mood cunningly planned' (ibid.: 373). Garry's ambition, constantly thwarted by his agent, is to play Peer Gynt, the man whose soul can be peeled like an onion to reveal nothing at all at its heart; the play has been labelled tragic – for example by John Lahr, who sees *Present Laughter* as exploring 'a dilemma: a man who dissimulates so eagerly that he has forgotten who he is' (Lahr 1982: 32). But this underestimates the reciprocal element Coward identifies in stardom. Garry is not solely responsible for his performing self. It is in the hands of the body of disparate individuals who look after it – producer, manager, secretary, scriptwriter, a group which resembles Coward's own trusted and much-loved entourage; they select his scripts, choose his venues, buy his dressing-gowns; they generally protect him from admirers, but occasionally punish his presumption in pretending to be too 'unspoiled by your great success' (Coward 1954: 339) by letting loose fans like the would-be playwright Roland Maule. *Present Laughter* ends happily not because Garry finds himself (though, arguably, Roland Maule finds *himself* after Garry's impassioned and witty lecture on theatrical craftsmanship), but because his entourage has resisted Joanna's attempt to break it up and his performing self is safe in their collective keeping.

The performing self inhabits the performing body and the audience is left in no doubt that it is as ordinary and vulnerable as their own. No one throws a custard pie at Coward's self-dramatizers, but the maintenance of style has a physical, often absurd price. Gilda, looking her most glamorous, moans that her feet hurt. Garry ponders the concept of a toupee like Hamlet confronting the skull. Even death does not bring dignity: when Judy Campbell created the role of the ghost Elvira in *Blithe Spirit* Coward instructed her not to waft gracefully but to stamp about as if wearing gumboots. As Coward grew older he reprised Edwardian plots with elderly characters far more down-to-earth than anything imagined by Pinero. The ladies in the home for aged actors in *Waiting in the Wings* (1960) suffer from rheumatism and Alzheimer's but deflate an emotional colleague with 'stop overacting' (Coward 1962: 517); Carlotta in *A Song at Twilight* (1966) uses compromising letters like an Edwardian adventuress, but without the glamour:

> In 1957 I lost my last remaining tooth in the Curran Theatre [. . .] it was a gallant old stump that held my lower plate together. I remember saying to my understudy one day, 'Sally, when this is out, you're on!' And sure enough a week later it was and she was. (Coward 1979: 178)

Coward's more serious plays are now clearly period pieces. *The Vortex* is still powerful but its characters are as alien to us as *The Second Mrs Tanqueray*; but his five favoured comedies have a curious modernity. While *The Vortex* shows characters using the sexual attitudes of their own social group as a vehicle for unconscious self-dramatization, the comedies of play strip down the business of loving to the basics. Here characters disregard gender; they do not have to worry about their economic status; they are artists who can afford to disregard social convention; they inhabit an almost abstract landscape in which the only matters under consideration are love and the lovers' way of acting out themselves. They do, however, have to consider us; we are fully involved in the process. Sex, gender, body and language are deployed by those performing selves so consciously that we are aware of their need for our desire and our laughter, even our money; the mocking on-stage self cannot function without these, but its reliance upon them means that it cannot take itself too seriously. Coward's reputation has fluctuated, but it is perhaps only in an age of spin, in which the media control the way that even minor celebrities are perceived, that his notion of the self as invention and artifice can be appreciated. His persona was part of his legacy, but it was one that could be adapted, enjoyed and laughed at, one that offered the actor a style, but also offered his audience a way of challenging and rendering poignant our understanding of how we present ourselves in our world.

PRIMARY READING

Coward, Noël (1934). *Play Parade I (Cavalcade, Design for Living, Bitter Sweet, Private Lives, Hay Fever, The Vortex, Post Mortem)*. London: Heinemann.

Coward, Noël (1939). *Play Parade II (This Year of Grace!, Words and Music, Operette, Conversation Piece, Easy Virtue, Fallen Angels)*. London: Heinemann.

Coward, Noël (1950). *Play Parade III (The Queen Was in the Parlour, I'll Leave it to You, Sirocco, The Young Idea, The Rat Trap, This was a Man, Home Chat, The Marquise)*. London: Heinemann.

Coward, Noël (1954). *Play Parade IV (Tonight at 8.30, Present Laughter, This Happy Breed)*. London: Heinemann.

Coward, Noël (1958). *Play Parade V (Blithe Spirit, Peace in Our Time, Quadrille, Relative Values, Pacific 1860)*. London: Heinemann.

Coward, Noël (1962). *Play Parade VI (Point Valaine, Ace of Clubs, South Sea Bubble, Nude with Violin, Waiting in the Wings)*. London: Heinemann.

Coward, Noël (1979). *Plays Five (Relative Values, Waiting in the Wings, Look After Lulu, Suite in Three Keys)*. London: Methuen.

Coward, Noël (1983). *Collected Short Stories*. London: Methuen.

Coward, Noël (1999). *Autobiography*. London: Methuen.

FURTHER READING

Beaton, Cecil (1954). *The Glass of Fashion*. London: Cassell.

Gray, Frances (1987). *Noël Coward*. London: Macmillan.

Hoare, Philip (1995). *Noël Coward*. London: Sinclair-Stevenson.

Holland, Peter (1994). 'Noel Coward and Comic Geometry' in M. Cordner, P. Holland and J. Kerrigan (eds.). *English Comedy*. Cambridge: Cambridge University Press.

Innes, Christopher (1992). *Modern British Drama: 1890-1990*. Cambridge: Cambridge University Press.

Kaplan, Joel (ed.) (2000). *Look Back in Pleasure: Noël Coward Reconsidered*. London: Methuen.

Lahr, John (1982). *Coward the Playwright*. London: Methuen.

Lesley, Cole (1976). *The Life of Noël Coward*. London: Jonathan Cape.

Luckhurst, Mary and Moody, Jane (2005). *Theatre and Celebrity in Britain, 1660–2000*. Basingstoke: Palgrave.

Mander, Raymond and Mitchenson, Joe (1957). *Theatrical Companion to Coward*. London: Rockliff.

Morley, Sheridan (1974). *A Talent to Amuse*. London: Penguin.

Tynan, Kenneth (1989). *Profiles*. London: Nick Hern.

19

Beckett's Divine Comedy

Katharine Worth

My title is not meant to point to a particular emphasis in this chapter on Dante's *The Divine Comedy* and Beckett's fascination with that great poem. Rather, the phrase sprang to mind in the course of pondering the critical difficulties raised by the placing of Beckett's dramatic oeuvre in the category 'comedy'. In some ways, of course, this is a natural placing. Beckett did at any rate describe the 1955 English version of *Waiting for Godot* (1953, Paris, in French[1]) on its title page as 'A tragi-comedy'. And there are lively comic elements in all three of the longer stage plays, from the knockabout turns of Vladimir and Estragon in *Godot* to jokes in *Happy Days* (1961, New York) about Willie's dirty postcard, which Winnie puts her spectacles on to pore over, avidly, while protesting 'No but this is just genuine pure filth!' (Beckett 1986: 144).[2] Such high spirits are more subdued in or absent from the later 'shorts'. But connections with comedy remain, if at times only in a droll turn of phrase or wry remark. In *Play* (1963, Ulm-Donau, in German) these build up into often very funny, though also agonized, recalls of sexual betrayals and jealousies of the past. Irish wit is always felt to be at work, enjoying the absurd whenever the situation allows.

The situations, however, are such as take us into a world beyond wit and worldliness. From *Godot* in 1953 to *What Where* in 1983 Beckett always makes us aware of an elusive spiritual dimension which the imagination continually seeks to express creatively. The difficulty of fitting this complex, haunted drama into the category of 'comedy' was accidentally highlighted by this volume's arrangement of playwrights in historical order, which has the droll effect of making Beckett's immediate predecessors Oscar Wilde and Noël Coward – unlikely bedfellows, though sharing with him a delight in absurdity. Clearly, some way of qualifying the generic term 'comedy' had to be found, to indicate what in Beckett's drama fits it for that category. His comedy is certainly of a rare, perhaps unique kind, co-existing as it does with intimations of a dimension I am calling divine.

That remote, mysteriously 'other' dimension is at times associated with religious thought and feeling. Beckett often has fun with the subject, as in the radio play *All*

That Fall (1957, BBC Third Programme), when he amuses us with the devout Miss Fitt's complacency about her religion. She failed to recognize her old acquaintance in church, she tells Mrs Rooney, because then she is so alone with her Maker that the verger taking the collection plate knows not to bother her: 'I simply do not see the plate, or bag, whatever it is they use, how could I?' (182). The amused tone turns sombre on the hard journey home of the Rooneys when she quotes from the psalm beginning 'The Lord upholdeth all that fall' and a silence falls upon them both, followed by wild laughter (198). In the television play *Eh Joe* (1966, BBC 2), Joe's surface piety is mocked by the voice of an invisible woman who compels him to listen while she describes the sad suicide of a girl he had abandoned, and taunts him with seeing himself as a suffering, Christ-like figure: 'The passion of our Joe' (364). He remains silent, leaving his feelings to be deduced from his face, which periodically enlarges till it fills the screen. Jack McGowran, the first Joe in 1966, presented a set, expressionless look, Patrick Magee in 1972 a stricken one.[3]

Of the stage plays, *Waiting for Godot* is most overtly concerned with religious issues, the Bible, the need to be 'saved'. At the start Vladimir is puzzling about the Crucifixion and how only one of the two thieves was saved; at the end he is exclaiming 'Christ have mercy on us!' (86). Estragon also has the Bible in mind, as we learn when he abandons his boots centre stage, citing Christ as his example for going barefoot: 'All my life I've compared myself to him' (49). In *Endgame* (1957, Paris, in French) prayers are heard at intervals, often in comical/satirical mode, as when Hamm's call, 'Let us pray to God', is received by Clov with a weary 'Again!' and by Nagg with a request for a bribe: 'Me sugar-plum!' Hamm's tart reply, 'God first!', keeps the comic note going, as does his reaction to the lack of divine response: 'The bastard! He doesn't exist' (119). Like many of the other black jokes or gibes in the play, this one reminds us of the Bible story while seeming to reject it. Prayers come in many different kinds of clothing in Beckett's theatre, from those in poetic cover, like Winnie's Miltonic line 'Hail, holy light' (160), to simple expressions of feeling for friends in trouble from the three women in the minuscule *Come And Go* (1966, Berlin, in German).

Beckett described *Godot* in its English version as 'A tragi-comedy in two acts' (7). What kind of comedy is it which comes so close to the tragic world while resisting fully tragic endings and opens up mystical dimensions while so enjoying the comical? It was at this point that the phrase 'divine comedy' suggested itself for a title. It seemed curiously appropriate, though difficult to apply in a modern context. Dante could use the term 'comedy' for an often terrifying, even gruesome, portrayal of humanity's spiritual existence because his Christian vision allowed for a Purgatorio as well as an Inferno and led to the unquestioned happy ending of a Paradiso. For Beckett, and no doubt for many in his audiences, that confident vision could not serve. James Knowlson has recorded how in his many re-readings of Dante, Beckett, unsurprisingly, focused on the purgatorial rather than the paradisiacal (Knowlson 1996: *passim*). Yet in changed form a positive vision made its way into the modern theatre through *Waiting for Godot*. Salvation is still the issue here, though the two hopefully waiting get no nearer the Saviour than a young Boy, unable to tell them much at all. It is a vision tuned to an age of doubt and scepticism. This 'tragicomic blend', to quote Ruby Cohn (and Beckett), has appealed to 'imaginations everywhere throughout "this bitch of an earth" ' (Cohn 2001: 179).

Estragon is always nearer to despair than Vladimir. When peering into the off-stage space, but finding it empty, he cries 'I'm in hell!' (67), bringing the dark side of the ancient vision into focus as a fierce personal distress. Hell is easier to modernize convincingly than heaven, Pozzo than Godot – though Pozzo is far from simple in his role as a false Godot. He is someone with total power over another person which he uses brutally. And yet he can make us laugh, as when he offers to have Lucky perform for the other two, feeling he hasn't done enough to reward their 'correct' behaviour to him: 'that's what tortures me, is it enough?' (37).

Heaven may be harder to dramatize than hell, but it is brought very near in Act II when Vladimir and Estragon move into a poetic rhythm of great beauty, conjuring up for us the mysterious presence of 'All the dead voices'. Beckett's stage direction requires a 'Long silence' following this high moment, before the two friends, deeply shaken, speak to each other, then return to the lively improvisations which feed the spirit of fellowship (57). The comic and the mystical require each other. Even the solitary tree, heavy with symbolism of crucifixion, is drawn firmly into the comic, not to say farcical, sphere when Estragon tries to use it as a way of hanging himself, forgetting that the trousers designed for a makeshift rope have fallen round his feet.

The word 'divine', used three times in the play, is spoken not by the seekers for Godot but by the slave commanded to 'think', the broken-down scholar, Lucky, in his wild meditation on the existence of 'a personal God quaquaquaqua with white beard' (40). Walter Asmus, when assistant to Beckett, who was himself directing the 1975 production of *Godot* (in German) at the Schiller-Theater, Berlin, was told by him that in his 'quaquaquaqua' Lucky was trying to pronounce the word 'quaversalis', referring to 'a god who turns himself in all directions at the same time' (McMillan and Knowlson 1993: 133). In this light Lucky's seeming bit of nonsense would express the difficulty of getting at that abstruse concept. Perhaps the problem of reconciling the idea of a 'personal God' with the infinite distances of the 'divine' condition is one that cannot be resolved. In his 'think', however, Lucky uses the word once more in referring to the 'divine Miranda', which points us to Shakespeare's heroine in *The Tempest*, someone able to suffer 'with those who for reasons unknown but time will tell are plunged in torment' (41). That she could so feel for total strangers understandably makes her 'divine' for the maltreated Lucky.

When he and his master make their final exit they could seem equally victims of a compulsion to travel on, always harshly connected. Also connected by need, though so differently, are Didi and Gogo (to use the pet names which express their closeness). Didi placing his coat over the sleeping Gogo is a touching image of the relief each provides for the other, as are their exchanges of wit and inventive fun. The comic context is never lost but has surely acquired a touch of the divine by the time they stand together at the end, still disappointed, still sharing the need to be there.

In the harsher comedy of *Endgame* there might seem little sense of the divine. The bare room with its two small windows out of reach except by a ladder, the blind man in the wheelchair, the crippled servant, the old parents consigned to dustbins; all this might rather suggest a kind of hell. Hamm sees it that way, as being 'down in a hole' while 'beyond the hills' it may still be green and flowering (111). He makes it so himself, we might think, with his contemptuous treatment of his own parents, his bullying of Clov, his way of turning 'divine' precepts such as 'Love your neighbour as yourself' into coarse caricature: 'Lick your neighbour as yourself!' (125).

It is not quite so simple, however. The dice are loaded against the inhabitants of the 'shelter' in their afflictions, to an extent which induces sympathy for them all, though Hamm often risks losing it. As for the parents, brusquely pushed down in their bins by Clov, we can tell ourselves they are not 'really' there, in their absurd nightcaps – or not as Hamm and Clov seem to be there. Yet their being so visually comical doesn't, so it proves in performance, rule out feeling for the nightcapped pair. A fine balance is maintained here, as throughout the play, between a sombre and a comic perspective. We are invited to be amused by the opening conversation of Nagg and Nell, checking on their latest symptoms of physical decay:

NAGG: I've lost me tooth.
NELL: When?
NAGG: I had it yesterday.
NELL: [*Elegiac.*] Ah yesterday!
(99)

This generally draws a laugh in the theatre despite the elegiac note on the word 'yesterday' called for by Beckett's stage direction. When they agree that their sense of sight is failing, melancholy strengthens for both audience and characters. But the comic perspective holds. Nell's 'Yes' to Nagg's query whether she can hear him elicits his triumphant 'Our hearing hasn't failed', at which she replies: 'Our what?' (99). Again we laugh, while also perhaps feeling a sense of chill developing. It's when responses have been refined to this extent that the comedy takes on a touch of the divine, filtering through Nagg's growing concern for Nell and his attempts to cheer her. His telling the story of the tailor and the trousers, which always delights a theatre audience and, he says, made her laugh on their honeymoon, leaves her cold: 'It's not funny' (102). She recalls laughing, not at his story, but only because she 'felt happy' – not quite what he wants her to say, but touching all the same. Their separateness as individuals, highlighted by the separate dustbins, is qualified throughout by such moments. They allow her death to be more than just macabre when Hamm gives the order 'Clear away this muck!', and the 'bottling' is duly carried out by Clov (103). It becomes instead something rare on the stage: a death which is tender and haunting while being also broadly, even grotesquely comic.

The more complex pair, Hamm and Clov, have a master–servant relationship comparable to that of Pozzo and Lucky, but here the servant plays a crucial part in the witty exchanges and repartee that keep them going. Though dressed to go at the close of the play, would Clov really be able to leave? He stands on the opposite side of the stage from the only door, the one leading to his kitchen. 'A second door is very wrong', Beckett wrote, on my referring once to a production I'd seen which had one.[4] The feeling must be that Clov can't go. Each of the pair needs the other to galvanize the witty exchanges and drily comic rituals which keep them going. Hamm's assertion 'I love the old questions' (110) rings true, as also, behind the play-acting, does the sense of movement towards some truth which they understand, though we the audience may not. The 'small boy' seen approaching by Clov on his ladder is one such veiled event. Hamm seems indifferent, but we may guess at something concealed, as we surely do when he says 'It was I was a father to you', at which Clov looks at him 'fixedly' (110). There are dark areas of consciousness here, in a relationship that is often uneasy or fractious. But stronger is the sense of their reliance on each other for relief, often in comic form, as when Clov punctures Hamm's mournful rhetoric about his longing to be by the sea, 'when the tide would come', with one of his pithy negatives: 'There's no more tide' (122). The audience is left unsure quite how to take Hamm's outpourings. (Such an impression was conveyed in the production at the Albery Theatre, London, in 2004 with particular sparkle and finesse by Michael Gambon, as Hamm, and by Lee Evans, a young actor well experienced in comic turns, as Clov.) Nell's reflection 'Nothing is funnier than unhappiness' (101) shocks Nagg but could well be thought of as germane to what Beckett is doing in this testing comedy. For 'comedy' it is, one that enables us to enter with sympathy into the darkness of 'down in the hole'.

Happy Days begins with what could seem mild mockery of the divine, given the comical gap between Winnie's opening line and the astonishing scenic image. Audiences unsurprisingly tend to laugh at the first view of the well-preserved woman of about 50, wearing a pearl necklace on her big bosom (Beckett's early stage direction), so grotesquely embedded up to her waist in a mound of earth, yet announcing rapturously: 'Another heavenly day'. How seriously can we be expected to take the inaudible praying that follows, of which we hear the pious close: 'World without end Amen' (138)?

Yet we soon find we must do so. Her wish to see the best of things, so overdone as to be a great source of fun for audiences, co-exists with a sharp awareness of how things really are, as when she strains to read the words on her toothbrush: 'genuine … pure … what? – [lays down brush] – blind next – [takes off spectacles] – ah well – [lays down spectacles] – seen enough' (139). Similarly amusing is her extravagant delight when Willie bestows on her a grunt or a line from the newspaper he is absorbed in for most of Act 1: 'Oh this *is* a happy day! This will have been another happy day!' But she adds between pauses (particularly meaningful in this play): 'After all. So far' (159). And at the close of the act she is telling herself: 'Pray your old prayer, Winnie' (159).

In Act II, now sunk up to her neck, unable even to turn her head, more fiercely than ever trapped in the unrelenting bright stage light, she is still uttering a kind of prayer, though not the 'conventional doxology', which, as Mary Bryden has shown,

Beckett seldom uses in his writings (Bryden 1998: 117). Winnie's opening line 'Hail, holy light' (160) is drawn not from the gospels, but, significantly, from *Paradise Lost*.

Throughout Act II Winnie uses this power to conjure up absent Willie, appealing to him as a listener, his customary role. When he does finally appear, grotesquely in his wedding clothes, with a bushy white battle-of-Britain beard, she upbraids him for being so slow to respond. Perhaps her power to evoke has faltered because she asks so much more of it where he is concerned. She had easily conjured up for us in the previous act the 'Mr Shower ... or Cooker' who had stared at her so rudely. But though she can call up Willie's 'look' on their wedding day she can't hold it: 'What day? [*Long pause.*] What look?' (166). Something similar happens with her 'story' about little Millie and her doll. Told in a curiously artificial narrative style, it seems at first to reflect the Winnie who wants everything to be happy. But it won't go that way. The emphasis on the doll's 'undies' hints at a sexual unease which intensifies when the undressing of 'Dollie' in the story is violently interrupted by the appearance of a mouse, which later runs up Millie's 'little thigh'. Winnie's 'piercing' screams at this point attach the teller to the tale in a rather terrifying way (165).

Significantly, it is then that she calls again for Willie. Whatever went wrong between them is nothing compared to her need for him now. Just what did go wrong we don't know, but there was a crisis, as she reminded Willie in Act 1, when he begged her to take his revolver away 'before I put myself out of my misery'. '*Your* misery!', she had said then, 'derisively' (151). Now it is a different misery and she seems to have acquired new strength to deal with it. Her tone on sexual matters is calm, even amused, as she talks out to a still absent Willie, about the 'sadness' after 'intimate sexual intercourse' that 'one is familiar with of course', adding, teasingly, 'You would concur with Aristotle there, Willie, I fancy' (164). When he does appear and starts crawling up the mound, we could be as unsure as she is about what he is aiming at, Winnie herself or 'something else', maybe the revolver, so conspicuously placed near her. Beckett's comically sinister stage direction tells us he is '*dressed to kill*'. Such doubts make all the more affecting the one word he speaks, the '*just audible*' sound of his pet name for her, 'Win'. Now she can convincingly use the present tense, as only once before, to express her joy – 'Oh this *is* a happy day' (with the usual postscript 'After all. (Pause.) So far') (166–8).

Then she is able at last to sing her song. This is one of the great, unforgettable scenes of theatre. Sung by actors as different as Madeleine Renaud (in French) or Peggy Ashcroft or Billie Whitelaw, I have never known it fail to produce in the audience a hushed silence, as if it were a miracle. So, in a way, it is. The banal words of *The Merry Widow* waltz are lifted, by its lilting tune and the shocking contrast between the song and the brutally immobilized singer, into another dimension where the dance might go on forever, like the memory of the wedding day and the words of love once spoken. Doubt remains about what might follow. Winnie's smiles go off, the two remain simply looking at each other. It is still recognizably the world of comedy, with Willie unromantically frozen in a crawling position. But it trembles on the edge of the divine in that long look, the song which evoked it, and the sense of need for each other that has somehow survived all that has gone wrong in their lives together.

I turn now to the shorter plays, omitting only a few, such as the early 'Roughs' and the later *Catastrophe* (1982, Avignon, in French), which fall rather outside the category bounds I am tracing; also the radio plays *Words and Music* (1962, BBC) and *Cascando* (1962, RTF, in French).

Of the plays written for television, only *Eh Joe*, already discussed, and *Quad* (1982, Süddeutscher Rundfunk) call for mention in the terms of this discussion. The latter conveys a sense of mysterious compulsion to enact a ritual, yet when the four dancers in their brightly coloured, cowled gowns enter one by one, to bustle along intricate set courses, always swerving to avoid the centre, they produce a clockwork effect, a droll neatness, which amuses before it begins to command a response to its formidable sense of purpose. It is a shock when there follows a shorter version of the permutations, with the colour drained away (an accidental result of Beckett seeing the rushes). Loss of colour darkens the mood without extinguishing the suggestion already conveyed; this is the comedy of life, driven by some force, perhaps divine, into predetermined 'courses'.

Can this concept of 'divine comedy' be applied equally to the shorter stage plays? Perhaps not to all, though surely to *Krapp's Last Tape* (1958). Here Beckett's use of a tape recorder brilliantly allows for a fusion of the comic and the lyrical in a process of self-exploration. Farce comes close at times, as in the business with the bananas, greedily relished by old Krapp just before Krapp on tape is heard resolving to 'Cut 'em out!' (217). Krapp's tendency to pomposity amuses while also bringing out the gulf between him and his later self in their attitude to spiritual mysteries. Krapp the elder brushes away more than the sanctimonious tone of his predecessor when he switches him off impatiently: 'Just been listening to that stupid bastard I took myself for thirty years ago' (222). He also dismisses the 'vision' the voice on tape claimed to have had, on a memorable night in March, 'when suddenly I saw the whole thing' (220).

What he does not dismiss are the more hesitant gropings of his younger self towards recognition of what constitutes the 'grain' of his life, 'those things worth having when all the dust has – when all *my* dust has settled' (217). The memories that constitute this 'grain' present themselves in a simple style far removed from that used to describe the 'vision' directly. They might seem random: old Miss McGlome singing songs of her girlhood; an idyllic love scene. But the naturalness of their recall gives them poignancy for the Krapp who listens as for the Krapp who recorded them. Finally there is an overwhelming impression of the mystical silence associated with the memory of lying, very still, with the girl in the punt, being gently moved by quiet waters. Old Krapp's lips are to be seen moving soundlessly while Krapp on tape reflects: 'Never knew such silence. The earth might be uninhabited' (223). A moment of highest pitch, surely bordering on the divine.

Among the later 'shorts' the delicate balance between comical and mystical is struck with a difference in *Play* (1963, in German), where the divine element, if such it be, is overwhelmingly associated with a sense of judgement. Comedy might seem the last thing to expect when the curtain rises on the three heads in their separate urns, gabbling under the command of a faint spotlight. When the spotlight, in fuller strength, mercilessly switches from one head to another to draw out their story of jealousy and adultery, judgement is still uppermost but comedy makes its way in. We can't but laugh at reactions such as M's to his wife's manoeuvres: 'She put a bloodhound on me, but I had a little chat with him. He was glad of the extra money' (309). Nothing tragic here nor much sign of moral anxiety. But we do begin to notice hints at serious consequences to come, even in M's conventional use of the word 'pardon', following the hiccups to which he is subject (a touch of real farce here).

W2 is sure in this first round that, with M, there was no danger of 'the … spiritual thing' (309). But we hear that taking over in the second phase, set in another, more inward dimension, where among the first words spoken is a call for 'Mercy, mercy' (312). Throughout what follows memories merge with anxious speculation on what 'change' in them is demanded by the spotlight. Would the inquisitorial light cease, W1 wonders, if she could some day tell the truth? Perhaps, as M says, all that went before was 'just play' (313). W2 remains doubtful about her ability to change, but it is already happening in the other two: in W1's new sympathy for all the 'Poor creatures' and in M's vision of the three coming together, in harmony, on a May morning (316). It happens in the audience too, surely, during the extraordinary repeat of the whole play, word for word (a unique theatrical experience). After experiencing the painful soul-searching of the second 'round' it is less easy to take the first one as 'just play'. The comedy remains, but has taken on a touch of the 'divine' in those fragile yearnings for friendship and harmony.

The sense of being under some kind of divine judgement and pressure for psychic change takes a more melancholy form in *Not I* (1972, New York). The Mouth suspended in dark space high above the stage, pouring out a breathless account of a miserable life, never knows that she is being heard by a cowled, silent figure on the opposite side, an Auditor (title suggesting both judge and listener) who throws out his arms '*in a gesture of helpless compassion*' (375) each time she refuses to acknowledge the story she tells as her own. The cutting of the Auditor from the televised version of 1991, though required by the change of medium, removed the stage effect of a mysterious other dimension, to do with judgement but also with kindly listening. In the first production, as I recall it, the listener's presence partially softened the harsh shock effect of the speaker's fearful solitude, though Billie Whitelaw, the first Mouth, has recorded the terror, for her as actor, of being so totally cut off physically from stage company and audience alike (Whitelaw 1995).

Can *Not I* be discussed at all in terms of comedy? Only perhaps in the specialized sense of the Dantesque kind which allows for a benign outcome after purgatorial experience. Mouth still offers prayers, we learn, though of a negative kind: 'begging it all to stop' (382). Perhaps because so negative, they remain, as she says, 'unanswered' or 'unheard' – or were they 'too faint'? Maybe she doesn't really want life to stop, for all that is wrong with it. Whether the inner struggle will ever be resolved we can't know. The weakening gestures of support from the Auditor may suggest not. But there is a hint of hope continuing in her last words, as the curtain comes down: 'keep on ... hit on it in the end ... then back ... God is love ... tender mercies'. And the play ends with her retrieval of her vision of the April morning and her voice telling herself to 'pick it up' (383).

In the brief plays following, that delicate balancing of comic and mystical elements yields to meditative, lyrical forms with little space for comedy, though humour never quite goes. The usually solitary speakers are always in some way retreading their past. In *Footfalls* (1976) the focus is on a spectral world evoked by the grey-haired figure in a worn grey wrap (exquisite in Jocelyn Herbert's design for Billie Whitelaw, the first May). In a world of ghostly walking May paces a narrow strip of stage; her mother's voice is heard saying 'I walk here now'; a 'semblance' is perceived (401). No place here for comedy, we might suppose, and it's true that there is not much. Yet after the intensity of the 'walking' sequences the atmosphere lightens, if oddly, when May creates a brighter story for herself and her mother about 'Old Mrs Winter, whom the reader will remember', 'doing' her mother's voice as well as her own and taking her to a church service in daylight, not the moonlight of the ghostly vision (402). And though the wished-for happy ending recedes, the touches of comic warmth may imply hope for some kind of divine peace when the stage light returns after a blackout to show '*No trace of May*' (403).

Towards the end of the oeuvre comic notes are few: the black joke, 'Birth was the death of him', that opens *A Piece of Monologue* (1980, New York); the startlingly unexpected 'Fuck life' from the 'prematurely old' woman in *Rockaby* (1981, Buffalo, New York); in *Ohio Impromptu* (1981, Ohio State University) the Reader's droll lapse into pedantry with his 'symptoms described at length page forty paragraph four' (446).

The note of the divine – of mystical experience, or meditation on spiritual dimensions – may strengthen in these last plays to the point where comedy retreats into the background. But the humorous view of things usually makes itself felt still, if only in a quiet change of tone, a comical eccentricity or *en passant* joke. In the earlier plays, as I have sought to show, comedy and a sense of the divine are wonderfully intertwined, making the mystical seem strangely real and the comical a saving grace.

NOTES

1 Dates after the titles of plays in the body of the chapter refer to the dates of their first performances. Except where indicated these are on stage, in English, and in London.

2 All further references to Beckett's plays are to this edition.

3 The production of *Eh Joe* which Beckett gave me permission to make for teaching

material was filmed by David Clark of the
University of London Audio-Visual Centre in
1972.

4 Samuel Beckett, letter to the author, 12 July
1973, saying also that Clov's door should be a
'simple aperture'.

PRIMARY READING

Beckett, Samuel (1986). *The Complete Dramatic Works*. London: Faber and Faber.

FURTHER READING

Ben-Zvi, Linda (1990). *Women in Beckett: Perform-ance and Critical Perspective*. Urbana: University of Illinois Press.

Bradby, David (2001). *Beckett: 'Waiting for Godot'*. Cambridge: Cambridge University Press.

Bryden, Mary (1998). *Beckett and the Idea of God*. Basingstoke: Macmillan.

Cohn, Ruby (2001). *A Beckett Canon*. Ann Arbor: University of Michigan Press.

Kalb, Jonathan (1989). *Beckett in Performance*. Cambridge: Cambridge University Press.

Knowlson, James (1996). *Damned to Fame: The Life of Samuel Beckett*. London: Bloomsbury.

McMillan, Dougald and Fehsenfeld, Martha (1988). *Beckett in the Theatre*. London: John Calder.

McMillan, Dougald and Knowlson, James (eds.) (1993). *The Theatrical Notebooks of Samuel Beck-ett: 'Waiting for Godot'*. London: Faber and Faber.

McMullan, Anna (1993). *Theatre on Trial: Samuel Beckett's Later Drama*. London: Routledge.

Oppenheim, Lois (ed.) (1994). *Directing Beckett*. Ann Arbor: University of Michigan Press.

Oppenheim, Lois (2004). *Samuel Beckett Studies*. Basingstoke: Palgrave Macmillan.

Stewart, Bruce (ed.) (1999). *Beckett and Beyond*. Gerrards Cross: Colin Smythe.

Whitelaw, Billie (1995). *Billie Whitelaw . . . Who He?*. London: Hodder and Stoughton.

Wilmer, S. E. (ed.) (1992). *Beckett in Dublin*. Dub-lin: Lilliput Press.

Worth, Katharine (1999). *Samuel Beckett's Theatre: Life Journeys*. Oxford: Oxford University Press.

20

Form and Ethics in the Comedies of Brendan Behan

John Brannigan

In *Regarding the Pain of Others*, Susan Sontag considers that certain images or emblems of suffering 'can be used like memento mori, as objects of contemplation to deepen one's sense of reality', perhaps even to galvanize active protest against it, but they would demand 'a sacred or meditative space upon which to look at them' (Sontag 2003: 119). 'Space reserved for being serious is hard to come by in a modern society', Sontag writes, and the image in particular, to convey its 'gravity' and 'emotional power', competes against the proliferation of images, in settings in which contemplation is inhibited, perhaps even deterred. Sontag draws our attention to the ethical problem of representing suffering as a spectacle, when images of suffering might be experienced as entertainment, even moral entertainment: 'There is the satisfaction of being able to look at the image without flinching. There is the pleasure of flinching' (Sontag 2003: 41). She also addresses this problem as one of form, however – the particular form which the representation of suffering might take in order to achieve its emotional impact. At stake in this relationship between ethics and form is the question of how the atrocity can be made meaningful, memorable, or imaginable, and to what ends, for the remote spectator.

The same question animates the two plays *The Quare Fellow* and *The Hostage*, Brendan Behan's most successful contributions to modern theatre. In *The Quare Fellow*, we are repeatedly told the manner in which condemned men are executed, a situation presented to us as the atrocity of legalized murder. The condemned man is absent from the action of the play, however, his last hours alive imagined and recounted for us by the prison warders and inmates. In *The Hostage*, a captive British soldier is pushed on stage blindfolded at the end of the first act, and learns that he is to be shot in reprisal for the death of an IRA prisoner about to be executed in Belfast. The play shows his remaining hours of life, his humane interactions with his captors, and his final tragic death, accidental after all, but none the less the product of belligerent political ideologies. In both plays, we have the symbolic image of suffering, the condemned man, an image refracted in post-9/11 mug-shots of suspected terrorists awaiting death sentences, and the grainy videos of blindfolded hostages kneeling before their masked captors. Such images attest to what Judith Butler has characterized as the limits of the human, centred on the 'differential allocation of grievability': 'what counts as a livable life and a grievable death?' (Butler 2004: xiv–xv). In Behan's plays, the political ideologies of either the state or fugitive nationalism put into lethal practice exclusionary conceptions of what constitutes a narratable or grievable subject, with tragic consequences. But the form of Behan's plays is not tragedy: the subtitle of *The Quare Fellow* is 'A Comedy Drama', and *The Hostage* is essentially a farce, heavily indebted to the influences of cabaret and music-hall. Behan's medium for the representation of atrocity was comedy, and it is this apparent paradox in these two plays which I explore in this chapter.

Behan (b. 1923) was renowned for interrupting the performances of his own plays with jokes, songs and boisterous antics *ad libitum*, but he did little to explain the comedic forms his plays took. His understanding of theatre owes much, in his own view, to the work of his uncle, P. J. Bourke, actor and manager of the Queen's Theatre in Dublin, renowned as 'the poor man's Abbey'. When *The Quare Fellow* opened successfully in November 1954, Behan recalls proudly 'I stood there thinking of my uncle, Paddy J. Bourke, and the times I watched him performing in his own melodramas and in the plays of Dion Boucicault' (Behan 1985: 258). Behan frequented the theatre in the 1920s and 1930s, when Bourke's repertoire of plays consisted essentially of political melodramas, welding the various elements of the Victorian melodramatic form – romantic, didactic, sentimental, spectacular and moral – into a powerful tool for promoting the cause of Irish nationalism on the stage. Dion Boucicault's plays were popular throughout the 1930s, while the nationalist dramas of J. W. Whitbread, H. C. Mangan and Bourke himself continued to appeal to postindependence audiences. The heroes of the Queen's melodramas were invariably nationalist heroes, but although Behan clearly derived both pleasure and pride from his theatre-going experiences in the Queen's, his own plays took very different forms, at best subverting the conventions of melodrama with comic and tragic deflations of nationalist rhetoric and iconography (see Brannigan 2002: 100–25).

Behan's only reflection on his own theatrical forms comes in *Brendan Behan's Island*, in which he distanced himself from the 'Abbey Theatre naturalism' of mainstream Irish theatre, and professed instead his admiration for music-hall, and the emphasis on diverting the audience which he attributed to T. S. Eliot:

I've always thought T. S. Eliot wasn't far wrong when he said that the main problem of the dramatist today was to keep his audience amused; and that while they were laughing their heads off, you could be up to any bloody thing behind their backs; and it was what you were doing behind their bloody backs that made your play great. (Behan 1965a: 17)

If there is direct allusion to Eliot's thoughts on the theatre, it appears to be to the levels of meaning layered behind the mask of theatrical entertainment which Eliot espouses in *The Use of Poetry and the Use of Criticism* for the poet-dramatist seeking 'the satisfaction of having a part to play in society as worthy as that of the music-hall comedian' (Eliot 1975: 95). As an explanation for the forms of entertainment in *The Quare Fellow* and *The Hostage*, however, for the repetitive interspersal of jokes, dances and songs amongst the tragic and serious depictions of atrocities, Behan's description of his theatrical method is misleading. The comedic forms of both plays are not simply diversions, behind which the serious action takes place. The argument of this chapter is that the comic 'interludes', dancing and singing performed in both plays are essential to their styles, and that style, as Martha Nussbaum maintains, is vital to the expression of 'a sense of life and of value, a sense of what matters and what does not, of what learning and communicating are, of life's relations and connections' (Nussbaum 1992: 5). The comedic forms of Behan's drama, in other words, are essentially ethical in purpose, and work to construct an alternative sense of moral values to the necrophiliac tendencies of the political ideologies satirized in the plays. If both plays take as their centre the spectacle of human suffering, this is inseparable from the alternative spectacles of carnivalesque celebration which are performed throughout, and which indeed form the conclusion to both plays. The hanged man and the butchered hostage become memento mori, not through the achievement of ethical and political gravity, but through the counter-discourses of comedy and music.

When *The Quare Fellow* was first performed in the Pike Theatre in Dublin in November 1954, one reviewer, Lennox Robinson, complained that the absence of 'the quare fellow' himself robbed the audience of a necessary sense of grief: 'A canary is going to expire from lack of water. We feel nothing more poignant' (Robinson 1954: 9). This is to miss the point of the play, which is that for the prisoners, warders, politicians and the public, and therefore also for the audience, the condemned man's death is ungrievable. A 'bog-man' has been cast out – we are not expected to feel poignancy. He has been banished, and his death is reported in the clipped, lifeless prose of the evening newspaper: 'Condemned man entered the hang-house at seven fifty-nine. At eight three the doctor pronounced life extinct' (Behan 1978: 45).[1] Behan's play shows no interest in enlisting the sympathy of the audience for the condemned man as tragic hero, or even as an individual. Instead, it mirrors the degree to which, in the public discourse surrounding capital punishment, the life of the condemned man is rendered less than human, his death unmarkable, and his burial, as the play shows at the end, an expedient form of disappearance.

The play mirrors this dehumanization of a life in order to show more effectively the means by which some lives are understood to be more livable, more human, than others. Indeed, this is the rationale by which the prisoners understand the decision to hang 'the quare fellow', who chopped up his brother with a butcher's knife, but reprieve 'silver-top', who beat his wife to death with his 'silver-topped cane'. The difference, it seems, is one of class, since 'silver-top' is 'a cut above meat-choppers whichever way you look at it' (42), and, as Patrick Colm Hogan argues, 'the quare fellow' is 'less a separate individual than a role which each member of the oppressed class may at some time be forced to play' (Hogan 1983: 139).

There is no central character, then, even and especially 'the quare fellow' of the title. There is also no suspense in the play. In the opening dialogue between prisoners, we learn that 'the quare fellow' will certainly be executed, and nothing to follow in the play suggests that we should expect anything else. Contrasting sharply with the melodramas of Behan's childhood fascination, the static plot and the minute observance of the routines and chores of prison life give the play the sense of absolute realism which Stephen Lacey notes is almost 'untheatrical' (Lacey 2001: 54). Séamus De Búrca, who attended the opening night, described the experience of seeing the play performed at the Pike as one of claustrophobia, which left him unable to rise from his seat at the end (De Búrca 1993: 23–4). So too, Alan Simpson recalled that several of Behan's 'old-lag' friends 'declared that they really felt they were "inside" again while watching *The Quare Fellow*' (Simpson 1962: 8). This was the effect partly of the Pike's small stage and auditorium, partly of Simpson's much-acclaimed gifts for set and lighting design, and partly of the play's static, hero-less form.

No heroes are to emerge, no one is to be saved, nothing will interrupt the tragic fate of the condemned man. Our sympathy and attention are drawn away from the 'meat-chopper' who is to be executed, to the reactions of the prisoners and warders, to the ways in which they amuse and entertain themselves to help pass the time. This is the basis upon which Anthony Roche considers *The Quare Fellow* comparable with Beckett's *Waiting for Godot*, and both plays exemplary of a 'comedy of survival' (Roche 1994: 36–71). If Roche works to establish that the correspondences between Beckett's and Behan's plays 'mark out the terrain of a contemporary Irish drama' (ibid.: 47), he also suggests that their common inheritance as influential Irish playwrights was the powerful uses to which Sean O'Casey put the form of music-hall comedy in serious theatre.[2]

The influence of music-hall on *The Quare Fellow* is not nearly so well established as it is in the case of *The Hostage*, but Roche is persuasive in maintaining that the comic banter and contrived routines (such as Dunlavin's crafty method of swigging methylated spirits under the cover of a medicinal rub) clearly resemble music-hall theatrics. In the absence of plot, the stuff of tragedy and melodrama which is all taking place off-stage, seemingly frivolous comic exchanges and theatrical action are interspersed with stories about hanging to fill the void. Even these grim stories serve a dual purpose; not only do they present grotesque images of the reality of hanging to the audience, but for the characters the stories are evidently forms of entertainment. Even the more frivolous comic banter and action are also shown to have a moral purpose from the beginning. Before the curtain rises on Act I, a prisoner sings the first verse of 'The Old Triangle', and the singing becomes richly defiant of the penal regime when the curtain rises and the audience can see the word 'Silence' printed on the wall. It is briefly defiant, because the warder threatens to leave the singer 'bloody well weeping if you don't give over your moaning' (Behan 1978: 40), but the Brechtian counterpoint of aural and visual signs serves to highlight the notion that the prison regime is not total in its power, and can be cheated, however contingently.

The Quare Fellow abounds with such counterposed signs, and in particular counterposed metonyms: the 'silver-topped' cane contrasts with the 'meat-chopper' of 'the quare fellow'; the cigarette butts left by the condemned man in the yard are as much a sign of humane compassion as the warder's gesture of removing their watches; the open grave at the centre of the stage for much of the play, which Lacey argues is a metonym for the 'entire judicial process' (Lacey 2001: 56), is juxtaposed with the cigarettes, bacon and letters which are the currency of the prisoners digging the grave. Each such metonymic sign, however, yields ambivalent moral implications: that the prisoners squabble for possession of the condemned man's letters, for example, might reveal their dehumanized and immoral disregard for the death of their fellow inmate, but it is no more immoral than the silence to which the warders wished to confine the condemned man by burying his letters with him. In this sense, the notice commanding 'silence' which dominates the set when the curtain rises has more profound implications than simply to highlight the prisoners' defiance: it is also metonymic of the death to which the prison regime can deliver any of those prisoners. The principal metonymic device used in the play is, of course, the old triangle. In the song which punctuates the play, it frequently denotes the prison regimen, for the triangle calls the prisoners to order, and that it can be heard along the banks of the canal suggests that it serves to warn even those outside the prison walls of the discipline to which the law constrains them. The key point here, however, is that by the end of the play 'the old triangle' is also a metaphor. The final verse suggests an altogether different meaning for 'the old triangle':

> In the female prison
> There are seventy women
> I wish it was with them that I did dwell,
> Then that old triangle
> Could jingle jangle
> Along the banks of the royal canal.
> (124)

Here, without spelling out the bawdy implication too far, 'the old triangle' becomes a metaphor for the ways in which the prisoners continue to find pleasure despite and because of the disciplinary apparatus of incarceration. That the prisoners convert signs of oppression into signs of defiance and even pleasure is indicative of a much wider process at work in *The Quare Fellow*. In the course of the play we find prisoners converting a medicinal rub into drink, the pages of the Bible and mattress coir into cigarettes, the dead man's letters into currency, and, of course, the hanging itself into an entertaining racing commentary. As soon as the play begins, the hanging is the focus of entertainment, 'a friendly subject of mutual interest' (75). To counter the silence and bleak regimen of prison life, anything which can be turned into talk and entertainment is welcome. This process of conversion extends deep into the language: the hanging is referred to as a 'haircut and shave' (40), the cell is known as a 'flowery dell' (43), the condemned man is 'the quare fellow' (42), while the homosexual character is known as 'the other fellow' (52). The hanging especially, as might be expected, is often denoted by euphemism, metonymy or metaphor, although the play also reserves its most literal language and representation for hanging, including in particular the attempted suicide by hanging of 'silver-top' at the end of Act I, which is a prefiguration of the execution at the end of the play. The literal descriptions of hanging ('the doctor slits the back of his neck to see if the bones are broken' (46), for example) serve to place the hanging as a grotesque spectacle before the audience, and provide what Sontag describes as the 'space reserved for being serious' about the immorality of capital punishment. It is through the figurative language, however, usually forming a kind of patois between the prisoners, but also sometimes between the warders, that an altogether different tone is set, mainly by the prisoners, one of entertainment and comedy.

The use of euphemisms, metaphor and metonymy, even to express the bleakest aspects of prison life and capital punishment, signals an inventiveness in language and communication which defies the penal system. Moreover, the play shows that the roots of this inventiveness lie outside the prison, in the equally punishing regimes of existence for the homeless 'lobbywatchers', one of whom recalls how 'you'd fall down and sleep on the pavement of a winter's night and not know but you were lying snug and comfortable in the Shelbourne' (60). The illusion is short-lived, of course, as is the notion of the prison cell as a 'flowery dell', but the play points to such necessary fictions as evidence of the vibrant affirmation of a sense of life antithetical to the corrupt and hypocritical morality which sponsors capital punishment, and which punishes a class for its social position. In the spirit of such affirmation, and true to the demands of its paradoxically comic form, *The Quare Fellow* ends not with the memento mori of a squalid, grotesque hanging, but with the prisoners-turned-gravediggers gambling for the dead man's letters, and the sexual innuendo of the last verse of the signature song. The atrocity to which such levity directs our attention is not the spectacle of the execution, but instead the fact that this man's death is shown to be beyond grief, his death merely the source of entertainment, his grave improperly marked and soon to be overgrown with cabbages, for as one prisoner says, 'They're not likely to be digging him up to canonize him' (124).

In contrast, in *The Hostage*, the death of Leslie Williams is properly mourned. Teresa, his new-found lover, weeps over his corpse, and tells him, 'I'll never forget you, Leslie, till the end of time' (237). This proper lament formed the tragic conclusion to Behan's original Gaelic version of the play, *An Giall*, but when he translated and revised the play for Joan Littlewood's Theatre Workshop production in London in October 1958, Leslie was given a theatrical afterlife, immediately leaping up from his corpse-like state, and, in a ghostly green light, singing the curtain song:

The bells of hell,
Go ting-a-ling-a-ling,
For you but not for me,
Oh death, where is thy sting-a-ling-a-ling?
Or grave thy victory?
If you meet the undertaker,
Or the young man from the Pru,
Get a pint with what's left over,
Now I'll say good-bye to you.

(236)

Like *The Quare Fellow*, then, *The Hostage* ends happily, by taking the sting out of death, and relieving the tragedy of a young man's death with comedy and song. Much of the humour of *The Hostage* is similar in kind to this closing song, a poignant sentiment pricked by frivolity. In the opening scene, a wild Irish jig is followed immediately by the strained sound of a lament played on bagpipes, and a conversation about the IRA boy about to be hanged in Belfast is interrupted by a gay prostitute who jokes about earning his rent from his next client. Early reviews tended to see this abrupt shift from solemnity to comedy, a recurrent characteristic of the form of the play, as a technical flaw. Milton Shulman, for example, writing for the *Evening Standard*, complained that '[Behan] is constantly interrupting the action with irrelevant ballads and he would rather burst than sustain a mood' (Shulman 1958: 13). But *The Hostage*, even more so than *The Quare Fellow*, is designed to pit song against action, laughter against mourning, and dancing against marching. This is inherent in the hybrid style of the play, which orchestrates music-hall comedy and songs, alongside a melodramatic plot and pantomimic caricatures. The effect of this hybrid style can be disorientating, as Michael Patrick Gillespie argues, because it makes it difficult for 'an audience trying to form a unified view of the play', but Gillespie attributes any resulting confusion not to the technical merits of the work but to the audience's 'mistaken intolerance for ambiguity' (Gillespie 1994: 93). *The Hostage* is, in this view, a radically decentred play, which allows no genre or discourse to obtain dominance. Just as any tragic or sombre moments are relieved by comedy or song, so too the farce and slapstick routines are undercut. The wild dance towards the end of Act II, in which anthems, flags and banners denoting political identities are made the objects of farce and ridicule, is immediately interrupted by the news that Leslie is to be shot. But rather than follow Gillespie's argument that the play offers a kind of unity, in that 'all figures combine to form a single, choric identity articulating the dilemma of the Ireland that they inhabit' (104), *The Hostage* seems to me to present contending moral arguments, and to affirm, through the carnivalesque, the values of dance, song, conversation and love.

One of the most direct ways in which it does this is by making an English soldier not just the central character, but the hero.[3] Leslie is thrust on stage at the end of Act I, as the other characters are caught up in a dance. His immediate reaction when his blindfold is removed is to protest, 'Don't stop. I like dancing' (169), and he leads them into song, 'There's no place like the world', which makes clear that, English or Irish, they all belong to the same planet, threatened by the H-bomb. Leslie is thus understood to be the voice of unity, and more specifically of fun, romance and reconciliation. Like Warder Regan in *The Quare Fellow*, another unlikely choice of hero given Behan's experiences in prison, Leslie articulates the moral arguments which are central to the play's critique of political ideologies. In his affable relations with his captors, his apparently naïve participation in dancing, singing and cheery conversation, and his willingness even to applaud the rebel songs which depict English soldiers as the hated enemy, he is depicted as almost unequivocally 'good'. In the system of melodramatic signification, Leslie takes the place ironically of a Robert Emmet or Wolfe Tone, the object of sympathy for all in the play except for the puritanical henchmen of the IRA, who are of course the 'persecuting villains' of the piece. In this sense, Leslie becomes, perhaps along with Teresa, the embodiment of the alternative moral values of forgiveness and love. He contrasts sharply with the image of English atrocities presented in Irish rebel songs, and even sympathizes with the plight of the IRA boy whose fate will determine his own.

Leslie functions in the play, then, to unsettle the politics of identity underpinning the murderous actions taking place in Belfast and in the brothel in Dublin. *The Hostage* mobilizes contradiction as the principal instrument for displacing the politics of identity. Sometimes, these contradictions take the form of inconsistencies. Meg is shocked when told that Monsewer's father was a bishop, but later admits casually that her father was the parish priest, for example; Teresa complains prudishly when Leslie attempts to touch her, then leaps jauntily into bed with him; she also understands Cockney dialect at one moment and not at another. Such inconsistencies destabilize the fixity of character in the play, and undermine the conventions of naturalist drama. At other times, the play stresses the ironic or paradoxical as forms of contradiction which reveal comic fallacies in the characters' own self-awareness: Monsewer as the rabid Irish nationalist nostalgic for Eton and the colonial service; Miss Gilchrist as the puritan Irish Catholic who adores English monarchy and sings patriotic English songs. Irony and contradiction are deployed frequently and effectively in *The Hostage*, and are used to dislodge the melodramatic and sentimental tendencies of the plot.

Behan's play counters the force of nationalist and imperialist myths with such contradictions. But the style of the play achieves more than this. Performed and continually improvised as a music-hall romp, a succession of cabaret acts linked through the occasional compère-like commentary to the audience, *The Hostage* thrusts the irrepressible joviality of Leslie, the determined innocence of Teresa and the sardonic wit of Meg and Pat, let alone the comic escapades of the various prostitutes and queers, against the forces of political violence. The comedy and music-hall antics of the play do not just serve to relieve the serious political critique, but engage the audience in frivolity. This is evident at various moments in the play, when Mulleady, Rio Rita and Princess Grace sing 'We're here because we're queer / Because we're queer because we're here' (225), for example. There is no point to this song. The point is simply that song functions through the play as expressive not of a political or moral standpoint, but of character or mood. And the mood of frivolous entertainment established by songs such as 'We're here because we're queer' (225), or 'There's no place on earth like the world' (169), or 'Don't muck about with the moon' (222) challenges the 'sense' of political ideologies like nationalism or imperialism. *The Hostage* inclines frequently towards frivolity, a mode of comedy which delights in the pursuit of laughter for its own sake. The play abounds with examples, from the opening scene in which Pat tells us, for no apparent reason, that 'Killymanjaro' is 'a noted mountain off the south coast of Switzerland' (131), through to the conclusion in which Mulleady declares 'I'm a secret policeman and I don't care who knows it' (235).

Behan's songs and jokes are often ludicrous or inane, played for momentary effect, such as the song Miss Gilchrist and Mulleady sing in Act I, consisting of the line 'Our souls. Our souls. Our souls', which the stage directions indicate should be *'slurred to sound – "Our souls. Are souls. Arseholes" '* (152). The frivolous instances of *The Hostage* work within an aesthetic of 'pure' theatre, which privileges spectacle and catharsis over the demands of a political theatre. The atrocity of Leslie's death, like the atrocity of the hanging in Belfast, are not trivialized by the play's loose structure and rapid effusion of gags, bawdy songs, dances, farcical action and quick-witted dialogue. Instead, the carnivalesque elements of the play serve further to underline the tragedy and futility of such atrocities. In the final scene of the play, Teresa may be the vehicle of both tragic sentiment and rational critique, as she weeps over Leslie's corpse and blames his death upon those like Pat whose injuries are used to fuel the vicious cycle of violence, but it is Leslie's jubilant rise from tragic death to comic life which signals the moral bearing of *The Hostage*.

Behan wrote or attempted to write several other plays, some of which, such as *The Landlady* and *Richard's Cork Leg*, remained incomplete at the time of his death (1964), and several short plays, including *The Big House*, *Moving Out* and *A Garden Party*, which are interesting as light comedies. In *The Quare Fellow* and *The Hostage*, however, he experimented with the dramatic possibilities of tragicomedy, and specifically of representing political and ethical atrocities within predominantly comic frames. In both plays, the ethical issues at stake could hardly have been more timely or more significant to the author and intended audiences. *The Quare Fellow* was written on the basis of Behan's familiarity with hanging in Irish prisons. Nine of his IRA comrades were hanged, some for similar offences to his own. It was also produced at a time when the abolition of capital punishment was being debated in both Ireland and Britain. *The Hostage* was also the product of Behan's experiences as an IRA member, and reflects his intense disillusionment with the justifications both for nationalist terror campaigns and for the terrors of the numerous colonial wars still being fought in the 1950s. Behan chose to represent these ethical questions about violence, law, justice and political identity not through the naturalist or melodramatic forms familiar from his youth, but through the effective use of carnivalesque comedy in his plays. The comic and music-hall forms of Behan's drama were not amusing diversions from the spectacles of suffering, but instead served to heighten the awareness of such suffering as unjustifiable. Both plays advance rational critiques against the logic of political execution, but the more effective means by which this logic is undermined is through the mode of living and being expressed through song, dance and often frivolous humour. If there is, as Sontag ponders, 'an antidote to the perennial seductiveness' of violence and war (Sontag 2003: 122), Behan's plays sought it out in the refashioned forms of music-hall and burlesque comedy.

NOTES

1 All references to *The Quare Fellow* and *The Hostage* are to the versions contained in the Methuen edition of *The Complete Plays*, introduced by Alan Simpson, published first in 1978.

2 Aside from the obvious influences O'Casey had on Behan in terms of representing tenement life and critical perspectives on Irish nationalism, O'Casey's use of farce, music, character types and symbolism in *Red Roses for Me* (1942) and *Cock-a-doodle Dandy* (1949) are worth examining as possible sources of influence for the forms Behan adopted in *The Quare Fellow* and *The Hostage*.

3 In *An Giall*, and in the first published version of *The Hostage* (1958), Leslie enters to the tune of a hornpipe tune, 'The Blackbird', a Gaelic metaphor for the hero.

PRIMARY READING

Behan, Brendan (1961). *Borstal Boy*. London: Corgi.

Behan, Brendan (1964a). *Brendan Behan's New York*. London: Hutchinson.

Behan, Brendan (1964b). *The Scarperer*. New York: Doubleday.

Behan, Brendan (1965a). *Brendan Behan's Island*. London: Corgi.

Behan, Brendan (1965b). *Hold Your Hour and Have Another*. London: Corgi.

Behan, Brendan (1978). *The Complete Plays*. London: Methuen.

Behan, Brendan (1981a). *After the Wake*, ed. Peter Fallon. Dublin: O'Brien.

Behan, Brendan (1981b). *Poems and a Play in Irish*. Oldcastle: Gallery Press.

Behan, Brendan (1985). *Confessions of an Irish Rebel*. London: Arena.

Behan, Brendan (1987). *An Giall/The Hostage*, ed. Richard Wall. Washington, DC: Catholic University of America Press.

Behan, Brendan (1997). *The Dubbalin Man*. Dublin: A. and A. Farmar.

FURTHER READING

Boyle, Ted E. (1969). *Brendan Behan*. New York: Twayne.

Brannigan, John (2002). *Brendan Behan: Cultural Nationalism and the Revisionist Writer*. Dublin: Four Courts Press.

Butler, Judith (2004). *Precarious Life: The Powers of Mourning and Violence*. London: Verso.

De Búrca, Séamus (1993). *Brendan Behan: A Memoir*. Dublin: P. J. Bourke.

Eliot, T. S. (1975). *Selected Prose*, ed. Frank Kermode. London: Faber and Faber.

Gillespie, Michael Patrick (1994). 'Violent Impotence and Impotent Violence: Brendan Behan's *The Hostage*', *Eire-Ireland* 29:1, 92–104.

Grene, Nicholas (1999). *The Politics of Irish Drama: Plays in Context from Boucicault to Friel*. Cambridge: Cambridge University Press.

Hogan, Patrick Colm (1983). 'Class Heroism in *The Quare Fellow*', *Etudes Irlandaises* 8, 139–44.

Kearney, Colbert (1977). *The Writings of Brendan Behan*. New York: St Martin's Press.

Kiberd, Declan (1995). *Inventing Ireland: The Literature of the Modern Nation*. London: Jonathan Cape.

Lacey, Stephen (2001). 'Brendan Behan' in John Bull (ed.). *Dictionary of Literary Biography: British and Irish Dramatists since World War Two*, 233. Detroit: Gale, 50–9.

Littlewood, Joan (1995). *Joan's Book: Joan Littlewood's Peculiar History As She Tells It*. London: Minerva.

Mikhail, E. H. (ed.) (1979). *The Art of Brendan Behan*. New York: Barnes and Noble.

Mikhail, E. H. (1980). *Brendan Behan: An Annotated Bibliography of Criticism*. New York: Barnes and Noble.

Mikhail, E. H. (ed.) (1982). *Brendan Behan: Interviews and Recollections*. London: Macmillan.

Mikhail, E. H. (ed.) (1992). *The Letters of Brendan Behan*. Basingstoke: Macmillan.

Murray, Christopher (1997). *Twentieth-Century Irish Drama: Mirror up to Nation*. Manchester: Manchester University Press.

Nussbaum, Martha (1992). *Love's Knowledge: Essays on Philosophy and Literature*. Oxford: Oxford University Press.

O'Connor, Ulick (1993). *Brendan Behan*. London: Abacus (1st edn. 1970).

O'Sullivan, Michael (1997). *Brendan Behan: A Life*. Dublin: Blackwater Press.

Robinson, Lennox (1954). 'Acting was Superb in Behan Play', *Irish Press* 20 November, 9.

Roche, Anthony (1994). *Contemporary Irish Drama: From Beckett to McGuinness*. Dublin: Gill and Macmillan.

Shulman, Milton (1958). 'Mr Behan Makes Fun of the I.R.A.', *Evening Standard* 15 October, 13.

Simpson, Alan (1962). *Beckett and Behan and a Theatre in Dublin*. London: Routledge and Kegan Paul.

Sontag, Susan (2003). *Regarding the Pain of Others*. New York: Picador.

Swift, Carolyn (1985). *Stage by Stage*. Dublin: Poolbeg Press.

Watt, Stephen (2000). 'Love and Death: A Reconsideration of Behan and Genet' in Stephen Watt, Eileen Morgan and Shakir Mustafa (eds.). *A Century of Irish Drama*. Bloomington: Indiana University Press, 130–45.

Witoszek, Walentyna (1986). 'The Funeral Comedy of Brendan Behan', *Études Irlandaises* 11, 83–91.

21

Joe Orton: Anger, Artifice and Absurdity

David Higgins

Joe Orton began his career as a dramatist in August 1963, when the BBC accepted his radio play *The Boy Hairdresser* (later retitled *The Ruffian on the Stair*). Between then and his death (aged 34) four years later, he wrote three other short plays, three full-length plays and a film script.[1] Orton's oeuvre is fairly small, but it is of a remarkably high quality: in particular *Entertaining Mr Sloane* (1964), *Loot* (1965) and *What the Butler Saw* (1969) are among the most important and innovative dramatic works of the 1960s. Orton's mockery of bourgeois mores and his provocative attempts to shock his audience contributed to his significant commercial success and his status as one of the bright young things of 'Swinging London', but also led to expressions of outrage from some reviewers and theatre-goers. If he had been alive to see the first performance of *Butler* in 1969, he would no doubt have been delighted by the booing and catcalls from the gallery. More recently, critical controversy has centred on the relationship between his homosexuality, his murder by his partner Kenneth Halliwell, and the anarchic sexuality and taboo-smashing apparent in his best work. While it is important to engage with these issues in order to provide a framework for understanding Orton, I want also in this chapter to think about the philosophical assumptions that lie behind his plays, assumptions that may well be equally disconcerting to both conservative and liberal critics.

Genre and Style

Much of Orton's reading as a young man was directed by Halliwell, who was seven years older and considerably better educated than his partner.[2] Orton's work is highly intertextual, alluding to and pastiching a wide range of sources and influences, from Aristophanes and Euripides to Oscar Wilde and the early twentieth-century comic novelist Ronald Firbank. For all Orton's innovation and apparent modishness, he was keen to position himself within the European comic tradition, as is shown by Sergeant

Match's appearance from the skylight in a parodic *deus ex machina* at the end of *Butler*, and the reworking of Euripides' *The Bacchae* in *The Erpingham Camp* (1966). Among contemporary writers, Orton was most influenced by Pinter; this is almost embarrassingly apparent in the 1964 television version of *The Ruffian on the Stair*, although less so in the revised 1967 play (Lahr 1978: 156–9). There is the odd echo of Pinter in *Sloane*, but in this play, his first major success, Orton began to find his own style: a mixture of farcical action and dialogue that combined epigrammatic wit with bourgeois clichés.

As in Wilde, speech in Orton's drama often has less to do with the revelation of character than with parodying the way in which people of a certain social class speak to one another. His characters are frequently reliant on words and phrases taken from popular culture and their language is often devoid of meaningful content. Orton identifies cliché in particular as symptomatic of the hypocrisy and stupidity of modern life: Kath, fantasising about Sloane, states that 'you have the air of lost wealth' (Orton 1976: 67; all further references to Orton's plays are to this edition); McLeavy, mixing his metaphors in *Loot*, suggests that the police are 'hamstrung by red tape' (206); Mike tells Joyce in *Ruffian* that 'I'm a powerfully attractive figure. I can still cause a flutter in feminine hearts' (32). Orton gets much humour from the obvious contrast between the moralistic platitudes spoken by the characters and the transgressiveness of their motivations or the action taking place. Sometimes this contrast manifests itself as innuendo; for example, Ed tells Sloane: 'Your youth pleads for leniency and, by God, I'm going to give it' (120). It is also an important part of Orton's satirical purpose: at the end of *Butler*, a play in which all the 'decencies' of British society have been thoroughly ridiculed, Sergeant Match's patriotic rhetoric on finally discovering the missing penis from Winston Churchill's statue can only seem utterly absurd (Match is wearing a torn leopard-spotted dress and is covered in his own blood): 'The Great Man can once more take up his place in the High Street as an example to us all of the spirit that won the Battle of Britain' (447).

Butler combines, as do *Loot* and the television play *Funeral Games* (1968), sophisticated dialogue with complex plotting and action in order to create an innovative form of black farce.[3] Historically, farce has been held in low critical esteem, often seen as an unsophisticated form of comedy that relies on improbable plotting and physical humour, and which has no serious intent. Modern critics, however, have suggested that it offers a space in which desires that are usually repressed can be represented and released: the normal conventions of society are transgressed and, perhaps, questioned (Smith 1989: 1–16). Farce, therefore, is festive, but it can also be aggressive. Although he admired the Aldwych farces of Ben Travers, Orton argued that the 'boundaries he set to present day farce are really too narrow [. . .] As I understand it, farce originally was very close to tragedy, and differed only in the *treatment* of its themes – themes like rape, bastardy, prostitution' (quoted in Lahr 1978: 225). Farce suited Orton because he saw modern life – in particular, its attempts to conceal and control humanity's animal desires through various structures and ideologies – as both cruel and funny.

In contrast to traditional farce, Orton emphasized that his work should be performed realistically for maximum impact: for example, in the production notes to the Royal Court for *Ruffian*, he wrote that there should be 'no attempt [. . .] to match the author's extravagance of dialogue with extravagance of direction. REALISTIC PLAYING AND DIRECTING' (quoted in Lahr 1978: 157). Heavy stylization is likely to diminish his plays' transgressiveness and, therefore, much of their power. Peter Wood, who directed the unsuccessful first production of *Loot* at the Cambridge Arts Theatre 'with a kind of cod formality', later admitted that 'it was a mistake not to have plumped for absolute realism' (quoted in Lahr 1978: 241). Douglas Hickox's kitschy 1969 film version of *Sloane* has little of the play's menace because it is constantly winking at the audience, and also because it weakens the impact of Sloane's murder of Kemp by letting it take place off-camera. Orton's only 'serious disagreement' with the director of the first American staging of *Sloane*, Alan Schneider, was because Schneider wanted to bring the curtain down before Kemp's murder (Lahr 1978: 215).

For Orton's use of farce techniques – cross-dressing, concealment, rapid entrances and exits, slapstick, and so on – has a highly serious purpose: a destructive critique of social conventions that suggests that they are ultimately without foundation. And although farce has generally been seen as downplaying the importance of verbal humour, Orton's dialogue is absolutely crucial to this critique. His transformation of traditional farce, exemplified by the French dramatist Georges Feydeau, has been interestingly described by C. W. E. Bigsby:

> The mistaken identities of French farce, the sexual taboos that are broken and the social etiquette that is momentarily abandoned are customary stages in a familiar and frivolous exercise. The indiscretions are themselves recognizable ploys in a game that will inevitably end with social roles happily reasserted, with broken relationships restored. But where such endings occur in Orton's work they are painfully ironic. Where Feydeau has flirtation, Orton has rape; where Feydeau has sexual misadventure, Orton has incest. In Feydeau sensibilities are offended, in Orton physical injuries are sustained. Feydeau's characters are driven to comic despair and momentary desperation, Orton's are driven to madness and death. Where Feydeau depends on the existence of a structured society, with its recognized codes and values, Orton presents a world in which normative values no longer exist, in which anarchy is the only dependable reality. (Bigsby 1982: 56)

Bigsby's account, though acute, is overstated. Clearly Orton's endings do ironize any notion of a return to 'normality'; in particular, he avoids outcomes that could be seen as morally appropriate in conventional terms. And, yes, there are plenty of references to murder, rape, incest, and so on. But the ending of *Butler*, for example, can hardly be described as 'painful'. This is a play that torments its characters but does not seriously damage them. The various misunderstandings and complexities that have threatened their lives and sanities are ultimately resolved, and in fact all of them have gained significantly from the play's events: Prentice and his wife have been reconciled and have found their children; Geraldine and Nick have discovered that they are brother and sister and have found their parents; Rance has salacious material for his book – 'Double incest is even more likely to produce a best-seller than murder' (446) – and Sergeant Match has successfully retrieved the missing penis from Churchill's statue. Orton is here parodying traditional farce's restoration of normality, but the tone of this parody is remarkably good-humoured. The endings of his other plays are, perhaps, darker. In *Loot*, McLeavy, an innocent man, is dragged off to prison, where he will probably be murdered by the police (although he is such a ridiculous figure that it is hard to imagine that anyone in the audience will particularly care about his fate). And although an equilibrium of sorts is established at the end of *Sloane*, there is also considerable doubt as to whether the 'sharing' arrangement between Ed and Kath will work – and will Sloane kill again? I am not suggesting that Orton was somehow 'mellowing' in his final play, but simply that it shows that his farce is not as utterly black as Bigsby's comments might suggest.

The point about 'normative values', though, is spot on. As has been widely noted, farce, in part because of its lack of association with naturalism and 'deep' characterization, is a tactic employed by absurdist playwrights such as Beckett and Ionesco, who use it to emphasize humanity's helplessness and alienation within a meaningless universe. There is no adequate critical account of the relationship between Orton's plays and the 'Theatre of the Absurd', and yet I would argue that the ontological assumptions that lie behind his work are fundamentally absurdist. Orton presents a Godless universe in which there are no transcendent values and human beings have little control over their lives. Like the absurdists, he also satirizes society's attempts to avoid facing up to these unpalatable facts by putting its faith in fictitious idols. So when McLeavy says that 'the police are for the protection of ordinary people', Truscott responds, 'I don't know where you pick up those slogans, sir. You must read them on the hoardings' (274). Key differences between Orton's work and absurdist theatre are the consistent artificiality of his dialogue, his complex plots and, perhaps most crucially, his lack of interest in metaphysics. What I mean by this is that although he shares absurdist assumptions, his plays, and in this sense they are completely unlike Beckett's, are not *troubled* by these assumptions. There is no striving in Orton, no desperation, no compassion for humanity's plight. For him, the absurd is a premise, but *not* an issue. His easy acceptance of this lack of 'metanarratives' and his happy exploitation of the comic possibilities created by the consequent moral anarchy, as well as his delight in parody and pastiche, make him arguably the first truly postmodern playwright.[4]

Orton and Homosexuality

It has been argued, with some justification, that the telling of Orton's life story by John Lahr and others has been warped by the prejudice that homosexuals are deviants and that their relationships are doomed to destruction, and that Lahr in particular does not understand how Orton's sexuality, placed in its historical context, informed his writing (Shepherd 1989; see also Clum 1992; de Jongh 1992; Nakayama 1993; Van Leer 2003).[5] It is certainly the case that Orton's life and work tend to provoke some critics into crude moralizing: Martin Esslin remarks that the life story is 'a cautionary tale of the highest order' (Esslin 1981: 96); and Christopher Innes goes even further, describing the murder of Orton by Halliwell as the 'logical result' of Orton's 'egoistic view' of life (Innes 1992: 271–2). In contrast to such reductive assertions, critics like Simon Shepherd and Alan Sinfield have focused productively on the relationship between Orton's sexuality and his writing (Shepherd 1989; Sinfield 1992, 2003). The most interesting question here is the extent to which Orton can be seen as a forerunner of gay liberation through his stage depictions of sexual freedom, or, alternatively, the extent to which he was 'trapped' by the repressive cultural assumptions about homosexuality that were still prevalent in the 1960s.

During Orton's lifetime, homosexuality was not only illegal (it was legalized for men over 21 a few days before he died in 1967), but also subject to a great deal of social prejudice. Repression of homosexuals was justified on the grounds that they were selfish and undisciplined, and that they formed a subversive group in society: these factors, it was argued, meant that homosexuality was likely to cause 'national degeneracy'. This, inevitably, had its effect on the self-image of homosexual men, who were told not only that their sexuality was 'unnatural and sick' but that it was 'anti-social, dangerous and criminal'. Therefore, they were likely 'to develop a sense of guilt': 'Pushed into furtive sex and vulnerable to blackmail, the homosexual learnt to connect his sexuality with insecurity. And always underlying these attitudes and ideas were the very real activities of a police force that hounded and exposed homosexuals' (Shepherd 1989: 15). Homosexuality might be 'tolerated', perhaps, if conducted behind closed doors, but public display and 'effeminacy' were deemed unacceptable. Homosexuals were under a great deal of pressure to show 'manly' self-control and to discipline their sexuality either by being a part of a marriage-type relationship or by being celibate. Orton's sexuality is interesting in this context because although he eschewed campness and presented himself as a very masculine figure, he was also highly promiscuous and saw no virtue in self-restraint. His sexual licence in life and art was in itself subversive; a refusal to control himself, literally and metaphorically, in a socially acceptable way: 'sex', he once said to Halliwell, was 'the only way to smash the wretched civilization' (Orton 1986: 125).[6]

One way in which homosexuals were oppressed in the postwar period was through stage censorship (which, of course, affected many other areas, such as politics). Before 1958, the lord chamberlain banned *all* stage references to homosexuality. In practice, as Nicholas de Jongh and others have shown, there were oblique representations of homosexuality on stage earlier in the twentieth century: these tended to reflect the widespread assumption that it was a social and moral evil. In engaging with the subject of homosexuality, a liberal commercial playwright like Terence Rattigan (who admired Orton's work) was faced with the triple deterrent of censorship, the conventionality of his audience (or, at least, his *belief* in their conventionality), and the fact that he was a closeted homosexual (de Jongh 1992: 54–8). But it is apparent from two plays of the late 1950s that the climate was changing: Roger Gellert's *Quaint Honour*, performed at the Arts Theatre club in 1958, represented 'adolescent homosexuality as uncorrupting and beneficial to consenting adolescent parties' (de Jongh 1992: 63); and although Geof in Shelagh Delaney's *A Taste of Honey* (1959) is stereotypically effeminate and frequently mocked by Jo, he is a highly sympathetic character because of his altruism and his heroic unconventionality.[7]

In 1958 the lord chamberlain conceded that plays that were 'sincere and serious' in their treatment of homosexuality would be allowed; 'salacious or offensive' references, though, would not be tolerated (de Jongh 2000: 116). The fact that Orton's notably non-serious depictions of homosexuality were allowed to appear in the commercial theatre (although some cuts were imposed on him by the lord chamberlain's office) is a good example of the way in which censorship was becoming increasingly toothless during the 1960s, as dramatists pushed at the boundaries of acceptability. Yet, ironically, it is exactly the fact that Orton does not seem to have been 'serious' about the role of the homosexual in the 1960s that has troubled critics like Sinfield and Clum, who suggest that he was not particularly interested in gay liberation per se and 'had difficulty conceiving a positive view of the homosexual' (Sinfield 1992: 182; see also Clum 1992: 133). On the other hand, Nicholas de Jongh describes Orton as 'the theatre's first homosexual revolutionary', the first British playwright 'to reject the dominant myth of homosexuality as sickness and sin and to live without the oppression of guilt' (de Jongh 1992: 94); writing in a similar vein, Dominic Shellard suggests that *Loot's* 'quiet celebration of the normality of homosexual relationships [is] *the* innovation of [the] work' (Shellard 1997: 123).

So how *did* Orton portray homosexuality on stage? To focus on *Loot*, in the US production notes Orton emphasized that the relationship between Hal and Dennis should not be presented as 'queer or camp or odd . . . they must be perfectly ordinary boys who happen to be fucking each other' (quoted in Lahr 1978: 248). Both characters are, in fact, bisexual: Hal spends his time 'thieving from slot machines and deflowering the daughters of better men than [him]self' (199), and, following Dennis's admission that he has made five women pregnant, Truscott tells him that 'you scatter your seed along the pavements without regard to age or sex' (244). Dennis is in love with Fay (a mass murderer who has blackmailed her way into a share in the boys' stolen money), and at the end of the play it is suggested that the two boys are going to be separated:

FAY: (*sharply*) When Dennis and I are married we'd have to move out.
HAL: Why?
FAY: People would talk. We must keep up appearances.

(275)

If this *is* a 'celebration' of homosexuality, then it is a curiously ironic one. Orton's true sexual subversiveness lies, rather, in his refusal of society's repressive categorization of sexual conduct as 'normal' or 'deviant', and his mockery of its attempts to pigeonhole individuals as one or the other. This is most apparent in *Butler*, which has been well described as 'a kind of orgy of cross-dressing, gender confusion, and hierarchical inversion' that insists 'on the arbitrariness and narrowness of gender roles, and that they are socially ascribed rather than naturally given' (Dollimore 1991: 315–16). It is fitting that in this play Rance describes 'heterosexual' as a 'Chaucerian' word (411) and dismisses as a 'folk-myth' (413) the idea that male heterosexuality necessarily has anything to do with virility. Perhaps Sinfield is right that Orton's refusal of 'nature, depth and sincerity' in his representation of homosexuality, and his failure to engage with gay stereotypes, shows a failure to face up to society's treatment of homosexuals (Sinfield 1992: 182). But I don't think that Orton would have concurred with Sinfield's leftist assumptions about the social role of art. Of course he saw his plays as a way of challenging the assumptions of what he believed to be a corrupt civilization, but he also had a strong streak of aestheticism and childish glee in shocking the bourgeoisie that prevented him from taking up coherent political positions. His refusal of homosexual stereotypes was innovative in the context of the 1960s, but there was also something profoundly *irresponsible* about his treatment of the subject.

Satire and Shock

Orton's satirical targets went beyond sexual repression. *Loot*, for example, mocks society's mystification and fetishization of death by subjecting the corpse of Mrs McLeavy to various farcical indignities, and takes numerous pot shots at Catholicism for good measure. Truscott represents not only police malpractice but also the way in which a corrupt state oppresses people in the name of law and order:

> TRUSCOTT (*shouting, knocking* HAL *to the floor*):   Under any other political system I'd
>   have you on the floor in tears!
> HAL (*crying*):   You've got me on the floor in tears!
>
>   (235)

McLeavy exemplifies the way in which people collude in their own oppression; his view of the police is made up of strung-together tabloid clichés, a sure sign of its absurdity: 'I'd like to see them given wider powers. They're hamstrung by red tape. They're a fine body of men. Doing their job under impossible conditions' (206). He is punished not simply for being stupid enough to trust those in authority, but for his *sincerity*. He really believes in the clichés that he spouts; the other characters know that the system is corrupt and yet they end up pretending to follow social norms – 'We must keep up appearances' – because they know that it is in their interest to do so (275).

Sinfield notes how exciting Orton's treatment of the police in *Loot* was for young left-liberals in 1965 (Sinfield 1992: 176–7). Forty years on, his satire inevitably seems rather tame. And yet *Loot* still has the power to shock. Towards the end of the play, Hal promises that he will take Dennis to 'a remarkable brothel [...] run by three Pakistanis aged between ten and fifteen. They do it for sweets. Part of their religion. Meet me at seven. Stock up with Mars bars' (257). This is jarring for a modern audience, with its reference to paedophilia and its arguable racism. It is also funny, though, and not simply because of its transgressiveness. Hal's vague claim about 'their religion' comically reveals his own ignorance, and, along with the boyish phrase 'Stock up with Mars bars', draws attention both to the *unreal* nature of his suggestion and to its very gratuitousness as a piece of dialogue, for it is required neither by the plot nor by the themes of the play. Its sole purpose seems to be to disgust some members of the audience, whilst allowing those who aren't shocked to feel knowing and sophisticated. When a customer wrote to the management of the Jeanetta Cochrane Theatre to register his outrage at the first act of *Loot*, Orton replied supportively in the guise of 'Edna Welthorpe':

> I myself consider it to be the most loathsome play on in London at the present moment [...] When I tell you that in the second act [...] there was a discussion upon the raping of children with Mars bars with other filthy details of a sexual and psychopathic nature I'm sure you'll pardon my writing. (Orton 1986: 289)

Typically, Orton, through 'Edna', makes the passage sound even worse than it is in the play by drawing on the disturbingly phallic connotations of 'Mars bars'. However, this is also to make a serious point about the prurient hysteria and hyperbole often apparent in the claims of self-appointed moral guardians.

There is, no doubt, a rather childish streak in Orton, a desire to shock for shock's sake, but I cannot agree with Esslin that his 'rage' is always 'purely negative' and 'unrelated to any positive creed, philosophy or programme of social reform' (Esslin 1981: 96). Orton's satirical attacks imply, by their very existence, a desire for a more liberated society. He clearly felt strongly, for example, about the way in which authority sought to control people's private lives. In *Loot*, Truscott is able to invade McLeavy's home and search it without a warrant by pretending to be from the Water Board; in *The Good and Faithful Servant* (1967), Orton's melancholic television play attacking the stifling work routines of modern life, Mrs Vealfoy tells Buchanan that 'Should your private life be involved, we shall be the first to inform you of the fact' (159). Buchanan, like McLeavy, believes in 'the system' (in this case represented by work) and suffers for it. Ray, his illegitimate son, on the other hand, lives 'for kicks' (168), much to Buchanan's horror, although he is eventually forced to take on a steady job because of his love for the pregnant Debbie. Love and family are prime Orton targets – both are, after all, crucial parts of bourgeois ideology – and in this case they lead to imprisonment in a stultifying work routine. But they can also lead to violent chaos: the Dionysiac attack on authority in *The Erpingham Camp* is prompted mainly by the campers' self-righteous horror that a pregnant woman might have been 'insulted': as her husband Kenny, who is also the ringleader of the revolt, says, 'I'm going to give you a good hiding, Erpingham. I'm going to smash your face in for the gratification of those in the family way everywhere' (317).[8]

Attitudes to the family are satirized in a different way in *Butler*, which is, among other things, a brilliant *reductio ad absurdum* of Freud's sexualization of parent–child relations. Intensely self-conscious, it both celebrates and parodies the 1960s' interest in sexuality and sexual liberation – hence Rance's absurd attempts to make sense of events through a mishmash of misplaced psychoanalytical assumptions and popular anthropology. Although a self-proclaimed 'representative of order' (417), Rance, like Truscott, is in fact the cause of anarchy, and his conservative rhetoric fails to mask his prurient and self-interested fascination with transgression: 'The whole treacherous avant-garde movement will be exposed for what it is – an instrument for inciting decent citizens to commit bizarre crimes against humanity and the state!' (428). *Butler* has less to say about religion than *Loot* or *Funeral Games* (where Christianity is memorably described as 'a bird of prey carrying an olive branch'; 355), but its sexual chaos is clearly in the service of Orton's anti-religious agenda. Rance notes that 'civilisations have been founded and maintained on theories which refused to obey facts' (383): that, indeed, was Orton's problem with what he describes in his diary as 'fucking Judeo-Christian civilisation' (Orton 1986: 251), for he believed that it fails to recognize the extent to which human beings are motivated by various forms of sexual desire and to understand that there is nothing harmful about this.

The ending of *Butler*, therefore, with Match holding aloft the penis from Churchill's statue, can be seen as an imaginative triumph, a saturnalian celebration of pagan sexual freedom and fertility that mocks attempts by church, state and the medical establishment to define and control sexual behaviour. It also shows Orton simultaneously undercutting and endorsing Churchill's status as a secular saint. Although on one level *Butler* clearly attacks the virile nationalism with which Churchill was associated (Shepherd 1989: 150), is there not also a sense in which the ending celebrates, however ironically, masculine power and authority? Whatever the transgressiveness of the play's themes and action, as Orton noted in his diary, 'the Euripidean ending works, surprisingly, as "all is forgiven" ' (Orton 1986: 242). Orton was a powerful satirist but he also had a strong impulse towards aesthetically pleasing structure and dialogue; he was too self-conscious an artist to have ended *Butler* differently, even at the cost of reducing its subversiveness.

Conclusion

Orton was clearly angry about many aspects of modern society, but at the same time his work seems often to be based on absurdist or materialist assumptions: that people are selfish, alienated, lost, unable to communicate with each other, exploited and exploiting. Farce, with its lack of interest in character and its emphasis on the unwindings of the plot, suited his fatalism perfectly. We might, therefore, identify three conflicting forces at work in his drama: anger, manifested in satirical attacks; a sense of absurdity, manifested as comic irresponsibility; and aestheticism, manifested in literary allusion and a concern with polished language and structure. The tension between these forces is highly creative, but it also makes Orton much harder to pigeonhole as a 'progressive' writer than, say, Wesker, Delaney or even Pinter. This is most apparent in the case of homosexuality, but it affects a number of other areas. If it is true that 'he had difficulty conceiving a positive view of the homosexual' (Sinfield 1992: 182), then it is also true that his plays, at least, have great difficulty in conceiving a positive view of anything or anyone. What they do celebrate is their own irresponsible mockery of a world that tries to avoid facing up to the meaninglessness of existence through the stultifying rituals of religion, government, domestic life, and work.

NOTES

1 Two early plays, *Fred and Madge* and *The Visitors*, and two novels, *Head to Toe* and *Between Us Girls*, were published posthumously.

2 During the 1950s, Orton and Halliwell wrote several unpublished novels in collaboration, and Halliwell continued to have an impact on Orton's writing until their deaths; for example, in his diary for 11 July 1967, Orton wrote, 'Yesterday Kenneth read the script [of *Butler*] and was enthusiastic – he made several important suggestions which I'm carrying out' (Orton 1986: 237).

3 Maurice Charney uses the suggestive term 'quotidian farce' in his discussion of *Loot*; see Charney (1984: 80–96). Although there are farce elements in *Sloane*, it is perhaps best described as a 'comedy of manners'; see Hirst (1979: 96–110) for a discussion of Orton's work in terms of this genre.

4 See Page (1992) for a thoughtful discussion of Orton and postmodernism.

5 This criticism does not of course invalidate Lahr's biography *Prick Up Your Ears* (1978) as a crucial source for the study of Orton, but it needs to be supplemented by Shepherd's *Because We're Queers* (1989).

6 For a more detailed account of Orton's sexuality, see Shepherd (1989: ch. 3).

7 The sexual politics of theatre in the late 1950s and early 1960s is a complex subject. It has been argued, for example, that the 'New Wave' attacks on the commercial theatre were fuelled by homophobia. For a judicious discussion of this issue, see Sinfield (2003).

8 As Patricia Juliana Smith has pointed out in an interesting essay, the bacchantes in *Erpingham* are 'little more than conservatives in revolutionary trappings' (Smith 2003: 28).

PRIMARY READING

Joe Orton Collection (University of Leicester Library).

John Lahr Collection (Mugar Memorial Library, University of Boston).

Orton, Joe (1976). *Complete Plays*. London: Methuen.

Orton, Joe (1979). *Up Against It*. London: Methuen.

Orton, Joe (1986). *The Orton Diaries*, ed. John Lahr. London: Methuen.

Orton, Joe (1990). *Head to Toe*. London: Minerva.

Further reading

Bigsby, C. W. E. (1982). *Joe Orton*. London: Methuen.

Casmus, Mary (1980). 'Farce and Verbal Style in the Plays of Joe Orton', *Journal of Popular Culture* 13, 461–8.

Charney, Maurice (1984). *Joe Orton*. Basingstoke: Macmillan.

Clum, John (1992). *Acting Gay: Male Homosexuality in Modern Drama*. New York: Columbia University Press.

Coppa, Francesca (ed.) (2003). *Joe Orton: A Casebook*. New York: Routledge.

Dean, Joan F. (1982). 'Joe Orton and the Redefinition of Farce', *Theatre Journal* 34, 481–92.

de Jongh, Nicholas (1992). *Not in Front of the Audience: Homosexuality on Stage*. London: Routledge.

de Jongh, Nicholas (2000). *Politics, Prudery and Perversions: The Censoring of the English Stage 1901–1968*. London: Methuen.

Dollimore, Jonathan (1991). *Sexual Dissidence: Augustine to Wilde, Freud to Foucault*. Oxford: Clarendon Press.

Esslin, Martin (1981). 'Joe Orton: The Comedy of (Ill) Manners' in C. W. E. Bigsby (ed.). *Contemporary English Drama*. London: Edward Arnold, 95–107.

Hirst, David L. (1979). *Comedy of Manners*. London: Methuen.

Innes, Christopher (1992). *Modern British Drama: 1890–1990*. Cambridge: Cambridge University Press.

Lahr, John (1978). *Prick Up Your Ears: The Biography of Joe Orton*. Harmondsworth: Penguin.

Nakayama, Randall S. (1993). 'Domesticating Mr. Orton', *Theatre Journal* 45, 185–95.

Page, Adrian (1992). 'An Age of Surfaces: Joe Orton's Drama and Postmodernism' in Adrian Page (ed.). *The Death of the Playwright? Modern British Drama and Literary Theory*. Basingstoke: Macmillan.

Shellard, Dominic (1997). *British Theatre since the War*. New Haven, CT: Yale University Press.

Shepherd, Simon (1989). *Because We're Queers: The Life and Crimes of Kenneth Halliwell and Joe Orton*. London: Gay Men's Press.

Sinfield, Alan (1992). 'Who Was Afraid of Joe Orton?' in Joseph Bristow (ed.). *Sexual Sameness: Textual Differences in Gay Writing*. London: Routledge, 170–86.

Sinfield, Alan (2003). 'Is there a Queer Tradition, and Is Orton in It?' in Francesca Coppa (ed.). *Joe Orton: A Casebook*. New York: Routledge, 85–94.

Smith, Leslie (1989). *Modern British Farce*. Basingstoke: Macmillan.

Smith, Patricia Juliana (2003). 'You Say You Want a Revolution: Joe Orton's *The Erpingham Camp* as the *Bacchae* of the 1960s' in Francesca Coppa (ed.). *Joe Orton: A Casebook*. New York: Routledge, 27–44.

Stirling, Grant (1997). 'Ortonesque/Carnivalesque: The Grotesque Realism of Joe Orton', *Journal of Dramatic Theory and Criticism* 11, 41–63.

Van Leer, David (2003). 'Saint Joe: Orton as Homosexual Rebel' in Francesca Coppa (ed.). *Joe Orton: A Casebook*. New York: Routledge, 109–40.

22

Alan Ayckbourn: Experiments in Comedy

Alexander Leggatt

Sir Alan Ayckbourn (b. 1939) is artistic director of the Stephen Joseph Theatre in the Yorkshire seaside town of Scarborough, where nearly all of his plays have received their first productions under his direction. This arrangement gives him a remarkable – and in our time probably unique – degree of control over the production of his own work. The conditions of Scarborough are special. Though an end-stage auditorium was added recently, most productions are theatre-in-the-round; and there is no star system. These conditions encourage ensemble work and a close connection between actor and audience and actors and each other, and are ideal for Ayckbourn's drama of interpersonal relations. Yet his plays are remarkably adaptable: beginning from an apparently small, local base, they have travelled the world, and they have been translated into many languages, flourishing on proscenium stages as they do in theatre-in-the-round.

Though he spends much of his time directing, Ayckbourn has written to date over 60 plays. His first major success, *Relatively Speaking* (1967), was written for Scarborough at the request of his mentor Stephen Joseph, who wanted 'a play which would make people laugh when their seaside summer holidays were spoiled by the rain' (Ayckbourn 1968: 4). The success of its London transfer launched him on a career as a writer of popular commercial comedies, with a corresponding tendency on the part of some critics to dismiss him as a lightweight entertainer, as though commercial success and entertainment value were incompatible with artistic achievement (so much for Shakespeare, Dickens, Verdi). He has never ceased to entertain; but it is through (not as well as or in spite of) entertainment that his work provokes and disturbs us, hits us where we live.

He began with comedies of sexual intrigue and misunderstanding, like *Relatively Speaking* and *How the Other Half Loves* (1969); but as he went on, the comedy darkened as the plays exposed the cruelties of marriage and the emptiness of the characters' lives. From *Way Upstream* (1981), in which the squabbling of a boat crew headed for Armageddon Bridge can be taken as a metaphor for the state of England, Ayckbourn's horizons broadened from the domestic focus of the early plays to the state of society. His generic range also expanded, to include futuristic science fiction and the thriller. *The*

Revenger's Comedies (1989) borrows the plot of *Strangers on a Train* (you do my murder, I'll do yours) and *FlatSpin* (2001) involves an unsuspecting woman in a dangerous sting operation. He has also written a number of family plays (a term he prefers to children's plays, since he wants the whole family to enjoy the play at different levels; Glaap and Quaintmere 1999: 133) which deal with many of the same issues as the adult plays. Susan in *Woman in Mind* (1985) retreats from an intolerable family into a fantasy life; so does Mary in the family play *Invisible Friends* (1989); both fantasies turn sinister.

Inevitably, this summary simplifies. We do not have to wait for *Way Upstream* to find Ayckbourn commenting on society: in *Absurd Person Singular* (1972) it matters that Sidney Hopcroft is not just a domestic bully but a sleazy property developer. By the same token, in the title of *A Small Family Business* (1987) the words 'family' and 'business' are equally important. The network of corruption the play exposes is a family network, and the descent of the honest businessman Jack McCracken begins when, yielding to family pressure, he submits to blackmail to get his daughter Samantha out of a shoplifting charge. Private relationships, and the state of society, inform each other.

To speak of Ayckbourn's work in generic terms can also be misleading. From the beginning he has made audiences laugh, and as a matter of convenience he appears in the comedy section of this Companion, with the word 'comedy' in my title. But labels applied to his work tend to come unglued. Comedy, farce, black comedy, social play, thriller, comedy thriller, science fiction, science fiction with comic elements and music written for family audiences – working out what to call an Ayckbourn play may be a way to spend a rainy afternoon, but the time is better spent on the play itself. With the publication of *Sisterly Feelings* and *Taking Steps* in 1981, Ayckbourn formally declared that in the future he would simply call his plays plays, and leave the pigeonholing to others (Ayckbourn 1981: ix).

In particular, he takes the laughter we expect in comedy and exposes the cruelty that lies behind it, to the point where he seems to be breaking the border that defines the form. As a member of the Scarborough audience said of *Absent Friends* (1974), 'If I'd known what I was laughing at while I was watching it, I wouldn't have laughed' (Allen 2001: 145). In the second act of *Absurd Person Singular* Eva, hiding in her kitchen during a Christmas party, makes several attempts to commit suicide, with her guests intervening. She lies down with her head in the oven; Jane, a compulsive tidier, assumes she is trying to clean it and does the job for her. Eva tries to hang herself; Roland, assuming she is trying to change a lightbulb, takes over the job, getting a severe electric shock in the process. Seeing various jobs to be done in the kitchen (all of them Eva's suicide attempts, misread) Sidney, always the manager, writes instructions on the backs of her suicide notes, not bothering to read them. At what point does the laughter stop? Julia McKenzie, preparing to play Susan in *Woman in Mind*, asked Ayckbourn the same question of that play – understandably, since the play ends with Susan's descent into insanity. Ayckbourn replied, 'ideally on the last page, a second before the last line' (Glaap and Quaintmere 1999: 101). In performance, the laughter is unpredictable: as Ayckbourn has noted, 'there'll be a completely different set of laughs on any two consecutive nights' (Allen 2001: 270). The laughs reflect not planted gags but a developing sense of character and situation. His plays are not laugh machines designed to trigger automatic responses; they are living organisms, inter-acting with that other, always unpredictable organism, the audience. The question of what to call them – comedies, or plays too dark to be comedy – is finally academic, that is, meaningless. They are what they are, and they do what they do.

One thing they do, quite persistently, is experiment: not just with genre but with time, place and action (in the sense of storytelling) – the basic conditions of theatre itself. Ayckbourn is constantly challenging himself, trying out new devices – as he puts it, surprising himself (Glaap and Quaintmere 1999: 5) – and this is one reason his work has remained fresh over a long career. His experiments with space and time go back to one of his early commercial successes, *How the Other Half Loves*, in which the set shows two living rooms overlapping in the same space, and we see two dinner parties, taking place on different nights, staged simultaneously. *The Norman Conquests* (1973) shows six characters going through a simultaneous action in three different plays, each with its own unchanging setting. In *Table Manners* (1973) we watch the part of the action that takes place in the dining room; in *Living Together* (1973), the sitting room; in *Round and Round the Garden* (1973), the garden. Each play provides its own perspective on the developing story; none is complete. In the process we are alerted to how much of getting through a day, or a relationship, depends on what we know and what we don't know, on things happening elsewhere when people we know are out of our sight. *House & Garden* (1999) returns to the experiment, reducing the plays and the settings to two: an eighteenth-century country mansion and the wild corner of a garden, with characters moving from one play, and place, to another and back again as a single story unfolds. The house belongs to Teddy, who has inherited a successful business and the Conservative political tradition of his predecessors. He is also having an affair with Joanna, wife of the local doctor Giles. Everyone knows but Giles. (At the end of Act I there is a great off-stage scream from Giles, emanating from the other setting and the other play, that tells us he has found out.) Teddy's wife Trish deals with the situation by refusing to speak to Teddy or even to see him; when they are alone together she treats the room as empty. Gavin, who has come from London to invite Teddy to stand for Parliament, is looking for a candidate who is 'squeaky clean'. We know where this is going. Teddy, practising his acceptance speech, is betrayed by slips of the tongue: 'I sit here your standing mem – no, no, no ... your fully erected member – oh, bloody hell' (Ayckbourn 2000: 57). Gavin himself starts a flirtation with Teddy's daughter Sally, beginning as a lesson in wine-tasting, and going on to a sexual fantasy about what they will do when they spend the night together. Sally initially responds, until Gavin's imagination suddenly turns crude and violent – he will tear off her clothes and spank her with a Bible for being a 'smug little prick-teaser' (88) – and she flees the room in shock. After a few drinks over lunch Teddy and the French actress Lucille, unable to speak each other's languages, banter loudly in nonsense-French (Teddy) and nonsense-English (Lucille). They go off to the garden together, and when Teddy next appears he is without his trousers. Gavin withdraws his offer of a seat in Parliament, and Trish leaves him.

In the house, we encounter silence, repression, desperation and sex that consists of nasty talk. In the garden, which is being prepared for the village fête, Teddy and Lucille, instead of shouting manic nonsense at each other, speak openly of the frustrations of their lives and Teddy, who has seemed an ordinary womanizer and politician on the make, emerges as a man who, simply and wistfully, misses the fun of life. This does not replace the other impression; it creates an alternative. Lucille, in French, makes a similar confession about the frustration of her dreams as an actress. They still do not understand each other's languages, but they have created a shared mood in which they understand each other. They make love in a tent; another character cuts the ropes and as the tent collapses on them Lucille calls out, 'Oh, mon Dieu! Quel amant! Qui dit que les anglais sont frigides!' (199). Sex in the garden is not talk but action, not nasty but funny and marvellous. There is also madness in the garden: Joanna, only glimpsed in *House*, becomes unhinged when Teddy rejects her. She imagines her husband Giles has been replaced by someone called Harold, her son Jake by Gordon. Her fantasy has a point: her real husband and her real son would not treat her as these two have. It also gets laughs: when Joanna addresses the others by their fantasy names and they instinctively respond, she cries, 'Gotcha!' In the garden there is frankness, fun and madness. There is even a spot of Morris dancing. But at the end, with Trish gone and Lucille off to a clinic to dry out, Teddy is left sitting alone, repeating the line with which Trish ended *House*, 'Ah, well. That's life, I suppose' (111, 222). Decisively separated, the characters are linked by resignation.

While the plays of *The Norman Conquests* (1973) are played one after another, *House* and *Garden* were written to be played simultaneously in different theatres. It is not just the characters but the actors who move from one play to another. Around the time Teddy speaks his last line on one stage, Trish is speaking the same line on the other. Ayckbourn's device of simultaneous performance does more than create a stage-manager's nightmare: it uses the circumstances of the performance itself to give a sharper awareness to the transformation of character by setting and to the knowledge that there is more going on in the lives around us than we can ever see at one time.

Other space experiments follow *How the Other Half Loves*, bringing different lives and settings on stage at once. *Things We Do for Love* (1997) uses Scarborough's recently opened end-stage auditorium to show a complete view of one room, the bottom of the room above, and the top of the room below. Dropped clothes in the room above show that a couple is having sex; in the room below another character is painting an erotic mural on the ceiling. The staging suggests the question, if we took off the side of a block of flats, what secrets would be revealed? And what would we see if we could look around time as we look around space? In *Time of My Life* (1992) we follow Glyn and Stephanie into the future, watching their relationship deteriorate; and we follow Adam and Maureen, whose relationship is in ruins at the play's beginning, into the past. Their story, told backwards, becomes increasingly charming and funny. But we know that this engaging couple is doomed, and as we move back and forth through time, there is a sense of entrapment no matter which way we go.

Communicating Doors (1994) and *Whenever* (2002) experiment with time to very different effect. In *Communicating Doors* we are in the same hotel room throughout the play, in 1974, 1994 and 2014. At the opening, in 2014, Reese has engaged Poopay, a prostitute (sorry, 'Specialist Sexual Consultant'), to witness his confession. Not only has he made his fortune spreading ruin and misery through the world; he has had his two wives murdered by his partner Julian. Travelling back to 1994 Poopay warns the second wife, Ruella, that Julian is about to kill her; Ruella in turn travels to 1974 to warn the first wife, Jessica. This creates an alternative action in which, with Ruella taking the lead and Poopay showing increasing courage and resourcefulness, both wives are saved and it is the sinister Julian who dies. This action ends with Reese transformed into a decent man and a force for good in the community, and Poopay, no longer a prostitute, as his adopted daughter – a much happier 2014 than the 2014 in which the play began. The family play *Whenever* begins in 1886 with Emily as a frightened, put-upon Victorian child terrorized by evil relations. She watches her uncle Martin, who has invented a time-machine, murdered by her uncle Lucas, who wants to use the machine to get money and power. Emily escapes through the time-machine, first of all into a future dominated by Lucas and his kind: in 1940, at the height of the Blitz, Lucas is collaborating with the Nazis; in 2010 most of the human race has been wiped out by war; at the end of time Emily encounters a shaggy, inarticulate creature whose language consists of one repeated word, 'Hoombean'. He is the last human being. Emily then uses the time-machine to return to 1886, where she prevents Martin's murder, Lucas is stymied, and a new version of human history is created in which, far from being annihilated by war, the human race has spread through the universe and Hoombean, fully articulate and gorgeously costumed, is an ambassador. Emily herself has been transformed from a frightened Victorian child into a modern young woman with short hair and trousers, who at the end of the play looks over Martin's plans for a flying machine and determines to be the first person to fly. As the play ends, she raises her arms with an exultant cry: 'Yes!' Both plays are optimistic, showing the world put to rights by women who clean up the mess created by men. And both plays have the same wry undercurrent beneath the optimism: to put the world to rights, you have to get into a different reality.

The time-travel plays show alternate stories, asking what would have happened with different choices, different circumstances. This links with another Ayckbourn experiment, alternate actions. In the family play *Mr. A's Amazing Maze Plays* (1988), as Suzy and her dog Neville search the house of Mr Accousticus for the voices he has stolen, there are points at which the audience votes on where the characters go next; different scenes are played according to the results of the vote. At the end of the first scene of *Sisterly Feelings* (1979) the subsequent action hinges on the toss of a coin, which is intended to be real; it determines which of two women Simon will go with. Later scenes end with choices, and the action continues to branch, but the various versions of the play have a common ending, in which the same characters are together, having got there by different routes, not quite satisfied but making the best of it.

In *Intimate Exchanges* (1982) there is no audience vote or coin-toss to introduce genuine chance into the performance; but there is no common ending either. At the beginning of the play Celia lights, or does not light, a cigarette. If she sits down to smoke it, she hears the doorbell and answers it, admitting Lionel. If she does not have the cigarette but disappears into the garden shed, she misses Lionel's call, he goes away, and her first encounter is with Miles. Each of the following scenes ends with a moment of choice, and a further branching, until there are sixteen possible endings. Each ending takes place outside the village church, where some form of communal occasion is going on – a christening, a wedding, a funeral, a school anniversary – but the stability the church represents is countered by the tremendous variety of possibilities for the characters, who end up successful or washed up or married to one person or to another, or separated or dead. Sometimes chance takes a hand: Miles goes home with his wife Rowena, or falls off a cliff in a fog and dies. But for the most part the alternatives stem from the characters' conscious choices, and they reflect their own mixed, conflicted natures. Lionel is a dabbler who tries various jobs; Sylvie tries to make herself over as a sophisticated woman. Sometimes they succeed, sometimes they fail – the common factor is the way they experiment with their own lives, just as the play is experimenting with their different stories. As *The Norman Conquests* and *House & Garden* make us aware of other actions beyond the actions we see at any one time, *Intimate Exchanges* alerts us to the shadow-lives that lie just beside the lives we have made: the offers we didn't take, the people we didn't marry, the play of freedom and fate that makes up any human story.

The ten roles in *Intimate Exchanges*, five men and five women, are intended to be played, as they were in the first production, by a grand total of two actors. This creates a theatrical self-consciousness as we admire the versatility of the performers, and it bears on the play's story experiment: the actors' ability to transform themselves mirrors the transformations in the characters' own lives. This and other uses of doubling (a favourite device of Ayckbourn's) activate the audience's awareness of the duality of actor and character, an awareness aided by the intimacy of theatre-in-the-round, the main form of staging in Scarborough. This may help to explain Ayckbourn's fascination with robots, who have haunted his work since *Henceforward* . . . (1987). The stage robot is an experiment with another of the conditions of theatre, the living body of the actor. In the performance, a live human plays a mechanical one; in the play, a mechanical human takes on the characteristics of a live one. In the first act of *Henceforward* . . . Jerome, a composer who lives a reclusive life surrounded by electronic equipment, is served (inefficiently) by a robot, NAN 300F, whose face he has made over to resemble that of his estranged wife Corinna. He hires an actress, Zoë, to pretend to be a companion with whom he has a loving, stable relationship so that the authorities will allow him to see his daughter, who has been kept from him. When Zoë walks out on him – he has recorded the sounds of their love-making for use in a musical composition, and she is furious – he makes NAN over into a replica of Zoë for the second act, so that the robot can do the job intended for the woman. In Act I, Nan is played by the actress who plays Corinna in Act II; and in Act II she is played by the actress who played Zoë in Act I. (Our awareness of the live performer gives a twinge of discomfort to the moment in Act I when Jerome puts his hand up NAN's skirt to adjust the mechanism.) The relationship of robot and woman – the woman who impersonates it, and the woman it impersonates – makes Jerome's dealings with the robot into a sign of his dealings with women: manipulating, imposing, mechanizing. The real woman the robot impersonates is always absent in the play during the impersonation, and present in the person of the actress. Jerome cannot deal with human reality, and excludes it from his life; in the end, caught up in composing a piece expressing love, he misses a chance to be reunited with his wife and daughter. Yet the reality he tries to exclude is there for us to see, in the form of the women who play their own mechanized substitutes.

In the family play *My Sister Sadie* (2003) the title character is a robot; while NAN has two external appearances, Sadie has two personalities: her creator Caroline gave Sadie her own loving nature; the authorities (represented by another woman, Thora) have turned her into a killer. In the end Sadie's Caroline-nature wins out, and she is adopted by a human family, suggesting, as the title does, the humanization of the robot and reversing Jerome's project of mechanizing the human. In *Comic Potential* (1998) the robot Jacie astonishes her handlers by laughing, crying and falling in love. The fact that her lover is called Adam takes us back to the prototype of the robot play, Karel Čapek's *R.U.R.* (1921), which ends with Adam and Eve robots setting out to repopulate a ruined world.

The duality of the robot also reflects, especially in the case of Sadie, a human capacity for duality that Ayckbourn explores elsewhere, locating it most often in women. In *Drowning on Dry Land* (2004) Marsha, a children's entertainer, is inarticulate with shyness in her own person, wildly aggressive in her professional role as Mr Chortles the clown. Charlotte in *Private Fears in Public Places* (2004) is a practising Christian full of kind thoughts and good works, and an equally practising porn actress, her roles linked by her habit of smiling enigmatically. Once again we are alerted to the duality of character and actor; Marsha and Charlotte both transform themselves through performing.

The robots of *Comic Potential* are also actors: they represent the future of television drama and their mechanized nature suits the scripts they are given. This brings us to another duality, and another form of alternative action: the difference between the complexity of actual human lives and the simplified versions created by the media. When *Man of the Moment* (1988) begins, it has been 17 years since the event that determined the lives of its principal characters. Vic Parks was holding up a bank, taking the beautiful teller Nerys as a human shield. Douglas Beechey, who had worshipped Nerys hopelessly from afar, went wild when he saw her in danger, charged Vic and overpowered him. For a short while Douglas was a hero in the press; then he lapsed into obscurity. He now lives with Nerys in a shabby house, working in double glazing. Vic, released from prison, has become a popular television celebrity, living high; the play is set in his Mediterranean villa. Genial in public, he is a vicious bully in private. The television presenter Jill Rillington contrives a meeting between the two men. The way she wants to spin the story is to draw out Douglas's envy and resentment at the unfairness of his fate and Vic's. She gets nowhere: Douglas is incapable of resentment, and innocently delighted by the splendour in which Vic lives. Jill's attempt to draw predictable emotions out of him are baffled by his intractable good nature. Not only does Jill fail in her attempts to distort Douglas's story; she misses a subtler, sadder story that the audience pieces together from Douglas's words, the story of Nerys. When Douglas made his heroic charge Vic fired, hitting Nerys in the face and leaving her permanently disfigured. Her engagement to another man was broken off, her friends deserted her, and in the end she was left with Douglas. He describes their relationship as a contented one, but the facts slip out: Nerys is self-conscious about her disfigurement, and never leaves the house for months on end. The marriage is childless, their sex life having stopped shortly after it began. Douglas reports that she never complains. Asked if she fell in love with him, he replies, 'I don't know. ... And I didn't ask her' (Ayckbourn 1995b: 539). The story Douglas cannot or will not tell is that his heroic act consigned the woman he loved to a living death.

In the end history repeats itself, with variations. Sharon, a pathetic fat girl who has idolized Vic and whom he taunts with relentless cruelty, tries to drown herself in the swimming pool, *'a tragi-comic, fat, black, rubber-clad figure'* (543). Vic refuses to save her – 'I'm not diving in there. Not in these clothes' (547) – and suggests the way to bring her to the surface is to sprinkle it with rum babas. His wife Trish, provoked beyond endurance, attacks him. Seeing Vic throttle her, Douglas, for the second time in his life, goes berserk, charges, and knocks Vic into the pool where with Sharon standing on him he drowns. Then television takes over. The play ends with a replay of the final action as a television show, with different actors playing the characters (the new Sharon's wetsuit shows off her svelte figure) and the grotesque black comedy of the original reduced to tacky pathos. The theatre audience becomes the studio audience; in applauding when the play is over, it is following orders from the stage to applaud the broadcast, and becomes complicit in the deception it has just witnessed.

The sense of entrapment this leaves us with goes with Ayckbourn's general preference for uncomfortable endings. His early and middle plays generally end bleakly, with characters frozen in various kinds of unhappiness. In his more recent work – and the more upbeat family plays bear some part in this – the bleak endings are not replaced but supplemented by endings that hold out hope or comfort. In *Body Language* (1990), *Sugar Daddies* (2003) and *Private Fears in Public Places* (2004) characters who have been in various ways put-upon and abused bond with each other. The bond is usually between two women; in the last-named play it is between a brother and a sister. It is as though Ayckbourn's career as a whole is *Intimate Exchanges* writ large, a trying-out of possibilities. At the end of *Drowning on Dry Land* (2004) there is an odd, teasing echo of Emily's flying gesture at the end of *Whenever*. The play's setting includes a strange folly tower in which, by an optical trick, a person entering the tower seems to be climbing stairs, but ends up still on ground level. No one has ever climbed to the top. It is an image of two Ayckbourn conditions, entrapment and frustration. At the end Charlie (like Vic a media celebrity, but one whose fame is based on the fact that he never wins anything) has lost his career, his reputation and his family. He makes one last attempt to climb the tower – and finds himself at the top. How did it happen, and what do we make of it? Ayckbourn answers neither question, though an answer to the second suggests itself: in a world in which success brutalizes, to fail as Charlie has failed is a grace that is for once rewarded. But that is more than the play actually says; Ayckbourn's way is not to point morals, but to show situations, play with possibilities, and in the process raise our awareness of the conditions of both theatre and life. And it seems fitting that in a career of constant experimentation at least one play of his should end not as so many do with clear images of despair or (less commonly) hope, but with an unsolved mystery.

PRIMARY READING

Ayckbourn, Alan (1968). *Relatively Speaking*. New York: Samuel French.

Ayckbourn, Alan (1972). *How the Other Half Loves*. London: Evans Books.

Ayckbourn, Alan (1973). *Time and Time Again*. London: Samuel French.

Ayckbourn, Alan (1977). *The Norman Conquests*. London: Penguin.

Ayckbourn, Alan (1979a). *Joking Apart and Other Plays (Just Between Ourselves, Ten Times Table, Joking Apart)*. London: Chatto and Windus.

Ayckbourn, Alan (1979b). *Three Plays (Absurd Person Singular, Absent Friends, Bedroom Farce)*. London: Penguin.

Ayckbourn, Alan (1981). *Sisterly Feelings and Taking Steps*. London: Chatto and Windus.

Ayckbourn, Alan (1982). *Season's Greetings*. London: Samuel French.

Ayckbourn, Alan (1983). *Way Upstream*. London: Samuel French.

Ayckbourn, Alan (1985). *Intimate Exchanges*. 2 vols. London: Samuel French.

Ayckbourn, Alan (1986). *Woman in Mind*. London: Faber and Faber.

Ayckbourn, Alan (1989). *Mr. A's Amazing Maze Plays*. London: Faber and Faber.

Ayckbourn, Alan (1991). *The Revenger's Comedies*. London: Faber and Faber.

Ayckbourn, Alan (1993a). *Time of My Life*. London: Faber and Faber.

Ayckbourn, Alan (1993b). *Wildest Dreams*. London: Faber and Faber.

Ayckbourn, Alan (1995a). *Communicating Doors*. London: Faber and Faber.

Ayckbourn, Alan (1995b). *Plays One (A Chorus of Disapproval, A Small Family Business, Henceforward . . . , Man of the Moment)*. London: Faber and Faber.

Ayckbourn, Alan (1998a). *Plays Two (Ernie's Incredible Illucinations, Invisible Friends, This is Where We Came In, My Very Own Story, The Champion of Paribanou)*. London: Faber and Faber.

Ayckbourn, Alan (1998b). *Things We Do for Love*. London: Faber and Faber.

Ayckbourn, Alan (1999). *Comic Potential*. London: Faber and Faber.

Ayckbourn, Alan (2000). *House & Garden*. London: Faber and Faber.

Ayckbourn, Alan (2001). *Body Language*. London: Samuel French.

Ayckbourn, Alan (2002a). *Damsels in Distress (GamePlan, FlatSpin, RolePlay)*. London: Faber and Faber.

Ayckbourn, Alan (2002b). *Whenever*. London: Faber and Faber.

Ayckbourn, Alan (2003a). *The Crafty Art of Play-making*. New York: Palgrave Macmillan.

Ayckbourn, Alan (2003b). *My Sister Sadie*. London: Faber and Faber.

Ayckbourn, Alan (2003c). *Orvin – Champion of Champions*. London: Faber and Faber.

Ayckbourn, Alan (2005). *Plays Three (Haunting Julia, Sugar Daddies, Drowning on Dry Land, Private Fears in Public Places)*. London: Faber and Faber.

FURTHER READING

Allen, Paul (2001). *Alan Ayckbourn: Grinning at the Edge*. London: Methuen.

Allen, Paul (2004). *A Pocket Guide to Alan Ayckbourn's Plays*. London: Faber and Faber.

Billington, Michael (1990). *Alan Ayckbourn*, 2nd edn. Basingstoke and London: Macmillan.

Dukore, Bernard F. (ed.) (1991). *Alan Ayckbourn: A Casebook*. New York and London: Garland.

Glaap, Albert-Reiner and Quaintmere, Nicholas P. (eds.) (1999). *A Guided Tour Through Ayckbourn Country*. Trier: Wissenschaftlicher.

Holt, Michael (1999). *Alan Ayckbourn*. Plymouth: Northcote House.

Kalson, Albert E. (1993). *Laughter in the Dark: The Plays of Alan Ayckbourn*. Rutherford, Madison and Teaneck: Fairleigh Dickinson University Press; London and Toronto: Associated University Presses.

Watson, Ian (1988). *Conversations with Ayckbourn*, rev. edn. London: Faber and Faber.

White, Sidney Howard (1984). *Alan Ayckbourn*. Boston: Twayne.

23

'They Both Add up to Me': The Logic of Tom Stoppard's Dialogic Comedy

Paul Delaney

Tom Stoppard burst onto the theatrical scene in 1966 when an amateur student production on the Edinburgh Festival Fringe caught the eye of a London reviewer. Ronald Bryden's prescient review for the *Observer* hailed *Rosencrantz and Guildenstern Are Dead* as 'the most brilliant debut by a young playwright since John Arden's'. Bryden praised the play's witty 'stream of ironic invention, metaphysical jokes and linguistic acrobatics', but he also described the play a bit more ponderously as 'an existentialist fable' with 'allegoric purposes' (Bryden, *Observer* 28 August 1966, 15). Bryden's review caught the eye of Kenneth Tynan, then literary manager at the National Theatre, who immediately cabled Stoppard to request a script. And in April 1967 the 29-year-old Stoppard, a Czech immigrant who had been a refugee in Singapore and India, became the youngest playwright to have a play performed by the prestigious National Theatre. Writing for the *Sunday Times*, Harold Hobson called the London production 'the most important event in the British professional theatre of the last nine years' (Hobson, *Sunday Times* 16 April 1967, 49) – that is, since Harold Pinter's debut with *The Birthday Party*. By November *Rosencrantz* had embarked for Broadway – the first National Theatre production to cross the Atlantic – and the hitherto obscure author found himself the toast of two continents, winning the *Evening Standard* drama award in London and the Tony award for best play on Broadway.

The sudden attention lavished on the play left the young playwright confounded by repeated questioning as to what *Rosencrantz* was 'about'. At one level the play is about two Elizabethan courtiers who have been summoned to centre stage where they make increasingly desperate attempts to delve and glean what afflicts Hamlet, to find out 'what's going on' (Stoppard 2000a: 58) in the mystifying world of Elsinore. Their fumbling efforts to understand their situation make them sympathetic, even endearing, characters. The courtiers flip coins, volley questions, and toy with getting caught up in the action when they encounter The Player and his tragedians. Their banter is never less than engaging and frequently laugh-out-loud funny. But amid the laughter, the very amorphousness of their identity and the irony of their situation make it easy for viewers to suppose that Stoppard's hapless courtiers must be emblematic of *something*.

Bryden's 'existential' label was much repeated as were terms like 'Beckettian', 'Pirandellian' and 'absurdist', all of which would prove equally inaccurate and irrelevant. Although Stoppard was not going to refute anyone who wanted to see his play as 'an existentialist fable' and get it produced on the South Bank or Broadway, a few years later he confessed 'I didn't know what the word "existential" meant until it was applied to *Rosencrantz*.' For good measure he added that 'even now existentialism is not a philosophy I find either attractive or plausible' (see Hudson in Delaney 1994: 58). What Stoppard had stumbled on in *Rosencrantz* was not a philosophy but a comic stratagem. What came through more strongly than in previous writing was the playwright's gift for badinage, repartee, verbal byplay:

> GUIL: What's the first thing you remember?
> ROS: Oh, let's see . . . The first thing that comes into my head, you mean?
> GUIL: No – the first thing you remember.
> ROS: Ah. (*Pause.*) No, it's no good, it's gone. It was a long time ago.
> GUIL (*patient but edged*): You don't get my meaning. What is the first thing after all the
>   things you've forgotten?
> ROS: Oh I see. (*Pause.*) I've forgotten the question.
>
> (Stoppard 2000a: 6–7)

Playing at 'words, words' in a kind of verbal tennis, young Stoppard was ready for Centre Court at Wimbledon. Even the earliest of interviewers found him, as Clive James would say, 'a dream interviewee talking in eerily quotable sentences' (James 1975: 70). While his conscious purpose in *Rosencrantz* may have been to amuse a roomful of theatre-goers, in the banter between Ros and Guil he found the kind of ironic juxtaposition that would be characteristic of his comedies – both high and low, both trivial and serious – throughout his career. Only in retrospect did he recognize the extent to which he was being self-revelatory not just in the substance but in the manner of the persistent crosstalk. 'They both add up to me in many ways in the sense that they're carrying out a dialogue which I carry out with myself', Stoppard said. 'One of them is fairly intellectual, fairly incisive; the other one is thicker, nicer in a curious way, more sympathetic. There's a leader and the led. Retrospectively, with all benefit of other people's comments and enthusiasm and so on, it just seems a classic case of self-revelation' (see Gordon in Delaney 1994: 19).

In the endless banter of the two courtiers, which he describes as 'a sort of infinite leap-frog' (see Hudson in Delaney 1994: 58), Stoppard had found a way of putting on stage something of the inner debate that he already carried on with himself: 'I write plays because dialogue is the most respectable way of contradicting myself.' The play, Stoppard affirmed, 'had nothing to do with the condition of modern man or the decline of metaphysics' (see Bradshaw in Delaney 1994: 99, 95). In Stoppard's hands such a comic stratagem proved so effective that he would use it again in his next play, which, as it turned out, dealt with the decline of metaphysics.

Kenneth Tynan famously described *Jumpers* (1972), Stoppard's next full-length play, as 'something unique in theatre: a farce whose main purpose is to affirm the existence of God' (Tynan 1989: 327). Although Stoppard denies that conveying a philosophical message was any part of his conscious purpose in *Rosencrantz*, he acknowledges that 'quite early on . . . I found that philosophical questions occupied me more than any other kind. I hadn't really thought of them as being philosophical questions, but one rapidly comes to an understanding that philosophy's only really about two questions: what is true, and what is good?' (Bedell, *Observer* 17 July 2005, Review, 5). After mulling over – during the five years after *Rosencrantz* – what is true and what is good, Stoppard decided that his next play needed to move on from Wimbledon:

> I wanted a device enabling me to set out arguments about whether social morality is simply a conditioned response to history and environment or whether moral sanctions obey an absolute intuitive God-given law. I've always felt that whether or not 'God-given' means anything, there has to be an ultimate external reference for our actions. Our view of good behaviour *must* not be relativist. The difference between moral rules and the rules of tennis is that the rules of tennis can be changed. I think it's a dangerous idea that what constitutes 'good behaviour' depends on social conventions – dangerous and unacceptable. That led me to the conclusion, not reached all that willingly, that if our behaviour is open to absolute judgement, there must be an absolute judge. (see Kerensky in Delaney 1994: 86)

Belief in the existence of an absolute judge provided, Stoppard explains, the motivation to write 'a theist play':

> I felt that nobody was saying this and it tended to be assumed that nobody held such a view. So I wanted to write a theist play, to combat the arrogant view that anyone who believes in God is some kind of cripple, using God as a crutch. I wanted to suggest that atheists may be the cripples, lacking the strength to live with the idea of God. (see Kerensky in Delaney 1994: 86–7)

Although Stoppard did have a philosophical message to convey in *Jumpers*, he used the same kind of ironic juxtaposition as in *Rosencrantz*. *Jumpers* pits a laughably dowdy professor of moral philosophy against a dapper shaman of a showman. Preparing for a symposium on the topic 'Man – Good, Bad or Indifferent', the moral philosopher George Moore is such a fumbler that he can't even get the pages of his lecture in order (striking a pose to begin he intones: 'Secondly! . . . '). Absorbed in trying to prove the existence of moral absolutes, George remains oblivious to his beautiful and occasionally naked wife in the next room, who is trying to hide the corpse of a murder victim.

George's antagonist in the play, the vice-chancellor Sir Archibald Jumper, is a jack-of-all-disciplines. Besides being 'a doctor of medicine, philosophy, literature and law, with diplomas in psychological medicine and PT including gym', he heads an acrobatic troupe comprised of 'the more philosophical members of the university gymnastics team and the more gymnastic members of the Philosophy School' (Stoppard 1986: 52, 41). Archie's versatility in leaping from one discipline to another is paralleled by his versatility as to what constitutes truth, his epistemological relativism. Archie is slick and suave, a stylist who is never at a loss for words and a showman who has his jumpers neatly choreograph – to the tune 'Sentimental Journey' – the removal of the corpse in Dotty's bedroom, giving graphic illustration to the Rad-Lib philosophy: 'No problem is insoluble given a big enough plastic bag' (ibid.: 31). In the verbal panache and dazzling virtuosity of Archie's showmanship, it is certainly possible to see something of Stoppard's own sparkling theatricality. But in *Jumpers* Stoppard was seeking to write about 'what is true and what is good', and *Jumpers* leads us to recognize the truths in what George is affirming even if we also see the culpability in George's obliviousness, insensitivity, and moral cowardice. In juxtaposing George and Archie, Stoppard may be deftly dividing his own verbal adroitness from his moral perception of what is right. But even if we see two sides of Stoppard in the moral affirmations of George and the stylistic panache of Archie, Stoppard gave such flair and savoir-faire to Archie, the amoral villain, that a few observers mistakenly regarded him as a spokesman for Stoppard himself.

That phenomenon repeated itself in *Travesties*. Well, no one has ever regarded Vladimir Lenin as a spokesman for Stoppard. But Tristan Tzara – the Dadaist, sonnet-scissoring, artist manqué – has been regarded by some as a sympathetic character. Like *Jumpers*, *Travesties* (1974) begins with a *mélange* of disparate images that at first seems incoherent. With something of the flamboyance of Archie, Tzara begins the play by pulling words out of a hat as an exercise in randomness, an attack on artistic order and design. Meanwhile, the novelist James Joyce is dictating the fragments that will form the earliest recollections of the protagonist in *Ulysses*, and Lenin and his wife are having an animated exchange in Russian. The words of Lenin, Joyce and Tzara may be equally incomprehensible on first hearing. But Lenin's words make coherent sense in Russian. Joyce's words make sense in the context of *Ulysses*. And from the first, Stoppard slyly subverts Tzara's presumed nonsense: the words Tzara pulls out of a hat as an exercise in randomness make coherent sense – unbeknownst to Tzara – as a transliterated limerick in French.

Stoppard sets *Travesties* in Zurich, Switzerland, where, historically in 1916, the political revolutionary Vladimir Lenin, the Dadaist performance artist Tristan Tzara, and the novelist James Joyce were all in residence. But Stoppard puts this historical convergence in the memory of one Henry Carr, a British expatriate and minor consular official who once sued Joyce for the cost of a pair of trousers worn in a production of *The Importance of Being Earnest*. The historic Carr made a cameo appearance in Joyce's *Ulysses* as a foul-mouthed, bullying British army private, but in Stoppard's play he becomes the narrator, the central consciousness for a kaleidoscope of memories. In Carr's mind such Wildean characters as Cecily and Gwendolen sweep on-stage and *Travesties* becomes as much a fantasia on Wilde's *Earnest* as *Rosencrantz* is a refraction of *Hamlet*. In the conflict between Tzara — who seeks to destroy art, reason, order, causality — and Joyce, Stoppard declares that he not only finds Joyce 'infinitely the most important' but that he 'loaded the play' for Joyce: 'When they have that argument about art at the end of the first act, notice that Joyce has the last word. I wanted him to murder Tzara, and he does' (see Wetzsteon and Eichelbaum in Delaney 1994: 82–3 and 105). If Stoppard is torn, and he is, it is between the extraordinary artist James Joyce and the claims of the ordinary, mundane individual Henry Carr who here serves as the unreliable, memory-slipping narrator. In the conflict between Joyce's claim that he need not justify himself in political terms at all, and Carr's affirmation of patriotism, duty, love and freedom, Stoppard says he finds himself on both sides of the debate: 'my answer to that question is liable to depend on the moment at which you run out of tape' (see Hudson in Delaney 1994: 69).

At the same time that Stoppard was seeking, in works of dazzling virtuosity like *Jumpers* and *Travesties,* to contrive 'the perfect marriage between the play of ideas and farce' (ibid.: 59), he was also turning his hand to more lightweight fare. *After Magritte* and *Travesties* may both begin with a bizarre 'pig's breakfast' of images that will subsequently be explained as making coherent sense. But while *Travesties* engages with questions regarding the role of the artist and the potentially competing claims of aesthetic and political freedom, Stoppard happily lumps *After Magritte* with his 'plays which are farcical and without an idea in their funny heads' (ibid). Stoppard distinguishes such rompy farces, which he calls entertainments, from his serious plays (however funny they may be). Confections like *The Real Inspector Hound* and *After Magritte* are intricately plotted pieces of stage machinery that 'attempt to bring off a sort of comic coup in pure mechanistic terms' (ibid.). By contrast, '*Jumpers* is a serious play dealt with in the farcical terms which in *Hound* actually *constitute* the play' (ibid.: 63, emphasis in original). 'The confusion arises', Stoppard acknowledges, 'because I treat plays of ideas in just about the same knockabout way as I treat the entertainments' (see Gussow in Delaney 1994: 130). But towards the end of the 1970s even Stoppard's shorter plays began to evince more substantial concerns. The origin of *Every Good Boy Deserves Favour* (*EGBDF*) (1977) was André Previn's query as to whether Stoppard might want to write a play that included a symphony orchestra. Confessing that 'before being carried out feet first, I would like to have done a bit of absolutely everything,' Stoppard says 'I find it very hard to turn down offers to write an underwater ballet for dolphins or a play for a motorcyclist on the wall of death' (see Bradshaw in Delaney 1994: 98). The chance to play with a full symphony orchestra — even if he couldn't play a note — was too playful an opportunity to pass up. Stoppard first conceived of *EGBDF* as a play about a Florida grapefruit millionaire, which sounds like an entertainment, a play without an idea in its funny head. But in the meanwhile Stoppard had been speaking out on behalf of Soviet dissidents and Czech survivors of Eastern-bloc repression. About the time Stoppard realized that the symphony orchestra in *EGBDF* could be in the mind of his protagonist, Stoppard was meeting with political prisoners who had been confined to Soviet psychiatric hospitals for their political beliefs. *EGBDF* may have begun as an entertainment, but by its first performance in 1977 the piece had greater resonance than even its tympani could provide. Stoppard's play sounds the dangers that an overly orchestrated society poses to individual human rights, political freedom and moral good.

Stoppard's subsequent plays are frequently playful, but they're never just playful. In *Professional Foul* (1977), Stoppard has a bit of fun with the way academics (and footballers) can talk past each other. But Stoppard's 1997 television play essentially picks up where *Jumpers* left off, with a moral philosopher confronting injustice and attempting to come to terms with 'the way human beings are supposed to behave towards each other' (see Hebert in Delaney 1994: 127). Prof. Anderson arrives at a Prague philosophy colloquium intending to give a paper on 'Ethical Fictions as Ethical Foundations' but has his own ethical foundations shaken when he encounters his former graduate student, Pavel Hollar, who has written a doctoral thesis arguing that 'the ethics of the State must be judged against the fundamental ethic of the individual' (1978: 55). Anderson at first refuses Hollar's appeal to take his thesis – which Czech authorities would regard as contraband – to the West. In the confrontation between a young Czech dissident who cannot escape repression and a complacent Englishman who has not had to consider what life is like for his East European counterparts, Stoppard finds himself on both sides of the Iron Curtain. After brushing up against the reality of Soviet-era repression as experienced by Hollar's son, a 10-year-old boy, Anderson gives a ringing public affirmation of 'a sense of right and wrong which precedes utterance' and argues that ethics are based on what is right in 'one person's dealings with another person' (1978: 90). In rejecting any 'collective or State ethic which finds itself in conflict with individual rights' (1978: 91), Anderson clings to a truth that Herzen would salvage from the shipwreck of utopian philosophy at the end of *The Coast of Utopia* (2002), Stoppard's magisterial trilogy on nineteenth-century Russian thinkers and artists.

Just as the protagonist of *The Real Thing* (1982) will affirm 'I don't think writers are sacred, but words are' (Stoppard 1988b: 54), *Night and Day* (1979) celebrates the freedom of the press while acknowledging the misuse of that freedom by some practitioners. 'People do awful things to each other,' says the photojournalist Guthrie, implicitly acknowledging that there is a way human beings are supposed to behave towards each other, 'but it's worse in places where everybody is kept in the dark. It really is. Information is light. Information, in itself, about anything, is light' (Stoppard 1979: 92). Stoppard has repeatedly insisted that the affirmation of a free press and Guthrie's blazing affirmation that information is light 'utterly speak for me' (see Berkvist in Delaney 1994: 137).

The Real Thing attempts to distinguish the genuine from the ersatz in romantic relationships and in writing – and the real link between writing that works and relationships that work. With a playwright as a protagonist, *The Real Thing* is the most autobiographical of Stoppard's plays. In writing, Henry reveres 'well chosen words nicely put together'; in relationships Henry values 'a sort of knowledge': 'what lovers trust each other with. Knowledge of each other, not of the flesh but through the flesh' (1988b: 51, 63). But just as Anderson in *Professional Foul* is 'educated by experience beyond the education he's received from thinking' (see Gollob in Delaney 1994: 155), Henry in the course of *The Real Thing* receives an education by experience that leaves him in 'tears, pain, self-abasement' (1988b: 72) prior to the final reconciliation. The extent to which art imitates life here is exceeded only by the degree to which life imitates art. Whether Henry's play-within-the-play is 'about self-knowledge through pain', as he describes it, or 'about did she have it off or didn't she' (ibid.: 62), as his daughter describes it, the autobiographical implications ripple outward.

In *Hapgood* (1988) Stoppard uses the quantum mysteries of particle physics and the twists and turns of a multinational spy caper as metaphoric equivalents for the mysterious complexity of personality, temperament and human identity. The spy caper hinges on the realization that Ridley, a suspected double agent, has an identical twin. Like light, Ridley can appear to be 'here' at the same time he is 'there'; he can be particle pattern or wave pattern, and investigators seeking to find one or the other invariably get what they interrogate for. But the buttoned-down professional Elizabeth Hapgood also appears to have a twin who is anything but buttoned-down. And as much as Hapgood exemplifies prudence, professionalism and propriety, she discovers a different side to herself when her 11-year-old son's life is on the line. Stoppard's play demonstrates that 'we're all doubles', that it is an oversimplification to think 'you're this or you're that' (Stoppard 1988a: 72, 73). The one who puts on the clothes in the morning may be 'the working majority' but at night 'we meet our sleeper – the priest is visited by the doubter, the Marxist sees the civilizing force of the bourgeoisie, the captain of industry admits the justice of common ownership' (ibid.: 72). And, as Stoppard says of Ros and Guil, it takes both to 'add up to me' (see Gordon in Delaney 1994: 19).

The radio play *In the Native State* (1991) and its much revised stage avatar, *Indian Ink* (1995), explores cultural imperialism and the ways in which a postcolonial mindset can be even more confining than constraints imposed by fiat. *Arcadia* (1993) weaves an intricate skein of past and present in a play that contrasts romantic and classical temperaments, Newtonian physics and chaos theory, the arts and sciences, the desire to know intellectually and the desire to know and be known in the biblical sense. Although Hannah may demonstrate classical reserve in stark contrast to Bernard's impetuous privileging of passion, Stoppard demonstrates again that temperament is a matter of 'both/and' rather than 'either/or'. Hannah largely refrains from asserting truth claims that go beyond demonstrable proof, but there does come a point where she trusts her gut instinct and asserts that she knows more than she can prove. Set in a Derbyshire stately home, Stoppard's play celebrates what endures as the genius of the place in the infallible mute witness of Gus – as well as celebrating Thomasina, a nineteenth-century prodigy who does not endure to see the dawn of her seventeenth birthday.

The Invention of Love (1997) dramatizes the conflict between restraint and release in the poet and classics scholar A. E. Housman, whose profoundly felt impulse towards restraint works against his passionately felt but almost wholly unexpressed ardour for Moses Jackson.

Using the vast canvas of a trilogy of full-length plays, Stoppard in *The Coast of Utopia* (2002) offers a panoramic view of Russian thinkers in the nineteenth century, wheeling from Chekhovian estates to Tsarist Moscow, from philosophic to political to poetic precepts. In the sweep of the trilogy, Stoppard pits ideological appeals to a utopian culmination of history against a more measured sense of the worth of particular persons. Stoppard ultimately appeals to the ineluctably moral value of the individual human life given 'our dignity as human beings' (Stoppard 2002c: 118), as opposed to any utilitarian view of the masses. If Stoppard is continuing to reflect on 'what is true, and what is good', he concludes in *The Coast of Utopia* that good is not to be found in some distant future. Stoppard rejects as a bloodthirsty Moloch the promise 'that everything will be beautiful after we're dead' (ibid.: 118). If life is to be valued, it is to be valued in the here and now, before Rosencrantz and Guildenstern are dead, not in some utopian future, whether con-ceived of as a Marxist march of history, or a Muslim paradise of martyrs, or 'the great celestial get-together for an exchange of views' (Stoppard 1993: 75). *The Coast of Utopia* offers Stoppard's full-length response not only to Marxism but to all ideology that calls for self-sacrifice, from *revolutsia* to jihad, from proletariat apparatchiks to suicide bombers. What Stoppard leaves us with instead is Herzen's much more modest affirmation that 'the end we work for must be closer, the labourer's wage, the pleasure in the work done, the summer lightning of personal happiness' (Stoppard 2002c: 118).

And what waves washing upon the *Coast of Utopia* can be traced back to ripples in *Rosencrantz and Guildenstern Are Dead*? In the long voyage of Stoppard's plays the pulse that continues is a sense of the value of the individual human life, the worth of particular persons, yes, even such nonentities as the laughably forgetful Henry Carr, the dowdy George Moore, or the inauspicious Ros and Guil. For all of the majestic sweep of Hamlet's tragic demise, it is also true that by the end of Shakespeare's play Rosencrantz and Guildenstern too are dead. In Stoppard's canon, even their little lives matter. While Ros and Guil are dying to know 'what was it all about?' (Stoppard 2000a: 116), Hannah assures Valentine that 'it's wanting to know that makes us matter' (Stoppard 1993: 76). Foreseeing the heat death of the universe, Thomasina says 'Yes, we must hurry if we are going to dance' (ibid.: 94). She waltzes fluently with Septimus through the time left, for 'it is God-given' (ibid.: 91). Carr dances with Cecily (Stoppard 1975: 97). Anderson retrieves Hollar's manuscript (Stoppard 1978: 93). Gus picks up what has been let fall by others (Stoppard 1993: 96–7).

Primary reading

Stoppard, Tom (1970). *The Real Inspector Hound*. London: Faber and Faber.

Stoppard, Tom (1975). *Travesties*. London: Faber and Faber.

Stoppard, Tom (1978). *Every Good Boy Deserves Favour* and *Professional Foul*. London: Faber and Faber.

Stoppard, Tom (1979). *Night and Day*. London: Faber and Faber.

Stoppard, Tom (1980). *Dogg's Hamlet, Cahoot's Macbeth*. London: Faber and Faber.

Stoppard, Tom (1985). *Rough Crossing*. London: Faber and Faber.

Stoppard, Tom (1986). *Jumpers*. London: Faber and Faber.

Stoppard, Tom (1988a). *Hapgood*. London: Faber and Faber.

Stoppard, Tom (1988b). *The Real Thing*. London: Faber and Faber.

Stoppard, Tom (1991a). 'Going Back', *Independent Magazine* 23 March, 25–30.

Stoppard, Tom (1991b). *In the Native State*. London: Faber and Faber.

Stoppard, Tom (1991c). *Rosencrantz and Guildenstern Are Dead: The Film*. London: Faber and Faber.

Stoppard, Tom (1993). *Arcadia*. London: Faber and Faber.

Stoppard, Tom (1994a). *The Plays for Radio, 1964–91* (*The Dissolution of Dominic Boot*, *'M' Is for Moon Among Other Things*, *If You're Glad I'll Be Frank*, *Albert's Bridge*, *Where Are They Now?*, *Artist Descending a Staircase*, *The Dog it Was That Died*, and *In the Native State*). London: Faber and Faber.

Stoppard, Tom (1994b). *The Television Plays, 1965–84* (*A Separate Peace*, *Neutral Ground*, *Teeth*, *Another Moon Called Earth*, *Professional Foul*, and *Squaring the Circle*). London: Faber and Faber.

Stoppard, Tom (1995). *Indian Ink*. London: Faber and Faber.

Stoppard, Tom (1997). *The Invention of Love*. London: Faber and Faber.

Stoppard, Tom (1999a). 'On Turning Out To Be Jewish', *Talk*, September, 190–4, 241–3.

Stoppard, Tom (1999b). *Shakespeare in Love: A Screenplay* (with Marc Norman, co-author). London: Faber and Faber.

Stoppard, Tom (2000a). *Rosencrantz and Guildenstern Are Dead*. London: Faber and Faber (1st edn. 1967).

Stoppard, Tom (2000b). 'The Invention of Love: An Exchange', *New York Review of Books* 21 September, 104.

Stoppard, Tom (2002a). *Voyage, The Coast of Utopia Part I*. London: Faber and Faber.

Stoppard, Tom (2002b). *Shipwreck, The Coast of Utopia Part II*. London: Faber and Faber.

Stoppard, Tom (2002c). *Salvage, The Coast of Utopia Part III*. London: Faber and Faber.

Further reading

Brassell, Tim (1985). *Tom Stoppard: An Assessment*. London: Macmillan.

Bull, John (2003). 'From Illyria to Arcadia: Uses of Pastoral in Modern English Theater', *Triquarterly* 116, 57–72.

Corballis, Richard (1984). *Stoppard: The Mystery and the Clockwork*. Oxford: Amber Lane Press.

Delaney, Paul (1990). *Tom Stoppard: The Moral Vision of the Major Plays*. London: Macmillan.

Delaney, Paul (ed.) (1994). *Tom Stoppard in Conversation*. Ann Arbor: University of Michigan Press.

Fleming, John (2001). *Stoppard's Theatre: Finding Order amid Chaos*. Austin: University of Texas Press.

Gussow, Mel (1995). *Conversations with Stoppard*. London: Nick Hern.

Hynes, Joseph (1995). 'Tom Stoppard's Lighted March', *Virginia Quarterly Review* 71:4, 642–55.

James, Clive (1975). 'Count Zero Splits the Infinite', *Encounter* 45, 68–76.

Jenkins, Anthony (1987). *The Theatre of Tom Stoppard*. Cambridge: Cambridge University Press.

Jernigan, Daniel (2003). 'Tom Stoppard and "Postmodern Science": Normalizing Radical Epistemologies in *Hapgood* and *Arcadia*', *Comparative Drama* 37:1, 3–35.

Karwowski, Michael (2003). 'All Right: An Assessment of Tom Stoppard's Plays', *Contemporary Review* 282:1646, 161–6.

Kelly, Katherine E. (1991). *Tom Stoppard and the Craft of Comedy*. Ann Arbor: University of Michigan Press.

Kelly, Katherine E. (ed.) (2001). *The Cambridge Companion to Tom Stoppard*. Cambridge: Cambridge University Press.

Kramer, Prapassaree and Kramer, Jeffrey (1997). 'Stoppard's *Arcadia*: Research, Time, Loss', *Modern Drama* 40:1, 1–10.

Melbourne, Lucy (1998). ' "Plotting the Apple of Knowledge": Tom Stoppard's *Arcadia* as Iterated Theatrical Algorithm', *Modern Drama* 41:1, 557–72.

Nadel, Ira (2002). *Double Act: A Life of Tom Stoppard*. London: Methuen.

Nadel, Ira (2004a). 'Tom Stoppard: In the Russian Court', *Modern Drama* 47:3, 500–24.

Nadel, Ira (2004b). 'Writing the Life of Tom Stoppard', *Journal of Modern Literature* 27:3, 19–29.

Pearce, Howard D. (1979). 'Stage as Mirror: Tom Stoppard's *Travesties*', *MLN* 94, 1138–58.

Rabinowitz, Peter J. (1980). ' "What's Hecuba to Us?": The Audience's Experience of Literary Borrowing' in Susan R. Suleiman and Inge Crosman (eds.). *The Reader in the Text: Essays on Audience and Interpretation*. Princeton: Princeton University Press, 241–73.

Russell, Richard B. (2004). ' "It Will Make Us Friends": Cultural Reconciliation in Tom Stoppard's *Indian Ink*', *Journal of Modern Literature* 27:3, 1–18.

Ryan, Carrie (2000–1). 'Translating *The Invention of Love*: The Journey from Page to Stage for Tom Stoppard's Latest Play', *Journal of Modern Literature* 24:2, 197–204.

Sternlieb, Lisa and Selleck, Nancy (2003). ' "What Is Carnal Embrace?": Learning to Converse in Stoppard's *Arcadia*', *Modern Drama* 46:3, 482–502.

Thirlwell, Adam (2005). 'Adam Thirlwell Talks with Tom Stoppard' in Vendela Vida (ed.). *The Believer Book of Writers Talking to Writers*. San Francisco: Believer, 349–77.

Tucker, Herbert F. (2005). 'History Played Back: In Defense of Stoppard's *Coast of Utopia*', *Raritan* 24:4, 149–69.

Tynan, Kenneth (1989). *Profiles*. London: Nick Hern.

Wheatley, Alison E. (2004). 'Aesthetic Consolation and the Genius of the Place in Stoppard's *Arcadia*', *Mosaic* 37:3, 171–84.

24

Stewart Parker's Comedy of Terrors

Anthony Roche

In the introduction to the three history plays he conceived and wrote between 1983 and 1987, Stewart Parker described them as 'a continuing comedy of terrors' (Parker 2000b: xiii). Comedy rather than tragedy had always been Parker's chosen theatrical mode, but it was a comedy of the darkest hue. In a lecture given at Queen's University Belfast in 1986, he outlined what he believed to be the alternatives facing a dramatist from Northern Ireland during the decades of 'the Troubles':

> Writing about and from within this particular place and time is an enterprise full of traps and snares. The raw material of drama is over-abundant here . . . an explosion, a shot, a tragic death: another Ulster play written. . . . And yet if ever a time and place cried out for the solace and rigour and passionate rejoinder of great drama, it is here and now. There is a whole culture to be achieved. (Parker 1986: 18–19)

To write a tragic play about Northern Ireland is for Parker to accept its status quo, the doomed inevitability of violent, sectarian conflict; instead, he skilfully, even surgically deployed as his weapon a honed and playful wit. In so doing, he also challenged the negative image of the Northern Protestant community, from which he came, as dour and humourless, countering it with a comic exuberance and a fertile imagination.

Stewart Parker died of cancer on 2 November 1988, at the young age of 47. Did he know when he wrote those last three history plays that, like the lead characters in *Northern Star* (1984) and *Heavenly Bodies* (1986), he was facing imminent extinction? Or as in his most Beckettian play *Nightshade* (1980), where the central figure is a funeral hall director, was death a constant companion? Parker had his brush early on, with a bout of pleurisy and a leg amputation while still in his teens. But beyond his personal biography there was the daily death toll on the streets of his birthplace. In *Northern Star*, the central character is given a privileged dramatist's-eye view of Irish history past and future and sums it up in the same phrase Parker used in his introduction and which supplies my title: 'the cycle just goes on, playing out the same demented comedy of terrors from generation to generation' (Parker 2000b: 69). There is something incomplete about Stewart Parker's achievement. He died at the height of his powers, having just written his most profound and moving play, *Pentecost* (1987), with the sense that he had much more to give – and that wholeness of culture he gestured at in relation to Northern Ireland is still some way from being achieved. Parker left a large body of work behind him, including award-winning TV and radio scripts. But it is his writing for the stage that comprises the centre of his achievement and legacy, sustained as it has been since his death by the productions of his niece Lynne Parker and her company Rough Magic in Dublin and by the Tinderbox Company in Belfast, and it is on those plays that this chapter will concentrate.

Spokesong, premiered in 1975 at the Dublin Theatre Festival, announced the arrival of a major new talent and introduced some of his signature dramatic elements. Paramount among these is music. The play features a series of songs with music by Jimmy Kennedy, a Northern Irish octogenarian writer of such popular ballads as 'Red Sails in the Sunset', and lyrics by Parker which indulge his love of outrageous puns and excruciating rhymes. They give vent to the central character Frank's love affair/obsession with the bicycle and his efforts to keep his family bicycle shop open in the face of two adversaries: the modernizers who are determined to tear down the historic Belfast and the bombers who are no less determined to blow it up. But this is not a musical; rather, the songs function as Brechtian devices to comment on the situations dramatized, to disrupt the conventions of realism. As Parker makes clear in a note, 'realism is only one mode among several adopted during the action' (Parker 2000a: 3). When a paramilitary figure arrives in the shop seeking protection money, *'dressed in a leather jacket and wearing dark glasses'* (Parker 2000a: 49), he is represented by the Trick Cyclist who introduces the 'show', acts as master of ceremonies and plays many of the secondary roles.

The complication for Frank is that this thug is his potential father-in-law. For Frank is attracted to a woman called (wait for it) Daisy Bell, who comes into Frank's shop to repair her bicycle when her car is blown up. As a couple, they provide one of the classic contrasting double-acts encountered in Parker's theatre, the romantic/dreamer/fantasist and the realist, the person of practical affairs: the dialogue between a man and a woman in which radically contrasting points of view are expressed simultaneously and convey an increasing sense of erotic attraction. The relationship between Frank and Daisy is deepened and contextualized by the play's conscious structural parallel with his Victorian grandparents, Francis and Kitty, who raised him when he was orphaned in World War II and are still alive as old people in the 'present' of the play. Francis and Kitty change ages, re-enacting scenes from their own courtship 60 years earlier. Here, as he was to do so often, Parker is writing a history play, enriching the present by bringing it into meaningful connection with the past. Francis and Kitty come from the same Protestant middle classes as Parker himself, but Kitty has converted to Irish nationalism where her husband-to-be remains a staunch unionist, albeit one whose truest allegiance is to the bicycle. The Victorian scenes of *Spokesong* make delightfully explicit Parker's own interest in and indebtedness to the writings of Oscar Wilde, not least in the courtship scenes. They also render more explicitly than Wilde's own writings the dialectic between Irishness and Englishness in his work, which is an important dual allegiance for Parker himself. The deployment of Wildean pastiche in a surrealistic play set in and commenting on the present also indicates another important resource for Parker's comic writing – Tom Stoppard, his contemporary. Stoppard's is a more ambiguous influence for Parker than Wilde, as I will examine later. The romantic plot is resolved by Daisy deciding not to leave for London but to stay with Frank in Belfast. There will be no conventional romantic denouement, the realist Daisy explains to the dreamer: 'No wedding bells, Frank. I'm not being responsible for another child growing up in this town. Without kids there's no point' (73). In a play which has set so much store by generations and legacy, the present contrasts most sharply with the past in this decision not to continue the line. The issue of giving birth, as both metaphor and a dramatic element, is one that resonated throughout Parker's plays.

His second play, *Catchpenny Twist*, premiered at Dublin's Peacock Theatre in 1977, focuses on a young and struggling Northern Irish male songwriter working with a double-act of composer and lyricist. This duplicates the process by which the songs for the play were written, with musician-composer Shaun Davey supplying the melodies and Parker the words. It also reflects the impact of contemporary popular music on Northern Ireland in the 1960s, where Derry man Phil Coulter twice co-composed the winning entry in the Eurovision Song Contest. The commerce–art debate is central to the play, for what complicates the scenes showing the two men struggling to write their songs is the number of different masters they are trying to serve and the different markets in which they are trying to compete. There is, first of all, the strictly commercial imperative to survive financially, which dictates that they write jingles for commercials: they are offered 'Brady's Frozen Chickens' (Parker 2000a: 91). Then there is the commercial jackpot of the European Song Contest or, in this instance, the Ettebruck Song Contest in Luxembourg. Parker has great fun writing their losing entry but even more, I suspect, with the lyrics for the song which goes on to win: 'Sing hello the Zig Zag song / Sing bye-bye the Zig Zag song / It's a song that all can sing / Come along and let it ring / . . . La-la-la-la-la-la-la / La-la-la-la-la-la-la' and so on (154). Their musical mainstays are contemporary romantic ballads sung by one of the two women members of their college gang, Monagh, for whom the writer Martyn carries a (largely unrequited) torch. The other woman from their gang, Marie, resurfaces in their lives as a member of the IRA and suggests that they might contribute patriotic ballads to the cause. They struggle to oblige:

> What rhymes with McVeigh?
> ROY: Slay.
> MARTYN: Pray? . . . Obey?
> ROY: Decay.
> MARTYN: Great. Thanks, That's terrific. 'He gave his life for Ireland, On account of tooth decay.'   (87)

The plot develops when they receive two bullets in the post, since they have also been writing ballads for Protestant paramilitaries and are suspected by both sides of informing. As a result, the musical trio leave town and Northern Ireland, seeking refuge first in the south of Ireland and later in London. In the end Martyn is moved to protest: 'We always seem to be on the run. I need to find some bearings' (130). Where they try most to live is in the romantic ballads they compose for Monagh, songs of emotional loss and masochism. The romantic paranoia in Martyn's lyrics provides a much more accurate representation of the politics in which they are enmeshed than the past-fixated patriotic ballads: 'Somebody out there loves you, sugar / Somebody out there wants to know you . . . / Yes, there's somebody out there / Somebody out there' (119–20), the stage lighting diminishes to the point where *'they all three stare fearfully out into the surrounding darkness, as they sing the final repeated line. Black out'* (120). The play concludes with the two writers waiting in limbo, in the transit area of an airport; they open a package they have recently been handed, which triggers the explosion prefigured earlier by the two bullets. But their musical number is not quite up. In the last and blackest ironic juxtaposition, Monagh sings the banal lyrics to their song-contest entry 'Crybaby' to the visual accompaniment of Roy and Martyn *'on their knees, hands and faces covered in blood, groping about blindly'* (159).

Parker was to follow *Catchpenny Twist* with a full-blown musical, *Kingdom Come* (1980), which received a dual production at the King's Head in London and the Lyric in Belfast, but which has neither been published nor revived (Harris 1997: 284). In the face of the negative reviews, music disappeared from Parker's next play; but it could not remain absent for long and it powerfully re-emerges in his later plays, serving to underscore and deepen the on-stage action.

Nightshade, staged at the Peacock Theatre in 1980, is Parker's most self-consciously theatrical play and the most removed from the immediate context of Northern Ireland. The drama is set in a firm of undertakers and their conversations forcefully bring to mind the daily removal of dead bodies from the streets: 'People need waking up. [. . .] While we're out scooping their son's intestines back into the stomach cavity, with all due reverence and dignity, of course' (Parker 2000a: 167). The main character, Quinn, keeps his job as mortician at bay by adopting a modernizing, technological approach (a visitor remarks that the morgue looks like a brothel) (202), but even more by practising his second profession, that of magician. Dressed in a variety of conjuror's outfits, Quinn performs magic acts throughout, most of them involving his beautiful bespangled assistant, 16-year-old daughter Delia. At one level, the magic fails to work, rather in the manner of Tommy Cooper, only to succeed at a more sophisticated level and disclose a deeper psychological truth. When Quinn plunges a sword into the box enclosing Delia, blood suddenly spurts out. It is opened to reveal the young woman inside, clutching her stomach, her face contorted in pain. Then, to the roll of drums, she leaps to her feet, unharmed (165). In this play, as in the three following, Parker found a way to make self-conscious theatrical artifice address and give expression to emotion. The father–daughter relationship between Quinn and Delia is at the core of *Nightshade*; the magic gag attests to the wounds he has inflicted on her – and even more on the wife-mother Agnes, who vanished from their lives a year earlier. When Quinn wants to test a straitjacket for its escapology potential, he straps Delia into it, not as aware as she is of the awful echo this act provides of her mother's psychological condition (189).

Delia is also the principal source of the fairy tales and biblical stories in which the play abounds. She is particularly drawn to the Old Testament and the story of Jacob wrestling with an angel. This finds surreal expression on the stage with two of the mortuary workers stripping off and having a wrestling match (echoing a Monty Python sketch where the existence of God is established by two falls and a submission). Delia has her own demons to wrestle with, especially when she finds that her mother's death in London (most probably suicide) has been kept from her. The question of whether the angel with whom Jacob wrestles is god or man continues to resonate throughout the play, and allows Parker to address one of his favourite themes, the split between body and soul. Delia wants to imagine a god that is close up and personal – 'A God you could get your mitts on. Feel him squirming in your gut. Face up to him in your own reflection' (189) – but in the meantime has to face her father and the fact that he is cracking up. Her diagnosis comes in the form of a lethal but truthful pun: 'He's come to grief, that's all. He's finally come to grief' (218). The relationship between Quinn and Delia reverses the familiar gender dynamic from earlier Parker plays. The woman is now at the centre, the man much more decentred and destabilized; and the straight opposition between dreamer and realist is more complicated and interknit. The final question posed by this play set in a funeral home is not how to die but how to live; as Delia remarks in one of her precocious school essays: 'For a person begins to die at the moment of birth. So dying is an action that we perform throughout our lives' (232). The echo of Beckett's *Waiting for Godot* (1955) here is unmistakeable and his spirit palpable throughout this most theatrically inventive of black comedies.

Pratt's Fall (1983) is the least well-known of Parker's comedies. It is as full of wit and inventiveness as one had come to expect, and has most to offer in its treatment of the relationship between the English and the Irish, but it suffers from a failure to find a satisfactory form for its concerns. The play hinges on the discovery of a map which would appear to indicate that the Irish discovered America, and Parker has a great deal of fun with the question of whether the map is authentic or not. To no one's great surprise, it is finally revealed as a fraud, though we do learn that 'there's a lecturer in Wisconsin who's currently claiming that the map is really genuine after all' (Parker 2000a: 331). But three years earlier Brian Friel's *Translations* had swept the boards when it came to placing map-making at the centre of an Irish play. The scene which works best in *Pratt's Fall* is the debate between the Irishman George Mahoney, who claims to have discovered the map, and the Englishwoman Victoria Pratt (or Queen Victoria, as George refers to her), who has come over to Ireland in an effort to authenticate it. His angry exchange with her hinges on the colonial relationship and is shadowed by their growing sexual and romantic interest in each other:

> this island you're on now is where it started and this is where it's drawing to a close, this is where you've always come to unleash your most damnable nightmares and devils. [...] I read once about an instruction in an old mapmaker's handbook: 'Where you know nothing, place terrors.' (283–4)

Yet the Irishman defending this ground is a Glaswegian with an Irish Catholic mother and a Scottish Presbyterian father. And the ground itself only temporarily shifts to Ireland. In the main, the play is set in England and is narrated in retrospect by George's best friend, Godfrey Dudley, an English academic, on the occasion of his marriage to Victoria. Godfrey has lusted after her since their student days at Oxford twenty years earlier and, Victoria's temporary relationship with the Hiberno-Scot now terminated, he is about to be rewarded. Godfrey still harbours a fear that Mahoney may show up like 'the ghost at the wedding feast' (251). And this is the problem. For too much of its length, *Pratt's Fall* plays like an academic English comedy, with the Irish characters and subject as a side issue. The spirit of Tom Stoppard is all too present, not least when Victoria's sister shows up with an absurd detective in tow straight out of *The Real Inspector Hound* (1968). George Mahoney is described as a man of 'no fixed abode' (267). Drifting in and out of the play, he pauses only long enough to express his sense of his own life as a form of latter-day pilgrimage which seeks to recapture 'the wild surge of faith...the rapture of it, the blind leap into the dark' (270). For the most part, *Pratt's Fall* remains an earthbound ersatz English comedy of academic life, with some good jokes: 'those who can, do, those who can't, teach. As to those who can't teach, there's always administration' (311).

For his next three plays, Stewart Parker was to turn back to Ireland, and to Belfast in particular. Ireland becomes his central subject and Irish drama the means by which his political vision is to be realized. *Northern Star* (1984) was the first play of Parker's to be commissioned and premiered in his native city at the Lyric Theatre, Belfast. What actor-director Stephen Rea has described as Parker's 'powerful preoccupation with the specifically Protestant republican and radical tradition of Belfast' (Parker 2000b: xi) provides the narrative through-line. Henry Joy McCracken, a leader of the United Irishmen in the north of Ireland during the 1798 Rebellion, begins by directly addressing the 'citizens of Belfast' (Parker 2000b: 4). His opening speech indicates that the play is framed not only by the historical context of the 1798 Rebellion but by a contemporary Northern Irish setting in which the political issues relating to the two communities remain no less relevant and fraught: 'I stand guilty of nurturing a brotherhood of affection between the Catholics of this town and my fellow Protestants..., confident in the blind belief that you will all unite together in freedom this week next week sometime never' (5; see also Richtarik 2000: 267).

Northern Star makes its way by means of theatrical pastiche of the entire Anglo-Irish dramatic tradition: Farquhar from the eighteenth century (and Northern

Ireland); the melodrama of Boucicault, the verbal wit of Wilde and the dialectic of Shaw from the nineteenth; the Hiberno-English dialect of Synge and the elaborate Dublinese of O'Casey from the Abbey Theatre tradition; the gallows humour of Behan's prisoners in *The Quare Fellow* (1954) and an appropriately brief sample of Beckett's theatrical and verbal endgames. The pastiche is in each case recognizable and brilliantly sustained. The funniest and most political is that of O'Casey with McFadden and Gorman, two doubles of Captain Boyle and Joxer from *The Plough and the Stars* (1926), arriving from Dublin to swear McCracken into membership of the Defenders. When their political ardour is roused, they both inveigh against Orangemen: 'By God I can feel the blood of past ages straining at me weskit buttons, till I could step out now this very minute and tear the throats out of any sixteen Orange craw-thumpers with me bare hands, and be back in a hour for further orders!' (65). When McCracken insists it must be understood 'that there is no vendetta against the Orange Society' (65), the two Dublin men execute the kind of verbal volte-face that is one of the hall-marks of an O'Casey play: 'I'm not afraid to tell whoever's asking, that your Orangeman is as stout a patriot as the next wan, and a sight more honest than plenty of pious Papists I could name' (66). What makes these passages more than an exercise in style and gives them edge is the way they etch the subsequent fate of republican politics in Northern Ireland. Discernible through the various pastiches is the historical process by which the brief utopian moment of 1798 is extinguished by increasing sectarianism: Orangeism moves to the fore with the Protestants and a republican Ireland becomes unequivocally identified with Catholicism. Beckett has almost the last word: 'Finish soon now, it must be nearly now, never soon enough, for me to finish, to be finished' (78). But the final lines go to Henry Joy McCracken in the play of *Northern Star*, which for all of its pastiche remains Parker's most original and distinctive play to date: 'Why would one place break your heart more than another? [. . .] And yet what would this poor fool not give to be able to walk freely again from Stranmillis down to Ann Street?' (81). In 1998, on the second centenary of the 1798 Rebellion, Stephen Rea directed a joint Field Day–Tinderbox production of *Northern Star* in which Henry Joy McCracken and Stewart Parker once more spoke to the citizens of Belfast, now both from beyond the grave.

One of Parker's theatrical progenitors from *Northern Star*, the nineteenth-century Dublin-born writer of melodrama Dion Boucicault, takes centre stage in *Heavenly Bodies* (1986). The play was staged only once, at the Birmingham Repertory Theatre, on 21 April 1986, and after the production Parker wrote a revised version which had to wait until 2004 for its premiere. It was staged at the Peacock in the summer of the Abbey Theatre's centenary year, in a production by Lynne Parker which helped her win as best director in the *Irish Times*/ESB (Electricity Supply Board) Theatre Awards. In her acceptance speech she spoke of how much it meant to her that she was being given the award for directing her uncle Stewart's work. *Heavenly Bodies* provides the bravura opportunity for a company of actors to engage in witty multiple casting and to play in a variety of theatrical styles, from nineteenth-century melodrama, with its declamatory style and strong exit lines, through to a contemporary farce like Michael

Frayn's *Noises Off* (1982). Parker's drama resembles the latter with its framing of an old-style play within a frenetic contemporary style in which chaos keeps threatening to erupt. In one rapidly accelerating and triply repeated scene, Boucicault arrives at a London theatre as a brash 20-year-old with a first script in his hand, each time getting his foot further in the door while the doorman/porter resists his best efforts: 'Soliciting is prohibited, whether from hawkers, beggars, pedlars, ponces, would-be players or self-styled playwrights, thank you and good morning' (Parker 2000b: 105). The production provided the opportunity for Lynne Parker and her talented Rough Magic theatre troupe, with their strong contemporary focus on physical mime and *commedia dell'arte* traditions, to get their foot in the door of Ireland's National Theatre and bring to its stage a range of skills honed on contemporary English playwrights like Frayn, Howard Brenton and Caryl Churchill.

Heavenly Bodies is a play about the theatre, about a life spent in the service of the theatre, and about the issues such a pursuit poses to a writer. In an Irish context, and that of a national theatre in particular, there is the question of whether a dramatist expresses or exploits the people he represents. This debate is fully engaged in by the dramatist Boucicault and his alter ego, Johnny Patterson the Stage Clown. When first travelling to London, Boucicault seeks to follow in the tradition of such Anglo-Irish predecessors as Goldsmith and Sheridan, writing comedies of manners with 'wit, elegance, refinement of feeling' (108), but increasingly finds himself reduced to hack work, seizing on and reworking pre-existent scripts rather than writing anything fresh, distinctive or Irish. Patterson, on the other hand, claims that he has kept faith with his people by staying close to the working-class roots of music-hall and singing such stage Irish ballads as 'The Garden Where the Praties Grow'. The two men share more common ground in the later stages of Boucicault's career, where his spell in America results in the adoption of a self-consciously Irish subject matter and the stage roles of Myles na Gopaleen and Conn the Shaughraun. In the face of Patterson's criticism that 'you conjured up a never-never Emerald Island' (155), Boucicault retorts that Patterson offered them the same thing. With this admission, Boucicault's high-minded claims are levelled, as Patterson concludes: 'There you are, now. You and me both. Paddy the Clown. Will we call it a day?' (155). In this comic version of Faust, where Patterson plays Mephistopheles, the dying Boucicault seems destined for hell; but the wake scene in *The Shaughraun* (1874), with which Parker's play concludes, earns him admission to heaven. In the closing *coup de théâtre*, his deathbed begins to ascend to the starry sky until, true to his and the play's comic origins, the heavens open and he is drenched in water. The staging of *Heavenly Bodies* at the Peacock provided a subtle and sustained contribution to the vexed question of art versus commerce during the Irish National Theatre's centenary year.

During the 1980s, the key theatrical movement in Ireland was the Field Day Theatre Company, co-founded by playwright Brian Friel and Stephen Rea. In 1987, Field Day made its strongest rebuttal of the charge that it favoured Irish Catholic nationalism when it staged Stewart Parker's last play, *Pentecost*. The play was about the Belfast of the recent past; in it, Parker eschewed the theatrical pastiche of his previous two plays for what he termed 'a form of heightened realism' (Parker 2000b: xiv). It was his most Protestant play, showing a concern with the life of the spirit which is signalled in its title. The play from the Irish theatrical canon with which *Pentecost* has the greatest affinity is his own *Spokesong*. Fittingly, Parker's last play revisits his first, to pay testimony to his abiding themes, loves and obsessions (Belfast, music, mismatched couples, comedy), but also to show the distance he had travelled in both personal and theatrical terms. *Pentecost*, written in 1987, is no less a history play than its two predecessors and is given the precisely historicized time-frame of the Ulster Workers' Strike of 1974, when a general strike was called by a body of Protestants to bring down the recently established power-sharing executive. The play is set during this historic week, though, as Lenny remarks, 'Every bloody day in the week's historic, in this place' (Parker 2000b: 200).

Marian and Lenny are the most complex and dramatically balanced of Parker's mismatched romantic couples. Here, they are not about to marry but to separate. The woman is now at the centre of the play, and her amiable trombone-playing husband Lenny has to play dramatic second fiddle (Eileen Pollock and Stephen Rea were equally strong and complementary in their playing of the roles). Lenny lets slip to another character that he and Marian had a baby, something he and she never mention to each other when discussing their marriage. The irony is that they only married because Marian was pregnant and then, in having the baby, discovered that they loved each other: 'For five months. That was how long it lasted... [...] At that point he checked out, he'd seen enough' (205). The image of the dead child, which runs throughout Parker's work as a metaphor for the failure of hope and possibility in Northern Ireland, here receives its most complex and moving articulation, as Marian and Lenny work to revive the love relationship which lasted a mere five months. At first appearance, he is the perennial dreamer, the musician still playing his saxophone on an amateur basis in low dives and dreaming of the big break; she is the practical one, the moneyed professional who wants the terms of their final separation agreed upon. But the main action of the play sees Marian engage on an enterprise closer to that of the dreamer Frank from *Spokesong*. As settlement she asks for a house Lenny has inherited which, far from selling as a valuable piece of Belfast real estate, Marian wishes to hold on to and restore as an example of a working-class Protestant community from the early years of the century. Instead, the house comes to function as a place of refuge, both for its estranged couple and for two other characters: Ruth, a friend of Marian's from ten years earlier, is on the run from her psychotic policeman husband; and Peter is an old friend of Lenny's, just returned from a long spell in England. All four characters are equally in need of what the play terms 'a refuge' (225) in which their psychological and spiritual wounds can be healed.

The cast of four is complicated by the presence of a fifth, the ghost of the house's previous occupant, Lily Mathews, who died at 74 from natural causes. Parker's previous ghosts have been theatrical or historical figures; Lily is a real person, an anonymous figure in historic terms but one whose life is representative of many aspects of Northern Ireland across the century. Parker can and does bring Lily directly on-stage through the magic art of theatre, to protest at the presence of these profane (that is, Catholic) characters in her respectable Protestant house. But Marian counters this opposition by drawing Lily into a dialogue about her suppressed past, encouraging her to speak for the first time about the lover she has taken and the child she has given away for adoption. This sets the scene for the arrival of Pentecost Sunday, in which the ghost of Lily does not appear. Marian as actress/playwright now takes on her role and speaks of the child Lily has never been able to acknowledge. Through this surrogacy Marian is released to speak of her own dead child, Christopher: 'I denied [. . .] the ghost of him that I still do carry, as I carried his little body' (224). As she finishes speaking, Lenny picks up his trombone and plays *a very slow and soulful version of "Just a Closer Walk with Thee"* ' (245).

This last scene received some criticism, in the context of the overall praise *Pentecost* attracted, and Parker was accused of imposing an overly didactic and religious conclusion. But the ending is absolutely in line with the play's overall dramaturgy, with the way its apparent realism soon yields to other dramatic possibilities. There is the extraordinary presence of the ghost of Lily Mathews, bringing to bear an earlier generation's experience on the present. Lenny fuses the secular and the sacred in the music he plays. Marian discovers her buried self through the ghost of her dead child. In turn that dead child evokes all those who have died in the recent history of Northern Ireland, 'our innocent dead' (Parker 2000b: 2, 245), who call on the living to redeem them. *Pentecost* is Stewart Parker's most eloquently humane play, a passionate call for personal and cultural renewal. Along with his entire dramatic output, which deserves to be better known, it makes for a powerful legacy.

PRIMARY READING

Parker, Stewart (1986). *Dramatis Personae*. Belfast: John Malone Memorial Committee.

Parker, Stewart (2000a). *Plays: 1*. London: Methuen.

Parker, Stewart (2000b). *Plays: 2*. London: Methuen.

FURTHER READING

Harris, Claudia W. (1997). 'Stewart Parker (1941–1988)' in Bernice Schrank and William M. Demastes (eds.). *Irish Playwrights 1880–1995: A Research and Production Notebook*. Westport, CT, and London: Greenwood Press, 279–99.

Richtarik, Marilynn (2000). ' "Ireland, the Continuous Past": Stewart Parker's Belfast History Plays' in Stephen Watt, Eileen Morgan and Shakir Mustafa (eds.). *A Century of Irish Drama: Widening the Stage*. Bloomington and Indianapolis: Indiana University Press, 256–74.

PART V
War and Terror

25

A Wounded Stage: Drama and World War I

Mary Luckhurst

The Great War . . . reversed the Idea of Progress.

Fussell (1975: 8)

One's revulsion to the ghastly horrors of war was submerged in the belief that this was the war to end all wars and Utopia would arise.

Corporal J. H. Tansley, quoted in Fussell (1975: 32)

World War I, the 'Great War' of 1914–18, cost a staggering ten million lives, overwhelmingly men aged between 16 and 30, brought emotional and social torment to millions bereaved and injured, and left political and social scars that have not healed. Historian John Keegan has no doubt that it 'inaugurated the manufacture of mass death', and with many European historians also knows it to have 'damaged the rational and liberal civilization of the European enlightenment, permanently for the worse and, through the damage done, world civilization also' (Keegan 1999: 4, 8). Despite the rhetoric of the time it proved not only not 'the war to end all wars' but rather a forceps for the bloodiest century in human history: World War II, from 1939 to 1945, 'five times more destructive of human life and incalculably more costly in material terms', was also 'the direct outcome of World War I, and in large measure its continuation' (Keegan 1999: 3, 9). Armistice Day 1918, marked by ceremonies throughout Britain (and continental Europe) on 11 November, remains the primary commemoration of all war- and service-dead, and published or broadcast military and social histories remain genuinely popular, partly on account of the many recent ancestors among the dead and partly because the gruesome conditions of 'trench warfare' on the Western Front have become emblematic, of military fatuity and as the original locus of neurasthenia or shell-shock, now better known as 'post-traumatic stress disorder'.

In this context the critical neglect of plays about the Great War is perplexing. War poetry and novels, from the war years to the present day, abound and are part of the

national literary consciousness. Poets Siegfried Sassoon and Wilfred Owen are standard fare for British schoolchildren, and novels or memoirs of the war, from Ford's *The
Good Soldier* (1915), Barbusse's *Under Fire* (1916), Graves's *Goodbye to All That* (1929),
Remarque's *All Quiet on the Western Front* (1929) and Brittain's *Testament of Youth*
(1933) to Barker's *Regeneration* trilogy (1991–5), are accepted modern classics.[1]
Furthermore, World War I fiction, poetry and life-writing are usually considered
intrinsic to modernism, and a critical catalyst of its aesthetic revolutions – yet theatre
is generally left out of the equation. Most critics who confidently describe a crisis of
representation brought about by World War I, reflecting on the relations of trauma to
artistic creation or the politics of witnessing, memorializing and realizing wartime
experiences, simply ignore drama; at best, R. C. Sherriff's *Journey's End*, premiered in
1928, and Joan Littlewood's *Oh What a Lovely War* (1963) serve as token offerings. But
the record is considerably more complex, often marked by paradox, and deserves much
more specifically dramatic attention.

The Theatres of War, 1914–18

For W. A. Darlington, who became a theatre reviewer for the *Daily Telegraph* in 1919
after serving in the war, it was 'obvious' that 'the art of the theatre dropped dead when
war was declared'. 'Serious theatre' he argued 'found itself with nothing to say and
[. . .] nobody was in the mood to listen to it':

> Although the nation had been warned often enough that Germany would not hesitate to
> start a war, nobody had really believed it, and soon after the incredible truth had been
> assimilated there came another equally unlooked for, that this was not a professional soldiers'
> war of the old romantic pattern, but a citizens' war of a new kind never even visualized
> before, and a grim utilitarian kind at that. This was something for which the new breed
> of realist dramatists had been no more prepared than their audiences – except for Bernard
> Shaw, and he was now talking a brand of detached commonsense which sounded danger-
> ously like treason to an over-excited and wholly bewildered public. (Darlington 1960: 70–1)

By comparison with pre-war repertoires, productions of realist plays and experimental
dramas were drastically reduced, especially in London's West End. This was partly
economics: London theatres had become sources of income for a new breed of business
magnate, who replaced the old actor-managers and were more interested in revenue than
repertoire (Marshall 1947: 14–16; Shaw 1931: 32–4). It was also to do with a new
composition of audiences and their tastes: revues, music-hall, farce[2] and musicals –
openly escapist 'good nights out' – dominated and were hugely popular with audiences
of soldiers and women of all classes.[3] Plays that did attempt relevance were constrained
in their approach: Lechmere Worrall's and J. E. Harold Terry's *The Man who Stayed at
Home* (Royalty Theatre, 1914; filmed 1915) was a spy-thriller celebrating the self-
sacrifice and bravery of ordinary civilians; and *General Post* (Duke of York's Theatre,

1917) emphasized that combatants from the lower classes were capable of both great
gallantry and leadership. Both plays were patriotic propaganda, transferring to Broadway in 1917–18, and played perfectly into what Darlington called the 'war-time
neurosis' of theatre audiences – a resistance to realistic representation of the fear and
suffering the population was enduring (Darlington 1960: 73).[4] *The Man Who Stayed at
Home* enjoyed a run of 584 performances, but the smash-hit of the period was Oscar
Asche's *Chu Chin Chow* (His Majesty's Theatre, 1916), which ran for 2,235 performances before closing in 1921. A version of *Ali Baba and the Forty Thieves*, it offered
spectacular sets and sumptuous costumes, unprecedented levels of nudity, show-stopping songs (to music by Fred Norton), and wit (though its imperial messages, like
Gilbert and Sullivan's operettas, sent out conflicting signals). It was not so much
Darlington's prejudices about 'serious' theatre that stopped him from going, 'but that
my battalion band played its music in the anteroom of the mess every Friday, by general
request, and I was sick of it' (75). Asche's show profited from the scandalous reputation
it acquired for nudity and innuendo, but the draw of sex was hardly unusual in this era;
as Clive Barker has pointed out, bare flesh was 'the common denominator for drama in a
time when previous modes of behaviour and conformity were thrown overboard in the
social chaos provoked by war' (Barker and Gale 2000: 13).

Whilst the West End shows increasingly became escapist, revue material and
music-hall comedy were in great demand in smaller venues and in reserve areas
behind the front, and could be decidedly confrontational. A satirical newspaper, the
Wipers Times, was produced in extraordinarily grim conditions by British soldiers at
the front in France: it borrowed directly from music-hall turns and publicity styles,
demonstrated a gung-ho gallows humour, and was highly subversive.[5] Concerts
behind the lines incorporated music-hall acts and sketches. Theatre was a major
preoccupation with British soldiers in particular, many looking to the intensity of
performance as a way of making sense of their own political identities as combatants
in the theatre of war. Paul Fussell has explained the obsession with theatre as follows:
'There are two main reasons for the British tendency to fuse memories of the war with
the imagery of theatre. One is the vividness of the sense of the role enjoined by the
British class system. The other is the British awareness of possessing Shakespeare as a
major national asset' (Fussell 1975: 197). Fussell invokes Shakespeare not as a distant
icon of national literature but as the creator of a powerfully populist theatre tradition,
and it was to popular forms of theatre that the vast majority turned during the Great
War. Critics were hostile – as G. E. Morrison wrote: 'To millions who had rarely or
never visited the theatre before, the war made it a solace almost as familiar as their
newspaper or their pipe. [...] Our managers have not risen to the occasion, rather
may some of them be said to have stooped to the opportunity' (Barker and Gale 2000:
13). Only recently have such biases been challenged and the labels 'high' and 'low' art
judged suspect. A great many revue scripts and music-hall sketches have been lost
either because they could not easily be transcribed or because they were not valued as
'literature'. It is important to remember, therefore, that comedy, and music-hall in
particular, could evade or defeat censorship mechanisms by inserting physical and

verbal gags that had not been submitted to the lord chamberlain for vetting, and it should not be assumed, despite the well-recorded look of the West End, that audiences for popular shows were uninformed or politically blunted.

Conventional dramas expressing opposition to the war, however, generally did *not* get past the censor or the theatre producers. In the provinces plays also overwhelmingly supported military action and denounced the enemy (Gardner in Kershaw 2004: 75–8). Rather remarkably John Drinkwater's $X = 0$ played at the Birmingham Rep in 1917; its strongly pacifist message stressed the futility of war but was apparently veiled behind its classical setting of the Trojan War. Furthermore, Drinkwater's status as a Georgian poet and pioneer in the revival of English verse drama seemed to put him beyond the suspicion of the lord chamberlain's office. Shaw, on the other hand, lost repeated battles against the censor but regarded the skirmish itself as performance. Written in 1915, his play *O'Flaherty V.C.*, subtitled 'A Recruiting Pamphlet', was a brilliant, devastating attack on both the war and British consideration of conscription in Ireland that stood no chance whatever of performance in Britain. He wrote later in the preface to *Heartbreak House*:

> When men are heroically dying for their country, it is not the time to shew their lovers and wives and fathers and mothers how they are being sacrificed to the blunders of boobies, the cupidity of capitalists, the ambition of conquerors, the electioneering of demagogues, the Pharisaism of patriots, the lusts and lies and rancors and bloodthirsts that love war because it opens their prison doors, and sets them in the thrones of power and popularity. (Shaw 1931: 39)

That he thought the war neither heroic nor noble is clear, and he compensated for the ban on his play by denouncing the British at war at every available opportunity. *O'Flaherty V.C.* is a trenchant send-up of British attempts to recruit Irishmen of the south, who broadly saw the war as a British not an Irish affair, and commonly viewed it in the context of the nationalist cause.[6] British plans to introduce conscription in Ireland were opposed, the campaign not helped by the refusal to give commissions to Catholic officers or to allow distinct Irish units. In his preface to the play Shaw revels in the absurdity of the British army signing up Irishmen loyal to Ireland and 'for the most part Roman Catholics', whom as colonizers they simultaneously regarded as 'heretics and rebels' (1931: 193).

The play evolves as a dialectical debate between O'Flaherty and the British general, Sir Pearce, and parodies both the imperialist's self-regard and racist stereotypes of the Irish warrior. Sir Pearce's pomposity and dullness of mind are relentlessly exposed by O'Flaherty's pragmatic responses:

SIR PEARCE: [. . .]   Does patriotism mean nothing to you?
O'FLAHERTY: It means different to me than what it would to you, sir. It means England and England's king to you. To me and the like of me, it means talking about the English just the way the English papers talk about the Boshes. [. . .] What better is anybody?

SIR PEARCE: I am sorry the terrible experience of this war – the greatest war ever
   fought – has taught you no better, O'Flaherty.
O'FLAHERTY: (*preserving his dignity*) I don't know about it's being a great war, sir. It's a
   big war; but that's not the same thing.

(Shaw 1931: 202)

O'Flaherty's rejection of the term 'great' underlines the ideological divide between the
two: Britain's defeat would hardly be a matter of mourning to him. He may have been
accorded a military honour, the Victoria Cross, for his 'heroism' (his mother is disgusted
by this alliance with the enemy), but to the Irishman it is meaningless as a national
symbol, and he is, at any rate, contemptuous of propagandistic discourses of comrade-
ship, bravery and sacrifice: 'all the lying, and pretending, and humbugging [. . .] your
comrade is killed in the trench beside you, and you don't as much look round at him
until you trip over his poor body' (203). He also destroys the myth of volunteering for an
exalted, spiritual cause, revealing that his mother bullied him into it for fear he would
dishonour the line of fighting O'Flaherties: 'I'd have fought the divil himself sooner
than face her after funking a fight. That was how I got to know that fighting was easier
than it looked' (200). O'Flaherty's bellicosity parodies the racial constructions of the
Irish as essentially bloodthirsty, an equation which is but a short step from constructs of
innate barbarism, as Joanna Bourke has discussed (Bourke 2000: 118–21). The bullish
ruthlessness of his mother and lover disturb O'Flaherty a good deal more than the
killing fields, and he is soon longing for the peace of the front line: 'I'd give five
shillings to be back in the trenches for the sake of a little rest and quiet' (198). Indeed, at
the end of the play the only shared ground between the two men is a tacit acknowledgement that the motives of many soldiers lie more in the desire to escape their
domestic life than in their devotion to defending their country – a secret which Shaw
wickedly offers up in aid of the recruitment campaign.

A deliciously scurrilous piece, *O'Flaherty V.C.* seemed little short of treasonable
to those in power in Britain, and just as unpalatable to managers of the Abbey Theatre
in Dublin – not least because of its subtitle (Morash 2002: 158). Shaw was far
from deterred but subsequently made his anti-war message more general in *The
Inca of Perusalem* (1917), *Annajanska, The Bolshevik Empress* (1918), and *Augustus
Does his Bit*, a merciless satire of a buffoonish '*member of the {English} governing
class*' on military duty in Little Pifflington (Shaw 1931: 253) – which omitted
reference to Ireland and was performed by the Court Theatre in 1917. Augustus in
some ways anticipates Colonel Blimp, David Low's famous cartoon-soldier of the
1920s–30s, yet Shaw's 'unperformable' wartime work is even now silently omitted
from standard biographical sketches that jump from *Androcles and the Lion* and
Pygmalion (both 1913) to *Heartbreak House* (1920), and the continuing *de facto*
suppression of a body of contemporary dramatic work on the war, though by a
major playwright, seems troublingly indicative of a pervasive sanitization of national
history.

The Once and Future War: Combatants' and Non-Combatants' Plays, 1919–39

Plays representing the varied experiences of the war began to appear only slowly and, unlike the most famous war poetry, were not graphic. The liveness of theatre and the deprivation and trauma suffered by so much of the populace made managements very cautious, and the censorship imposed on mainstream theatres also prevented play-wrights from conjuring representations and dialogue that might be regarded as too subversive. Shaw's *Heartbreak House* reached the London stage in 1921, having been performed in New York the year before. It is a Chekhovian study of the decadent English upper classes on the eve of the war. Paralysed by their own self-obsession, indolence and futility, the inhabitants of Heartbreak House are doomed, and the play ends with the sounds of bombs exploding, one landing perilously close to the house itself. The last line is pointedly given to Ellie, a young impoverished visitor, who responds with rhapsodic delight to her hostess's joke that the bombs might strike them directly the following night: 'Ellie: (*radiant at the prospect*) Oh, I do hope so.' Those bombs signal both destruction and revolution, and for Shaw the socialist end of Edwardian England is only to be welcomed; but the bombs are heard, not seen, and Shaw never did represent World War I soldiers in actual combat. Social and political dissection interested him more, and representing events (increasingly widely under-stood – if rarely discussed – as profoundly traumatic) of which he had no first-hand experience was perhaps a challenge too far.

But the crisis of how to represent the real was a larger issue – it was already a major question for modernists, and it only intensified during and after the war. How could such trauma be described? How could the horrors of Passchendaele or the Somme be captured? There was a further problem in a pre-televisual age: most had not seen acts of war but relied on personal testimony, newspaper reports and photographs. But even soldiers in trenches at the front and pilots flying over war zones could not actually see what was happening. Fernand Léger, a French painter who fought at Verdun, found the experience visually bamboozling, describing it as 'a life of the blind, where everything the eye could perceive and gather hid itself and disappeared. Nobody had seen the War – we lived hidden, concealed, stooped and the useless eye saw nothing' (Kosinski 1994: 58). What is seen and what concealed is particularly telling in J. R. Ackerley's *Prisoners of War* (1925), in part based on his own experiences. Set in 1918 in the Swiss Alps, it presents a group of POWs, mostly RAF men, awaiting their turn before the Repatriation Board: though their stultifying boredom and claustrophobia, anxiety about the future, and experiences of internment are alluded to superficially, a fretful intensity in their friendships signals inner tumult. Captain Conrad's agonizingly slow spiral into inarticulacy and breakdown is set against the perversely piercing beauty of the mountain scenery, where the sun has a '*burning, eye-wearying brilliance*' and '*the snow seems more white, the rocks more black, and the glaciers more green than is natural*' (Ackerley 1925: 2, 99). Ackerley's non-naturalistic stage directions describe a grotesquely and invasively vivid landscape that is lethal in its lure – Conrad's breakdown comes at the moment he realizes Adelby has deliberately walked to his death (97). In the last moments of the play Conrad retreats to the veranda and symbolically sits watching the pink flames of the sunset creep up the summits and turn to shadows, his face *'expressionless'*, now *'a creature obscure, apart'* (99, 109). If Conrad has been internally devastated by the war and suffers post-traumatic stress disorder (the reading of 'neurosis' was prevalent at the time), he can also be understood as a repressed homosexual, an orientation both criminalized and pathologized from 1885 to 1967, but which often found heightened expression in the altered and extreme conditions of war (de Jongh 2000: 95–8). His final renunciation of all company at the end comes after Grayle, with whom he has been obsessed, once again repulses him. Behind the surface banter and camaraderie Ackerley exposes harrowing pain, demonstrating that it is not simply combat that can kill, maim and destroy, that trauma also has many ways of creating scars.

The claustrophobia and terror of an enemy invisible yet horrifyingly close are also poignantly depicted by R. C. Sherriff in *Journey's End*. Rejected by a succession of theatre managers, Sherriff's play was finally given a single Sunday performance at the Apollo Theatre in 1928, with Laurence Olivier playing the lead role, Captain Stanhope. Two actors who had fought in the war and were cast in it implored Darlington to attend on the grounds that 'here, for the first time in the theatre, the spirit in which our men had fought in the First World War had been truly caught and honestly rendered. For anybody who, like themselves had fought in the war, the play, would, they were sure, be an unforgettable experience.' The actors were also convinced that because it was 'unheroic' and 'uncompromisingly grim' it would not be given a run. Darlington found it 'one of the most completely absorbing plays ever written', understood that it had a 'huge, ready-made audience', but discovered that theatre managers thought its stress on the anti-heroic would not appeal to women and would thereby affect its box office draw (Darlington 1960: 153–4). In the event theatre impresarios proved a great deal more conservative than theatre-goers: Shaw helped in the negotiations for a mainstream production at the Savoy Theatre in 1929, and the play's success in London, on the continent and then in the US amassed its author more than enough money to become a full-time writer.[7]

The image of trench warfare has come to symbolize the horror of World War I more than conditions on any other front (Fussell 1975: 36–74), and *Journey's End* is set in a dugout in the last two days before a group of officers lead their men to almost certain death. The protagonist is Captain Stanhope, fêted as a 'hero' in patriotic rhetoric (he has received the Military Cross) and particularly by Raleigh, new to the trenches, a former school-mate of Stanhope's and the brother of his girlfriend. Stanhope, we learn, came to the front 'straight from school' and has served three years, the last one 'without a rest', and has survived longer than any: 'There's not a man left who was here when I came' (Sherriff 1983: 13, 31). Stanhope's 'heroism', as Raleigh rapidly learns, is entirely fuelled by an alcoholism developed to enable him to endure the terror, death, misery and squalor of the everyday. Such is the gravity of his drink problem that it has become 'a kind of freak show exhibit' which affords amusement to others (12). His nerves 'all to blazes' (13), and essentially unfit for duty, Stanhope's pathological determination to push himself beyond the limits of his mental and physical health is precisely what the military rewards and needs; and his belief that 'breaking the strain' (32) and taking a rest is a sign of moral failure only reflects the success of the British army's inculcatory machinery.[8] Stanhope explains that his choice is madness or alcoholic haze (32), but like his superiors he regards mental strain as weakness, not illness or injury. Confronted by Hibbert's gradual collapse into neurosis, Stanhope ruthlessly refuses to accept it is authentic, threatening him at gunpoint and insisting that the shame of pulling out is worse than death: that 'sticking it [. . .] is the only thing a decent man can do'(58). Piqued by Raleigh's hero-worship and conscious of his own decline, Stanhope despises his former schoolmate's naïveté and romanticism of combat. But when Raleigh is fatally injured by shelling Stanhope tenderly cares for him in his last minutes of life. Raleigh dies emitting a sound *'something between a sob and a moan'*, and after a few moments of exhausted, silent reflection Stanhope is called away and exits into intense shelling and machine-gun fire, the dugout caving in behind him (94–5). The bleakness of the ending sends an unequivocal message that war wastes lives, especially young lives, and our compassion for the situation of Stanhope – whose misfortune has been to live for too long – is overwhelming. That anti-war message has lost none of its resonance, as the long, extended West End run of *Journey's End* proved in 2005 (Iraq no doubt in many people's minds).

Even the bleakness of *Journey's End*, however, pales beside Sean O'Casey's extraordinarily nightmarish *The Silver Tassie*, which represents its protagonist Harry Heegan at the peak of his athleticism as a footballer before enrolment, as a soldier on the battlefield, and in the aftermath of war as a survivor – disabled, wheelchair-bound, his life destroyed. To some extent the play was born of O'Casey's determination to outdo Sherriff both representationally and politically, of a conviction that the working-class soldier's story needed to be told more than the officer's (he once blusteringly referred to *Journey's End* as that 'backboneless and ribless play').[9] *The Silver Tassie* bamboozled Yeats, who in 1928 infamously rejected it for performance at the Abbey Theatre, finding it 'all anti-war propaganda to the exclusion of plot and character'.[10] For Yeats O'Casey's haunting concoction of song, incantation, everyday speech and poetry, as well as his melding of realism with an expressionist Act II, had nothing about it that was recognizably 'Irish' (that is, in the tradition of Synge) in either form or content, and its politics did not therefore fit what he saw as an Abbey play. There was also the blasphemous critique of Christianity pointedly integrated into the war zone in Act II: a figure of a Virgin, a life-size crucifix, the jagged and lacerated ruin of a monastery punctuate a grotesquely devastated landscape which includes dead hands protruding from heaps of rubbish, shell-holes, barbed wire, and a large howitzer gun (O'Casey 1959: s.d., 35). O'Casey's condemnation of Christianity's militancy is also evident in the organ music, dialogue, liturgical echoes and incantations of Act II: 'Christ, who bore the cross, still weary / Now trails a rope tied to a field gun'(53). These hellish visions and soundscapes constitute one of the most theatrically excessive creations in twentieth-century drama; aesthetically hallucinogenic, unearthly and blood-curdling, it is also a profoundly affecting political and religious counterblast to the war. The central focus in Act II is clearly the soldiers, an eerie chorus of exhausted, blood-spattered and grave-faced figures:

1ST SOLDIER: Cold and wet and tir'd.
2ND SOLDIER: Wet and tir'd and cold.
3RD SOLDIER: Tir'd and cold and wet.
4TH SOLDIER: Twelve blasted hours of ammunition transport fatigue!
1ST SOLDIER: Twelve weary hours.
2ND SOLDIER: And wasting hours.
3RD SOLDIER: And hot and heavy hours.
1ST SOLDIER: Toiling and thinking to build the wall of force that blocks the way from here to home.
2ND SOLDIER: Lifting shells.
3RD SOLDIER: Carrying shells.
4TH SOLDIER: Piling shells.
1ST SOLDIER: In the falling, pissing rine and whistling wind.
2ND SOLDIER: The whistling wind and falling, drenching rain.
3RD SOLDIER: The God-dam rain and blasted whistling wind.
1ST SOLDIER: And the shirkers sife at home coil'd up at ease.

(37–8)

O'Casey's poetic rhymes and repetitions emphasize the crushing physicality of their lives, as the best memorial statuary does: huddled around a brazier as they try to warm themselves, they narrate their own lives; brain-numbed and reaching out for a descriptive vocabulary, they become more than the choric witnesses of Greek drama – they are unwilling perpetrators, victims and witnesses. In 1935 the Abbey finally recognized the singularity of *The Silver Tassie* and staged it. O'Casey, however, could not forget the episode and never offered them a play again.

The caution about staging plays interrogating the war did not dissipate in the 1930s, even as the dread of renewed war grew steadily greater. The 'interwar years' of 1918 to 1939 never escaped the memory and fear of war, yet theatre managements and censors preferred to distil the brutality of it in a steady stream of horror, crime, grand guignol and spy plays rather than confront it directly (Barker and Gale 2000: 229). Noël Coward enjoyed tremendous popularity, but tellingly his play about the Great War, *Post-Mortem*, is still waiting for a professional premiere.[11] Coward wrote it in 1930 shortly after he had played Captain Stanhope in *Journey's End*.[12] *Post-Mortem* contains vitriolic attacks on church and state; on the stupidity of the English, civilian public, who 'must enjoy its war; and [. . .] reconcile it with a strong sense of patriotism and a nice Christian God. It couldn't do that if it had the remotest suspicion of what really happens'; and on the politically slavish and unreflective media machine that ensures 'the newspapers still lie over anything of importance'

(Coward 1999: 285, 329). The blatancy and viciousness in *Post-Mortem* bemused readers, who could not reconcile it with the playwright's previous work. The English, Coward's mouthpiece Perry rages contemptuously, had learned no lessons, and furthermore were on course to repeat the same mistakes:

> They'll never know whichever way it goes, victory or defeat. They'll smarm over it all with memorials and Rolls of Honour and Angel of Mons and it'll look so noble and glorious in retrospect that they'll all start itching for another war, egged on by dear old gentlemen in clubs who wish they were twenty years younger, and newspaper owners and oily financiers, and the splendid women of England happy and proud to give their sons and husband and lovers, and even their photographs. You see, there'll be an outbreak of war literature in so many years, everyone will write war books and war plays and everyone will read them and see them and be vicariously thrilled by them, until one day someone will go too far and say something that's really true and be flung into prison for blasphemy, immorality, lèse majesty, contempt of court, and atheism. (285)

Sheridan Morley is right to point out that *Post-Mortem* has a violence found nowhere else in Coward's work (Coward 1999: xii). Coward later argued that it contained some of his best writing and some of his worst, claimed that it was 'confused and unbalanced', and seemed anxious to bury it. This is perhaps not surprising for a man acutely conscious of his public image and whose celebrity was based on a certain kind of Englishness that depended on just the sort of stereotypes he describes above. None the less, it is fascinating that he did write *Post-Mortem*, and it is significant that he described the process as 'purging' him of 'certain accumulated acids' (xiii).[13] The British soldiers who performed it at their prison camp in Germany in 1944 were perhaps trying to vent similar emotions (xii).

Somerset Maugham fared badly with his treatment of 1920s England. *For Services Rendered* (Globe Theatre, 1932) did get on but was closed after 78 performances and, in Clive Barker's words, 'ended his playwriting career', even though it was a 'masterpiece of textured dramaturgy' (Barker and Gale 2000: 227–8). The Ardsley family is depicted as slowly disintegrating and in a state of denial about themselves, the consequences of the war, and the contemporary political situation. The son, Sydney Ardsley, blinded by his war service, regards his life as over and is appalled that family members, especially his father, still glamorize the past: 'we were the dupes of incompetent fools [...] sacrificed to their vanity, their greed and their stupidity' (Maugham 1952: 164). The ending is a chilling exposé of utterly false promise, as his mentally disturbed sister, Eva, naïvely sings the national anthem *'in a thin cracked voice'*, after her father's deeply unconvincing speech about England's moral and economic health, while everyone stares at her *'petrified, in horror-struck surprise'* (181).

Another victim was Muriel Box's refreshing and original play *Angels of War*, published in 1935, but not performed until 1981 (by a feminist theatre company called Mrs Worthington's Daughters). Box became well known, penned nearly a hundred plays and 15 major film scripts, and won an Oscar with *The Seventh Veil* in

1945.[14] Focusing on a group of largely working-class women ambulance-drivers working at the front, *Angels at War* depicts the gruelling conditions of work and punctures the sanitized myth of 'Britain's brave and beautiful daughters' doing their bit without getting their hands dirty, swearing, or losing their virginity. Life involves 'swilling out your ambulance – blood and filth, till you vomit at the sight of the muck' and being 'terrified at every pot-hole in case you shake up some poor devil inside with his legs half off' (Box 1999: 121). If there is a positive side to their war experience it is the freedom that such work provides, and the confidence instilled in them that they can have identities which are not defined by men.[15] Informed that war has ended at the close of the play the women are left speculating about what peacetime will bring them. Jo is determined not to be 'fobbed off' with menial work having done a man's job; Vic can see little promise in the conventional solution of marriage:

> It's not a very bright prospect is it? Most of the men of our generation maimed in mind or body – the rest dead. A lot of us won't be able to marry, and if we don't, I can't see us settling down to fancy needlework or knitting after this, can you? (138)

Like Coward and Maugham, Box warns of further bloodshed, ending with Vic's conviction that 'there can never be another war after this' and that they cannot 'have been through it all for nothing' (139); but they had, and soon enough everyone would know it.

In sum, playwrights of the 1920s and 1930s struggled to get their plays about (the) war staged at all, and if they did reception was unpredictable. Britain's (and particularly England's) dramatic history once again seems bizarrely disjunct from its poetic and prosaic histories, for the war poems and warnings of Auden, Isherwood, Spender and their various allies and opponents, over Abyssinia and Spain and Manchuria, fill and richly texture the 1930s, and have become a very active academic field. Whatever the factors, theatre-practice always reflects particular decisions by particular individuals, and it is hard with hindsight to avoid a potent sense of their collective disinclination to promote a theatre with moral historical purpose, even when offered great plays and surprised by the success of the few they did let on.

The *First* War: Plays since 1945

More human beings have died in combat since 1945 than the estimated sixty million who died between 1939 and 1945, and a long list of other wars have vied for representation on the stage: World War II itself, the Korean War, Vietnam, the Falklands,[16] the Gulf War and Iraq represent significant new subjects, as do some re-envisioned historical conflicts, while at the 2005 Edinburgh Festival Fringe the ongoing 'War on Terror' predictably occupied the vast majority of theatre companies. Theatre's attention to combat is of course dwarfed by that of film, and there are substantial bodies of World War I drama on both celluloid and video, but the war also continues to receive live theatrical attention, sometimes in notable plays. Most obviously, Littlewood's *Oh What a Lovely War* (1963) brought a politicized and popular theatre into the mainstream when it transferred from the Theatre Royal, Stratford East, London, to the Wyndham's Theatre on the West End. Derek Paget has argued that although the interpretation of World War I in the play 'as a catastrophic blunder by the "old" ruling classes' has become an orthodoxy, 'it was new in the 1960s' (Kershaw 2004: 398). Perhaps it was, to especially conservative audiences, but socialist ideas were far from new; the army (and all associated with it) had long learned from the murderous blunders of 1914–18, and had shown in 1939–45 that it would not repeat them (Dunkirk was especially critical); and it was Littlewood's upbeat mixture of documentary footage, song, music-hall and other comic genres which really caught imaginations. That it was upbeat, if at the same time savage in its denunciation of heroizing and patriotic rhetoric, is perhaps why it tends to be given a privileged place in the modern canon – as the great comic British novels of World War II, Evelyn Waugh's *Sword of Honour* trilogy (1952–61), are privileged above their great tragic counterparts, Paul Scott's *Raj Quartet* (1966–75). Comedy is still for the English a more palatable way to digest dramatic representations of both world wars, and *Oh What a Lovely War* turns on a show-stopping musical format that can make it very safe entertainment. John Wilson's *Hamp* (1964), on the other hand, which played at the Theatre Royal, Newcastle, was a relentlessly horrifying journey to the execution of a young, idealistic Lancashire-born private who is court-martialled and shot for desertion. Wilson's play offers no relief of any kind, the firing squad botching the execution.

Three plays in the 1980s brought other narratives to the stage. Peter Whelan's *Accrington Pals* (Royal Shakespeare Company, 1981) focuses on the effects of government propaganda and recruiting strategies on a community, and the heartache caused when they realize only a handful of their soldiers have survived combat. Whelan draws the portraits of the women with particular care, emphasizing the mental and physical hardships they face while their menfolk are at the front. In *Not About Heroes* (Edinburgh Festival, 1982) Stephen MacDonald represents the encounter between soldier-poets Siegfried Sassoon and Wilfred Owen as they recover from shell-shock, Sassoon later learning of Owen's death; the subject was also dramatically redacted in Allan Scott's screenplay for Gillies Mackinnon's 1997 film of Pat Barker's *Regeneration*. The most accomplished play of recent years is Frank McGuinness's *Observe the Sons of Ulster Marching Towards the Somme* (Abbey Theatre, 1985), a visually and lyrically powerful piece exploring the despair, desperation, faith and hope of a group of Ulster men caught up in the Somme, one of the bloodiest battles of the war. More recently Nick Whitby's *To the Green Fields Beyond* (Donmar Warehouse, 2000), directed by Sam Mendes, told the story of recruits in the Tank Corps, and represented a West Indian and an Indian soldier in the cast, thereby reminding us of the (overlooked) contributions and sacrifice of men from the Commonwealth, especially the Indian subcontinent: more than 250,000 served overseas, and of 947,000 imperial war-dead about 49,000 were sepoys of the Indian Army.[17] The contribution of the Australian and New Zealand troops and the appalling scale of their needless losses at Gallipoli, however, always seem to surprise Britons when the annual ANZAC ceremonies at the Gallipoli memorials appear on the news. Perhaps diagnostically, in 2005 Tom Stoppard's translation of Gérald Sibleyras' *Heroes* (starring the formidable assembly of Ken Stott, John Hurt and Richard Griffiths) depicted forgotten veterans of World War I in an old people's home, counting out the days to their death and fantasizing about escape.

Yet the neglect clustering about Britain's continuing political refusal genuinely to confront the worst of its late imperial history must co-exist with an enduring popular memory of a colossal trauma, the brunt of which was borne by ordinary people from every walk of life. The dwindling band of veterans are venerated more than ever, but as living testimonies of a known horror that cannot be imagined yet is almost never slighted, rather than as heroes; the haunting lines 'I missed the 14–18 war / But not the sorrow afterward' are not from mid-century, but from the Clash's 'Something about England' (1980), and a respect for veterans was a notable undercurrent in much late twentieth-century popular culture. In that context an important British dramatic treatment may well be Richard Curtis's and Ben Elton's six 30-minute scripts for *Blackadder Goes Forth* (BBC TV, 1989), the final instalments of a farcical, politically combative sitcom that saw a remarkable Edmund Blackadder (1485–1917) traverse Tudor and Hanoverian history in three series between 1983 and 1987. As those personal dates suggest, *Blackadder Goes Forth* finally brought the doubtable hero and cohorts to the Western Front – in itself an achievement, World War I having until then been notably unused for a sitcom, despite the enduring successes of *Dad's Army*, *It Ain't Half Hot, Mum!* and *'Allo, 'Allo* with World War II situations. And the final *Blackadder* episode, 'Goodbyee', went a good deal further than any other sitcom or comedy, by terminally sending pretty much the entire cast over the top in 1917, into a silence that has (saving a brief Blackadder film at the Millennium Dome in 2000) endured ever since. Many millions of viewers were shocked, and almost all taken aback by the abrupt realization of tragedy amid much-loved national television and after riotous laughter to that sudden and bitter end; as with the death of Dickens's fictional and infinitely more sentimental Little Nell, the public remembers its bereavement, and Blackadder (buoyantly available on DVD) has in death impossibly mutated his short, dark, comedic self, with his notably stupid and disgusting servant Baldrick, into English versions of Brecht's *Good Soldier Schweyk* meeting an implacable history. Read in retrospect the four series effectively assume Keegan's belief that a culture, perhaps even a civilization, died in the trenches, and indict with some savagery and relentless laughter the whole of English (and latterly British) history that came to such a pass – so it may also be that notwithstanding the forces of personal dramatic testimony and preventive moral witness, the real reluctance, or difficulty, of dramatizing 1914–18 lies in the sheer scale of the trauma and outright losses that British theatre, and everything else, suffered in that bloody and seminal chaos.

NOTES

1 Dates for novels are publishing dates, dates cited after plays refer to premieres – except, of course, in the bibliography.
2 The most successful farce during the war period was *A Little Bit of Fluff* by Walter E. Ellis, which ran for 1,241 performances.
3 One manager of a London theatre estimated that 90 per cent of theatre-goers were soldiers and their friends (Barker and Gale 2000: 11). See also Shaw's commentaries in the preface to *Heartbreak House*: 'For four years the London theatres were crowded every night with thousands of soldiers on leave from the front' (Shaw 1931: 36–9). James Ross Moore writes that World War I 'extended the length of show runs to exaggerated proportions' (Barker and Gale 2000: 90).
4 Darlington argues that J. M. Barrie's *Dear Brutus* (1917) was one of the best plays of the era. Symbolically it is about a man who is given a second chance in life.
5 'Wipers' was slang for Ypres, the site of three significant battles, the last also known as Passchendaele. Advertisements included: 'A Stirring Drama entitled / MINED / A most Uplifting Performance' and 'MISS MINNIE WERFER / Always Meets with a Thunderous Reception' (Fussell 1975: 194–5).
6 Yeats, for example, remained detached from the war; see Jacqueline Genet in Devine (1999: 36–55). Many Irishmen from the south did volunteer, though not in the same numbers as unionists from the north.
7 Findlater (1952: 117) claims that Sherriff earned an extraordinary £300,000 from *Journey's End*.

8 See Tate (1998: 10–40); Deborah Parsons (2004). 'Trauma and War Memory' in Laura Marcus and Peter Nicholls (eds.). *The New Cambridge History of Twentieth-Century English Literature*. Cambridge: Cambridge University Press, 175–96.
9 *The Letters of Sean O'Casey 1910–1941*, ed. David Krause. London: Cassell (1975), I, 822.
10 See *The Letters of W. B. Yeats*, ed. Allan Wade. London: Hart-Davis (1954), 743.
11 The BBC filmed a shortened version of it and broadcast it in a series called *The Jazz Age* in 1968.
12 For a touring company, the Quaints, in Singapore.
13 Coward wrote a World War II film, *In Which We Serve*, which was made with official backing in 1942.
14 She often co-authored scripts with her husband Sydney Box.
15 For background see: Janet Watson (2000). 'The Paradox of Working Heroines: Conflict Over the Changing Social Order in Wartime Britain, 1914–1918' in Douglas Machaman and Michael Mays (eds.). *World War I and the Cultures of Modernity*. Jackson, MI: University Press of Mississippi, 68–85; Claire Tylee (1990). *The Great War and Women's Consciousness*. London: Macmillan; Richard Wall and Jay Winter (eds.) (1988). *The Upheaval of War: Family, Work and Welfare in Europe 1914–18*. Cambridge: Cambridge University Press.
16 Britain never officially declared war.
17 See David Omissi (ed.) (1999). *Indian Voices of the Great War: Soldiers' Letters, 1914–18*. London and New York: Macmillan.

PRIMARY READING

Ackerley, J. R. (1925). *The Prisoners of War*. London: Chatto and Windus.
Box, Muriel (1999). *Angels of War* in *War Plays by Women: An International Anthology*, eds. Claire M. Tylee, Elaine Turner and Agnès Cardinal. London: Routledge.
Coward, Noël (1999). *Collected Plays: Two* (including *Post-Mortem*). London: Methuen.
Drinkwater, John (1925). *Collected Plays*. Vol. 1. London: Sidgwick and Jackson.

Littlewood, Joan and Theatre Workshop (1965). *Oh What a Lovely War*. London: Methuen.
Macdonald, Stephen (1983). *Not About Heroes*. London: Faber and Faber.
Maugham, Somerset W. (1952). *The Collected Plays*. Vol. 3 (including *For Services Rendered*). Melbourne, London and Toronto: Heinemann.
McGuinness, Frank (1996). *Plays 1* (including *Observe the Sons of Ulster Marching Towards the Somme*). London: Faber and Faber.

O'Casey, Sean (1959). *Collected Plays*. Vol. 2 (*The Silver Tassie, Within the Gates, The Star Turns Red*). London: Macmillan.

Shaw, George Bernard (1931). *Heartbreak House, Great Catherine, Playlets of the War* (including *O'Flaherty V.C.*). London: Constable.

Sherriff, R. C. (1983). *Journey's End*. London: Penguin.

Sibleyras, Gérald (2005). *Heroes*, trans. Tom Stoppard. London: Faber and Faber.

Whelan, Peter (2003). *Plays 1* (including *The Accrington Pals*). London: Methuen.

Whitby, Nick (2000). *To the Green Fields Beyond*. London: Faber and Faber.

Wilson, John (1966). *Hamp*. London and New York: Evans.

FURTHER READING

Barker, Clive and Gale, Maggie B. (eds.) (2000). *British Theatre Between the Wars, 1918–1939*. Cambridge: Cambridge University Press.

Bourke, Joanna (2000). *An Intimate History of Killing*. London: Granta.

Collins, L. J. (1998). *Theatre at War 1914–18*. London: Macmillan.

Darlington, W. A. (1960). *Six Thousand and One Nights*. London: Harrap.

de Jongh, Nicholas (2000). *Politics, Prudery and Perversions: The Censoring of the English Stage 1901–1968*. London: Methuen.

Devine, Kathleen (ed.) (1999). *Modern Irish Writers and the Wars*. Gerrards Cross: Colin Smythe.

Findlater, Richard (1952). *The Unholy Trade*. London: Gollancz.

Fussell, Paul (1975). *The Great War and Modern Memory*. Oxford: Oxford University Press.

Keegan, John (1999). *The First World War*. London: Pimlico.

Kershaw, Baz (ed.) (2004). *The Cambridge History of the British Theatre*. Vol. 3. Cambridge: Cambridge University Press.

Kosinski, D. (ed.) (1994). *Fernand Léger 1911–1924*. Munich: Prestel.

Marshall, Norman (1947). *The Other Theatre*. London: Lehmann.

Morash, Christopher (2002). *A History of Irish Theatre 1601–2002*. Cambridge: Cambridge University Press.

Tate, Trudi (1998). *Modernism, History and the First World War*. Manchester and New York: Manchester University Press.

26

Staging 'the Holocaust' in England

John Lennard

Nach Auschwitz ein Gedicht zu schreiben, ist barbarisch.
[After Auschwitz to write a poem is barbaric.]

Theodor Adorno

What must it be then to stage a *Sho'ah*? Adorno's fierce declaration denounces an inevitable, intolerable aestheticization in art.[1] If here specifying poetry, Adorno inhibits artists in all media. Many accept the impossibility of adequately representing the 'black sun of Auschwitz',[2] and all Holocaust art begins in aesthetic and moral crisis.

Even terminology is problematic. A holocaust (Gk, 'holo' + 'kaustos') is 'a sacrifice wholly consumed by fire': '*the* Holocaust', eclipsing others, reaches hideously to animal sacrifice – hence I use the word *Sho'ah*, adopted from 1940 in Palestine (Young 1990: 85–9), and internationalized from 1986 by Claude Lanzmann's documentary film. In Hebrew it meant 'destruction' without particular reference; its use expressly rejects religious construction,[3] enabling more careful response, but offers no help in theatre, where (for example) most who have seen 1945 film of survivors will not accept evidently well-fed actors as skeletal victims[4] – even if the wire they stand behind is real. Related moral anxieties attend portrayals of recovered survivors and, inversely, with severe complications, representations of Hitler.

Intrinsic internationalism also means *Sho'ah* reception cannot sensibly be restricted to any simple national focus, and in so far as England *has* confronted the *Sho'ah*, theatrically or otherwise, it has been in evolving international contexts. Until the 1980s the *Sho'ah* was in the West commonly supposed transcendent, uniting all in condemnation. It may be still, but many now struggle with the politics of *Sho'ah* memorialization. Hannah Arendt's *Eichmann in Jerusalem* (1963)[5] seemed clarion; more recent witnesses expose themselves with success to celebrity and hostile deconstruction, as Lanzmann, Art Spiegelman, Daniel Goldhagen, Gitta Sereny and

Daniel Liebeskind variously testify. As history slips from living memory, tainted transparency and vulnerable convictions obtrude.

There is, however, a particular English context of episodic denial: rarely of the *Sho'ah* itself, rather of implication in Nazi war-crimes and of much late-imperial history and its continuing consequences. Considering the attitude of all postwar British governments to apology for past massacres or expedient sacrifices,[6] especially wartime ones, it is no surprise that all efforts to consider British (or English) complicity with Nazi eugenics and racial policy receive a withering reception; nor that for theatres this can cause problems if a play (supposedly) impugns British policy or kindness.

Additionally, *Sho'ah* awareness in England remains thin by comparison with continental Europe. There is no major public memorial to its victims (nor has there been the accompanying debate), and only a nascent practice of specific annual remembrance. The English did not until the 1990s pursue perpetrators at home, nor as often struggle with the *Sho'ah* as others. For artists, moral and aesthetic problems reductively overstated by Adorno are sharpened in theatre by its intrinsic need for sensual representation, and reinforced by the conservatism of much mainstream theatre.[7] English writers or performers of *Sho'ah* material whose documentation I have seen or heard have all found themselves in greater, more distinctive struggles than with other shows – often, despite everything, unexpectedly so.

After the Nuremberg trials in October 1946 little was said about the bitterest events of 1933–45 before the later 1950s, when the term 'Holocaust' came into use. In England many heard Richard Dimbleby's 1945 radio-reports from Belsen, but few could have found it easy to ask questions and none able to answer would have been encouraged to do so. Yet most knew and tens of thousands had witnessed *something*. Old soldiers mention their inability to bear and unwillingness to hear witness – a context relevant to Charles Wood's war-plays *Dingo* (wr. 1961; perf. Bristol/Royal Court Theatre (RCT), 1967) and *Jingo* (Royal Shakespeare Company (RSC), 1975); therapy was neither expected nor available, and traumata suffered by or through eyewitness of the camps almost unimaginable. Austerity remained a byword and privation commonplace well into the 1950s, until they were abruptly succeeded by wilful optimism as economic recovery began to pay war's technological dividend. Even – especially – in Israel, people were for years after its foundation in 1948 unable or unwilling to articulate what they could never forget (Gouri 1994: 153–4).

The first significant Anglo-American stage work is John Van Druten's adaptation of Christopher Isherwood's Berlin tales as *I am a Camera* (US/UK, 1951; filmed 1955) – set in 1929–34 and never reaching past 1938, when Isherwood left Berlin: knowing audiences knew what followed his curtain, Van Druten let them supply the agony. Joe Masteroff's Book for the 1966 Broadway musical by John Kander and Fred Ebb, and Bob Fosse's 1972 film-adaptation of it, both *Cabaret*, equally concentrate on foreboding; as does Frances Goodrich's and Albert Hackett's *The Diary of Anne Frank* (US/UK, 1955–6; filmed 1959), all but finally concerned with life in hiding, not the place or means of death. This strategy of encompassing 'dramatic irony' still worked superbly in 1981 in C. P. Taylor's play *Good* and Hungarian film-maker István Szábo's *Mephisto* (adapting Klaus Mann's 1935 novel), but as history recedes audiences grow less reliably apt to their task.

Despite elaboration of Isherwood's narratives there is in all versions of his work a strategy of (at one level) simplicity, a direct voice of witness as valid on stage as in court. A witness under moral self-compulsion may defy Adorno, as the survivor-poet Paul Celan did, commanding any medium to testify; some continental European witness-drama began among survivors and their kith immediately after 1945. In Anglo-American theatre the seminal work was *Anne Frank*, the published *Diary* (then free from deconstructive scrutiny) acting to guarantee authenticity, whereby necessary fictionalizations of dialogue and action were rendered acceptable because forged 'in good faith' from a totemic mass-distributed record. Goodrich's and Hackett's redemptive hagiography exemplifies 'Americanization of the Holocaust' (Langer 1995) and shares the term's religiosity, but Frank's representative status went largely unquestioned before the 1980s. Plays lacking a documented protagonist of such repute – Millard Lampell's *The Wall* (US, 1960), dramatizing John Hersey's novel about the Warsaw ghetto uprising, or Shimon Wincelberg's *The Windows of Heaven* (wr. US, 1962; pub. UK, 1964; perf. Sweden, 1969),[8] inspired by Łodz survivor Rachmil Bryks's *A Cat in the Ghetto* – had less success.

What changed things from 1960–1 was the kidnapping, trial and execution of Adolf Eichmann by agents of the Israeli state. Public attention was internationally sustained throughout the 1960s by the first wave of *Sho'ah* historiography, German trials, Willy Brandt, and on stage Erwin Piscator's direction of two docudramas, Rolf Hochhuth's *Der Stellvertreter* (*The Representative* or *Deputy*, 1963), on Vatican complicity, and Peter Weiss's *Die Ermittlung* (*The Investigation*, 1965), reporting the 'Auschwitz trial'.[9] The politically active of the 1960s did not open their eyes primarily to look at horror, but they did open them to the *Sho'ah*, and everywhere began promoting the idea (entrenched in Germany by de-Nazification) that public and educational witness to 'the Holocaust' must constantly be borne.

Despite Weiss's insistence that in staging *The Investigation* 'no attempt should be made to reconstruct the courtroom before which the proceedings [. . .] took place' (Weiss 1967: xi), realist court-room sets were common, as fidelity to transcripts was implicit. Stage-evidence could remain in hard copy, carried by dialogue; documentary footage or stills could but need not be projected; and the set was staple for many English-language theatres. Robert Shaw dramatized Eichmann's trial in *The Man in the Glass Booth* (UK/US, 1967): his play, like the trial, explicitly grapples with history and justice; his audiences, like Weiss's, undergo obligation of witness, and usually accept that duty. But his example did not prosper in London, where the next relevant English examples of transcriptive docudrama are *Nuremberg* (Tricycle, 1996), Richard Norton-Taylor's closest approach to the *Sho'ah* in his outstanding practice of contemporary political docudrama,[10] and Anthony Sher's *Primo* (National Theatre (NT), 2004).

Robert Shaw's Broadway production, conversely, was among a spate in/directly confronting the *Sho'ah* and Arendt. A first wave in 1963–4 included Max Frisch's *Andorra*,

Mary Drahos's *Eternal Sabbath*, Bertolt Brecht's *The Resistible Rise of Arturo Ui*, Harold Leivick's *The Sage of Rottenberg*, Arthur Miller's *After the Fall* and *Incident at Vichy*, Ben-Zion Tomer's *Children of the Shadows*, Rolf Hochhuth's *The Deputy* and (in Washington) a revision of Lampell's *The Wall*. A second wave, in 1967–8 following *The Investigation* (and the Arab–Israeli War), included Shaw with Jakov Lind's *Ergo*, George Tabori's *The Cannibals*, Stanley Eveling's *The Strange Case of Martin Richter*, John Allen's *The Other Man*, Kander's, Ebb's and Masteroff's *Cabaret*, and another *Arturo Ui* (Isser 1997: 21–2). Interest abated as Vietnam intensified, and many of these works exhibit problematic 'Americanization', but also represent (whatever their failings) a concerted attack on the theatrical problem for moral as well as political reasons: a call variously heeded.

In England, there was by the late 1960s fertile ground for ideas of a duty to guard against repetition – and for an English stage ever inclined to comedy, genuine possibilities might have been swiftly suggested by the use of a 'counter-genre' (partly theorized in Dürrenmatt 1976), often comedic, to act something as Perseus's shield did in confronting the Medusa. The inset musical *Springtime for Hitler* in Mel Brooks's cult classic *The Producers* (1968), like Fosse's *Cabaret* (1972), pointed the way; Joan Littlewood's *Oh What a Lovely War* (Theatre Royal, Stratford East, 1963; filmed 1969) had tried it with notable success in a related cause. Yet within the 1960s any potent sense of theatre's duty to bear continuing pedagogic witness seems to have passed to a largely undocumented, voluntary school-practice of screening Alain Resnais's *Nacht und Nebel* ('Night and Fog', 1955, with footage from 1945), typically for 16–18-year-olds.

This acceptance that film carries the primary pedagogic duty is telling; cinematic 'authenticity' (however mis/understood or too easily supposed)[11] was preferred to theatrical engagement with problems of representation, and obviated any theatrical duty to moral/ized public pedagogy. For those nevertheless determined on a theatrical attempt it also contributed to a degree of dramaturgical liberation, slowly enabling non-naturalistic strategies and modes of representation in the medium that, lacking cinematic authenticity, needed them – but well into the 1970s, while political theatre ran strong, notably with Edgar's *Destiny* (NT, 1977) about English neo-fascism, the English stage largely kept *Sho'ah* silence. Even Shakespearean *Sho'ah* work by two established playwright-citizens, Tabori's *I Would my Daughter were Dead at my Feet and the Jewels in her Ear* (1975), a *Shylock Variation*, and Arnold Wesker's *The Merchant* (1976), played in Berlin and New York but not London.

The protracted English delay in theatrical confrontation explains the extremity of the Pip Simmons Group's *An die Musik* (1975) – a touchstone of moral unease. What tends to be remembered is the use of nudity (particularly a uniformed guard fondling a stripped prisoner's breast) and the ending, a tableau-blackout with visibly spouting vents, making the stage momentarily a Birkenau gas-chamber. There has been some extreme theatre in Germany and Poland (where site-specificity is demanding), but rarely this; for good reason. No poetry, even Celan's, can so speak for these dead, who cannot be re-embodied, rekilled, or rekindled without offence. English delay explains political frustrations that explain the attempt, but comparison with Tabori's intelligent, cruel *Cannibals* – where only enforced cannibalism permits survival, dragging audience sympathy towards the abyss (Skloot 1987: 346) – suggests incapacitating crudity.[12] The small-scale show was word-of-mouth notorious at the Nancy and Avignon Off festivals; the capacity for blasphemous anger it represented exploded two years later with punk, producing Johnny Rotten's delivery (at the last Sex Pistols gig, in San Francisco's Winterland Ballroom in January 1978) of a song probably by Sid Vicious,[13] 'Belsen was a gas, I heard the other day' – 'a musical version of the punk swastika' (Marcus 1990: 117), and in all its crassness probably the most famous English *Sho'ah* performance on record.

Amid the shake-up provided by punk, counter-generic strategy at last flowered in three major plays: Peter Barnes's *Auschwitz* (part of *Laughter!*, RCT, 1978), Martin Sherman's *Bent* (RCT, 1979) and Taylor's *Good* (RSC, 1981).[14] *Laughter!* paired *Auschwitz* with *Tsar*, about Ivan the Terrible, but historical comparison mattered less than riffs from TV sitcom applied to Eichmann's fellow bureaucrats. Barnes's ending and epilogue echo extremity, but his gassed corpses disentangled by mute 'Sanitation Men' are explicitly *'wet straw dummies* [. . .] *painted light blue* [that] *have no faces'*, and in the epilogue, while *'music has faded out imperceptibly into a hissing sound'*, implicitly gas, stage visuals are a follow-spot turning blue and fading while the 'Boffo Boys of Birkenau, Abe Bimko & Hymie Bieberstein [. . .] *cough and stagger* [. . .] *fall to their knees* [. . .] *collapse* [. . . and] *die in darkness'* (Fuchs 1987: 138, 144–5). Highly theatrical 'revelation' of the reality behind the form-filling (civil-service construction standards for crematoria) is the calculated point of distracting chat and office politics between Cranach and Gottleb, but it is Barnes's didactic need, not Gottleb's established character, that authorizes an outburst packing summary facts into crude variations of register (with the mime of straw dummies, once the filing-cabinet set splits open, as backdrop). The purpose was honourable, the play a long step forward for English theatre, but neither consideration can disguise the weakness in the script.

Sherman's far subtler *Bent* has enjoyed prolonged success. American by birth, he had bad experiences with a staged reading (Eugene O'Neill Theater Center, Waterford, CT, 1978) generating advice to scrap Act II; but the play had been written for Gay Sweatshop in London, who engineered an RCT co-production (with Ian McKellen and Tom Bell) that transferred to the West End while another (with Richard Gere) opened on Broadway. A fusion of gay liberation with *Sho'ah* material was – before AIDS – a high-risk trope, and use of the pink triangle by gay activists may still seem crass,[15] but homophobes echo Nazi characterizations and *Bent* carefully runs both issues in tandem within history. The camp represented in Act II is Dachau, a *Konzentrationlager*, and Horst and Max suffer lone deaths by electrocution, not in crowded chambers as at Birkenau or Treblinka; the play is set in 1934 and the *Todeslager* (whose sole purpose was facilitation of genocide through assembly-line reception, mass murder and cremation) did not then exist. Debts to *Cabaret* (Act I) and Beckett (Act II) are clear ; Act II also recalls Athol Fugard's, John Kani's and Winston Ntshona's *The Island* (Cape Town and RCT, 1973; New York, 1974),[16] devised to represent Robben Island – another *Konzentrationlager* with paired men subject to similarly spirit-breaking (not industrially productive) work routines.

Bent requires a domestic set in Act I, but only a fence, stones, emblematic costume and sound and light in Act II. Beckettian minimalism is apparent, suggesting actors may properly play doomed prisoners or damned guards if suppositious realism and stage flummery are avoided; the impossibility of adequate representation is acknowledged in every bare moment, and imaginative witness borne as needs must. Minimalism stages the script's limitations to Dachau, 1934, and murders falling short of genocide; gathered senses of reticence additionally align with gay self-repression in hostile cultures, allowing Sherman to fuse commemoration with activism. His strategy is tremendous, but hard to develop in representing the *Sho'ah*.

Taylor spent his career writing youth plays in north-east England, finding major success only with *Good*. Halder, a bourgeois Goethe scholar and teacher, becomes actively complicit with euthanasia programmes and eventually Auschwitz: Taylor anticipated Joshua Sobol's famous *Ghetto* (Haifa, 1984; US, 1986; NT, 1989) in making stage apparatus an extension of his protagonist's head, allowing Halder (like Srulik in *Ghetto*) to inhabit multiple times, scripting, casting, enacting and narrating (with commentary) his own protracted damnation. The plays share music, but Sobol's point is always that Lithuania's Vilna ghetto theatre and musicians were real (see Rovit and Goldfarb 1999: 111, 136), while Taylor's on-stage musicians are repeatedly identified visibly and in dialogue as Halder's fantasies: '*A street musician*, HITLER, *dressed in tweed plus-fours takes up his stance* [. . . and] *plays the first few bars of a Yiddish folksong*' (Taylor 1990: 23). Sobol's songs were 'actually composed in the ghettos and camps' (Fuchs 1987: xix), but Halder's head holds classical lieder and popular songs of the 1920s–40s; where the *Ghetto* orchestra performs always in the ghetto, immanent in Srulik's living room, Halder's 'marvellously useful neurosis' (Cushman 1981: 458) allows his musicians to be anywhere his mind goes – until his body, at last in SS uniform, goes in 1942 to Auschwitz:

> The funny thing was . . . I heard this band. Playing a Schubert March. 'Oh,' I registered to myself. 'We're having Schubert, now.'
> . . . Then I became aware that there was in fact a group of prisoners . . . maybe in my honour. I'm not sure . . . The important thing was . . . The significant thing: the band was *real*.
> *Up band* . . . HALDER *watching them* . . .
> . . . The band was *real!*
> *Up music.* (Taylor 1990: 69)

The dramaturgical ethics of this restorative twist to Taylor's use of Scheherazade's 1,001 nights repays thought. *Ghetto* plays Scheherazade straight, music keeping musicians alive day by day; *Good*'s songs serve Halder in maintaining his self-exculpating perpetrator's grasp on unreality. Wide-ranging sound includes fragments of Sobol's reclaimed music of Yiddish affirmation, but summons the deep horror of educated European aesthetics *and* popular culture hand in glove with genocide – an approach to Adorno comprehending the music of Celan's *Todesfuge*, the greatest artistic utterance from within the *Sho'ah* and written, unbearably, amazingly, in metrically jaunty German (Felstiner 1995: 26–41). Compare Szábo's ending in *Mephisto*, also 1981: a whiteout as actor-protagonist Höfgren is thrust onto the new Nuremberg party-stage – Speer's 'Cathedral of Ice', awaiting in 1936 an opening performance Höfgren has 'despite himself' signally assisted.[17]

Taylor found a highly stageable means of embodying the question music asks of the *Sho'ah*, and pitched a perfect play to the RSC, outside his usual circles. Using prescribed music to stunning effect, the extended London (and Broadway) production of 1981–2 (during which Taylor died) saw Alan Howard and Joe Melia memorably explore the roles of Halder and Maurice; the Donmar revival in 1999, with Charles Dance and Ian Gelder, stranded itself by incomprehensibly and mortally cutting musicians and much music.[18] There are amateur revivals and the play has recently been anthologized in Canada (Watts 2004b),[19] but has not in a quarter-century of acute relevance entered its own national repertoire.

Two further plays at the NT in 1982 pointed in opposite but complementary directions. Edward Bond's *Summer*, a holiday meeting between women with a history and a former soldier, considers the age of surviving victims and perpetrators, foreseeing what would happen as (approaching) death/s loosened tongues – the controversy of revealed pasts, renewed judicial process and rising exhaustion. Christopher Hampton's *The Portage to San Cristobal of A. H.*, rapidly dramatizing George Steiner's 1981 novella, was a mouthpiece for Steiner's theory of the *Sho'ah* as punishment for philosophically 'intolerable demands' levied by Judaism, but showed young revengers sitting in expedient judgement on old history, a rising generation trying to know against Bond's passing generation unable to forget. That Steiner's novella (controversially giving Hitler centre-stage) was so promptly mounted at the NT testifies to Hampton's bankability and Steiner's reputation (Hampton 2005: 110); in contrast, another displaced court-room drama, Anthony Shaffer's *This Savage Parade* (King's Head, London, 1987), received only fringe production despite Shaffer's credentials – fairly, maybe, for it is very odd; but so is Steiner's fantasy of a geriatric Hitler, which wasn't even a play.

Differently displaced, Jim Allen's court-room drama *Perdition* (1987), based on a 1955 libel action by Israel Rudolf Kasztner against another survivor, Malkiel Gruenwald, but 'written in direct response to the 1982 Israeli invasion of Lebanon' (Isser 1997: 135), was cancelled in production at the Royal Court after organized Jewish protests. Allen's handling of Zionist organization in pre-war and wartime Hungarian ghettos develops accusations of wilful individual and institutional Zionist collaboration in the *Sho'ah*, and he found insufficient defenders. Given that Kasztner (murdered on his doorstep in 1957 by someone who believed Gruenwald) was posthumously exonerated by the Israeli Supreme Court in 1958, and considering the anti-semitism readily attending any attempt to assert Jewish *responsibility* for the *Sho'ah*, that seems right; for an agonizing moral triage patently liable to explosive mis/interpretation, stringent minimalist docudrama might properly have been defended against moral or political objections – but docudrama has never been the Court's game, and Allen had his own agenda.[20]

(Inter)generational issues limned by Bond and Steiner have since informed most *Sho'ah* plays, notably Peter Flannery's energetic *Singer* and Howard Brenton's extraordinary *H.I.D. (Hess Is Dead)* (both RSC, 1989),[21] Bernard Kops's *Dreams of Anne Frank* (Polka Theatre, London, 1992), Diane Samuels's *Kindertransport* (Cockpit, London, 1993) and Sherman's refreshingly incorrect *Rose* (NT, 1999). In Ronald Harwood's *The Handyman* (Minerva Theatre, Chichester, 1996) the issue is explicitly the War Crimes Act 1991, a desperately belated start to British prosecution of resident perpetrators; Harwood's *Taking Sides* (Minerva, 1995) debates a prosecution of conductor Wilhelm Furtwängler in 1945–6, but neither opposition to the Act in the House of Lords nor half-hearted enforcement (there has been one conviction) has otherwise been much noticed outside crime fiction.[22] Comparably, David Irving's dishonourable libel action against Deborah Lipstadt and Penguin in 1999, the first British case centred on *Sho'ah* denial, remains undramatized despite an excellent prose account (Guttenplan 2001).

Use of counter-genres continues, internationally reinforced in the 1980s by *Ghetto* and Spiegelman's *Maus*, and later by films, notably Roberto Benigni's *Life is Beautiful* (1997), Radu Mihaileanu's *Train of Life* (1998) and Peter Kassovitz's remake of *Jakob the Liar* (1999).[23] *Singer*, however, like Julia Pascal's *Holocaust Trilogy* (1990–2) and David Edgar's monumental *Albert Speer* (2000), shows new strategies, perhaps indebted to Taylor but rooted in Brecht and responding to the fractal passage of generations. The broadest view to date is James E. Young's in *At Memory's Edge: After-Images of the Holocaust in Contemporary Art and Architecture* (2000), investigating formal traces of a witnessing artist's generational displacement from the heat of the black sun; the devolved cornerstone of witness is inclusion within a work of how the *Sho'ah* was learned – in filial exasperation from a parent-survivor, as by Spiegelman, or forcibly, variously the *donnée* of *Kindertransport*, *The Handyman*, *Theresa* (Pascal 2000: 4) and, very differently, *Albert Speer*.

The fullest English response has been Pascal's, exposing overt censorship. *Theresa* (Gulbenkian Studio Theatre, Newcastle, 1990) deploys with great sophistication in 'living newspaper and documentary theatre techniques, musical theatre, cabaret, and dance' (Luckhurst 2001: 257) an unpalatable factual narrative – Jews in the Channel Islands not only not evacuated in 1940, but held as 'enemy aliens' and after occupation handed over to the Gestapo. Pascal's fictions of greater age and professional rank for the historical Theresa Steiner, who had found British sanctuary yet died in Auschwitz, balanced the embodied truth of actor Ruth Posner, creating the role, who escaped the Warsaw ghetto as a child. Yet in a much less notorious case far worse than *Perdition* and supporting Pascal's *J'accuse*, her play was and is banned in Guernsey, ostensibly for 'distasteful language'; despite continental success and a BBC radio production in 1996, it has had only two fringe productions in England, achieved largely through Pascal's personal efforts (a BBC film was aborted). The trilogy – including *A Dead Woman on Holiday* (Holborn Centre for Performing Arts, 1991), about translators at the Nuremberg Trials, and *The Dybbuk* (New End Theatre, London, 1992), using Anski's classic Yiddish play as a totem of cultural continuity in suffering – was staged at the New End in 1995, and belatedly published by Oberon in 2000, but has critically been neglected (Luckhurst 2001: 266). By comparison, Moira Buffini's politically correct *Gabriel* (Soho Theatre, 1997), exploring female relationships in wartime Guernsey, ignores deported Jews (though four of six were women, and two wives of British citizens) and avoids collaboration and the *Sho'ah*. It is hard not to credit active obstruction of Pascal's play, rising in Guernsey to outright suppression, and the case of *Theresa* should highlight the anti-semitism revealed in the Channel Islands, as continuing prosecutions for homosexuality revealed an unacceptable bigotry in the Isle of Man: but on that the government acted.

Related pressures were exerted on Edgar's *Albert Speer* (NT, 2000), adapting Sereny's *Albert Speer: His Battle with Truth* (1995), but the issues were murkier and the show, as a main-stage production directed by Trevor Nunn, less vulnerable. One line of attack found humane portrayal of Hitler (in Speer's memory and imagination) unacceptable; another charged Edgar (and Nunn) with covering up Sereny's duping by Speer in the interviews underpinning her biography.[24] What none seemed to celebrate was the technical ethics of script and production alike: Sereny was never, at her insistence, to figure in the dramatization as in her book; Edgar and Nunn always worked around as much as with her, and multiple framing and post-Brechtian techniques, more formally articulated than in *Good* or *Theresa*, brilliantly accommodated many moments of *Sho'ah* transmission or denial within (explicitly) reflexive awareness of generational passage. Sereny, whatever her faith in Speer, has no copyright on such issues, nor on what Speer's life may mean; such problems as may beset her biography were well within the production's theatrical and moral scope. Edgar could easily have used a Nuremberg court-room format, but, drawing like Pascal on many techniques, bypassed documentary stasis to include the evolving balance and worth of Speer's desire to stay alive even as an admitted perpetrator. In a strong sense *Albert Speer* begins where *Good* ends – the band was real and Halder knew it, but when, exactly? – and despite its scale was swiftly produced in Germany and the US.

In 2004 Anthony Sher performed *Primo* at the National Theatre, a solo narrative he edited from Stuart Woolf's translations of Primo Levi's *Se questo è un uomo* (*If This is a Man*, 1958/69) and *La Tregua* (*The Truce*, 1963/5). The production transferred to Cape Town, is available on DVD and is documented in *Primo Time* (2005), a selection from Sher's diaries. Sher's performance (directed by Richard Wilson) was beautifully restrained – exemplified by a simple gesture, hand over crotch, to indicate forced nudity. The contrast with *An die Musik* could hardly be greater, but if minimalism was absolutely right, there is something troubling in Sher's documentation, combining a story of reading Levi, writing the script, and only then securing rights from Levi's wary family, with a battle against stage-fright. One locus is Levi's eventual suicide, another the inevitable self-dramatization of Sher's complex psychic and theatrical identity (including *Singer*), and a third the pseudo-realism of workshops in which he and another were subject to sadistic and irrational command by actors in

SS uniforms. Self-effacing performance is thrown into relief by knowledge of Sher's rehearsal experiences and personal terror, a difficulty that joint marketing of the DVD and *Primo Time* sustains: so that despite clear efforts to withstand it, occlusion of Levi begins. This, as much as Adorno's contempt for aestheticization, was what the minimalism restrained, but it could do so only in performance; and whether the show can be revived by other actors remains to be seen.

Restatement of Levi's testimony nearly twenty years after his more than unbearably sad death is welcome and necessary. His unflinching, calm insistence is rightly a touchstone for the weary or innocent of witness: this happened, like this; know; watch and ward: taught in many places, he should be everywhere as celebrated as Ghandi or Mandela. It is an English irony to have celebrated him, yes, at the National Theatre with a prestigious actor, but incidentally, in a one-man show driven by complex personal witness; and in isolation, amid intense silence about war-crimes whose relevance to ourselves we still refuse to recognize.

NOTES

1 The original remark was in *Prismen* (Adorno 1974: vol. 10a, 30); see also *Ohne Leitbild* (vol. 10a, 452–3), *Negative Dialektik* (vol. 6, 355–6) and *Noten zur Literatur IV* (vol. 11, 603).

2 The analogy 'black sun : Auschwitz :: white sun : Hiroshima' is powerful. Imagine staging nuclear annihilation.

3 It replaced *der dritter cherbm* (Yiddish, 'the third *cherbm*'); biblical *cherbm*s destroyed the Temples.

4 Weight-management is a paradigm of Strasberg's Actor's Studio 'Method' – consider the reception of Robert DeNiro in *Raging Bull* and Tom Hanks in *Castaway*.

5 Written 1962, serialized in the *New Yorker* February–March 1963, published in May with the influential subtitle *A Report on the Banality of Evil*.

6 For example, field general courts martial (1914–18), the Amritsar Massacre (1919) and the treatment of Russian and Yugoslav refugees (1945), on which see Mitchell (1998).

7 For a view more explicit on anti-semitism see 'Bernard Shaw and British Holocaust Drama' in Isser (1997: 44–61).

8 Later titled *Resort 67*, as in Skloot (1982); see Skloot (1987: 345).

9 *Die Ermittlung* was premiered in 17 cities in East and West Germany on 19 October 1965; Piscator directed at the Freie Volksbühne. Weiss's royalties went to a fund for survivors and their children.

10 Norton-Taylor's Tricycle Theatre work includes *Half the Picture* (1994), *Srebrenica* (1997), *The Colour of Justice* (1998) and *Justifying War* (2003); his model was used by Brittain and Slovo for *Guantanamo* (Tricycle, 2004).

11 It was cut by a censor who found it showed naked corpses too immodestly, while Resnais's inevitable choices/exclusions of footage are more consequential than transparent.

12 In 2000 a touring Romanian revival of *An die Musik* played at the Tricycle (and in Reading, Warwick and Cardiff) to renewed offence.

13 John Simon Ritchie (1957–79).

14 Both Royal Court plays were programmed during the artistic directorship of Stuart Burge (1977–9).

15 The yellow Star of David armband has not been rehabilitated, nor other colour-coded camp symbols.

16 In Athol Fugard (1993). *The Township Plays*. Oxford and Cape Town: Oxford University Press.

17 The camera points into floodlights against which Höfgren disappears – as Max does ending *Bent*; the life and character of Höfgren were based on those of Gustaf Gründgrens, Klaus Mann's sometime brother-in-law and reputedly, as the great Mephisto (in Goethe's *Faust*) of his generation, Göring's favourite actor. 'Cathedral of Ice' was the British ambassador's description of Speer's plans.

18 Both productions used (with variant doubling) ten actors, but the RSC also had five musicians permanently on stage; at the Donmar 'Instruments and other parts' (programme) were played by members of the company.

19 The text in Watts (2004b) lacks the final stage direction.

20 I do not suggest Allen might not properly have written and the Court presented an anti-Israeli drama; only that he could not properly freight an anti-Israeli drama with Kasztner materials, engorging a contemporary political case with implications and applications of the *Sho'ah*. Isser (1997) compares *Perdition* with Arthur Giron's *Edith Stein* (US, 1969), revised 1988–93 to intervene in the controversy about Carmelite nuns at the Auschwitz site.

21 *H.I.D.* was developed at the Mickery Theatre, Amsterdam.

22 The Act made possible prosecution, for warcrimes committed outside British jurisdiction, of British residents or citizens.

23 Jurek Becker's 1969 novel was first filmed in 1974.

24 See 'Author's Note' and 'Afterword' in Edgar (2000); White (2001).

PRIMARY READING

Collections of Holocaust plays

Fuchs, Elinor (ed.) (1987). *Plays of the Holocaust: An International Anthology*. (Nelly Sachs, *Eli*; Liliane Atlan, *Mister Fugue*; Peter Barnes, *Auschwitz*; József Szajna, *Replika*; Joshua Sobol, *Ghetto*; James Schevill, *Cathedral of Ice*.) New York: Theatre Communications Group.

Skloot, Robert (ed.) (1982). *The Theatre of the Holocaust. Vol. 1: Four Plays*. (Shimon Wincelberg, *Resort 76* [*The Windows of Heaven*]; Harold and Edith Lieberman, *Throne of Straw*; George Tabori, *The Cannibals*; Charlotte Delbo, *Who Will Carry the Word?*) Madison: University of Wisconsin Press.

Skloot, Robert (ed.) (1999). *The Theatre of the Holocaust. Vol. 2: Six Plays*. (Roy Kift, *Camp Comedy*; Leeny Sack, *The Survivor and the Translator*; Bernard Kops, *Dreams of Anne Frank*; Donald Margulies, *The Model Apartment*; Christopher Hampton, *The Portage to San Cristobal of A. H.*; Howard Brenton, *H.I.D.*) Madison: University of Wisconsin Press.

Watts, Irene, (ed.) (2004a). *A Terrible Truth: Anthology of Holocaust Drama*. (David Edgar, *Albert Speer*; Joshua Sobol, *Ghetto*; Martin Sherman, *Rose*; Anne Szumigalski, *Z*; Eugene Lion, *Sammy's Follies*.) Toronto: Playwrights Canada Press.

Watts, Irene (ed.) (2004b). *A Terrible Truth. Vol. Two: Anthology of Holocaust Drama*. (C. P. Taylor, *Good*; Jason Sherman, *None is Too Many*; Arthur Miller, *Playing for Time*; Theresa Tova, *Still the Night*; Jonathan Garfinkel, *The Trials of John Demjanjuk*.) Toronto: Playwrights Canada Press.

Individual Holocaust plays

Allen, Jim (1987). *Perdition*. London: Ithaca.

Barnes, Peter (1989). *Auschwitz* (1978) in *Plays: 1*. London: Methuen.

Bond, Edward (1992). *Summer* (1982) in *Plays: 4*. London: Methuen.

Brenton, Howard (1989). *H.I.D. (Hess Is Dead)*. London: Nick Hern.

Buffini, Moira (1998). *Gabriel*. London: Faber and Faber.

Edgar, David (2000). *Albert Speer*. London: Nick Hern.

Flannery, Peter (1990). *Singer*. London: Nick Hern.

Goodrich, Frances and Hackett, Albert (1956). *The Diary of Anne Frank, Dramatized*. New York: Random House.

Hampton, Christopher (1983). *George Steiner's The Portage to San Cristobal of A. H*. London: Faber and Faber.

Harwood, Ronald (1995). *Taking Sides* in *Plays: 2*. London: Faber and Faber.

Harwood, Ronald (1996).*The Handyman*. London: Faber and Faber.

Hochhuth, Rolf (1964). *The Deputy.* As *Der Stell-vertreter*, 1963; trans. Richard Winston and Clara Winston. New York: Grove Press.

Norton-Taylor, Richard (ed.) (1997). *Nuremberg.* London: Nick Hern.

Pascal, Julia (2000). *The Holocaust Trilogy.* London: Oberon Books.

Samuels, Diane (1995). *Kindertransport.* London: Nick Hern.

Shaffer, Anthony (1988). *This Savage Parade.* Oxford: Amber Lane Press.

Shaw, Robert (1968). *The Man in the Glass Booth.* New York: Grove Press.

Sher, Anthony. *Primo.* (2004; unpublished; released on DVD, 2005).

Sherman, Martin (2004). *Bent* (1979) and *Rose* (1999) in *Plays: 1.* London: Methuen.

Tabori, George (1974). *The Cannibals.* London: Davis-Poynter.

Tabori, George (1979). *Ich wollte meine Tochter läge tot zu meinen Füssen und hätte die Juwelen in den Ohren: Improvisationen über Shakespeares Shylock: Dokumentationen einer Theaterarbeit.* Munich: C. Hanser.

Taylor, C. P. (1990). *Good* and *And a Nightingale Sang. . . .* London: Methuen.

Van Druten, John (1954). *I am a Camera.* London: Gollancz.

Weiss, Peter (1967). *The Investigation.* As *Die Ermittlung,* 1965; trans. Jon Swan and Ulu Grosbard, New York: Atheneum.

Wesker, Arnold (1980). *The Merchant* (1976) in *Collected Plays Vol. 4.* Harmondsworth: Penguin.

FURTHER READING

Adorno, Theodor (1974). *Gesammelte Schriften.* 20 vols, Frankfurt: Suhrkamp.

Arendt, Hannah (1965). *Eichmann in Jerusalem: A Report on the Banality of Evil.* Harmondsworth: Penguin.

Burt, Richard (2002). 'Shakespeare and the Holocaust' in Richard Burt (ed.). *Shakespeare After Mass Media.* London: Palgrave, 295–329.

Cushman, Robert (1981). Review of *Good, London Theatre Record* 27 August–9 September, 458.

Dürrenmatt, Friedrich (1976). 'Theatre Problems', in *Writings on Theatre and Drama.* London: Jonathan Cape, 59–91.

Felstiner, John (1995). *Paul Celan: Poet, Survivor, Jew.* New Haven, CT, and London: Yale University Press.

Gouri, Haim (1994). 'Facing the Glass Booth' in Geoffrey H. Hartman (ed.). *Holocaust Remembrance: The Shapes of Memory.* Oxford: Blackwell, 153–60.

Guttenplan, D. D. (2001). *The Holocaust on Trial: History, Justice and the David Irving Libel Case.* London: Granta Books.

Hampton, Christopher (2005). *Hampton on Hampton,* ed. Alistair Owen. London: Faber and Faber.

Isser, Edward R. (1997). *Stages of Annihilation: Theatrical Representations of the Holocaust.* Madison and Teaneck, NJ: Fairleigh Dickinson University Press; London: Associated University Presses.

Langer, Lawrence L. (1995). 'The Americanization of the Holocaust on Stage and Screen' in *Admitting the Holocaust: Collected Essays.* New York and Oxford: Oxford University Press, 157–77.

Luckhurst, Mary (2001). 'The Case of Theresa: Guernsey, the Holocaust and Theatre Censorship in the 1990s' in Edward Batley and David Bradby (eds.). *Morality and Justice: The Challenge of European Theatre.* New York and Amsterdam: Rodopi, 255–67.

Marcus, Greil (1990). 'The Last Sex Pistols Concert' in *Lipstick Traces: A Secret History of the Twentieth Century.* London: Secker and Warburg, 27–152.

Mitchell, Ian (1998). *The Cost of a Reputation: Aldington versus Tolstoy.* Edinburgh: Canongate.

Rovit, Rebecca and Goldfarb, Alvin (1999). *Theatrical Performance during the Holocaust: Texts, Documents, Memoirs.* Baltimore and London: Johns Hopkins University Press.

Russell, Susan (2001). 'Holocaust History as Postmodern Performance', *Essays in Theatre* 19:2, 127–39.

Schumacher, Claude (ed.) (1998). *Staging the Holocaust: The Shoah in Drama and Performance.* Cambridge: Cambridge University Press.

Sher, Anthony (2005). *Primo Time.* London: Nick Hern.

Skloot, Robert (1987). 'The Drama of the Holocaust: Issues of Choice and Survival', *New Theatre Quarterly* III:12, 337–48.

Skloot, Robert (1988). *The Darkness We Carry: The Drama of the Holocaust*. Madison: University of Wisconsin Press.

White, Nick (2001). 'Gitta Sereny and Albert Speer's "Battle with Truth" on the London Stage', *New Theatre Quarterly* XVII:2, 170–85.

Young, James E. (1990). *Writing and Rewriting the Holocaust: Narrative and the Consequences of Interpretation*. Bloomington and Indianapolis: Indiana University Press.

Young, James E. (2000). *At Memory's Edge: After-Images of the Holocaust in Contemporary Art and Architecture*. New Haven, CT, and London: Yale University Press.

27

Troubling Perspectives: Northern Ireland, the 'Troubles' and Drama

Helen Lojek

Traditionally, Northern Ireland has been the forgotten branch of British and Irish theatre, fully integrated neither into the Irish Republic's theatrical scene (developed as a way of investigating and shaping Irish culture) nor into the British theatrical scene (which seldom returns the gaze from the 'province' of Northern Ireland). When playwrights began to respond to the 'Troubles' which re-emerged in 1968, however, it was no longer possible to forget the region or its increasingly compelling theatre. The Troubles were a painful conjunction of cultural, economic, political and social forces, and plays dealing with them often reach well beyond the provincial to touch basic issues of human conflict and freedom. It was as though, to paraphrase Auden's poem 'In Memory of W. B. Yeats', mad Ireland had hurt the writers into drama. As they sought to transform the hurt into effective drama, playwrights were forced to confront the relationship of literature and culture, and to discover ways of sufficiently distancing the subject of sectarian tension for their work to promote not further factionalism but genuine discussion.

Various strategies were adopted, often simultaneously, to achieve perspective – humour, even-handedness and balanced character portrayals, for example. With surprising frequency, playwrights modelled cross-cultural understanding by creating sympathetic portraits of communities to which they did not belong. The most common strategy was use of the past, and in their concern with history the plays converge with contemporary theories of feminism, postcolonialism and postmodernism. Some writers were more self-consciously influenced by cultural/literary theories than others, but the theories were thick in the air, and plays of the Troubles are helpfully considered in the light of them. Both nationalists and unionists, for example, felt dispossessed and resisted domination. Local language and history are central concerns, and the plays often validate local performance traditions. In both subject and style they resist the pull of current established views in favour of demythologizing the past and moving forwards. One sign that playwrights, while looking back, were interested in the future is the overwhelming use of urban settings, a sharp break with traditional Irish play settings in the rural west. A significant number of women playwrights (previously rare in male-dominated Irish theatre) emerged and gained broad audiences. Both theatres and funding organizations supported productions focusing on the Troubles, indicating that the arts community in general felt the need to engage in cultural discussion. The result is dramatic work that surprises, and that incorporates voices from various economic, religious, cultural and gender categories.

Dramatic responses to the Troubles came predominantly from Northern Ireland, in part because comfortable residents of a Troubles-free Republic preferred not to think about the situation.[1] The plays position themselves at various points along the continuum from direct engagement with specific political issues to assumption of a cultural realm within Ireland but outside politics. They generally assume a primarily Irish audience, and naturalism remains the norm. Within that norm, the plays display various approaches to playwriting and performance, and a willingness to experiment. What Northern Irish poet Seamus Heaney termed 'the quarrel between free creative imagination and the constraints of religious, political, and domestic obligation'[2] led playwrights to consider Ireland's continuous past, seeking not to produce historically accurate docudramas, but to consider how history and the myths of history shed light on Northern Ireland's present difficult struggle to determine its cultural and political future.

In addressing uncomfortable truths, playwrights upset myths around which various factions had united. Divided communities tended to respond most immediately by categorizing the drama according to the perceived cultural identifications of the authors, and part of the story of Northern Ireland and the Troubles is a narrative of how playwrights found ways to reach across cultural divides and engage mixed audiences in discussions that went beyond tribal loyalties. None of these texts, however, is disinterested, and audiences needed to be (and generally were) alert to ways they were being asked to perceive the Troubles.

The nature of the problem is revealed by reactions to Brian Friel's *The Freedom of the City* (1973), a play clearly based on the events of Bloody Sunday, 1972, when British troops killed 13 unarmed civil rights marchers in Derry. (A fourteenth died later in hospital.) Friel, a Catholic with roots in Derry and County Donegal (just across the border in the Republic), carefully dates the play in 1970, before Bloody Sunday, but it remains his most overt consideration of the Troubles and is commonly referred to as 'Friel's Bloody Sunday play'. An English judge, an American sociologist, an Irish priest, a Dublin television commentator, an Irish balladeer and a British soldier provide differing interpretations of events, all of which contrast sharply with the less shaped, less articulate voices of those who died. Despite Friel's focus on the difficulty of discerning 'truth' - and despite his contention that the play is really about poverty[3] – it was widely judged to have a 'green' or republican view of events, and it did not play in Belfast.

In 1973 Friel noted: 'This play raises the old problem of writing about events which are still happening ... because we're all involved in the present situation people are going to say "this is a very unfair play." ' He went on to note the 'trouble' of 'cliché articulation ... we have all got answers for everything' (Murray 1999: 58, 60). A decade later Friel described *The Freedom of the City* as 'a reckless play ... [an] ill-considered play because it was written out of ... anger at Bloody Sunday events in Derry. I don't say I regret it but I certainly wouldn't do it now.'[4]

Playwrights of the Troubles are overwhelmingly aware of the challenge Friel noted. Pushed, and pushing themselves, to address the Troubles, they wanted to avoid narrow political agendas. One strategy was to use familiar dramatic forms to approach new subjects. John Boyd's *The Flats* (1971), for example (the first Troubles play by a local writer to be staged in Belfast), used a straightforward naturalistic mode with which audiences were comfortable to emphasize not the sectarian divide, but the divide between privileged and underprivileged. It attracted less traditional theatre audiences, often people from outside the middle classes who shared the Belfast street idiom the characters used. The play's staging at Belfast's Lyric Theatre indicated that a conservative theatrical establishment also felt responsible for expanding cultural discussion.

Similarly, Belfast playwright Graham Reid approached the Troubles in television plays that coupled conventional form with painful subject matter. The three *Billy* plays (1982–4, adapted for the stage in 1990) and the six plays in *Ties of Blood* (1985) put the Troubles in numerous living rooms on both sides of the Irish Sea. (John McGahern, Frank McGuinness and Anne Devlin also produced television dramas dealing with Northern Irish tensions.) Reid's stage play *The Death of Humpty Dumpty* (1979) slightly obscures its connection to Belfast, as does *Dorothy* (1980), but *Hidden Curriculum* (1982) specifically critiques the disconnection between Northern Irish secondary education and the lives students could expect, suggesting that the failure of education helped push young loyalists into paramilitary activity. The well-intentioned teacher who emphasizes the war poets, encouraging students to recognize that their ancestors fought the battle of the Somme, is unwittingly using history not to enable but to cripple. Reid's weaknesses are easy to spot, but his work constitutes a brave confrontation of issues and represents the first major dramatic response to the Troubles. Reid's plays were less threatening because of his conventional forms, even-handed treatment and establishment Protestantism.

Another strategy playwrights adopted to emphasize that they were not advocating any particular political position was to allow characters from various factions to articulate different perspectives. Martin Lynch's *The Interrogation of Ambrose Fogarty* (1982) presented a Belfast interrogation (by Protestant police) of an unemployed Catholic suspected of armed robbery. Lynch, a Catholic who noted that he had himself experienced such an interrogation, specified that he wanted to reach across community divisions: 'I want Catholics to have a better understanding of the police and I want Protestants to have a better understanding of how people end up Republican' (quoted in Byrne 2001: 62). The play was premiered just after the hunger strikes in which Bobby Sands and nine other republican prisoners died, and the Lyric's decision to mount it evidenced continued commitment to discussions that sought to go beyond the tribal. Ron Hutchinson's *Rat in the Skull* (1984) also depicts an interrogation, this one in a London police station, where an IRA suspect is being interviewed by a Belfast policeman and a young English police constable. Contrasting accents are theatrically effective in presenting a debate that most critics found even-handed. *Rat in the Skull* played in London and New York, but was not staged in Northern Ireland until 1987. *Interrogation* differs from *Rat* in its skilful incorporation of Belfast humour, which is fiercely black, colloquial, uninhibited. The humour moderates the pain of the subject. Hutchinson's play is just painful.

Belfast humour also characterized the works of Charabanc Theatre Company (1983–95), whose success was further evidence that new audiences were ready for new ways of thinking about community, and for new kinds of drama. The company was founded (without a particular agenda) by five Belfast women actors who were tired of being unemployed. Working initially with Martin Lynch the actors researched Belfast's 1911 linen-mill strike and collaboratively developed *Lay Up Your Ends* (1983), which focuses on poverty and its connection to gender. Collaborative development, including first-hand research and the creation of roles they could play themselves, became hall-marks of Charabanc's script development, and they soon embraced the designation 'feminist'.

In addition, the company worked to recover forgotten segments of local history and to validate local idiom. Colloquialisms, slang and gritty, vibrant, uncompromised accents marked their performances. They softened the accents when performing abroad, but never in Ireland. The idiomatic language, cutting across the sectarian divide, had not often been heard from characters meant to be taken seriously. Charabanc also validated local performance traditions, emphasizing not only Belfast's black humour, but also the mixture of song and satire found in the city's popular pantos. Their low-budget, easily toured productions abandoned strict naturalism: men's roles were played by women, and costume changes (typically stylistic, like the donning of a shawl, for example) were made in full view. A focus on women's forgotten history provided additional perspective on tribal divisions.

Charabanc's *Now You're Talking* (1985) and *Somewhere Over the Balcony* (1987) focus not on history, but on the unrecorded realities of women's lives in the present. They achieve perspective by combining humour with diverse voices. In *Now You're Talking* women from both communities meet in a Northern Irish Reconciliation Centre and dismiss the American facilitator with irreverent humour. Out-group negotiator breeds in-group solidarity. *Somewhere Over the Balcony* represents a more daring decision. Charabanc's principal members were Protestant, so their representation of Catholic women living in Belfast's infamous Divis Flats (a public housing tower with a British army post on its roof) was itself a model of cross-cultural understanding. Charabanc conducted extensive interviews with Divis residents and produced a black comedy emphasizing the powerlessness and endurance of women at the bottom of the economic and social hierarchy. The play's anarchic humour reflects its origins in a surrealistic dream of company member Carol

Scanlan (Moore), and it is one of the few plays about the Troubles that completely eschews the conventions of naturalism. Like other Charabanc plays, it is closer in style to panto than to a well-made play. *Somewhere Over the Balcony* sees the Troubles from the point of view of poor and powerless women, rather than from a sectarian point of view, generally ignoring the binary division of Irish culture into unionist and nationalist and demonstrating that slicing community in different ways leads to different understandings.

Venues as well as subject matter for Charabanc plays moved beyond the middle classes and attracted audiences unaccustomed to theatre-going. Charabanc toured on both sides of the border, often playing in parish halls and leisure centres. Audiences could attend performances in familiar venues close to their homes. The company succeeded in reaching wide audiences with plays that were topical but not polemical or narrowly political.

Marie Jones, who emerged as Charabanc's principal writer, went on to a solo playwriting career. Her 'one-hander' *A Night in November* (1994) is based on the 1993 World Cup qualifying match between Northern Ireland and the Republic of Ireland, during which spectators exhibited rancorous sectarianism. The play's lone character, a Protestant (like Jones), is attracted to Catholic culture, and in the process of moving towards appreciation of the 'other' he analyses the stereotypes of both factions. Jones later won the John Hewett Award for her contributions to the cultural traditions debate. Like the Charabanc plays that preceded it, *A Night in November* uses raucous humour to engage audiences in serious subject matter.

A Night in November was produced by DubblJoint (the name plays on Dublin/ Belfast) and directed by Pam Brighton, who had directed Charabanc's first play. DubblJoint and Brighton also produced the controversial *Binlids* (1997), which elicited heated debate about the role of the arts (and of government funding agencies) in addressing sectarianism. The play's multiple authors included well-known republican spokesperson and former Maze prisoner Danny Morrison. Set during the period of 1970s internment, when nationalists beat trashcan lids on the pavement to warn of approaching danger, it re-enacted the Springhill and Ballymurphy massacres and played to sell-out audiences, some of whom cheered the depiction of a British soldier's murder. *Binlids* continued the pattern of breaking from procedures of establishment theatre, using historical research, collaborative development and a mixture of community and professional actors. DubblJoint's *Forced Upon Us* (1999), a play about the history of the RUC (Royal Ulster Constabulary, the Northern Irish police force), began with the rape of a Catholic by a Protestant, and used extracts from unionist speeches to parallel individual force and bias with the group force and bias of Protestant leaders. The Northern Irish Arts Council pulled funding from the production, insisting they did so not for political reasons, but because the play failed to meet acceptable professional standards. The Arts Council decision elicited protests, including a letter signed by prominent theatre professionals like Marina Carr, John McGrath, Frank McGuinness, Neil Donnelly and Marie Jones, who 'regretted' the continuation of Ireland's 'sorry history of censorship'.[5] Most of the funding was restored. Neither play is in print, and neither gained critical accolades. Both have heavy political agendas, and both represent continued dramatic experimentation in approaching the Troubles.

Far less controversial are the short dramatic monologues (some broadcast on the radio) by Jennifer Johnston, an established novelist. Individually the pieces present the view of one faction or the other, but as a whole they illuminate various perspectives and the dominant tone is one of sadness for lives spun out of control. *Twinkletoes* (originally *O Ananais, Azarais and Miseal*, 1993) is delivered by the wife of an imprisoned IRA member. *Mustn't Forget High Noon* (1989) is the lament of Billy, a Protestant, for a friend shot by the IRA. *Christine* (1989) is the lament of Billy's widow (who is from the Republic) for a sterile life of wasted opportunity. Published together as *Three Monologues*, the dedication reads: 'to all the men, women and children who have been victims of violence and intolerance, for so long, in this country, Ireland'.

Northern Ireland's other well-known women playwrights, Christina Reid and Anne Devlin, come (like Marie Jones) from working-class Belfast backgrounds. Reid is Protestant and Devlin Catholic. Both moved to England in the 1980s, but Belfast continues to be the powerful setting for their basically realistic works, which draw inspiration from the writers' biographies and centre on women's lives. Reid's *Tea in a China Cup* (1983) spans three generations of women, centring on Beth, who struggles to move beyond her family's 'respectable' traditions while preserving something of their history. In *The Belle of the Belfast City* (1989) several generations of Protestant/unionist women come together during the anti-Anglo-Irish Treaty demonstrations, and the play explores how the men in their lives control them with 'surveillance' as surely as British army surveillance seeks to control political dissent. *Did You Hear the One About the Irishman...?* (1985) explores the symbiotic relationship of extremist nationalists and extremist unionists. Parallel scenes and speeches emphasize the mutual dependence of opposing bigots, a point driven home by the double casting of an actor who plays a terrorist from each side.

Perhaps her most interesting play, *Joyriders* (1986) grew out of Reid's work with Divis Flats young people, who composed songs for the play. Reid was working at Divis at roughly the same time as Charabanc; like them, she was a Protestant in Catholic territory. A black comedy, *Joyriders* opens with Belfast teenagers watching a production of Sean O'Casey's *The Shadow of a Gunman* (1923), thus linking generations of Irish theatre and generations of British army involvement in Ireland. The teens are enrolled in a useless government training scheme whose inadequacies reflect more general problems in Northern Irish government and education.

Anne Devlin, from the opposite side of Belfast's sectarian divide, shares with Reid a concern with the lives of women and families, rather than a focus on the more stereotypically political issue of who should control the government. The title of *Ourselves Alone* (1985) refers to the usual translation of 'Sinn Féin'. The play, however, focuses on the loneliness of working-class women who, Devlin says, 'were in some ways living without men'[6] – despite the fact men constantly invade the private spaces which are at the centre of the play. Like Charabanc, Devlin created an ensemble piece, with major roles for women. Like Lynch and Hutchinson, she provided characters who voiced fiercely differing views, a theatrical practice she describes as rooted in her inherited 'word culture, which was about arguments and debates'. Her forthright exploration of parallels between social/political patriarchy and familial patriarchy was unusual at the time. History, she says, 'was a big huge character [. . .] before we can put down this particular burden that is our history we have to recall certain things that have not been visible'.[7] The play, however, was not widely known in Northern Ireland – nor was Devlin's *After Easter* (1994), a far less naturalistic work that was premiered shortly after the 1993 Downing Street Declaration and not long before the IRA ceasefire. In it Devlin again examines parent–child relationships and the lives of Belfast women, depicting the fates of sisters who dealt with the Troubles in radically different ways, and joining religious and political implications in the title's reminder of the 1916 Easter Rebellion.

The number of women playwrights who emerged in Northern Ireland during this period is noteworthy, since women continue to be relatively rare on the Republic's playwriting field. Voicing important challenges to received orthodoxy about sectarianism and about women's place, they presented alternatives to prevailing male discourse. Furthermore, their concentration on the 'typically female' domestic scene represents not an escape from politics as usual, but an exploration of the inseparability of politics and domesticity. The ultimate impact of these female voices is difficult to assess. Reid and Devlin, whose careers seem to have wound down, use the most traditional dramatic forms, relying on conventional realism and autobiographical material. Charabanc, which represented a subversive challenge to conventional subject matter and to establishment conventions of dramatic form, production and company organization, ceased to exist in 1995. Little of their important early work is in print, and almost none has been performed by anyone other than the women who devised it. Marie Jones continues to write and enjoy commercial success, but her recent work has shown little development.

Whether or not the plays survive, their impact not just on Northern Irish theatre but on Irish theatre in general has been considerable. Women playwrights weighed in on compelling cultural and political issues, demonstrating the value of women's voices and rejecting the convention that only men should address 'public' issues. They exploded the notion that the private and the public can in fact be divided, expanded the way their culture thought about the connection between the arts and social/political issues, and provided evidence that women could succeed as playwrights, directors and theatre company managers.

The company whose work is most widely known – and known specifically in relation to the Troubles – is Field Day, founded in 1980 by playwright Brian Friel and actor Stephen Rea. ('Field Day' is a play on 'Friel' and 'Rea'.) Friel and Rea were soon joined on the Field Day board by Seamus Heaney, Seamus Deane, Tom Paulin and David Hammond, and the company's male focus is an interesting balance to Charabanc's focus on women. The board was evenly split between Protestants and Catholics, and the company based itself in Derry, a town with an evenly split population, a border location distant from both Dublin and Belfast, and a contested name ('Londonderry' to unionists; 'Derry' to nationalists). From the start, the company toured, playing (like Charabanc) in regional theatres, parish halls and leisure centres. The touring was linked to the company's clearly articulated sense of purpose:

> the political crisis in the North and its reverberations in the Republic had made the necessity of a reappraisal of Ireland's political and cultural situation explicit and urgent. All of the directors are northerners. They believed that Field Day could and should contribute to the solution of the present crisis by producing analyses of the established opinions, myths, and stereotypes which had become both a symptom and a cause of the current situation.[8]

Field Day's first production was Brian Friel's hugely successful *Translations* (1980), set in 1833, when the British army is mapping Donegal and translating Irish place names into English. The hedge-school set focuses attention on control of education as well as the relation of language to nationality. Language, never a neutral medium, is a site from which nationalist, postcolonial authors often speak. In Ireland that site is 'nonnative' English. Friel famously establishes the convention that most of his characters are speaking Irish, though the play is written entirely in English (except for passages in Greek and Latin that are part of the curriculum). Characters speak powerfully on all sides of the issues, and the irony that most Irish audience members (regardless of their emotional attachment to the Irish language) would have been unable to understand a play performed in Irish brings home the complexity.

Friel's play was judged remarkably 'fair', considering the fact the author was a Catholic with nationalist tendencies. Using the past as a distancing device enabled him to avoid the polemical risk of a more contemporary setting. Unlike *The Freedom of the City*, *Translations* could not be connected to a particular current event. Friel (and the audience) could examine the past without being in thrall to it. On the other hand, Friel felt the play was 'offered pieties that I didn't intend for it',[9] and he produced a balancing farce for his next Field Day offering. *The Communication Cord* (1982), sometimes described as an 'antidote' to *Translations*, mocks the contemporary reverence for the past which 'restores' rural cottages into museum-like second homes. Friel's third Field Day play, *Making History* (1988), focuses on seventeenth-century Ulster lord Hugh O'Neill, who led a rebellion against the English. These plays share awareness of the past, and of the need to come to terms with the past in order to comprehend the present. They note the reality that all versions of the past are shaped, so that agreement on history's meaning is hard to come by, and they warn of dangers involved when people are imprisoned by language or history: 'it is not the literal past, the "facts" of history, that shape us,' says Hugh in *Translations*, 'but images of the past embodied in language'.[10]

Field Day's habit of reconsidering the past was not limited to Friel. In 1983 Field Day commissioned David Rudkin's *The Saxon Shore*, which paralleled Northern Irish

Protestants with Saxons transplanted to Roman Britain. Field Day eventually opted not to produce *The Saxon Shore*, fearing it would be perceived as too nationalist, despite Rudkin's Protestantism, but this play too used history to analyse current cultural conflicts and identities. Such issues also inform Tom Kilroy's *Double Cross* (1986). Kilroy's play is based on the lives of two Irishmen who re-created themselves during World War II, one becoming the British minister of information, the other a Nazi radio broadcaster. The double casting of Stephen Rea in both parts emphasized parallel opposites (as had double casting in *Did You Hear the One about the Irishman . . . ?*). Kilroy's *The Madame MacAdam Travelling Theatre* (1991) was likewise set during World War II. Field Day also found relevance in adaptations of classical texts. Russian, French and Greek texts adapted by well-known Irish writers (Tom Paulin, Seamus Heaney, Derek Mahon, Brian Friel) made deliberate use of Northern Irish vernacular to explore non-parochial issues with parochial implications.

Field Day used history and the classics to distance immediate issues of identity, language and cultural conflict, so that these concerns could be considered without the usual sectarian clichés. When the results focused on division and opposition it was never precisely the division and opposition tearing the society around them, but the plays were aimed specifically at illuminating that contemporary society. Like Charabanc, Field Day toured widely throughout Ireland and England. The touring was a matter of practical finances and an essentially political recognition that the Troubles had both causes and implications that lay well outside Northern Ireland. Those tours drew appreciative attention from both the Republic and England and raised the profile of Northern Irish drama.

The influence of contemporary cultural and literary theory on Field Day's texts was direct. The company's specific, detailed cultural debate evolved into extensive programme essays, pamphlets, and eventually an anthology of Irish literature. Three of the board members were academics, and discussions of postcolonialism and postmodernism spilled over not only into their pamphlets, but also into their board meetings and into the plays they wrote and produced.

Next to *Translations* the best-known Field Day play is *Pentecost* (1987), by inventive, imaginative Belfast Protestant Stewart Parker. Parker's *Spokesong* (1975), a musical set in a Belfast bicycle shop, traces eighty years of history in the city where the pneumatic tyre was invented. *Catchpenny Twist* (1977), also a musical, follows the careers of a Protestant composer and a Catholic lyricist who collaborate on songs for both loyalists and republicans. *Northern Star* (1984) and *Heavenly Bodies* (1986) deal with Irish history, with particular attention to Irish theatrical history, incorporated by means of parodic references to canonical texts and performance styles. *Pentecost*, whose title, like *After Easter*, indicates its focus on events after the Easter Rebellion, is the only Field Day play to deal directly with relatively contemporary Troubles. But this play too uses the past to illuminate the present. The 1987 play is set during a 1974 unionist strike that eventually succeeded in destroying a power-sharing agreement crafted to end the Troubles. It focuses on four young people – two men, two women; two Protestants, two Catholics. And one ghost from the past. Into a realistic, contemporary setting Parker brings an equally realistic ghost from the previous generation, juxtaposing World War I concerns with the 1970s and 1980s. The play focuses on private struggles within the larger sectarian context, seeking a usable past on which to build a future.

Parker's exploration of historical theatrical styles, as well as his extensive use of music, gives his plays an exciting performance aspect. Like Charabanc, he often operates outside the bounds of conventional naturalism. The same is true of Vincent Woods's *At the Black Pig's Dyke* (1992), which incorporates music, myth, fairy tales and (most powerfully) the ancient tradition of mumming to create a highly theatrical examination of three generations of a family in the border area.

It was Frank McGuinness, though – a Catholic from Donegal, just a few miles from the Northern Irish border – whose play became an icon of cross-cultural understanding. *Observe the Sons of Ulster Marching Towards the Somme* (1985) follows eight Protestant Ulstermen as they fight (and mostly die) in the World War I battle of the Somme. Dublin reviews routinely mentioned the fact that a Catholic nationalist had created an understanding portrait of Protestant unionists.[11] The response was overwhelmingly positive, and the play has been revived numerous times. Like *Translations*, it breaks down the grand narratives of the past and deliberately undermines stereotypical understandings of sect and violence – and sex, since the play has gay characters. Difference, it reveals, is not synonymous with opposition. Because the play is a memory play, it also examines the ways in which past and present shape each other. McGuinness's *Carthaginians* (1988), sometimes seen as a companion piece to *Observe the Sons of Ulster*, focuses on Catholic responses to Bloody Sunday. Seven people in a Derry cemetery come to terms with their individual pasts and with Bloody Sunday, now 15 years behind them. There is no direct depiction of Bloody Sunday, and characters' narratives of the day focus on individual experiences that parallel public events but are not directly part of them. The play assesses the role of the arts in confronting the Troubles: a play-within-the-play mocks conventional depictions of the Troubles and parodies a section of Sean O'Casey's *Juno and the Paycock* (1924). Dido, the central character, is a gloriously self-dramatizing Irish queen, his outsider sexuality and non-involvement in Bloody Sunday providing perspective and a possible way forward. Rejecting binary categories of sexuality, McGuinness also rejects binary sectarian categories. Both *Sons of Ulster* and *Carthaginians* use examination of the past as a way to confront current Troubles. Both also use humour and gay sexuality to achieve perspective.

A year after *Sons of Ulster*, Robin Glendinning pleased English critics and shocked Northern Irish audiences with an explicit presentation of gay sexuality in *Mumbo Jumbo* (1986), set in a Belfast boarding school that simultaneously inculcates standard loyalist political propaganda and provides an opportunity for students to explore sexuality many people would regard as non-standard.

By October 1994, when first the IRA and then the combined Loyalist Military Command (Ulster Defence Association, Ulster Volunteer Force and the Red Hand Commandos) announced ceasefires that led eventually to a fragile peace agreement, most of these dramatic voices had ceased, or ceased to dwell on the Troubles. For all practical purposes, Charabanc and Field Day no longer existed. Stewart Parker had died. Graham Reid, Christina Reid and Anne Devlin were writing little. Brian Friel and Frank McGuinness had turned their creative energies elsewhere. New voices focused on the Protestant community long stereotyped as hostile to the arts. *The Mourning Ring* (1995), a Protestant community play (directed, as almost everyone noted, by a Catholic), juxtaposed scenes from seventeenth-century history with scenes set in the present. And Gary Mitchell produced *In a Little World of Our Own* (1997), the first of several dramas focusing on the Protestant Belfast community from which he came.

Increasingly, though, dramatic attention was shifting from the Troubles to reconciliation of the sort dealt with early on by Charabanc and represented later by McGuinness's *Sons of Ulster*. Several innovative productions sought to promote healing. In *Loved Ones* (1995), a play based on interviews, Damian Gorman created parallel grieving mothers, one of whom lost her son to a bomb planted by the other son, who is now in prison – a sort of updating of Sean O'Casey's *Juno and the Paycock*, except that the mothers attempt a direct reconciliation.

Marie Jones and Martin Lynch, who first noted the similarity of their cross-cultural working-class backgrounds when they were involved with Charabanc, collaborated with community actors to develop *The Wedding Community Play* (1999). The tale of a cross-cultural marriage was played in real time, and audiences were bussed between four actual Belfast locations. The short physical distance between Protestant and Catholic communities emphasized the far larger political/cultural distance. More notably, *convictions* (2000) combined seven short plays (by Daragh Carville, Damian Gorman, Marie Jones, Martin Lynch, Owen McCafferty, Nicola McCartney and Gary Mitchell) with art installations in the Crumlin Road Courthouse and Jail, the site of numerous trials, convictions and imprisonments. The production, an extraordinary reclaiming of space, brought audiences to a controversial site to examine present and past attitudes to the building's physical, political and cultural heritage. Neither production is repeatable in any real sense, but both represent extraordinary uses of theatre to address issues of cultural concern.

As the thematic focus of plays shifted from the Troubles to reconciliation, it shifted as well from the past – which, after all, provided few models of healing. It did not shift from the urban landscape that had been a primary site of the Troubles. Nor did playwrights abandon the use of regional humour and language. Unlike novels or television, drama is a community experience, demanding public engagement and reaction. Plays of the Troubles pulled important issues from obscurity into light. To do so without exacerbating tensions required writers to discover vantage points from which to identify important features of the cultural typography around them. They did not answer the eternal question of whether humans repeat the past because they have forgotten it, or because they cannot forget it. And plays, like poetry, may make nothing happen. But at their best, which came frequently, plays of the Troubles grappled powerfully with what it means to be human, and with what the arts can do to make us more so.

NOTES

1   Tom Murphy's *The Blue Macushla* (1980) and *The Patriot Game* (1991), though, are essentially Troubles plays by a writer from deep in the Republic.
2   Seamus Heaney (1983). 'Introduction' in *Sweeney Astray: A Version from the Irish*. London: Faber and Faber, n.p.
3   See, for example, 'In Interview with Eavan Boland' (1973), repr. in Murray (1999: 58).
4   'In Interview with Laurence Finnegan' (1986), repr. in Murray (1999: 125).
5   'An Off-Stage Irish Drama', *Guardian*, Saturday 31 July 1999.
6   Anne Devlin (1986). *Ourselves Alone* (with *A Woman Calling* and *The Long March*). London: Faber, 10.
7   'In Conversation with Enrica Cerquoni' in Lilian Chambers, Ger FitzGibbon and Eamonn Jordan (eds.) (2001). *Theatre Talk: Voices of Irish Theatre Practitioners*. Dublin: Carysfort Press, 107–23, esp. 108, 117.
8   Preface in *Ireland's Field Day* (1985). London: Hutchinson, vii.
9   'In Interview with Fintan O'Toole' (1982), repr. in Murray (1999: 107).
10 Brian Friel (1981). *Translations*. New York: Samuel French, 80. Hugh is echoing George Steiner's (1975) *After Babel: Aspects of Language and Translation* (Oxford: Oxford University Press), a work that heavily influenced Friel.
11 The Abbey Theatre Archives hold copies of most reviews of the theatre's productions. Copies are also in the Tilling Archives, privately held by Philip Tilling in Coleraine, Northern Ireland.

PRIMARY READING

Most plays discussed here are readily available, and only those appearing in less obvious places are listed below. Complete publication information on all Irish plays produced after 1950 is available at www.irishplayography.com. *State of Play*, edited by Ophelia Byrne (2001), has publication information on all twentieth-century Ulster plays. Belfast's Linen Hall Library (www.linenhall.com) has an extensive theatre archive, including unpublished scripts, and programme materials. The Irish Theatre Archives in Dublin hold some of the same material.

Carville, Daragh, Gorman, Damian, Jones, Marie et al. (2000). *convictions*. Belfast: Tinderbox Theatre Company.

Charabanc (2001). *Somewhere Over the Balcony* in Helen Gilbert (ed.). *Postcolonial Plays: An Anthology*. London: Routledge, 443–69.

Woods, Vincent (1998). *At the Black Pig's Dyke* in John Fairleigh (ed.). *Far from the Land: Contemporary Irish Plays*. London: Methuen, 1–61.

FURTHER READING

Byrne, Ophelia (ed.) (2001). *State of Play: The Theatre and Cultural Identity in 20th Century Ulster*. Belfast: Linen Hall Library.

'Conflict and Politics in Northern Ireland (1968 to the Present)'. Conflict Archive on the Internet (CAIN). University of Ulster/Magee: cain.ulst.ac.uk.

Murray, Christopher (1997). ' "A Modern Ecstasy": Playing the North' in *Twentieth-Century Irish Drama: Mirror Up to Nation*. Manchester: Manchester University Press, 187–222.

Murray, Christopher (ed.) (1999). *Brian Friel: Essays, Diaries, Interviews: 1964–1999*. London: Faber and Faber.

Pilkington, Lionel (2001). *Theatre and State in Twentieth Century Ireland: Cultivating the People*. London: Routledge.

Richards, Shaun (ed.) (2004). *The Cambridge Companion to Twentieth-Century Irish Drama*. Cambridge: Cambridge University Press.

Richtarik, Marilynn (1995). *Acting Between the Lines: The Field Day Theatre Company and Irish Cultural Politics, 1980–1984*. Oxford: Oxford University Press.

28

On War: Charles Wood's Military Conscience

Dawn Fowler and John Lennard

What we must understand is precisely what it means when somebody says we are now going to go to war with another country, because that war may be considered just but as soon as the first shot is fired it becomes unjust. That is the character of war. As soon as you start killing justice goes out the window.

(Wood 2005a: 16)

Charles Wood is Britain's most perceptive and prolific dramatic interrogator of soldiering, military leadership and the politics of war, yet he figures little in received British theatre history. His stage and screen plays have often been controversial – Richard Findlater argued of *Dingo* (1967) that Wood had 'more trouble with the Lord Chamberlain than any other dramatist' (Findlater 1967: 178). In the preface to Wood's *Plays One*, Richard Eyre, a director long associated with his work, declares:

There is no contemporary writer who has chronicled the experience of modern war with so much authority, knowledge, compassion, wit and despair, and [. . .] received so little of his deserved public acclaim. [. . .] If John Osborne was always looking forward to the past, Charles Wood has always looked the present in the face through the prism of the decline of the British Empire, the legacy of the First World War, the vainglory of the Falklands War, or the immutable stalemate of Northern Ireland. (Wood 1997: 8–9)

Later in his preface, however, Eyre admits his own 'faint-heartedness' in not having done more 'to argue the case for Charles' work in the theatre', and supposes Wood's work is unfashionable because it is 'uncompromisingly painful and tells such uncomfortable truths' (Wood 1997: 9). From a sometime director of the National Theatre, subject to more pressures than most of us can imagine, this is a bleakly pragmatic admission; but given how politically challenging and aesthetically inventive Wood's plays are his critical marginalization is very odd.

Born in Guernsey in 1932 into a theatrical family on tour, Wood spent a peripatetic childhood and adolescence in England observing and working in the repertory theatres at which his parents were employed. He thus lived through the war of 1939–45 as an increasingly responsible observer and participant in productions practically dependent on and properly sensitive to audiences of serving soldiers and their kin. More traditional education at Chesterfield Grammar, at King Charles I School, Kidderminster, and in a foundation year at Birmingham College of Art was overmatched in 1946–9 by intensified family demands when Wood's father became theatre manager at the Kidderminster Playhouse:

> I would do the get-out and the get-in and the build up when I could. That meant getting out the set on Saturday night, taking it up to the station, getting it onto a carriage. They had special carriages for moving scenery you know at that time. Then the new show would come in either on the Sunday or the Monday early in the morning. And if I wasn't at school, and sometimes I would not go to school, I would help get the set in and build it up. That was the exciting time of my life and we saw some wonderful productions. I saw a whole range of scenic design from the very bad to the absolutely brilliant. And I'd worked on setting them up, building them up and lighting them, then at night I used to work on the switchboard or wherever I was needed on the floor. Sometimes if it was a ballet company or an opera company, I would work on the floor changing all the gels and the floods and other things on the stage. And that was my life for quite a while. In between that I would do my revision and my homework up on a perch in the switchboard [*laughs*]. (Wood 2005a: 3)

The other necessity, of course, was the repertoire itself:

> I played everything. [...] all the juvenile leads in things like *The Winslow Boy* and *The Corn is Green* and [...] daft things in melodramas like *Sweeney Todd* and *East Lynne* and *Maria Marten* [...]. Dad even got me to play a sixty-two-year-old doctor in *The Cat and the Canary* – I still have a photograph of me made up looking just like a sixteen-year-old with a lot of hair on his face. [...] The important thing is I was seeing a lot of good stuff. I rarely saw anything from the front, from the audience. I couldn't because I was working, but I absorbed everything. I didn't see a play once: I saw it and I heard it for nine performances throughout the week. I heard the lines going on, and whatever that is, from rubbish to wonderful stuff, Shakespeare to any kind of other drama, you begin to get an idea of the form and you begin to understand what it is that makes a play work. And that was my grounding. I did that every night. [...] I knew that this was what actors did. This was what mum and dad did all the time and it wasn't strange to be asked to do it. (Wood 2005a: 4–5)

But at the same time 'I didn't like acting – I hated it. I found it too exposing. That's the point of acting, of course. But I had no choice. My parents were actors and I was expected to go on and do my bit' (Wood 2005b: 3). At 18, with his one-year student grant for art college expiring, Wood became liable for two years of National Service. Taking the bull by the horns (which allowed him to choose his regiment), Wood pre-empted his call-up and enlisted for a five-year tour with the 17th/21st (now Queen's Royal) Lancers (1950–5), and for seven further years remained in the Reserve. Biographical sketches sometimes describe his joining the army as rebellion against the theatrical career that would reclaim him, but it was more a mix of need and young male passion – 'I joined the army to get some sort of order into my life [. . . and] because I liked the idea of being a soldier' (Wood 2005a: 5) – reflecting Wood's forcible connection to militarized reality as much as to dramatized imagination and theatrical grind.

Nor should his choice of regiment be forgotten. The 17th/21st Lancers, whose motto is the death's head with 'Or Glory' slung beneath, had a long and distinguished history as cavalry, but (like other lancer regiments) of necessity became a tank unit – finally bowing in 1938 to the brutal lesson that began when the Light Brigade led by the 17th Lancers charged the Russian guns at Balaclava in 1854, losing 247 of 670 officers and men, and prompting Maréchal Bosquet to remark 'C'est magnifique, mais ce n'est pas la guerre.'[1] The social patterns and inherited traditions of such a regiment are strong, and Wood, though serving principally as a tank-radio operator, was lectured about Balaclava and other regimental history, and was at the annual regimental memorial celebrations of the charge; but tanks are (like submarines) a modern branch of service with peculiar combat-horrors, and Wood was also serving with and under men who had seen hard action against the Germans in North Africa and Italy (1942–5), and subsequently been in Greece (1946), Egypt (1947) and Palestine (1948) – where the regiment lost two officers and fourteen other ranks. Most of Wood's own service was with the British Army of the Rhine, clanking through early Cold War exercises and manoeuvres, and latterly in Britain as an instructor, but the realities of combat were never far away. Other British units were in those years deployed to Korea, the Middle East, Malaya (where a very bitter clandestine war was brewing) and Kenya; the army as a whole took regular, sometimes substantial casualties, especially in Korea, and as Wood left regular service in 1955 the Cyprus emergency was beginning. While stationed in England in 1954 he had married Valerie Newman, an actress, so there were family matters and obligations to consider. As a husband of 23, and after five years of real soldiering, the needs that had driven Wood to enlist were assuaged, but in re-entering civilian life he took with him not only experience of the Lancers and their history, but military contacts and a focus of emotional concern with continuing British military deployments that have informed his best drama.

Professional theatre offered only poverty, and for a year Wood worked in Bristol in missile manufacture, using his army training. He then went with his family to Canada for 18 months, working as a commercial artist and learning the newspaper side of that business, before returning to London in 1957 and finding a job as stage manager at Theatre Workshop with John Bury and Joan Littlewood. If exhilarating and instructive, it also paid very badly, and after trying freelance work as a scenic artist for a while, Wood moved back to Bristol and an art job on the *Evening Post* that he held until 1963. He was acquainted there with Tom Stoppard, also on staff, but his real prompt to becoming a writer seems to have been a realization (as Paddy

Tim Preece, Alfred Lynch and Norman Rossington in Wood's *Prisoner and Escort* (1964). Photo: ABC Television.

Chayevsky and the revolutionary new capacity of video-tape arrived in Britain) that there could be decent money in *television* drama.

Wood wrote *Prisoner and Escort* in 1959 as a screen play, but it had an initial airing on radio, and then needed to be adapted for the stage (with *John Thomas* and *Spare*) as part of Wood's *Cockade* trilogy at the Arts Theatre in 1963, before finally being produced in its intended medium by ITV in 1964. By then *Dingo* had started its tortuous path to production, and Wood's dual mark – as a 'difficult' stage writer and as a television writer – was already manifest. His attitude to his various media, moreover, was unusual:

> dramatic writing is dramatic writing and I never found any difficulty in going from radio to the stage to film, and even to television [. . .] The only difference between a film and a television-film is you put your shoulders back and breathe more deeply if you are going to write a film. That's all you do, you just expand. Even if you only have three

characters in a room you feel that there is a greater dimension if you are writing for film, that's all. But it is exactly the same kind of dramatic writing and good dramatic writing fits everything. (Wood 2005a: 7)

These academically unpalatable propositions are powerfully borne out in Wood's career, which includes a sequence of plays staged at major theatres[2] as well as many original films and adaptations, and original television plays and adaptations. After cataloguing 17 stage plays or adaptations, 14 films or adaptations, and 20 television plays or adaptations (but, tellingly, only 10 publications), *Who's Who* calmly gives Wood's recreations as 'military and theatrical studies; gardening' and his clubs as 'Royal Over-Seas League, British Playwrights' Mafia' – the tokens of an identity, devotions and a humour that have simply not been critically understood.

Theatrically and dramatically, three most interesting tropes overlap: a grounding in pre-war repertory, a visual sensibility extending from set-painting and design to cinematic framing, and a career strung between old and new media of performance. That most critics and scholars fall between poles or know only fragments explains some of the neglect; another factor is a defensive tendency to construe Wood's stage drama as satirical, and hence to set his theatrical and military careers at odds – which is absurd. Regimental military life is intrinsically theatrical, and most military life full of amateur dramatics – as Wood understood before, during and after his service. Blunt labelling of his work masks the deployment of modes such as camp concerts, socialist drama, pantomime, music-hall and cinematic abbreviation. Polemicism also misses the deep respect Wood has for serving soldiers, including those in command, however he may represent individuals, and theatre historians have too often misunderstood and mangled the theatrical modalities of Wood's stage work.

The best of Wood's plays are characterized both by experimental ambitiousness in form and visual invention, and by representation of compelling linguistic worlds. From the squaddie-dialects of *Cockade* and *Dingo*, Victorian intonations of *H*, collapse-of-empire slang of *Jingo* and distinctive Gielgud voice in *Veterans*,[3] Wood is in the very best sense a stage Kipling, experimenting with speech-patterns and idioms deployed within varying theatrical parameters. Richard Eyre, drawn to Wood's work by his own strongly visual directorial imagination, eloquently describes the multiplicity:

> You could call Charles Wood a playwright, poet, and a painter. The playwright speaks for himself on the stage and on the screen; the poet is revealed in the text through the repeated rhythms, the hint of rhyme, the stylized translation of conversation, and in the emergence of an idiosyncratic and obsessional voice; the painter is latent in the stage directions: indelible images of a sandhill and a tank in the desert; [...] a moonlit soldier stumbling through a perpetual night under the burden of his full kit [...]
> (Wood 1997:7)

In addition to these performative complexities, Wood's reputation for controversy has as much to do with his refusal to compromise in politics as with the unflinching portrayals of the brutal and futile aspects of war on which the press have intermittently seized. Wood admits being uninterested in writers who are not in some sense subversive, and sees it as the playwright's role to challenge conventions of form and content, but never advocates shock for shock's sake (Wood 1987: x). He does, however, consistently deconstruct myths of infallible heroism bestowed on historical figures like Winston Churchill, parodied by the comic in *Dingo* urinating on the West Wall of Hitler's Germany, and General Havelock, shown delirious and dying of dysentery in *H*. And Wood's simultaneous movements beyond acceptable realism baffle and outrage: in *Dingo* an audience hears 'Chalky' White burning to death in a tank before his charred corpse is brought on as a grotesque ventriloquist's dummy, and in *H* the practical Surgeon Sooter performs an impromptu amputation by biting off a man's gangrenous finger – but these kinds of things are quite mild (if very effective) distortions of routines beloved in the music-hall, pantomime and Grand Guignol.

The breadth and variety of Wood's work demand a proper assessment, at full biographical and critical length, but with the scholarly and historical grounds of consideration cleared a little, our initial proposition can serve as a guide to that core of Wood's stage work directly concerning military life and actions. Film and television work must sometimes be admitted, following Wood's own lack of distinction, but what is dramatically at stake is an extended, coherent and badly neglected part of Britain's theatrical struggle since 1945 to represent and understand the state of affairs in which it has devastatingly found itself.

Wood's military-theatrical career began with *Cockade* (Arts Theatre, London, 1963), a trilogy of short plays about postwar army life adapted from material written over several years, for which he won the *Evening Standard Award* for Most Promising New Writer in 1963.[4] The swearing and barrack-room slang weaving through the dialogue of *Prisoner and Escort*, *John Thomas* and *Spare* was a part of army life previously unheard on the stage: 'no one had told the truth about life in the army quite like this before. Wood signalled the rise of 1960s iconoclasm' (Chambers 1997: 115). But the dominant theme of the three plays is not verisimilar obscenity but articulate protest at the cyclical nature of war. In *Prisoner and Escort*, the detainee Jupp is sent to military prison for urinating on the boots of a German officer on parade; this was not childish petulance, as his escorts believe, but a political protest at what he sees as the futility of uniting with the previous enemy against the previous ally (Russia) in a never-ending vicious circle:

> Standing there – rank on rank of wet khaki simpletons – none of you saw. None of you felt a thing. Standing there – best boots gleaming – buffed up like a lot of thick as muck guardsmen. Medals out too – that's what got me – bloody medals. (Wood 1962: 18)

It emerges that most men in his family have died horrifically in recurrent conflict, and his action stands as an ultimately futile protest at this injustice. *Prisoner and Escort*,

Wood admits, was 'a kind of reaction'[5] to a farcical popular comedy, *The Army Game*, five series of which ran on the ITV network from 1957 to 1961. It focused on a group of incompetent National Service recruits presided over by the appropriately named Sergeant-Major Bullimore, and treated its army subject matter with a distinct British absurdity that Wood stripped away to much darker effect. His Corporal Blake, in charge of Jupp, tortures and goads him to pathetic submission in a brutalizing and merciless environment.

In *Spare*, the last play, Wood reinforces Jupp's bleak views by dispensing with naturalism in favour of a more impressionistic representation of military life when one of the soldiers goes to his death by jumping off the stage into smoke, only to return as another soldier, suggesting he is bound to a wheel of death. The title insinuates an endless stream of dispensable lives, where spares can instantly replace fallen soldiers in a boundless cycle, and it is the pointlessness of killing measured against the individuality of living soldiers that informs *Dingo*, Wood's first full-length play, written in 1961.[6]

Its development can equally be traced in shorter army plays, some performed, some not, in which Wood can be seen developing his voice and experimenting with different scenarios. What emerges throughout this early work is exploration of the British attempt to gloss negatives in a soldier's existence with gallant stereotype.[7] In the irreverent comedy *Don't Make me Laugh* (Aldwych Theatre, 1966), for example, part of the *Cockade* trilogy before giving way to *Prisoner and Escort*, a corporal shows a sergeant his severely injured leg: 'see that … look at that … I've lost a packet of ginger hairs. Makes you sick.' He later argues that his injury 'Could go cancerous … might well be on the way to poisoning the whole system.'[8] Wood explicitly uses the injury as a symbol for the harsh realities of soldiering that civilians and some soldiers would prefer to ignore. The corporal's wife orders him to keep his leg 'out of sodding sight out of sodding mind', while the sergeant concludes 'It's not all nice curtains in the windows and good furniture – you've got to be tough.'[9] What this and other plays show is a writer exposing truths usually hidden inside barracks, and a preoccupation, like Kipling's but more personally experienced, with working-class NCOs and private soldiers going about their business.

Wood's experience with Theatre Workshop led him to hope that Littlewood would like *Dingo*, and it is written to benefit from the improvisation and intense rehearsal characteristic of her preparation. But Littlewood did not like *Dingo*, and pursued a quite different production, *Oh What A Lovely War* (1963, filmed 1968), a satirical musical about World War I that for Wood simply missed his point:

> you can't find anybody who says: 'Yes, that war was worth fighting.' You can find people who say the Second World War was worth fighting and in lots of ways it was. Whereas *Dingo* isn't at all about the reasons for fighting the Second World War, *Dingo* is a representation of the things we have been told about what that war was about. (Wood 2005a: 12)

Disappointed in Stratford East, Wood came close to production at the National Theatre in 1964, but the lord chamberlain refused a licence, and a member of the National's Board threatened to resign if it went on 'because he thought it subversive' (Wood 1999: 7). A memorandum by Kenneth Tynan, then literary manager, summarizes the objections: aside from demands to cut obscene language and blasphemy, other problems relate to the representation of 'George VI not wanting to be king'; concern that the General is too identifiable as Viscount Montgomery;[10] and the representations of Chalky's death, bayonettings and 'blood pouring out of Scot's mouth' as 'needlessly horrific'.[11] *Dingo* was also regarded as politically dangerous (or felt as emotionally unacceptable) because it directly played against the received ideologies of British valour in war, and appeared to impugn Churchill. It might have become the first new play staged at the National Theatre (opened in 1963), but was eventually performed in 1967 at the Royal Court under club conditions to evade censorship.

Behind the fate of becoming a cause before it was fully a play is *Dingo*'s grounding in the experience of living soldiers. Willis Hall's *The Long and the Short and the Tall* (Royal Court, 1959), set in a Malayan jungle during the Japanese advance on Singapore in 1942, savagely critiques military action, but Wood alone among the emerging English playwrights of the 1960s seriously attempted to represent the horrors of the modern battlefield and inventively attacked the bland rhetorics of its public heroization. In Act 1 Scene 5, when the eponymous Dingo placates Tanky, losing his mind after witnessing Chalky burning, he suggests the charred corpse could not possibly be a British soldier:

> Do you think we'd risk offending every mother here tonight with unlikely looking material. Highly upset they'd be. That's enemy. People out there lost their dear ones – that's enemy. No British soldier dies like that. That's enemy. You won't find a photograph, a statue, a painting of a British soldier like that. (Wood 1999: 304)

Dingo's assertion and the gruesome image of Chalky's corpse are reminders that the adversary's pain and suffering often mirror one's own. Shielding ourselves from the deathly reality of war, Wood suggests, is a dangerous business serving only to promote future conflicts.

Eyre emphasizes Wood's interest in 'the profession of soldiering, and the point of being a soldier is to break the ultimate taboo – the point is to destroy the enemy on our behalf, to kill people' (Wood 1997: 8). *Dingo* presents this 'ultimate taboo' from the viewpoint of both the British and their erstwhile enemies. It opens in the Western Desert in October 1942, where Dingo and Mogg, in sun-bleached khaki, have a conversation which has been compared to the banter between Beckett's Vladimir and Estragon in 'arch literariness', 'vaudeville skittishness and the comic pointlessness of everything that is being done' (Hayman 1979: 65):

DINGO: The thing about fighting in the desert is that it is a clean war – without brutality. And clean-limbed – without dishonourable actions on either side.
MOGG: They say.
DINGO: And there are no civilians.
MOGG: Except me – I'm a civilian.
DINGO: What am I then?

(Wood 1999: 268)

Here as elsewhere *Dingo* mixes elements of absurdism, music-hall, expressionism, the comedy skit and realism, as army theatricals and many other kinds of popular theatrical evening often do without much caring about it, but Wood has rarely been extended either the understanding or the baffled respect that Beckett won as *Waiting for Godot* and *Endgame* settled into the repertoire.

One block that should not be underestimated (certainly where the National Theatre is concerned) was disrespectful representation of Churchill, whose state funeral in 1965 would for some have put *Dingo* even further out of the question. Wood was partly responding to his own knowledge of the dubious mechanisms used in wartime to promote unquestioning loyalty such as newspapers urging the 'duty of the nation' to rally around Churchill, while proclaiming him 'one of those who have never been deceived by the character and purpose of our treacherous enemy'.[12] He also drew a Churchill quite recognizable from the ranks (and Churchill had been prime minister for the last time in 1951–5), in popular caricatures predating his post-World War II canonization as the Great Leader, and in more revisionist modern histories – a leader with significant addictions who could be both domineering and impetuous, and who sometimes had to be managed and dissuaded. In Act III he is seen in 'A Forward latrine somewhere in France. 1944' as a petulant drunk declaring:

I want a battle now. I am determined to get as much fun and personal satisfaction as I possibly can out of this war and bring my rich and rousing personality to bear upon the men and women engaged in the day-to-day jobs of battle. (Wood 1999: 346)

This scene is followed by a blackout in which a doctor is heard treating a young soldier with unimaginably horrific injuries amidst the sounds of battle; he orders any missing body parts found and preserved, and instructs 'the boy's' head be held up so he does not swallow blood: 'Of course he is screaming' he says (ibid.: 346). Scenes are juxtaposed in ways familiar from epic drama to contrast the politicians who send to war and those who are sent, and in the Royal Court club production Wood used two 10-minute intervals to show original news footage. Two years later Joe Orton would manage popularly to dismember Churchill in effigy in *What the Butler Saw* (Queen's Theatre, 1969), but without any hint of military accountability, and Wood's attack probably remains an impediment to the play's revival.

The working title, 'I Don't Hold with Heroes', changed at Kenneth Tynan's suggestion, had better pointed the play's stance against the unproblematic, politically mediated representation of World War II in popular culture. Wood remained dismayed by ideologically suspect historicizations and heroizing discourses of World War II that, *Dingo* insinuates, ultimately serve a war-enhancing purpose. Cinema also frequently falsified war in a way that Wood found offensive. He had already provided two successful screen plays for the director Richard Lester, *The Knack* (1965) and *Help!* (1966), which became emblematic of countercultural 'swinging London' – so in 1967 Wood wrote *How I Won the War* for Lester, a surreal parody of war films close in content and theme to *Dingo*. The joke in *How I Won the War* is that the inept second lieutenant played by Michael Crawford has not the slightest idea how to lead men, but at one point the cameraman is told to stop shooting, to which John Lennon, playing Private Gripweed (in a major triumph for Lester), responds 'No, let the bastards see', as though he is determined not to let the audience remain in an easy state of ignorance. A cult success in its day, the film remains helpful as a gloss on aspects of *Dingo*, and its success soon provided Wood with a major film vehicle – *The Charge of the Light Brigade*, with Trevor Howard as Lord Cardigan and John Gielgud as Lord Raglan, directed in 1968 by Tony Richardson.

Wood's script recounts a true story of the disastrous leadership of the 17th Lancers fighting on a confused day in 1854 in the indecisive and very costly Crimean War (which also generated the image of Florence Nightingale). Vanessa Redgrave, one of its starring actors, declared it 'a masterpiece of all time. I think it's one of the best films ever made about the British Empire and about the horror of war' (McFarlane 1997: 470). Certainly it is unsparing in condemning the incompetence that led to the disastrous charge at Balaclava – but Wood had detailed and exacting knowledge far superior to Redgrave's, and his script is equally scathing, for example, in its treatment of the British press, who instead of calling for calm heads and a halt to war are seen in quirky animated scenes stirring the nation with bloodthirsty calls for conflict. The film was released amid the turmoil of Vietnam and was a timely condemnation of the role in war of the news media – but for many critics these elements proved obstacles to understanding the remarkable theatricality of Wood's characterizations. Fascinatingly, Wood was on site during filming to monitor the dialogue, having researched period vernacular to create a florid speech full of Victorian colloquialisms and 'constructed it in such a way that it couldn't really be paraphrased' (Wood 2005a: 14). The film's panoramic composition, however, seems also to have invigorated the scene-designer and set-painter in Wood, with startling results.

Wood is interestingly credited with substantial contributions to Peter Brook's massive semi-devised Vietnam anti-war piece for the National, *U/S* (1968), but the play that is sharply remembered by all who saw it is *H: or Monologues at Front of Burning Cities*, an account of certain events during the Indian Mutiny, principally in 1857, staged at the National Theatre in 1969. One dramaturgical axis was language:

> I'd tried to invent this kind of language for *The Charge of the Light Brigade*, the inversions and the tricks of grammar. And mostly it goes back to the regiment I served in which was the 17th/21st Lancers. The 17th Lancers were in the Crimea and on the

charge and after the Crimea they went to India and were on the Indian Mutiny. I got interested in the war that came after the Crimea so I started to read up on the mutiny and I found this General Havelock, who seemed to me the epitome of the Victorian Christian who could nevertheless fight the most savage war with incredible ruthlessness. I was thinking about the problems between being a good Christian and being a good soldier. (Wood 2005a: 13)

The play begins with a superbly complex speech and set of observations by a bombardier of mixed race whose voice scorns and fears much that he sees but slides seamlessly between colloquial and imperial registers: the audience had to remain aurally alert, and readers of the play often have difficulty imagining the ease with which *H*'s complexities can be clarified on stage. The other axis was the gorgeous 'set-drops' against which all the dialogue was posed. An epic play that for *Sunday Times* critic Harold Hobson (1969) 'marks the National Theatre's return to form; and not to form only, but to ambition', *H* also ingeniously used the ornate frame of a Victorian toy-theatre to contain a series of tableaux presenting General Sir Henry Havelock.

This real-life Victorian war-hero is shown as a man whose heroic Christian ideals crucifyingly contrast with the brutal realities of his command. Havelock remains patriotic to a point of modern absurdity, fiercely believing that his Christian beliefs will guide him to victory:

> Soldiers. There is work
> before us. We are bound on
> an expedition whose object
> is to restore the Supremacy of
> British rule and avenge the
> fate of British men and women.
> (Wood 1999: 38)

The rhythm of this and many epic speeches in the play is set against the rough dialects of the ordinary soldiers, snatches of Hindi and terrible English maulings of it, and other complex distinctions of verbal identity. A resemblance to Shakespeare's masterpiece of military rhetoric, *Henry V*, is plain,[13] and like Henry before Agincourt Havelock believes that it is not only the soldier's job to obey orders (defeat rebels and restore order in India), but also their moral obligation to their commanders, although their killings lie on their own heads. He gives a speech to the troops comparing them to religious crusaders: 'The soldier can be a Saviour, should be a Saviour, in India is now a Saviour' (48). His son Harry provides a more practical, level-headed voice; he says of the mutineers: 'I am not able to even order them hanged, for I cannot order what I cannot do myself' (162) – a statement that both shows the difference between those who give and those who have to carry out orders, and suggests that however 'just' a war is considered, it should not be undertaken without moral heartache nor concluded without remorse. Wood extends *Dingo*'s condemnation of glorifying war to imperial ambition and colonization, as Captain Jones Parry sums up: 'I am sure every soldier feels his war to be the most interesting and famous, I should hope he do, he will not do much if he do not' (152).

One recurrent motif is the image of a violated woman, and Havelock urges the soldiers to remember the 'British ladies; our tenderly nurtured countrywomen' who are 'Innocents!' (Wood 1999: 38). Corporal Forbes Mitchell is less delicate when he finds the body of a naked girl after the relief of Cawnpore (Kanpur):

> We will cut the hairs from
> her head, you shall each man
> have a portion to send home
> and the rest we shall count hair
> by hair, every hair on this young
> white woman's head, and for every
> hair counted we vow that one of the
> rebels shall die.
>
> (Wood 1999: 87)

This (and the underlying supposition of pre-mortem rape) fills exhausted troops with hate and anger, fuelling desire for revenge and capacity for barbarism. The thought of foreigners who are heathens violating and killing 'their' women appeals to an exaggerated masculinity, partly in a soldier's function but corrupted by the psycho-politics of this imperial emergency to inspire a mob in the service of supposedly justified and exemplary militant-Christian vengeance. These scenes, unpalatable and 'surely' false to many, are in fact sharply historical, and attempts politically to understand events at Cawnpore equally inform Forster's *A Passage to India* (1924) and Scott's *The Jewel in the Crown* (1966).[14] As Harry Havelock puts one side of it, 'Hate is a powerful aid to marching / I am sure, when the spirit is strained / out' (Wood 1999: 90) – but *H* as a whole insists on the consequences of that hate, and anticipated the most popular modern history, Christopher Hibbert's *The Great Mutiny: India 1857*,[15] in openly asking the hard questions about British conduct.

Havelock eventually dies on the bare boards of the stage holding his son's hand and begging that his grave will not become 'a shrine to me'. Instead he asks 'put up the simple words of Christ' (172). Hobson wrote that Wood 'makes Havelock's greatness more palpable, not less, by having him die on the stage whilst relieving his bowels' (*Sunday Times* 16 February 1969), as the staged elements of Victorian theatre are removed to show a hero as vulnerable and mortal as any person. But *H* is a hugely ambitious project for any theatre company, and the National Theatre struggled with costs. Where *Dingo* thrives in 'warehouses, drill/church halls, small ramshackle theatres that are simple performing spaces' (Wood 1999: 7), *H*'s epic scale needs a large space and painstaking direction.

A further and consequent correction can be seen in Wood's next stage play, *Veterans* (Royal Court, 1972), his greatest financial stage success.[16] He had written the part of

Havelock for John Gielgud, who turned it down, supplying Wood in his refusal with the subtitle 'Monologues at Front of Burning Cities' (Wood 2005a: 16–17). Wood then wrote another Gielgud part in *Veterans*, this time parodying the great actor's speech-patterns, and to Wood's surprise Gielgud agreed to play Sir Geoffrey Kendle alongside John Mills as 'Dotty' D'Orsay, two elderly actors waiting around on a film-set where something like *The Charge of the Light Brigade* is being made. The play incorporates jokes about the cost of such an epic, and condemns the media's concentration on trivial spin-offs of war rather than the thing itself. The same theme emerges in Wood's last play for the National Theatre, *Has Washington Legs?* (1978), which concerns itself with the problems of making a film about the American War of Independence. But the earlier and greater *Veterans* works predominantly as a homage to Gielgud – scion of the Terry dynasty and a product of theatre life like Wood himself – and through him to qualities that might seem most to be mocked by the satirical elements of Wood's dramaturgy. 'Future students of acting', wrote Ronald Bryden, 'who wish to understand [Gielgud's] peculiar grace will refer, not to *The Charge [of the Light Brigade]*, James Agate's notices or Rosamund Gilder's line-by-line analysis of his Hamlet, but to this [...] most endearing portrait of an actor ever drawn' (Roberts 1989: 71). Despite Wood's delicious characterization of Kendle as foul-mouthed and lewd, an iconoclastic send-up of Gielgud's received image at which critics predictably rebelled, audiences did not, as Gielgud had not, and the small-scale self-deprecation allowed an intensity of historical criticism and evaluation as well as celebration of a perfectly British character.

With his next play, *Jingo* (Royal Shakespeare Company (RSC), 1975), Wood turned to the fall of Singapore in 1941, which marked the end of British dominion in South Asia. It is set among the British officer class in the luxurious Raffles hotel, where 'frightfully flighty' Gwendoline is a serial officer's wife (Wood 1999: 185), as yet from choice rather than bereavement. Current husband George is disastrously (but again historically) blasé about danger: 'Who is going to bomb us, the little yellow men? Like to see them try' (ibid.: 192). Ex-husband Ian, a major in the Royal Engineers, also reveals this racist underestimation of the Japanese, which resulted in the mass surrender of more than 100,000 British and Indian troops, the largest Allied capitulation of the war, with political consequence throughout the empire. Again, while the incompetence, horrifying xenophobia and blind stupidity of those who gave orders is made plain, Wood insists that one of the tragedies in the fall of empire is the tragedy of those who believed in it.

Towards the end of the play Percy, a colonel who is pursuing Gwendoline, demands she thrash him for a long list of failures during the fighting: 'Blame me for the whole wretched business, I would wish to be blamed. I am responsible for the end of the British Empire as we know it' (ibid.: 238). Gwendoline eventually obliges, but Wood lets her condemn herself with the last word: 'Well, all in all, I hope this play has made you feel that in spite of the troublous times we live in, it is still pretty exciting to be English' (259). Wood was partly continuing and extending the imperial South Asian legacies of Cawnpore by tying in the masochism once internationally known as 'the

English disease', and interestingly parallels J. G. Farrell's movement from *The Siege of Krishnapur* (1973), based on the Mutiny Siege of Lucknow, to *The Singapore Grip* (1978), but also broaches the wider topic of imperialism and sexuality, explored in Caryl Churchill's *Cloud Nine* (1972). The hotel itself, named after imperial adventurer and founder of Singapore Sir Stamford Raffles (1781–1826), but also invoking the gentleman-burglar created by E. W. Hornung (1866–1921) in four novels of 1899–1909,[17] remains even today a byword for bygone elegance and archaic grandeur drenched in oriental promise, and if the set of *Jingo* properly evokes the place, questions should be asked about the geography and situation these British exports were placed in as much as about the exports themselves.

Yet again, by now unsurprisingly, *Jingo*, like *Dingo*, was a play more appreciated by actors and directors than audiences. Patrick Stewart glossed its complexity in saying it 'moved me deeply and with a complicated mixture of nostalgia and affection, rage and loathing'.[18] The RSC's then artistic director, Trevor Nunn, pondered the fact that *Jingo* was 'an original, distinctive, apposite, funny play', but wrote to Wood shortly afterwards, saying the RSC 'wants to do your work' but was looking for 'a big popular success that would run for a year! [. . .] the Ben Jonson in you [. . .] the breadth of your *Light Brigade* script, the scale of *H*'.[19] In short, Wood's prodigious talent was clearly recognized – adaptations by him were to be staged at the National Theatre in 1989 and 1993, and at the Almeida in 1995 – but fears of an unreliable box office prevented any warmer theatrical embrace, even from a subsidized company.[20] After 1979, when the 'Winter of Discontent' swept Margaret Thatcher to power, and her 'Khaki' re-election in 1983, the jaws of enforced commercialization and a great political arousal of jingoism inexorably foreclosed on the opportunities the author of *Jingo* could find in live theatre.

Wood has continued to write about the army in various media, and with *Tumble-down* (BBC, 1989), which won a BAFTA for Best Single Drama, achieved perhaps his greatest success. Based on the life of Robert Lawrence, an officer horrifically injured in the Falklands-Malvinas War of 1983, *Tumbledown* is one of the definitive British television dramas of the later century, and became notorious via a right-wing press (already stirred by the row over Ian Curteis's *The Falklands Play*) who called on the BBC not to show it because it included the army's dismissive treatment of the partially paralysed Lawrence. Highly placed army officers and governmental officials also objected to its implicit and explicit critiques of strategy, tactics, logistics and personnel management, raising questions about the propriety of filming the story so soon after events. Wood, moreover, apportioned no blame to the Argentine sniper who caused the injury, and whom Lawrence came to realize was only doing the same job as himself – not a view appreciated by Thatcher's government, though common among professional soldiers. That there was at least some command-level disquiet seems clear, and Lawrence was personally 'ostracized by his regiment' (Wood 2005a: 19), but no real research has yet been done on how British or Argentine veterans of the conflict might understand the play, or what presently serving officers and other ranks might think.

For Wood himself, far more personally than with Havelock in *H*, *Tumbledown*'s focus on an officer also represented an evolution in his personal understanding and consequent dramaturgy:

> Robert is a dear friend of ours. [...] Yes I felt very protective but I could do little. Robert thank God was a big enough chap – he knew how to deal with it. The interesting thing about Robert is when I first met him I thought I hated everything he stood for. [...] As far as I was concerned he came from a privileged background, he was a guards officer (who really are on the whole pretty awful) – all he cared about was women and fast cars and all that. But by the time I got to know him I absolutely adored him – I thought he was a marvellous young man. And I think it shows in the piece that I got to know him rather well and admired him tremendously because he was a very courageous chap. Not in the accepted sense shall we say, in the sense of being a courageous soldier, but being a courageous man. The way he dealt with his injuries was I think quite admirable. (Wood 2005a: 19)

Officers too, especially in action and not necessarily in the end, are individuals, and though Wood did not himself see combat, it is a measure of the understanding of it the army instilled in him that his acknowledgements of Lawrence's individual worth and military shortcomings could co-exist with a far more hostile political analysis of the forces that brought Lawrence to his doom.

In the light of recent international politics, Wood's plays remain as bitingly pertinent as ever. Yet he does not presume to offer us any solutions to the soldier's problems, or hint of a brighter future, or attempt to suggest a way to change the established order of things. Orders must still be followed, the army is a vital institution and Wood has never pretended otherwise. An efficient military, he argues however, demands a competent and moral leadership, and if we are to send soldiers out to fight in our (supposed) defence, we must fully understand what it is they endure, outgrowing past glorifications of war. In his plays, as we watch ordinary soldiers of many ranks and variant identities attempt to make sense of their experiences, to impose reason on their surroundings, we also witness the full tragedy of warfare, which eventually instils a sense of hopelessness into its recruits. Thus scrutinizing the military, Wood reminds us that while the army must work as a unit it is made of people as idiosyncratic, idealistic and individual as any citizen should hope to be.

NOTES

1 After the battle of Inkerman two weeks later Bosquet described the fiercely contested Sand Bag Battery as an abattoir.

2 Including the Royal Court (*Meals on Wheels*, 1965; *Dingo*, 1967; and *Veterans*, 1972, starring John Gielgud and John Mills); the National Theatre (*H: or Monologues at Front of Burning Cities*, 1969; and *Has Washington Legs?*, 1978); the Nottingham Playhouse (*Fill the Stage with Happy Hours*, 1967); an RSC production at the Aldwych Theatre (*Jingo*, 1975); and the Comedy Theatre (*Across from the Garden of Allah*, 1986).

3 Wood wrote the part specifically for Gielgud.

4 Wood shared the award this year with James Saunders for *Next Time I'll Sing to You*. Joe Orton came second with *Entertaining Mr Sloane* (but won Best Play).

5 Charles Wood, email to Dawn Fowler dated 13 July 2005.

6 For the manuscripts see the Charles Wood Papers (CW), in the Samuel Storey Archives (SSA), Borthwick Institute, University of York: *Dingo*, 1967: CW/2/27/1/1, W/2/27/1/2, CW/2/27/1/3, CW/2/27/1/4 (script annotated with inserts), CW/2/27/1/5 (script annotated with inserts).

7 See in particular the army plays, SSA, University of York: *The Princess and the Rifle*, 1960 (CW/2/85/1/1); *Step Short in Front*, 1961 (CW/2/101/1, CW/2/101/1/1); *The Drill Pig*, 1964 (CW/2/32/1/1 (early draft, undated), CW/2/32/1/1 (draft with annotations and amendments, undated), CW/2/32/1/3 (full script, 1964)); *Traitor in a Steel Helmet*, 1961 (CW/2/108/1/1 (full script with rehearsal and transmission information, August–September 1961)).

8 Charles Wood, *Don't Make Me Laugh*, SSA, University of York (CW/2/30/1/1), n.p.

9 Ibid., n.p.

10 On Montgomery's oddity see, Ronald Hyam (1990). *Empire and Sexuality: The British Experience*. Manchester and New York: Manchester University Press.

11 The memorandum is dated 11 February 1965. CW, SSA, University of York. As yet this item is uncatalogued.

12 *Daily Mirror*, Saturday 11 May 1940. CW, SSA: not yet catalogued.

13 This play depicting a nation fighting a legally and morally questionable war has inspired much of Wood's theatre work, and he cites the 1944 film adaptation directed by and starring Laurence Olivier as the most notable film he ever saw. 'The first real film I saw,' he declares, 'the first impressive film I saw where my brain said to me this is a good film you are seeing, and impressed me, was *Henry V*' (Wood 2005a: 2).

14 For grim details and analysis see Andrew Ward (1996). *Our Bones are Scattered: The Cawnpore Massacres and the Indian Mutiny of 1857*. London: John Murray.

15 Hibbert (1980); paperback edn. Harmondsworth: Penguin.

16 A rehearsed reading of *Veterans* was part of the Royal Court's celebration of its 50 years from 1956 to 2006.

17 *The Amateur Cracksman* (1899), *The Black Mask* (1901), *A Thief in the Night* (1905) and *Mr Justice Raffles* (1909).

18 CW, SSA, Patrick Stewart, letter to Charles Wood, 14 September 1975: as yet uncatalogued.

19 CW, SSA, letter from Trevor Nunn to Charles Wood, 3 November 1975: as yet uncatalogued.

20 In Wood's manuscripts there are letters from his agent, Peggy Ramsay, expressing concern about how his plays can be placed with theatres because of their unorthodoxy. CW, SSA, as yet uncatalogued.

Primary reading

The Charles Wood Papers form part of the Samuel Storey Archives (SSA) in the Borthwick Institute for Archives at the University of York. They include drafts of performed and unperformed scripts, publicity material and programmes, letters, directors' notes, film stock, and photographs from the late 1950s to the present.

Wood, Charles (1962). *Prisoner and Escort*. SSA: CW/2/86/1/1.

Wood, Charles (1965a). *Cockade: Prisoner and Escort, John Thomas* and *Spare* in *New English Dramatists 8*, 19–97. London: Penguin.

Wood, Charles (1965b). *Don't Make Me Laugh*. SSA: CW/2/30/1/1.

Wood, Charles (1978). *Has Washington Legs?* and *Dingo*. London: Methuen.

Wood, Charles (1987). *Tumbledown: A Screenplay*. Harmondsworth: Penguin.

Wood, Charles (1997). *Plays One: Veterans* and *Across From the Garden of Allah*. London: Oberon.

Wood, Charles (1999). *Plays Two: 'H', Jingo* and *Dingo*. London: Oberon.

Wood, Charles (2005a). Interview with Dawn Fowler, 30 March.

Wood, Charles (2005b). Interview with Mary Luckhurst, 4 December.

FURTHER READING

Brandt, George W. (1993). *British Television Drama in the 1980s*. Cambridge: Cambridge University Press.

Chambers, Colin (1997). *Peggy: The Life of Margaret Ramsey, Play Agent*. London: Nick Hern.

Croall, Jonathan (2001). *Gielgud: A Theatrical Life 1904–2000*. London: Methuen.

de Jongh, Nicholas (2000). *Politics, Prudery and Perversions: The Censoring of the English Stage, 1901–1968*. London: Methuen.

Eyre, Richard (2003). *National Service: Diary of a Decade at the National Theatre*. London: Bloomsbury.

Eyre, Richard and Wright, Nicholas (2000). *Changing Stages: A View of British Theatre in the Twentieth Century*. London: Bloomsbury.

Findlater, Richard (1967). *Banned! A Review of Theatrical Censorship in Britain*. London: Macgibbon and Kee.

Hall, Willis (1959). *The Long and the Short and the Tall*. London: Evans Brothers.

Hayman, Ronald (1979). *British Theatre since 1955*. Oxford: Oxford University Press.

Hobson, Harold (1969). 'Soldiers of the Queen' (review of Charles Wood's *H*), *Sunday Times* 16 February.

Hobson, Harold (1972). 'Review of Charles Wood's *Veterans*', *Sunday Times* 12 March.

Howard, Tony and Stokes, John (eds.) (1996). *Acts of War: The Representation of Military Conflict on the British Stage and Television since 1945*. Aldershot: Scolar Press.

Johnston, John (1990). *The Lord Chamberlain's Blue Pencil*. London: Hodder and Stoughton.

Lewenstein, Oscar (1994). *Kicking Against the Pricks: A Theatre Producer Looks Back*. London: Nick Hern.

McFarlane, Brian (1997). *An Autobiography of British Cinema*. London: Methuen.

Nichols, Peter (2000). *Diaries 1969–1977*. London: Nick Hern.

Nicholson, Steve (2003). *The Censorship of British Drama, 1900–1968*. Exeter: University of Exeter Press.

Roberts, Peter (ed.) (1989). *The Best of Plays and Players. Vol. Two: 1969–1983*. London: Methuen.

29

Torture in the Plays of Harold Pinter

Mary Luckhurst

Since World War II torture has become a major international human rights issue, as attested by the United Nations Declaration against Torture[1] and the work of charities such as Amnesty International. From his earliest dramas in the 1950s Nobel Prize-winning playwright Harold Pinter[2] (b. 1930) has shown an increasing interest in depicting torture, campaigning against it since the 1970s, and examining it overtly in his plays since the early 1980s – viewing it not just from a writer's perspective, but also as an actor and director.[3] Torture, as far as the United Nations understands it, is not intrinsically wrong provided it is carried out within the rule of law: it can be defined as the use of extreme stress or physical pain to make the subject willing to provide information, and to test the maximal truthfulness of what is said. There is, in the context of international law, a level of stressing during interrogation that is both morally and legally acceptable. But Pinter's concerns reflect research over the last decades by various human rights organizations whose conclusions may surprise and should appal: that torture is usually 'part of state-controlled machinery to suppress dissent', and that it is 'most often used as an integral means of a government's security strategy' (Amnesty International 1984: 4). He is particularly preoccupied with the hypocrisies of western democracies in relation to torture, especially those among the 150 nation-state signatories of the Geneva Convention in 1949 who renounced torture as criminal in both international and non-international armed conflicts, yet continue to turn over massive profit by producing and exporting the implements of torture. Western democracies themselves, especially the USA, Pinter has argued, increasingly abuse the very human rights they have instigated (*Various Voices*, 1998, and *War*, 2003). Scandals surrounding Iraqi detainees in Abu Ghraib (2004), as well as the incarceration of 'terrorists' at Guantanamo Bay (starting in 2002), have only served to fuel global controversy about the political ethics of torture and have reasserted its legality.[4] Pinter has been outspoken in his denunciation of both.

   Pinter's fascination with power politics, cruelty and violence is clear in his earliest plays: *The Birthday Party* (Arts Theatre, Cambridge, 1958), *The Room* (first staged by

Bristol University Drama Department, 1957; then Hampstead Theatre, 1960), *The Dumb Waiter* (premiered in Germany, 1959; Hampstead Theatre, 1960), *The Caretaker* (Arts Theatre, London, 1960) and *The Hothouse* (wr. 1958; premiered Hampstead Theatre, 1980). Martin Esslin has rightly argued that 'recurring figures of terrorists, torturers, and executioners' are located at the centre of Pinter's work, making him a playwright who has a particular resonance for the modern age, in an era 'of the Holocaust, genocide, and the nuclear bomb' (Burkman and Kundert-Gibbs 1993: 28). Even in the plays which do not directly represent torture and interrogation, Pinter is persistently intrigued by the role of cruelty and power in familial and erotic relationships.[5] Violence, he has acknowledged, 'has always been in my plays, from the very beginning [. . .] We are brought up every day of our lives in this world of violence' (Smith 2005: 93). But the brutality in his first plays was disturbing because – whilst realist conventions were recognizable – the psyches of perpetrators and victims remained unexplained, and the acts of cruelty were sudden and motiveless. If Pinter was initially interested in pitting apparently powerful figures against apparently helpless ones, his later scenarios have dispensed with ambiguity and become more extreme. Since *One for the Road* (Lyric Theatre Studio, 1984), the empowered and the victimized are identifiable from the start, their roles are not reversible, and they are symbolic of a larger picture of state oppression and abuse: the issue is only in what manner and over what period of time the victim will be systematically broken down and destroyed.

Pinter's first professionally performed play, *The Birthday Party* (1958), bemused its director Peter Wood as much as its critics and audiences. Wood thought the play flawed because Stanley does not justify his actions and fails to provide reasons for his vulnerability to the terror tactics of his unexpected visitors, the sinister duo of Goldberg and McCann (see Pinter's pre-rehearsal letter to Wood; Pinter 1998b: 8–11).[6] Wood also struggled with the style of the play, which draws on traditions of absurdism, realism, English comic revue and the grotesque surrealism of Franz Kafka. Stanley is a long-term lodger at a seaside boarding house run by Petey and his simple-minded but disturbingly flirtatious wife Meg; Stanley seems to fear discovery, and Goldberg and McCann promptly arrive, menacingly circling and closing in on him, subjecting him to bizarre interrogations before isolating him for their final assault. In under 24 hours Stanley disintegrates verbally, mentally and physically and is finally removed from the house by his interrogators to be taken to 'Monty', who will provide 'special treatment' (Pinter 1991a: 79). Petey tries to intervene as Goldberg and McCann take Stanley away, crying 'Leave him alone!' (79), but he is unequal to their threats of dispatching him as well and '*broken*' by what he is witnessing; so he merely implores: 'Stan, don't let them tell you what to do!' (80). Goldberg and McCann are recognizably generic heavies with characteristics familiar from 1950s thrillers, but they also indulge in verbal routines from music-hall (Billington 1996: 76–85). Their authority as mobsters is contradicted too by their ethnicities, one as a Jew and the other an Irishman (England knew virulent racism against both in the postwar years), and both have a tendency to launch into cod rhetoric about their blissful ethnic pasts. But their comedy is also counterpoised with ominous verbal and physical codes, which imply more than a waiting and baiting game; perpetrators and victim may also share secrets from the past. McCann's meticulous ripping of a newspaper into strips hints at a carefully controlled violence (31); his whistling of 'The Mountains of Morne' (in which Stanley joins) creates a tense stand-off between the two, suggesting that they have met before or once worked for the same organization (32); and Goldberg's symbolic snapping of Stanley's spectacles during a game of blind man's buff – itself a metaphor for a ludic ritual of displacement and dispossession (57) – comes after a prolonged play of suspense foregrounding Stanley's eyesight as an obvious locus of physical vulnerability. Goldberg and McCann's style of interrogation involves grotesque rounds of rapid-fire questions, all of which seem abstract yet also hint at a shared understanding of Stanley's fraudulence, inadequacy and criminality. In this scene, as in all of Pinter's interrogation scenarios, there is no interest in 'confession' or information-gathering: the tormentors indulge in an exercise of cruelty and destruction with the intent if not of complete elimination, then of permanent damage.

GOLDBERG: You stink of sin.
McCANN: I can smell it.
GOLDBERG: Do you recognize an external force?
STANLEY: What?
GOLDBERG: Do you recognize an external force? [...] No society would touch you.
   Not even a building society.
McCANN: You're a traitor to the cloth.
GOLDBERG: What do you use for pyjamas?
STANLEY: Nothing.
GOLDBERG: You verminate the sheet of your birth. [...] Why did the chicken cross
   the road?
STANLEY: He wanted...
McCANN: He doesn't know. He doesn't know which came first!
GOLDBERG: Which came first?
McCANN: Chicken? Egg? Which came first? Which came first? *Stanley screams.*

                                                                        (44–6)

Inclusion of old jokes aside, it is Stanley who is the butt of the real joke as far as the interrogators are concerned. He is accused of betraying religious, state, sexual, familial and basic ethical codes. Prevailing opinion has already sentenced Stanley to death for refusing conformity and for running away:

GOLDBERG: What makes you think you exist?
McCANN: You're dead.

                                                                        (46)

Their methods, continued off-stage during the night, bring about a catastrophic collapse. By the end Stanley cannot utter words, has lost control of his body, trembles easily, and in his mental confusion has tried to screw the lenses of his spectacles into his eye sockets. His torturers' jaunty stichomythic exchange becomes a sadistic anticipation of their victim's destruction, their listing of the ways he will be 're-oriented' and 'adjusted' a ghastly promise of future horrors to be inflicted on him (77).

Pinter has identified Nazi Germany, and specifically the Gestapo, Hitler's secret police, as an important background to the germination of *The Birthday Party* (Gussow 1994: 71; Smith 2005: 83). A Jew himself who as a child witnessed the bombing of London's East End during World War II, Pinter had good cause to ponder the knock at the door that so many Jews in continental Europe experienced, not to mention their subsequent fate. But this play, like all of Pinter's, resists straightforward readings. Goldberg and McCann, Pinter has argued, represent 'the hierarchy, the establishment, the arbiters, the socio-religious monsters [who] arrive to effect alteration and censure upon a member of the club who has discarded responsibility' (1998b: 11). In other words, *The Birthday Party* can be mapped onto any political or religious systems, and as Pinter has pointed out: 'Couldn't we all find ourselves in Stanley's position at any given moment?' (ibid.: 11). If resistance to oppressive, dehumanizing structures maintains individual integrity, it makes sense that Pinter regards Petey's cry of 'Stan, don't let them tell you what to do!' as 'one of the most important lines I've ever written' (Gussow 1994: 71). The original director, worrying about realist stage-time and naturalism of character, may have found Stanley's submission to tyranny implausibly rapid, but Pinter is adamant that he has depicted a man who 'fights for his life' (1998b: 11). That fight may be short, and Stanley's tactics are mainly evasion and bluff, but in both the dialogue and the stage directions he does make acts of defiance, including taunting his visitants with another rendition of 'The Mountains of Morne' (Pinter 1991a: 41) and kicking Goldberg in the stomach (46). Nevertheless, by the end of Act II and the game of blind man's buff, Stanley's breakdown is fully apparent.

Much has been written about the importance of resistance in *The Birthday Party*. Billington celebrates Stanley as a 'defiant hero', arguing that his torturers are significantly 'exposed' by his collapse (Billington 1996: 80). Pinter is clear, however, that Stanley 'though nonconformist, is neither hero nor exemplar of revolt' (1998b: 9); he is a man who 'cannot perceive his only valid justification – which is, he is what he is – therefore he certainly can never be articulate about it' (ibid.: 9). The torture in *The Birthday Party*, as in all of Pinter's dramas that deal with the subject, is language-based, but Pinter considers this play to be most starkly about 'terrorizing through words of power' (Smith 2005: 83). Stanley's lack of articulacy is crucial, and though he is reduced to what Pinter describes as 'a rattle in the throat' (ibid.: 10), those last noises 'ug-gughh . . . uh-gughhh . . .' and 'caaahhh . . . caaahhh . . .' (Pinter 1991a: 79) are 'nearer to the true nature of himself than ever before and certainly ever after' (1998b: 10). Stanley is on the 'edge of utterance' and the very desire to speak out is what gives him tragic dignity (ibid.: 10). His destroyers are undoubtedly shaken by the event, McCann refusing to 'go up there again', Goldberg temporarily losing grip of his belief system, and the stage directions indicating transitions from 'vacant' to 'desperate' and 'lost', but both resume their mission of destruction only a short time afterwards, and whatever 'exposure' occurs is of no help to Stanley (Pinter 1991a: 67,72).

In the two-hander, *The Dumb Waiter*, contract-killers Ben and Gus are on a mission in which they themselves become the targets. Another comic double-act, they bicker, idly fritter away time, and rehearse their murder routine in a Birmingham basement whilst awaiting instructions on their next victim. Gus is an anxious chatterer, full of questions about the venue, the routine, the procedure and their employer, fretting as much about the toilet and the kettle (Pinter 1991a: 117, 125) as he does about 'who clears up after we've gone?', the girl they murdered who was 'a mess', 'didn't she spread, eh? She didn't half spread' (130–1), and 'his splitting headache' which causes him to 'hope the bloke's not going to get excited tonight, or anything' (137). In the twist at the end, it is not an unknown victim but Gus who comes flying through the door, stripped of his gun, his jacket, waistcoat and tie, and Ben who instinctively trains his revolver on him, the play ending with the directions 'A long silence. They stare at each other' (149). The drama's suspense is created by the increasing anxiety both killers suffer, Gus unhappy with inconsistencies he has noted in the routine, and both made ill-at-ease by the nearby yet invisible presence of the person or persons who issue their instructions. An envelope of matches is inexplicably poked under the door, while orders for the kitchen and items of food and drink arrive via the dumb waiter.[7] Certainly both seem to suspect from the start that something is up (and it is an interesting challenge for any director to decide how much they suspect), but at the denouement Ben has to make the logical connection that if he is expected to eliminate his partner then he may be next on the list. In *The Dumb Waiter* the torturers become the tortured, and if it is a homage to Beckett's *Waiting for Godot* (British premiere 1955), in which two men wait for an authority figure who never shows up, then Pinter has created a Godot who is decidedly present yet never seen, sadistic, ruthless, and apparently the head of a mysterious killing organization.[8]

The Caretaker, Pinter's first commercial and international success, does not feature torturers, but Aston's shocking monologue at the end of Act II represents him as the victim of a medical treatment which appears to be a pathologized, institutional form of torture intended to enable him to 'live like the others' (Pinter 1991b: 53). Aston explains that he did try to resist but that his mother had signed the consent forms, and in an attempt to avoid treatment he tried to saw through bars and murder hospital personnel (54). Aston describes a procedure that sounds like electro-convulsive therapy (ECT), quite widely used in psychiatric treatments during the 1950s and 1960s, during which patients (or victims) are held down, 'pincers' clamped to the sides of the skull, and electric currents passed through the brain. The monologue suddenly provides a context for Aston's eccentric behaviour up to that point and an explanation for his fixations. His extreme suffering also becomes evident:

The trouble was ... my thoughts ... had become very slow ... I couldn't think at all ... I couldn't ... get ... my thoughts ... together ... uuuhh ... I could ... never quite get it together. The trouble was I couldn't hear what people were saying [...] if I turned my head round ... I couldn't keep ... upright. And I had these headaches. I used to sit in my room. (55)

If Aston retains a fragile emotional state, limited independence, and a healthy sense of injustice, Lamb in *The Hothouse* blindly offers himself up for ritual slaughter. Set in a 'rest home' (Pinter 1991a: 232), otherwise a secret state-run facility which systematically tortures 'patients' (325) who are known by number not name, *The Hothouse* is a black comedy depicting the banal bureaucratization of flagrant human rights abuses. It is run by Colonel Roote, who has the speech-patterns of a pompous, old English colonial, persists in an absurd estimation of his predecessor, and is prone to ineptitude and sentimentality. Lamb accepts interrogation and electrocution with a servile desire to please:

GIBBS: ... if you'd give me a helping hand?
LAMB: I'd be quite delighted!

(237)

It leaves him in a state of catatonia, making him an obvious scapegoat for the riots, the massacre of the staff and Gibbs's suspicious takeover from Roote at the end. Miss Cutts, as her name suggests, extracts a sadist's pleasure from watching the agonies of others, experiencing sexual intoxication while working with her co-interrogator. Indeed, sex and power are interlinked for Miss Cutts to an extreme degree, the interrogation procedure itself becoming a form of sexual climax, 'the intimacy becomes unbearable [...] and it's question time, question time, question time, forever and forever and forever' (294). The torture and interrogation of Lamb covers 20 pages (234–54) and sits at the heart of the dramaturgical structure, a grotesque insight into the real abuses of power behind the bluff language of officialese, the filing systems and the discrepancies in Roote's diary-keeping. Under attack is Lamb's very individuality, especially his virginity – and in targeting his sexuality his assailants exploit a commonly used strategy of dehumanization (Forrest for Amnesty International 1996: 65–73). Next to Lamb, Stanley in *The Birthday Party* has decided spirit, and while Stanley tries to speak out against his tormentors to the last, Lamb is unaware of danger, yielding up passively, 'quite enjoying' himself and 'quite ready' for more questions (Pinter 1991a: 253). In the final image of the play, however, he is in a silent, vegetative condition (328).

The Hothouse demonstrates what Amnesty International recognizes as the 'bureaucracy of repression' needed for rule by terror (Forrest for Amnesty International 1996: 141). It evokes the medical experiments practised by Nazi doctors in the death camps and the terrifyingly meticulous bureaucracies deployed by both fascist and communist dictatorships in the twentieth century. The methods of torture and the medical terminologies also have echoes in testimonies published after it was written, notably

Alexander Solzhenitsyn's exposés of the Soviet Union's systematic human rights abuses against dissidents in psychiatric hospitals. Electroshock specifically as torture also has a gruesome topicality – after beating, it is the world's most common form of physical abuse (ibid.: 139), which is perhaps why Pinter pulled this play out of a bottom drawer in 1979 (Pinter 1991a:, author's note, 186). A fact also not lost on Pinter is that for some western democracies torture is big business: in 1995, for example, England's Ministry of Defence was at the centre of a massive scandal when Channel Four exposed their largest arms deal ever – a £20-billion package to sell electroshock batons to Saudi Arabia (Forrest for Amnesty International 1996: 144–5).

Despite having said after *One for the Road* that 'I can't go on writing plays about torture' (Pinter 1984: 18), Pinter has directly represented torture, tyranny and interrogation in much of his theatre work from 1984 to the present, and in ways – with the exception of *The New World Order* (Royal Court, 1991) and *Press Conference* (National Theatre, 2002) – that have tended to move away from the comic. The turn towards a more overtly political theatre can first be perceived in 1984 in *One for the Road* and continued in *Mountain Language* (National Theatre, 1988). As Billington has made clear, Pinter's decision to address these concerns unambiguously in his plays came out of pre-existing agendas, though the military coup in Chile in 1973 became his 'crux' moment for committing to greater activism (Billington 1996: 287). Two other factors were important in determining Pinter on this path: the Conservative party's regime, especially their economic and foreign policies under Margaret Thatcher from 1979 to 1990;[9] and the influence of his second wife, Lady Antonia Fraser, whom he married in 1980, and who comes from a family heavily engaged with political life. Pinter's activism has been born of certain causes and his allegiance to particular human rights organizations, notably the Campaign for Nuclear Disarmament (CND), the worldwide writers' association PEN, Charter 88 and Amnesty International.[10]

One for the Road was inspired by fury and written in one night. Pinter has described his rage against two Turkish women encountered at a party, who were not only unmoved by human rights abuses in Turkish prisons but tried to justify them (Gussow 1994: 87). The play depicts Nicolas in a series of one-to-one scenes interrogating three members of the same family, the father Victor, his wife Gila and their son Nicky. The physical abuse takes place off-stage though the effects of it are evident on the husband and wife: Victor is '*bruised*' and '*his clothes are torn*' (Pinter 1998a: 223); by the end he is struggling to move and speak, his tongue brutalized; Gila is mentally the most fragile, and carrying the marks of repeated rapes – so many she has lost count (243). At the end, when Victor asks about his son, Nicolas delivers the last line of the play: 'Your son? Oh, don't worry about him. He was a little prick' (247) – the clear implication being that he has been killed. *One for the Road* is relentless and harrowing, leaves its audiences silent and choked with horror, and caused the original actors such distress that they 'couldn't face the idea of doing the play again for anything but a very short run' (Pinter 1984: 17).[11] Shortly after the production, Pinter commented that he no longer felt comedy was 'appropriate' to the subject of torture, that *One for the Road* was 'past a joke': 'in 1957 the concentration camps were still an open wound which was impossible to ignore, whereas now it's only too easy to ignore what's going on around us' (ibid.: 9–11). He also argued:

> You can interpret reality in various ways, but there's only one. And if that reality is thousands of people being tortured to death at this very moment and hundreds of thousands of megatons of nuclear bombs standing there waiting to go off at this very moment, then that's it and that's that. It has to be faced. (21)

A few years later, Pinter explained that he was interested neither in propaganda nor in agit-prop, but was exploring the possibilities of a drama that was direct though not 'pursuing the normal narrative procedure' (Gussow 1994: 92).

If *One for the Road* is bleak, there is still a dignity in Victor's silence. An intellectual – he possesses 'lots of books' (Pinter 1984: 228) – and apparently an opponent of the regime, Victor uses silence as his only remaining means of protest. But Victor's silences vary in their emotional pitch. In contrast to Lamb in *The Hothouse*, he can resist complicity in the interrogation and refuse to answer questions:

> NICOLAS: You do respect me, I take it?
> *He stands in front of Victor and looks down on him. Victor looks up.*
> I would be right in assuming that?
> *Silence.*
>
> (226)

He can undermine the terrorizing purpose of the interrogation:

> VICTOR: Kill me.
> NICOLAS: What?
> VICTOR: Kill me.
>   (232)

And he can express his numb horror at the abomination of his son's murder: after Nicolas's last line the stage directions read '*Victor straightens and stares at Nicolas. Silence. Blackout*' (247). Victor's silence is always balanced against Nicolas's logorrhoea, and if Pinter was aware from the first of the abuse of power through speech alone (1998b: 19), he demonstrates it chillingly in Nicolas's encounter with Gila, using the word 'fuckpig' to devastating effect (1984: 240). Far from finding resistance in silence, Gila is so traumatized that she loses her verbal and mental grip, as her screaming testifies (ibid.: 239). If Pinter shows that torture is ultimately language-destroying, and that for Stanley and Gila, self is destroyed as their power over language wanes, Elaine Scarry has come to the same conclusions in her book *The Body in Pain: The Making and Unmaking of the World*. Scarry has argued that the purpose of torture and interrogation is 'the transformation of body into voice': 'The goal of the torturer is to make the one, the body, emphatically and crushingly *present* by destroying it, and to make the other, the voice, *absent* by destroying it' (Scarry 1985: 45, 49). This is always true of Pinter's interrogation scenes, in which confession is irrelevant. There is no interest in extracting information, because the judgement on the victims is a foregone conclusion and their crime more about who they are than what they might have done. In *One for the Road*, interrogation is another instrument of sowing personal and political terror and securing further state control. In Scarry's words, both torture and interrogation lead to the 'undoing of civilization' (Scarry 1985: 38).

In *Mountain Language* Pinter moves beyond interrogation as an instrument of suppression by exploring the devastating consequences of a militarily enforced silence through the outlawing of a language and thereby its speakers (a narrative with dark resonances for England's colonial past). The denial of the right to speak a language becomes legitimized state torture and symbolically marks the beginning of genocide. *Mountain Language* was inspired by torture victims whom Pinter met in Turkey. He has described the play as 'a series of short, sharp brutal events' which could take place anywhere but are 'very close to home' (Smith 2005: 82–3). The scenes are set in and outside a torture camp, where the female Mountain people struggle to gain access to their incarcerated male relatives, to whom they are not permitted to speak in their own language. At the end, a male prisoner has a violent fit when he realizes that his mother has become mute with terror even though the language ban has suddenly been lifted (Pinter 1998a: 267). In scene three, a young woman with an anglicized name, Sara Johnson, sees her imprisoned, hooded husband from a distance. They do not speak but a tender lovers' dialogue between them plays in oversound before the man collapses and he is dragged away (263). Similarly in scene two, though not permitted to speak their language, a voice-over dialogue between the prisoner and his elderly mother indicates that they are thinking of one another, and that she is hopeful of his release (261). Pinter deploys voice-over as a device to highlight that, however stark the circumstances, colonization of the mind is ultimately not possible and that an individual's love and memories can be powerful aids in resisting oppression. At the same time, he is deploying it to emphasize precisely the individuality that is being suppressed and denied. For Pinter the enforced erasure of a language is historically one of the great examples of human rights abuse.

In 1991, Pinter moved back to representing interrogation directly in his sketch *The New World Order*, which prefaced performances of Ariel Dorfman's *Death and the Maiden*. The comic aspects of Lionel and Des recall Goldberg and McCann as well as Ben and Gus, but ideologically the implication of ethnic cleansing is clear – they are 'keeping the world clean for democracy' (Pinter 1998a: 277) and are constructed to critique western nations that pursue aggressive domestic and foreign policies to maintain the principle of 'freedom'. In the same year *Party Time* (Almeida Theatre, 1991) explored the chilling 'society of beautifully dressed people', connoisseurs of 'elegance, style, grace, taste' (Pinter 1998a: 299), who are implicated in the state-sponsored brutality happening outside on the streets, a situation which one party-goer refers to as a set of 'problems' to be 'resolved very soon' (313). Dusty refuses to behave according to form and breaks protocol by persistently asking about what has happened to her missing brother Jimmy. Her husband Terry is unable to silence her, despite insisting that Jimmy is 'not on anyone's agenda' and threatening to have Dusty and 'all her lot' slaughtered (296, 302). Jimmy's entrance and monologue at the end of the play set up a devastating contrast to all that has been euphemistically skirted. A survivor of horrific torture, and no doubt one of the 'problems' who has already been 'resolved', Jimmy scarcely recognizes himself as human:

> I had a name. It was Jimmy. People called me Jimmy. That was my name. [. . .]
>   Sometimes a door bangs, I hear voices, then it stops. Everything stops. It all stops. It all closes. It closes down. It shuts. It all shuts. It shuts down. It shuts. I see nothing at any time any more. I sit sucking the dark.
>   It's what I have. The dark is in my mouth and I suck it. It's the only thing I have. It's mine. It's my own. I suck it. (313–14)

This is the only moment in a Pinter play where a victim articulates the aftermath of torture, describing the process as one of reduction from subject to object: 'I had a name', 'What am I?' (313–14). Framed by a doorway and backlit by a burning light (s.d., 313), itself a reference to torture techniques which injure or blind their victims, Jimmy and his shadow loom over the shocked party guests, momentarily eclipsing their world of surface chat. A second door on set, '*never used*', yet always '*half open in a dim light*' (281), implicates the 'dark', the world of secret terrors known by Jimmy and sustained by the 'beautifully dressed'. Pinter has described this juxtaposition of revelling champagne drinkers with military and police repression as 'an image of universal reference':

> I believe that there *are* extremely powerful people in apartments in capital cities in all countries who are actually controlling events that are happening on the street in a number of very subtle and not so subtle ways. But they don't really bother to talk about it, because they know it's happening and they know they have the power. It's a question of how power operates. (Smith 2005: 92)

Austin Quigley has rightly argued that plays such as *One for the Road* demonstrate Pinter's primary concern to explore 'the pre-supposition and self-justification' of powerful persecutors, especially those employed by governments (in Raby 2001: 10). Pinter hints at rationales for his tormentors. He is quite clear that Nicolas is 'deluded', 'possessed' and 'an absolute disaster' (his constant drinking is a clear pointer towards his implosion), but at the same time he recognizes the 'plight' in which his religious and political pathologies place him (1998b: 62). Quigley once again gives a sharp analysis:

> Rather than showing that the personal is the political by dissolving the personal into the political, Pinter has, effectively, dramatized the converse: that the political is, among other things, the personal. As such it is as complex and dangerous and as worthy

of our scrupulous attention as any other sphere of social interaction [. . .] What is dramatized is not the physical torture, murder and rape so frequently referred to in critical discussion, but the processes of self-justification they promote and the differing consequences for the oppressors and the oppressed of their limited persuasiveness. (Quigley in Raby 2001: 10)

Pinter is also fundamentally concerned with his torturers' different styles of rhetoric: in *Party Time* what is so disturbing is not that Terry tries to justify state terror but that he takes it entirely for granted and that his rhetoric is one that assumes club membership to mean unquestioning and, above all, silent support. It is significant that in *Voices*, written in 2000 but first broadcast on BBC Radio in 2005 to mark his seventy-fifth birthday, Pinter begins and ends with Jimmy's last monologue in *Party Time*. A selection of excerpts from various plays, *Voices* overwhelmingly focuses on tormentors and the tormented, but allows the victim's words to frame – what Paul Allain, the post-performance presenter, called – this 'journey into human hell'. Michael Billington echoed Quigley when he spoke of *Voices* portraying 'a world of public terror, nightmare and persecution' which 'merges indissolubly' with the private world of 'our daily life and its elements of treachery, betrayal and domination' (BBC Radio, 10 October 2005). Accompanying music by James Clarke made the broadcast all the more visceral and harrowing.

In his most recent sketch, *Press Conference* (2002), Pinter presents a master torturer, a minister of culture and former head of Secret Police, who dismisses the mass murder of women and children in his press-briefing. He also makes it clear to the assembled journalists that they can expect interrogation, torture and rehabilitation (one suspects at best) should they criticize the regime:

> We need critical dissent because it keeps us on our toes. But we don't want to see it in the market place or on the avenues and piazzas of our great institutions. We are happy for it to remain at home, which means we can pop in at any time and read what is kept under the bed, discuss it with the writer, pat him on the head, shake him by the hand, give him perhaps a minor kick up the arse or in the balls and set fire to the whole shebang. By this method we keep our society free from infection. There is of course, however, always room for confession, retraction and redemption. (Pinter 2003: 4)

Apparently civilized, polished and affable, the minister is an apologist for state terror. That *Press Conference* is a critique of the political rhetoric of western democracies such as Britain and the USA is clear, and the parodic swipe at the Blair government and their notorious use of the media to spin propaganda is brutally effective. Pinter himself played the minister,[12] reminding audiences of an opinion he has expressed many times before: that Britain, like any other western democracy, 'can easily employ totalitarian measures' – especially when seeking to combat terrorism (Smith 2005: 103). In his performance Pinter once more resorts to comedy, and that this piece is aimed at Bush and Blair is nowhere clearer than when Pinter gives an avuncular smile as he tells the press that he sees children as a threat. After 9/11, questions of what state measures might be morally and legally necessary rather than amorally and ideologically expedient are particularly pertinent.[13] Countries such as Britain, the USA, France, Germany and Spain gain substantial boosts to their economies through the selling of arms and trade in what Pinter has called 'repressive, cynical and indifferent acts of murder' (1998b: 65). If Pinter has been viciously attacked for the directness of his most recent plays and for his willingness to use his celebrity as one of the world's great playwrights to voice his political views, it is perhaps all too understandable that he feels present times do not call for subtlety.

> Political theatre is even more important than it ever was, if by political theatre you mean plays which deal with the real world, not with a manufactured or fantasy world. We are in a terrible dip at the moment, a kind of abyss, because the assumption is that politics are all over. That's what the propaganda says. But I don't believe the propaganda. I believe that politics, our political consciousness and our political intelligence are not all over, because if they are, we are really doomed. (Smith 2005: 92–3)

NOTES

1 General Assembly resolution 3452 (XXX) of 9 December 1975; see Ian Brownie (ed.) (1992). *Basic Documents on Human Rights*, 3rd edn. Oxford: Clarendon Press, 35–52.

2 Pinter was awarded the Nobel Prize in 2005. He has also been knighted and is a Companion of Honour.

3 Pinter initially trained as an actor and worked in repertory theatre.

4 See Ken Booth and Tim Dunne (eds.) (2002). *Worlds in Collision: Terror and the Future of Global Order*. Basingstoke and New York: Palgrave; Karen J. Greenberg and Joshua L. Dratel (eds.) (2005). *The Torture Papers: The Road to Abu Ghraib*. Cambridge: Cambridge University Press.

5 See, for example, *A Slight Ache* (radio, 1959; stage, 1961), *The Homecoming* (1965), *Landscape* (radio, 1968; stage, 1969), *Betrayal* (1978), *Ashes to Ashes* (1996).

6 See also Pinter's poem 'A View of the Party' (1998b: 135–7).

7 A service-hatch with an interior lift.

8 Samuel Beckett and Franz Kafka have been strong influences on Pinter. See Smith (2005: 53).

9 Pinter formed the June 20 Group opposing Thatcherism, 'which was destroying so many institutions and convictions' (Pinter in Smith 2005: 101).

10 For information on the organizations and campaigns with which Pinter is involved see www.haroldpinter.org.

11 *One for the Road* is rarely performed and presents such emotional challenges to actors that it is particularly vulnerable to bad productions, as Pinter has noted. See Gussow (1994: 152).

12 Generally when acting in his own dramas he plays torturers not victims. In the premiere BBC radio broadcast of *Voices* (10 October 2005), Pinter played Nicolas. The presenter of the post-show discussion, Paul Allain, remarked on Pinter's 'appeal as the fiercest of interrogators', and Michael Billington commented that whilst Nicolas 'represents the antithesis of all that Pinter believes in', he could still play him 'with demonic conviction'.

13 See Michael Ignatieff (2005). *The Lesser Evil: Political Ethics in an Age of Terror*. Edinburgh: Edinburgh University Press, for a provocative debate on the issues faced by liberal democracies after 9/11: 'What lesser evils may a society commit when it believes it faces the greater evil of its own destruction?' (1).

Primary reading

Pinter's manuscripts are housed in the British Library, London.

Pinter, Harold (1984). *One for the Road*. London: Methuen. (Including interview between Pinter and Nick Hern, 7–23.)

Pinter, Harold (1991a). *Plays 1*. London: Faber and Faber. (Includes *The Birthday Party, The Dumb Waiter, The Hothouse*.)

Pinter, Harold (1991b). *Plays 2*. London: Faber and Faber. (Includes *The Caretaker*.)

Pinter, Harold (1997). *Plays 3*. London: Faber and Faber. (Includes *The Homecoming*.)

Pinter, Harold (1998a). *Plays 4*. London: Faber and Faber. (Includes *One for the Road, Mountain Language, The New World Order, Party Time*.)

Pinter, Harold (1998b). *Various Voices: Prose, Poetry, Politics 1948–1998*. London. Faber and Faber.

Pinter, Harold (2002). *Press Conference*. London: Faber and Faber.

Pinter, Harold (2003). *War*. London: Faber and Faber.

Further reading

Amnesty International Report (1984). *Torture in the Eighties*. London: Amnesty International Publications.

Batty, Mark (2005). *About Pinter: the Playwright and the Work*. London. Faber and Faber.

Billington, Michael (1996). *The Life and Work of Harold Pinter*. London: Faber and Faber.

Burkman, Katherine H. and Kundert-Gibbs, John L. (eds.) (1993). *Pinter at Sixty*. Bloomington and Indianapolis: Indiana University Press.

Esslin, Martin (2000). *Pinter the Playwright*, 6th edn. London: Methuen.

Forrest, Duncan (ed.) for Amnesty International (1996). *A Glimpse of Hell: Reports on Torture Worldwide*. London: Cassell.

Gordon, Lois (ed.) (2001). *Pinter at 70*. New York and London: Routledge.

Gussow, Mel (1994). *Conversations with Pinter*. London: Nick Hern.

Kane, Leslie (ed.) (2004). *The Art of Crime: The Plays and Films of Harold Pinter and David Mamet*. London and New York: Routledge.

Merritt, Susan Hollis (1990). *Pinter in Play*. Durham, NC, and London: Duke University Press.

Peacock, D. Keith (1997). *Harold Pinter and the New British Theatre*. Westport, CT, and London: Greenwood Press.

Raby, Peter (2001). *The Cambridge Companion to Harold Pinter*. Cambridge: Cambridge University Press.

Scarry, Elaine (1985). *The Body in Pain: The Making and Unmaking of the World*. Oxford: Oxford University Press.

Silverstein, Marc (1991). '*One for the Road, Mountain Language* and the Impasse of Politics', *Modern Drama*, December, 422–40.

Silverstein, Marc (1993). *Harold Pinter and the Language of Cultural Power*. London: Associated University Presses.

Smith, Ian (ed.) (2005) *Pinter in the Theatre*. London: Nick Hern.

30

Sarah Kane: From Terror to Trauma

Steve Waters

The opening of *Blasted* on 17 January 1995 in the Theatre Upstairs at the Royal Court has achieved a secure place in theatre mythology. It is tragically mirrored by an answering mythical moment, the suicide of the author of the play, aged 28, in February 1999. These events and what lies between them continue to bear a traumatic force. Sarah Kane opened up a wound in the theatre that has yet to be healed (see Luckhurst 2005).

It is illuminating if wearying to go back to the reviews of that foundational moment. Consulting *Theatre Record* yields few surprises bar a startlingly open reaction from the *Daily Mail* ('They will call her mad but they said that about Strindberg'; *Mail on Sunday* 22 January 1995),[1] or the *Observer*, which describes *Blasted* as 'at once cool and classical' (*Observer* 5 February 1995). But beyond that the monologic voice of English theatre criticism is all too audible. The play presents violence but does not explain it, refusing to annotate itself: 'the final scenes never clarify' (*The Times* 20 January 1995); 'It would have helped to have known how the characters are related to each other' (*Time Out* 25 January 1995); 'what is going on?' (*Financial Times* 23 January 1995). Elsewhere the play is deemed infantile: 'puerile tosh' (*Guardian* 20 January 1995), '[this] very silly play' (*Sunday Times* 22 January 1995), '[displays] abject puerility' (*Independent* 20 January 1995). It is pilloried for sheer bad craft, creating '[its] own lawless environment' (*Daily Mail* 19 January 1995) with 'writing so bad it is almost touching' (*Daily Telegraph* 22 January 1995). In addition the critics compete to itemize in fancy Latinate terms the horrors awaiting the audience, the long ascent to the Theatre Upstairs is wielded as a further cruelty, and one walk-out is ceaselessly noted.

What makes these reviews fascinating now is the way they register the foundering of a theatre settlement, as *Blasted*'s first director James MacDonald, an associate of the Royal Court Theatre at the time, has generously noted: 'It's easy to misread a tone you don't recognize and completely new forms often create a strong emotional and intellectual response' (*Observer* 28 January 1999). Especially revealing are the observations of the critic Michael Billington, whose comment, 'the reason the play falls apart is that there is no sense of external reality', clarifies the specific threat *Blasted* presented to the then dominant social realist tradition. Billington later develops this point, by noting how Kane's refusal to specify the context of *Blasted* deviates from 'a run of outstanding plays at the Theatre Upstairs based on exact social observation' (*Guardian* 20 January 1995). This particular heresy, the refusal to specify, is reiterated elsewhere; Nick Curtis asks: 'Is Kane talking about Ireland? Bosnia? Leeds? Try as you may to contextualize it her catalogue of inhumanity ultimately provokes revulsion rather than thought' (*Evening Standard* 19 January 1995). Jane Edwardes echoes this angry confusion: 'what war is being waged and why... are we really in Leeds?' (*Time Out* 25 January 1995); David Nathan has a go at providing the missing context himself: 'For all the talk of Bosnia, it is not related to Bosnia in any specific way' (*Jewish Chronicle* 27 January 1995). A brief glance at the text of course reveals not a single reference to Bosnia.

In a retrospective piece written just after Kane's death, James MacDonald offers a useful diagnosis of this traumatized commentary, arguing that what critics were after was a type of play which *Blasted* was to expel from the stage: 'The Royal Court play of the Seventies and Eighties, driven by a clear political agenda, kitted out with signposts indicating meaning, and generally featuring a hefty state-of-the-nation speech somewhere near the end. More than anyone, she knew this template is no use to us now' (*Observer* 28 February 1999). Macdonald himself was an artistic associate of the team at the Royal Court which did indeed cast such plays into oblivion under the aegis of artistic director Stephen Daldry. When in 1999 Sarah Kane's career was so tragically cut short that tendency had hardened, her work increasingly uncoupled from political intentions and salvaged instead as poetry or as an anatomy of passion. Mark Ravenhill's moving obituary for Kane in the *Independent* presents her, perhaps in the light of her revision of *Phaedra*, as 'a contemporary writer of classical sensibility'; *Blasted* had become a play chiefly concerned with 'great passions locked in a small room' (*Independent* 23 February 1999). For Macdonald she was remarkable for writing about 'the possibilities of love', and for 'saying the unsayable in beautiful English' (*Guardian* 23 February 1999); whilst critic Lyn Gardner added that Kane 'wrote about a world in which love and violence were deeply entwined' (*Guardian* 23 February 1999). Bosnia, horror, shock were now deemed secondary to the drama of private pain, of states of love, of obsession; Kane's own narrative – from incendiary origins to her terrible end – had blotted out the questions her work had earlier raised.

Ten years on from its debut, *Blasted* looks as robust as ever and seems truer than ever. It is certainly more performed than ever – if not in its country of origin. Indeed, a repentant Michael Billington noted this irony in the *Guardian* (23 March 2005) in response to a revival directed by Thomas Ostermeier in Berlin. In the new century Kane didn't survive to witness, her work is more likely to be seen in Chile, Poland or Denmark than in Britain. Ostermeier offered a convincing case for her ubiquity in the world repertoire: 'The startling thing about *Blasted* is that it makes more sense now than it did ten years ago... it is about something we currently understand: the fear that at any moment, our whole society can be ripped apart' (*Guardian* 23 March 2005).

Ostermeier's production at the Schaubühne banished the disputed ghost of Bosnia for a more alarming contemporary specification: Fallujah in Iraq. Yet both his approach and observations reveal that much of the power of *Blasted* and later *Cleansed* (1998) derive from their tendency to enact a kind of aesthetic terror on the audience. There are of course many precedents for such assaults both in art and in life. During the Vietnam war Situationists in Paris sprung corpses of South East Asian origin from morgues, covered them in theatrical gore and floated them down the Seine. Their desire to fuse art and life in outrage claimed ancestry from the Surrealists: indeed André Breton, the self-proclaimed theorist of Surrealism, asserted in his manifesto that the primary Surrealist act consisted of going into the street with revolvers in your fists and shooting blindly into the crowd.[2] More controversially, the German composer Karl Heinz Stockhausen characterized the crashing of two passenger jets into the iconic Twin Towers on September 11, 2001, as 'the greatest work of art ever'.[3] In the furore that followed this comment, few remarked on the fact that this action itself was indeed dubbed by Al-Qaeda as a 'spectacular'. What these actions or works share with terrorism proper is their desire to confound expectation by means of short-circuiting expectation. Whatever the deeper didactic intent, artistic terror and actual terror seek to jolt the world from its habitual mode, and usher in a state of perpetual uncertainty. They seek to undermine everyday life and its deemed complacencies; and whilst terrorism might have commenced as the military action of the weak, it has mutated into something much more inexplicable.

It is startling to think that Sarah Kane did not live to see the events of 9/11 and the ensuing open-ended 'war on terror'. Indeed at the end of Kane's all too short life terrorism in its more conventionally understood form, by non-state agents, seemed to be on the wane (witness the peace process in Northern Ireland and the Oslo accords still in effect in Israel/Palestine). The dominant mode of violence in the 1990s was in fact internecine war – conflicts in the former Yugoslavia, inter-ethnic conflicts in the former Soviet Union, the first invasion of Chechnya and the horror of the Rwandan genocide. Violence, for the West at least, was elsewhere, done to others by others.

A central concern in Kane's work, however, is a passionate, almost pathological identification with pain and trauma and a concomitant desire to communicate the horror of pain in its own idiom. To achieve this end she shaped a writerly practice which sought to shatter the social realist certainties of British theatre and the pieties of the new consensus known as political correctness; her plays resisted ideology at all levels in response to political conflicts enacted in the name of fixed identities and categories. *Blasted* proved to be the acme of this approach.

Before examining this thesis more closely it is useful to rehearse once more the facts about Kane's life and work. Born in 1971 near Brentwood in Essex, she had an ostensibly unremarkable childhood, despite a phase of extreme religiosity which her entire family embarked on in her teens; her father was a journalist, at one point writing for the *Daily Mirror* – something that proved crucial in her latter-day demonization. She read drama at Bristol University in a cohort that included other key playwrights of the 1990s, David Greig and Mark Ravenhill (though she had no contact with Ravenhill at the time). Despite maintaining an offensive against the complacencies of her lecturers she achieved a first class degree, acting in and directing numerous works, notably *Victory* by Howard Barker (Barker was to prove something of a touchstone for Kane). In 1992 she attended David Edgar's MA in playwriting at the University of Birmingham, where again she was a controversial student, most notably and symptomatically picking a fight with director and playwright Terry Johnson during a weekend examining the director Max Stafford-Clark's methodology – both apogees of a theatre establishment she would continue to chafe against. Her degree show unveiled Act I of *Blasted*; it arrived after a rehearsal process of unprecedented tension, with much mutinous talk by the undergraduate performers concerning the racist jokes and extreme sexuality. Its debut was witnessed by agent Mel Kenyon, whose strong links with the Royal Court were to prove pivotal for the play's professional exposure 18 months later. After graduation Kane entered the new writing scene in London like a heat-seeking missile; as a reader she proved a key figure at the Bush theatre under director Dominic Dromgoole. Then, on a cold January night in 1995, *Blasted* opened.

To link the writing of a play with an act of terrorism is tendentious to say the least. But (and it's an impossible but) if one could screen out the physical mayhem and torment activated in the name of terror and examine the intent of the act in itself, the shock of *Blasted* and the impact of terrorism have more in common than might at first be assumed. Firstly one should consider the perpetrators themselves – it is a cliché of counter-terrorism that the violence of the terrorist act arises from social isolation. Certainly, terrorists often hail from unassimilable minority groups who despair of the vehicles of protest or change available in the mainstream and stand at odds with or in advance of the majority – terrorists are always to this extent 'avant-gardists'; and the extremity of Kane's writing speaks of the gulf between her and both her notional audience and the theatre establishment of the day. Her work was not destined for the West End, but it also sat uneasily within the official fringes of the metropolitan scene; for all its latter-day infamy *Blasted* played for three weeks in a 60-seater theatre in its first incarnation, its audience barely exceeding 1,000 viewers. Equally *Cleansed* in 1998, her first main-stage show, made little impact on the vast auditorium of the Duke of York's Theatre – especially if compared with the Court's other great hit of that year, the transferred production of Conor McPherson's *The Weir*. Conventional politics aim to reach and persuade majorities and theatre audiences, but in their disregard for conventional audience pleasure or approbation, Kane's plays mirror terrorism's disdain for rhetoric and the numbers game. Her plays seek not to persuade but to present.

One way of understanding the terror aesthetic is to see it as a repudiation of humanism. Humanist politics is embodied in the credos of liberalism and pluralism; in aesthetic terms it is best expressed in a resonant line from Jean Renoir's great film

La Règle du Jeu (1939), 'everyone has their reasons'. In theatrical terms humanism gently proposes that these reasons might be articulated within the play – indeed that a play is a place to air and voice reasons in order to reveal the characters as complex, yet reasonable beings, driven by motives that can be *understood*. Humanism, evidently, has its blind spots: it does not interrogate violence with sophistication. In fact humanist theatre or indeed social realist theatre only represents violence through a desire to rationalize it as something soluble and comprehensible. Terrorism dispenses with humanism from the outset. Terrorism asserts that it is too late for reasons, too late for debate. The Chechen woman who informed a captive in the Dubrovka theatre in Moscow that the fear she was experiencing was the fear Chechens experienced *daily* is indicative of the way terrorism eschews words for didactic deeds.[4]

This rebuttal of humanism helps explain the source of the cold power of *Blasted* and *Cleansed*; in these two plays Kane offers a world without explanations, both within the text at the level of motive and through generic precedent – settings, for instance, mutate into their opposite, and that must simply be accepted as a challenge to the rules of theatrical engagement. Actions and relationships lack prehistories or refuse to elucidate them. Gestures generate incomprehensible responses. The brutal exchanges between Ian and Cate have a flat, uninflected logic to them; they reveal little behind themselves and the emotion they inspire verges on numbness:

IAN: Why did you come here?
CATE: You sounded unhappy.
IAN: Make me happy.
CATE: I can't.
IAN: Please.
CATE: No.
IAN: Why not?
CATE: Can't.
IAN: Can.
CATE: How?
IAN: You know.
CATE: Don't.
(Kane 2001: 23)

The actor of course can supply subtext; yet this tone marks the beginning of a refusal of dialogic norms that Kane would take further in *Cleansed*. Language is subjected to a reduction, the dialogue refuses to advance story, circling back on itself, refusing to elucidate. Movement and revelation, so central to humanist dramaturgy, are disavowed. When the Soldier arrives in Act II his itemization of the cruelties he has engaged in does not serve as such to make sense of his rape and mutilation of Ian, but is merely present for its inexorable logic:

It's nothing. Saw thousands of people packed into trucks like pigs trying to leave town. Women threw their babies on board hoping someone would look after them. Crushing each other to death. Insides of people's heads came out their eyes. Saw a child most of his face blown off, young girl I fucked hand up inside her trying to claw my liquid out, starving man eating his wife's leg. Gun was born here and can't die. Can't get tragic about your arse. (Kane 2001: 50)

None of this is present in order to explain or make sense of anything. Violence has permeated the world with numbness, with a failure of evaluative language – notably, as with Kane's tendency to offer subjectless titles, the dialogue is often devoid of personal pronouns. Actions are separated from subjects and nothing seems personal. Even when he is on the brink of raping Ian, Kane gives the Soldier a line of devastating affectlessness: 'Can't get tragic about your arse.' Indeed the Soldier's partiality for synecdoche (Ian as 'arse', violence as 'gun') is an endemic tendency in a world where parts have thoroughly displaced the reality of wholes.

In *Cleansed* Kane develops this process, and the flat, italicized statement of violence is both deliberate and casual at the same time. Tinker's nonchalant doling out of mayhem is without malice; even as he despatches Graham he delivers a banal truism: 'Life is sweet' (Kane 2001: 108). What is even more disturbing in this play is Kane's removal of any resistance bar a kind of placid stoicism, summed up in the reiterated word, 'lovely'. This is horror become routine and there's nothing to be done about it. At this point we are back to the unrecuperable nature of violence which Kane more than ever *expresses* in her work: despite all the comparisons with the Jacobeans or the Greeks its meaning resides precisely in its lack of meaning. In *Cleansed* there is no sign-system of violence to map the acts onto, unlike the systems which lie behind *The Duchess of Malfi* or *Agamemnon*. The latter plays function in a context where redemption and catharsis have literal analogues, or take part in a moralized schema of the body. But the application of such terms to Kane's texts is quite anachronistic.

If terror speaks at all then its message is devastatingly simple; it seeks to reveal the vulnerability of those far from combat zones who deem themselves immune to violence. It is no coincidence that it emerges at precisely the point when developed nations live in unprecedented prosperity and security, far from what the philosopher Ted Honderich has called 'a world of bad lives'.[5] This notion was highlighted perceptively in one of the keenest defences of *Blasted* – a letter to the *Guardian* from her fellow playwrights Martin Crimp, Paul Godfrey, Meredith Oakes and Gregory Motton: 'the power of Ms Kane's play lies precisely in the fact that she dares to range beyond personal experience and bring the wars that rage at such a convenient distance from this island right into its heart' (*Guardian* 23 January 1995). In this light one has to assess Kane's grafting of atrocity onto the bland, normalized violence of the world of Ian and Cate, and epitomized by Ian's lazy recitation of a murder over the phone to his editor before he rapes Cate. The sublimely arrogant image of the New World Order proclaimed by the American diplomat Francis Fukuyama as the 'end of history' was horribly belied by the inter-ethnic slaughters of the 1990s; yet whether in Rwanda or Bosnia the gawping voyeurs of the West could look on and dub these eruptions of face-to-face violence atavism. Kane's project was to map one world onto another, to bring the violence home. Her major plays are profoundly preoccupied with the representation of violence, which has become a ubiquitous commodity in mainstream culture. Ian's 'story', for instance, is hilariously estranged by the mechanisms of dictated typographic realization and punctuation:

> A serial killer slaughtered British tourist Samantha Scrace, S-C-R-A-C-E, in a sick murder ritual comma, police revealed yesterday point new par. The bubbly nineteen year old from Leeds was among seven victims found buried in identical triangular tombs . . . Each had been stabbed more than twenty times and placed face down comma, hands bound behind their backs point new par. (Kane 2001: 12)

Ian sees his task of packaging violence ('Shootings and rapes and kids getting fiddled by queer priests and schooteachers') into viable tabloid 'stories' as quite separate from responding to the horrors the Soldier tells him about, which he claims lack a 'personal' dimension. Ian is, after all, a 'home journalist' who doesn't cover 'foreign affairs'. To this extent he speaks for a culture that refuses to read violence as part of social action, and which seeks to trivialize suffering through narrative convention and cliché. In the re-education of Ian, the play releases violence from limiting ideology and consoling frameworks: it makes it precisely gratuitous. The actions that occur are beyond description; they even seem to defy theatrical realization. They push representation to its limits and break given forms in the process.

It is useful to compare the impact of *Blasted* with its peer texts. The paradigmatic account offered in Aleks Sierz's *In-Yer-Face Theatre* (2000) stakes out the terrain, if rather too inclusively. It is necessary to separate Kane out from the company with which she has been grouped, the *enfants terribles* of the mid-1990s. The plays of David Eldridge, Joe Penhall, Simon Block, Patrick Marber and Jez Butterworth, for instance, bear little resemblance to the ambitions and formal violations that Kane's work proposes. These dramatists, who represent collectively a movement not dissimilar to the wave of New British Artists or the practitioners of Britpop, share a traditionalist outlook on theatre form that marks a revisiting of the devices and effects of British theatre in its 1960s heyday — social realism, albeit nuanced, heightened and transmuted through an affiliation to the dialogic stringencies of a Pinter or a Mamet, is the presiding aesthetic for such writers. It is hardly surprising that their curt, socially accurate, eminently actable early plays, which largely centre on male experience and wholly repudiate any epic or political legacies, have yielded careers that move seamlessly from theatre to television and film. It is hard to imagine a similar trajectory for Kane had she been granted the time to 'mature'. Equally, whilst the defining voices above moved without difficulty between new-writing theatres (the Royal Court, the Bush, the Hampstead), their 'authenticity' offered as an identity card, their audiences (so often mirroring the characters in their plays) might have felt refreshed by 'new', 'in-yer-face' contents, drug taking, sexual frankness and the poetics of obscenity, but they were rarely confronted at a fundamental, ethical and perceptual level. Indeed, these plays carried within them their ideal audience, using shock in turn with recognition; they sought to cultivate a new audience rather than excoriating audiences as such. Aesthetic terrorism was hardly their bag.

Even more alarming contemporaries such as Anthony Neilson, Mark Ravenhill or Philip Ridley worked much closer to the shore than Kane. Ravenhill's *Shopping and Fucking* (1996) depends upon genre and shared cultural references, which may make the play hermetic for some, but creates recognition at a deep level for others; pleasure, after all, is a defining programme for the queer theatre Ravenhill practises, even if that pleasure houses extremity and suffering within it. It is notable that much of Ravenhill's work, like that of say Martin McDonagh's, is unabashedly comic in form, offering queasy closures and aphoristic dialogue in the Wildean tradition. It is hard to imagine *Blasted* gaining three successive revivals and a British Council subsidized world tour as Ravenhill's play did, an emissary for 'Cool Britannia' despite its ostensible bleakness.

In retrospect it seems that many of Kane's contemporaries are dramatists who are seeking to uphold or gently nuance the given consensus of the stage rather than challenge it. The rimming, baby-burning and anal evisceration that constitute the shock semiotics of Ravenhill's work are not interchangeable with the amputations, deocularizations and graftings that litter Kane's. In much so-called 'in-yer-face' theatre, violence provides a site of ambiguous pleasure and narrative movement; it is part of the moral economy of the play. In fact, much of the impetus towards staging violence came from the contemporary film aesthetic epitomized by director Quentin Tarantino, who pronounced it to be an action interchangeable with any other, generating no moral backwash, simply one sign amongst others. The disturbing yet consumable drama of self-abuse in Mark Ravenhill, symbolized by Gary in *Shopping and Fucking* wishing upon himself a 'hurt' that unifies desire and punishment in one hit, certainly troubles the audience – but the same masochism evident in Grace's demands in *Cleansed* has a more enduring impact simply from its structural position, which is precisely bathetic and anti-climactic. Kane's signs of violence are literally show-stopping in their ponderous heaviness and their un-apologetic frequency. Linguistically too the 'in-yer-face' oeuvre is marked by its street-smart demotic, its unleashing of a highly self-conscious and intertextualized profane poetics of speech, which is largely connected to its staging of masculinity. Again Tarantino, himself a perhaps unwitting apostle of David Mamet, stands as a model, his films marked by a baroque, language-heavy idiom, emotionally cauter-ized and wilfully ironic. The citability of the dialogue of Penhall or Ravenhill is an index of their theatricality; whilst much of the dialogue in these plays is spare, it is punctuated by self-inventing, bizarre extemporizations, such as Robbie's fantasy after the club sequence in *Shopping and Fucking*. The vigour of the story-telling and the bravado of the reference-laden text outrun the limits of social realism and transcend the functions of narrative – these plays are marked by writers with 'voices'.

Again the contrast with Kane is apparent; there is scarcely a memorable line in her first two plays. Dialogue in the first half of *Blasted* is barely allowed to transcend the monosyllable; there is little pleasure to be derived from the wearying reflex of the obscenity, the racist jokes, the ceaseless rehearsals of spoken abuse – as in her model play Bond's *Saved*, the dialogue takes the form of a maze. In the second half of the play, language loses even the spine of give and take, whittled down to gruelling litanies of violence, then finally reduced to grunts and animalistic outbursts. For all the tragic potential and imagistic echoes, there is no *sophrosyne* for Ian, just 'horror on horror's head accumulating'. Few dramatists have dared to enact the banality of evil quite so thoroughly.

The wheeling out of uncomprehending critical jeremiads, such as Jack Tinker's dubbing of the play a 'feast of filth', is proof positive of Kane's success, and reveals that the play has an inner didacticism which resides precisely in its refusal to tell and its compulsion to show. It is notable that the play has rarely been revived on the British stage, for it bears within it a resistance to theatre itself. The title, with its often-remarked clenched echo of Bond's *Saved*, is intentionally vague in reference – who is blasted? Is it a shared state for the characters? Is it an intention in relation to form itself, which meticulously pursues naturalism to its limit only to discard it for fragments of lyrical horror? The play relies on the tragic impulse to create truth out of pain but then seeks only to show the effects of pain, as if they spoke just as eloquently. There is a curious optimism in this idea that unvoiced staged suffering and violence are expressive rather than simply a refusal of expression (violence is a silence, after all) – the same optimism that perhaps motivates terrorists to see random acts of destruction, unvoiced and unowned, as a form of communication.

Cleansed reveals more of this equivocal and dangerous sensibility and starts to turn it into a code of sorts, however naïve and spasmodic. In one of her rarely granted interviews Kane revealed that the play was a response to Roland Barthes's provocative comment in *A Lover's Discourse* that being in love was akin to incarceration in Dachau (Saunders 2002: 93); and that indeed the play itself was a testimony to the experience of love. If critics and commentators struggled to place *Blasted* in a consensual context and finally offered it at best as a response to the shocking rage of inter-ethnic violence in former Yugoslavia, *Cleansed* could only be attributed to a more interior disorder, a more private pain. As the text is dedicated to fellow inpatients and staff at the ES3 clinic, an acute psychiatric inpatient admission ward at the Maudsley Hospital in London, that reading seems borne out. For again Kane effaced the inner clues to the play's functioning, an effacement rendered even more baffling in James MacDonald's epic and laborious first production, which seemed to progress with the unhurried tempo of a nightmare. *Cleansed* departed from the legible context of English playwriting and broke up into an assemblage of images with a lineage in expressionism and performance art.

The defining heresy against audiences and critics alike was the continued abandonment of narrative gratification in favour of fragments of action; the images are pegged on a slender fable: the accession of Grace to some mystical institution (presided over by the mysterious Tinker) to retrieve the remains of her brother Graham. Kane's own direction of Büchner's *Woyzeck* at the Gate Theatre the previous year seemed to grant her a structure – but where Büchner's scenes are accidentally foreshortened and oblique because the play was unfinished, Kane's play repudiates development and action. Indeed she replaces action with violence, which in most narratives advances and catalyses action – that is, psychological and linguistic reactions – but here it merely forms a type of punctuation, expressive of states and processes beyond language. In turn, the dialogue is flat and enervated, which reduces characters to mere bodies and voices.

If *Blasted*'s world of violence draws its meaning and plausibility from the systematized outrages of war, the violence is presented as a code without a key. In *Cleansed* the institution Grace enters is described as a university with cricket grounds and medical rooms, but it functions like a site for animal experimentation such as Huntingdon Life Sciences (Kane herself was a vegan and opposed to vivisection). It is a death camp but also, in a contemporary twist, a rape camp, as in Omarska in the former Yugoslavian conflict. The play's title certainly echoes a key phrase of that war – 'ethnic cleansing'. However, the setting is also a house of correction, a prison and an asylum, comparable to those analysed in Michel Foucault's *Discipline and Punish*. The deliberate confusion of functions and spaces is critical to Kane's terrorism – by fusing the familiar with the unfamiliar, she reproduces the shock of the extempore use of social spaces such as the deployment of gyms in Bosnia as torture chambers. But again Kane's bleak vision dresses up the entire process of being social as a constant deformation and mutilation of the self which even the perpetrators do not transcend – witness Tinker, who, like Ian, reveals male sexuality as chiefly masturbatory and voyeuristic. The ambiguous past participle that hangs over the play is expressive again of a profound challenge to judgement and categorization.

It seems to me that Kane's progress and presence as a dramatist are still deeply traumatic to the English theatre. Having considered Kane in relation to her contemporaries, it is worth setting her against what comes before and trying to account for why her plays proved so profoundly unintelligible to critics, audiences and the theatre culture. *Blasted* emerged in several drafts, the first, as mentioned before, presented at the end of Kane's year on David Edgar's MA in playwriting studies in Birmingham. This context is significant – it is hard to imagine the play emerging through a process of commission, or indeed for it to be described in advance of its written form. The slightly abstract context of a writing course far from the exigencies of the commercial stage offered Kane a space to envision a play that would almost certainly have had no home on the English stage as it stood – with Max Stafford-Clark working out his tenure at the Royal Court (its most obvious destination). The consensual play emerging from Stafford-Clark's long spell as artistic director (1980–1993) (see Roberts 1999) was, broadly speaking, epitomized by the work of dramatists such as April de Angelis or Timberlake Wertenbaker, often honed and refined through the prism of Stafford-Clark's own sensibility – plays which could be defined as offering a sort of feminist humanism, with clear social conviction behind them, marked by a degree of optimism, seeking a consensus and speaking to an embattled minority of the left for whom the Court was the house theatre. This theatre of tact, socially focused even in its lyrical departures from naturalism, was marked by a refusal to represent violence in general, and rape in particular. Its strategies were inclusive, and its commitments to the suggestive. Indeed a key play in this tradition, *Low Level Panic* (1990) by Clare MacIntyre, Kane's own tutor at Birmingham, embodies these virtues – there is frank talk of sexuality but none directly represented; men's shadows fall everywhere but men themselves are absent from the stage. The dominant tone is comic and wry, self-deprecating; indeed, implicit in the play is a sense of a shared audience of women finding their voices and men experiencing transformation. That such a play is now inconceivable on the British stage is partly the legacy of Kane's work, and an indication of the sundering of the consensual model of theatre Stafford-Clark had nurtured. *Blasted*'s emergence on a writing course is equally significant; a course with David Edgar at its head, an icon of a type of socialist aesthetic, developing a workable dramaturgy which Kane's play systematically violates on every level. This is a particularly vivid example of an Oedipal struggle at work, also evident in *Cleansed* with its image of a campus presided over by an engineer of human souls, carrying a curious overtone of the very institutionalization of creativity which its promulgation necessitates. As one of Kane's peers during that fateful year (1992–3), I can bear witness to her constant struggle with what she saw as the normative culture of the course, of the theatre as such. That struggle bore fruit in the rage of *Blasted* – here sex in all its dangerous pain is staged; here the tact of what was dubbed 'political correctness' is gleefully broken; here masculinity re-enters the stage in the wounded form of Ian, anatomized, even celebrated before being brutally punished; here the theatre of humanism and consensus is abandoned for ceaseless confrontation.

The affront of Kane to British theatre was to attack the shared codes of legibility and value that had enabled this consensual practice. In that sense she was as much symptom as cause. The post-ideological dramatists of the 1990s, who shook themselves loose from the constraint of 'grand narratives', and who were dubbed patronisingly by Benedict Nightingale 'Mrs Thatcher's disorientated children' (Saunders 2002: 6), found themselves incapable of affirming the socialist and feminist underpinnings of the British stage that preceded them. In that sense Kane, their bravest and most radical voice, revealed formally the intimation of the politics that would occupy the ensuing vacuum – post-humanist, experiential, non-consensual. The chorus of stunned disapproval that marked Sarah Kane's entry into the annals of British theatre may have congealed into mythology, but the challenge presented by *Blasted* is still to be fully answered.

NOTES

1 For all reviews of *Blasted* see *Theatre Record* XV.
2 See André Breton (1930). 'Second Manifesto of Surrealism' in Richard Seaver and Helen R. Lane (eds.) (1969). *Manifestoes of Surrealism*. Ann Arbor: University of Michigan Press, 117–94.

3 The observation was made in a press conference in Hamburg; it is cited amongst other places in the website www.jahsonic.com/Stockhausen.html.

4 See Anna Politkovskaya (2004). *Putin's Russia*. London: Harvill, for more details.

5 Ted Honderich (2002). *After the Terror*. Edinburgh: Edinburgh University Press, 1–29.

PRIMARY READING

Kane, Sarah (2001). *Complete Plays*. London: Methuen.

FURTHER READING

Aston, Elaine (2003). *Feminist Views on the English Stage*. Cambridge: Cambridge University Press.

Aston, Elaine and Reinelt, Janelle (eds.) (2000). *The Cambridge Companion to Modern British Women Playwrights*. Cambridge: Cambridge University Press.

Dromgoole, Dominic (2000). *The Full Room*. London: Methuen.

Iball, Helen (2005). 'Room Service: En Suite on the *Blasted* Frontline', *Contemporary Theatre Review* 15, 320–30.

Innes, Christopher (2002). *Modern British Drama: The Twentieth Century*. Cambridge: Cambridge University Press.

Luckhurst, Mary (2005). 'Infamy and Dying Young: Sarah Kane, 1971–1999' in Mary Luckhurst and Jane Moody (eds.). *Theatre and Celebrity in Britain, 1660–2000*. Basingstoke and New York: Palgrave, 107–24.

Roberts, Philip (1999). *The Royal Court Theatre and the Modern Stage*. Cambridge: Cambridge University Press.

Saunders, Graham (2002). '*Love Me or Kill Me*': *Sarah Kane and the Theatre of Extremes*. Manchester: Manchester University Press.

Sierz, Aleks (2000). *In-Yer-Face Theatre: British Drama Today*. London: Faber and Faber.

PART VI
Theatre since 1968

31

Theatre since 1968

David Pattie

1968–79: State of Emergency

Like 1956, 1968 is a label, and like all labels it is artificial. It implies a sharp, clean break with what came before, and a new way of thinking and working that somehow sprang into existence overnight. These supposedly iconic dates, however, favour certain perspectives and ideologies. 'History' is created by contemporary generations and invariably rewritten by succeeding ones. By the end of the 1960s, sufficient time had passed for a narrative to have formed around 1956. This narrative, which cast male writers like Osborne, Wesker and Arden in the role of social analysts, providing dynamic, insightful reportage on the state of the nation, was in fact a narrow version of the complexity of the theatrical landscape in the 1950s. Its main objective was to privilege the Royal Court Theatre's new plays above others, exclude individuals (like Joan Littlewood) who did not subscribe to the Court's version of (white, male) realism, and marginalize writers like Orton, whose work was commercially successful (but even so subversive). It is a narrative that also excluded work produced outside London, tended to colonize writers from Wales, Scotland and Ireland, and deprivileged work that was non-realistic (Beckett and Pinter, for example, did not find long-term homes at the Court). Post-1968 revolt had become a communal, generational matter. Students in America protested against the Vietnam war. Students and workers came close to overthrowing the government in France, and in Czechoslovakia reforming communists stood up against the Soviet Union. British society too seemed to be on the brink of transformation, and a new, radical, communitarian socialist left seemed poised to play some kind of part in the change. More specifically, playwrights reflecting on a changing society (often inspired by Brecht) had two advantages over previous generations. Firstly, a growing network of venues and companies – described variously as the fringe or as comprising an alternative theatre – sprang up in the wake of 1968. Secondly, after a number of well-publicized confrontations, most notably over Edward Bond's *Saved* (1965), theatre censorship was abolished in 1968. From being perhaps the most heavily regulated of art forms, theatre became one of the most free.

The 1968 generation of playwrights came to maturity at a profoundly traumatic time in British social and political life. Apart from the conflict in Northern Ireland and IRA bombing campaigns in England, there were struggles between trades unions and the Conservative government in the early 1970s (culminating in a miners' strike, a three-day working week, and a rota of power cuts); the oil-price crisis hit in 1973; there was an inexorable rise in unemployment and racial tension, sparking into conflict during the Notting Hill Carnival in 1976; the International Monetary Fund had to intervene in the British economy; and in 1979, the Winter of Discontent – an iconic moment for both left and right – unions and government clashed over cuts in public expenditure. As Baz Kershaw has noted: 'conditions of continual crisis and confrontation created an unavoidable impression of social fragmentation and loss of control' (Kershaw 1992: 134).

An image common to many plays written during the decade was of a society trembling on the point of destruction. Howard Brenton's *The Churchill Play* (1974), *Magnificence* (1973) and *Weapons of Happiness* (1976) showed political tensions sparking into open conflict. David Edgar's *Destiny* (1976) anatomized the conditions under which the radical right might begin to assume power; and other plays – David Hare's *Plenty* (1978), Barrie Keefe's *Gotcha* (1976) – echoed a wider sense of social disintegration in stories of individual, personal despair. These texts, and others like them – Hare's *Teeth 'n Smiles* (1975), Trevor Griffiths's *The Party* (1973) and *Comedians* (1975) – have sometimes been called state-of-the-nation plays. But a truer term might be state-of-emergency plays. The cosily oppressive system that had cushioned Britain as it sank into political and social crisis had split apart, and the very integrity of the British Isles seemed to be under threat as Scotland began to rediscover a sense of national identity. In prolonged postcolonial crisis, the notion of 'Britain' seemed to be collapsing, and underlying social and economic tensions were encoded in many plays of the period. It would be wrong to assume, however, that the changes these writers discussed all moved in one direction. All the writers named above would describe themselves as socialist, but there was a world of difference between Trevor Griffiths's fundamentally optimistic view of the changes to come – 'My plays are never about the battle between socialism and capitalism. I take that as being decisively won by socialism' (Bull 1984: 131) – and Arthur, in Hare's *Teeth 'n Smiles,* uneasily aware of the British state's continued ability to outflank and neutralize dissent: 'One day it's a revolution to say fuck on the bus. Next day it's the only way to get a ticket' (Hare 1996: 124).

The general sense that things could not continue as they were did not just provide subject matter for playwrights who would describe themselves as being on the socialist left. The same atmosphere is readily discernible in the writing of Stephen Poliakoff (in plays such as *Hitting Town* (1975), *Shout across the River* (1978) and *City Sugar* (1975), he created an urban world populated by the disaffected and the alienated); and Tom Stoppard's *Jumpers* (1972), a philosophical farce, shows a Britain governed by the Radical Liberals – a catch-all political formation which exists purely to exercise power. It was present too in David Rudkin's *Ashes* (1974); in Peter Barnes's *The Ruling Class* (1968) and *The Bewitched* (1974); and in the anarchic dramas of Heathcote Williams, especially *AC/DC* (1970). A general atmosphere of social disintegration and transformation is also clearly apparent in the work of rather more mainstream dramatists. For example, at the end of Alan Ayckbourn's *Absurd Person Singular* (1972) the most ambitious, egotistical and anti-social character (who seems, from a contemporary perspective, a Thatcherite in the making) easily wins out over his less motivated and acquisitive fellows. In Ireland, of course, 1968 marked the beginning of the Troubles, which generated a significant number of strikingly powerful plays (Brian Friel's *The Freedom of the City* (1973) being one of the most notable examples). Other Irish writers such as Tom Murphy, Frank McGuinness and Stuart Parker found themselves involved in a re-examination of Irish history. Harold Pinter's work, however, seemed to move against this general trend. His plays of the 1970s, such as *Old Times* (1971), *No Man's Land* (1975) and *Betrayal* (1978), seemed in comparison rather domestic, the ambiguous conflicts now played out between characters, rather than between the individual and a threatening outside world.

It would be wrong to suggest that all drama in the 1970s tended towards apocalypse, in one form or another. The 1968 generation of writers had close contact with a developing network of touring theatre companies whose aim was to analyse political problems and pose socialist solutions. Writers such as David Edgar moved from small companies to the larger London stages; whereas John McGrath and John Arden moved in the opposite direction. McGrath in particular removed himself wholesale from the established theatre, forming and writing for his own company 7:84:

> We wanted to be able to tour plays which had a very strong and immediate contemporary connection, that would raise a socialist perspective on contemporary events, that would entertain people and would notably appeal to the working class and the supporters of the working class, who could be found amongst students and amongst the intellectual circles who hover, one foot in the middle class and one foot in a general liberal movement. (McGrath 2002: 48–9)

McGrath's description is worth recording at length because it neatly captures two unique elements of the time: firstly, it suggests that there was a network of audiences who could support and sustain the kind of work McGrath wanted to do; secondly, it implies that this audience was interested in work that 'raise[d] a socialist perspective', that is, work that posited a new, socialist society meant to replace and redeem a divided and decaying Britain. This optimism buoyed companies like 7:84 for much of the decade: it also threaded its way into the work of Edward Bond (amongst others), who, after a series of works that anatomized the impact of social change on the individual (*Bingo* (1973), *The Fool* (1975) and *The Woman* (1978)), turned his attention to what he called 'answer plays' – plays in which revolutionary violence would lead to a society that was, if not perfect, then at least better than the one it replaced.

The sense that a new world could be born from the ruins of the old was not simply the preserve of socialist writers and theatre-workers. A generation of women writers, influenced by the upsurge in feminist activism at the end of the 1960s and closely allied with the alternative theatre movement, also began to make an impact on the British stage. Feminist playwrights followed the same path as many of their male counterparts; their work was supported by a developing network of small-scale theatre companies who saw it as their mission to find an audience who could engage with such plays. A large number of women writers produced work in the 1970s, including Bryony Lavery, Michelene Wandor, Jill Posner, Claire Luckham, Mary O'Malley and Louise Page. Two stood out: Pam Gems and Caryl Churchill tended to overshadow their contemporaries and for too long were treated as token women playwrights by academics and critics. Both Gems and Churchill had begun to write before the events of the late 1960s and the birth of contemporary feminism. During the 1970s both turned to the theatre – at least partly because of the influence of the feminist movement's impact on the theatre of the time. Gems's work, after her breakthrough play *Dusa, Fish, Stas and Vi* (1976), dealt most notably with the lives of a series of iconic women – Queen Christina, Edith Piaf, Marlene Dietrich – who had to negotiate the difficult path between their private selves and a socially acceptable image of womanhood. Churchill's 1970s work blended a strong commitment to both socialism and feminism with an interest in experimentation. Her formally innovative plays combined an analysis of gender and economic oppression, both in contemporary Britain and in other historical ages – see, for example, *Owners* (1972), *Light Shining in Buckinghamshire* (1976), *Vinegar Tom* (1976) and *Cloud Nine* (1978).

Churchill, one of Europe's great living playwrights, developed much of her work in collaboration with, and supported by, new touring companies such as Monstrous Regiment (a feminist theatre group) and Joint Stock (a theatre company who evolved their shows through a process of collaborative research and workshopping). Other theatre companies (Gay Sweatshop, Black Theatre Co-operative, Temba, Tara Arts) supported other types of new writing and produced plays that explored gay and lesbian issues, or the position of ethnic groups in British society. All in all, the 1970s was a very fruitful time for new writers. But as the decade came to an end, the promise of potential transformation that had seemed at least partially attainable at the end of the 1960s now seemed to be receding. David Hare noted that the state of emergency that had been an integral part of British life during the 1970s had led, not to a raising of socialist consciousness, but to a pervasive cynicism in the nation's public life. It became harder, as the 1970s ended and the 1980s began, to voice a desire that the world should change with the same confidence that Griffiths and McGrath had manifested earlier. As Churchill put it in 1982:

> [I know] quite well what kind of society I would like: decentralized, non-authoritarian, communist, non-sexist – a society in which people can be in touch with their feelings

and in control of their lives. But it always sounds both ridiculous and unattainable when you put it into words. (Aston 1997: 3)

1979–89: Thatcherism and the Theatre

Thatcherism did not come out of nowhere: the political trends that led to the election of Margaret Thatcher in 1979 had already been identified by some on the left. An article in the journal *Marxism Today* written by Stuart Hall described a 'Great Moving Right Show' (reprinted in Hall 1988: 39–56) – a move away from the welfare state, towards a rather more traditionally authoritarian political style. The Conservatives were well placed to take advantage of this; even so, it was only after the industrial conflicts of the winter of 1978–9 that Labour finally lost the political initiative. Thatcher came to power promising change: Britain was to be freed from the shackles of the welfare state, and the naturally entrepreneurial spirit of the British people was to be unleashed; at the same time, society was to return to traditional values of self-reliance and individual prudence (there was, she famously proclaimed, no such thing as society – only individuals and their families). Thatcher frequently gave the impression that the British people were rather schizophrenic – able to compete ruthlessly in the marketplace during the day, and return home to a traditional family life in the evenings. This proved to be an unsustainable contradiction, and in power the traditional and free-market aspects of Conservative philosophy frequently clashed. However, facing a divided opposition, with some large-scale victories to its apparent credit (the Falklands conflict in 1982 and the bitter conflict with the National Union of Miners in 1984–5), and with the support of the newly elected right-wing American president Ronald Reagan, the Conservatives seemed to carry all before them.

The new political atmosphere affected the theatre both directly and indirectly. The arts were encouraged to pay their way: funding was curtailed and the Arts Council of England was brought into the ambit of Thatcherite philosophy. The Arts Council's traditional approach to arts funding – that money should be concentrated in 'centres of excellence', most of which happened to be in London – came to co-exist uneasily with the first stirrings of the idea that the arts were part of the Creative Industries, and were therefore worthy of inclusion in the free market. In this atmosphere, the kind of work done by small-scale theatre companies in the 1970s became increasingly difficult to sustain. The number of companies continued to increase for much of the decade, peaking at just over 300 in 1986, and the sector continued to evolve, as touring groups became more and more interested in the idea of working with specific communities rather than a loosely defined idea of the working classes and the intelligentsia. However, there is no doubt that the political atmosphere was against such work. Many companies had their funding cut: others found it increasingly difficult to develop and sustain their work. At the same time, the fortunes of the West End theatre revived. The most successful theatrical product of the 1980s was the spectacular musical; *Cats* (1982), *Les Misérables* (1987), *Starlight Express* (1984) and

The Phantom of the Opera (1986) were perhaps the most visible face of Thatcherite theatre – commodified, market-orientated, and (the most important criterion) self-financing. Indeed, the musical has firmly established itself as the only example of a genuinely mass theatre in the West.

Throughout Britain the consequences of Thatcherite policy were quickly felt (as severe recession was followed by unsustainable growth, which itself led only to yet another severe recession). Ideologically motivated funding cuts led not to a renewed spirit of experimentation, but to a greater uncertainty – and, consequently, artistic directors lost their appetite for risk-taking. In practice, this meant that a still-growing sector of the British theatre was strangled before its full potential had been realized, and that theatre companies were forced into a profoundly uneasy compromise between responding to a new political and social dispensation, and satisfying the new administration's desire for market solutions and traditional values. If the prototypical theatrical figure of the 1970s was the socialist agitator, in the 1980s it was the administrator – a necessary addition to many small and middle-scale companies: after all, someone had to hack their way through the jungle of funding applications and business plans that had sprung up in the wake of the government's policies. Doug Lucie's plays *Fashion* (1987) and *Doing the Business* (1990) explored the ruthlessness of the commercial world, the latter play offering a sardonic indictment of business sponsorship of the arts. On the mainstream stages, the 1980s were given over to the work of Frayn, Bennett, Stoppard and Ayckbourn. As John Bull noted in *Stage Right* (1994), their work represents a full-blown retreat from the idea that theatre could function as a diagnostic tool for those engaged in progressive politics. But Harold Pinter's and Caryl Churchill's work bucked the trend. Starting with *One for the Road* (1984), Pinter's plays became overtly political. Pinter in effect returned to an old theme – the way in which power distorts and deforms both the powerful and the powerless – and simply made the rationale employed by the powerful a little more explicit (without sacrificing the sense of uncontainable threat that marked his earlier work). Churchill's work increasingly examined war, genocide and man-made threats to future survival.

However, the 1968 generation did not cede ground without a fight. Indeed, they provided some of the decade's most memorable theatrical images: Anthony Hopkins, hair slicked back and gleaming, as Lambert Leroux in Hare and Brenton's *Pravda* (1985); the truck lights shining through the fence at Greenham Common in David Edgar's *Maydays* (1983); the trading-floor scene at the end of the first act of Churchill's *Serious Money* (1987). For much of the decade the writers formed by the events at the end of the 1960s provided an acute, incisive commentary on the new state of the nation, but they were aware that the political tide was now travelling in the opposite direction. This manifested itself in a number of plays: Brenton's *Greenland* (1988) posited a utopian world far beyond the end of capitalism, which could only be reached by the play's contemporary characters after they had been driven to suicidal despair: and in Hare's *The Secret Rapture* (1988), a wholly good character, Isobel, is marginalized and destroyed both by the social trends endorsed by

Thatcherism, and by something less definable – by the presence of evil in her world, a presence she finds almost impossible to recognize.

The 1968 generation, then, spent much of the decade fighting a losing battle against the ethos of the times: some, like Edgar, Churchill and Brenton, continued to anatomize the fault-lines that Thatcherism had opened; some, like Howard Barker and (arguably) David Hare, retreated from direct social engagement and took refuge in metaphysics; some, like Trevor Griffiths, found it increasingly difficult to gain access to production and were forced into a temporary silence. This was not entirely due to the ideological pressure exercised by the government: it was also due to the fact that the radical energy which had sustained the field in the 1970s had moved elsewhere. It had passed to community theatre (the first part of the decade saw a mini-boom in large-scale community dramas, based on the model established by Ann Jellicoe's Colway Theatre Trust in Devon). It had also passed to women's writing. Because feminism had grown up in opposition not only to capitalism, but also to some of the more patriarchal aspects of socialism, it was less vulnerable to the anti-leftist tenor of the times: writers like Sarah Daniels could mount a radical assault on the forces of patriarchy through plays such as *Masterpieces* (1983), *The Devil's Gateway* (1983) and *Neaptide* (1984), and do so with an ideological certainty that was not vulnerable to the charge that socialism was dead.

There were other points of growth and change. The country was splitting: by the end of the decade, the number of Conservative MPs in Scotland and Wales had dwindled almost to nothing. In both countries, the centre of political gravity was shifting to the left. Scottish theatre, for example, was firmly set on a different trajectory to theatre in England; the example set by John McGrath in the previous decade had been followed and expanded upon by a number of touring groups (Wildcat, Borderline, Communicado and others); major theatres such as the Citizens in Glasgow and the Traverse in Edinburgh continued to explore European theatre and to encourage both Scottish and international new writing. In Ireland, the activities of several new (or relatively new) touring companies – Druid, Charabanc, and most notably Field Day, established by Brian Friel and the actor Stephen Rea in 1980 – not only provided writers with a further outlet for their work (Charabanc, for example, staged Marie Jones's early work), but also were responsible for some of the most powerful re-examinations of Irish life and identity (Brian Friel's *Translations* (1980) and Stewart Parker's *Pentecost* (1987)). In Wales, the influence of the Cardiff Laboratory Theatre, Moving Being, and then in the 1980s the performance group Brith Gof meant that theatrical experimentation, and questions of culture and identity, were explored not in text-based theatre but in live and performance art. This proved particularly suitable for a country whose relation to the dominant language of the theatre, English, in many ways replicated that of a colonized nation; if the very nature of language itself was contested, then the debate could be conducted better through the creation of images that reflected on language and identity. All in all, the centre of theatrical gravity in the British Isles had, by the end of the decade, begun to move from London, more decisively than it had in previous decades.[1]

Wales at the time was running slightly ahead of the theatrical tide. The radical confrontational politics of the 1960s and early 1970s had almost exhausted themselves by the end of the 1980s, sapped by the 10-year-long confrontation with Thatcherism. At the same time, the radical certainties of the 1960s were being replaced by the all-pervasive sense that there were no certainties left to defend. Postmodernism had existed as a loose theoretical formation since the 1970s: the term – which at its simplest has served as a label for an age where there are no fixed points of reference, where representation has come to stand in for reality, and where the individual is cast adrift in a sea of depthless affect – came into its own in the 1990s. Some writers and groups in the 1980s had noticed that the world was changing; Caryl Churchill had begun to explore the construction of gender and social identity in a characteristically fragmented postmodern style (*A Mouthful of Birds* (1986), co–written with David Lan). Forced Entertainment, a performance group based in postindustrial Sheffield, created a number of devised works which explored the fragmented country created by the aggressive economic policies of the 1980s. In retrospect, after the events of 1989, this type of work seemed uncannily prescient.

1989–2001: The Happy World

In 1989 the Berlin Wall was torn down and with it the sense of a world shaped by two implacably opposed ideological forces. The collapse of the regimes in Eastern Europe and the apparent triumph of a particularly aggressive type of capitalism put paid to the hopes of the left in Britain and elsewhere. At the same time the continued economic pressure placed on the theatre and the arts by central government ensured that new work was far more difficult to sustain than it had been in previous decades. At the beginning of the 1990s, the mainstream British stage seemed to be the province of directors and designers. On the fringes, the initiative had passed from writers to performance groups whose work crossed generic and artistic boundaries (Forced Entertainment, Blast Theory, DV8 Physical Theatre and Theatre de Complicite). The work of these and similar companies had an explicitly international dimension. For example, Tim Etchells in Forced Entertainment has always acknowledged the debt the company owes to Elizabeth Lecompte and the Wooster Group; and Theatre de Complicite were schooled in performance techniques developed by Jacques Lecoq in France.

The end of communism in Eastern Europe inspired a number of dramas from the 1968 generation which rank alongside the best of their work in previous decades. Brenton's *Berlin Bertie* (1992), Churchill's *Mad Forest* (1990) and David Edgar's *The Shape of the Table* (1990) and *Pentecost* (1994) were intriguing works. David Hare created a state-of-the-nation trilogy – *Racing Demon* (1990), *Murmuring Judges* (1991) and *The Absence of War* (1993) – which took stock of the depredations the prevailing political climate had wreaked on the nation's institutions. But in general, those writers who were unencumbered by the troubling ideological baggage of socialism

– Stoppard, Frayn and Bennett – once again managed to sail through the 1990s without difficulty. Indeed, the 1990s saw some of their most notable successes – *Copenhagen* (1998) and *Arcadia* (1993). Caryl Churchill, whose work had anticipated the new cultural climate, continued to work successfully in the new, post-Cold War world. In retrospect, though, the beginning of the 1990s was as much of a point of transition as 1968 had been: a generation of writers, whose work had been closely tied to a particular political and social situation, found that the world had changed irrevocably – that the solutions which they had previously advocated no longer applied.

However, any sense that drama as an art form was dying in the postmodern 1990s was short-lived. The fringe network established in previous decades had been decimated by years of underfunding, but some London theatres (in particular the Royal Court and the Bush) continued to provide active support for new writing; and once again new writers were well placed to catch the prevailing cultural tide:

> The fall of the Berlin Wall and the exit of Margaret Thatcher showed those under twenty-five that, despite the evidence of political ossification, change was possible; the end of Cold War ideological partisanship freed young imaginations. Youth could be critical of capitalism without writing state-of–the-nation plays; it could be sceptical of male power without being dogmatically feminist; it could express outrage without being politically correct. Picking away the tattered remains of modernism, and encouraged by postmodernism's notion that 'anything goes', theatre shook off the style police and began to explore a new-found freedom. (Sierz 2000: 36)

The 1990s generation of writers were as heterogeneous as any such grouping: and the range of work they produced was as diverse as any produced by previous generations of writers – from Joe Penhall's naturalistic plays *Some Voices* (1994) and *Blue/Orange* (2000), Anthony Neilson's blackly surreal psychodramas *Normal* (1990) and *Penetrator* (1994), to the theatrically and textually inventive writing of Sarah Kane and Martin Crimp, who wrote respectively *4:48 Psychosis* (2000) and *Attempts on her Life* (1997). But the view of Britain in 1990s drama was a profoundly unsettling one: writers might have embraced the supposed freedom that Sierz describes above, but the Britain they explored was an unsettling, morally ambiguous place, locked into a killing compromise with the free market, and profoundly uncertain about the past, the present and the future. The Britain of the 1990s was memorably described in Mark Ravenhill's *Some Explicit Polaroids* (1999) as 'the happy land'; a land where it seemed momentarily possible to deny suffering through acts of willed self-definition. Most 1990s drama suggested this was impossible: sooner or later, the drugs would stop working and the walls would come down.

Other themes emerged in 1990s writing: a preoccupation with masculinity (in the work of Patrick Marber and Jez Butterworth); a welcome tendency to treat gay and lesbian relationships as entirely normal (as in the work of Phyllis Nagy, Mark Ravenhill and Jonathan Harvey); an interest in the marginalized and excluded

(Joe Penhall, Rebecca Pritchard, Judy Upton); and a wider exposure for writers from other parts of the British isles and Ireland (Chris Hannan, Liz Lochhead, David Greig, David Harrower, Nicola McDonald and Gregory Burke from Scotland; Sebastian Barry, Christina Reid, Conor McPherson, Marina Carr and Martin McDonagh from Ireland). Indeed, the mid-1990s marks the beginning of a period in British theatre in which the traditional London centres that nurtured new writing faced increasing competition from other venues and other parts of the country. Scotland in particular had moved further and further away from the political mainstream occupied by the rest of the country. Devolution, granted in 1999, merely cemented this trend; and it managed also to cement into place a social and cultural climate that was conducive to new writing for the stage. In the second half of the 1990s and the early 2000s, regional theatres have transformed the new writing renaissance: major projects in theatres like the Birmingham Rep, the Liverpool Everyman and the West Yorkshire Playhouse have established very successful new writing centres. Touring companies (Paines Plough, Out of Joint and the like) have also provided invaluable support for new writers. Changes in funding policy have made the theatre sector as a whole more audience-orientated, with initiatives to encourage the development of black and Asian theatres. The mid-1990s inaugurated a boom in new British and Irish writing for the stage which has yet to subside (Luckhurst 2006).

The subject matter of 1990s drama was immensely varied and resists easy definitions, particularly those which stressed the shock value of the texts. Terms like 'new brutalism', 'in-yer-face theatre' or, more picturesquely, 'smack and sodomy plays' might capture a pervasive sense of violence and desperation in new writing, but violence on stage is hardly new. Playwrights like Mark Ravenhill condemned the categorization of their work and argued that critical attempts to label them as sensationalist did not do justice to an underlying tone of moral seriousness in their plays. As Ravenhill said in 2004: 'Certainly I've always written against moral relativism. I want audiences to make choices: to decide moment by moment – intellectually and emotionally – whether what the characters are doing and the choices they are making are right or wrong' (Ravenhill 2004: 313). Ravenhill's dramas, which seemed so modishly shocking when they were first staged (the title of his first success, *Shopping and Fucking* (1996), encapsulated a mid-nineties trend towards obscenity for its own sake), now might be described as postmodern reimaginings of Brechtian epic theatre. Sarah Kane, the writer who excited the most virulent abuse from critics, has more in common with the last-ditch desperation of Samuel Beckett than she does with the stylish bloodletting of the films *Reservoir Dogs* and *Kill Bill* (Quentin Tarantino's films were a frequent and profoundly misleading reference point for critics).

In effect, then, the 1990s generation were for the most part as concerned with the position of the individual in society as the generation that they seemed to have replaced. What was different about their work, though, was the all-pervasive sense that grand narratives had died; that party politics were suspect and that there was no single 'British' community. In the 1990s, new writing caught and commented on an uneasy awareness that, in the happy post-Cold War world, isolated individuals would risk everything – including themselves – in the desperate attempt to connect. The question of identity, both personal and national, is anatomized again and again in contemporary British and Irish drama (Harvie 2005: *passim*).

2001 to the Present: Stuff Happens

Postmodernity has not aged well. A world which seemed denuded of meaning in the 1990s now seems as much in thrall to grand narratives as it ever was: witness the triumph (at least in the polls) of the religious right in America; the terrorist attacks on the World Trade Centre, and America's retaliation, first in Afghanistan, and then in Iraq; the growing awareness of endemic global poverty, created and sustained mainly by the economic choices made by rich governments; the first discernible signs that global warming is occurring. All have tended to undercut the postmodern claim that modern life is affectless, fragmented and contingent. Once again, the theatre has proved a reliable cultural barometer. Documentary drama (as written by Richard Norton-Taylor, promoted by the Tricycle Theatre in London, and bolstered by West End successes, not only of the Tricycle's work, but also of David Hare's *The Permanent Way* (2003) and *Stuff Happens* (2004)) is undergoing a resurgence. There have been a number of recent plays (by Roy Williams, Kwame Kwei-Armah and Gurpreet Kaur Bhatti, whose play *Behzti* (2005) was controversially taken off by Birmingham Rep after protests from the local Sikh community) which have addressed the contradictory complexity of British social life, as experienced by those groups who remain marginalized, even in a supposedly multicultural society. Gary Mitchell and Owen McCafferty have written incisively about the long transition from conflict to peace in Northern Ireland. In addition, some writers whose work has spanned the period under discussion (Harold Pinter and Caryl Churchill most obviously spring to mind) have become international symbols of the strength of British playwriting. It is, however, fascinating to note that neither Pinter nor Churchill, nor their successor Sarah Kane, owes much to the apparently ingrained idea in England that realism is superior to other forms of drama. Perhaps the most characteristic dramatist of the new millennium (at least so far) is the Scottish writer David Greig. As with so many of his contemporaries, he has written for a number of different stages (from his own theatre company Suspect Culture, co-founded with Graham Eatough, to the Royal Shakespeare Company). Greig's writing also does not conform to a strictly realistic format but is a compelling mixture of naturalism, Brechtian analysis and poetic meditation. Greig's work explores individual identity in a shifting political and social climate; his best work – *Europe* (1994), *The Cosmonaut's Last Message to the Woman he Loved in the Former Soviet Union* (1999), *Victoria* (2000), *Outlying Islands* (2002) – links him to a tradition of British playwriting which has been dominant arguably since World War II, and certainly since 1968: a tradition which regards theatre as perhaps the best vehicle for those who wish to show us, as powerfully as possible, what it feels like to live in a changing, uncertain world.

NOTE

1 See Kershaw (2004: 291–512) for informative essays on mainstream and alternative theatres, and theatre in England, Wales and Scotland; and Luckhurst (2006).

FURTHER READING

Aston, Elaine (1997). *Caryl Churchill*. London: Northcote House.

Aston, Elaine (1999). *Feminist Theatre Practice: A Handbook*. London: Routledge.

Aston, Elaine and Reinelt, Janelle (eds.) (2000). *The Cambridge Companion to Modern British Women Playwrights*. Cambridge: Cambridge University Press.

Bertens, Hans (1995). *The Idea of the Postmodern*. London: Routledge.

Bertens, Hans and Natoli, Joseph (eds.) (2002). *Postmodernism: The Key Figures*. Oxford: Blackwell.

Bolger, Dermot (2001). *Druids, Dudes, and Beauty Queens: The Changing Face of Irish Theatre*. Dublin: New Island.

Bull, John (1984). *New British Political Dramatists*. Houndmills: Macmillan.

Bull, John (1994). *Stage Right: Crisis and Recovery in British Contemporary Mainstream Theatre*. Basingstoke: Macmillan.

Eagleton, Terry (2003). *After Theory*. London: Allen Lane.

Goodman, Lizbeth (1993). *Contemporary Feminist Theatres: To Each Her Own*. London: Routledge.

Griffin, Gabriele (2003). *Contemporary Black and Asian Women Playwrights in Britain*. Cambridge: Cambridge University Press.

Hall, Stuart (1998). *The Hard Road to Renewal: Thatcherism and the Crisis of the Left*. London and New York: Verso.

Hanna, Gillian (1991). *Monstrous Regiment: Four Plays and a Collective Celebration*. London: Nick Hern.

Hare, David (1996). *Plays 1*. London: Faber and Faber.

Harvie, Jen (2005). *Staging the UK*. Manchester: Manchester University Press.

Innes, Christopher (2002). *Modern British Drama: The Twentieth Century*. Cambridge: Cambridge University Press.

Itzin, Catherine (1980). *Stages in the Revolution: Political Theatre in Britain since 1968*. London: Eyre Methuen.

Kershaw, Baz (1992). *The Politics of Performance*. London: Routledge.

Kershaw, Baz (1999). *The Radical in Performance*. London: Routledge.

Kershaw, Baz (ed.) (2004). *The Cambridge History of British Theatre*. Vol. 3. Cambridge. Cambridge University Press.

Luckhurst, Mary (2006). *Dramaturgy: A Revolution in Theatre*. Cambridge: Cambridge University Press.

McGrath, John (1989). *A Good Night Out*. London: Methuen.

McGrath, John (1990). *The Bone Won't Break: On Theatre and Hope in Hard Times*. London: Methuen.

McGrath, John (2002). *Naked Thoughts that Roam About*. London: Nick Hern.

Osment, Philip (1989). *Gay Sweatshop: Four Plays and a Company*. London: Methuen.

Poggi, Valentina and Rose, Margaret (2000). *A Theatre that Matters: Twentieth-Century Scottish Drama and Theatre*. Milano: Unicopli.

Rabey, David Ian (2003). *English Drama since 1940*. London: Pearson.

Ravenhill, Mark (2004). 'A Tear in the Fabric: The James Bulger Case and New Theatre Writing in the Nineties', *New Theatre Quarterly* 80, 305–14.

Rees, Roland (1992). *Fringe First: Pioneers of Fringe Theatre on Record*. London: Oberon Books.

Reinelt, Janelle (1994). *After Brecht: British Epic Theatre*. Ann Arbor: University of Michigan Press.

Richards, Shaun (2003). *The Cambridge Companion to Twentieth-Century Irish Drama*. Cambridge: Cambridge University Press.

Richtarik, Marilynn (1995). *Acting Between the Lines: The Field Day Theatre Company and Irish*

Cultural Politics, 1980–1984. New York: Oxford University Press.

Ritchie, Rob (1987). *The Joint Stock Book*. London: Methuen.

Sierz, Aleks (2000). *In-Yer-Face Theatre: British Drama Today*. London: Faber and Faber.

Stephenson, Heidi and Langridge, Natasha (eds.) (1997). *Rage and Reason: Women Playwrights on Playwriting*. London: Methuen.

Stevenson, Randall and Wallace, Gavin (eds.) (1996). *Scottish Theatre since the Seventies*. Edinburgh: Edinburgh University Press.

32

Lesbian and Gay Theatre: All Queer on the West End Front

John Deeney

1968 and All What?

In late 1967, when the lord chamberlain refused the Royal Court Theatre's licence application for Edward Bond's *Early Morning* (1968), the theatre censor's powers were already in terminal decline. The controversy over Bond's *Saved* (1965) had led the Labour home secretary to initiate an inquiry into theatre censorship. The final upshot of this process, the 1968 Theatres Act, revoked completely the lord chamberlain's powers in such matters, thereby removing a 231-year-old stranglehold. Whilst *Saved* is rightly seen as the catalyst here, *Early Morning* is significant for quite different reasons. A fantasized deconstruction of Victorian politics, ethics and the ruling elite, the play partly concerns Queen Victoria in the throes of a lesbian liaison with Florence Nightingale: 'I'm changed. Queen Victoria has raped me ... Her legs are covered in shiny black hairs' (Bond 1968: 28). We later see Nightingale in the national dress of Victoria's Scottish servant, John Brown, so that the queen can be perceived as 'a normal lonely widow' (ibid.: 71). Victoria is also represented in heaven, chewing contentedly on a bloodied human hand. Nicolas de Jongh has argued that such scenes seemed purposefully 'calculated to enrage the Chamberlain' (de Jongh 2000: 232) – and indeed depicting the sovereign as a cannibalistic lesbian did kick against everything that the chamberlain – as a member of the royal household – stood for.

It might seem somewhat incongruous to open a chapter on post-1968 'lesbian and gay theatre' with an allusion to *Early Morning*. The play is rarely invoked in commentaries on the dramatic representations of same-sex relations. We might presume that this is because Bond is identified as a heterosexual playwright, and/or that his dark yet farcical treatment of lesbianism in *Early Morning* is just one of many strategies for attacking the ethical system and discourses we have inherited from the Victorians (that is, this is not a play *about* lesbianism per se). Conversely, the development of a visible and contemporary lesbian and gay theatre in Britain (or more specifically England) has commonly come to imply that, variously:

its practitioners openly identify as lesbian or gay; the work this theatre produces is primarily *about* the cultural, historical, political, psychological and social configuration of those same identities; and this is a theatre principally *for* lesbian and gay audiences.

Whilst the genesis of such a theatre has been routinely contextualized around the aftermath of the 1968 Theatres Act, the forces that made this theatre possible extended well beyond that Act. Thus, repeatedly, the naissance of a contemporary lesbian and gay theatre has been viewed as a component of the 'fringe' or 'alternative theatre' movement from 1968 through to the 1980s, as part of the collective (though by no means consensual) drive towards overt political, feminist, and black and Asian theatre practices (see Chambers and Prior 1987; Itzin 1980; Shellard 1999). The playwright David Edgar positions such developments within a much broader time-frame:

The first wave of 1956 playwrights confronted the consequences of [. . .] working class empowerment [. . .] For the generation that followed, forged in the youth revolt of the late 1960s, the questions were much more aggressively political. They were about the limits of social democracy and the welfare state (in the jargon of the time, the debate between liberal reform and socialist revolution). While in the early 1980s the ground shifted once more, as women, black and gay playwrights confronted the questions of difference and identity which had emerged in the 1960s and 1970s. (Edgar 1999: 5)

Edgar argues that gay playwrights (though not lesbian – might lesbian be included with 'women'?) only come to the fore in the 1980s. So where might this leave the gay and lesbian theatre work that has emerged since 1968? Revealingly, Edgar's orderly narrative works only by exclusion. He is certainly attempting to make sense of particular connected patterns in postwar playwriting, but he can only do this by foregrounding the work that suits these patterns. Edgar is, it seems, primarily referring to those playwrights (such as himself, Howard Brenton, David Hare and Caryl Churchill) who have graduated from the fringe to the mainstream subsidized theatre: namely the Royal Court Theatre, the National Theatre and the Royal Shakespeare Company.

Whilst it is not the intention here to deny the importance of 1968 as a turning point in the overt politicization of theatre practice, this chapter will argue that its symbolic hold over our understanding of subsequent developments in lesbian and gay playwriting and its production now invites vigilant revisionism. In relation to this, Edgar's overview highlights the danger of divorcing playwriting from the sites of its production. And in terms of the historical mapping of lesbian and gay work this, as we shall see, is a critical matter. Most significantly, the confluence of 'lesbian' and 'gay' theatre – as with all forms of cultural production – has come to represent a theoretical and historical minefield. Alan Sinfield has latterly argued that all 'gay and lesbian theatre representations need to be considered together', refuting a previously held position that 'theatre was a distinctively male homosexual space'. Sinfield's change of position was made on the basis of evidence of 'overlapping milieux' of lesbians and gay men in inter-war English 'high society, the cultural establishment, the bohemian avant-garde' (Sinfield 1999: 4). Significantly, Sinfield's comments introduce what is (to date) the only study devoted to lesbian *and* gay theatre in twentieth-century London and New York theatres. But whilst Sinfield is careful to highlight the 'specificity of lesbian situations' (ibid.: 4), his attempt to conceive a historical continuum with a focus on 'representations' means that (*pace* Edgar) the production and modus operandi of such a theatre receive only secondary attention. Consequently, Sinfield fails to account properly for the evidential lacuna that has come to distinguish lesbian from gay theatre practice. Jeffrey Weeks, for example, has argued that the emergence of lesbian and male homosexual identities in twentieth-century Britain carry 'different social implications': 'For men, homosexuality is seen as a rejection of maleness, with all its socially approved connotations. For women, it can be an assertion of femaleness, of separateness from men, and of identity' (Weeks 1990: 101). In the theatre – just one of the cultural sites in which identity might be provided with a model – Weeks's distinction, as this chapter will demonstrate, does not entirely hold up.

Nevertheless, Weeks does highlight the importance of accounting for the contesting narratives, histories and discourses that inform lesbian and gay cultural production. It is simplistic to presume that the alliances between lesbians and gay men are founded on the notion of same-sex identification, and that political coalitions are forged in terms of how such identification stands in opposition to dominant ideology – an ideology that normalizes and perpetuates male heterosexual identities and practices. Whilst the advent of second-wave feminism in the 1970s provided a renewed political locus for lesbians, the early years of the liberation movement 'insisted on women as the same rather than different', and this 'generally meant that the lesbian position was overlooked' (Aston 1995: 102). Second-wave feminism initially emphasized the identity of the group over that of the individual, and thus the greater potential in collective action. The point here is that such marginalization further served to emphasize lesbian difference and outsiderliness. As Monique Wittig notably put it: ' "woman" has meaning only in heterosexual systems of thought and heterosexual economic systems. Lesbians are not women' (quoted in Freeman 1997: 3). Such analysis might yet imply a union of sorts with gay men. Yet male homosexuality has, as we have seen, been discoursed in terms of it being *contingent* on male heterosexuality; the thing, to quote Weeks, that it knowingly 'rejects'.

This invites a return to the 'problem' presented by a play such as *Early Morning*. Sinfield's foregrounding of 'representations' comes as part of a more concerted move by lesbian, gay and feminist scholars to investigate how 'theatre helped to establish, consolidate and challenge notions of lesbian and gay men which were held both *by them* and *in society at large*' (Sinfield 1999: 4, my emphasis). This presents a particular challenge in the historical mapping of lesbian and gay theatre. De Jongh states that an 'authentic gay theatre' emerged in the 1970s, 'created by companies presenting plays to gay audiences' (de Jongh 1992: 144). Correspondingly, but with more exactness, Sandra Freeman dates the 'beginning of lesbian theatre' to '1975' (Freeman 1997: 20). But if we characterize 1968 as a nodal point that generated a synchronic readjustment across theatrical, political and social spheres, then in lesbian and gay theatre we are also in danger of claiming that one set of preferred 'representations' replaced another – less preferred or even hostile. Sinfield (1999) and de Jongh (1992) have provided us with a much-needed account of the changing relationship between homosexuality and the stage in the twentieth century. Yet in assessing the impact of the thorny progress from subterfuge to tentative openness, from oppression to imperfect liberation, the 'purchase' of gay and lesbian representations by and within apparent heterosexually identified theatre spaces and contexts must be accounted for in any interpretative paradigm. Equally, from the 1980s to the present, one of the consequences of the political and cultural reappropriation of 'queer' – a term traditionally of heterosexist abuse – has meant that lesbians and gay men have arguably been able to re-enter strategically certain spaces – both virtual and actual – from which they were previously prohibited. And might this now mean that to continue to speak of a 'lesbian and gay theatre' is a redundant exercise?

In (and Out of) the Sweatshop

Established in 1975, Gay Sweatshop Theatre Company emerged from a lunchtime season organized by Ed Berman at London's Almost Free Theatre. An advertisement in *Gay News* put out a call for gay theatre workers and 'anyone with a play' (Osment 1989: vii). Gay Sweatshop was a product not only of the freedoms made possible by the Theatres Act, but equally of the gay liberation movement of the late 1960s and early 1970s. The 1967 Sexual Offences Act decriminalized 'private' same-sex relations between consenting adult males over the age of 21. Although an index of the changing attitudes and discourses towards and around male homosexuality – the view of homosexuality as a medical problem, immoral, sinful and so forth – the Act's 'restrictions were harsh from the start' (Weeks 1990: 176, 168–82). Particular concern centred on the meaning of 'private'; 'public' referred not only to municipal spaces but anywhere where a third person might be present. Over the next couple of years 'the number of prosecutions actually increased' (ibid.: 176). The new legislation therefore worked to give a reformist appearance whilst simultaneously promoting the increased policing and regulation of homosexuals and homosexual activity. The 1967 Sexual Offences Act, and its consequences, led in part to the establishment of the Gay Liberation Front (GLF) in 1970. Whilst legal reform had been facilitated through the cautious campaigning of groups such as the Homosexual Law Reform Society, the GLF sought not a compromise but a confrontation with the status quo. For the GLF, legal reform repositioned the homosexual inside the metaphorical 'closet'. The GLF took its inspiration from 1968, from the new political radicalism created by events on the world stage (such as the American war in Vietnam, the Paris riots, the

'Prague Spring') and the countercultural movement. Like the women's liberation movement, it moved to fight imposed stereotypes; so the choice, declaration and pride of one's homosexuality were themselves a revolutionary act (ibid.: 185–206). The GLF had folded by 1972, to be replaced by the Campaign for Homosexual Equality (CHE). If the GLF represented lesbian and gay 'difference', then the CHE represented 'sameness' with heterosexuality and a return to the reformist agenda of the 1960s.

Although Gay Sweatshop emerged in the aftermath of the GLF, the political and cultural residue of its labours was clearly felt in the company's early work. *Mister X* (1975, unpublished; see Osment 1989: xix–xxiv; Lucas 1994: 17–24; Sinfield 1999: 303–4) by Drew Griffiths (co-founder of Gay Sweatshop) and Roger Baker and *Any Woman Can* (1975) by Jill Posener appear at first glance to be sibling plays, both reflecting 'the maxim that "the personal is political" and that coming out is a necessary politicization of the self' (Lucas 1994: 17). Both pieces also use forms of direct address. The 'coming out' of the anonymous 'Mister X' involves the actor discarding his scripted 'role' and announcing his actual name and address to the assembled audience. *Any Woman Can* opens with Ginny declaring to her onlookers: 'You are looking at a screaming lesbian. A raving dyke, pervert, deviant . . . I'm everywhere . . . in seat D22, yes sir, right next to you' (Posener 1987: 15). Both plays might also be considered as didactic or agit-prop, in that they open up the socially imposed 'problem' of identifying as gay or lesbian and offer solutions to that problem. *Mister X* and *Any Woman Can* toured the UK and Ireland – sometimes together – throughout 1976, playing to largely gay and lesbian audiences and not infrequently encountering the wrath of local government and establishment figures (Osment 1989: xix–xxiv). This was the moment of de Jongh's 'authentic gay theatre' and Freeman's 'beginning of lesbian theatre'. Whilst there is no doubt about the plays' significance, *Mister X* and *Any Woman Can* also symbolized the fragile alliances that existed between lesbian and gay theatre and between the communities at large. And under the umbrella of Gay Sweatshop, lesbian and gay separatism was to prove an ongoing issue over the next few years, both in its organization and in its production work (ibid.: xxiv–xxx).

In broader terms, *Mister X* and *Any Woman Can* are also examples of types of theatre-making that in part came to characterize the alternative theatre movement. Whilst both plays had authors' names attached to them, both were also the product of close collaboration between playwrights and actors (Lucas 1994: 17; Posener 1987: 25). Subsequent developments in lesbian theatre in the 1970s and 1980s, as exemplified in projects such as Gay Sweatshop's *Care and Control* (1977) – about women involved in child-custody cases – and the Women's Theatre Group's *Double Vision* (1982) – concerning the relationship between two lesbians of conflicting class and politics – extended the use of such working practices (Gay Sweatshop and Wandor 1980; Women's Theatre Group with Mason 1987). Whilst these developments can be seen as part of lesbian theatre's interface with feminist theatre practices, in terms of 'lesbian and gay theatre' the implications were rather different: 1968 might have emphasized a broad-based revolutionary politics of collective action, but what followed was an individuation of issues along the frequently conflicting lines of race, gender, class and identity. Just as feminist theatre practice attempted to reflect the efficacy of feminism's own form of self-determined collective action, so too did lesbian theatre. This is where one can identify an important contra-flow with gay theatre. As the 1970s progressed, text-based gay theatre increasingly began to foreground the playwright over the ensemble; Noël Greig, for example, emerged as one of Gay Sweatshop's leading figures. And increasingly 'gay-friendly' venues such as the Traverse Theatre in Edinburgh and London's Almost Free and Royal Court Theatres staged the work of Michael Wilcox and the London-based American playwright Martin Sherman. With reasonable speed, the subsidized mainstream theatre began producing gay-themed work by gay playwrights.

If gay liberation had been primarily about empowering gay men and responding to *their* oppressions, then the theatre could be seen to be following a similar pattern. This is an important point. Lesbian disempowerment, as has already been mooted, was part and parcel of legalistic, cultural and historical discourses around invisibility. Lesbian sex did not need to be legalized in 1967, as it was never illegal in the first place. In *As Time Goes By* (1977) by Noël Greig and Drew Griffiths, each of three sections realizes a specific historical setting: late Victorian England, early 1930s Berlin, and late 1960s New York prior to the Stonewall riots (Greig and Griffiths 1981). The play represents three 'moments' that could be identified as catalytic in both unveiling a gay history and shaping contemporary attitudes towards homosexuality residing in heterosexual hegemony. Greig's *The Dear Love of Comrades* (1979) is set in the late nineteenth century and focuses on the British socialist Edward Carpenter in order to examine the relationship between socialism and the emerging homosexual political consciousness (Greig 1989). Such discernible histories are largely unavailable to lesbian playwrights. However, the gay playwright is enabled to process such material, both to make cognizant and to deconstruct the structures of oppression. Furthermore, though both plays might desist from classical realism and employ a Brechtian dramaturgy, they do make use of *available* dramaturgical strategies. In this respect at least, aspects of gay playwriting from the 1970s onwards would become allied with the wider movement in male-dominated political playwriting (Shellard 1999: 149–58).

Whilst lesbian plays, like gay plays, certainly had their targets in sight, one can discern in the former a response to the threat of invisibility in terms of a concerted experimentation with dramatic and performance forms. Such experimentation has been intimately connected with contemporaneous developments in feminist theatre practice, the makeup of audiences and the function of spectatorship. However, as Freeman has argued, building on the work of Jill Dolan (1990), once lesbian theatre made for lesbian audiences plays in venues dominated by heterosexual audiences, 'assimilation into the dominant culture' will occur, and this is most likely 'when the author makes concessions to realism' (Freeman 1997: 170). Bryony Lavery's *Her Aching Heart* (1990) takes the 'bodice-ripper' form of romantic fiction and dovetails two lesbian love stories, one in the 'real' present and the other a historical romance (Lavery 1998). The play was written for the Women's Theatre Group and is composed on the basis of using just two female actors/performers to adopt multiple roles. Significantly, therefore, the play's form is also indicative of the economic exigencies – diminutive public subsidy – that have continually impacted on lesbian theatre. Elaine Aston has argued that the play's 'comic energy comes from Lavery's multi-role composition and attendant performance register that gender-bends performatively to border on the frantic, the hysterical'. Thus, not only does the play provide 'a dramatic tracing of the historical "disavowal" of lesbianism', but the 'anarchic and celebratory' form means that 'lesbian desire bursts on to the stage, as a refusal of the heteropatriarchal fiction that gives lie [*sic*] to lesbian lives' (Aston 2003: 101–2). Aston's observations also point to how lesbian dramaturgical strategies can foreground the ludic via the performative – a means of dissuading from a *rational* thesis and critique. This has come to distinguish important aspects of lesbian playwriting from feminist playwriting. However, *Her Aching Heart* not only dramatizes and performs a 'refusal'; in the unfixing of 'disavowal' it is simultaneously constructing lesbian identities which, cumulatively, offer the possibility of a lesbian historiography (not a *re*-writing but a historical *inscription*) that works to stand outside 'heteropatriarchal fiction.'

Con/Testing Times and the Queer Deluge

The 1980s presented both gay and lesbian communities with a fresh set of challenges, both political and personal. It was not long after the advent of AIDS in San Francisco in the early part of the decade that increasing numbers of cases of infection were diagnosed amongst the United Kingdom's gay community. The Conservative government, installed under the leadership of Margaret Thatcher in 1979, made, at best, a muted response. But as the decade advanced, the government began showing its true colours. Section 28 of the 1988 Local Government Act prevented local authorities from 'promoting' homosexuality. Section 28 was avowedly homophobic, but is perhaps best understood in terms of Thatcherism's ideological imperative to couple the economic and political maxims of 'self-interest, competitive individualism, [and] anti-statism' with those of 'tradition, family and nation, patriarchalism and order' (Hall 1988: 42–8). Accordingly, Thatcherism would have no truck with gay and lesbian parenting rights or the legal recognition of same-sex partnerships. The measured achievements of the late 1960s and 1970s were under frontal attack.

It is piquant perhaps that in May 1979, as Thatcher was being elected into office, Martin Sherman's *Bent* was having its premiere at the Royal Court Theatre. Set in 1930s Berlin, the play adroitly examines the persecution of homosexuals under Nazism. It has also become celebrated for an intense and disturbing dramatic zenith; in Dachau concentration camp Max and Horst achieve orgasm through an erotic dualogue – a triumph of self and identity over tyranny (Sherman 1989). The play was originally intended for Gay Sweatshop. Not only did *Bent* attract the actor Ian McKellen to the role of Max, it also had a successful West End transfer (de Jongh 1992: 145–56). In the history of gay theatre, *Bent* has acquired an important status in terms of assessing the journey of postliberationist gay drama from the alternative theatre through to subsidized mainstream and into the commercial sector. De Jongh considers the play 'remarkable' as it 'illuminated what had previously been obscured' (ibid.: 145), but it has also been criticized, like its predecessors, for remaining 'locked largely into its own circumscribed area' (Chambers and Prior 1987: 117). These commentaries highlight the opposing (gay/straight) positions of the desired modus operandi of gay drama once it enters the mainstream. However, it is pertinent to note that the Royal Court produced *Bent* principally because it was 'one of those plays you do when you're short of money'; it was 'sensational' rather than 'great' (Stuart Burge, quoted in Roberts 1999: 167). Whilst it would be erroneous to view the appropriation of gay drama by the mainstream as entirely about economic gain or survival, *Bent* heralded another important development.

Although based in London, Sherman is an American playwright, and it was American responses to the AIDS crisis that came to figure significantly in the subsidized and commercial mainstream theatre in the 1980s and into the early 1990s. Sinfield cogently notes how plays such as Larry Kramer's *The Normal Heart* (1985) and Tony Kushner's two-part *Angels in America* (1991, 1992) foreground AIDS as creating a representational crisis in the theatre, not only around AIDS itself but around male homosexuality. These and other American plays, Sinfield argues, oscillate variously and uncomfortably between cathartic and political modes (Sinfield 1999: 317–26). In part, AIDS recast the homosexual as 'victim' and perpetuated previously held disease metaphors around homosexuality, and this may also partly explain the 'mainstreaming' of AIDS plays around this period. The homosexual once again becomes a figure who is simultaneously a threat and a threat that can be contained. In *My Night With Reg* (1994), by the British playwright Kevin Elyot, the conventions of the English drawing-room comedy are employed to explore a series of various couplings and decouplings in which Reg always seems to figure. Yet Reg is never actually seen in the play and dies from an AIDS-related illness (Elyot 1994). The play's use of realistic conventions combined with the non-staging of its protagonist promotes the Freudian 'Oedipal imperative' that separates 'identification from desire' (Savran 2003: 60). Rather than exploding the Oedipal myth, *My Night With Reg* reinforces the homosexual as 'other', not as one who can destabilize heteronormativity but as one who can be positioned, safely, within its discourses. This criticism might seem a little harsh, particularly as plays such as *My Night With Reg* offered a response to the AIDS crisis that was both needed and, in some ways, probing; the play does, for example – unlike many American AIDS plays – examine class conflict. Similarly, though dealing with a different subject matter, Jonathan Harvey's 'feel-good' comedy *Beautiful Thing* (1993) concerns an evolving gay relationship between two working-class adolescents (Harvey 1999). The play had particular cachet at the time of its production because of the campaign to reduce the age of homosexual consensual sex to 16, the same as that for heterosexuals. However, the success of such plays within mainstream theatre – both had successful West End runs – will reveal an important pattern.

In answer to the question 'whatever happened to gay theatre?' Brian Roberts has responded that 'it grew up . . . the best of gay theatre work in the last decade has become closer kin to the radical theatre of its origins' (Roberts 2000: 184). Roberts's grand historicizing makes reference not only to the aforementioned mainstream efforts of Elyot and Harvey, but also to the important work of individuals and companies such as Neil Bartlett and his company Gloria, the drag artists Bette Bourne and Bloolips, and choreographer Matthew Bourne and his ensemble Adventures in Motion Pictures. This presents a dilemma. The latter work belongs to a different tradition; not to an 'alternative' one in the sense that the term has been used in this chapter, but to a self-reflexive praxis that engages with performance and theatrical forms – such as the West End musical, drag, cabaret, ballet – that have been a significant part of twentieth-century gay culture. This is a tradition, more often than not, that foregrounds the performative over the textual. However, this work departs from the mainstream of Elyot and Harvey in that the evolution of the latter can be configured, relatively easily, within a linear and straight (*sic*) history. It is not surprising, for example, that plays as different in subject matter as *My Night With Reg* and Mark Ravenhill's 'in-yer-face' look at the interface between sex and consumerism, *Shopping and Fucking* (1996; Ravenhill 2001), are subsumed within groups of other plays by men that 'address masculinity and its discontents' (Edgar 1999: 27). And the plays themselves, their forms and the sites of their production, facilitate this appropriation. Conversely, the counter-tradition that is in operation in the work of Neil Bartlett, for example, is not about a writing *into* history but rather the *re*-writing of an already existing history.

This is where an important distinction from lesbian theatre emerges. With Lavery's *Her Aching Heart*, it was possible to discern not a writing into or a re-writing of history, but an inscription, the historiographical marking of the lesbian (in theatre). The work of Split Britches, a company founded in New York that established London as its 'second home', has exploited American popular culture to explore the political transgressiveness of butch/femme role playing (Case 1996). In Claire Dowie's *Why is John Lennon Wearing a Skirt?* (1987), the author performs solo 'stand-up theatre' to create a space for her own visibility and configuration of gender identity (Dowie 1996). It is pertinent to note the continued experimentation with dramatic and performance forms in lesbian practice, forms that contravene the established procedures of text-based theatre practice. Additionally, lesbian theatre has marked out its own identifiable territories, at venues such as London's Oval House and Drill Hall (Freeman 1997: 124–35).

This chapter has not yet noted how 'queer theory' might act as a corrective to many of the arguments, and particularly the distinctions between lesbian and gay theatre practice, thus far put forward. In the light of the work of scholars such as Judith Butler, Eve Sedgwick and Diana Fuss, queer theory proposes that gender is performative and, as such, has a radicalizing political and cultural potential. It deconstructs the binary oppositions of male/female, homosexual/heterosexual and lesbian/gay and maintains that compulsory heterosexuality is maintained by our regimes of knowledge. The performative dimension to queer theory has a demonstrable affinity with theatre practice and can be traced to much of the work discussed here (see, for example, Griffin 2004). It might indeed be suggested that, in some respects, this chapter offers a queer re-reading of a particular lesbian and gay theatre history. However, whilst queer theory has an important contribution to make to many of the issues raised, it is the author's view, following Stephen Seidman, that part of queer theory's error lies in presuming a 'deep cultural logic to explain the staying power of heterosexism' (Seidman 1997: 157). This chapter has in part attempted to demonstrate that the institutional analysis of theatre in terms of lesbian and gay practices and representations problematizes the notion of such logic. All, therefore, might not be so queer on the West End front.

PRIMARY READING

Bartlett, Neil (1990). *A Vision of Love Revealed in Sleep* in Michael Wilcox (ed.). *Gay Plays. Vol. 4.* London: Methuen, 81–112.

Bartlett, Neil (1993). *Night After Night.* London: Methuen.

Bond, Edward (1968). *Early Morning.* London: Caldar and Boyers.

Dowie, Claire (1996). *Why is John Lennon Wearing a Skirt? And Other Stand-Up Theatre Plays.* London: Methuen.

Elyot, Kevin (1994). *My Night With Reg.* London: Nick Hern.

Gay Sweatshop and Wandor, Michelene (1980). *Care and Control* in Michelene Wandor (ed.). *Strike While the Iron is Hot: Three Plays on Sexual Politics.* London: Journeyman Press, 63–113.

Greig, Noël (1989). *The Dear Love of Comrades* in Philip Osment (ed.). *Gay Sweatshop: Four Plays and a Company.* London: Methuen, 1–50.

Greig, Noël and Griffiths, Drew (1981). *As Time Goes By* in *Two Gay Sweatshop Plays.* London: Gay Men's Press, 5–70.

Harvey, Jonathan (1999). *Plays: 1.* London: Methuen.

Lavery, Bryony (1998). *Plays: 1.* London: Methuen.

Nagy, Phyllis (1998). *Plays: 1.* London: Methuen.

Posener, Jill (1987). *Any Woman Can* in Jill Davis (ed.). *Lesbian Plays.* London: Methuen, 13–27.

Ravenhill, Mark (2001). *Plays 1.* London: Methuen.

Sherman, Martin (1979). *Bent.* Oxford: Amber Lane Press.

Women's Theatre Group with Mason, Libby (1987). *Double Vision* in Jill Davis (ed.). *Lesbian Plays.* London: Methuen, 29–55.

FURTHER READING

Aston, Elaine (1995). *An Introduction to Feminism and Theatre.* London: Routledge.

Aston, Elaine (2003). *Feminist Views on the English Stage: Women Playwrights 1990–2000.* Cambridge: Cambridge University Press.

Bartlett, Neil (1996). 'What's Mainstream?' in C. Spencer with P. Heritage (eds.). *It's Queer Up North 1992–1996: A Catalogue of Queer Performance.* Manchester: It's Queer Up North, 47–53.

Brewer, Mary (1999). *Race, Sex and Gender in Contemporary Women's Theatre: The Construction of 'Woman'*. Brighton: Sussex Academic Press.

Butler, Judith (1990). *Gender Trouble: Feminism and the Subversion of Identity*. New York: Routledge.

Case, Sue-Ellen (ed.) (1996). *Split Britches: Lesbian Practice/Feminist Performance*. London: Routledge.

Chambers, Colin and Prior, Mike (1987). *Playwrights' Progress: Patterns of Post-War British Drama*. Oxford: Amber Lane Press.

Collis, Rose (1993). 'Sister George is Dead: The Making of Modern Lesbian Theatre' in Trevor R. Griffiths and Margaret Llewellyn-Jones (eds.). *British and Irish Women Dramatists Since 1958: A Critical Handbook*. Buckingham: Open University Press, 78–83.

Clum, John M. (1992). *Acting Gay: Male Homosexuality in Modern Drama*. New York: Columbia University Press.

Davis, Jill (1987). 'Introduction' in J. Davis (ed.). *Lesbian Plays*. London: Methuen, 7–12.

de Jongh, Nicholas (1992). *Not in Front of the Audience: Homosexuality on Stage*. London: Routledge.

de Jongh, Nicholas (2000). *Politics, Prudery and Perversions: The Censoring of the English Stage, 1901–1968*. London: Methuen.

Dolan, Jill (1990). ' "Lesbian" Subjectivity in Realism: Dragging at the Margins of Structure and Ideology' in Sue-Ellen Case (ed.). *Performing Feminisms: Feminist Critical Theory and Theatre*. Baltimore: Johns Hopkins University Press, 40–53.

Edgar, David (1999). 'Provocative Acts: British Playwriting in the Post-War Era and Beyond' in David Edgar (ed.). *State of Play: Playwrights on Playwriting*. London: Faber and Faber, 3–34.

Freeman, Sandra (1997). *Putting Your Daughters on the Stage: Lesbian Theatre from the 1970s to the 1990s*. London: Cassell.

Fuss, Diana (ed.) (1991). *Inside/Out: Lesbian Theories, Gay Theories*. London: Penguin.

Goodman, Lizbeth (1993). *Contemporary Feminist Theatres: To Each Her Own*. London: Routledge.

Griffin, Gabriele (2004). 'Troubling Identities: Claire Dowie's *Why is John Lennon Wearing a Skirt?*' in Maggie B. Gale and Viv Gardner (eds.). *Auto/Biography and Identity: Women, Theatre and Performance*. Manchester: Manchester University Press, 151–75.

Hall, Stuart (1988). *The Hard Road to Renewal: Thatcherism and the Crisis of the New Left*. London: Verso.

Itzin, Catherine (1980). *Stages in the Revolution: Political Theatre in Britain Since 1968*. London: Eyre Methuen.

Lucas, Ian (1994). *Impertinent Decorum: Gay Theatrical Manoeuvres*. London: Cassell.

Osment, Philip (1989). 'Finding Room on the Agenda for Love: A History of Gay Sweatshop' in Philip Osment (ed.). *Gay Sweatshop: Four Plays and a Company*. London: Methuen, v–lxviii.

Roberts, Brian (2000). 'Whatever Happened to Gay Theatre?', *New Theatre Quarterly* 62, 175–85.

Roberts, Philip (1999). *The Royal Court Theatre and the Modern Stage*. Cambridge: Cambridge University Press.

Savran, David (2003). *A Queer Sort of Materialism: Recontextualizing American Theater*. Ann Arbor: University of Michigan Press.

Sedgwick, Eve Kosofsky (1994). *Epistemology of the Closet*. London: Penguin.

Seidman, Stephen (1997). *Difference Troubles: Queering Social Theory and Sexual Politics*. Cambridge: Cambridge University Press.

Shellard, Dominic (1999). *British Theatre since the War*. New Haven, CT: Yale University Press.

Sierz, Aleks (2001). *In-Yer-Face Theatre: British Drama Today*. London: Faber and Faber.

Sinfield, Alan (1998). *Gay and After*. London: Serpent's Tail.

Sinfield, Alan (1999). *Out on Stage: Lesbian and Gay Theatre in the Twentieth Century*. New Haven, CT: Yale University Press.

Stephenson, Heidi and Langridge, Natasha (1997). *Rage and Reason: Women Playwrights on Playwriting*. London: Methuen.

Wandor, Michelene (2001). *Post-War British Drama: Looking Back in Gender*. London: Routledge.

Weeks, Jeffrey (1990). *Coming Out: Homosexual Politics in Britain from the Nineteenth Century to the Present*. London: Quartet.

33

Edward Bond: Maker of Myths

Michael Patterson

'Literature is a social act', proclaimed Edward Bond (Bond 1978a: xi). Indeed it is, and this is especially true of drama. It is impossible to gather members of the public together to observe performers interacting together without generating some social and political resonance. Even the most escapist comedy will at the very least confirm the status quo and reassure the audience that their 'normality' is superior to the eccentricities or malice of the characters they are laughing at. However, while theatre may possess an inevitably political dimension, it operates in a quite different way from conventional political debate.

Politics proceeds, or purports to proceed, by rational argument. It attempts to offer a coherent pattern of choice: in extreme cases, the choice between accepting continuing oppression or committing oneself to the violent overthrow of the oppressor; or, in the token freedom of western democracies, it may be the choice between lower taxation and improved public services. Above all, political argument will endeavour to persuade the potential insurgent or reluctant voter towards a particular course of action.

Theatre rarely offers rational arguments. There may be scenes in which issues are debated, but the great strength of theatre – and what makes theatre theatrical – is not political analysis but the creation of situations and images which provide reference points for political thought. Furthermore, only the most didactic of theatre pieces offer political solutions; the best theatre invites the audience to draw their own conclusions and to seek answers for themselves.

Edward Bond is a playwright who perhaps more than any other contemporary British and Irish dramatist throws into relief the differences between the modes of communication of conventional politics and of the theatre. Indeed, by combining uncompromising political views with a remarkably innovative use of the stage he has achieved a further distinction amongst his contemporaries: the darling of theatre scholars and academics who rate him one of the finest living dramatists in the English language, he remains a playwright who has never achieved much popularity amongst

British audiences. By contrast, the clever plays of David Edgar and Michael Frayn, and the more congenial domestic settings of most of Harold Pinter's and David Hare's work, have accorded them continuing public recognition and mainstream revivals, while Bond's plays now tend to be admired only on the continent and, in Britain, are now mainly performed by amateurs (a situation that, given his despair over the state of contemporary British professional theatre, is not wholly unwelcome to Bond). Bond is an intensely political figure, anti-authoritarian, utterly committed to the relief of human suffering and to the alleviation of man's cruelty to man, occupying a position that might be loosely termed humane Marxism. Furthermore, more than any British playwright since Shaw, Bond has theorized about society and its problems in numerous prefaces, interviews, essays and letters.

His basic political insight, which is the foundation of what he terms 'Rational Theatre', is that humankind is essentially peaceable and non-aggressive but that social conditions drive us to commit appalling acts of violence:

> We have a capacity for violence and, like many animals, are violent when we are afraid or frustrated. This is as natural as when a drowning man fights for his life. But it is not natural for him to keep falling in the water...Violence is like pain, not a normal condition but a sign that something is wrong. (Hay and Roberts 1978: 52)

We are like caged animals, but, instead of turning on our keepers, we fawn on them because they bring us sufficient food; so we vent our frustration and animosity on our fellow captives.

The traditional response, a Christian attitude embraced gleefully and understandably by the establishment, is that things have always been like this and that the way to rise above such suffering is through resignation and acceptance of the status quo. If the cage-door were left open, we would fear to step into freedom, because we would not know what lay beyond. So we acquiesce in our imprisonment, 'the fascism of lazy men', as Bond calls it (Bond 1978a: 4); or, worse, we actively support the system in order to oppress others and so feel slightly freer ourselves.

The function of 'Rational Theatre' is to urge us to seek a new existence for ourselves: 'Theatre is recreating what it means to be human, to redefine our relationship with the world...The dramatist's problem is: how do you speak sanity to the insane?' (Bond, in Theatre Voice 2005). In short, theatre exhorts us to break out of our cage. How this is to be achieved is never exactly clarified by Bond, and he presents a convincing argument for his vagueness: 'I have not tried to say what the future should be like, because that is a mistake. If your plan of the future is too rigid you start to coerce people to fit into it. We do not need a plan of the future, we need a method of change' (Bond 1978a: 11).

Wherever the future lies, Bond fears there is not much time left to steer towards it. Given the achievements of modern technology, whereby humankind faces imminent self-annihilation from nuclear weapons or through destruction of the environment, we are, in Bond's view, teetering on the edge of an abyss. Only immediate and radical change can save us; hence his frustration with critics: 'If a house is on fire and I shout "Fire! Fire!", I don't want people to commend my shouting ability, I want them to join in the firefighting' (see Hay and Roberts 1978: 71).

This is one reason Bond gives for writing plays rather than novels: 'when I write, the rhythm – the whole concentration of the writing – requires action. Finally, somebody has to get up and do something – mere words on paper are not expressive enough' (Bond 1972: 12). Only the theatre, which offers the immediacy of enactment in a public context, would seem to answer Bond's sense of urgency. However, it is precisely because of this urgent enactment in the present that theatre is not well suited to operate as a forum for cool rational debate. This account of Bond's work will therefore argue that rather than establishing a 'Rational Theatre' (in any conventional sense) he has created a body of myths for our age – a considerably more important achievement.

It is unfortunate that the word 'myth' is now often used as an equivalent for an untruth, as in dismissive phrases like 'That's a mere myth.' In fact, myth has traditionally embodied the most profound truths of humankind. Myths render into comprehensible stories and images insights into the relationship between individuals and their fellows and between individuals and a wider power, be that the gods, history or social forces. As George Steiner wrote in his *Death of Tragedy*, myth is 'a fable to help us to endure' (Steiner 1961: 5). Bond, in creating myths for our time, not only provides useful reference points for our political thinking; he also helps us to face up to the social evils with which we are daily confronted.

Bond's introduction to theatre, while still a schoolboy of 14, overwhelmed him:

> for the very first time in my life – I remember this quite distinctly – I met somebody who was actually talking about my problems, about the life I'd been living, the political society around me. Nobody else had said anything about my life to me at all, ever... I knew all these people, they were there in the street or in the newspapers – this in fact was my world. (Bond 1972: 5)

Significantly, this revelation for the disadvantaged lad from Crouch End Secondary Modern School had not been achieved by some avant-garde political group or contemporary kitchen-sink drama; the young Bond had witnessed the flamboyantly old-fashioned actor Donald Wolfit performing Shakespeare's *Macbeth*. The mythical images of violence in a piece over three centuries old could be immediately under-stood by Bond and recognized as being still all too relevant to the world about him.

When in the late 1950s he began to devote himself to writing, Bond's plays thus eschewed the overtly political and sought to tell stories with powerful images that would more potently convey a political message than the domestic naturalism familiar from Arnold Wesker and John Osborne. He was encouraged in this enterprise by the newly formed Writers' Group at the Royal Court Theatre, to which not only Arnold Wesker belonged but also the much more poetically orientated writer John Arden. Bond joined the group in 1959, although he did not become a full-time writer until 1965.

Bond's first performed play, *The Pope's Wedding*, was staged in 1962 at the Royal Court as a Sunday night production without decor. Right from the title (which indicates an impossible event), the play's portrayal of a group of feckless youths with little sense of direction is anything but naturalistic. The dialogue, based on East Anglian dialect, is terse and stylized; there is the curiously enigmatic figure of the hermit Alen (= alien?); and one of the youths, Scopey, develops a concern for Alen bordering on obsession, then finally murders him and dresses in the old man's clothes in a futile attempt to discover his secret. There is no secret, however – at least not one to be learned from this tetchy old recluse. Godot has not come to this Essex village, and uncomfortable as Bond might be with the idea of being compared to the absurdist Beckett, the anguish and silence of the ending of his first play place him closer to Beckett than to most contemporary political playwrights.

Bond's next play was to establish him as one of the most controversial writers of his generation. *Saved* (1965) caused a furore and is still most remembered for the scene in which a baby is stoned to death in its pram. Theatre has traditionally not been squeamish: Euripides Medea murders her children; Shakespeare's Lavinia in *Titus Andronicus* has her tongue cut out and hands severed; De Flores triumphantly appears with the finger cut from a dead man in Middleton and Rowley's *The Changeling*. But traditionally too, the theatre usually places the actual act of violence off-stage, and removes the action to a remote foreign location. While Bond does not actually show a baby, which remains concealed in its pram, the violence is acted out before us – and by the kind of youths that we might have passed on our way into the theatre. What is perhaps even more disturbing is that there is no malice in the youths' behaviour: it is simply a game that gets out of control, as casually carried out as kicking a ball. An act of deliberate cruelty might be healthier; at least the baby would be something other than an object.

This stoning of the baby was to be the first and most notorious of Bond's 'aggro-effects'. Taking issue with Brecht, whose 'V-effect' ('alienation' or 'distanciation') can too easily leave a contemporary audience unmoved, Bond urged more drastic tactics: 'Sometimes it is necessary to emotionally commit the audience – which is why I have aggro-effects. Without this the V-effect can deteriorate into an aesthetic style' (Bond 1978b: 34). Bond's intention was to shock the audience into examining the sources of violence in contemporary society:

> Clearly the stoning to death of a baby in a London Park is a typical English understatement. Compared to the 'strategic' bombing of German towns it is a negligible atrocity, compared to the cultural and emotional deprivation of most of our children its consequences are insignificant. (Bond 1977: 310–11)

As Mangan, with reference to Bond's *Lear*, perceptively puts it: 'the ways in which the moments of violence are staged are themselves analyses of violence' (Mangan 1998: 26).

Unfortunately for Bond and his message, the moral outrage felt by many of the audience at his depiction of violence obscured any consideration of the more significant atrocities of their century. Certainly, what was offered here was anything other than 'rational' theatre; it was a brutal confrontation with the sickness of our society. Significantly, however, while Bond continued to produce extremely violent images in his writing, they became more muted in comparison with the baby-stoning, thus inviting reflection rather than revulsion: the cannibalism of *Early Morning* is set within an overtly surreal context; in *Narrow Road to the Deep North* the five children are murdered off-stage; and *Lear* is similarly set in the past and has the precedent of Shakespeare's own play to make episodes like the blinding of Lear (*sic*) more acceptable.

Apart from the ritual quality of the baby-stoning scene, which regrettably still tends to dominate any discussion of *Saved*, there are many other elements in the play that go beyond naturalism. Once again, the dialogue is terse and elliptical; after Harry gets hurt in his fight with Len, he appears as a ghost-like figure in long white combinations and a skull-cap of bandages; the play ends in a long silent scene. It is these theatrical images that create an impact rather than any hint of political debate.

Bond's next play, *Early Morning*, was given two hurried performances at the Royal Court in 1968, its closure threatened by official censorship (which ironically ended later that same year). Making his mark as the *enfant terrible* of British theatre, Bond now enraged the English middle classes by representing one of their sacred cows, Queen Victoria, as a cannibal and rapist of Florence Nightingale. While the *Sunday Times* drama critic Harold Hobson dismissed the piece as a 'melodramatic farrago of the deliberately disgusting and obscene' (Roberts 1985: 18), Ronald Bryden in the rival *Observer* understood Bond's intentions much better, describing the play as 'a gargantuan Swiftian metaphor of universal consumption: a society based on cannibalism, in which all achievement, power, and even love consists of devouring other lives' (ibid.: 18).

Bond's next play, *Narrow Road to the Deep North* (1968), once again had a historical setting, one that is yet again deliberately imprecise. It is set in late seventeenth-century Japan, at the time of the great poet Matsuo Basho, and yet it also depicts nineteenth-century British imperialists, intent on violently freeing the populace from their 'barbarism'. It reveals more than most Bond plays the influence of Brecht (a direct influence that Bond hotly denies), especially a play like *Man's a Man*. Like Brecht's play, it has an oriental setting, thinly drawn characters, and violence coupled with humour. Bond goes further by presenting the dialectic between eastern brutality and western 'civilization', in which the former is perhaps preferable to the hypocrisy and sophisticated weaponry of the latter. Shogo, the Japanese tyrant, is ruthless and in no way idealized, but his behaviour seems less objectionable than that of the commodore who ultimately defeats him. Though written three and a half decades previously, Bond's play remains all too relevant to the invasion of Iraq in 2003.

Having cocked a snook at venerated figures from history in *Early Morning*, Bond now dared to take on the giant of English drama, William Shakespeare, and not in some minor work but in probably Shakespeare's greatest drama, *King Lear*. There were several reasons why Bond boldly accepted this challenge in his *Lear* (1971), creating arguably the finest dramatic revisiting of Shakespeare ever undertaken. First, Bond was regularly dismayed by the way critics and university lecturers paid homage to Shakespeare without recognizing his relevance to our own society. Secondly, Bond was dismayed by Shakespeare's social moral, which allegedly urged his audience to 'endure till in time the world will be made right' (see Hay and Roberts 1978: 53): 'Acceptance is not enough . . . you can sit quietly at home and have an H-bomb dropped on you. Shakespeare had time . . . But . . . for us, time is running out' (ibid.: 18). Thirdly, Bond needed to examine the processes of violent revolution and confront the disturbing fact that the idealism of Marxism-Leninism had led inexorably to the cruel oppression of Stalin: 'The simple fact is that if you behave violently, you create an atmosphere of violence, which generates more violence . . . So a violent revolution always destroys itself' (ibid.: 18).

Bond's re-writing of *King Lear* was characteristically radical and significantly dispenses with the 'King' of the title. Though set in some vague early Britain, the piece is full of anachronisms: rifles, photographs, knitting, an aerosol can, etc. There are no good characters in this version: no good daughter, no Gloucester, no Kent, no Edgar, not even an Albany. Lear is a tyrant, who does not give away his kingdom to his daughters, here named Bodice and Fontanelle, but has it wrested from him by them. Bond's Cordelia is no relation to Lear, but the raped widow of a young man, the Gravedigger's Boy, who is murdered by soldiers and reappears as a ghost. Cordelia leads a successful revolt against Bodice and Fontanelle, but then becomes as oppressive as they and their father. The major symbol in Bond's adaptation is the huge wall that Lear has built to keep out his enemies. After being driven mad, captured and blinded, he finally recognizes the futility of maintaining the wall. He finds his way towards it and, when he begins to dismantle it, is shot.

Once again, Bond presents us with a magnificent theatrical image: a huge wall dominating the stage, a constant reminder that our rulers need to keep us in a state of fearful defensiveness in order to justify their continuing failure to create an equitable society. At the time of writing *Lear*, the nearest equivalent was the threat of nuclear weapons, allowing both sides in the Cold War to stockpile an arsenal large enough to destroy the world several times in pursuit of a policy of mutually assured destruction, with its apposite acronym MAD. We have now moved on to paranoia about world terrorism, building a new wall to justify imprisonment without trial and psychological torture.

If we were to analyse coldly the role of the wall in Bond's *Lear*, then we should have to admit that it does not make logical sense. It has no geographical clarity (where is this wall, and what territory lies either side of it?). If Cordelia has defeated her enemies, why is the wall to be maintained in the same place: should she not now be considering coastal defences? However, these questions are inappropriate, since Bond is once again creating a powerful theatrical image, not offering rational argument.

The next major play by Bond was a radical departure from his earlier work: without violence or shocking effects, it comes as close as is conceivable for a writer like Bond to a comedy of manners. *The Sea* (1973) is dominated by two characters, the paranoid draper Hatch, convinced that his little coastal town is being invaded by aliens, and his counterpart, the no-nonsense Mrs Rafi, a kind of East Anglian Lady Bracknell. Only the wisdom of Evens, an eccentric old seaman, and the bravery of the young Willy Carson offer some hope that the world can be saved from its irrational terror. But even here Bond characteristically rejects facile optimism. Willy's last words to Rose, the fiancée of his drowned friend, break off in mid-sentence: 'I left the sentence of the play unfinished because the play can have no satisfactory solution at that stage. Rose and Willy have to go away and help to create a sane society – and it is for the audience to go away and complete the sentence in their own lives' (Bond in Roberts 1985: 30).

Bond's next play, *Bingo* (1973), returned to reassessing a great figure from the past, this time Shakespeare himself. However, it is not Shakespeare's greatness or creativity that is the focus of Bond's interest; what Bond examines in *Bingo* is the question of social responsibility: 'Shakespeare may be the greatest dramatist of all times, but he is subject to the same laws as you or I or the man who drives your bus' (Stoll 1975: 422). We encounter Shakespeare as an irascible old man, no longer writing plays. Despite his grand pronouncements of humanity in a play like *King Lear* ('O! I have ta'en / Too little care of this'), he acquiesces in the introduction of enclosures, which will drive the poor off common land and so lead inevitably to their destitution. Because Shakespeare is a writer of colossal influence, his silence is especially reprehensible. When he recognizes the extent of his betrayal, he commits suicide by taking poison. Apart from the image of a young woman hanged for burning farms, this play has fewer powerful images than most of Bond's work, and its overall mood is contemplative rather than theatrical.

From the world's greatest playwright Bond now turned his attention in *The Fool* (1975) to a lesser-known poet, with whom he felt great affinity: John Clare. Like Clare, Bond came from a humble rural background, and like Clare, found himself, for a time at least, lionized by 'cultured' society and then dropped when his radical ideas appeared too challenging for the chattering classes. But this play is much more than an autobiographical piece, for here once again Bond explores how any imaginative and creative impulses can be stifled in our perverted society. Clare is here, therefore, not far removed from the youths of *The Pope's Wedding* or *Saved*; all suffer from the same violence of the uncaring world in which they live. In Clare's case, he ends as a mute wreck in an asylum, finally silenced by the establishment. His counterpart in the play is the fictional character of the symbolically named Darkie, a rebellious labourer who leads a violent attack on the oppressive rich and is condemned to death. Both men are intent on changing their world, one with insight and understanding, the other with force; both are destroyed, one by hanging, one more subtly. As Bond said in an interview in 1981: 'both their lives are wasted and that's simply because the two necessary parts of action – understanding and whatever force is necessary to put that understanding into effect – are not joined' (see Roberts 1985: 36).

Emboldened by his success in reappraising significant historical figures, great writers and a major Shakespearian tragedy, Bond now turned to ancient Greek drama in *The Woman* (1978), a revisiting of Euripides' *Hecuba*. Like Euripides, Bond reflects on the cycle of violence and revenge that war engenders. But in the Greek tragedy Hecuba's motives are primarily personal in exacting a terrible revenge on Polymestor for killing her son. In Bond, Hecuba acts politically against the cruel tyranny of the Greeks' rule and their arrogant exercise of power. Although she is herself destroyed at the end, the principle of peaceful and reasonable conduct, somewhat stereotypically embodied in a woman, has been vindicated.

With the writing of *The Woman*, Bond felt that he had completed a cycle of three plays 'which dealt specifically with this problem of culture, with the problem of the past which makes change so difficult'. He now endeavoured to write dramas that 'try and look at what answers are applicable' (Bond in Hay and Roberts 1980: 266). The first of these, *The Bundle* (1978), revisits the territory of *Narrow Road to the Deep North*. This revised version begins again with the discovery of the baby by the riverside ('the bundle'), but this time the focus is on the poor Ferryman who humanely but unwisely rescues the child. The child grows into Wang, a revolutionary leader, who with humour and resourcefulness frees his people and ushers in a new and genuinely democratic society. With this vision of an attainable utopia, Bond went much further than the restoration of peace amongst the islanders at the end of *The Woman*; he also renounced the bleak vision of *Lear* by implying that violence may produce beneficial results.

Bond's optimism was short-lived. One might have imagined that in his next major play, *Restoration* (1981), Bob Hedges, the innocent servant who is condemned to be hanged for the murder of his mistress, would ultimately go free. But Bond is enough of a realist to know that the rich and powerful will always be able to manipulate the law to their own ends, especially when the illiterate Bob is a willing slave to the authority of his master, Lord Are, the actual murderer. As Bob's wife, the black servant-girl Rose, says: 'How can yer fight for freedom when yer think you've got it?' (Bond 1992: 254). The only hope of change lies in her rebellious spirit: as she says in the final scene, in a direct challenge to the audience: 'What have I learned? If nothing, then I was hanged' (ibid.: 275).

After this excursion into a modernized Restoration comedy, the ever versatile Bond continued to write plays both long and short, both historical and contemporary, sometimes for a bare stage, sometimes with full orchestra for opera and ballet. Most recently he has concentrated on writing for the relatively unspoilt minds of children. Surprisingly for a political dramatist, he also penned two so-called 'postmodern' plays.

It would be a bold individual who would claim to define postmodernism precisely, but its major characteristics include a rejection of conventional narrative, an embracing of deconstruction, an acquisitive exploitation of references and images (many from pop culture and 'cult' sources of the past), and a deliberate eschewing of overt meaning. Bond's play *Jackets* (1989) certainly does not fulfil these criteria. It portrays two cases of martyrdom, the first by a young boy who willingly surrenders himself to death to protect the emperor's son in an unnamed Asian country in the past; the second unwittingly by a young British soldier during urban riots in the England of the present. In both the narrative is crystal clear, and the effect is of concentrated minimalism, not the kaleidoscopic impulses characteristic of postmodernism. The meaning, while not spelled out, is by no means obscure: it is an echo of Brecht's *Galileo*, who declares 'Unhappy the land that has need of heroes': martyrdom is undeniably heroic and selfless, but Bond asks us to question the society which creates such waste out of noble and generous action.

The clue to Bond's understanding of the term 'postmodernism' is revealed in his *Notes on Post-Modernism* (1989). Citing various examples of modernism, he asserts 'all are icons of chaos' (Bond 1996: 23). It would seem that, far from embracing the even greater randomness of postmodernism, he seeks a new coherence in the rubble of modernism: his postmodernism is simply what follows modernism: 'Theatre . . . has to be both iconoclastic and iconographic because that is a function imposed on it by the mind's need to humanize itself' (ibid.: 31).

So we return to the opening remarks of this chapter. While Bond's facility with language is astonishing, it is unlikely that audiences will remember much of the dialogue of any of his plays. What will be branded on their minds is the sight of youths stoning a baby in its pram; Lear having his eyes gouged out by a crude scientific apparatus or struggling blindly up his wall in a futile attempt to remove it; Shakespeare encountering a hanged woman on the gibbet; the wonderfully articulate poet John Clare reduced to a dribbling idiot; Lord Are in a grotesque farce running around with the corpse of his wife in a desperate attempt to get his servant to strike her with a rapier. Whether shocking, moving or farcical, these images, these icons, are what make Edward Bond such a powerful writer for the contemporary theatre.

His 'Rational Theatre' is not the cold reasoning of conventional political discourse. It has its source in the rich rationality accessible through myth. To call Bond 'a maker of myths' is not to dismiss him as some mystical visionary; on the contrary, his playwriting, in his own words, stands as 'the demonstration of the human need for the rational' (Bond 1978a: xv).

PRIMARY READING

Bond, Edward (1972). 'Drama and the Dialectics of Violence: Edward Bond Interviewed by the Editors [Roger Hudson, Catherine Itzin, and Simon Trussler]', *Theatre Quarterly* 2:5, 4–14.

Bond, Edward (1977). *Plays: 1: Saved, Early Morning, The Pope's Wedding*. London: Methuen.

Bond, Edward (1978a). *Plays: 2: Lear, The Sea, Narrow Road to the Deep North, Black Mass, Passion*. London: Methuen.

Bond, Edward (1978b). 'On Brecht: A Letter to Peter Holland', *Theatre Quarterly* 8:30, 34–5.

Bond, Edward (1987). *Plays: 3: Bingo, The Fool, The Woman, Stone*. London: Methuen.

Bond, Edward (1992) *Plays: 4: The Worlds with the Activists Papers, Restoration, Summer*. London: Methuen.

Bond, Edward (1996). *Plays: 5: Human Cannon, The Bundle, Jackets, In the Company of Men*. London: Methuen.

Bond, Edward (1998). *Plays: 6: The War Plays: A Trilogy, Choruses from After the Assassination*. London: Methuen.

Bond, Edward (2002). *Plays: 7: Olly's Prison, The Crime of the Twenty-First Century, The Swing, Derek, Fables and Stories*. London: Methuen.

FURTHER READING

Coult, Tony (1978). *The Plays of Edward Bond*. London: Methuen.

Hay, Malcolm and Roberts, Philip (1978). *Edward Bond: A Companion to his Plays*. London: TQ.

Hay, Malcolm and Roberts, Philip (1980). *Bond: A Study of his Plays*. London: Methuen.

Hirst, David L. (1985). *Edward Bond*. Basingstoke: Macmillan.

Lappin, Lou (1987). *The Art and Politics of Edward Bond*. New York: Lang.

Mangan, Michael (1998). *Edward Bond*. Plymouth: Northcote House.

Patterson, Michael (2003). *Strategies of Political Theatre*. Cambridge: Cambridge University Press.

Roberts, Philip (1985). *Bond on File*. London: Methuen.

Scharine, Robert (1976). *The Plays of Edward Bond*. Lewisburg: Bucknell University Press.

Spencer, Jenny S. (1992). *Dramatic Strategies in the Plays of Edward Bond*. Cambridge: Cambridge University Press.

Steiner, George (1961). *The Death of Tragedy*. London: Faber and Faber.

Stoll, K. H. (1975). *The New British Drama*. Bern: Lang.

Theatre Voice (2005). 'Reputations: Edward Bond', discussion chaired by Aleks Sierz at the Theatre Museum, London, 11 March, *Theatre Voice*, www.theatrevoice.com.

Trussler, Simon (1976). *Edward Bond*. London: Longman.

34

John McGrath and Popular Political Theatre

Maria DiCenzo

The theatre can never *cause* a social change. It can articulate the pressures towards one, help people to celebrate their strengths and maybe build their self-confidence. It can be a public emblem of inner, and outer, events, and occasionally a reminder, an elbow-jogger, a perspective-bringer. Above all, it can be the way people can find voice, their solidarity and their collective determination. (McGrath 1981a: xxvii)

There is a need for a sharp, satirical theatre to scrutinize our values, to contest the borders of our democracy, to give a voice to the excluded, to the minorities, to guard against the tyranny of the majority, to criticize without fear, to seek true and multifaceted information, to combat the distorting power of the mass media, to define and re-define freedom for our age, to demand the equality of all citizens for the short time we have on this earth before we die. (McGrath 2001: 239)

Separated by almost three decades, these statements offer a key to understanding John McGrath's career-long commitment to harnessing the power of theatre as a public form to the processes of social change. Along with making significant contributions in the fields of television and film, McGrath remains best known as a playwright and founder of the 7:84 Theatre Company in 1971, its name deriving from a statistic published in *The Economist* indicating that 7 per cent of the population of Great Britain controlled 84 per cent of its capital wealth. Such profound inequities were the driving force behind McGrath's socialism and his determination to bring informed, critical and entertaining theatre to working-class audiences. McGrath's work with what eventually became two companies (7:84 England and 7:84 Scotland) represents a major development and tendency in postwar political theatre and signals the ways in which he remains an anomalous figure in the history of modern British theatre. While he is linked in many ways to other playwrights in this Companion, his work follows a different line of development, problematizing more conventional categories and genres, and his long list of published works accounts for only a small part of his important contribution. Tributes published after his untimely death in 2002 stressed the range of McGrath's achievements. Celebrated as a writer, director and producer, he was also remembered for being a passionate and outspoken critic of government, funding bodies and his contemporaries in the theatre world. He bridged the divides not only between different media (television, film and theatre), but also between national contexts. Michael Billington, in the *Guardian*, claimed that 'No one since Joan Littlewood did more to advance the cause of popular theatre in Britain than John McGrath' (24 January 2002), while Mike Wade in the *Scotsman* referred to McGrath as 'the architect of a Scots theatre revival', stating that his 'writing and directing talents shaped a generation of Scottish theatre' (24 January 2002). It is unusual for a non-Scot to become recognized as a major Scottish playwright, but Randall Stevenson notes that 'Scottish commentators and audiences are likely to forget this [how far his career extended beyond Scotland] simply because his work was so important within Scotland – so influential on Scottish theatre and so clearly shaped by it too' (Stevenson 2005: 73). Similarly, Nadine Holdsworth argues that 'Frequently relegated to a footnote of theatre history, 7:84 England has suffered an interesting reversal of the cultural imperialism that often leaves Scottish theatre overshadowed by its English counterpart' (Holdsworth 2005: 55). By documenting McGrath's involvement with 7:84 England and recovering some of the key plays, Holdsworth has been instrumental in bringing that material to light.[1]

Such efforts also remind us of how easily collaborative, often unpublished, touring theatre can slip between the cracks even in recent theatre history. As critics documented the expanding and evolving body of political theatre in Britain between the late 1970s and 1990s, the space devoted to McGrath's experiments has varied considerably in sources ranging from early landmark studies (Itzin 1980; Bull 1983) to more narrowly defined approaches (Peacock 1991; Kershaw 1992; Reinelt 1996), as well as broad overviews of modern British drama (Shellard 1999; Innes 2002). While political playwrights such as David Edgar and David Hare invariably get more detailed coverage, unorthodox figures such as McGrath and John Arden are treated less predictably. At the same time, in general studies, McGrath and the 7:84 companies are frequently used as examples of socialist or popular political theatre over the work of other companies in the 1970s. There are a number of reasons for this visibility. For one, 7:84 Scotland was one of the longest-surviving companies and its first production was very successful. The televised version of *The Cheviot* on tour, filmed for BBC's 'Play for Today' series in 1974, made a larger audience aware of this play and the company, and an illustrated edition of the play was published by Methuen in 1981, making it available to a wider readership, including researchers and teachers. Many of McGrath's other plays have also been published, in single and collected editions. His direct involvement in the critical debates about contemporary theatre practices in the pages of influential journals like *New Theatre Quarterly*, and his polemical and theoretical writing, most notably *A Good Night Out*, based on a series of lectures at Cambridge University, account in part for his prominence. It is crucial to acknowledge the role academics, theatre critics and practitioners play in canon formation (even in non-canonical areas) and the challenges some forms and practices represent in terms of documentation. In this sense, the position of McGrath's 'oeuvre' in the academy raises some interesting questions about how we categorize and assess theatre-work that is as noteworthy in terms of 'productions' and what it aimed to do in a particular context, developed with and for a specific company or groups of performers, as it is in terms of the 'texts' which have become a part of theatre history and the body of dramatic 'literature'.

If McGrath indeed remains best known as a playwright and, most notably in conjunction with 7:84 Scotland's famous production of *The Cheviot, the Stag and the Black, Black Oil*, understanding how he came to 'write' that play helps to explain both the ways in which he reversed the usual career pattern and why he warrants an unusual place in postwar theatre history. Accounts of his early work frequently highlight the fact that, unlike many of his contemporaries, McGrath began his career in the mainstream, writing and directing for television (*Z-Cars*) and film (*Billion Dollar Brain*, 1967; *The Bofors Gun*, 1968; *The Reckoning*, 1970). The commercial success helped to finance later alternative ventures. By 1975, when asked in an interview for *Theatre Quarterly* what he would do if Peter Hall were to commission a play from him for the National Theatre, he claimed he would 'run about twenty-five miles . . . I would rather have a bad night in Bootle' (McGrath 1975: 54). Reaching working-class audiences, about issues relevant to their lives, in their leisure and entertainment spaces – community centres and workers' clubs, not traditional theatre venues – became his artistic and political goal. It was there he believed that socialist theatre could be part of generating a genuine and effective counterculture. He later described this in terms of the fundamental decisions any practitioner must make, stating that 'a writer (or director, actor or technician) coming into the theatre has to make a choice between working in bourgeois theatre with bourgeois values for largely middle-class audiences – and I include the trendy, experimental bits of the National and RSC [Royal Shakespeare Company] as well as Bournemouth Rep. – and working in popular theatre with socialist values for largely working-class audiences' (McGrath 1981b: 95).

He experimented with plays at the Liverpool Everyman in the early 1970s, where artistic director Alan Dossor had been trying to build a community-based theatre that would attract local, working-class audiences – in the tradition of Joan Littlewood's Theatre Workshop. McGrath's works in this period include a series of short plays called *Unruly Elements* (1971), *Soft or a Girl?* (1971) and *Fish in the Sea* (1972) (Merkin 2005). The link to Joan Littlewood is significant and represents a particular trajectory of work (distinguished from that initiated by the Royal Court) which served as a major influence on theatre artists who were interested in working outside of conventional theatre structures and trying to reach non-theatre-going audiences. Littlewood's methods of working with actors, her interest in drawing on popular forms of entertainment, her approaches to staging, and even her character – charismatic, but authoritarian and determined – all had an impact on McGrath (who referred to himself as a 'benevolent dictator'), and the resonances with Theatre Workshop productions such as *Oh What a Lovely War* (1963) are most evident in *The Cheviot*. The productions at the Liverpool Everyman overlapped with the early ventures of the 7:84 Theatre Company, all of which provided opportunities to explore the use of different forms for different audiences, primarily in an urban, English context.

The decision to form a separate company to produce and tour plays in Scotland was a major turning point in McGrath's career. Scottish history, political culture, language and entertainment traditions made for particularly fertile ground for the kind of popular theatre he was interested in developing. Randall Stevenson traces and elaborates these features of the Scottish context in historical terms and argues that 'McGrath undoubtedly brought to Scotland a set of political interests and perform-ance idioms developed for himself, based on [earlier] work … Yet to an extent he arrived in Scotland to discover his idioms and interests got there before him or had always been there' (Stevenson 2005: 78–9). This is not to diminish McGrath's achievement, but rather to stress that the ability or effectiveness of oppositional theatre to engage its audiences is situated in historically, politically and culturally specific ways. *The Cheviot* is a case in point. The play traces the 'savage process of capitalism' on the Highlands from the time of the Clearances to the (then recent) takeover of North Sea oil by multinationals. All of its components – the Marxist analysis of the history of the exploitation of the region, the evocation of Gaelic culture and language, the satirical treatment of English and American capitalists, and the urgent call to unite and fight back, all delivered in the form of a ceilidh – had strong resonances for audiences, young and old, at the time. It is significant that the first read/run through of the play was done for a conference on 'What Kind of Scotland?' where participants from a variety of backgrounds (arts, politics, labour movement, public sector) were debating the future of Scotland. The company was able to tap directly into these passionate, public debates, even though their critical line on Scottish nationalism and the Scottish National Party was a source of controversy. The show toured venues such as community centres, village halls and schools all over Scotland, launching the beginning of what would become the company's Highland touring circuits, bringing plays to locations where professional theatre had never gone before.

McGrath and 7:84 Scotland drew from and elaborated existing models for com-munity documentary plays and collective approaches to the creation of scripts. He offers a detailed account of these processes in 'The Year of the Cheviot' (McGrath 1981a) by way of preface to the published edition of the play. He conceived of the play as a series of episodes from pivotal points in Highland history and then involved the company in the research and development. Even though McGrath remained clear about his role as 'writer', the intention was to establish an egalitarian working environment, as a deliberate response to and rejection of 'the insane hierarchies of the theatre' (McGrath 1981a: ix). The choice of the ceilidh – a gathering featuring story-telling, music, songs, and dancing – provided a suitable structure for the episodic components of the play, and a familiar, culturally rooted vehicle for the material. But it demanded a different style of performance from the actors and musicians, just as the collective approach to creation and production would require a broader set of responsibilities, before and during the tour, with members sharing in all aspects of pre- and post-production work. Not only did fluid movement between sketches, monologues and musical numbers mean that the actors would play multiple roles or characters, but they were also expected to step out of 'character' and address the audience, sometimes reading directly from historical sources. The presentational style of performance, and the effective blending of comic and satirical as well as serious and emotionally compelling elements, was crucial to generating a positive rapport between the performers and the audience. After the 'play' was over, the company became the Force Ten Gaels Dance Band, often playing music and interacting with audiences until the early hours. The play was adapted and new material inserted as information came to light through these informal gatherings in local communities. Building a relationship of solidarity with the audiences for whom the plays were created was a priority for McGrath and the company from the outset, and remained so.

There is much to be said about this rich and dynamic play and it has received extensive scholarly attention (see DiCenzo 2005; Kershaw 1992; Nelson 2005; Patterson 2003; Peacock 1991; Reinelt 1996). But for the purposes of this overview, it is important to stress that *The Cheviot* enjoyed the rare status of being both a significant departure from mainstream and even alternative forms of theatre, and a huge critical success (not unlike Joan Littlewood's *Oh What a Lovely War* a decade earlier). The problem was that it set up high expectations that many critics believed subsequent productions were unable to live up to. But McGrath's aim was not to keep doing the same thing, as was evident from his next play and the company's second major production, *The Game's a Bogey* (1974). While there are overlapping features with *The Cheviot*, this show was the first geared specifically to urban, industrial, working-class audiences in clubs and union halls, so its subject matter and its form were necessarily different. This play also makes historical connections, but this time it is the story of John MacLean, a socialist hero from the days of the Red Clyde, which is used as a framework for exploring contemporary problems in urban centres like Glasgow.[2] *The Game's a Bogey* is episodic and musical and addresses the audience directly, but draws on the variety show and club entertainment, rather than the ceilidh, for its particular idiom and gritty style.

These first plays helped to define the two separate strands of 7:84 Scotland's work in the 1970s and 1980s – the plays for the Highland and Islands (*Boom*, 1974; *The Catch*, 1981; *The Albannach*, 1985; *There is a Happy Land*, 1986; *Mairi Mhor, the Woman of Skye*, 1987) versus those for the urban, industrial belt (such as *Little Red Hen*, 1975; *Out of Our Heads*, 1976; *Joe's Drum*, 1979; *Blood Red Roses*, 1980) – but McGrath continued to experiment in his work for both 7:84 companies. Some of the developments occurred in the translation of a play from one medium to another, as Stephen Lacey's analysis of McGrath's 'practical realism' in the television adaptation of *Blood Red Roses* reveals (Lacey 2005). Even later examples such as the large-scale promenade play *Border Warfare* (1989), presented by Wildcat Stage Productions at Tramway

Theatre (formerly the Museum of Transport) in Glasgow, and the one-woman shows he wrote for his wife Elizabeth MacLennan in the 1990s are at opposite ends of the production spectrum, exploring new directions in themes, forms and venues. As with all his work, they are nevertheless underscored by a sustained interest in history, an international perspective, and an uncompromising commitment to and belief in socialism as a rational solution to the inequalities and injustices of capitalism.

Nowhere are these principles and their implications for cultural production more clearly articulated than in his book *A Good Night Out* (1981). Throughout his career, McGrath attempted to theorize and document his theatre practice, generating writings which are not only important to an understanding of his work, but also offer a valuable and provocative perspective on theatre in postwar Britain more generally. *A Good Night Out* derives from the first of two major lecture series at Cambridge University in 1979 (the second was published as *The Bone Won't Break* in 1990). In the interests of theorizing the relationship between theatrical form and social class, he engages in a materialist analysis of theatre and demonstrates how theatre works as a complex social event – from the price of tickets to post-production activity. At the core of the book is an attempt to identify and describe the characteristics and functions of working-class theatre, as distinguished from bourgeois forms of theatre, in order to demonstrate how the political and social values/meanings of plays are not the same for all audiences. His analysis of elements such as directness, comedy, music, emotion, variety, effect, immediacy and localism is illuminating, even if at times contentious. Just as the plays themselves must be understood in historically specific terms, so too must we situate *A Good Night Out* in the context of a diverse body of writing on working-class history and culture and the institutionalization of Marxist or more broadly left-wing discourses in the postwar period. The work represents, as Raymond Williams's foreword to the book notes, a rare bridge between theatre professionals and academics. As a personal account of the experiments of a particular practitioner and company, along with *The Bone Won't Break*, it reveals the internal workings of such groups and how their fates are inevitably tied to shifts in the larger social, political and economic structures in which they operate.

In these ways, McGrath holds a special position as a 'theatre activist', not simply in the sense of using theatre as part of a political, activist agenda, but also in the sense of agitating within the theatre world to force an interrogation of existing theatre practices and to challenge assumptions about who makes theatre, whom it is for, where it takes place, and ultimately, what role it can play in wider social and political processes. This role extended to independent film-making through the founding of Moonstone in 1997, an experimental laboratory for emerging film-makers – in fact film-makers may associate McGrath more with Moonstone in the 1990s than with *The Cheviot* or 7:84 in the 1970s. In addition to facilitating new work and writers, he was instrumental in the recovery of earlier ones. The Clydebuilt season mounted in 1982, based on research conducted by Linda Mackenney, revived a series of scripts that were part of an earlier tradition of popular political plays in Scotland, including Joe Corrie's *In Time of Strife* (1926) and Ena Lamont Stewart's *Men Should Weep* (1947).

Randall Stevenson refers to the Clydebuilt season as 'an act of auto-genealogy', stressing the significance of this act of recovery in bringing Scotland's theatrical past to light and shaping a new generation of playwrights in the process (Stevenson 2005: 80). Liz Lochhead recalls 'as a producer, [McGrath's] *Clydebuilt* series was a big influence on everybody of my generation. In the same way that *The Cheviot* restored a voice to us all, the *Clydebuilt* series restored this history' (see Brown 2005: 100–12).

The fact that it is difficult to avoid the use of the phrase 'McGrath's work' in describing these various endeavours only underscores the extent to which his contribution is about much more than writing (even than directing and producing); it is also about a larger sense of 'cultural work'. But McGrath's long-standing commitment to producing theatre for working-class audiences eventually came to be seen by some as increasingly problematic. For readers approaching him for the first time, the plays may present challenges; for instance, they feature memorable characters, scenes and songs, document powerful historical details, or use the stage to embody and communicate hard-hitting political analysis, but they are not and do not 'read' like more conventionally literary plays (realist or otherwise). In *A Good Night Out* he claimed that the 'act of *creating theatre* has nothing to do with the making of dramatic literature . . . it is fatal for playwrights to try to write "dramatic literature" ' (McGrath 1981b: 6). These plays also relied for much of their impact on the performers and musicians who were integral to their development and on the environments and circumstances in which the shows took place. The values and standards on which artistic work is based and the criteria by which it is evaluated became a major theme in *The Bone Won't Break*. The second set of Cambridge lectures forming the basis of the book took place after McGrath resigned as artistic director of 7:84 Scotland, which in turn followed a threat of complete withdrawal of funding from the Scottish Arts Council in 1988 (7:84 England had already been cut by the Arts Council of Great Britain in 1985). One of the main reasons cited for the threatened cut was the 'artistic quality' of the company's work.

Another challenge for readers now involves negotiating the terms of McGrath's Marxist discourse, since even by the 1980s the idea of 'socialist theatre' for 'working-class audiences' began to seem dated. It was a problem he was aware of as he addressed his second Cambridge audience:

> One of the main planks of the work [with 7:84] was the need for 'class-consciousness' in the working class, that is, knowledge of, solidarity with those with common interests and roles in society. Through the 60s and 70s this concept of 'class-consciousness' raised no problems: people knew what it meant, and knew it existed, and could chart its growth. Now, ten years later, the concept is unfamiliar, a word for something that no longer exists, something that failed. (McGrath 1990: 3)

But he continued to define 'popular' and 'popular cultures' in Gramscian terms, as rooted in 'the mass of working people in their areas', as the site of ongoing struggle (McGrath 1990: 57, 64),[3] with theatre – and the process of 'making' theatre – playing a central role in those contexts:

such a theatre [of popular celebration] could take its place among the organs of a
Resistance Movement that needs to find the popular imagination as well as express postindustrial reality. Of course theatre *alone* cannot, should not and never will achieve a
great deal politically; but in the process of trying to articulate a deeply felt complex of
thoughts, emotions and desires, and trying to explore and present a greater range of our
experiences of living, such a dramatising could bring some new life to our theatre, as
well as moving political awareness and giving some self-confidence to some otherwise
demoralised or silenced sectors of society – like the working class, those who care about
the natural and animal life around us, and those dispossessed of their full potential for
living. (McGrath 1990: 161)

McGrath's language may have been out of step with the changing discourses of
political debates (inside and outside the theatre world), but the fundamental inequalities he was trying to describe and address had not changed, nor had his own
determination to play a role in mobilizing people politically in order to change them.

David Edgar, with reference to his own heated debate with McGrath over the
viability of a socialist theatre project at the end of the 1970s (see Edgar 1979;
McGrath 1979), offered a retrospective assessment of some of these issues in 2002.
Recalling his last meeting with McGrath in 2000, he writes:

I thought then – and think even more now – that it's wrong to see him as a socialist
writer who sacrificed what could have been a distinguished and prosperous mainstream
career for his convictions. Superficially, John seemed to stick four-square in the Marxist
mainstream while all around him were deviating down the enticing tributories [*sic*] of
identity politics. But in fact John's best plays were all about the complex conflicts in the
contested borderlands between religions, nations, genders, and classes (in a sense the
title of *Border Warfare* could have been a fitting title for his work as a whole). (Edgar
2002: 306)

Perhaps even more poignant is Edgar's reminder of the changes that the 7:84 statistic
has undergone in the intervening years, concluding that 'however you define or
categorize them (and however they define or categorize themselves), the ninety-
three per cent are still out there' (Edgar 2002: 306).

NOTES

1 Holdsworth offers a detailed introduction
to the work of 7:84 England in McGrath
(2005).
2 'Red Clyde' or the 'Red Clydeside' (named for
the Clyde river and the industries surrounding
it) refer to the revolutionary activity of the
labour movement in Glasgow in the early decades of the twentieth century. John MacLean,

one of the most famous leaders of this movement, was instrumental in rallying workers to
protest and strike, and taught Marxist economics to classes of thousands. The play uses
MacLean's earlier call for a Scottish Workers'
Republic, and his appeals to the working
classes then, to rally exploited workers in the
present.

3 In both *A Good Night Out* (64) and *The Bone Won't Break* (52), McGrath refers to Antonio Gramsci's idea of the 'national popular' in order to explain his own use of the term 'popular culture', noting Gramsci's ability to see popular culture 'not as the inert object of sociological description, but as the site of a political struggle' (McGrath 1981b: 64). He also cites Brecht's definition as a particularly clear expression of the concept as McGrath himself employs it: 'Popular means: intelligible to the broad masses, adopting and enriching their forms of expression/assuming their standpoint, confirming and correcting it/representing the most progressive section of the people so that it can assume leadership' (McGrath 1981b: 63). In *The Bone Won't Break* he devotes a whole chapter to related concepts and offers a specific working definition: 'I use popular to distinguish these cultures [several differing low or working-class cultures] from the dominant high culture which the middle and upper-classes are mainly qualified to consume – through education, wealth and social conditioning – and which is aimed primarily at them. Popular cultures are similarly those of the mass of the working people in their areas, and are primarily made for and enjoyed by them. Popular culture, as I have argued at length, is the site of a long, ongoing struggle' (McGrath 1990: 57).

Primary Reading

McGrath, John (1975). 'Better a Bad Night in Bootle', *Theatre Quarterly* 19, 39–54.

McGrath, John (1979). 'The Theory and Practice of Political Theatre', *Theatre Quarterly* 9, 43–54.

McGrath, John (1981a). 'The Year of the Cheviot' in John McGrath. *The Cheviot, the Stag and the Black, Black Oil*. London: Methuen, v–xxviii.

McGrath, John (1981b). *A Good Night Out: Popular Theatre: Audience, Class and Form*. London: Methuen.

McGrath, John (1985). 'Popular Theatre and the Changing Perspectives of the Eighties', *New Theatre Quarterly* 1:4, 390–416.

McGrath, John (1990). *The Bone Won't Break: On Theatre and Hope in Hard Times*. London: Methuen.

McGrath, John (1996). *Six-Pack: Plays for Scotland*. Edinburgh: Polygon.

McGrath, John (2001). 'Theatre and Democracy' in John McGrath (2002). *Naked Thoughts that Roam About: Reflections on Theatre 1958–2001*, ed. Nadine Holdsworth. London: Nick Hern, 228–39.

McGrath, John (2002). *Naked Thoughts that Roam About: Reflections on Theatre 1958–2001*, ed. Nadine Holdsworth. London: Nick Hern.

McGrath, John (2005). *John McGrath: Plays for England*, selected and intro. Nadine Holdsworth. Exeter: University of Exeter Press.

Further Reading

Bradby, David and Capon, Susanna (eds.) (2005). *Freedom's Pioneer: John McGrath's Work in Theatre, Film and Television*. Exeter: University of Exeter Press.

Brown, Ian (2005). ' "Bursting through the Hoop and Dancing on the Edge of Seediness": Five Scottish Playwrights Talk about John McGrath' in David Bradby and Susanna Capon (eds.). *Freedom's Pioneer: John McGrath's Work in Theatre, Film and Television*. Exeter: University of Exeter Press, 100–12.

Bull, John (1983). *New British Political Dramatists*. New York: Grove Press.

DiCenzo, Maria (1996). *The Politics of Alternative Theatre in Britain, 1968–1990: The Case of 7:84 (Scotland)*. Cambridge: Cambridge University Press.

DiCenzo, Maria (2005). 'Theatre, Theory and Politics: The Contribution of John McGrath' in David Bradby and Susanna Capon (eds.). *Freedom's Pioneer: John McGrath's Work in Theatre, Film and Television*. Exeter: University of Exeter Press, 3–14.

Edgar, David (1979). 'Ten Years of Political Theatre, 1968–78', *Theatre Quarterly* 8:32, 25–33.

Edgar, David (2002). 'Views Across Borders', *New Theatre Quarterly* 72, 305–6.

Holdsworth, Nadine (2005). 'Finding the Right Places, Finding the Right Audiences: Topicality and Entertainment in the Work of 7:84 England' in David Bradby and Susanna Capon (eds.). *Freedom's Pioneer: John McGrath's Work in Theatre, Film and Television*. Exeter: University of Exeter Press, 55–69.

Innes, Christopher (2002). *Modern British Drama: The Twentieth Century*. Cambridge: Cambridge University Press.

Itzin, Catherine (1980). *Stages in the Revolution: Political Theatre in Britain since 1968*. London: Methuen.

Kershaw, Baz (1992). *The Politics of Performance: Radical Theatre as Cultural Intervention*. London: Routledge.

Lacey, Stephen (2005). 'A Practical Realism: McGrath, Brecht, Lukács and *Blood Red Roses*' in David Bradby and Susanna Capon (eds.). *Freedom's Pioneer: John McGrath's Work in Theatre, Film and Television*. Exeter: University of Exeter Press, 130–43.

MacLennan, Elizabeth (1990). *The Moon Belongs to Everyone: Making Theatre with 7:84*. London: Methuen.

Merkin, Ros (2005). 'A Life Outside 7:84: John McGrath and the Everyman Theatre, Liverpool' in David Bradby and Susanna Capon (eds.). *Freedom's Pioneer: John McGrath's Work in Theatre, Film and Television*. Exeter: University of Exeter Press, 25–38.

Nelson, Robin (2005). 'The Television Adaptation of *The Cheviot, the Stag and the Black, Black Oil*' in David Bradby and Susanna Capon (eds.). *Freedom's Pioneer: John McGrath's Work in Theatre, Film and Television*. Exeter: University of Exeter Press, 115–29.

Patterson, Michael (2003). *Strategies of Political Theatre: Post-War British Playwrights*. Cambridge: Cambridge University Press.

Peacock, D. Keith (1991). *Radical Stages: Alternative History in Modern British Drama*. Westport, CT: Greenwood Press.

Reinelt, Janelle (1996). *After Brecht: British Epic Theatre*. Ann Arbor: University of Michigan Press.

Shellard, Dominic (1999). *British Theatre since the War*. New Haven, CT: Yale University Press.

Stevenson, Randall (2005). 'Border Warranty: John McGrath and Scotland' in David Bradby and Susanna Capon (eds.). *Freedom's Pioneer: John McGrath's Work in Theatre, Film and Television*. Exeter: University of Exeter Press, 73–85.

For a more complete list of theatre, television and film credits see:

Horvat, Ksenija and McGrath, John (2001). 'John McGrath: An Updated Checklist and Bibliography', *International Journal of Scottish Theatre* 2:1, arts.qmuc.ac.uk/ijost/Volume2_no1/K_Horvat.htm.

See also tributes and articles in:

'The Theatres of John McGrath' (2002). *New Theatre Quarterly* 18:4, 299–333.

35

David Hare and Political Playwriting: Between the Third Way and the Permanent Way

John Deeney

David Hare (b. 1947) is one of the key figures in late twentieth- and early twenty-first-century English mainstream subsidized theatre. Recent productions of *The Permanent Way* (2003) and *Stuff Happens* (2004) relaunched Hare's career and also brought the perception of a waning political theatre back into the media limelight with fervent and furious discussion in the middle-class press about the function and funding of theatre in England. Whilst much of Hare's original output for the stage, particularly when viewed alongside that of his contemporaries such as Howard Barker, Howard Brenton, Caryl Churchill and David Edgar, has productively been critiqued in terms of 'self-consciously addressing the social, political and cultural state of the nation' (Edgar 1999: 5), Hare's various explorations in dramatic form and content, working method and theatrical style suggest a somewhat less schematic and more lateral critical approach. His early work is also vastly different from the later work, in terms of both aesthetic form and ideological fixity. In one respect at least, the route through Hare's oeuvre is a traceable journey from an alternative and Marxist-informed praxis to the mainstream of the political centre ground, a shift from a concerted engagement with the modus operandi of political play-making to a sometimes agonized collusion with the conventions of dramatic realism.

Hare's status within British theatre has changed considerably over a period of approaching forty years. As the co-founder of Portable Theatre in 1968 and the then innovative Joint Stock Theatre Company in 1975 (see Ritchie 1987), Hare quickly established himself as one of the leaders of the burgeoning and politically committed alternative theatre movement. His early work combined single-authored dramas with collaborative and workshop-based forms of play-making (typical of Joint Stock), and he also directed. As early as 1974 his comedy thriller *Knuckle* received a commercial West End production, and during the 1970s Hare became rapidly assimilated (in this respect not unlike many of his white, male, middle-class contemporaries) into the mainstream subsidized theatre sector, most notably, for Hare, the National Theatre (NT). Whilst directing much of his own work, Hare was also taken under the wing of directors who carried a particular cachet in terms of developing the work and repertoires of this sector; firstly by Max Stafford-Clark at Joint Stock (subsequently artistic director of the Royal Court) and then by Richard Eyre, who as artistic director of the NT during the 1990s provided Hare with the type of exposure that many of his contemporaries were increasingly denied. Significantly, the Eyre/Hare marriage also coincided with references to Hare in the press as 'the national playwright'. This media construction was a phenomenon which Hare always encouraged, aligning himself with a so-called 'tradition' and confessing that John Osborne's *Look Back in Anger* (1956) 'was the play whose effect I would most like to have provoked' (Hare 1997c: 14). Hare also argued that the new writers who had emerged at the Royal Court in the mid-nineties (a reference to figures such as Sarah Kane and Mark Ravenhill) had failed to offer that 'kind of rallying point that every generation needs to provide a focus for its own wishes and dreams' (ibid.: 14). This does not simply read as sheepishly self-canonizing, it discloses Hare's concern for constructing and preserving an absolutist position within the order of professional playwrights.

It was Hare's play *Plenty* (NT, 1978) that marked a formative turning point, both in terms of his maturation as a dramatist and in gaining a wider critical and public recognition that the NT exposure facilitated. Hare's work up to this point might best be typified as dramatizing 'England in microcosm'. Plays such as *Slag* (1970), *The Great Exhibition* (1972), *Teeth 'n' Smiles* (1975) and *Plenty* employ the milieu of postwar and contemporary England to discourse what C. W. E. Bigsby describes as 'a country in which private despair is the constant'. Furthermore, Hare 'is responding more directly to a national sense of failed purpose and moral attrition than those writers for whom a simple shift in the distribution of wealth and power constitutes a clear solution to problems which are perceived as primarily a product of late capitalism' (Bigsby 1981: 43). The notion that Hare's generation perceived an aperture within the postwar consensus for the discharge of a Marxist-informed praxis is an all too simplistic reading of this period in English theatre history. Hare's work from the 1970s acutely demonstrates as much. Nevertheless, the onslaught of Thatcherism in the 1980s represented the final dismantling of that consensus, and this necessitated reassessment and reorientation.

The 1980s saw Hare flexing his dramaturgical muscles, splitting his energies between playwriting, screenwriting and directing. Not only does *A Map of the World* (1982) place the dramatic action in Bombay rather than England, but its debate is located between left-wing idealism and the plight of the third world in a dialectic exploring the relationship between art and reality. Thematically connected, *The Bay at Nice* (1986) employs the context of Soviet Russia; an ex-student of Matisse's from 1920s Paris is invited to authenticate a painting said to be the work of her teacher – a springboard for the examination of the nature of authenticity, both in art and in life. In the 1980s Hare also revived his playwriting partnership with Howard Brenton (they had previously collaborated on *Brassneck*, 1974) and they co-authored *Pravda* (1985), a comedy about the newspaper industry. *Pravda's* unconcealed attack on Thatcherism was dismissed by Herb Greer as 'radical-chic agitprop' (quoted in Page 1990: 64), an indication of the problems encountered by political theatre in the 1980s. But if the dramaturgical kitbag was in need of new tools, or at least a fresher usage, Hare's final stage play of the decade marked a somewhat sullen return to more familiar territory. In *The Secret Rapture* (1988) two sisters, one a Conservative junior minister and the other a commercial artist, represent the bipolar opposites of contemporary Britain. Marion, ambitious, judgemental and sanctimonious, sets herself against the compassionate Isobel as the latter agrees in the wake of their father's death to care for their stepmother. Marion's scheming ultimately results in Isobel's murder. At the time of its opening Hare described *The Secret Rapture* as being 'about the intractability of goodness' (quoted in Boon 2003: 122), and it was this idea of 'goodness' that would prove to be one of Hare's main thematic preoccupations throughout the 1990s and into the new millennium.

If one can typify the 1980s as Hare's 'problem period', then the years since 1990 represent little short of a renaissance in his fortunes as a dramatist. By 1993 he had completed 'the trilogy', a five-year research project that culminated in Richard Eyre's simultaneous NT staging of *Racing Demon* (1990), *Murmuring Judges* (1991) and *The Absence of War* (1993). The Church of England, the English legal system and the Labour party provide the subject matter here for an examination of the allied crises facing English institutions. This 'state-of-the-nation' trilogy was heralded by many as the phoenix rising from the ashes of political theatre. And although indicative of Hare's increasing political and dramatic conservativism, the trilogy does represent a careful examination of the institutions. But in yet another turn-around – now an established pattern – Hare's next ventures represented a return to more scaled-down offerings. The austere realism of *Skylight* (1995) pits the recently widowed Tom, a restaurant entrepreneur and the embodiment of Thatcherite acquisitiveness, against his ex-lover Kyra, an idealistic East End teacher. *Amy's View* (1997) employs a 16-year time-frame and a 'well-made' four-act structure to provide a study of a volatile mother-daughter relationship set against the shifting values of England's socio-cultural landscape. Both *Skylight* and *Amy's View* transferred from the NT to the West End. By 1998 Hare, now in receipt of a knighthood from the recently installed 'New' Labour government led by Tony Blair, was proving unusually prolific. *The Judas Kiss* (1998) offered a re-examination of Oscar Wilde's relationship with Lord Alfred Douglas and *The Blue Room* (1998) freely transposed Schnitzler's *La Ronde* (1900) to the present day. With these last four works Hare had also managed to attract those members of the acting fraternity that roam the international circuit; respectively, Michael Gambon, Judy Dench, Liam Neeson and, in a major coup, Nicole Kidman. Not surprisingly, Broadway transfers were secured in each case.

It was also during this period that Hare found himself without a theatrical home. Richard Eyre had left the NT in 1997 and so Hare was effectively removed from his unofficial position as 'house dramatist'. Whilst Hare continued to satisfy expectation, there was also a search for a new focus. Thus in his next project Hare placed himself centre stage. Invited by the Royal Court Theatre's International Department to write a play about Palestine and Israel, Hare's response to visiting the region was to compose a monologue that he himself performed. Following a Royal Court opening, *Via Dolorosa* (1998) also transferred to Broadway. *My Zinc Bed* (2000) and *The Breath of Life* (2002) offered variations on realism – standing variously between the opaque and the transparent – for Royal Court and West End audiences respectively. But if *Via Dolorosa* seemed a concerted effort by Hare to re-establish his credentials as a 'political dramatist', then this was confirmed in all sorts of ways with *The Permanent Way* (2003). In part influenced by the resurgence of verbatim theatre[1] and the employment of real-life personal testimony in *Via Dolorosa*, Hare set about offering a dramatized account of the deleterious impact of privatization on the British railways. *The Permanent Way*, co-produced by Out of Joint and the NT, saw Hare rekindle some of the Joint Stock practices of the 1970s; not only was the piece directed by Hare's former Joint Stock associate Max Stafford-Clark, but also actors were utilized in the initial assemblage of personal testimony. And if *The Permanent Way* emphasized the efficacy of personal testimony, then Hare was to expand on this dramaturgical practice for his next project. The vast dramatis personae of *Stuff Happens* includes George W. Bush, Tony Blair and Saddam Hussein; a cast of real-life characters used to scrutinize the events leading up to the Anglo-American-led invasion of Iraq in 2003.

Splitting Hare/s

It would be entertaining though disingenuous to suggest that this laconic overview of Hare's work and career represents the dramatic and theatrical equivalent of multiple personality disorder. However, assessing Hare's standing as a political dramatist within such a mutating context is not without its problems. As early as 1978, Hare was himself complicating matters in a lecture given at Cambridge University:

> Over and over again I have written about romantic love, because it never goes away. And the view of the world it provides, the dislocation it offers, is the most intense experience that many people know on earth.
>
> And I write comedy because [. . .] such ideas as the one I have just uttered make me laugh.
>
> And I write about politics because the challenge of communism, in however debased and ugly a form, is to ask whether the criteria by which we have been brought up are right. (Hare 1991b: 35)

Hare later recounts how hecklers interrupted the lecture and that this marked his split with 'Marxist theatre' (Hare 1999: 37). Yet the lecture also suggests a self-styled vacillation combined with a rather schematic approach to his own dramaturgy. Accordingly, Richard Boon has argued that Hare's seemingly 'contradictory and paradoxical' accounts of the relationship between his playwriting and its interface with politics mask the fact that he is the dramatist of his generation who has persistently 'succeeded in capturing the *zeitgeist* . . . [he has] constantly set up, dismantled and set up again the "scaffolding" of his work' (Boon 2003: 5–6). Yet such an observation rests heavily on removing Hare's work from its theatrical and historical context. I would also suggest that the trajectory of Hare's career reveals a rather different teleology, one in which the dramatist has – by turns serially and simultaneously – placed himself (and indeed been placed) in the roles of 'outsider' and 'insider', both the 'enemy' and the 'guardian' of the dominant culture and ideology, and that this has now reached a critical impasse.

In assessing Hare's work it might be tempting to distinguish the more self-consciously 'political' strain in his playwriting (*Pravda*, the trilogy, *Stuff Happens*, etc.) from the work that takes a more overtly personal or domestic focus (*Skylight*, *Amy's View*, etc.). Commentators rightly intimate the self-defeating nature of such a strategy, suggesting like Boon that his canon demonstrates a purposeful engagement, not simply with the layers that constitute private, public and political life, but as much with the seepage that occurs between these various worlds. In *Plenty* the personal disintegration of its heroine Susan Traherne is set against a series of domestic and semi-public encounters in a time-frame covering the years 1943–62. Susan is first pictured in 1962, in a 'stripped bare' Knightsbridge room, sitting over a 'naked man' we later learn to be her estranged husband (Hare 1996: 377). The *mise en scène*, literally, is one of emptiness and loss. The play rewinds to 1943 and we see Susan working for British Intelligence in France. Hare then switches to 1947 and begins to chart Susan's descent, via employment in an advertising agency, a doomed marriage to a Foreign Office envoy, a liaison with a man whom she wishes – fruitlessly – to father her child, and a reunion with a wartime colleague. The action is closely played out against the euphoria and cataclysm of key national events such as the Festival of Britain and the Suez crisis. But the final scene of the play returns us to France, to liberation day in 1944. In the company of a French farmer, who protests that 'the land is poor' and who has 'to work each moment of the day', Susan proclaims that 'We will improve our world . . . There will be days and days and days like this' (ibid.: 477–8). Christopher Innes takes the somewhat unusual step of comparing *Plenty* to Hare's earlier Joint Stock piece *Fanshen* (1975), a work adapted from an actual account of the impact and efficacy of communism in a Chinese village. Innes argues that scenes in both plays:

> are organized as illustrations of different stages in a social process, rather than a naturalistic cause-and-effect sequence. Clusters of examples with wide gaps between are juxtaposed. The style of the two plays is also similar in the sense of spartan clarity that comes from reducing each situation to its essentials. (Innes 2002: 223–4)

Hare's manipulation of chronology and the epic characteristics of *Plenty* outlined by Innes point to a spectator engagement that opens up dialectical possibilities. On one level, *Plenty* might resist conventional 'naturalistic cause-and-effect', but its epic qualities cannot disguise the fact that Susan's psychological decline blandly promotes a 'subjective response in spectators' (ibid.: 224). *Plenty* might feign a discourse between the private and public realms, between the past and the present, but its heroine is persistently sequestered as the victim of history, not its interlocutor. And although the play's structure and Innes's comments suggest otherwise, *Plenty* represents a very English-styled aestheticization of the Brechtian epic form. The play's uncomplicated positioning of recognizable characters uttering recognizable dialogue within equally recognizable contexts – episodic as they might be – draws the play closer to the more familiar terrain of dramatic realism. Accordingly, Mary Luckhurst has argued that Hare's work fits neatly into the conventional history of twentieth-century British theatre, one that is 'constructed to form a series of repeated discoveries of certain types of realism' (Luckhurst 2002: 76). Moreover,

> [Hare's] work taps into a comfortingly familiar vein for the English and he closes the gap between the late-twentieth and late-nineteenth centuries with an uncanny virtuosity. The fact that many plays contain gentle disquisitions on Britannia's decline and at the same time celebrate what She once was serves to underline that much of Hare's appeal for the English is nostalgic. (ibid.: 74)

Colin Chambers and Mike Prior have argued that the 'nostalgia' of *Plenty* offers 'a readjustment of the past in ways which allow history to provide a security and comfort that the present denies' (Chambers and Prior 1987: 183). Such an analysis lends nostalgia a dubiously affirmative political dimension. But the nostalgia of *Plenty* is frighteningly formulaic: nostalgia = loss – critique. If *Fanshen* 'engages us in a genuine dialectic, prompting us to consider alternatives to the social and economic ordering of our world' (Patterson 2003: 137), then, in comparison, all *Plenty* seems to offer is a sub-Stanislavskian 'magic if'.

This reading of *Plenty* highlights a dramatic practice that is pulling in opposing directions; one towards a Brechtian-informed dialectic, the other towards the ingrained customs of realism in British theatre. Yet whilst the final scene suggests an attempt to interleave a dialectic, in the fissure between the farmer's pragmatism and Susan's idealism, it is also, curiously, the episodic(-cum-circular) structure of the play that militates against this. John Bull has celebrated the 'sabotage that Hare deploys on the expectancies of a straight-line plot development – the *status quo*, disruption of the *status quo* by a solvable moral dilemma, explication and resolution of situation – of the standard model' (Bull 1984: 61). Yet such an analysis ignores *how* the status quo can itself appropriate so-called sabotaging strategies. To appreciate Hare's practice as a political dramatist more fully, it is useful to consider his comments on adapting Brecht's *Galileo* (1994) and *Mother Courage* (1995). Hare dismisses the 'paraphernalia of Brechtianism – the placards, the announcements, the forties German music' in favour of 'sandblasting away some of the layers that now cover these plays... not to soften their politics but to reveal them' (see Boon 2003: 138). What is interesting here is that Hare perceives Brechtian practice not only in primarily presentational terms, but in *aesthetic* terms. He mistakenly reduces Brechtian *method* – distanciation, *gestus*, juxtaposition – to a succession of outmoded theatrical displays.[2] This is not to suggest that the problem with a play like *Plenty* lies in Hare's failing to submit himself unreservedly to a particular dramaturgical system. Rather, his plays have come increasingly to represent the embodiment of the very disabling aesthetic he mistakenly perceives in Brechtian practice. It is an aesthetic that one can now discern to be part and parcel of Hare's larger thematic concerns.

Hare 'the Good'

Part of Susan Traherne's tragedy lies in the political failure to create a 'common good' in the aftermath of World War II. In *The Secret Rapture*, the spiritual goodness of Isobel Glass cannot survive the culture of material individualism created by Thatcherism. Of the trilogy, Hare has asked 'if not through institutions, how do we express the common good?' (Hare 1993b: 8). In *Skylight*, Tom's promise of a better life is not enough to distract Kyra from 'helping these children . . . because they need to be helped' (Hare 1995: 79). In *Amy's View*, the death of a good person is the catalyst for an alienated mother and son-in-law to propose and perform mutual acts of kindness. In *The Judas Kiss*, the demobbed Oscar Wilde liberates Bosie from his misdeed with a kiss from the betrayer. What is Hare articulating here about goodness and acts of kindness, even as political discourses? Tracing a line between *The Secret Rapture* and *The Permanent Way*, Hare has stated that the plays are 'about realizing that good behaviour is not enough' (quoted in Sylvester 2003: 23). Is he therefore mourning the loss or absence of a consensual ethical system? Or is he emphasizing the gap between private and public morality? Finlay Donesky cogently argues that many of the plays from this period:

> appear to be revenge fantasies of the alienated [. . .] in which the spiritually and emotionally unenlightened gang up on saints whose spiritual powers are so awesome that all they have to do is exist to cause chaos and alarm. It is a dream of consolation in which one can only truly invest in one's self and all the dividends appear to be spiritual. (Donesky 1996: 155)

In similar fashion, Duncan Wu refers to Hare's heroines as 'spiritual extremists', but positions his work within the Romantic tradition (Wu 1995: 97–116). Wu's observations are revealing, and not only because they invite important questions about Hare's gender politics. As Boris Dewiel has argued, a major aspect of the Romantic tradition was 'the secularization of divine-command morality, and *the good would come to be seen as that which humans actively, wilfully valued*', as well as the fact that 'power would become associated with the creative will' (Dewiel 2000: 35, my emphasis). Indeed, Hare's conception of 'the good' is indivisible from his own manufactured status as an *author-god* figure. This is part of a process that has permitted his positioning as an insider/outsider, a process that reached its apotheosis with *Via Dolorosa*.

The Absence of War, the final play of the trilogy, is based on the unprecedented access Hare was granted to the inner circles of the Labour party for its 1992 election campaign, a campaign that resulted in Labour's fourth successive election defeat and the end of Neil Kinnock's leadership of the party (Hare 1993b). George Jones is Hare's Labour leader, whose substance lacks style, a figure whose idealism cannot be shaped into more votes at the ballot box. One of the key sequences in the play is when Jones – finally persuaded to utter his true passions before the party faithful: 'My socialism . . . it is concrete. It is real. *It is to do with helping people . . . It is an enabling philosophy*' – cannot complete and awkwardly has to return to the scripted speech (Hare 1993a: 95–6, my emphasis). David Edgar proposes that Jones's 'jaded failure' and 'deflated rhetoric' are an emblematic moment of post-Osborne 'social drama', whilst Boon argues that Jones's story 'is the tragedy of an honourable man who pays the price for not trusting in the power of "the old words" ' (Edgar 1999: 9–10; Boon 2003: 48). But it is equally possible to view Jones's speech as a failed effort to invent a new rhetoric within a transforming political landscape. Although it would be four more years before a rebranded 'New' Labour party would attain a landslide election victory under the leadership of Tony Blair, *The Absence of War* surreptitiously represents Hare's engagement with an emergent ideology within Britain and the Labour party.

Much of New Labour's public and economic policy has been identified as a 'Third Way' route in social democracy, a shift by the traditional left towards a centre ground that seeks to balance 'rights' with 'responsibilities' and globalized market forces with state intervention. Sarah Hale has observed how New Labour, as part of its communitarian-influenced agenda, has revived the notion of the 'good citizen'. Drawing from the work of the philosopher Charles Taylor, Hale argues, however, that for New Labour, 'community is not the framework which provides us with our bearings, but is itself a means to an end'; thus a 'society of self-fulfillers' is the consequence, and an 'atomistic outlook' is created, 'eroding the bases of community identifications' (Hale 2004: 93–4). Hale's analysis also suggests how Third Way conceptions of 'the good' can not only become dangerously rarefied and naturalized, but also function as a mediatized smokescreen. For David Hare, Tony Blair is 'a man who appears to be fundamentally decent and honest' (quoted in Boon 2003: 135). This is a revealing comment. Blair's qualities are a matter of appearance and spectacle; they have not been deduced from analysis and critique.

At the climax of *The Absence of War* the defeated George Jones emerges from the Cenotaph memorial service asking 'Could we have done more?' (Hare 1993a: 109–10). But this is mere rhetorical questioning, for Jones represents the epitome here of the castrated 'good man', framed by but isolated from the spectacle of a national ritual. The pattern is repeated in both *Racing Demon* and *Murmuring Judges*. Lionel, a do-gooding clergyman, and Irina, an idealistic barrister, both prove to be ineffective agents for change. The upshot is not simply that Hare 'has openly become the conserver and refresher of the status quo' (Donesky 1996: 183). Hare's slippery conception of 'the good' only finds resonance in these plays by extricating individual from institution, private from public.

A similar pattern is detectable in Hare's scaled-down offerings. Donesky notes how Kyra in *Skylight* 'reduces helping children to the apolitical simplicity of a personal preference' (ibid.: 192). The reconciliation in the final act of *Amy's View* involves Dominic, Esme's alienated son-in-law, leaving her a substantial monetary gift. The financially ruined Esme, a once famous West End actress, has returned to the theatre in the aftermath of her daughter's death. Although Dominic's gift represents a small salvation that Esme describes as 'My daughter's ashes' (Hare 1997b: 126), Hare seems to be suggesting here that giving, whether material (in Dominic) or loving (in Amy), has revocable value; and tellingly, in *The Judas Kiss* Oscar Wilde can only find salvation in the promise of an immaterial world (Hare 1998a: 118).

A riposte to the accusation that these plays represent an increasing sense of retrenchment by Hare arguably arrives with *Via Dolorosa*. Hare's decision to perform his own monologue about the Israeli-Palestinian crisis raises many questions. His own account of rehearsing and performing the piece in London and New York reveals as much, emphasizing his irritability at his lack of acting skills: 'I still can't *act*. I perform' (Hare 1999: 181). Ian McNeil, the designer of *Via Dolorosa*, observes the director Stephen Daldry's cunning stratagems, working on Hare *not* becoming 'too good' and 'too smooth', with result that his performance '*lived*' the material rather than 'depicted' it (quoted in Boon 2003: 199). However, as David Ian Rabey notes, *Via Dolorosa* exemplifies Hare's move from a 'demonstrative' to a 'presentational' form that 'involves no overt theatricalization', but rather pushes Hare closer 'to the status of social commentator' (Rabey 2003: 114–16). Yet *Via Dolorosa* does employ a veiled theatricality. Hare, the great 'creator of concepts', transforms himself into Hare 'the apologist', a globe-trotting 'do-gooder' who has no right to take to the stage space, yet needs *must* in order that he may rehearse his own moral crisis. But if Christ travelled the Via Dolorosa towards Calvary in order to save humankind, then Hare's journey can only return him to the comfort of Hampstead and his dog Blanche (Hare 1998b: 43). Hare's failure to 'act' and attempt to 'perform' are not only tantamount to feigning and failing to employ a practice that can gainfully invite fresh perceptions on his chosen subject. This is solipsism aestheticized and mediatized as political theatre, a disabling practice that really seeks to endorse the person at its centre.

Whilst the arguments put forward in this chapter might be countered by fore-grounding Hare's overt desire for justice and social democracy, it is insightful to note his take on the latter as 'the embodiment and expression of people's confusions and contradictions' (see Boon 2003: 173). So whilst Hare might see *Stuff Happens* and *The Permanent Way* as attempts to re-engage positively with 'the real' of the public and political spheres, he cannot help but see the connection between individuals and 'the great events of history' as 'apparently irresoluble' (Hare 2005a: 7). And if we might think that these works offer a critique of global imperialism and the modus operandi of nation-states, *Stuff Happens* suggests otherwise:

> IRAQI EXILE: . . . Iraq has been crucified. By Saddam's sins, by ten years of sanctions, and then this. Basically it's a story that failed in only one thing. But it's a big sin. It failed to take charge of itself [. . .]
>
> I mean, Iraqis say to me, 'Look, tell America.' I tell them: 'You are putting your faith in the wrong person. Don't expect America or anybody will do it for you.'
>
> If you don't do it yourself, this is what you get.
>
> (Hare 2004: 120)

Hare's playwriting from the late 1970s onwards can in fact be seen to be an extended mourning for the loss of human agency that the Iraqi Exile intimates. In the move away from the politics of collective action, the opportunity for change has gone and the dialectical possibility of alternative choices is now a redundant exercise. Yet what this has partly led to with Hare is the elevation of a notion of goodness that has become precariously ubiquitous, and its mediation unquestioned. What separates the 'decency' of Tony Blair from the quasi-Christian metaphors of the Iraqi Exile? In Hare, very little; in reality, quite a lot. I would like to end by suggesting that Hare's dramaturgy is the cultural microcosm of what Terry Eagleton has perceived in broader terms:

> The liberal state provided a space for limited plurality in which interests could be bred which then rationally challenged, in the name of justice or the good life, that state itself. But if it is merely a space of incommensurable interests, between which there can be no rational negotiation, there can be no question of any particular set of these interests submitting the other, and the very structures which enable them, to rational critique. (Eagleton 1994: 10)

This is not to suggest that 'rational critique' is the dramatist's only route out of this impasse. Dramatists such as Caryl Churchill and Howard Barker have radically proved otherwise, but Hare remains trapped within his theatre of 'incommensurable interests'. That is his failure and, paradoxically, his success.

NOTES

1 For example, Richard Norton-Taylor's *The Colour of Justice* (Tricycle Theatre, 1999) and *Justifying War* (Tricycle Theatre, 2003) employed entirely word-for-word testimony from, respectively, the Stephen Lawrence inquiry into the racist murder of a black teenager and the Hutton inquiry into events leading up to the Anglo-American invasion of Iraq in 2003.

Alecky Blythe's *Come Out Eli* (Recorded Delivery, 2003) and Robin Soans's *Talking to Terrorists* (Out of Joint/Royal Court Theatre, 2005) employed recorded personal testimony that was performed verbatim by actors.

2 For a recent reassessment of Brecht's theory and practice see Fredric Jameson (2000). *Brecht and Method*. London: Verso.

Primary reading

David Hare Collection (personal papers). Harry Ransom Humanities Research Centre, University of Texas, Austin.

Hare, David (1984). *The History Plays (Knuckle, Licking Hitler, Plenty)*. London. Faber and Faber.

Hare, David (1986). *The Asian Plays (Fanshen, The Year of the Cat, A Map of the World)*. London: Faber and Faber.

Hare, David (1990). *Racing Demon*. London: Faber and Faber.

Hare, David (1991a). *Murmuring Judges*. London: Faber and Faber.

Hare, David (1991b). *Writing Left-Handed*. London: Faber and Faber.

Hare, David (1993a). *The Absence of War*. London: Faber and Faber.

Hare, David (1993b). *Asking Around: Background to the David Hare Trilogy*, ed. L. Haill. London: Faber and Faber.

Hare, David (1995). *Skylight*. London: Faber and Faber.

Hare, David (1996). *Plays One*. London: Faber and Faber.

Hare, David (1997a). *Plays Two*. London: Faber and Faber.

Hare, David (1997b). *Amy's View*. London: Faber and Faber.

Hare, David (1997c). 'A Defence of the New' in *Platform Papers 9: David Hare*. London: Royal National Theatre/Almeida Theatre, 5–17.

Hare, David (1998a). *The Judas Kiss*. London: Faber and Faber.

Hare, David (1998b). *Via Dolorosa and When Shall We Live?* London: Faber and Faber.

Hare, David (1998c). *The Blue Room*. London: Faber and Faber.

Hare, David (1999). *Acting Up: A Diary*. London: Faber and Faber.

Hare, David (2000). *My Zinc Bed*. London: Faber and Faber.

Hare, David (2002). *The Breath of Life*. London: Faber and Faber.

Hare, David (2003). *The Permanent Way*. London: Faber and Faber.

Hare, David (2004). *Stuff Happens*. London: Faber and Faber.

Hare, David (2005a). 'Guide to Reality', *Guardian Weekend* 30 April, 7.

Hare, David (2005b). *Obedience, Struggle and Revolt*. London: Faber and Faber.

Further reading

Bigsby, C. W. E. (1981). 'The Language of Crisis in the British Theatre: The Drama of Cultural Pathology' in C. W. E. Bigsby (ed.). *Contemporary English Drama*. London: Edward Arnold, 11–51.

Boon, Richard (2003). *About Hare: The Playwright and the Work*. London: Faber and Faber.

Bull, John (1984). *New British Political Dramatists*. Basingstoke: Macmillan.

Chambers, Colin and Prior, Mike (1987). *Playwrights' Progress: Patterns of Postwar British Drama*. Oxford: Amber Lane Press.

Dewiel, Boris (2000). *Democracy: A History of Ideas*. Vancouver: UBC Press.

Donesky, Finlay (1996). *David Hare: Moral and Historical Perspectives*. Westport, CT: Greenwood Press.

Eagleton, Terry (1994). 'The Right and the Good: Postmodernism and the Liberal State', *Textual Practice* 8:1, 1–10.

Edgar, David (1999). 'Provocative Acts: British Playwriting in the Postwar Era and Beyond' in David Edgar (ed.). *State of Play: Playwrights on Playwriting*. London: Faber and Faber, 3–34.

Hale, Sarah (2004). 'The Communitarian "Philosophy" of New Labour' in Sarah Hale, Will Leggett and Luke Martell (eds.). *The Third Way and Beyond: Criticisms, Futures, Alternatives*. Manchester: Manchester University Press, 85–107.

Homden, Carol (1995). *The Plays of David Hare*. Cambridge: Cambridge University Press.

Innes, Christopher (2002). *Modern British Drama: The Twentieth Century*. Cambridge: Cambridge University Press.

Luckhurst, Mary (2002). 'Contemporary English Theatre: Why Realism?' in M. Rubik and E. Mettinger-Schartmann (eds.). *(Dis)Continuities: Trend and Tradition in Contemporary Theatre and*

Drama in English. Trier: Wissenschaftlicher, 73–84.

Olivia, Judy Lee (1990). *David Hare: Theatricalizing Politics*. Ann Arbor: UMI Research Press.

Page, Malcolm (1990). *File on Hare*. London: Methuen.

Patterson, Michael (2003). *Strategies of Political Theatre: Postwar British Playwrights*. Cambridge: Cambridge University Press.

Pattie, David (1999). 'The Common Good: The Hare Trilogy', *Modern Drama* 42, 363–74.

Peacock, D. Keith (1999). *Thatcher's Theatre: British Drama and Theatre in the Eighties*. Westport, CT: Greenwood Press.

Rabey, David Ian (2003). *English Drama since 1940*. London: Longman.

Ritchie, Rob (ed.) (1987). *The Joint Stock Book: The Making of a Theatre Collective*. London: Methuen.

Sylvester, Rachel (2003). 'Nothing Works in Blair's Britain', *Sunday Telegraph* 16 November, 23.

Wu, Duncan (1995). *Six Contemporary Dramatists: Bennett, Potter, Gray, Brenton, Hare, Ayckbourn*. Basingstoke: Macmillan.

36

Left in Front: David Edgar's Political Theatre

John Bull

David Edgar is a prolific, wide-ranging playwright with more than 50 stage plays produced since 1970, and extensive work in journalism and drama education. He has chronicled and analysed the postwar political landscapes of Britain, extending attention to continental Europe, Africa and North America and engaging with many topics, always as an acute political observer fully engaged in a serious task *and* well able to reflect on its humorous potential.

Born in 1948 in Birmingham, where he still lives, Edgar was educated at Oundle School and, just as thoroughly, by the socialist liberalism of the 1960s and the extraordinary, tempering events of 1968. After completing a drama degree at Manchester University, he found work as a journalist in Bradford and came into contact with the university drama group there, at first as a reviewer. In 1970 he began to write for groups associated with Bradford University. His initial efforts drew heavily on journalistic experiences and desire to write from a socialist perspective:

> I don't feel that until I left university my socialism developed beyond combining being quite a good public speaker and quite a good polemical writer with a sense of social injustice, emerging from horror at the hydrogen bomb, plus a sense of disillusion with the Labour government and of outrage at the Vietnam war. (Barker and Trussler 1979: 4)

Edgar began to explore agit-prop, searching for a theatrical form that would allow him to present the immediacies of local political struggles in a larger socialist context.

From 1970 to 1974 Edgar had an astonishing 30 pieces produced, most one-act plays, many at Bradford and other universities, but from 1972 increasingly complex work for Birmingham Repertory Theatre and established fringe venues in Edinburgh and London.[1] *The National Interest* (Bradford University, 1971) tackled the new Conservative administration of Edward Heath, presenting Tory MPs (after Brecht's *Arturo Ui*) as Chicago gangsters. In the same year *Tedderella* (Pool Theatre, Edinburgh) put pastiche pantomime to work on Heath's European difficulties, and in all Edgar's work he mixed serious political content with slapstick and other humours drawn from popular cultural models. *Rent, Or Caught in the Act* (General Will Theatre Company, 1972) utilized carefully slanted music-hall turns; *Dick Deterred* (Bush Theatre, 1974), about Nixon and Watergate, pastiched Shakespeare's *Richard III* ('Dick de turd'). Edgar also collaborated, notably with Brenton on *England's Ireland* (Mickery Theatre, Amsterdam, 1972) and *A Fart for Europe* (Royal Court Theatre Upstairs, 1973), but political sympathy was insufficient to make collaboration attractive and Edgar's theatrical socialism was becoming distinctive. The great thread through all his work was politics, individual and collective, but the overall effect of his dramaturgies was to steer him away from the kind of socialist realism that had been a staple of the earlier generation of committed leftist writers such as Arnold Wesker, and left him with no obvious English model.[2]

In 1974 *The Dunkirk Spirit* – 'a history of British capitalism since the war' (Bull 1984: 162) – was successfully toured by General Will, but Edgar increasingly felt he had exhausted his possibilities in that mode and things had anyway changed:

> What happened was that after *Dunkirk* I got obsessed with slickness. I was fed up with seeing agitprop plays that were messy, and also I was increasingly thinking that the politics you could get across were very crude, whereas the world about us was getting more complicated. (Barker and Trussler 1979: 13)

The new apprehension of difficulty is evident in *Ball Boys* (Birmingham Rep, 1975, and with other works as *Blood Sports*, Bush Theatre, London, 1976), one of a series of shorts dealing comically with the class aspects of national games and sports from hunting to tennis. Two rebellious ball boys murder a famous Swedish tennis star during Wimbledon; introducing the published text, Edgar pointed out (almost keeping a straight face) that this murder has a far larger significance:

> *Ball Boys* is an attempt, through the story of two unlovely orphans in a tennis club locker-room, to expose the essential contradictions inherent in late monopoly capitalism, to analyse the role of neo-colonialism in confirming the repressively-tolerant ideological interface between superstructure and base (while remaining not unmindful of the need to be fully cognizant of the essential dualism of the decaying bourgeois apparatus), to express implacable hostility to the running dogs of craven reformism in the labour bureaucracies, and to stress the vital need for alternative modes of leadership to pose the essential question of state power. (Edgar 1978: i)

The joke is partly on an audience of his own generation, well versed in the sophistications of Marxist dialectics, and partly on himself, author of *The Case of the Workers' Plane*, about Concorde (Bristol New Vic, 1973), and the even more snappily titled *Events Following the Closure of a Motorcycle Factory* (Birmingham Rep, 1976). The humour stays dead-pan to the final sentence – 'It is arguable that in this project the play is not totally successful' – but Edgar now understood that agit-prop theatre is admirably suited to periods of intense political activity, when its simple message can readily be assimilated, but much less effective in dealing with more complicated situations and analyses, when it may leave large sections of its audience in blank incomprehension. Much of the humour in *Ball Boys* comes from a character with a political vocabulary that is out of place, as his companion notes:

ONE-EYE: What are you talking about?
RUPERT: Been reading.
ONE-EYE: What?
RUPERT: Marx. The theses on Feuerbach.
ONE-EYE: You who?

(Edgar 1989: 41)

Just so, and although Edgar continued to write agit-prop, from 1975 he moved decisively beyond the understandings of 1968, and with continued commitment to a politically effective theatre looked to develop a drama capable of 'dealing with complexity, contradiction and even just plain doubt' (Edgar 1988: 230).[3]

The play that introduced Edgar to a mainstream theatre-going public, *Destiny* (Royal Shakespeare Company (RSC), 1976), grew directly from his career as a journalist:

My interest in the far right had begun five years earlier when I was a reporter on the *Bradford Telegraph and Argus*, and covered meetings of an outfit called the Yorkshire Campaign to Stop Immigration. Its leader was a rather dapper ex-Conservative councillor, who presided benignly over chaotic meetings in which films were shown upside down and without sound. Later the group merged with the National Front. But for its leader and his followers, it addressed many real needs and some real fears. When the National Front won 16% in the 1973 West Bromwich by-election, I decided to write a play about it. (Edgar, *Guardian* 14 September 2005)

Destiny opens in India on Independence Day 1947, introducing Indian and British characters who develop the political and narrative threads, culminating in a bitterly fought election coincident with a strike by Asian workers at a local foundry. The play exhibits some features of agit-prop: in one scene, two young men, once friends, are in the same cell pending formal arrest. They share social origins, but one has moved towards an extreme right-wing position, the other to a militant socialist one, and their walled debate is a working model of formal debate, not resulting in dialectical conclusion but in opposition:

PAUL: All history's the struggle of the classes.
TONY: No. All history's the struggle of the races.
PAUL: The workers of all races must unite
TONY: The workers of all classes must unite.

(Edgar 1987: 391)

This formal stichomythia can find its powerful place in *Destiny*, but other legacies of agit-prop could not. It was initially too long, particularly in including a long sequence dealing with the Court of Enquiry about the strike, and Edgar pragmatically reworked the sequence as a play in its own right (*Our Own People*, Pirate Jenny Theatre Company, 1977). In reshaping to secure mainstream production, Edgar's fictional narratives became increasingly sophisticated in claiming from neutral audiences simultaneous acceptance of self-relishing theatricality and of historically, socially and politically cogent verisimilitude.

Some half-ironically call such combinations of fiction and fact 'faction', but in *Destiny* and all Edgar's later works, as I have stated before, political thinking and dramaturgy go far beyond the partisan.

> [*Destiny*] is not an attempt to reproduce history as such, but involves the creation of a fictional set of characters to demonstrate the workings of the meticulously researched material. His general model is a variant of the epic, with frequent changes of location, and a series of jumps through history before eventually concentrating on a brief period in contemporary England. The effect is to show the way in which a current political reality is a product both of previous history and of the particular interventions and interrelations of individuals acting within that history. The objective history is enmeshed with subjective responses. So, although Edgar is scarcely more interested in individual psychology here than in his earlier plays, more scope is allowed for the development of character. The use of epic-devices, in particular the continual breaks in the action, does, however, prevent such development from taking the edge off Edgar's insistence on a material and social explanation of behaviour. (Bull 1984: 170)

In scale and sophistication *Destiny* marked a departure towards large epic pieces designed for subsidized theatres and satisfying Edgar's confessed desire for 'slickness' (though the word does his craftsmanship no justice). But, as 'epic' implies, Edgar while in no sense Brecht's disciple has learned much from him, and never equates mainstream success with selling out; quite the opposite: democratic political commitment means reaching out as widely as possible, and no form of theatre should be lightly discarded from a playwright's armoury.

Edgar continued to write for theatrical groups seeking direct political intervention at community level: *Wreckers* (1977) for 7:84 England in Exeter, *Our Own People* (1977) for Pirate Jenny in London, and, with Susan Todd, *Teendreams* (1979) for Monstrous Regiment in Bristol. But *The Jail Diary of Albie Sachs* (RSC, 1978), his most influential play of the later 1970s, commissioned for the Warehouse in London, showed Edgar's acceptance of the challenge of international socialism. Peter McEnery gave a brilliant performance as the white South African lawyer (now an internationally honoured judge) imprisoned under the Ninety-Day Law for his anti-apartheid stance and support of the African National Congress (ANC) – a performance made possible because Edgar did not attempt an epic account of the South African struggle, but dramatized the experiences of one privileged yet pressurized, strikingly honest and articulate participant. The effect is to suggest, by careful understatement, the full horror of the situation, and goes beyond *Destiny* in that Edgar's desire to present a more complicated account of political struggle began to transform his desire to remove from audiences the possibility of primarily psychological explanations, and develop his interest in the relationship between politics and individual psychology. While this has never resulted in plays truly privileging personal relationships among stage characters, *Mary Barnes* (Birmingham Rep, 1978), about the work of psychologists Laing and Cooper, is based on a historical account of a schizophrenic's diagnosis and treatment. Audiences almost always become aware that characters represent different political positions, in a manner not systematically attempted on the British stage since Shaw, but (as with *The Jail Diary* and the historical presence of Albie Sachs) an apprehended reality accompanies fictions of dialogue and dramatic arrangement, and human individuality is not lost to political symbolism – though some characters may wish that it were.

The strength of these plays points to Edgar's developing skill as an adaptor of material, and in 1980 the RSC commissioned him to dramatize (in two parts) Dickens's whopping novel *Nicholas Nickleby*. It proved a triumph in Edgar's career and the company's: success certainly owed much to the continuing popularity of Dickens, particularly on television, but skilled evocation of nineteenth-century life, in a relatively down-market, mainstream, costume-drama format, with biting social comment and a cast of brilliantly rounded if frequently grotesque characters, went far beyond the BBC:

> Nicholas's adventures take him through acquaintance with all levels of English class society in the second decade of the nineteenth century when the action of the novel takes place. Yet the most important fact about David Edgar's adaptation is that its locality was the Aldwych Theatre and its time setting, the present. Its true political dimension was that of the first term of the Thatcher government. (Painter 1996: 67)

Sheer scale, 45 actors playing about three times as many characters, encouraged Edgar to continue to think in broad social and Brechtian epic terms, and its enormous appeal as a piece of genuinely popular theatre (there were American and Australian productions as well as assorted revivals and tours) encouraged the RSC to offer a further commission. Edgar had found an unimpeachable way of vigorously, enjoyably and effectively politicizing a runaway nine-hour mainstream success; the very excess of triumph proved a burden, and unusually for a playwright who had always produced at a prodigious rate, notwithstanding his insistence on proper research, it would be three years before the commission bore fruit; 1981–2 were the first years since 1970 to see no premieres, and a more measured (though still relentless) pattern of creation has since prevailed.

Maydays (RSC, Barbican, 1983) eventually continued where *Destiny* had left off. After *Nickleby*, Edgar was able to use a panoply of new technology for an original play, and, again drawing on Brechtian ideas, *Maydays* is structurally and innovatively epic, one scene developing from another as lights cross-fade and trucks are moved in and out. The effect is a continuity of action that plays against historical and geographical jumps in narrative, flowing more smoothly than *Destiny*. Like many state-of-the-nation plays of the period – Brenton's *The Churchill Play* (1974), Howard Brenton and David Hare's *Brassneck* (1973), Hare's *Plenty* (1978), and Edgar's own *Destiny* – it opens in 1945, the last year of World War II, tracing events towards the present. But Edgar's concern is with a specifically socialist and hence supra-national postwar history, and in linking British locations with Eastern European ones.

The play thus also pits itself against *Destiny*, moving past national parochialism, and in its willingness to confront the malaise of the left under Thatcher attempted something new in modern British theatre. Edgar works consciously for the audience to connect various parts of the play through deployment of interrelated plots and character groups. His political landmarks are still public – May Day 1945 (though significantly opening not with the British Labour victory, but with a communist rally); Hungary in 1956; the beginnings of CND in 1962; events between the spring of 1968 and the Vietcong victory of 1974; and a sequence that moves from the immediate lead-in to the 1979 general election to the (then) present day and Greenham Common – but Edgar is now far more concerned with the thinking behind individual choices and actions.

Of primary interest is (in British terms) what happened to Edgar's contemporaries, youthful activists of the late 1960s, and (in European terms) how this might connect with a general movement to overthrow communist oppression. Two readings of left-wing thought are in conjunction as the play considers reactions by three individuals from different generations to this socialist history, parts of which each has variously entered, and out of which each moves towards a more right-wing stance. The dominant concern is defection from left to right and the individual reasons for it.

The young man addressing the communist rally at the beginning is Jeremy Crowther, who leaves the party in the aftermath of Hungary – direct experience of which starts a second man, Pavel Lermentov, a dedicated Russian party member, on his own road to defection. Drifting into teaching (in a public school where a third man, Martin Glass, will be radicalized by opposition to nuclear warfare), Crowther still regrets being too young to fight in Spain and enters academic life in 1968 (when Glass begins moving to a revolutionary position). He ends in a hard-right stance as part of a caucus intent on consolidating an anti-socialist future for Britain, in which he will be joined by Glass, disillusioned with revolutionary politics and safely ensconced with the *Sunday Times*; but not Lermentov, who has left Russia after many years in labour camps but will not support their movement. Glass is most developed, for his experiences come closest to Edgar's, but the whole play questions, disturbingly and with the wicked humour of hindsight, what happened to the revolutionary urges of an entire generation. In the final scene, Glass meets his old comrade and lover, Amanda, ironically just after he has repurchased his family home, a vicarage where his father led protests at the first generation of nuclear weapons, and that is now part of the Greenham Common women's peace camp.

That Edgar's play should, like Brenton's *The Genius* (1983), end at Greenham Common is not coincidence – in the next decade female writers would largely shoulder the task of generating new kinds of political drama – but as Edgar starts his play with a communist rally and incorporates the descent into Stalinism, the local and British are always seen within a larger context. International connections are continually made, and parallels stressed between the communist move from revolutionary party to orthodox bureaucracy, and the tension in modern British socialism between the desire for individual spontaneity and the need for collective organization. The play concludes in Moscow as freedom struggles continue: two men have arranged to meet at night so one can take to the West the manifesto published by the other for his unofficial trade union.

KOROLENKO:	Well, then?
PUGACHEV:	How long?
KOROLENKO:	How long?
PUGACHEV:	Do you think you'll last. A week, a month, a year?
KOROLENKO:	Maybe. Who knows? 'May Days'.

(Edgar 1983: 69–70)

European events were shortly to provide some brisk answers, and it indicates Edgar's quality as an analyst of the contemporary world that he should as early as 1983 have raised the issue the West would understand through Lech Wałęsa and Solidarity.

Edgar's next project was an enormous community play, *Entertaining Strangers: A Play for Dorchester*, produced in 1985 with a cast of more than 100 in St Mary's, Dorchester, and miniaturized at the National Theatre (NT) in London two years later. He was invited to undertake the project by Ann Jellicoe as one of a series of site-specific community shows of which she had become the 'only begetter'. The play used local citizens as cast and crew, a primary strategy in these projects, and offered itself as a critical celebration of Dorchester's people and history. Reshaping it for the opportunities and limitations of the NT was demanding, and comparison of the texts is an object lesson in Edgar's formidable dramaturgical skills; the primacy for him of Jellicoe's communal, local project also offers a political lesson, and his ability to connect that project with the NT is both a striking instance of pragmatic capacities and a stunning demonstration of theatrical range and connected efficacy.

Returning to domestic politics at large in *That Summer* (Hampstead Theatre, London, 1987), Edgar reflected on the 1984–5 miners' strike, concentrating less on public facts or political interpretations of the strike, and more on the way in which meetings between working-class strikers and the 'networks of supporters that sprung up around the country' (Edgar 1991: xii) effected considerable changes in both sides' lifestyles and personal politics. This important subject has (like the strike itself) been woefully under-dramatized – partly as a result of the political climate that Thatcherism generated, and the commercial pressures to which Thatcherite arts policy subjected theatres, partly because of a growing apoliticism in theatre and theatre audiences – and Edgar sought to shed much-needed light. Yet as the 1980s came to an end, the freedom movement in the Soviet empire gained critical momentum, climaxing in the pulling down of the Berlin Wall in November 1989, and presented a compelling international socialist dilemma in reciprocal tension with the bitter and stale domestic dilemma posed by Thatcherism's artistic illiberality and cultural philistinism. Edgar's remarkable response involved two projects that would co-exist for a decade: a trilogy of explicitly international-political plays for the national stage, and a negotiated appointment as Britain's first director and professor of playwriting studies at his home-town university, Birmingham.

The influence of Edgar's MA programmes in playwriting and in dramaturgy are startlingly suggested by the list of his graduates, including Sarah Kane and Steve Waters, and when a history of British drama education is written he will have a notable and honourable place. Space precludes analysis here, but the politics of giving a decade of one's prime to home-town provision of a superior education in dramatic craftsmanship and professionalism deserves respectful thought, and in combination with continuing access to provincial stages and London's flagship theatres sketches Edgar as very fully Brechtian. He left the chair in 1999, but the programme and the careers of his pupils continue.

The first of the trilogy, *The Shape of the Table* (NT, 1990), was necessarily concerned with the immediacy of 1989. After the celebrations came the need to redraw borders and attempt the reconciliation of political and ethnic differences forcefully smoothed over since the Yalta Conference partitioned Europe:

> There are two great political stories. One is about how you give up power – the story of *Richard II* and *King Lear*. The other is about how, when you've got power, you avoid turning into the people you've taken it from – *Henry IV*, I suppose. Both of these were present and people were concentrating on the second one – which comes into the second half of the play – but apparently ignoring the first. That's where I started from. (Clement 1990: 7)

What fascinated and continues to fascinate is the minutiae of negotiation: how people actually behave in political situations, not how they ought. There is considerable flow between events in and around the closed negotiating room, and reports of activity brought in from outside:

> Since the fall of the Berlin wall, I have been fascinated by the process of politics, by negotiations, the drafting of documents, strategizing, role-play and ceremony. This is, I suppose, political theatre in its narrowest definition: plays about politics as work. (Edgar, *Guardian* 19 April 2003)

Edgar does not offer a specific location for events in the play, but allows his audience to imagine as it will: there is implicitly sufficient common ground in post-Soviet Eastern Europe to allow a presentation of history that is adequately specific even as it refuses to be wholly so.

This sense of a potently archetypal locus is illustrated by the opening quotations in the published text of the play completing the trilogy, *The Prisoner's Dilemma* (RSC, The Other Place, 2001). Though it begins at the same point as *Shape*, in 1989, Edgar's epigraph quotes the Downing Street Declaration of December 1993:

> The British Government agree that it is for the people of the island of Ireland alone, by agreement between the two parts respectively, to exercise their right of self-determination on the basis of consent, freely and concurrently given, North and South, to bring about a united Ireland, if that is their wish. (Edgar 2001: n.p.)

On the same page he refers directly to the Israeli–Palestinian conflict: plainly the negotiations taking place have general currency across Eastern Europe, but equally serve as a model – good or bad – for what is happening nearer home. In the later play, audiences need no longer rely on reports from the outside being brought into the negotiation site, but are shown the brutal realities of ethnic and political separation, and such creation of a realized space for the oppressed helps for some to make the second play in the European trilogy, *Pentecost* (RSC, The Other Place, 1994), Edgar's greatest achievement.

Set amid the conflict of Soviet collapse – not far, perhaps, from Sarajevo – the play concerns the discovery in an old church of a painted Deposition (that is, the taking down of Christ from the Cross) that, if authenticated and dated, will significantly anticipate the 'invention' of perspective in Renaissance Italy. In context, this discovery of perspective also has a specific contemporary significance, offering realism in place of idealism. In the opening scene a local curator, Gabriella, brings an English art-historian to view her find:

> GABRIELLA: Because if I am right that painting with perspective even kind of painted before Giotto born, then I think I make pretty damn substantial finding here.
>
> (Edgar 1995: 9)

The historian's scepticism arises partly, as Gabriella notes, from his inbuilt bias against something of such monumental importance occurring in a country that 'make such botch of everything it touch' (ibid.: 10). The response to her bitter retort is interesting:

> It's just basic British insularity. It's suddenly the papers are full of places one had vaguely thought to be made up. If not Slovenia, then certainly Slavonia. And then suddenly concentration camps start springing up all over pastoral Shakespearian locations. (ibid.: 10)

Shocked audiences realize they are in contemporary Bohemia, one not of the gold-touched shepherds in Acts III–IV of Shakespeare's *Winter's Tale* but of bloody fighting, massacres, ethnic cleansing and torture in internment camps. And at the end of this scene Gabriella asks the historian why he has suddenly agreed to help her prove her case: 'Because . . . because . . . This is Illyria, lady' (ibid.: 13).

At this point pastoral intrusions may seem merely ironic. The blood-bath of the post-Soviet Balkans hardly squares with Shakespeare's imaginations of half-magical reconciliation; the narrative continues with arguments about the painting's provenance, the efficacy of restoration, and the possibility of removing it to a museum to be venerated as a target for cultural tourism. Although audiences are aware that didactic debate, dialogue and characterization broadly conform to naturalism until towards the end of Act I, the church is abruptly broken into by a bunch of deliberately representative political refugees in search of asylum: any intertextual sense of two languages on stage – the educated English of Oliver (an intruding court-figure) and Gabriella's (a native 'shepherdess') mixture of her own tongue and an imperfectly learnt American English – is disturbed by a host of languages competing for attention: the cacophony of Babel, language as division rendering mutual communication and understanding impossible.

The disputing art-folk are taken hostage by the refugees and forced to change clothes with them in a pastoral switch: 'you should know – you are a different people now' (ibid.: 52), the Palestinian refugee tells them. The first act ends with an off-stage loudspeaker appealing to the hostages to come out; the second opens with emergent dialogue between refugees and hostages, intermingled with plans to escape and accounts of atrocities, the debate about the painting interwoven with one about the fate of intruders.

What follows is an extraordinary scene in which surface naturalism gives way to a visionary sequence deploying music and dance to create a very different mood. It is an equivalent to the pastoral scene in *A Winter's Tale*, and similarly offers hope for a future by mixing the events of the day with the play's title, Pentecost – when the apostles met after the resurrection and spoke in tongues. Edgar's tongues are not of Christian apostles, but of languages represented in the church, which has historically served many different functions and cannot be neatly tied to simple Christian significance. A story of suffering, torture and murder is told that crosses language barriers, and leads to the possibility of an optimistic ending – mirrored in the painted Deposition – where belief in common humanity might gestate a better world. In the published text translations are given after each speech to assist actors, guiding them towards gestural articulation of various strands of the story in a way that will be decipherable not only for characters on stage but for the paying audience.

There is no equivalent epiphany in *The Prisoner's Dilemma*, and the trilogy is not as a whole optimistic, but Edgar's major adaptation of the 1990s, *The Strange Case of Dr Jekyll and Mr Hyde* (RSC, Barbican, 1991; revised, Birmingham Rep, 1996), necessarily found resolution, and a dark echo of *Pentecost* appeared in *Albert Speer* (RNT, Olivier Theatre, 2000), a massive epic dramatization of Gitta Sereny's biography of the most famous Nazi penitent, into which Edgar plunged after leaving his teaching post. The major conundrum is Speer's simultaneous admission of guilt and denial of knowledge – what constitutes responsibility? – and the narrative (superbly handled on many scales) drives to a resolution concerning Speer's ability to desire to continue to live. The climax involves Speer in a deathbed vision of Hitler openly scornful as he never was in Speer's gilded memories (staging which drew some bitter criticism), and the play is a major contribution to British works on the Holocaust, testing audiences powerfully and subtly with the full resources of the NT's largest stage. Edgar's focused interest in Speer as an individual anticipated his decision to adapt Brecht's *Life of Galileo* (Birmingham Rep, 2005), and suggests the continuing evolution of his dramatic concern with individuals.

Edgar was commissioned, for the 2003 Oregon Shakespeare Festival, to write two linked plays about contemporary America, *Mothers Against* and *Daughters of the Revolution*, collectively *Continental Divide*; both came to the Barbican in 2004. As with *Maydays*, one prompt was fascination with what had happened to the idealism of the 1960s:

> I was twenty in 1968, and so I felt a part of the same story. For many years, I'd wanted to write a quest play, in which a former sixties activist would investigate and come to terms with his own past, with all its heroism, passion and betrayal. As the baby-boomer generation began to run for high political office, I realized I could set a play about the legacy of the 1960s against the background of a conventional political campaign. (Edgar 2004: 4)

One play presents a Republican perspective, the other a Democratic one, translating the socialist calendar of Edgar's generation into domestic American terms. He is again fascinated by the details of political struggle, but without the context of European socialism the party strife seems more obviously about naked desire for power. Yet for all the wheeler-dealing and chicanery, Edgar is eager to point to elements of political idealism on both sides. What optimism the plays possess derives from the eco-warriors in the forest in *Daughters of the Revolution* (lovingly created in production): that the trees they seek to preserve, and from which they construct a spiritual ritual, are the same trees the Republican family in the first play mourned losing to the blindness of capitalism echoes Chekhov's *Cherry Orchard*. The sense of an irrecoverable, seductive past, a problematic and divided present, and a future always just out of reach, in which optimism tinges with inescapable *realpolitik*: these are the essential components of all Edgar's mature plays.

Playing With Fire (NT, 2005) provides admirable opportunity to consider the magnitude and scope of Edgar's achievements to date. Its opening placement is quite specific – 'Apart from one scene in London, the play is set in and around a town in west Yorkshire, during an early term of a current Labour Government'[4] – and means that audiences confront, as often in Edgar's work, a play set in a present conceived in directly political terms. The narrative is concerned with interventions by representatives of 'southern' New Labour into the workings of a 'northern' town run by a somewhat non-New Labour council. In the confrontation that ensues, racial divisions within the community are exacerbated and, in the context of the local rise of a nationalist party committed to white supremacy, a riot occurs. In writing the play, which was rigorously researched, Edgar had in mind:

Britain's worst ever race riots [in 2001] . . . in three northern towns that were not so much multicultural as duocultural, Bradford, Oldham and Burnley [which] had geographically concentrated Muslim communities of Pakistani/Bangladeshi origin who had felt threatened by far-right groups which held increasing sway over poor white working-class communities next door. (Edgar, *Guardian* 14 September 2005)

The second act consists largely of a public inquiry, the position an inquiry once had in *Destiny*. Edgar's note in the stage directions – 'The feel, structure and ground-rules of the dramatization follow those of the tribunal plays at the Tricycle Theatre, the Manchester Library and elsewhere' – invokes the docudrama of Richard Norton-Taylor, presenting actual testimonies in a formal theatrical mode, as famously in *The Colour of Justice* (Tricycle Theatre, 1999; BBC TV, 2000). But it is less an acknowledgement of debt than an effective shorthand, and Edgar's confident use now of the inquiry format he had to jettison from *Destiny* more than 30 years ago is testimony, far beyond neat coincidence, to his political and theatrical constancy: 35 years after his first play was performed, he is still there, in the thick of the debate, his political fire and his eagerness to engage unquenched.

NOTES

1 1970: *A Truer Shade of Blue* (Bradford University), *Two Kinds of Angel* (Bradford University); 1971: *Acid* (Bradford University), *Bloody Rosa* (Manchester University, Edinburgh Fringe), *Conversation in Paradise* (Edinburgh University), *The National Interest* (Bradford University), *The Rupert Show* (General Will), *State of Emergency* (General Will), *Still Life* (Pool Theatre, Edinburgh), *Tedderella* (Pool Theatre, Edinburgh); 1972: *Death Story* (Birmingham Repertory), *The End* (Bradford University), *England's Ireland* (Shoot Theatre Company, Mickery Theatre, Amsterdam; with Brenton, Hare and others), *Excuses, Excuses* (Belgrade Theatre, Coventry), *Not With a Bang But a Whimper* (Leeds Polytechnic), *Rent, Or Caught in the Act* (General Will), *The Road to Hanoi* (Paradise Foundry Theatre Company); 1973: *Baby Love* (Soho Polytechnic), *The Case of the Workers' Plane* (Bristol New Vic), *The Eagle Has Landed* (Liverpool University), *A Fart for Europe* (Royal Court Theatre Upstairs; with Brenton), *Gangsters* (Soho Polytechnic), *The Liberated Zone* (Bingley College of Education), *Operation Iszra* (Paradise Foundry Theatre Company), *Up Spaghetti Junction* (Birmingham Repertory); 1974: *The All-Singing All-Talking Golden Oldie Rock Revival Ho Chi Minh Peace Love And Revolution Show* (Bingley College of Education), *Dick Deterred* (Bush Theatre, London), *The Dunkirk Spirit* (General Will), *Man Only Dines* (Leeds Polytechnic), *The & Show* (Bingley College of Education).

2 On the early plays, see Painter (1996: 13–27) and Bull (1984: 151–69).

3 Edgar was also responding to the political shift marked by the two general elections of 1974, Heath's defeat by Wilson, and his subsequent loss of the Conservative party leadership to Thatcher.

4 I am grateful to David Edgar for his provision of a working draft.

PRIMARY READING

Plays by David Edgar

Edgar, David (1977). *Wreckers*. London: Methuen.

Edgar, David (1978). *Ball Boys*. London: Pluto.

Edgar, David (1979). *Mary Barnes*. London: Methuen.

Edgar, David (with Susan Todd) (1979). *Teendreams*. London: Methuen.

Edgar, David (1982a). *The Jail Diary of Albie Sachs*. London: Rex Collings.

Edgar, David (1982b). *Nicholas Nickleby*. Dramatists' Play Services.

Edgar, David (1983). *Maydays*. London: Methuen.

Edgar, David (1986). *Entertaining Strangers*. London: Methuen.

Edgar, David (1987). *Plays I*. London: Methuen. (Includes *Destiny*.)

Edgar, David (1989). *Shorts*. London: Nick Hern.

Edgar, David (1990a). *Plays II*. London: Methuen.

Edgar, David (1990b). *The Shape of the Table*. London: Nick Hern.

Edgar, David (1991). *Plays III*. London: Methuen. (Includes *That Summer*.)

Edgar, David (1992). *The Strange Case of Dr Jekyll and Mr Hyde*. London: Nick Hern.

Edgar, David (1995). *Pentecost*. London: Nick Hern.

Edgar, David (2000). *Albert Speer*. London: Nick Hern.

Edgar, David (2001). *The Prisoner's Dilemma*. London: Nick Hern.

Edgar, David (2004). *Continental Divide*. London: Nick Hern.

Edgar, David (2005). *Playing with Fire*. London: Nick Hern.

Criticism and interviews

Barker, Clive and Trussler, Simon (1979). 'Towards a Theatre of Dynamic Ambiguities: Interview with David Edgar', *Theatre Quarterly* IX: 33.

Edgar, David (1973). 'Green Room: Against the General Will', *Plays and Players*, May.

Edgar, David (1977a). 'Exit Fascism, Stage Right', *Leveller*, June.

Edgar, David (1977b). *Racism, Fascism, and the Politics of the National Front*. London: Institute of Race Relations.

Edgar, David (1977c). 'Theatre, Politics and the Working Class', *Tribune* 22 April.

Edgar, David (1978). 'Political Theatre, Part I and Part II', *Socialist Review* 1 April and 2 May.

Edgar, David (1988). *The Second Time as Farce: Reflections on the Drama of Mean Times*. London: Lawrence and Wishart.

David, Edgar (ed.) (1999). *State of Play: Playwrights on Playwriting*. London: Faber and Faber.

FURTHER READING

Bull, John (1984). *New British Political Dramatists*. London: Macmillan.

Clement, Martin (1990). 'Table Talk', *Plays and Players,* November.

Itzin, Catherine (1980). *Stages in the Revolution*. London: Methuen, 139–51.

Page, Malcolm and Trussler, Simon (eds.) (1991). *File on Edgar*. London: Methuen.

Painter, Susan (1996). *Edgar the Playwright*. London: Methuen.

Rubin, Leon (1981). *The Nicholas Nickleby Story*. London: Heinemann.

Swaine, Elizabeth (1986). *David Edgar: Playwright and Politician*. New York: Peter Lang.

37

Liz Lochhead: Writer and Re-Writer: Stories, Ancient and Modern

Jan McDonald

Liz Lochhead (b. 1947) is a two-faced iconoclast. The cultural icons she challenges are the myths, historical and contemporary, that have accumulated around Scottish national identities, and traditional ideologies of gender, specifically those engaging with the concept of 'sisterhood', and with women as creative artists or in positions of power. Her approach is 'two-faced' because she displays sympathy, even, in her own words, 'a love which goes beyond judgement' (Lochhead 1991b: 75), for aspects of the cultural narratives she seeks to revise.

In this chapter, I examine Lochhead's major plays, exploring them first in terms of her reassessment of popular mythologies, perceived cultural certainties and contemporary attitudes, and secondly by interrogating her dramaturgical strategies, namely her use of language and visual signifiers and the modes of theatrical presentation she deploys to achieve her effects. She is a 're-writer' of both the subject matter and the means of expression in contemporary Scottish drama.

Scotch Myths and Misses

In *Mary Queen of Scots Got her Head Chopped Off* (*MQS*) (1987), La Corbie, the choric crow, Spirit of Scotland, begins her narration in the classic fairytale manner, 'once upon a time'. This is emphatically not, according to the author, 'a history play'. 'It's really about Scotland, more about the present than the past, how those myths of the past have carried on into the present malaise of Scotland today' (Harvie 1996: 97–8). Lochhead offers a re-vision not of Mary and Elizabeth, the closed historical characters, but rather of the accretions which popular culture has built around them, and shows how the warring sectarian factors within Scotland and between Scotland and England in the sixteenth century are re-enacted in a school playground in the twentieth, as 'Proddies' and 'Papes' engage in a violent game of bigotry and sexism.

Scots were ready to adopt Mary as an iconic heroine because she was a Stuart, the last Stuart to be the ruler solely of Scotland, and part of the mythic status that dynasty acquired, particularly in defeat. She may easily be constructed as a victim, a beautiful young Catholic woman brought up in a foreign land, 'exiled' to her own cold, unwelcoming and turbulent realm and set in political and personal opposition to Elizabeth, the successful Protestant queen of England, Scotland's neighbour and traditional enemy. To destabilize the myth, one must critique the characteristics that made Scotland so eager to embrace it – romanticism, inferiorism, defeatism, the servility and resentment inherent in the mentality of the culturally colonized, and, as La Corbie puts it, the 'National pastime: nostalgia' (Lochhead 1989: 11). Lochhead's play exposes the deficiencies in the received interpretation of one of Scotland's privileged historical moments, implicitly through a revising of the 'Mary' myth and explicitly in the opening lines of La Corbie, who introduces the historical characters to enact their (hi)story as animals in a grotesque circus parade.

MQS also engages with the constraints power can inflict on a woman's personal agenda, the negotiations she must make between her gender and her public role, the sacrifices that are expected of her, and the attempts of the patriarchy to marginalize and suppress her. The play was written in the heyday of Thatcherism and is often cited, along with Caryl Churchill's *Top Girls* (1980), as a pertinent and topical comment on 'the regiment of women'.

In an early manuscript version of the play, Elizabeth says of Mary: 'I hate her for trying to be a woman-queen' (Harvie 1996: 111). Lochhead explores the dilemma of a woman being a queen and a queen being a woman, and demonstrates how the sociopolitical contexts in which women exist and/or reign impinge on their lives.

Elizabeth rejects the man she loves, Dudley, earl of Leicester, because he is a commoner and she fears that: 'If we lay down together as King and Queen, then we would wake as plain Mister and Mistress Dudley. The nation would not have it' (Lochhead 1989: 24). Mary's marriage to Henry Darnley, also a commoner, sees her fulfil Elizabeth's prophetic nightmare: Darnley seeks to take precedence over Mary; he encourages the squabbling factions among the nobles; the Scottish nation *is* set at risk.

Elizabeth, the 'Virgin Queen' who was *not* a virgin, and Mary, cast by her enemies as a French whore, who *was* one, respectively sacrifice personal happiness to political duty, and the welfare of the realm to individual satisfaction. Both lose, but neither is condemned. Such choices should not be demanded of women.

The last scene of the play, the contemporary playground, is subtitled 'Jock Tamson's Bairns' – an affectionate nickname for Scots by Scots – and used again ironically as the title of Lochhead's devised piece with Communicado Theatre Company in 1990. At a parodic Burns (or 'burnt') Supper the 'Drunk Man', the anti-hero of Hugh MacDairmid's poem *A Drunk Man Looks at the Thistle* (1926), is turned into a haggis, which on closer inspection is seen to contain the full gamut of objects redolent of 'Scotch' kitsch and tartanry; for example, Bonnie Prince Charlie, the Loch Ness Monster, 'The Stag at Bay' and a Tartan gonk. The traditional reading of 'Tam O'Shanter' is performed with a twist, because Tam is not saved by his faithful mare, but defeated in combat by the bonny wee witch, Cutty Sark. *Jock Tamson's Bairns* is an anarchic romp. The scenario debunks a series of Scottish shibboleths and is an amusing satire, but lacks the multi-layered complexity of Lochhead's major dramas.

Quelques Fleurs (1995), like *Perfect Days* (1998), explores the effects of increased financial prosperity (for some) in Scotland in the late twentieth century, the flourishing of materialism in a culturally impoverished community, and the search for personal fulfilment in a society obsessed by rampant consumerism. The heroine, Verena, first appeared in two monologues, 'Security' and 'Anklebiters', in *True Confessions and New Clichés* (1985) and resurfaced in *Bagpipe Muzak* (1991), delivering an extended series of monologues under the title *Quelques Fleurs (A Tale of Two Sisters)*. In 1995, a full production of the play incorporating a series of parallel monologues by Verena's husband, Derek, was mounted at the Citizens Theatre, Glasgow. The characters make no contact with each other: Verena remains isolated in the sitting room of her suburban bungalow; Derek is seen travelling on trains between Glasgow and Aberdeen, where he is an oilrig worker, absent from home for extended periods. Lochhead engaged with the monologue form very successfully in her revues, performing many of them herself. She aims for verisimilitude, 'what the person would actually say', but is fascinated by 'the unreliability of the narrator' (Crawford and Varty 1993: 87–8). The speakers reveal more in what they omit from, or merely hint at in, their speeches than in the actual words spoken. Further, as Robert Crawford points out, in Lochhead's monologues, 'there is not just the voice we hear, there is also the implied voice which is being argued against and talked about' (ibid.: 70).

On the surface, Verena is doing well, comfortably off, able to indulge her taste for luxury furnishings and kitchen gadgets and relishing her good fortune in being independent, without children or an ever-present husband to make demands. She considers herself more fortunate than her sister, Joy, whose chaotic lifestyle in Easterhouse, a rundown housing estate, with five children and an unemployed husband, she ostensibly pities and deplores. What emerges in the interstices of the couple's 'solo turns' is that Verena is lonely and bored, that she is very jealous of Joy, and that she desperately wants to have a child. She is first presented as a selfish, vacuous, self-deluding woman but unconsciously reveals herself as a pitiable creature, isolated and bitter, particularly after her attempt to 'buy' Joy's sixth baby fails. Verena finally explodes in a tirade of violent abuse against the sister in relation to whom she has always measured herself, who is the other 'implied voice' in the monologue.

There are two strands in the text of *Perfect Days*: the first continues Lochhead's challenge to current cultural myths, with its satirical portrayal of the 'new' Glasgow, a rebranding of the 'old' city of slums and gang warfare, born in the 1988 Garden Festival, bred in the heady atmosphere of 1990 when Glasgow was European City of Culture, and blossoming in the stylish City of Architecture and Design in 1999. In *Bagpipe Muzak* Lochhead had turned her attention to the re-imaging of Glasgow, lamenting (nostalgically) the passing of the city's industrial heritage, the emasculation of its proud tradition of labour, notably in the shipyards of the Clyde, and the 'rusting skeletons of cranes' that have become mere exhibits in 'A Disneyland where work disnae exist' (Lochhead 1991a: 29). The second strand is concerned with 'the romantic comedy' – as the play is subtitled – starring Barbs, a 39-year-old hairstylist, who is determined to have a baby by any man with an acceptable genetic profile, a 'designer' baby for a 'designer' lifestyle. One of the problems with the text, however, is that the respective modes of satire and romance do not always sit comfortably together.

Perfect Days is set in a chic loft apartment, decorated in minimalist style, in the refurbished Merchant City, a favoured location for upwardly mobile young professionals. The environment fits well with the conventions of romantic (or more precisely 'screwball') comedy in that it typifies 'the elegance of the urban playground' (Gehring 1986: 45) and shows 'beautiful people in beautiful settings' (ibid.: 154). One such 'beautiful person' is Barbs, partner in the Razor City beauty salon and celebrity hostess of the *Morning Makeover* television programme. Glasgow's earlier notoriety for engaging with razors for rather less salubrious purposes than hairdressing has been thoroughly 'made over'. As Randall Stevenson describes in his essay on the play (in Poggi and Rose 2000: 111–19) the part of Barbs was written for the actor Siobhan Redmond, and both the character and the performer relate to the galaxy of screwball screen heroines, Myrna Loy, Carole Lombard and Katharine Hepburn. Nevertheless, Barbs is more of a Barbie Doll than an icon of liberation. She is certainly smart enough to be sceptical about the reality behind the glitzy facade. In response to a question about whether Glasgow is indeed 'your European regional capital', she replies: 'Are we buggery, it's all a lot of bollox, but am I complaining?' (Lochhead 1998a: 43), yet she still condones it and visibly benefits from it.

While Barbs is funny and charming and not without affection and generosity, her insouciant triviality, her predilection for luxury consumables and her obsession that she must breed at any cost attracted adverse criticism from feminists, in that Lochhead appeared to be presenting a negative image of women. Although she has argued that 'you don't have to write positively about women or create heroines' (Lochhead 1991b: 74), nevertheless in 'loving' Barbs but satirizing her lifestyle, the dramatist does not altogether succeed in maintaining the balance between iconoclasm and sympathy that she achieves elsewhere. Barbs's close friend, Brendan, a gay man, the 'best cutter' in the salon, can be read as the non-assertive male of the screwball genre, and their relationship, which privileges fun and friendship, 'love-companionship' (Karnick and Jenkins 1995: 325) over sentimental romance is conducted in witty, fast dialogue (barbed, perhaps). 'Verbal wrangling was the characteristic sound of screwball comedy' (ibid.: 330). None the less Brendan and his unseen sexual partner, Cammy the Stripogram, can be read as crude stereotypes of homosexual men and such representation was found offensive. The fusing of genres works well to a point, but is ultimately reductive.

Barbs and Brendan, together with Barbs's ex-husband, Davie, who is 'into retro' and is about to launch a new business in interior design, form the nucleus of the 'new' Glasgow set. 'Old' Glasgow is represented by Barbs's mother, Sadie, who describes the trendy Merchant City as being 'Back o' Goldbergs' (Lochhead 1998a: 41), and who sullies Barbs's loft with choice pieces of kailyard and kitsch, copies of the *People's Friend* and a light-up novelty talking Christmas tree. Sadie is described by Barbs as 'the biggest bigot in the West' (57), a rigid upholder of old-fashioned social values. Another traditional character is Alice, Barbs's ex-sister-in-law, who favours Marks and Spencers rather than Armani, and a 'neat' hairstyle rather than a Razor City *'fabulous special'* (10). But the divisions between the 'new' and the 'old' Glaswegians are not as firmly drawn as it appears. Alice and Sadie were victims as well as citizens of the old city, with its narrow puritanism and its demeaning poverty. Alice was forced to have her illegitimate baby adopted, her 'shameful' pregnancy cruelly hushed up by her family, and Sadie suffered material deprivation as the single parent of two children which has left her bitter and resentful. Some things have improved by being 'made over'.

The conclusion of screwball comedy is designed as a liberation from an overly rigid code of values. Barbs does, in the end, have her baby, artificially inseminated by the gorgeous Cammy, and the last scene shows her with the child, Grace, and Brendan, happy in a new-style family trinity. The ghost of Sadie, as a young mother, gives her blessing from the grave. As Gehring observes, it is dangerous to attack the endings of romantic comedies. 'To do so contradicts the fundamental pattern of comedy itself' (Gehring 1986: 157).

Reconstructing Monsters: *Blood and Ice* (1982, 1986) and *Dracula* (1985)

Each of the above plays is closely linked to (and in the case of *Dracula*, adapted from) a celebrated nineteenth-century novel, Mary Shelley's *Frankenstein* (1815) and Bram Stoker's *Dracula* (1898). Both novels have inspired a plethora of dramatizations on stage and film, and their respective 'monsters' have become bywords in western culture. Both novels – and both plays – are engaged with the unnatural, the perversion of natural order. In the Frankenstein story, a man assumes the divine role of creator of life: in *Dracula*, the vampire puts himself beyond death, preserving himself through feeding on the lifeblood of others.

Lochhead in her 'transcreations' of these sources retains much of their ethos, but makes a major shift in emphasis, by placing women at the centre of the narratives. In *Blood and Ice*, the focus is not on Mary Shelley as the author of *Frankenstein*, but on Mary Shelley as the author of her own story. In the later version (1984), Lochhead discarded her strategy of linking the characters in Mary's novel to those in her life. Rather they become facets of Mary herself in a drama that is, in effect, a stream of subconsciousness. Mary sees herself as Frankenstein *and* the monster *and* the female monster (Crawford and Varty 1993: 129–30), and concludes:

> But now I see who I am in my book. I am Captain Walton, explorer.
> Survivor. My own cool narrator. (Lochhead 1988: 115)

In Lochhead's *Dracula*, Stoker's representation of an evil vampire preying on young women, awakening in them desires that were best left dormant, is altered to reflect the view that the vampire could be regarded as an empowering agent to those women who freely decide to admit him into their lives, liberating them from sexual and psychological repressions induced by the tyranny of a patriarchal culture. Both Lucy and Mina Westerman superficially represent Victorian constructions of womanhood; Lucy, the 'waif', immature, frivolous, vulnerable, hysterical, and Mina, the 'good wife', caring, loyal and obedient. But the advent of Dracula puts paid to such clichés.

Little Lucy on becoming a vampire is 'lovely, terrifying and ethereal' (Lochhead 1989: 134). She is transformed, not into Stoker's creature of pure evil, but into a mature woman, initiating sexual union with her chosen partners.

Mina's 'awakening' by Dracula is not to sexual maturity, but to power. The brute force of the men cannot move the gates of the vampire's castle, but one word from Mina and 'the gates fly open wide', revealing *'Mina, wrapped in furs and deathly pale, blindfolded, reaching out straight ahead of her'* (Lochhead 1989: 143–4). Iconically reconfigured as Nemesis/Justice, Mina is implacable. This is the gift of Dracula – it was what she wanted.

Lochhead makes it clear that Dracula is merely the trigger for transformation. The audience has already seen Lucy as the vampire bride who tempts Jonathan in Dracula's castle, and even Mina, whom Jonathan vehemently seeks to distance from these highly sexualized women, is described ironically as *'a very recently powdered one of them'* (Lochhead 1989: 101). In general feminists have eschewed vampire mythology, disliking the image it presented of women as either victims or predators. By expanding the mythology to include the idea of women being transformed by the exposure of a transgressive impulse, Lochhead has added a new dimension to the legend. It is important to her that Dracula cannot enter unless first invited. Lochhead's women subconsciously desire his intrusion. Terrifying as it may be, it signals liberation and empowerment (Crawford and Varty 1993: 133).

Although Lochhead engages with the socio-political historical backgrounds that contextualize each of the plays – Romanticism and its radicalism in *Blood and Ice,* and imperialism and fears of its passing in *Dracula* (Harvie 1996: *passim*) – the two dramas have, for the most part, domestic settings, the Shelley house by Lake Geneva, and Heartwood, the Westermans' home in Whitby. Each household has two sisters (half-sisters in *Blood and Ice*), a 'bonded' male community and a maid. Each set of sisters is characterized as 'somewhat alike' but also as different as 'chalk and cheese' or 'night and day' (Terry 1995: 1–24). Mary Shelley and Mina Westerman are 'good' in the sense that they have a strong sense of duty, are aware of social proprieties and seek to act in a responsible manner. Yet each embarks on a dangerous moral and psychological journey: Mary Shelley's fictional quest with/as Captain Walton to find her 'monster'/herself, and Mina's subconscious travels with Dracula across sea and land, to death and rebirth. Lucy and Claire are the 'bad' sisters, self-absorbed, unstable, immature and dangerous. Both are also victims, a role given visual expression in the velvet band each wears around her throat. Lucy wears the ribbon to conceal Dracula's penetration of her body: Claire grossly affects the fashion of imitating those women guillotined in the Reign of Terror after the French Revolution. The accessory is appropriately called '*à la victime*' (Lochhead 1988: 88).

The maids, Elise in *Blood and Ice* and Florrie in *Dracula*, provide a social context, notably a class context, by exposing the inconsistencies between the lip service their mistresses pay to liberal idealism and the way in which they treat their servants. Elise has been taught to read and write by Mary, who sees it as a 'duty to educate her, enlighten her' (ibid.: 96) – an attitude viewed sceptically by Byron, in whose opinion this benevolence is nothing less than cultural imperialism ('I won't tyrannize the world', he says, 'by force-feeding it freedom'; 96). Elise has read *A Vindication of the Rights of Woman*. When she is dismissed by Mary and told sharply that a mere maid cannot understand such sentiments as are enunciated in the book, she responds violently:

> Indeed I understood it very well. The Rights of Woman. The marvellous Mary Wollstonecraft was very keen on freedom for Woman. At least freedom for the woman with six hundred a year and a mill-owning husband to support her – and a bevy of maidservants sweeping and starching and giving suck to her squalling infants – not to speak of her rutting husband.
> *Mary slaps her hard. Elise and Mary looking at each other...*
> Don't you think we are sisters? Are we not somewhat alike? (107)

In *Dracula*, Mina also tries to be 'friends' with Florrie, to admit her to 'the cliché – one big happy family' (Lochhead 1989: 96). Mina 'doesn't believe in servants' (96) but, moments later, she reverts to her role as mistress, imperiously instructing Florrie to clear up the mess in the room. Florrie recognizes that for all the fine words, she is still a maid at the mercy of her mistress's whims.

> Don't believe in servants! Oh, don't believe in servants, don't you, that's very interest-ing. Better pinch yourself, Florrie my girl, look in the mirror, pinch yourself to see if you're real. (98)

The concept of the 'sisterhood' of women is challenged: there are 'bad' sisters, and social hierarchy can be stronger than gender solidarity.

The men in each play form a triad: in *Blood and Ice* there are Shelley, Byron and the unseen but ever present William Godwin; in *Dracula*, there are Jonathan Harker, Arthur Seward and the mysterious 'healer' and putative double of Dracula, Van Helsing. Each group seeks to set the agenda for the female characters, laying out the parameters of their co-existence. The idealistic but impractical tenets of the male Romantic philosophy of individualism and self-indulgence threaten Mary's life and sanity: the stifling conventions of late Victorian society cause the men in *Dracula* to abandon Lucy and Mina to the vampire because they fear their own sexual desires. The women succeed in breaking through these constraints and recover the authorship of their own stories.

Strategies of Re-Writing

Language

Lochhead's use of language is a constant reminder that she was a poet first and a dramatist later; indeed much of her poetry inspired, or was inspired by, her playwriting; for example, 'Dreaming Frankenstein' and 'What the Creature Said' (Lochhead 1984: 11–13) and 'Lucy's Diary' and 'Renfield's Nurse' in *Bagpipe Muzak* (Lochhead 1991a: 60–4). Her plays abound in polyvalent imagery, frequently clustered around flowers and food (Crawford and Varty 1993: 124–47), metatextual references, ironic double entendres and playful puns within a frame of eminently speakable dialogue (McDonald 1993: 99–101; McDonald in Poggi and Rose 2000: 89–110). She swings skilfully from the shorthand of casual idiomatic conversation, replete with contemporary brand labels and familiar place names, to a higher register of stylized referential discourse. She is comfortable with both Scottish colloquial speech and her own devised version of a past Scottish language.

In *Blood and Ice*, a play about poets, poetry and the creation of a literary masterpiece, 'there is a deliberate overemphasis on the importance of words' (Scullion 1994: 149). A reading of Coleridge's *The Ancient Mariner* is intertextually positioned between passages of nuanced rhetoric and mundane references to childcare, clothing and household chores. Dracula keeps Jonathan Harker at his castle so that he can learn the 'wonderful English language', including 'A good slanging! The lifeblood of the language' (Lochhead 1989: 93–4). Language will confirm him as 'a good Englishman', and 'the lifeblood' of Lucy and Mina will revitalize him in his uncanny eternal life. Much of Dracula's humour and irony is contained in double entendres and punning around blood, food and drinking.

In *MQS* the languages of the two queens serve to highlight the differences between the women and between their realms. As Lynda Mugglestone observes (Crawford and Varty 1993: 93–108), Mary's speech is flexible, largely Scots but peppered with French phrases. Elizabeth's is more rigid, even archaic, with the use of words such as 'methinks' and the royal 'we'. She indicates that *she* has command of the (superior) English language: Mary may write poetry, but that is 'In French. And in "Scots" [*scornful laugh*]' (Lochhead 1989: 17–18). As La Corbie points out, the two queens only speak 'the wan language – mair or less' (15). *Quelques Fleurs* and *Perfect Days* exploit the richness of Glasgow's distinctive 'patter'. Verena describes her sister Joy's lifestyle:

> Five weans. Man that's no worked since nineteen-canteen.
> Stays in a three-up in Easterhoose that's that bogging damp the paper's curling aff the walls, has to humph that pram doon three flights past pish, broken gless, and hypodermics and Alsatian-shite.
> Excuse my French. (40–1)

Barbs warns her ex-husband of the problems of launching a new enterprise:

> I don't like to piss on your parade Davie, but, I tell you the banks at the moment are basically being bastards. (37)

('Basically' pronounced 'bazically' was introduced by Siobhan Redmond as a ubiquitous and misused adverb in everyday Glasgow speech.) This is the language of the Glasgow pantomime, only slightly heightened from the language of its citizens.

Lochhead's 'Glasgow' plays give an immediacy to the streets, the shops and the quotidian life of the city. Verena frequents Princes Square, buys her sister's Christmas present at Arnott's, and takes husband Derek to Queen Street for the Aberdeen train. The rather more stylish Barbs favours Armani Emporio and the West End boutique Moon. City and citizens are paradoxically reified by featuring in a literary fiction, one reason, perhaps, for the popularity of the play. Verbal language, colloquial and imagistic, is enriched by the use of sound, music and songs, from the strange, sad or wild tunes of the Fiddler and the ironic ballads in *MQS* to the judiciously selected pop hits that punctuate the dialogue of *Perfect Days*.

Making pictures

Lochhead's training in the visual arts has had as much influence on her dramaturgy as has her early career as a poet. She favoured poetry over painting as a student at Glasgow School of Art because she found visual art lacked narrative. The fashion of the time was for abstract rather than figurative work, and she believed that the medium was inadequate for her to articulate what she wanted to say. None the less, she maintained that 'Writing plays feels like making pictures' (Crawford and Varty 1993: 5). Her dramas are stories told in (and with) pictures. Historical paintings are realized on stage; for example, in the opening scene of the 1986 *Blood and Ice*, Mary Shelley is discovered in the ghostly nursery, asleep on a chaise longue '*in a classic nightmare pose*' from Fuseli's painting *Nightmare*. She has '*her own book open on her chest (where Fuseli's . . . homunculus lies in the painting)*' (Crawford and Varty 1993: 154). The metatextual reference immediately sites Mary and displays her ambivalence towards her 'hideous progeny' (Shelley 1831: xii).

The first scene in *Dracula* 'pictures' Lucy on a swing in the Edenic garden of Heartwood, an image reminiscent of Fragonard's *The Swing*, not least because of the salacious menace of the voyeuristic lover looking up the girl's frilly petticoat and the sinister priest pushing her ever upwards. Neither Fragonard's garden nor Lochhead's is free of serpents. Also in *Dracula* are two visual references to a pietà; when Dracula cradles Jonathan, and when the Nurse(s) lay out the body of Renfield. Jonathan and Renfield in their sacrificial, Christ-like poses are presented as both victims and martyrs, the double reference linking them as instruments in Dracula's predatory pursuits. Dracula's holding of Jonathan also signifies the ambivalent gender identity of the vampire and the complexity of his feelings for his prisoner.

La Corbie in *MQS* likens herself to 'a skating minister' (Lochhead 1989: 11), an iconic painting attributed to Henry Raeburn, an enigmatic representation of a strait-laced Protestant Man of God indulging in a frivolous activity. La Corbie's 'blackness' comes with subversive glee. At the queen's progress through Edinburgh, Mary's subjects, a vital part of the context in which she has to rule, are described as '*a whole set of Breughel grotesques*' (32). In addition to the pictorial reference, the grotesque nature of the historical crowd is a reminder of a circus parade of actors who open the play.

Lochhead also creates her own pictures on stage, one excellent example of a 'talking picture' being the composite scene in *Dracula* which presents to the audience, in one *mise en scène*, Heartwood, the asylum and Dracula's castle (Lochhead 1989: 98–101). Each image complements and is a commentary on the others, destabilizing geographical location and temporal linearity to bring all the characters together in the same mental space. But she also uses her palette to pictorial and symbolic effect, nowhere more powerfully than in the closing scene of *Dracula*:

> *Our lovers entwined on Dracula's {black} cloak, white snow begins to fall, then blush-pink petals like apple blossom and confetti, darker pink and finally red, red petals as the curtain falls.* (147)

Items of costume are important signifiers: John Knox's bowler hat and rolled umbrella situate him in the contemporary context of an Orange Walk; Riccio's embroidered brocade waistcoat is a reminder of the decorative sophistication of Europe which Mary has lost. To cover his nakedness after swimming, Shelley drapes himself in a lace tablecloth, a prefiguring of his shroud.

A variation of being framed within a stage picture is framing oneself, either in a photograph – an image given to or taken by a photographer – or in a mirror. In the mirrors which are frequent stage properties in Lochhead's dramas, one may see oneself, or a performative version of oneself, as Lucy does when she '*kisses her own lovely reflection*' (Lochhead 1989: 73) while dreaming of marriage; or one may see another, a quasi-sister, an unwanted aspect of oneself, as Mary Shelley does when she and Claire each brush their hair on either side of the tilted mirror; or one may not see what one assumes will be reflected, as Dracula's image is absent from Jonathan's shaving mirror. Jonathan sees only himself, an upstanding young man: his Dracula-self who lusts after Lucy and Florrie, his vampire brides, is not reflected, but is present.

A variation of the mirror image is the double-sided doll in *Blood and Ice*, Mary on one side, and on the other Elise, which makes Mary understand that servitude is the common lot of all women, maids and mistresses alike. In Mary's nightmare, the doll, grown to life size, becomes herself and Claire. Through the dolls, Mary/Claire/Elise are all linked to the female 'monster' to whom Frankenstein (and Mary, Frankenstein's creator) denied life.

Lochhead's deployment of her actors is frequently imagistic, as is evident in her non-naturalistic technique of leaving a 'silent' character on-stage whose physical presence has a choric function, embodying an alternative narrative to the spoken dialogue. She also, through her use of doubling, presents the audience with a series of 'visual puns'. In *MQS*, the actors playing the queens also play their respective maids *and* Edinburgh whores *and* modern children. Mistresses, maids, queens and whores are thematically and structurally intertwined. Although Mary and Elizabeth never met, on stage the actors 'going as' the queens are in constant proximity, leading to moments of ironic tension. These changeovers in characterization are effected by the interpolations of La Corbie, often accompanied by a crack of the whip, a drumbeat or a flash of lightning, cueing the dissolution of one 'character' into another, the differences and the similarities of each being physically embodied in one performer.

Lochhead's major plays demonstrate her command of a range of theatrical languages. *Perfect Days* is largely naturalistic, although borrowing elements of farce and fantasy from the filmic genre of romantic comedy. *MQS* is non-naturalistic, engaging with metatheatrical devices, a choric narrator, circus parades, an interpolated Mummers' play, multiple role playing and interpolated songs. In *Blood and Ice* and in *Quelques Fleurs* two women tell their own stories with contrasting degrees of self-awareness and 'reliability'. In the Scottish theatre of the 1980s and 1990s, Lochhead's 'playfulness' was both an innovation and a challenge.

PRIMARY READING

Lochhead, Liz (1984). *Dreaming Frankenstein and Collected Poems.* Edinburgh: Polygon.

Lochhead, Liz (1985a). *Tartuffe.* Edinburgh: Polygon.

Lochhead, Liz (1985b). *True Confessions and New Clichés.* Edinburgh: Polygon.

Lochhead, Liz (1988). *Blood and Ice* in Michelene Wandor (ed.). *Plays by Women. Vol. 4.* London: Methuen, 81–118. (Revised version of the play in a new edition of this volume.)

Lochhead, Liz (1989). *Mary Queen of Scots Got her Head Chopped Off* and *Dracula.* Harmondsworth: Penguin.

Lochhead, Liz (1990). 'Interview with Rebecca E. Wilson' in Gillean Somerville-Arjat and Rebecca E. Wilson (eds.). *Sleeping with Monsters: Conversations with Scottish and Irish Women Poets.* Edinburgh: Polygon, 8–14.

Lochhead, Liz (1991a). *Bagpipe Muzak.* Harmondsworth: Penguin.

Lochhead, Liz (1991b). 'Women's Writing and the Millennium' in Janice Galloway (ed.). *Meantime: Looking Forward to the Millennium.* Edinburgh: Polygon, 71–5.

Lochhead, Liz (1992). 'Interview with Emily B. Todd', *Verse* 8:3 and 9:1, 83–95.

Lochhead, Liz (1992). 'Knucklebones of Irony' in Colin Nicholson (ed.). *Poem, Purpose and Place: Shaping Identity in Contemporary Scottish Verse.* Edinburgh: Polygon, 202–23.

Lochhead, Liz (1998a). *Perfect Days.* London: Nick Hern.

Lochhead, Liz (1998b). *Quelques Fleurs* in Philip Howard (ed.). *Scotland Plays.* London: Nick Hern, 261–90.

Lochhead, Liz (2000). *Medea.* London: Nick Hern.

Lochhead, Liz (2003). *The Thebans.* London: Nick Hern.

Lochhead, Liz (forthcoming). *Good Things*. London: Nick Hern.
Note: The Scottish Theatre Archive in Glasgow University Library holds scripts of several of Lochhead's plays, including 'Jock Tamson's Bairns' (STA SAC 3) and her preferred script of 'Blood and Ice' (STA Jd 5/5).

FURTHER READING

Cousin, Geraldine (1996). 'Retellings' in Geraldine Cousin (ed.). *Women in Dramatic Place and Time*. London: Routledge, 127–37.
Crawford, Robert and Varty, Anne (eds.) (1993). *Liz Lochhead's Voices*. Edinburgh: Edinburgh University Press.
(Included in this collection is a checklist by Hamish Whyte of Lochhead's works and critical and biographical material before 1992.)
Gehring, Wes D. (1986). *Screwball Comedy: A Genre of Madcap Romance*. New York, Westport, CT, and London: Greenwood Press.
Harvie, Jennifer (1993). 'Desire and Difference in Liz Lochhead's *Dracula*', *Essays in Theatre/Etudes Théatrâles* 11:2, 133–43.
Harvie, Jennifer (1996). 'Liz Lochhead's Drama'. Special Collections Department, Glasgow University Library, unpublished PhD thesis.
Karnick, Kristine Brunovska and Jenkins, Henry (1995). *Classical Hollywood Comedy*. London: Routledge.
McDonald, Jan (1993). 'The Devil is Beautiful: *Dracula*: Freudian Novel and Feminist Drama' in Peter Reynolds (ed.). *Novel Images: Literature in Performance*. London: Routledge, 80–104.
Poggi, Valentina and Rose, Margaret (eds.) (2000). *A Theatre that Matters: Twentieth-Century Scottish Drama and Theatre*. Milan: Edizioni Unicopli.
(Essays in this collection which are relevant to a study of Lochhead's work include: Laura Caretti, 'Mary Queen of Scots and the "Siren's Song of Tolerance" '(41–56); Sara Soncini, 'Liz Lochhead's Revisionist Mythmaking' (57–88); Jan McDonald, 'Food as Signifier and Symbol in the Work of Contemporary Scottish Women Dramatists' (89–110); Randall Stevenson, 'Perfect Days? Scottish Theatre at the Millennium' (111–19), and an interview with Lochhead (252–5).)
Scullion, Adrienne (1994). 'Liz Lochhead' in K. A. Besney (ed.). *Contemporary Dramatists*. London, Washington, DC, and Detroit: St James Press.
Scullion, Adrienne (2000). 'Contemporary Scottish Women Playwrights' in Elaine Aston and Janelle Reinelt (eds.). *The Cambridge Companion to Modern British Women Playwrights*. Cambridge: Cambridge University Press, 94–118.
Shelley, Mary (1831). *Frankenstein: Or the Modern Prometheus*. London: Henry Colburn and Richard Bentley.
Terry, Helen (1995). 'The Representation of Sisters and Sisterhood in the Plays of Liz Lochhead'. University of Glasgow, unpublished MPhil dissertation.

38

'Spirits that Have Become Mean and Broken': Tom Murphy and the 'Famine' of Modern Ireland

Shaun Richards

What binds Murphy's work together is that 'it forms a kind of inner history of Ireland since the momentous changes which were set in motion in 1959' (O'Toole 1987: 16). This locates his work in the crucial aftermath of the 1958 *Report on Economic Development* with its directive that 'It would be well to shut the door on the past and to move forward' (Whitaker 1958: 9), and Murphy, perhaps even more than his contemporary Brian Friel, provides insights into Ireland's engagement with the forces of economic modernization. The description of his plays as 'screams in the night' (Stembridge 1987: 61) suggests a discontent with this process, but his concern is only partially with the material consequences – and inequalities – of Ireland's political liberation and subsequent modernization. His drama engages with an Irish state which, while nominally decolonized, retained a class-based exclusion which is exacerbated by 'mentalities that have become distorted, spirits that have become mean and broken' (Murphy 1992: xi), for Murphy's concerns are with spiritual as well as material well-being. Mommo's description of the characters in *Bailegangaire* (1985) as 'Poor banished children of Eve' (Murphy 1993: 169), the use of Gigli's 'O Paradiso' in *The Gigli Concert* (1983) and Peggy's singing of 'All in the April Evening (I thought on the lamb of God)' (Murphy 1993: 81) in *Conversations on a Homecoming* (1985) evoke a desire for redemption which is spiritual as much as material. This emerged, however, as his drama developed and it is the discontents of society, rather than the soul, which are addressed most overtly in his first play, *On the Outside* (1959), and the companion work *On the Inside* (1974).

On the Outside focuses on the lack of entrance money which leaves young men outside a village dance hall, but that exclusion has wider social and political resonances. As Murphy's description of Frank makes clear, he is 'aware of the very rigid class descriptions that pervade a small, urban community and resents "them" because he has not got the same' (Murphy 1997: 170). His response to exclusion is a complex interaction of envy and disdain, for while his dominant impulse is to acquire the money for the dance and meet his date, his vision of society has a revolutionary force:

The whole town is like a tank . . . And we're at the bottom, splashing around all week in their Friday night vomit . . . And the bosses – and the big shots – are up around the top, looking in, looking down . . . Spitting. On top of us. (180)

However, as is clear from *On the Inside*, Murphy's perception is that increased prosperity alone will not produce more than a comfortable conformity. The setting is the dance-hall from which the characters of the earlier play were excluded. The salary of Kieran's teacher exceeds that of Frank but he still occupies a culture in which 'There's nothing happening' (Murphy 1997: 220), and sexual solace has a furtiveness in which lovers are 'lurking somewhere; in doorways, or dirty old sheds, or mucky old laneways' (199). Kieran's desire to be 'FREE! Free, free!' (217) captures all the anguished desire for a meaningful life which torments Murphy's characters; a condition fully investigated in the thematically twinned *A Whistle in the Dark* (1961) and *A Crucial Week in the Life of a Grocer's Assistant* (1962).

In *A Whistle in the Dark*, Michael Carney's rejection of a family who 'don't know how to live' (Murphy 1997: 57) has taken him into exile in England, where he has superficially adapted to a life defined by the nuclear family and personal advancement. But Michael's Irish past haunts him in the form of his brothers, who use his home as the base for their violent and criminal lives, and the arrival from Ireland of his father, Dada, and youngest brother, Des. The torment which produces the cry 'I want to get out of this kind of life' (57) is born of Michael's entrapment within a family whose primitive tribal loyalties sit awkwardly in an Ireland where the mark of success is now the acquisition of a professional position. Michael is riven by his desire to modernize his family, particularly by making Des into 'something'. What Murphy dramatizes through Michael's struggle is analogous to the trauma of modern Ireland; for the domestic setting stages in microcosm 'the tensions of a society on the brink of civilization, about to become belatedly "civilized" ' (O'Toole 1987: 46).

In Ireland, class envy has driven Dada into petty theft in attempted revenge on the professional men at the golf club where the offer of a caretaking job has demonstrated the actuality of social division, just as it is class which, as recalled by Harry, scarred his school-days through the callous superiority of the teacher. Murphy is dramatizing the breakdown of a system of loyalties which, brutal and petty as they are in the self-aggrandizement of Dada, also have 'a touch of nobility' (3) in the character of Iggy and, in Harry, give rise to a moving expression of the plight of those marginalized by the ethic of success. The power of the play resides in Murphy's ability to invest his characters with an almost tragic dignity as they fall victim to processes beyond their ability to comprehend or Michael's ability to control.

Yet, while Murphy in *A Whistle in the Dark* successfully stages the trauma of this transitional social moment, he has not yet found the means of dramatizing its transcendence. When Michael kills Des at the play's conclusion it is a moment born of his disgust at the past's seemingly inescapable power. For Michael and Ireland the problem is that there is no substantial vision of a future other than that of social and material advancement, with embourgeoisement producing only the guilt and frustration out of which failure is bred. Michael's lament 'I don't want to be what I am' (57) is paralleled in Dada's despairing moan 'Oh, I wish to God I was out of it all. I wish I had something, anything. Away, away, some place' (61). In this bleak world the only confident self-assertion is found in Harry's 'I know where I stand. And I like it' (44). But his savage resistance to 'THEM! Them shams!'(44) provides only a temporary point of personal resistance. However, there is an honesty within his brutality, and it is the ability to articulate the unpalatable truth which suggests one of the directions in which Murphy's subsequent work advanced, from a despair located deep within selves whose redemption lay beyond the power of purely economic palliatives.

If Michael's escape from the past cannot be effected by emigration alone, John Joe Moran in *A Crucial Week* articulates a dawning sense that Ireland's limitations must be confronted. As his final triumphant emphasis on financial and emotional self-determination makes clear, the problem is that there is 'Never the freedom to decide and make choices for ourselves. And then we're half men here, or half-men away, and how can we hope ever to do anything' (Murphy 1997: 162). Here, Murphy determinedly locates the cause of these stunted lives deep in the past, as suggested by the description of John Joe's mother as 'a product of Irish history' (94).

In his violent and misogynistic behaviour, *A Whistle in the Dark*'s Dada embodies 'hypermasculinity' (Nandy 1988: 9), a compensation for colonial subordination which extends into the nominally decolonized Ireland of the Republic. Michael's and John Joe's situations are framed by the same historical determinants, for while John Joe's mother is full of comfort and consolation, his dream-state evocation of her concerns captures the equally repressive reverse of Dada's violence, as both define the child in terms of a predetermined pattern of behaviour: 'Off-to-America, that's where he was going!...Leaving us here in the lurch. Deserting his mammy and daddy and uncle that's good to him. That's gratitudinous!' (93). Dada and John Joe's mother are products of an emotional impoverishment which has outlasted the historical circumstances which were its initial cause. The term Murphy uses is 'famine'.

In his preface to *Famine* Murphy expands on the contemporary implications of that nineteenth-century catastrophe. Noting that the absence of food is only one aspect of famine, he asks:

> What about the other 'poverties' that attend famine? A hungry and demoralized people becomes silent...Intelligence becomes cunning. There is a poverty of thought and expression. Womanhood becomes harsh. Love, tenderness, loyalty, generosity go out the door in the struggle for survival. Men fester in vicarious dreams of destruction. (Murphy 1992: xi)

Above all, famine does not end when food returns and health is restored, for 'Famine is a racial memory, it provides a debilitating history and that it has left its mark I have no doubt' (xi). Murphy's work is concerned with a double debilitation, that of the famine which produced 'the desiccated determination to survive even at the expense of emotional starvation' (O'Toole 1987: 101), and a modern materialism which leads the 'Irish Man' of *The Gigli Concert* to mental breakdown and despair at a world of 'corruption, brutality, backhanding, fronthanding, backstabbing' (Murphy 1994: 173). However, while the latter is never entirely absent from Murphy's drama, it is 'emotional starvation' which is the major concern of his plays, and, as evidenced in *A Crucial Week*, so too is a concern with the means by which 'Eden' can be re-entered.

The town in the play could, like Murphy's home town, be described as being 'at the epicentre of Irish conservatism, darkness and pain' (Waters 1986: 26). Here, the description of the mother as 'harsh in expression and bitter' matches the environment, as both she and Ireland are scarred by 'poverty and ignorance' (Murphy 1997: 94). Stage directions state 'appearance is slovenly – she wears too many clothes, and these are drab and old' (94), but John Joe's dream illustrates that she had a life before the onset of drab bitterness: 'She told me she smelt the primroses once, a print dress and her hair, walking Cloonasscragh' (117). When the mother finally declares 'But isn't it a lovely Spring morning!' (163), the implication is that she is now free from a famine of the imagination in which denial of self and others has become a way of life. What is rendered with absolute clarity is the lesson to be learnt from Uncle Alec's lament over his lost life: 'I was too late in learning to speak out my mind when it was needed' (60). Individuals can confront and overcome their historically determined limitations, but while John Joe raises the possibility that the causes of the mother's narrowness 'came from a hundred years ago' (159), the impetus is towards a future which transcends historically imposed limitations.

However, while Murphy charted the range of poverties suffered by Ireland in the aftermath of a protracted famine, he was equally alert to the void which could lie at the heart of a progress which was purely material. The allusions to these limitations which permeated the plays of the 1960s culminated in *The Blue Macushla* (1980), whose thematic point is that Ireland, like the night club of the title, plays host to a class of entrepreneurs while, beyond the doors, the sub-proletariat is riven by unemployment, prostitution and drug addiction. Eddie the night-club owner's description of the country as a place in which people are 'eatin'' one another, all walks of life 'n' 'joyin' the taste!' (220) encapsulates Murphy's sense of a profound corruption stretching from the night club to the highest levels of government. In the play, as in the Ireland defined by Murphy as a place where 'Nothing was transparent' (Murphy 1992: xx), the corruption of politics is so absolute as to taint all those engaged with it. When Eddie cries 'I want to be a person again' (202), he articulates the perception which informs the subsequent plays.

In a 1991 interview Murphy acknowledged the devastating consequences of the loss of absolute convictions: 'when the disenchantment sets in then the person becomes increasingly dangerous as he/she kicks out in agony, against the loss of all these certainties' (Jackson 1991: 19). While his comments were directed at Ireland's progressive loss of Catholic faith, his plays engaged with the disintegration of a sustaining raft of certainties across the social and economic domain as Ireland became a commodity on the global market, for sale 'to any old bidder with a pound, a dollar, a mark or a yen' (Murphy 1993: 80). The concern of his plays was now the question of how meaning could be sustained in a world of vanishing certainties while resisting the temptation to retreat into modes of thought and behaviour which, as his earliest works demonstrated, were the consequences of famine.

Two plays, *The Gigli Concert* (1983) and *Conversations on a Homecoming* (1985), define the problem and the potential solution in a society where 'This kind of – life – isn't it at all' (Murphy 1993: 28). The drama is provided by the search for meaning; in *Conversations* that of the 'homecoming' Michael Ridge for the fulfilment of the frustrated idealism of the 1960s, in *The Gigli Concert* of all three characters for the ability to 'sing like Gigli': a desire which functions as the metaphor for the achievement of beauty. While both plays are set in 1980s Ireland, *Conversations* has a social and historical precision which defines the context in which much of Murphy's later work can be read.

The fact that Ireland has become economically dominated by a pseudo-American lifestyle and the valuation of human relationships in terms of economic gain is satirized through Liam: 'He is a farmer, an estate agent, a travel agent, he owns property...he affects a slight American accent; a bit stupid and insensitive – seemingly the requisites of success' (4). Liam has introduced a partition into the White House pub in which the play is set and so overthrown its founding principles that 'there should be no public bar, no divisions or class distinctions' (38). He is 'the worst type of a ponce of a modern fuckin' gombeen man' (72), but one to whom there is no evident alternative, for Ireland's embrace of 'American politics or business methods...images: fuckin' neon shadows' (57) has seemingly removed all indigenous cultural and political resistance.

The ideals for which Michael Ridge returned from America were born of Ireland's 1960s embrace of modernity, which, coinciding with the inspirational American presidency of J. F. Kennedy, provided a short-lived prelude to the corrupt decades of disillusion captured in *The Blue Macushla*. As Michael has found America to be lacking the idealism for which it was once, briefly, the source, his homecoming is based on the expectation of idealism remaining in Ireland. However, the 'rising culture' of the sixties is now revealed to have been merely the first stage of Ireland's embourgeoisement.

Michael is a development of *A Whistle in the Dark*'s Michael Carney in that he finds an answer for his anguish. Having started out saying 'I'm not sure what I came home for, but I think I'm finding out' (59), he concludes 'I know what I came home for' (86) – namely an end to his confusion and uncertainty. Exposure to the reality of Ireland determines his return to America, a seeming victory for Tom's cynical demolition of his ideals. But Tom should not be read as a guiding intelligence set against the naïve idealism of Michael and the naked materialism of Liam. In his mockery of the idea of returning to 'drink from the wellsprings' (40), he not only undermines Michael's vain quest for idealism but simultaneously denies all sustenance for himself. 'I can't feel anything about anything anymore' (65) he confesses, and his denunciation of 'those honest and honourable men who are cutting down the trees for making – Easter-egg boxes!' (80) is a harsh expression of the devastation of an Ireland for which it appears there will be no resurrection. Indeed, the apparent absence of all the promise of the past and the impossibility of a future determine Michael's return to America, as 'They've probably cut down the rest of the wood by now, anyway' (87). Michael is unable to grasp the import of Anne's rejoinder to his nihilism: 'There's still the stream' (87), a whispered possibility captured in the final stage directions which focus on Anne 'smiling her gentle hope out at the night' (87). What Murphy's drama required was a realization of the possibility of hope at both thematic and dramatic levels – one more forcefully realized than in stage directions alone.

Murphy had already essayed an exploration of the search for meaning in a world without faith in *The Sanctuary Lamp* (1975; revised 1984) which focused on the situation of three *marginaux* becalmed in an empty church. While there is an ever-present threat of violence between Harry and Francisco because of the latter's affair with Harry's wife, they gradually move towards a reconciliation effected through visions of human harmony. As Harry conceives the fate of the soul after death, it moves out 'to take its place in the silent outer wall of eternity' (Murphy 1994: 158). And should any of the silhouettes of souls become damaged then it is repaired by using another soul, which has been stacked softly like a cloud until needed: 'And whose silhouette is the new one? The father of the damaged one. Or the mother's, sometimes. Or a brother's, or a sweetheart's. Loved ones. That's it. And one is implanted on the other' (159). Harry's ideal of harmony is imagined through the souls of predecessors who heal those of a subsequent generation, and it is echoed in *The Gigli Concert*, where the 'Irish Man' is maimed by despair: 'This – something – cloud has come down on me' (Murphy 1994: 172) he cries, as he seeks solace in the ability to sing like Gigli; 'No inverted commas' (175) – for he desires the actual achievement of beauty and not its approximation. But while the use of Gigli's version of 'O Paradiso' carries clear echoes of *The Sanctuary Lamp*'s dream of redemption, the latter's geographical indeterminacy in 'a church in a city' (Murphy 1994: 98) gives way to everyday Dublin, and redemptive action replaces philosophical speculation.

More overtly than in any of Murphy's other works, *The Gigli Concert* addresses the utopian impulse which enables individuals to realize their own suppressed desire for beauty, and carries a socially transformative capacity suggested in JPW King's concluding act of releasing the voice of Gigli through the open windows into the sleeping world of Dublin. In his assertion that 'There's more to life than working myself to death or wheeling and dealing with that band of criminals of would-be present day little pygmy Napoleons we've got at the top' (224), the 'Irish Man' lays bare the weakness in Ireland's embrace of modernity and materialism. This society also scars Mona, whose round of alcohol and casual sex expresses an equally desperate attempt to escape an emptiness which sees her translate Gigli's song into an expression of her own desired future: 'A baby. That's what it's all about' (69). While the song functions as the aural manifestation of Mona's individual desire, it also articulates the thematic heart of Murphy's work to this point: the future as predicated not on material progress, but on the realization of human potential.

While the stage directions state that the aria heard in the final moments of the play is Gigli's own solo recording, they are equally clear that before his final drug-and-drink-induced recital JPW 'switches off the record player, and unplugs it from its power-point as a double precaution (and proof)' (238). Then, having sung 'like Gigli', 'He remembers record-player: checks to find that it is indeed disconnected from its power-point', after which he gives a 'laugh of achievement' (239). Within the realist set of a dingy Dublin office, Murphy gives expression to a transcendence of limitations which dispenses both with abstract discussion and with symbolic representation, committing himself to making audiences see that 'the romantic kingdom *is* of this world' (190). In setting *Bailegangaire* in 'a country kitchen in the old style' (Murphy 1993: 91), Murphy determined to ensure that audiences familiar with the cultural centrality of that set were left in no doubt as to which world was the focus of his desire for transformation.

Bailegangaire is contained within two time scales: the modern moment of the play's location is 1984, in which the downside of Ireland's economic expansion is signalled by the closure of the Japanese-owned computer plant, and the pre-expansion period of horse-drawn carts and country markets is referenced in Mommo's story. As the off-stage world of capitalism makes clear, Murphy is alert to the actuality of global economic forces and equally aware of the material and emotional poverty of the insular world they displaced; one captured in Mommo's account of lives 'wretched and neglected, dilapidated an' forlorn' (164).

The heart of the play resides in the endlessly incomplete story of Mommo, whose inability to draw it to a conclusion and admit the reality of the death of her grandchild freeze-frames past and present without admitting an ending which will liberate the future. As her granddaughter Mary's first imitation, and then repetition, of Mommo's demand for home demonstrate, the play is informed by the journey to redemption encapsulated in the lines of Mary's final speech, which opens 'To conclude', and closes with the welcoming of the new baby as 'another chance' (170). The drama focuses on the personal dramas of three women from one family, but their experiences of a journey from peasant poverty to material prosperity make their lives paradigmatic of the Irish experience; a fact highlighted through the character of Mommo.

W. B. Yeats's and Lady Gregory's *Cathleen ni Houlihan* (1903) concludes with the transformation of the old woman into 'a young girl, and she had the walk of a queen' (Yeats 1997: 220), but that drama of liberation from colonization is mocked by Mommo's senility within an Ireland dictated by the logic of a global market. Mommo has been scarred by physical poverty and, more devastatingly, by emotional starvation in a marriage with a husband who would 'rise in the mornin' [and] not give her a glance. An' so long had it had been he had called her by her first name, she'd near forgot it herself... Hah?' (140). That people in Ireland live at such a low emotional ebb is central to the drama, for Mommo's contribution to the death of her own grandson echoes in her recollections of a wider national culpability for 'The unbaptised an' stillborn in shoeboxes planted' (164). Murphy's demand is that all truths must be told in order that freedom can be achieved.

Mary's resolution to 'move on to a new place' (153) drives her to help Mommo acknowledge a reality presented as both release and renewal, for it is Mary's active participation in the traditional story form which enables her 'homecoming'. *Bailegangaire* closes on a totalizing harmony in which Mommo finally recognizes Mary, just as the latter agrees to take her sister Dolly's illegitimate baby. The child is to be called Tom, a name which projects a now unified past and present into a potential future, for Tom was the grandchild whose death Mommo was unable to acknowledge. The final image of Mary and Dolly sharing Mommo's bed draws all Murphy's shattered families together and extends hope to the equally sundered nation.

This, however, marks the culmination and termination of Murphy's dramas of redemption, for Christopher, the protagonist of *Too Late for Logic* (1990), condemns the 'complicated thorns of kindred in my side' (Murphy 1990: 8) and, failing in his attempt at 'Finding and restoring my true self' (7), commits suicide. The cause of Christopher's suicide is his abandonment of the power of love and family which led to the harmony of *Bailegangaire*; indeed his desire 'To escape, *ease* the pain of boundless love' (41) is a retreat from the human interdependency which Murphy has advanced as means of enabling a future. While dramatic tension is reduced through the immediate awareness of Christopher's suicide (the causes of which are analysed in the play), it still functions as a clear, if negative coda to the earlier work in suggesting that Christopher is in thrall to careerism and unable to produce a meaningful alternative. Given this dramatic autopsy on a life ended because of a self-absorbed abandonment of love, it might have been anticipated that Murphy's subsequent work would address not simply the cause of contemporary disillusion but its correction. However, in *The Wake* (1998) Murphy dramatizes a family so dedicated to material gain that all connections and emotions are abused in the search for profit. While there are echoes of *Bailegangaire* in Vera's account of sharing her grandmother's bed, her return to Ireland from America carries no reprise of that play's drama of reconciliation: 'The thought of here hasn't kept me going: the thought of here cripples me' (49).

The Wake is unsparing in its antipathy towards an Ireland perceived as unchanged from the repressive, petit-bourgeois Free State founded in 1921. Class again comes to the fore with the stage directions for Finbar, recalling the brutal treatment of Harry in *A Whistle in the Dark*: 'Lifted as a boy by "the authorities" and put into care, brutalized there and sexually abused by the Christian brothers' (9). But the earlier play's sympathy for the excluded is now extended into a positive preference for 'the Punjab', the working-class estate where you can get 'a breath of fresh air' and reject what '*they*' had on offer' (58).

The Wake revisits earlier themes, but with a jaundiced eye whose gaze acknowledges little possibility of a national redemption. While initially acknowledging that 'They mean an awful lot to me. So they do. They keep me going' (42), Vera's rebellion against the family unites her with her brother-in-law Henry, who leaps on her suggestion that her 'last throw in the game of family' (50) might be to burn down the hotel she has inherited: 'By Jesus yes!...Put it to the torch, leave it in ashes and I'll purify myself in the flames with you bejasus!' (50) – a desire born of the fact that 'The culture has defeated him. He does not know who he is' (22). Character, as in the case of Vera's brother Tom, is 'ingrained in him from the culture' (26), and against that determining power Murphy's characters only engage in the self-defeating resistance of alcoholism or, in Vera's case, a return to America.

This preoccupation with the still unredeemed nature of Ireland continued in *The House* (2000), where the allusions to a class-ridden country which informed *A Whistle in the Dark* are realized in grim actuality. Set in the 1950s in the immediate aftermath of the declaration of the Republic – a nominal shedding of the last vestiges of colonialism – the play focuses on Christy, who returns to his home town, with other economic migrants, for the ritual summer visit. However, far from being welcomed, the group are seen as 'outcasts, white trash' (Murphy 2000: 37), and Christy is condemned by Kerrigan, the lawyer who has risen from an equally impoverished background, as 'You – *scruff* – back from England!'; an insult followed by the brutal 'Look, why don't you go and – before we do it for you – put a bullet in your head!' (111). The consequence of social marginalization in Christy's childhood, and subsequent enforced migration, is an obsessive, almost psychopathic, identification with the country: 'I'd kill for here! Would you kill for here? I'd kill' (43). And when the possibility of, literally, locating himself at the social centre of the community presents itself through the purchase of the house of the de Burcas – 'a veritable, veritable Ireland in itself' (81) – he kills the youngest daughter of the family when, as his account of the event suggests, 'She said my mother scrubbing your floors...She said choice things' (100); in other words, reiterates her earlier description of him as 'Heathcliff' and 'A servant boy' (29). While Christy succeeds in his purchase, the play ends with him 'close to tears', 'standing in the setting sun. He chokes back a sob' (113).

Both *The Wake* and *The House* problematize Murphy's assertion that 'I'm at that stage that I don't want down endings...there's always hope at the end of the play...I seem to be looking for hope, always' (Waters 1986: 28). Up to this point he had produced powerful plays which moved from analysis to antidote, finally dramatizing the belief that the romantic kingdom is of this world. However, these last two plays suggest that the bite of the old narratives is deep and corrosive. Far from the world of globalization and the Celtic Tiger, Murphy sees 'famine' as the determining force on an Ireland still exiled from 'Eden'.

PRIMARY READING

Murphy, Tom (1990). *Too Late for Logic*. London: Methuen.

Murphy, Tom (1992). *Plays: 1*. London: Methuen.

Murphy, Tom (1993). *Plays: 2*. London: Methuen.

Murphy, Tom (1994). *Plays: 3*. London: Methuen.

Murphy, Tom (1997). *Plays: 4*. London: Methuen.

Murphy, Tom (1998). *The Wake*. London: Methuen.

Murphy, Tom (2000). *The House*. London: Methuen.

FURTHER READING

Grene, Nicholas (1999). *The Politics of Irish Drama: Plays in Context from Boucicault to Friel*. Cambridge: Cambridge University Press.

Grene, Nicholas (ed.) (2002). *Talking About Tom Murphy*. Dublin: Carysfort Press.

Grene, Nicholas (2004). 'Tom Murphy and the Children of Loss' in Shaun Richards (ed.). *The Cambridge Companion to Twentieth-Century Irish Drama*. Cambridge: Cambridge University Press, 204–17.

Jackson, J. (1991). 'Making the Words Sing' (interview with Tom Murphy). *Hot Press* 4, 18–19.

Murray, Christopher (ed.) (1987). *Irish University Review* (Tom Murphy special issue) 17:1.

Murray, Christopher (1997). *Twentieth-Century Irish Drama: Mirror Up to Nation*. Manchester: Manchester University Press.

Nandy, Ashis (1988). *The Intimate Enemy: Loss and Recovery of Self Under Colonialism*. Delhi: Oxford University Press.

O'Toole, Fintan (1987). *The Politics of Magic: The Work and Times of Tom Murphy*. Dublin: Raven Arts Press.

Richards, Shaun (1989). 'Refiguring Lost Narratives – Prefiguring New Ones: The Theatre of Tom Murphy', *Canadian Journal of Irish Studies* 15:1, 80–100.

Roche, Anthony (1994). *Contemporary Irish Drama: From Beckett to McGuiness*. Dublin: Gill and Macmillan.

Stembridge, Gerard (1987). 'Murphy's Language of Theatrical Empathy' in Christopher Murray (ed.). *Irish University Review* (Tom Murphy special issue) 17:1, 51–61.

Waters, John (1986). 'The Frontiersman' (interview with Tom Murphy), *In Dublin* 15 May, 24–9.

Whitaker, T. K. (1958). *Report on Economic Development* (Pr4808). Dublin: Irish Government.

Yeats, W. B. (1997). *W. B. Yeats: A Critical Edition of the Major Works*, ed. Edward Larrissy. Oxford: Oxford University Press.

39

Caryl Churchill: Feeling Global

Elin Diamond

Caryl Churchill's plays create a stunning record of historical reflection and theatrical exuberance. The lineaments of her career are well known: since 1965, she has written some 35 dramatic works for radio, theatre and television. A formally adventurous writer, she thrives on collaboration and in recent years has opened her theatrical texts to modern dance and opera. Yet however much her plays and their expressive media vary, Churchill (b. 1938) has had from the outset two abiding 'obsessions' – the exploration of 'mental states' and the critique of capitalism (Thurman 1982: 54). In Walter Benjamin's words, she is interested in our 'historical existence' (Nägele 1988: 10) – what it feels like in the nervous system to live in times of social and political struggle, or, as in the last decades, at a time when multinational capital, not political debate, destabilizes the psychic and social frameworks of human connection. In earlier satiric plays (*Vinegar Tom*, 1976; *Cloud Nine*, 1979), Churchill drew inspiration from socialist feminist critiques of patriarchy and imperialism. In *Fen* (1983) and *Serious Money* (1987), and later in *The Skriker* (1994) and *Far Away* (2000), Churchill explores a darker emotional zone: what her Skriker drolly calls 'feeling global'.

These days the term 'globalization' has all but lost any resemblance to the McLuhanesque utopia of a world made closer and more harmonious through technology (McLuhan 1964, 1967). Globalization now denotes the rapid, internet-driven integration of markets around the world such that national economies and workforces are subsumed by supra-national circuits of financial activity. This intensified form of capitalism – some call it 'turbo capitalism' – has expanded the reach of western power across regions and continents into distant locales, fuelling reactionary politics and divisiveness, and exacerbating, rather than relieving, the miseries of poverty (Luttwak 1999). For many ecologists, globalization means that nature is being 'pushed inexorably back by a rising tide of population, pollution, and developmental pressure' (Motavali 1999: 14). Since the 1980s globalization has been linked to our 'postmodern condition', of which there have been many interpreters. David Harvey describes the 1980s and 1990s as 'an intense phase of time-space compression' – the time taken to traverse space has shrunk more and more, which has accelerated the collapse of borders and facilitated cultural globalization (Harvey 1990: 284). Arjun Apparduri writes with measured admiration of the possibilities inherent when 'ideas, ideologies, people, goods, images, technologies and spatial flow across national borders seemingly independent of traditional constraints of information transfer [and] national regulation' (Apparduri 2001: 3). Saskia Sassen argues that the discourse of 'flows' submerges gender differences and charges us to ferret out the 'geography behind globalization', the global cities where capital circulates and the human infrastructure (often women's labour) that enables the flow (Sassen 2002: 257). Fredric Jameson describes the dystopian horror of 'our insertion as individual subjects into a multidimensional set of radically discontinuous realities, whose frames range from the still surviving spaces of bourgeois private life all the way to the unimaginable decentering of global capital . . . [This results in] the fragmented and schizophrenic decentering and dispersion' of the subject (Jameson 1991: 413). Yet for Hal Foster, this description of the postmodern is too 'spatialistic'. He focuses on the 'different speeds' as well as the 'mixed spaces of postmodern culture', and links the crisis of subjectivity to the way individuals experience time under conditions of globalization: 'There is no simple Now: every present is nonsynchronous, a mix of different times' (Foster 1993: 5).

This chapter will argue that Caryl Churchill, despite working in a theatre redolent of humanist tradition, recharges dramatic form such that audiences can apprehend the link between 'the still surviving spaces of bourgeois private life . . . [and] the unimaginable decentering of global capital itself'. Even before confronting global capital explicitly in *Serious Money* and *Fen*, Caryl Churchill found formal ways of grappling with the historical pain of fragmentation. In *Top Girls* (1982), she began the practice of modifying dramatic speech. With punctuation slashes, she signals moments when characters interrupt and overlap each other's speech, such that (the illusion of) individual subjectivity dissolves into near-cacophonic vocalizations. And Churchill's plays are at times aggressively non-synchronous. *Traps* (1977) uncouples the fantasy of forward-moving dramatic time from the 'real time' of a clock on the wall. Clock time advances, but dramatic time slips back or skips ahead unpredictably, and a given stage encounter, while internally logical, cannot be placed in sequence, hence is impossible to apprehend as coherent action. In *Cloud Nine* time shifts are politically revelatory. Collapsing Victorian time with the mid-1970s – that is, stipulating that a hundred years pass between Acts I and II, while the characters age only 25 years – the play provides a vision of gender structuration over the long durée. And *Vinegar Tom* intercalates scenes of seventeenth-century witch-hunting with contemporary rock and feminist lyrics, showing the long legacy of the demonization of women.

In effect Churchill calibrates dramatic time to the complexity of her historical moment. Here she echoes Brecht's 'historicization', his technique of widening the spectator's perception by revealing the constructedness of the present and its dialectical relation to the past. *Serious Money* begins with a scene in full Restoration dress from Thomas Shadwell's *The Stockjobbers* (1692), a play that satirizes the sharp practices of members of the Stock Exchange who 'turn[ed] a penny' by dealing in

stocks on behalf of themselves or their clients. According to Corfield and Harte, by
the late seventeenth century England was 'subordinated to the capitalists' and the
burgeoning economic growth of London was unbalancing the economy of England as
a whole.[1] No sooner do Shadwell's bewigged stockjobbers leave the stage than
Churchill's satire on the greed of contemporary stock traders and corporate raiders
roars into life – or rather LIFFE (pronounced 'life'), the London International Financial Futures Exchange, under whose banner the action occurs. A tour de force in fancy
iambics, *Serious Money* makes the Brechtian gesture of educating its audience: we learn
that after 'the Big Bang' – the deregulation of the London stock market in October
1986 – capital investment boomed and old ways of conducting business almost
instantly died. As the elder trader Frosby regretfully explains: 'Since Big Bang the
floor is bare, / They deal in offices on screens. / But if the chap's not really there / You
can't be certain what he means' (Churchill 1987: 29). Turbo capitalism trounces old-
boy networks, and the culture of disconnection reverberates in the larger economy.
Historian Perry Anderson writes that after deregulation London, already a global
financial centre, became 'denationalized . . . no longer merely disconnected from domestic industry but . . . estranged from any linkage with the national economy at all'.[2]
Indeed British manufacturing declined after deregulation, generating lay-offs and
bankruptcies. Then as now, London's wealth did not raise the country's prosperity, but
as Shadwell's stockjobbers show us, traders deal in greed, not fairness.

Churchill's traders ply the phones and their rapid-fire dialogue imitates instantaneous computerized transactions, while their feverish competition is expressed in Ian
Drury's obscene lyrics at the end of Act I: 'Money-making money-making money-
making caper / Do the fucking business do the fucking business do the fucking
business / And bang it down on paper' (ibid.: 61). The upper-crust Grevilles mingle
with the brash 'oiks' on the floor, and a British corporate raider plans a hostile
takeover of a traditional British company, appropriately named Albion, with the
help of young Jake Greville's insider-trading tips and World Bank funds siphoned off
by Jaccinta Condor, a Peruvian copper heiress who bribes the CIA and launders her
money through an American arbitrageur. In other words global financial activity is
inevitably criminal activity, but only if you get caught holding the bag. Enacted in
flashbacks, the plot turns on Jake's death, or suicide, but his sister Scilla's search for
the facts so piques her own ambition that she loses interest in the truth and seeks only
a piece of the serious money Jake was leveraging. By the end she has joined Marylou
Baines, the Ivan-Boesky-like arbitrageur, to become a 'rising star' on Wall Street. In
the play's final moments the cast unites on-stage to celebrate the re-election of
Margaret Thatcher's Tories: 'Five more glorious years . . . my new Ferrari has
just arrived, these pleasures stay unqualified . . . send her victorious for five fucking
morious / five more glorious years!' (ibid.: 111).

So what does *Serious Money* tell us about 'feeling global'? That depends on whether
one has, as gilts trader Grimes says, a 'feel for the market' (ibid.: 21). Sexual
assignations on the trading floor and in hotel lobbies are hilariously cross-switched
with the language of deal-making ('Zac, you're so charming. I'm almost as fond / Of

you as I am of a eurobond') (ibid.: 21). Fuelling the rush of sexy global feeling, banker Zackerman woos Jaccinta with exoticized, commodified nature – 'a small aviary...of parrots, cockatoos and lovebirds', for which he stipulates not bird compatibility but 'good bright colours' (ibid.: 34). Still, 'what really matters', says Zackerman, in an uncharacteristically unrhymed line, 'is the massive sums of money being passed round the world, and trying to appreciate their size can drive you mental' (ibid.: 109). Addressed to the audience, this line feels dialectical – it asks for a countervailing system. But, as is Churchill's wont, the play refuses to provide one. Where, then, are the consequences of globalization? In *Serious Money*, decidedly off-stage. Jake's unexplained death is made to stand for the mystified, silent numbers of global capital's road-kill, those who lose jobs across the world when corporations are taken over, closed or traded.

Four years earlier, Churchill subtly tackled globalization from the perspective of the powerless and the silenced. For this task, historicization, Brecht's means of educating spectators to understand historical change – and even perform it – was not enough. The year 1982 was a depressing one for the British left. The Falklands War gave Margaret Thatcher a huge victory in 1983 (and, as *Serious Money* predicted, it happened again in 1986), serving as endorsement of her politics of privatization. In 1982, Churchill read Michel Foucault's *Discipline and Punish* and found a discussion that helped explain what she was already interested in: the 'softer' methods by which discipline becomes part of an internal feedback system, a 'technology' of the body essential for the operations of modern society. Foucault was not endorsing political reform, but it is clear that the power relations he describes, which 'invest [the] body, mark it, train it, torture it, force it to carry out tasks, to perform ceremonies, to emit signs', are embedded in everyday social structures, from the family to schools, to the military, to cultural institutions and governments. In order to make human beings productive, society must first make us 'docile' (Foucault 1979). If Foucault was criticized for seeming to abolish agency and resistance, he was deeply suggestive to Churchill, for economic determinants alone could not explain the social inertia of Thatcherite Britain.

With *Fen* Churchill was remarkably prescient about globalization – the reach of finance capital across continents always has local effects, including the demand for docile productive bodies. In the first of its 28 scenes, a Japanese businessman appears, in 'a fen' and 'a fog', and in satirically clipped second-language English he recounts the history of this marshy region of East Anglia, making common cause with the 'rich lords...thinking men, brave investors' who hired a Dutchman to drain the swamps for agricultural production (Churchill 1983: 5). It wasn't easy: 'Wild people, fen tigers, King Charles wanted dry land...Fen people supported Cromwell. Didn't like drainage. Smashed dykes, broke sluices...Wanted to keep fishes and eels to live on, no vision...Problems. Windmills. Problems' (ibid.: 5). In a darkly comic demonstration of a history written by the winners he concludes: 'But in the end we have beautiful black earth. Very efficient, flat land, plough right up to the edge no waste. This farm, one of our twenty-five farms, very good investment. Belongs to Baxter

Noelsford Ltd. which belongs to Reindorp Smith Farm Land trust, which belongs 65% to our company.' The Japanese businessman is now among the new landowning aristocracy of 'Esso, Gallagher, Imperial Tobacco, Equitable Life [who] all love this excellent earth'. Because it's 'too foggy to take pictures', he heads for a 'teashop, warm fire, old countryman to tell us tales' (ibid.: 5).

Churchill is masterful at reducing history's amplitude to the language of blissful self-interest. Yet the businessman speech is rich in vivid, dialectical images: wild nature (tigers, eels) and regional myths (web-footed fen dwellers) are linked to an uprising against early modernity's entrepreneurs and, by implication, to today's multinational cartels. Capital's advance, fuelled by 'vision' and 'bravery', is the figure of Enlightenment progress that, 'in the end', results in 'efficient land management' and productivity (ibid.: 5). The 'rich lords' of old, whose dominion over their peasantry seemed eternal, give subtle ballast to the notion that the princely multi-national corporation may not rule forever. Nevertheless, local knowledge and folklore, unique to a region, have become fodder for cultural tourism: 'old countryman's tales' from a misty past to distract a jet-lagged corporate executive. In a visually stunning juxtaposition, the gap between over there and over here, foreign investment and local labour, the curtain rises, and with the businessman's reference to global capital ('Esso . . . Imperial Tobacco') freshly in mind, we meet the fen women *'working in a row, potato picking down a field'*, an immemorial image of peasant labour (ibid.: 5). As Saskia Sassen (2002) has shown, in every globalization story, poor women are the group most severely 'disciplined' as productive bodies. With no social or political means of resistance, Val and her 'gang' of labourers are dependent for subsistence wages on the farmer Tewson, who is himself bought out by foreign capital and forced to become a tenant on land owned by his family for generations.

Churchill never sentimentalizes her underdogs: in near monosyllabic exchanges between three generations of fen women, body-wracking labour and child-rearing chores form part of an endless cycle of denial, guilt and rage. When Churchill and her actors went to interview contemporary fen labourers, they heard of the women's pride in their toughness – they worked even with icicles on their cheeks – another testimony to the docility inscribed in Val and her co-workers. Val's lover Frank provides an even more alarming vision of internalized discipline, when he imagines himself slapping the boss, and slaps himself instead. The only escape for the women comes when narrative logic is upended: Val asks Frank to kill her since she is unable to choose between him and her children. He murders her with an axe, stuffs her in a cupboard, then she immediately walks out to describe, in contrast to the cyclical despair and inertia depicted in the play, a vivid swirl of undisciplined atemporal activity. Val: 'There's so much happening' (ibid.: 23). She describes a girl from 'a long time ago when they believed in boggarts' seeking sustenance from a revivifying earth. Nell crosses the stage on stilts, an image of the ancient fen people, and, no longer merely a 'trouble maker' and teller of grimly sadistic folk tales, she now defies nature with a new-found political agency: 'The sun spoke to me. It said, "Turn back, turn back." I said "I won't turn back for you or anyone" ' (ibid.: 24). In the wet fens, the weather changes at last from the misty and mystified fog of the opening to a salutary green mist, and Val's old mother, who wants to sing but never could, arrives and sings. But the 150-year-old ghost has no need of afterlife redemption. She confronts Tewson in scene nine after he sells the land: 'We are starving, we will not stand this no longer' (ibid.: 12). And when farmer and spectre agree that nothing will change for the poor when capital moves from private families to multinationals, Ghost pronounces a curse that, in typical Churchill fashion, gestures beyond individual agency: 'Get home then. I live in your house. I watch television with you. I stand beside your chair and watch the killings. I watch the food and I watch what makes people laugh. My baby died starving' (ibid.: 12). With these words, given to a ghost rather than a living person, Churchill reveals the complexity of ethical witness in a world where unregulated global capital moves effortlessly and, as the murders in *Fen* and *Serious Money* suggest, with fatal consequences.

Fen offers a treasure trove of images and ideas that inspired Churchill's treatment of globalization in *The Skriker*. In *Fen*, for the first time, she joins time shifts to a new kind of dramatic space, an atemporal zone after narrative death that makes room for a non-human spirit world of gods, legends and folklore. We might say that globalization, a world-shaping discourse, needs its own dramatic vocabulary, one that escapes too-strident registers of finger-pointing and protest. This is what Churchill finds in British folklore: a repository of types, motifs and narratives that are both local and infinitely extensible, reaching back to a region's earliest oral traditions but able, like global capital, to take on new shapes and traverse national borders. In a sense, folklore might be understood as the first global discourse, home-grown but dynamically mutating to accommodate the hungers and terrors of localities far from its place of origin. Of course traditional folk tales, dances and melodies travelled not instantaneously, by computer networks, but in the memories and gestures of the earliest travellers, both the voluntary adventurers and those suffering forced migrations (slaves, victims of religious or ethnic persecution). Yet they travelled, inexorably. Rawheadandbloodybones, an ancient Lancashire goblin in *The Skriker*, appears in the black American novelist Zora Neale Hurston's *Mules and Men* of 1936. Folklore is always on the move. It builds on motifs already laid down, but, like capitalism, is constantly innovating. Yet it carries connotations that seem the very obverse of capital. For Marx the dynamism of capital depends on a marketplace that mystifies or erases the social labour of commodity production. Folklore, by contrast, carries the patina of sturdy authenticity; its roots are deep in the soil of its locality, in its relation to nature and nature's continuities. Still, the continued life of folklore depends on its historical performers, those who recreate it with each recitation. Fairy tales belong to the present as well as the past.

This is, in any case, Churchill's rather brilliant wager: fairies and goblins and boggarts may belong to the misty nostalgic past, but they are too charged by their human creators with desire and meaning to stay there. If our historical existence under conditions of globalization is marked by temporal discontinuities and by the disruption of local communities and traditions, why not put such discontinuities on stage and let those erased traditions speak – and shriek? To put it another way, the historical force-field, which Brecht's drama foregrounded and made available for audience critique, has been modified by Churchill to include anti-rational forces: magic, possession and regular appearances of the hybrid and the non-human. These elements and figures are not used as stand-ins for ideological oppression, but rather as prosthetic figures of desire and *knowledge* unarticulable by individual subjects. For example, *Mouthful of Birds* (1986), a play of seven discrete stories involving contemporary Londoners, is invaded by Euripides' *The Bacchae*. That is, the terror and possession of the Bacchantes, Pentheus, Agave and Dionysos infect the contemporary characters, an infection that Churchill and her collaborator David Lan describe as 'something not invented by us or by Euripides . . . something that bursts from the past, *into* these people open to possession . . . first the voice of an a unquiet spirit telling of a murder, finally the murder itself happening as the climax to all their stories' (Churchill 1986: 5). In this play Dionysian possession is signalled not by dialogue but by dance, an expressive medium that slips the noose of rational discourse. In the penultimate scene, a stultifyingly hot day in an apartment block, two women cross the line from impotent rage into magical agency. While one reads out newspaper stories of horrific murders, these contemporary Bacchantes suddenly become capable of telepathically hurling objects and ejecting an intrusive male from their midst. In *Mad Forest* (1990), a play 'documenting' the confusion surrounding the bloody, if brief, Romanian revolution that led to the arrest and murder of Stalinist strong-man Nicolae Ceasescu and his wife, Churchill confines the paranormal to an archangel, a well-dressed vampire and a talking dog played by a trembling naked man. The vampire is drawn to the revolution by the smell of blood: 'You begin to want blood. Your limbs ache, your head burns, you have to keep moving faster and faster' (Churchill 1990: 50). The play shows, in snapshot-like scenes, the intertwining lives of two Romanian families (one working-class, the other middle-class) in the days before, during and after the revolution. In this new season of liberation, where the characters feel utterly uncertain about whether a revolution happened, or only a political putsch that installed another communist apparatchik, the archangel and the vampire appear to dance at a wedding that unites the families. Do these non-human wedding-crashers express a desire for moral guidance? For old-fashioned, blood-spilling revenge? Or is Churchill seeking to give theatrical shape to the irrational energy released in violent events, the frightening feeling of 'moving faster and faster' (ibid.), of being swept up and deposited in a new world order whose social arrangements are as yet undecided? The archangel and the vampire are out of temporal order, making the Romanian 'now' feel disturbingly, if exhilaratingly, non-synchronous.

The Skriker takes us further. Instead of gracefully lifting the veil of urban anomie to reveal metaphors of anti-social rage and mythic power (*Mouthful of Birds*), instead of a dapper Vampire commenting on the murderous thrill of revolution ('You begin to want blood'; ibid.), Churchill populates her stage with restless fairies, spirits, goblins and monsters led by the shape-shifting Skriker, 'ancient and damaged'. In the first moments of the play, Johnny Square foot, a pig-like, stone-throwing man, crosses a dark stage, then suddenly the Skriker rises from a trapdoor underworld, shrieking like the Lancashire goblin and death portent after which she is named. The Skriker's companions, as any compendium of British folklore reveals, are unequivocally malevolent – Yallery Brown (an evil fairy), Black Dog (the Skriker's other shape), Jennie Greenteeth (a bogey that drags children into ponds), Kelpie (a bogey/water-horse and body eater) and Rawheadandbloodybones (a water demon that drags children into ponds and devours them – in Samuel Johnson's dictionary, a 'spectre, mentioned to frighten children'; see Briggs 1976: 338–9). Outnumbered by hungry displaced fairies are two young women, Lily and Josie, the first pregnant, the second an infanticide, who, in swiftly moving scenes, interact with the Skriker as the latter morphs from old crone, to disturbed child, to loud American, to enraged male stalker. Hundreds of years old, the Skriker needs the young women's love – and blood – and, like dark fairies of legend, craves a human baby to regenerate an earth so damaged that not even fairy 'glamour' can hide its decay. Shouts the Skriker in her American shape: 'You people are killing me, do you know that? I am sick, I am a sick woman' (Churchill 1994: 15). While the Skriker enables Lily to spit coins and support herself and the baby, strange sickly spirits come and go, like after-images of ecological disaster. In the form of the male stalker, the Skriker dismisses all current chatter about environmental sensitivity or sustainable development:

> Have you noticed the large number of meteorological phenomena lately? Earthquakes. Volcanoes. Drought.... The increase of sickness. It was always possible to think whatever your personal problem, there's always nature. Spring will return even if it's without me. Nobody loves me but at least it's a sunny day. This has been a comfort to people as long as they've existed. But it's not available any more. Sorry. Nobody loves me and the sun's going to kill me. Spring will return and nothing will grow. (ibid.: 43–4)

'Postmodernism', writes Fredric Jameson, 'is what you have when the modernization process is complete and nature is gone for good' (Jameson 1991: ix). But the notion of 'gone for good' spurs Churchill to fresh invention. Bursting through barriers, ever mutating, manipulating the desire of Josie and Lily and turning them into consumers of fairy glamour, the Skriker incarnates, in the words of Deleuze and Guattari, 'the awesome schizophrenic accumulation of energy [in] capitalism' (Deleuze and Guattari 1983: 12). Like the television technology she tries to understand, the Skriker is both here *and* there; indeed, like capitalism, she is everywhere and *in* everyone. But if she figures capitalism's versatility and ubiquity, she also figures its pathology. The 'discontinuous realities' that fragment subjectivity are embedded in the Skriker's speech. Language has always been Churchill's subtle register for pain and confusion: here she writes a kind of virtual double-talk wherein the last word of one phrase becomes the switch point for another, such that discontinuous realities are continually created:

> Revengeance is gold mine, sweet. Fe fi fo fumbledown cottage pie crust my heart and
> hope to die. My mother she killed me and put me in pies for sale away and home and
> awayday. Peck out her eyes have it. I'll give you three wishy washy. An open grave must
> be fed up you go like dust in the sunlight of heart. Gobble gobble says the turkey
> turnkey key to my heart, gobbledegook de gook is after you. Ready or not here we come
> quick or dead of night night sleep tightarse. (Churchill 1994: 5)

Amid the witty cacophony of alliterative echoes, rhymes, obscenities and biblical and
proverbial puns, the Skriker's multiple semantic worlds convey torrents of feeling.
Certainly her pain is as palpable as her rage. She impersonates the Christian God
('Vengeance is mine') but also the dead child put in pies, and 'pie crust' blurs into the
clichéd but suicidal 'crust my heart and hope to die'. The open grave of a depleted
earth must be 'fed', yet 'fed up', the spirits seek 'revengeance' for their damage (the
gobbledegook – the Skriker's own speech? – is after you). 'Dust in the sunlight of
heart' foreshadows the death of Lily, for a common motif of fairy tales is that a mortal
who has visited fairy land will, upon return, eat mortal food and turn immediately to
dust. It is indeed tempting to label the circuit-switching in the Skriker's discourse as
'schizoid' – the term popularized by Deleuze and Guattari and reused by Jameson to
mean a break in the signifying chain of conventional speech, leaving 'a rubble
of distinct and unrelated signifiers' (Deleuze and Guattari 1983: 1–9, 273–382;
Jameson 1991: 28ff., 297–418). But in the Skriker's garbled speech, there are
relations and associations and affective if not logical meanings. Bits of fairy tales
and high and popular culture sit beside, and inside, signifiers of everyday life to
render a comic and terrible vision of the end of things: 'Everything gone with the
window cleaner' (Churchill 1994: 3).

We should not be surprised that Churchill was particularly attracted to the
temporal disorder in fairy land:

> I got very taken with … fairy stories [in which] two different things happen with time
> when fairies take people off to the underworld. One is where you go off and you think
> you've spent years and years and it's actually the same second. And the other is […]
> where you think […] you've only been away a second and when you come home it's a
> hundred years later and everyone is dead.[3]

The fairy-land conceit allows Churchill to explore simultaneity: like the instantaneous
signals of televisual existence, we are here and there. Yet the worlds are not the same.
While the 'human' world is visibly depleted, the fairy underworld is set as an opera
with a banquet table covered in glamour – that is, fairy enchantment – not unlike
Marx's phantasmagoria of commodities which lure Josie. But because the underworld
is dependent on the human world, the fairy glamour is *'not working – some of the food is
twigs, leaves, beetles, some of the clothes are rags, some of the beautiful people have a claw hand
or hideous face'* (Churchill 1994: s.d., 29). Josie, though she asked to come, refuses to
eat, for to eat means to stay. The Skriker urges:

Don't you want to feel global warm and happy every after? Warm the cackles of your heartless. Make you brave and rave. Look at the colourful, smell the tasty. Won't you drink a toasty with me, Josie, after all we've done for? *JOSIE drinks.* (ibid.: 30)

Warmth and sensuous beauty now belong to the 'global', to the underworld. There is no other discourse, thus no resistance to its discipline. The young women can neither leave the Skriker nor survive her. To experience the goblin's fake nurture is to accept utter temporal disconnection, to lose not only one's past life, but the possibility of a future where conditions might be changed. Josie experiences the first kind of fairy time-warp – she believes she has been gone for a lifetime but returns to find that not one second has elapsed – and the feeling of discontinuous realities, a postmodern nightmare writ large, tortures her. That the gentle Lily suffers the other temporal trick – 'where you think . . . you've only been away a second and when you come home it's a hundred years later and everyone is dead' – is Churchill's decisive judgement on the ameliorative possibilities of kindness and love. There is no saving this world: Lily is greeted by her granddaughter, now an ancient woman, and her deformed great-great-granddaughter, who *'bellows wordlessly at Lily'*. Her past gone, her future stolen, Lily eats a mortal sandwich and, in the words of the Skriker who concludes this ghastly tale, 'she was dustbin' (ibid.: 52).

Far Away must serve as our conclusion. Churchill has written a chilling postscript to the social conditions of global capital run amok. No more goblins heralding a decaying nature, but in their place a fully rationalized and disciplined world population engaged in a global war in which animals, birds, humans, nations, insects and even the weather are 'mobilized' for mutual extermination. Voices of moral witness – the girl Joan questioning her aunt about the prisoners she sees being herded from a truck to a barn and beaten bloody by her uncle – are silenced by lies. (But Churchill knows her audience will recall television images of ethnic cleansing or of the brutal treatment of migrant labourers.) The next scenes show capitalism's beginnings in cottage industry (without the cottage), but here the girl, now grown, has become an expert designer of hats to be worn by prisoners on their way to execution. A dazzling scene follows showing a stage full of bloodied prisoners on parade, each wearing a hand-crafted, unique, ostentatious hat, a parody of the individuality that has been taken from them. Churchill's plays never feature artists, but in *Far Away*, aesthetic questions – should hats be abstract or representational? – and thus her own labour are implicated in global destruction. And this self-criticism should not surprise us. To penetrate the meaning of our historical existence is to attempt to connect the familiar (family, work, love, death) to the 'far away' and unimaginable, like the 'massive sums of money being passed around the world'. To see these connections might, as Zackerman in *Serious Money* puts it, 'drive us mental' (Churchill 1987: 109). But in the presence of Churchill's prodigious theatrical imagination we will enjoy the journey, laughing out loud through clenched teeth.

Ben Tyler-Wray in the silent parade scene of Churchill's *Far Away*, directed by Mary Luckhurst, York Theatre Royal, 2005. Photo: Rob Weaver

Jim Stevenson, Kai Low, Alex Crampton, Fran Trewin, Fiona Cooper and Lewis Charlesworth in the silent parade scene of Churchill's *Far Away*, directed by Mary Luckhurst, York Theatre Royal, 2005. Photo: Rob Weaver.

NOTES

1 P. J. Corfield and N. B. Harte (eds.) (1990). *London and the English Economy 1500–1700.* London: Hambledon Press, 135, cited in Judith Bailey Slagle (1996). 'Shadwell's *Volunteers* through the Centuries: Power Structures Adapted in Scott's *Peveril of the Peak* and Churchill's *Serious Money*', *Restoration: Studies in English Literary Culture, 1660–1700*, 20:2, 237.

2 Perry Anderson (1992). *English Questions.* London: Verso, 181, cited in Linda Kintz's fine 1999 essay, 'Performing Capital in Caryl Churchill's *Serious Money', Theatre Journal* 51:3, 253.

3 Caryl Churchill in interview with Nicholas Wright (1996), excerpted from 'The Platform Discussion at the Royal National Theatre of Great Britain', *Public Access* 2:7, 40, cited in Diamond (1997: 100).

PRIMARY READING

Churchill, Caryl (1982). *Top Girls.* London: Methuen.

Churchill, Caryl (1983). *Fen.* London: Methuen.

Churchill, Caryl (1985). *Caryl Churchill Plays One: Traps, Vinegar Tom, Cloud Nine.* London: Methuen.

Churchill, Caryl (1986). *Mouthful of Birds.* London: Methuen.

Churchill, Caryl (1987). *Serious Money.* London: Methuen.

Churchill, Caryl (1990). *Mad Forest.* London: Nick Hern.

Churchill, Caryl (1994). *The Skriker.* London: Nick Hern.

Churchill, Caryl (2001). *Far Away.* New York: Theatre Communications Group.

FURTHER READING

Appadurai, Arjun (ed.) (2001). *Globalization.* Durham, NC: Duke University Press.

Aston, Elaine (1997). *Caryl Churchill.* Plymouth: Northcote House.

Briggs, Katherine (1976). *A Dictionary of Fairies, Hobgoblins, Brownies, Bogies and Other Supernatural Creatures.* London: Allen Lane.

Deleuze, Gilles and Guattari, Felix (1983). *Anti-Oedipus: Capitalism and Schizophrenia.* Minneapolis: University of Minnesota Press.

Diamond, Elin (1997). *Unmaking Mimesis: Essays on Feminism and Theatre.* London and New York: Routledge.

Foster, Hal (1993). 'Postmodernism in Parallax', *October 63*, 3–20.

Foucault, Michel (1979). *Discipline and Punish*, trans. Alan Sheridan. New York: Vintage.

Harvey, David (1990). *The Condition of Postmodernity.* Cambridge, MA, and Oxford: Blackwell.

Jameson, Fredric (1991). *Postmodernism or, The Cultural Logic of Late Capitalism.* Durham, NC: Duke University Press.

Kritzer, Amelia Howe (1991). *The Plays of Caryl Churchill: Theatre of Empowerment.* New York: St Martin's Press.

Luttwak, Edward (1999). *Turbo-Capitalism: Winners and Losers in the Global Economy.* New York: HarperCollins.

McLuhan, Marshall (1964). *Understanding Media.* London: Routledge.

McLuhan, Marshall (1967). *The Medium is the Massage: An Inventory of Effects.* New York: Random House.

Motavali, Joe (1999). '2000: Planet Earth at the Crossroads', repr. in Edward Moran (ed.). *The Global Ecology.* New York and Dublin: H. W. Wilson.

Nägele, Rainer (1988). *Benjamin's Ground.* Detroit, MI: Wayne State University Press.

Reinelt, Janelle (1994). *After Brecht: British Epic Theatre.* Ann Arbor: University of Michigan Press.

Sassen, Saskia (2002). 'Global Cities and Survival Circuits' in Barbara Ehrenreich and Arlie Hochschild (eds.). *Global Women: Nannies, Maids, and Sex Workers in the New Economy.* New York: Henry Holt.

Thurman, Judith (1982). 'Caryl Churchill: The Playwright Who Makes You Laugh about Orgasm, Racism, Class Struggle, Homophobia, Woman-Hating, the British Empire, and the Irrepressible Strangeness of the Human Heart', *Ms* (May), 51, 54, 57.

40

Howard Barker and the Theatre of Catastrophe

Chris Megson

Theatre might be viewed [. . .] as a de-civilizing experience, a series of permissions to transgress, an act of indiscipline or a mutiny whose forms are inverted reflections of conventional morality or moral speculations given entitlement of expression by virtue of the physical and emotional barriers separating it from the world.

Barker (1997: 110)

Howard Barker's theatre of challenging and unflinching moral exploration occupies a unique position in postwar European drama. Through four decades of sustained theatrical activity, his playwriting has moved from early experiments in social realism and satire that encapsulate his despair of parliamentary politics and the stagnation of state institutions, to a distinctive creed of tragedy, comprised of intense historical and metaphysical speculation, which finally attests to the transformative possibilities of sexual desire. Barker's plays are notoriously complex and replete with ambiguity, yet this should not eclipse their consummate theatrical accomplishment. His work is charged with stunning visual images that at once disturb and compel, with a sweeping poetic language, and with moments of brittle, frequently scatological comedy. Most distinctively, his plays attain theatrical force through their focus on protagonists whose insistent reach for self-definition catapults them beyond the socially regulated parameters of 'conventional morality'.

Since the late 1960s, Barker (b. 1946) has written over 70 plays for theatre, television and radio. Numerous collections of his work – including six volumes of poetry – have been published, many fronted with Barker's own drawings. *Arguments for a Theatre*, a key text in which he sets out the aesthetic and philosophical imperatives that have informed his dramaturgy, was first published in 1989 and has since been revised and expanded. The conjunction of intellectual rigour and theatrical ambition at the heart of Barker's playwriting has proved attractive to actors; indeed, it was a group of performers, led by Kenny Ireland and Hugh Fraser, who founded The Wrestling School in 1988 in order to counter the increasing neglect of Barker's work in the repertoires of British commercial and subsidized theatres alike. The Wrestling

School has its administrative offices in London, but it is effectively a 'buildingless' company solely committed to touring productions of Barker's plays. Funded by the Arts Council of England and representing a bond of allegiance between practitioners and playwright that is unrivalled in contemporary theatre, the company has made a major contribution to establishing Barker's reputation, especially in continental Europe. Since 1994 Barker has also directed numerous productions of his own plays for The Wrestling School – revivals as well as new work – throughout Europe and in Australia. The savage intensity of his stage poetry and his uncompromising approach to theatrical representation have profoundly influenced the provocative aesthetics of younger dramatists who emerged in the 1990s, particularly Sarah Kane.

Yet in spite of his undoubted impact, the complexity and expansiveness that characterize Barker's dramatic worlds have ensured that, for many years, he has remained a controversial and isolated figure in British theatre culture. Often his work has been received with marked circumspection if not outright hostility by reviewers and, with occasional exceptions, has been rejected by major theatre establishments, most notoriously the National Theatre.[1] In the academy, he has been accused, variously, of promoting a reactionary 'mystical anarchism' (Gottlieb 1988: 103), of promulgating a 'cult of the author' (Shaughnessy 1989) and, in his disavowal of collective politics, of offering a dubious theatrical endorsement of neo-liberal individualism (Tomlin 2000). This is symptomatic of the fact that Barker's plays remain resistant to both definitive critical exegesis and easy political categorization, largely because they eschew the twin shibboleths that, in his view, have spavined much postwar British drama: namely, Stanislavskian naturalism and Brechtian dialectical theatre.

Instead, Barker's theatre is conceived as an unashamedly privileged and mysterious space where the force of the writer's imagination, aligned with the skills and commitment of the actor, work to corrode received moral and political pieties: 'I would like to propose', Barker has written, 'that the value of works of art, in social circumstances such as the present, lies not in their entertainment value, nor in their ability to "change perceptions" in pursuit of some common purpose, but in their power to devastate the received wisdom of the collective, which conspires to diminish individual experience at all levels' (Barker 1997: 93). In his mature plays, spectators are exposed to the transformation that occurs when an individual's will to action, fermented within scenarios of crisis, collides with the habitual moral or ideological prohibitions of liberal humanist society. If this is the philosophical terrain of Barker's drama, then it has inexorably brought his playwriting into the orbit of tragedy – the only form of theatre, in his view, which takes moral revaluation as its first principle. His signal achievement is to have developed and theorized a new paradigm for contemporary tragedy, the 'Theatre of Catastrophe', which aims to inculcate a state of anxiety in the audience, an anxiety that is a precondition for witnessing the moral dislocation that lies at the heart of his drama.[2]

Barker's gravitation towards Catastrophism originated in a distrust of political ideology that emerged gradually from his deeply felt despair with the failures of Wilsonian social democracy in the 1960s and, later, with the populist reflexes of successive Thatcherite governments in the 1980s. His early work in the 1970s, much of it unpublished, is responsive to the political retrenchment of the left at a time of intensifying industrial crisis and class conflict. One such example, *Edward, the Final Days* (1972), is an extended theatrical lampoon on Edward Heath, the then prime minister, and is described by Barker as 'my best piece of unadulterated satire [...] heaving out of the pain of an oppressed English youth' (Hay and Trussler 1981: 5). Like those of Howard Brenton and others of the iconoclastic, post-1968 theatrical generation, Barker's early plays are shot through with mordant satire and sanguine comedy that register a profound disillusionment at the failing prospects of revolutionary socialism, in a moribund political culture marked by institutional ossification and intellectual recidivism.

While Barker's facility for penetrating wit and linguistic dexterity found an early outlet in satire, it is, more fundamentally, the tension between 'the ambiguous state of power, its mediation, [and] the complicity of victims' that is calibrated in much of his early playwriting (Dunn 1984: 34). In this respect, *Claw* (1975) represents the first major turning point in Barker's trajectory: although the satiric impulse is strong in the first two acts of this play, its final scene is characterized, presciently, by what Lamb calls 'tragic intensity' (Lamb 2005: 12). Set in working-class south London, the play focuses on Noel Biledew – born illegitimately during the war and held in contempt by his Marxist father – who sets himself up as a pimp for Nora, a fiery young communist. The two are immediately victimized by a policeman, which prompts Noel to rename himself 'Claw' and seek vengeance on the establishment. He begins procuring for Clapcott, one of the sardonic and languidly corrupt politicians who figure in Barker's plays of the 1970s, but subsequently becomes obsessed with the minister's wife, Angie. Their sexual liaison in a lay-by threatens her husband's career, and she eventually betrays Noel, who is forcibly interned in an institution for the mentally ill. Motivated by a vision of his dying father, Noel pleads for clemency in a powerful oration directed at his two psychotic guards:

> Because our little squabbles and our playground fights and little murders in the entrances of flats are hardly crimes compared to that crime they are working on us, all of us driven mad by their brutality and no coppers to protect us against their claws! Their great claw, slashing us, splitting our people up, their great claws ripping our faces and tearing up our streets, their jaguars feeding on our lazy herds! (*Pause*) And we have nothing except each other. Our common nothingness [...] (*Pause*) Defend me. Don't murder me. (Barker 1990a: 71).

This startling denouement raises and then dashes the possibility of redemption in a situation that becomes manifestly hopeless. His appeal for class allegiance falls on deaf ears: a bath is lowered onto the stage, Noel undresses, and is then drowned by his two wardens. This lengthy sequence, at once disturbing and visually electrifying, unfolds without any dialogue. After the subsequent blackout, the lights are raised briefly on Clapcott addressing the House of Commons: he dismisses Noel's death as accidental and attributes it, with a carefully honed sense of the banal, to 'staff shortages' (ibid.:

72). As one contemporary reviewer put it, '[*Claw*] is a piece which says more about the state of England than anything John Osborne has written in many a long day.'[3]

Claw prefigures Barker's later theatrical preoccupations in a number of significant ways. The focus on endemic corruption in state institutions, the crushing effects of hegemonic power on the individual, and the infelicity of conventional class rhetoric in addressing new political realities throws into relief the degradation and impotency of political ideals in a postwar society seemingly mired in intractable decline. These concerns resurface in Barker's next tranche of work, dating from 1975 to the production of *Downchild* 10 years later, which offers a robust theatrical dissection of 'the state of England'. Unlike the contemporaneous plays written by Howard Brenton, David Edgar and Trevor Griffiths, Barker's plays of the late 1970s and early 1980s – including *That Good Between Us* (1977), *The Love of a Good Man* (1978) and *The Hang of the Gaol* (1978) – are not orthodox social realist plays driven by an engagement with historical dialectics and an impulse to foster debate on pressing topical issues. Instead, they deliberate on, as Barker puts it, the 'melancholy of defused ambitions rather than any rage that might attach to them'.[4]

Barker's 'state-of-England' dramas generally instantiate a recognizable socio-political milieu, embedding heightened satirical elements within quasi-realistic scenarios. However, they also dispense categorically with the characteristic tropes and preoccupations of theatrical naturalism. The strategic rupturing of naturalism is primarily achieved through Barker's fragmented dramatic structure, his deployment of an intensely concentrated form of poetic dialogue and his unusual choice of settings. Structurally, while there is narrative cohesion in these plays, the action is splintered into short, episodic scenes punctuated, variously, by monologues, voice-overs and, in the case of *A Passion in Six Days* (1983), songs and choric interludes. The effect of this is deliberately disruptive and disorientating, compelling spectators to aggregate associative correspondences between sequences that are not always linked explicitly by the linear progression of plot. Barker's approach to dialogue, meanwhile, is best exemplified in the opening exchange of *The Hang of the Gaol*, in which Cooper, the governor of Middenhurst prison, and his wife ruminate on the possible causes of a devastating fire in C Block. The action commences, unforgettably, with the duo surveying the ruins:

COOPER: A bucket-shitter did this. In some kidney of the wing. In some pissy, toxic corner of the night. Plotted it. Just look.
JANE: Taxpayer's ulcer bursts. John Betjeman prostrate with shock.
COOPER: My lovely ringing corridors of English iron. Struck sparks off the heels of warders' boots.
JANE: Probably what started it.

(Barker 1982a: 9)

The dialogue crackles with an incandescent emotional force and shrapnel-like velocity that place it at some distance from the measured mimetic cadences of naturalist speech. Barker has said of his playwriting that 'within a scene or two [the audience] is invited to discard its normal assumptions about the manner in which reality is reproduced' (Barker 1997: 29). In this respect, the expansive settings of this play – ranging from the burned-out shell of C Block to the isolated moors surrounding the prison – are similarly axiomatic of Barker's shift towards a more overtly metaphoric and elliptical register of writing. For him, the outright rejection of the hermetic domestic carapace within which most naturalist drama is contained – a manoeuvre that he has since described as the 'effective banning of the room' from his playwriting – is part of a much broader theatrical mission:

> There are rooms in my plays but they are peculiar rooms, rarely domestic and usually varieties of torture chambers [. . .] There are gymnasiums, banqueting halls, castles, burned-out gaols, but few domestic interiors. Unconsciously, I was resisting the reconciliation that the home enforces, for behind all domestic drama lies the spectre of reconciliation. Once the walls were taken down and the home abolished, imagination was liberated and speculation became possible. (Barker 1997: 33)

Unsurprisingly, then, these 'state-of-England' plays are studded throughout with set-piece iconic sequences that breach the boundaries of naturalism in order to adumbrate fully Barker's sense of English political malaise. Such moments range from the darkly comic ceremonial of the Ancient Order of Savages that opens *The Loud Boy's Life* (whose upper-crust members, as one of the attendant waiters pithily observes, 'drop pound notes like dung at a gymkhana'; Barker 1982b: 13) and the hoisting of a prostitute's skirt as the flag of 'New England' in *Crimes in Hot Countries* (1983), to the vertiginous rhetorical tirades of police inspector Croydon and his coup-plotting fascistic cabal in *Birth on a Hard Shoulder* (1982). Barker's acknowledged sense of a bitter 'melancholy' born from profound despair reaches an apotheosis in the desolating accusation levelled at the corrupted civil servant Jardine at the end of *The Hang of the Gaol*: 'England', asserts Matheson, his colleague, 'brings you down at last' (Barker 1982a: 82). While Barker is not the only member of his generation of playwrights to give theatrical expression to the failures of English, and particularly leftist, politics at the end of the 1970s, the stark pessimism that rises from his plays is unmatched in the drama of this period. Barker's achievement, however, is to make the experience of pessimism theatrically exhilarating.

In a landmark interview for *Theatre Quarterly*, published in 1981, Barker elaborated on his frustration more fully: 'The tension in the plays often comes from knowing what I don't like, what offends my sensibilities, but at the same time not being able to pose an alternative' (Hay and Trussler 1981: 7). Indeed, it is precisely this sense of political disillusionment tilting into existential despair that infuses the triptych of plays written in the early 1980s – *The Loud Boy's Life* (1980), *A Passion in Six Days* (1986) and *Downchild* (1985). In their evocation of suffocating English parochialism and errant politicians hamstrung within an interminably reformist party political culture, these plays work cumulatively to strip away the delusions that oxygenate political idealism, contrasting this with the radically destabilizing force of sexual passion. Importantly, it is the dynamics of sexual desire, and its painful but redemptive possibilities, which furnished Barker with the requisite 'alternative' subject matter that propelled his theatre away from contemporary political realities, towards historical speculation and, ultimately, tragedy, in the 1980s.

Barker offers his own retrospective rationale for his rejection of satire and realism in the following terms:

> I had discerned that what I required was a narrative about the *evasion* of authority and not the exercise of authority. Until then, English political types figured extensively in my work because the failure to be heroic – surely what characterized all English politics in the 1970s – brought these individuals into the scope of satire. I was a satirist because I was trying to evade social realism. I had not found an aesthetic that would edge me beyond satire, and when I found it, the objects of the satire disappeared with it.[5]

The evolution of such an aesthetic, which Barker describes as a gradual, chaotic and instinctive process, is set out in *Arguments for a Theatre*. In this compilation of articles, essays and polemical provocations, Barker contends that the proliferation of mega-musicals and the unremitting adherence to naturalism in contemporary theatre has eviscerated its capacity to engage an audience in speculative inquiry. Both the commercial West End and the subsidized theatres (it is notable that Barker reserves particular rhetorical firepower for the Royal Court) have flattered the liberal predilections of the audience by pandering routinely to the mantras of 'accessibility' and 'clarity' that are the sanctified watchwords of left and right alike. Catastrophist tragedy, in this context, is posited as an uncompromising riposte to an increasingly shrill, homogenized and market-driven theatre culture held in thrall to Thatcherite populism, and too often content to shore up the stultifying shibboleths of liberal humanist ideology. In Barker's final analysis, this has worked to shrink the scope of the spectator's imagination and delimit the radical expressive potential of the actor working on complex text in performance.

Barker's writings on theatre, to be sure, are occasionally sustained by an admixture of hyperbolic conceit and sheer epigrammatic panache that can make an evaluation of his claims, especially about the ecology of contemporary theatre and the impact of his work in performance, problematic. This is a deliberate strategy, opening up much of his theoretical writing to the free play of interpretative possibility that characterizes his plays. The challenge he makes is to establish terms for a new kind of tragic theatre, a theatre that addresses not an 'audience' as such (the singularity of the word implies a misleading notion of assumed solidarity), but a gathering of potentially divided spectators who are drawn to the work of necessity and whose relationship with it is uneasy, wholly unpredictable, but marked fundamentally by a willingness to collaborate in the imagined enactment of 'feelings [. . .] explored beyond the point of social legitimacy' (Barker 1997: 143). Scholarship on Barker, which has proliferated only in the past 15 or so years, is beginning to test the viability and implications of these claims. None the less, Barker's playwriting has sought consistently to undermine the expectations of its spectators by confronting them with narrative complexity and ambiguity of meaning: 'In a culture now so rampantly populist that the cultural distinctions between left and right have evaporated, the public have a right of access to a theatre which is neither brief nor relentlessly uplifting, but which insists on complexity and pain, and the beauty that can only be created from the spectacle of pain' (Barker 1997: 54).

If the 'spectacle of pain' is the aesthetic preoccupation of the Theatre of Catastrophe, then it attains a dramatic focus in the travails of the desiring subject. In this respect, his work finds a corollary in the taxonomy of desire rendered with acute perspicacity by Roland Barthes in *A Lover's Discourse* (1990, first published 1977). In this study, Barthes offers a dissection of the various discourses that constitute the desiring – or, in his formulation, 'amorous' – subject. Barthes notes that the lover experiences desire and attempts to comprehend it, in chaotic 'fragments of discourse' which he calls '*figures*' (Barthes 1990: 3). He posits that these figures are, in essence, 'gymnastic or choreographic' – 'gesture[s] caught in action' (ibid.: 3–4) – which, since they are mediated through the body, have indelible signifying properties that are intrinsically performative. Barthes proceeds to identify a range of specific figures in his analysis, but it is useful to isolate three in particular. The first, introduced as 'I am engulfed, I succumb', is described as an 'Outburst of annihilation which affects the amorous subject in despair or fulfillment [*sic*]' (ibid.: 10). Intriguingly, another of Barthes's figures is labelled 'Catastrophe': a 'Violent crisis during which the subject, experiencing the amorous situation as a definitive impasse, a trap from which he [*sic*] can never escape, sees himself doomed to total destruction' (ibid.: 48). Finally, a third figure is designated 'Ravishment': 'The supposedly initial episode (though it may be reconstructed after the fact) during which the amorous subject is "ravished" (captured and enchanted) by the image of the loved object (popular name: *love at first sight*; scholarly name: *enamoration*)' (ibid.: 188).

In essence, Barthes argues that the lover's discourse is comprised of an 'image repertoire' – a series of choreographed figures that map the complexion of desire at the moment of its performative exposure (ibid.: 4). These insights, I argue, help establish parameters for appraising how Barker negotiates similar concerns in his Catastrophist drama. In many of his mature plays, desire is (con)figured as an overwhelming impetus to action that destabilizes perceptions and compels the 'enamorated' subject to grope, blindly but determinedly, towards self-reconstruction. As Barker puts it: 'What lies behind the idea of catastrophe is the sense of other varieties of the self repressed or obscured by politics, social convention, or simple fear' (Barker 1997: 194). However, this process, which is the substance of tragedy and the effect of 'ravishment', brings the desiring subject into conflict with normative political mores to the point at which shameless transformation potentially affronts, even jeopardizes, the social order. *Judith* (1990), for example, is a short play which draws on the famous narrative of the Apocrypha. In Judith's attempted seduction and eventual murder of the loathed military leader Holofernes, ostensibly in the interests of national security, Barker traces the gradual emergence of her desire for him, which, as her Servant repeatedly opines, is politically untenable and so morally outrageous. The following words (spoken by Judith in an early exchange with

Holofernes), and the ensuing cavernous silence, offer a Catastrophist embodiment of Barthes's figure of 'Ravishment':

> Am I talking too much? You have revealed so much I feel I should also, but perhaps that's wrong. You might wish me to be silent. You might wish to imagine me rather than to know me. That is the source of desire, in my view. Not what we are, but the possibilities we allow to others to create us. Silence, for example. Might be judged as mystery. *(Long pause. They look at one another.)* (Barker 1990b: 55)

Barker's concern is not only to expose the extent to which the state routinely co-opts the body, sexualizing it and deploying it for strategic advantage, but to indicate that intoxicating 'enamoration' has the capacity to overwhelm ideological injunctions and repudiate its conscription by authority. In this, Judith herself is only partly successful, and the play enacts her struggle.

In the series of ground-breaking plays written by Barker in the 1980s, the 'image repertoire' of his desiring subjects is played out in the shadow of seismic historical convulsion: *Victory* (1983) is set in the aftermath of the Restoration, *The Power of the Dog* (1984) during the Soviet advance on Poland at the end of World War II, while *The Castle* (1985) commences with the return of a beleaguered group of Crusaders to their (unrecognizable) homestead. Importantly, these plays are marked by their refusal of documentary approaches to the staging of historical material. Barker's interest is not to 'reconstruct' history dramatically, but to subject its constitutive discourses, and their deleterious effects on the individual, to voracious imaginative scrutiny. The historical framework of these plays establishes a context of unthinkable extremity within which the provisionality and instability of humanist ethics can be gradually tested and laid bare. This, in effect, enables Barker to locate ostensibly irrational behaviour – what he calls moments of 'wrong action' (Barker 1997: 59) – at the centre of the theatrical experience. These are moments when characters, fortified by their proximity to Barthes's 'Catastrophe', insist on choices that directly and defiantly contravene prevailing ideological orthodoxies. In so doing, Barker's protagonists struggle to resist the absorption of their experiences by forms of authority: Katrin, for example, surrenders her child to the Turks at the end of *The Europeans* (1987) in order to confound attempts by the triumphalist state to recast her suffering within the grand narratives of imperial history, while, in *The Possibilities* (1988), Barker sets out a series of crisis situations in which the socialized conscience disintegrates and 'wrong action' becomes, shockingly, not only viable and legitimate but potentially seductive.

Consequently, Barker's Theatre of Catastrophe is marked by a denial of reconciliation, of the appropriation or amelioration of pain, which he discerns to be a staple ingredient of humanist tragic form. The reinscription of the social order that concludes classical tragedy is, for Barker, nothing less than a suspect moral capitulation to the hegemonic ethical values that the protagonist has been compelled to transgress. His plays, in contrast, resist closure largely because his characters cling to their suffering as the principal catalyst of their own transformation. With this in mind, Barker has subjected a series of talismanic canonical plays to Catastrophist renegotiation. These include a version of Middleton's *Women Beware Women* (1986) and, more recently, his 'annexation' of *Hamlet*, entitled *Gertrude – The Cry* (2002). The latter, in placing the emphasis squarely on the 'fatal eroticism' that binds Hamlet's mother to Claudius, stands directly counter to Shakespeare's 'sketchily-described' Gertrude, 'soddened with shame and regret'.[6] As its title indicates, Gertrude's reiterated 'cry' is both the auditory sign of her all-consuming 'enamoration' and the leitmotif of the play. Perhaps Barker's most spectacular reworking, however, is his *(Uncle) Vanya* (1996), which is set in an abstracted domestic space that gradually but tellingly falls apart: early on, there are ominous sounds of wood splintering and glass breaking, and the iconic veranda itself subsides (Barker 1993b: 311). Later, we hear falling masonry and a desolating wind cutting through what, in the final sequence of the play, has become 'the ruins of the house' (ibid.: 338). In demolishing the repressive domestic patina that, for Barker, prevents Chekhov's characters from acting on their own latent desires, the play also, of course, literally collapses the infrastructure upholding the naturalist visual aesthetic. Amongst the rubble, and in a strident assertion of Nietzschean will power, Vanya's final, and indeed heroic, act is to evacuate the domestic space. Barker has written of his contempt for 'the odour of the Chekhovian room, stale with frustrated decision and annihilated will' (Barker 1997: 168), and, indeed, Vanya's exodus is so profoundly disruptive that it triggers a splintering of his conditioned identity: '**Where am I going**', he finally cries, '**Where am I**' (Barker 1993b: 341). Barker's comment (1997: 170) on the metaphoric significance of this sequence penetrates to the core of his formal and philosophical priorities: 'what is the price that must be paid to leave the room, rather than describing the melancholy of remaining in it'?

Barker's versatility as a theatre artist is demonstrated in the prolific range of work that he has produced in recent years. This includes plays for marionettes, *All He Fears* (1993) and *The Swing at Night* (2001); a one-woman monologue, *Und* (1999); and large-scale kaleidoscopic pieces of stunning poetic density, most notably *The Ecstatic Bible* (2000). Throughout this period, he has also developed a distinctive signature as a director with The Wrestling School in productions marked by meticulously choreographed composition, austere expressionist design and discordant, unsettling soundscapes. His is a theatre of savagery and sensuousness, poetry and 'ravishment', which exposes disorder as the primary condition of social and individual experience. His most recent collection of writings, *Death, the One and the Art of Theatre* (2005), affirms the subversive erotic appeal of tragedy and the insuperable longing for dissolution that underscores the encounter with 'the One', the desired other. It is a text that further corroborates Barker's enduring sense of the disturbing but ultimately exquisite capacity of theatre to push the limits of human tolerance and understanding:

> In the *art of theatre* beauty is characterized by its brevity, its instability, its *ill-health*. Whereas death is the nightmare of cheerless democracies, abolished from consciousness by the nauseating complicity of medicine and leisure, death in *the art of theatre* is the

condition of beauty and anxiety the price of its revelation. Would you be seduced effortlessly? (Barker 2005: 25–6)

NOTES

1 None of Barker's plays has been staged at the National Theatre, a fact that has attracted much critical comment, most recently from Lamb (2005: 158).
2 Barker sets out the principles of his Theatre of Catastrophe in *Arguments for a Theatre* (1989, 3rd edn. 1997). See, in particular, 'Beauty and Terror in the Theatre of Catastrophe' (55–60) and 'The Deconse-

cration of Meaning in the Theatre of Catastrophe'(79–84).
3 Jack Tinker, *Daily Mail* 31 January 1975.
4 Howard Barker, letter to the author, 13 October 1996.
5 Ibid.
6 Programme note by Howard Barker, *Gertrude the Cry*, Wrestling School (dir. Howard Barker, 2002), n.p.

PRIMARY READING

Barker, Howard (1980). *That Good Between Us/ Credentials of a Sympathiser*. London: John Calder.

Barker, Howard (1982a). *The Hang of the Gaol & Heaven*. London: John Calder.

Barker, Howard (1982b). *Two Plays for the Right: The Loud Boy's Life & Birth on a Hard Shoulder*. London: John Calder.

Barker, Howard (1984). *Crimes in Hot Countries & Fair Slaughter*. London: John Calder.

Barker, Howard (1985). *A Passion in Six Days/ Downchild*. London: John Calder.

Barker, Howard (1990a). *Collected Plays. Vol. One* (includes *Claw, Victory, The Castle*). London: John Calder.

Barker, Howard (1990b). *The Europeans/Judith*. London: John Calder.

Barker, Howard (1993a). *All He Fears: A Play for Marionettes*. London: John Calder.

Barker, Howard (1993b). *Collected Plays. Vol. Two* (includes *The Love of a Good Man, The Possibilities, (Uncle) Vanya*). London: John Calder.

Barker, Howard (1996). *Collected Plays. Vol. Three* (includes *The Power of the Dog, The Europeans, Women Beware Women, Judith*). London: John Calder.

Barker, Howard (1997). *Arguments for a Theatre*, 3rd edn. Manchester: Manchester University Press.

Barker, Howard (1998). *Collected Plays. Vol. Four*. London: John Calder.

Barker, Howard (2001). *Collected Plays. Vol. Five* (includes *Und*). London: John Calder.

Barker, Howard (2002). *Gertrude – The Cry/Knowledge and a Girl*. London: John Calder.

Barker, Howard (2004). *The Ecstatic Bible: A New Testament*. London: Oberon.

Barker, Howard (2005). *Death, the One and the Art of Theatre*. London: Routledge.

FURTHER READING

Barnett, David (2001). 'Howard Barker: Polemic Theory and Dramatic Practice. Nietzsche, Metatheatre and the Play *The Europeans*', *Modern Drama* 44:4, 458–75.

Barthes, Roland (1990; first pub. 1977). *A Lover's Discourse*, trans. Richard Howard. London: Penguin.

Cornforth, Andy and Rabey, David Ian (2001). 'Kissing Holes for the Bullets: Consciousness in Directing and Playing Barker's *Uncle Vanya*', *Performing Arts International* 1:4, 25–45.

Donesky, Finlay (1986). 'Oppression, Resistance, and the Writer's Testament', *New Theatre Quarterly* 11:8, 336–44.

Dunn, Tony (ed.) (1984). *Gambit: International Theatre Review* (Howard Barker special issue) 11:41.

Gottlieb, Vera (1988). 'Thatcher's Theatre – Or After *Equus*', *New Theatre Quarterly* 4:14, 99–104.

Grant, Steve (1975). 'Barker's Bite', *Plays and Players* 23:3, 36–9.

Hay, Malcolm and Trussler, Simon (1981). 'Energy – and the Small Discovery of Dignity', *Theatre Quarterly* 10:40, 3–14.

Hutchings, William (1988). ' "Creative Vandalism": Or, a Tragedy Transformed – Howard Barker's "Collaboration" with Thomas Middleton on the 1986 Version of *Women Beware Women*' in Karelisa Hartigan (ed.). *Text and Presentation*. Maryland: Lanham, 93–101.

Klotz, Günther (1991). 'Howard Barker: Paradigm of Postmodernism', *New Theatre Quarterly* 7:25, 20–6.

Lamb, Charles (1984). 'Howard Barker's *Crimes in Hot Countries*: A Director's Perspective' in Leslie Bell (ed.). *Contradictory Theatres: The Theatre Underground and the Essex University New Plays Scheme – Critical and Theoretical Essays with Documentation*. Essex: Theatre Action Press, 113–31.

Lamb, Charles (2005). *The Theatre of Howard Barker*. London: Routledge.

Rabey, David Ian (1989). *Howard Barker: Politics and Desire: An Expository Study of his Drama and Poetry, 1969–1987*. Basingstoke: Macmillan.

Rabey, David Ian (1992). ' "What Do You See?": Howard Barker's *The Europeans*: A Director's Perspective', *Studies in Theatre Production* 6, 23–34.

Rabey, David Ian (1996). 'Howard Barker' in William W. Demastes (ed.). *British Playwrights, 1956–1995: A Research and Production Sourcebook*. Westport, CT: Greenwood Press, 28–38.

Shaughnessy, Robert (1989). 'Howard Barker, the Wrestling School, and the Cult of the Author', *New Theatre Quarterly* 5:19, 264–71.

Thomas, Alan (1992). 'Howard Barker: Modern Allegorist', *Modern Drama* 35:3, 433– 43.

Tomlin, Liz (2000). 'The Politics of Catastrophe: Confrontation or Confirmation in Howard Barker's Theatre', *Modern Drama* 43:1, 66–77.

Wilcher, Robert (1993). 'Honouring the Audience: The Theatre of Howard Barker' in James Acheson (ed.). *British and Irish Drama since 1960*. Basingstoke: Macmillan, 176–89.

41

Reading History in the Plays of Brian Friel

Lionel Pilkington

Part of the appeal of the drama of Brian Friel (b. 1929) is that it deals with a widely shared transnational experience – the impact of capitalist modernity on a traditional society – by means of recognizably national characters and settings. In particular, it chronicles the period of Ireland's economic modernization in the second part of the twentieth century, when, beginning in the late 1950s, government thinking shifted sharply from a policy of economic self-sufficiency to what is now western capitalism's overwhelming orthodoxy: encouraging a profit-orientated export economy through multinational inward capital investment. Whether in *Philadelphia, Here I Come!* (1964), which deals with emigration from the peripheral north-western county of Donegal in the 1960s, or in *Translations* (1980), which is concerned with the changes brought about by the loss of the Irish language in the 1830s, or in *Dancing at Lughnasa* (1990), which deals with the calamitous effects of modernization on the domestic and personal lives of five sisters in Donegal in the 1930s, the preoccupying theme of Friel's plays is the effect on the individual of such broader social, political and economic changes.

The majority of Friel's plays are set in the localized but fictional area of Ballybeg (or 'Baile Beag', meaning 'small town') in County Donegal. Fitting easily into Ireland's dominant twentieth-century literary and theatrical aesthetic of naturalism (see Cleary 2004: 232–8), Friel's drama tends to take place at a moment contemporaneous with the play's production ('the present in Ireland') as, for example, in *Volunteers* (1975), *Living Quarters* (1977), *The Communication Cord* (1982) and *Wonderful Tennessee* (1993), or at a precisely specified date, as in autumn 587 for *The Enemy Within* (1962), August 1936 for *Dancing at Lughnasa*, or 1970 for *The Freedom of the City*. Repeatedly, however, the significance of these settings is shown as lying less in their historical or cultural particularity than in their role as background for a universal condition. A characteristic feature of Friel's treatment of Ireland, in other words, is that it is offered less as a social analysis and more as a metaphor for an overarching existential concern. *Philadelphia, Here I Come!*, for example, is not so much a play about emigration as it is about the male protagonist's crisis of loss and separation from his parents. Similarly, *The Freedom of the City*, set in 1970 in Derry city, exists only superficially as a satire of the British government's official exoneration of the soldiers who shot 13 civilians dead in Derry on Bloody Sunday (30 January 1972; a fourteenth civilian died later in hospital). Its more profound concern is what it regards as the tragic gap between the plenitude of individual experience and what is seen as the distorting effects of representing that experience in language. In *Translations* Friel's concern with the loss of the Irish language under the impact of colonial modernity also conceals what is revealed by the third act as a deeper truth: a perennial existential crisis in which the privacy of the individual is never fully expressed by language. Again, in *Dancing at Lughnasa*, the tragedy of the five Mundy sisters in 1930s County Donegal is offered not so much as a product of a particular history (and, therefore, as a situation that could be changed), but as a metaphor for a universal gap between desire and realization. In Friel's plays, as Fintan O'Toole puts it succinctly, 'the times and reason, the historical context, matter hardly at all. What matters is the image' (O'Toole 1993: 203).

And yet the point remains. An impression of historical verisimilitude – the depiction of a socially and chronologically identifiable Ireland – is crucial to the persuasive effect of Brian Friel's plays. Certainly, Friel's plays end up repudiating the thematic importance of the specificity of Irish history and politics except as an illustration of general trends, and to this extent Friel indeed may be considered as an 'anti-historical and anti-political writer' (O' Toole 1993: 205). But this manoeuvre is achieved on the basis of a reiterated claim, reinforced by the naturalism of the plays' dramaturgy, and in some cases by the accompaniment of elaborate, historically detailed programme notes:[1] that this history is known and knowable in the first place. What then is the reason for Friel's strikingly ambivalent attitude to Irish historical and cultural difference, and how, if at all, does it illuminate the relationship between Friel's plays and their contemporary contexts?

The 1958 publication of the white paper *Economic Development* – authored by the civil servant economist T. K. Whitaker and promoted by the Fianna Fáil minister Seán Lemass – proposed a radical change of direction in Irish government thinking on the economy. It argued for export-orientated manufacturing concentrated in regional growth centres and funded by foreign investment and state intervention. Keynesian in its approach, Whitaker's and Lemass's new economic policy favoured centralized industrial planning, gave primacy to private enterprise over state-owned, promoted mechanized agriculture and applauded the benefits of multinational inward capital investment (see Whitaker 1986). The result was a 4 per cent growth in Ireland's GNP and a general fall in emigration figures, except among small farmers and agricultural workers in peripheral rural areas in the south and west. Within the context of this export-orientated economic expansion, there was an increased emphasis on institutional culture in Ireland as a potential tourism asset (the Dublin Theatre Festival, for example, was established in 1957), and on the writing and production of plays amenable to performance abroad as well as nationally (see Pilkington 2001: 149–50).

Friel's celebrated early play *Philadelphia, Here I Come!* is part of this changing economic and cultural landscape. First performed as part of the Dublin Theatre Festival in September 1964, the play was transferred to New York in 1966, where it was widely acclaimed and became the longest-running Irish play on Broadway. It deals with the emotionally and politically sensitive topic of emigration. But whereas John B. Keane's popular musical *Many Young Men of Twenty* (1961) attacks the inability and unwillingness of Irish governments to address this problem properly in rural areas, and Peadar O'Donnell's *There Will Be Another Day* (1963) celebrates a tradition of activist resistance to the conditions that generate emigration, Friel's play adopts an altogether different approach. His protagonist, Gareth (Gar) O'Donnell, is shown as having to emigrate not so much for economic reasons as because of a social world that is stultifyingly conservative. Gar does not belong to that pre-1958 category of small farmers and rural unskilled labourers from the west of Ireland that had been so marginalized by the government's Whitaker reforms, and for whom emigration was still chronic. On the contrary, Gar belongs to a rural middle class, albeit at the lower end of its scale. His father is a shopkeeper, a local County Donegal county councillor, and has a housekeeper; Gar himself is described as having spent a year at university. In this respect, and in his railing at those conventions that curtail or ignore male libido, Gar is like a 1950s angry young man, a softer Irish analogue, perhaps, of Jimmy Porter in John Osborne's landmark play *Look Back in Anger* (1956).[2] Indeed, what *Philadelphia, Here I Come!* presents as by far the most important reason for emigration is not so much the dismal employment prospects experienced by so many in the western counties in this period, but rather sexual immiseration. Ironically, given that the play concentrates so exclusively on the trauma of its male protagonist, emigration from the west of Ireland in this period was particularly severe amongst women, and was motivated as much by *their* dismal marriage prospects as it was by economics (see Moser 1993).

The trauma that triggers Gar's decision to emigrate, however, is an Oedipal one. This is evident in his hapless succumbing to his Aunt Lizzie's invitation to live in her home in the United States because of his perception of her as a substitute for his deceased mother (Friel 1965: 64), and in his distress and rage against his father for his lack of affection. In contrast to the emotional abstemiousness of Donegal, the United States is presented as a fantasy world of libidinal and consumer fulfilment. Just as the Donegal of *Philadelphia, Here I Come!* is absurdly out of place in a world increasingly dominated by the idioms of Anglo-American popular culture, there is in Ireland no public language in which Gar can express his private world of desire. For Gar, a realization of desire entails, above all, a complete submission of the self to the play of international market forces; thus Ireland, like Gar, can become modern only by abandoning the essential markers of distinctiveness. What is lamented by Friel's play is both traditional Ireland's failure to adapt quickly enough to the fast pace of a US-dominated international capitalism *and* the necessity and human cost of this adaptation. If the protagonist is to achieve the psycho-sexual fulfilment that he desires then he will have to emigrate, but this, it is implied, will involve a coarsening – a further falling off from the originary plenitude that Gar associates so elegiacally with his dead mother. The tragic irony of the play, and one that Friel exploits and develops in *The Loves of Cass McGuire* (1966) and in many of his later plays, is that the changes necessary for personal fulfilment (in this case, emigration) entail a fundamental loss of plenitude. As Nicholas Grene points out, Friel's play affirms the absolute rightness of Gar's decision to emigrate (Grene 1999: 205). Identity can be realized only through its loss and, in the face of an older, traditional Ireland that is unable or unwilling to meet the needs of modernity, emigration is offered as a kind of ontological inevitability.

Given the compelling nature of this narrative, it is interesting to consider that County Donegal in the late 1950s and early 1960s was also the location for vigorous challenges both to the inevitability of rural emigration from western counties and to the main thrust of the Whitaker reforms. In the early 1960s, at approximately the same time as the composition of *Philadelphia, Here I Come!*, Father (Fr) James McDyer of the parish of Glencolumkille in County Donegal organized and co-ordinated a range of local initiatives, in conjunction with the industrialist General Michael Costello (chairman of Erin Foods and director of the Irish Sugar Company) and the prominent republican writer and intellectual Peadar O'Donnell (see McDyer 1982: 83–5). For Costello, McDyer and O'Donnell, Whitaker's reorientation of government policy towards an aggressive integration of Ireland into what was in effect a US-dominated international capitalism had served to hasten rather than stem emigration, especially among the children of small farmers and agricultural labourers. Motivated in part by 'traditional nationalism' (ibid.: 49), McDyer and his colleagues considered emigration as a legacy of British rule and as a failure of successive Irish governments since independence. Vigorously opposed to the Keynesian principle of centralized state planning or, in McDyer's words, 'state paternalism' (ibid.: 68), a 'Save the West' campaign was established. This was a broad-based umbrella group that called on local initiative for the establishment of agricultural co-operatives as well as small-scale industries. It was designed to foster increased local democracy, local agricultural and industrial co-operatives, and an alliance between industrial workers and small farmers (see Ó Drisceoil 2001: 119–20), and was opposed to the drive for multinational capitalist investment as a panacea for Irish economic difficulty. With a strong socialist dimension, McDyer's campaign offered an alternative modernity for Donegal, one that harnessed industrial development to the traditional needs of the community.

> [M]y dream differed radically from private enterprise. Mine was community enterprise through which the curse of dependence on the investor and the bureaucrat would be lifted so that the future could be planned in dignity and equality [. . .].
>
> My strategy was to build a chain of small industries funded by the shareholding of the local people; the profits of the first two industries would prime the creation of other small factories, until a cordon enclosed the community to trap emigration and farm redundancy at its source. (McDyer 1982: 74–5)

Looked at in relation to its historical context, then, *Philadelphia, Here I Come!* may be considered as one response, but by no means the only one, to the social crisis posed by emigration. What for McDyer's 'Save the West' campaign was a motivating force for an activist politics critical of the state and fostering local democracy and community initiative, Friel's play presents elegiacally as the only possible escape from an enervating libidinal frustration. The despairing restrictiveness of this conception of Irish history and politics is even more evident in a lesser-known Friel play, *The Mundy Scheme* (1969). This is a farcical treatment of what Friel presents scathingly as the impossibly limited political options for an Ireland facing modernization. Confronted with impending national bankruptcy and World Bank humiliation, the government, led by its Taoiseach F. X. Ryan, opts to sell off the entire western part of the country as a US-owned funerary plot.

But to remark on the despair of Friel's early plays is not to accuse Friel of political bad faith. It is likely that many young men did emigrate from County Donegal in the early 1960s in order to escape a prevailing claustrophobic moral atmosphere. The authenticity of Friel's vision is not what is at issue. Instead what I want to argue is that Friel's negative political vision arises not only from a view of history that sees tradition and modernity in opposition to each other, but also from the way in which this view of history is fostered and reinforced by naturalism. For example, the fundamental theatrical premise of *Philadelphia, Here I Come!* is that the protagonist, Gareth O'Donnell, is represented on stage by two characters, Public Gar and Private Gar. Public Gar is visible to the other characters on stage whereas Private Gar, described by Friel's stage directions as 'the man within, the conscience, the *alter ego*', is visible only to the theatre audience. A condition of the play's performance, therefore, is the audience's sense of the irreconcilability of these two characters: on stage they are, literally, two different people. Theatrical convention in this instance reinforces the play's thematic emphasis on the fixed and permanent separation between Gar's public and private selves, between desire and fulfilment. If nothing can unify the two Gar characters, then nothing can reconcile the fantasy world of Private Gar with his father, the schoolteacher or anyone else. This then is the play's structural basis for the view that since tradition and modernity are incompatible, emigration is an ontological necessity. Imagining anything different means imagining a different kind of theatre.

A further case in point is Friel's 1973 play *The Freedom of the City*. Set in February 1970 in the aftermath of a banned civil rights march in Derry, many of the details of *The Freedom of the City* evoke the events that took place on Bloody Sunday. In addition, the play quotes directly from the British government's subsequent and now widely discredited official inquiry, the Widgery Report. The play's three protagonists (Lily, Michael and Skinner) have taken part in the banned protest and, in order to escape from CS gas and rubber bullets, they take refuge in what they later discover is the mayor's parlour in the City Guildhall. Their accidental occupation of the Guildhall prompts an accumulation of rumour, speculation and exaggerated news reports. A journalist cites 'unconfirmed reports . . . of about fifty armed gunmen', a nationalist balladeer alludes to 'a hundred Irish heroes' (Friel 1974: 29–30), and a British army press officer makes reference to 'a band of terrorists... [of] up to forty persons' (ibid.: 39). Surrounded by an array of army and police, Lily, Michael and Skinner are largely oblivious to what is taking place outside. The British officer in charge of the military siege orders the three to surrender, but when they do finally emerge, with their hands raised above their heads, they are summarily gunned down. Presented as a sequence of flashbacks presided over by a Widgery-like judge, the play ends with a speech by the Judge exculpating the army and suggesting that the three may have emerged firing from the Guildhall. The audience is cast in the role of adjudicator and is encouraged to compare what can be seen and heard to take place in the mayor's parlour with the many verbal commentaries and assessments that are made from the outside. Thus what the audience can see and hear in the final scene in the theatre is contradicted by the Judge's conclusions: the spectator witnesses Lily and the others with their hands above their heads – clearly unarmed – and then a 15-second burst of gunfire.

Friel's technique of placing the shooting immediately after the Judge has finished his magisterial-sounding conclusions reinforces an impression that the three civilians have been killed partly because of the Judge's *parti-pris* assumptions. But Friel's play also suggests that distortion is inextricably involved in *any* attempt at description or assessment, and that this extends to Derry's nationalist population as well. Priest, Balladeer, Journalist and people on the street are shown as participating in various forms of representation of the incident that are just as inaccurate. It is not just the Judge's inquiry that is complicit in the killings of Lily, Michael and Skinner, but the general tendency to stand back from a situation and represent it, for which Irish nationalists are just as culpable. The cumulative effect of these distortions, so the movement of the play suggests, is the killing of the three civilians. Thus the fact-finding objectivity of the Judge (or the Widgery Report) cannot be singled out for condemnation or satire because, Friel's play insists, it is just one version of the distorting process of representation in general. This impression of tragedy and political paralysis is most powerfully conveyed by the scene in which Lily, Michael and Skinner explain their reasons for taking part in the civil rights march, and, in each case, their stated reasons are revealed as subterfuges for a more complex humanity. Even Skinner, whose socialist rhetoric is the most eloquent and convincing ('It's about us – the poor – the majority stirring in our sleep'; ibid.: 77) is silenced by Lily's disclosure that she takes part in the civil rights marches out of an irrational 'motherly' concern for her son, who has Down syndrome. In this, the most moving and revelatory scene of the play, authenticity resides in tradition: Lily's preliterate feminine irrationality. But in so far as Lily is portrayed as longing herself for self-representation (Friel 1974: 72), the audience is left with a sense that tradition and modernity are fundamentally incompatible and that tradition must always yield to modernity.

The Freedom of the City can also be read, like *Philadelphia, Here I Come!*, as a rebuttal of specific forms of contemporary activism and militancy. Unlike, for example, the activism of Derry-based socialists such as Bernadette Devlin MP and People's Democracy founder Eamonn McCann (see Pilkington 2001: 200), not to mention the guerrilla tactics of the Provisional IRA, Friel's play suggests that despite the flagrant injustices of British rule in Northern Ireland, nothing can be done to change the situation. That nothing can be done about the three civilians and, by extension, about the conflict in Northern Ireland as a whole is as obvious as our existence as spectators when, in the final tableau of *The Freedom of the City*, the three protagonists stare out at the audience with their hands over their heads. This scene, like the play as a whole, has a dual function: it presents conclusive evidence that the Judge's inquiry is a cover-up, and it confronts the audience with its own passivity. In so far as the three characters stare directly out at the auditorium – the same direction from which the shooting comes – we the audience are indicted for complicity. In other words, the same objective passivity that is the basis for our empirical conclusion that the three civilians are innocent is here also presented as an emblem of political despair. But such a conclusion is no more than the logical extension of the play's theatrical premise. The political hopelessness of the play is grounded, tautologically, in an assumption that is presented as the play's fundamental condition: that the role of a theatre audience is to witness, not change, the action presented on stage.[3]

Friel's later plays and, in particular *Volunteers, Faith Healer* (1979), *Translations* and *Making History* (1988), show an increasing thematic self-consciousness with the problem of representing history. Their preoccupation is with the idea that history is constructed by narrative, and narrative is contingent partly on the charisma and authority of the narrator and partly on cultural predisposition. 'It is not the literal past, the "facts" of history, that shape us', remarks the schoolteacher Hugh towards the end of *Translations*, 'but images of the past embodied in language' (Friel 1981: 66). But whereas for *The Freedom of the City* the problem of representing an event in history is construed as a kind of existential impossibility leading only to political paralysis, for plays such as *Volunteers, Translations* and *Making History*, it forms the basis for a revisionist cultural project directed against what is portrayed as the entrenched beliefs of Irish nationalism. Thus, the title of *Volunteers* reflects ironically on the name given to IRA activists, while the play's action as a whole suggests that what motivates republican militancy is not injustice, but an atavistic clinging to nationalist ideology. Performed at the height of an IRA war of insurgency in Northern Ireland and at the beginning of the British government's policy of criminalizing that insurgency (see O'Dowd et al. 1982), *Volunteers* is Friel's most overtly anti-republican play. It leaves its audience with the impression that IRA actions are motivated by a pathologically myopic commitment to ideas of victimhood and self-sacrifice, and that such ideas need to be seen not as the verities of a campaign of anti-colonial resistance, but as dangerously misleading constructions.

Historical demystification is also a key idea for the Derry-based Field Day Theatre Company and for Friel's *Translations*, performed, in September 1980, as Field Day's inaugural production. Described by Field Day board member David Hammond as having grown out of 'despair with unionist and nationalist outlooks, and a mistrust of politicians, political systems' (quoted in Richtarik 1994: 103), Field Day's stated objective was the search for a solution to the Northern Ireland crisis through a cultural 'fifth province' that would transcend political differences. *Translations* begins with a contrast between the philistine red-coated British soldiers of the Ordnance Survey and the Latin-speaking but indigent peasant members of a Donegal hedge school. By the third act, however, the audience is made to recognize that it is precisely the familiarity and reassurance of this contrast that is the problem. The hedge school may well be characterized by an attractive quixotic panache, but it is so out of touch with quotidian domestic realities that, as a society, it is incapable of a future. And while the richness of an Irish-speaking vernacular is deeply attractive, especially to audiences sympathetic to Irish nationalism, this too must be seen as a delusive quixoticism. In the context of an inexorable modernity associated with British imperialism and the consequent need for adjustment amongst peripheral or dependent communities, Hugh's proposal at the end of the play that the English language should be accepted is presented as the only compelling alternative to the IRA-like tactics of militant resistance. And yet, like Friel's plangent treatment of emigration in *Philadelphia, Here I Come!*, there is also an impression that such a change will involve an unquantifiable ontological loss. In the final moments of the play, Maire – a young woman who wants to learn English so that she can emigrate – asks Hugh to teach her. She asked the same question in Act I, but had been dismissed. Now, however, Hugh agrees to the request. He tells Maire that he will provide her with 'the available words and the available grammar', but then adds that he has no idea whether this will allow her to interpret 'between privacies' (Friel 1981: 67). Written and performed at a time when Provisional Sinn Féin, as well as IRA and other republican prisoners, were mobilizing both the Irish language and a colonial interpretation of the conflict in Northern Ireland as part of a lexicon of political resistance (see Pilkington 2001: 219–20), *Translations* is a play that is directed precisely against such a campaign of resistance. And yet, here again the persuasiveness of *Translations*'s conclusion, especially in relation to the view that recovering the Irish language as a spoken vernacular is misguided, rests, tautologically, both on Friel's exclusion of the Irish language from *Translations*, except as place names, and on what the play offers as a coup of theatrical expediency: that we understand English as spoken by the Irish characters in the play as a theatrical convention for Irish (see Pilkington 2001: 210–20).

Friel's plays deal with the relationship between what is portrayed as an inexorable and dehumanizing modernity and a benighted but ontologically rich traditional culture. Succumbing to the lure of the latter, as in the case of the insurgent figures in *Translations* (Owen, Doalty and the Donnelly twins) or the eccentric priest Fr Jack in *Dancing at Lughnasa*, is associated with a dangerous recidivism, while the alternative – accepting Ireland's relationship of dependent development – is associated with plangency and loss. The political restrictiveness of this choice, I have argued, is a product both of the dichotomous terms in which Friel casts the relationship between modernity and non-modernity (a move which occludes a wide range of historically specific strategies of resistance that are themselves a complex interpenetration of tradition and modernity), and of Friel's commitment to the dominant naturalistic conventions of the institutional theatre.

ACKNOWLEDGEMENT

I am very grateful for the advice provided by Dr Caoilfhionn Ní Bheacháin and Dr Tony Varley in preparing this chapter.

NOTES

1 Two excellent examples of this are the 1980 Field Day programme for *Translations*, which contains extracts from various historical works and documents including P. J. Dowling's *The Hedge Schools of Ireland*, William Careleton's *The Autobiography of William Careleton* and Thomas Colby's *Ordnance Survey of Ireland*, and the 1991 Abbey Theatre programme for *Dancing at Lughnasa*, which is illustrated with photo-graphs from the folklore collection at University College Dublin and contains an extract from Maire MacNeill's respected monograph *The Festival of Lughnasa*.

2 In a 1964 interview with Peter Lennon, Friel himself describes *Philadelphia, Here I Come!* as 'really an angry play' (see Murray 1999: 3).

3 For a discussion of spectatorship and agency in Irish theatre, see Pilkington (1998).

PRIMARY READING

The Brian Friel papers 1960–2001 are held in the National Library of Ireland, Kildare Street, Dublin 2. A summary of the archive (MS collection list 73) can be accessed on line at www.nli.ie/pdfs/mss%20lists/frielb.pdf. The manuscript numbers are MSS 37,041–37,806.

Friel, Brian (1965). *Philadelphia, Here I Come!* London: Faber and Faber.

Friel, Brian (1967). *The Loves of Cass McGuire.* London: Faber and Faber.

Friel, Brian (1969). *Lovers.* London: Faber and Faber.

Friel, Brian (1970a). *Crystal and Fox.* London: Faber and Faber.

Friel, Brian (1970b). *The Mundy Scheme* in *Two Plays.* New York: Farrar, Straus and Giroux.

Friel, Brian (1973). *The Gentle Island.* London: Davis-Poynter.

Friel, Brian (1974). *The Freedom of the City.* London: Faber and Faber.

Friel, Brian (1978). *Living Quarters.* London: Faber and Faber.

Friel, Brian (1979a). *The Enemy Within.* Dublin: Gallery Press.

Friel, Brian (1979b). *Volunteers.* London: Faber and Faber.

Friel, Brian (1980a). *Aristocrats.* Dublin: Gallery Press.

Friel, Brian (1980b). *Faith Healer.* London: Faber and Faber.

Friel, Brian (1980c). *Fathers and Sons.* London: Faber and Faber.

Friel, Brian (1980d). *The Three Sisters.* Dublin: Gallery Press.

Friel, Brian (1981). *Translations.* London: Faber and Faber.

Friel, Brian (1983). *The Communication Cord.* London: Faber and Faber.

Friel, Brian (1988). *Making History.* London: Faber and Faber.

Friel, Brian (1990a). *Dancing at Lughnasa*. London: Faber and Faber.

Friel, Brian (1990b). *The London Vertigo*. Dublin: Gallery Press.

Friel, Brian (1992). *A Month in the Country*. Dublin: Gallery Press.

Friel, Brian (1993). *Wonderful Tennessee*. Dublin: Gallery Press.

Friel, Brian (1994). *Molly Sweeney*. Dublin: Gallery Press.

FURTHER READING

Brown, Terence (1993). 'Have We a Context?: Transition, Self and Society in the Theatre of Brian Friel' in Alan J. Peacock (ed.). *The Achievement of Brian Friel*. Gerrards Cross: Colin Smythe, 190–201.

Cleary, Joe (2004). 'Towards a Materialist-Formalist History of Twentieth-Century Irish Literature', *Boundary 2: An International Journal of Literature and Culture* 31:1, 207–41.

Grene, Nicholas (1999). 'Versions of Pastoral' in *The Politics of Irish Drama: Plays in Context from Boucicault to Friel*. Cambridge: Cambridge University Press, 194–218.

Harris, Claudia W. (1997). 'The Engendered Space: Performing Friel's Women from Cass McGuire to Molly Sweeney' in William Kerwin (ed.). *Brian Friel: A Casebook*. New York and London: Garland, 45–75.

Kerwin, William (ed.) (1997). *Brian Friel: A Casebook*. New York and London: Garland.

McDyer, James (1982). *Fr McDyer of Glencolumkille: An Autobiography*. Dingle: Brandon.

McMullan, Anna (1999). ' "In Touch with Some Otherness": Gender, Authority and the Body in *Dancing at Lughnasa*', *Irish University Review* 29:1, 90–100.

Moser, Peter (1993). 'Rural Economy and Female Emigration in the West of Ireland 1936–1956', *UCG Women's Studies Centre Review* 2, eds. Anne Byrne, Jane Conroy and Sean Ryder, 41–51.

Murray, Christopher (ed.) (1999). *Brian Friel: Essays, Diaries, Interviews: 1964–1999*. London: Faber and Faber.

O'Donnell, Peadar (1963). *There Will be Another Day*. Dublin: Dolmen Press.

O'Dowd, L., Rolston, B. and Tomlinson, M. (1982). 'From Labour to the Tories: The Ideology of Containment in Northern Ireland', *Capital and Class* 18, 72–90.

Ó Drisceoil, Donal (2001). *Peadar O'Donnell*. Cork: Cork University Press.

O'Toole, Fintan (1993). 'Marking Time: From *Making History* to *Dancing at Lughnasa*' in Alan J. Peacock (ed.). *The Achievement of Brian Friel*. Gerrards Cross: Colin Smythe, 202–14.

Pilkington, Lionel (2001). *Theatre and the State in Twentieth-Century Ireland: Cultivating the People*. London and New York: Routledge.

Pilkington, Lionel (1998). 'Irish Theatre Historiography and Political Resistance' in Jeanne Colleran and Jenny S. Spencer (eds.). *Staging Resistance: Essays on Political Theatre*. Ann Arbor: University of Michigan Press, 13–30.

Richtarik, Marilynn J. (1994). *Acting Between the Lines: The Field Day Theatre Company and Irish Cultural Politics 1980–1984*. Oxford: Clarendon Press.

Roche, Anthony (1985). *Contemporary Irish Drama: From Beckett to McGuinness*. New York: St Martin's Press.

Whitaker, T. K. (1986). 'Economic Development 1958–1985' in Kieran A. Kennedy (ed.). *Ireland in Transition: Economic and Social Change since 1960*. Cork and Dublin: Mercier Press, 10–18.

42

Marina Carr: Violence and Destruction: Language, Space and Landscape

Cathy Leeney

Marina Carr's gradual accession to her current place as the most visionary Irish playwright of her generation is marked by huge creativity, restless courage and epic ambition. The poet Eavan Boland talks about the 'lived vocation' of the writer or the artist and Carr's work in theatre exemplifies this ideal (Boland 1989: 11). Her plays have attracted the best directors, performers and designers in theatre both in Ireland and abroad. Her journey thus far has had its nightmares, for her plays pose challenges to style and staging as they demand representation that is extreme. Born in 1964 and brought up near Tullamore, County Offaly, in the Midlands of Ireland, Carr self-consciously places herself within a tradition of inspired authorship (Carr 1998). This is a highly unfashionable stance at the beginning of the twenty-first century, and Carr has attracted a great deal of controversy pertaining both to her Romantically inspired self-construction and to her plays. Carr's respect for the crafts of writing and performance is allied powerfully with a daring imagination and intoxicating energy. As Frank McGuinness has argued: 'In confrontation with terror, she is without fear' (see Leeney and McMullan 2003: 87).

Her use of an idiomatic, heavily accented form of English, as it is spoken in the Midlands of Ireland, marks most of her plays. The eccentric spellings in the quotations that follow are not misprints, but markers of a very particular and muscular engagement with language. Early works, such as *Low in the Dark* (1989), *Ullaloo* (1991) and *The Mai* (1994), are, more or less, in standard Hiberno-English. From *Portia Coughlan* (1996), through to *By the Bog of Cats* (1998), *On Raftery's Hill* (2000) and *Ariel* (2002), Carr's strategy with dramatic language changes. McGuinness describes this as a 'physical attack on the conventions of syntax, spelling and sounds of Standard English' (Leeney and McMullan 2003: 78). Although he is referring specifically to *Portia Coughlan*, McGuinness's insight also applies to her subsequent plays. The first edition of *Portia Coughlan*, in the collection entitled *The Dazzling Dark* (1996), is an extreme example of heavily accented speech. It is tenaciously true to an aural vision for performance which impacts physically on audiences: they are refused clarity and drawn into a struggle to expand imaginative engagement with every aspect of the play beyond the ordinary. This linguistic contest becomes a parallel for a broader representational contest that is being played out. Later, Carr re-wrote *Portia Coughlan* in an effort to make it more accessible, yet she did not surrender the on-stage dramatic language that emphasizes the physicality of performance, and that heightens the audience's awareness of the limits of words to express, their tendency to lie and to haunt, and their power over mind and body. Carr chooses the landscape of the Midlands, neglected by tourist advertisements and calendar photographers, to create a territory that accommodates a kind of Irish heart of darkness. The geography in her plays works on many levels, paralleling emotional states in the characters, opening Ireland out into a metonym for the world as the vulnerable home and sanctuary of the human race: 'Carr's Irish Midlands', as Claudia Harris has said, 'are her passageway into an ancient new imaginative world' (Leeney and McMullan 2003: 217).

As the best-known woman playwright currently working in Ireland, Carr has been the subject of considerable critical attention, and as Clare Wallace has written, 're-sponses have seldom been lukewarm, and are regularly hyperbolic' (Leeney and McMullan 2003: 43). Her gender has been used to market her work (ibid.: 45), and she is sometimes perceived as bearing a burden of representing women and women's experience. On many levels this is undoubtedly true. Feminist readings of her plays reveal the gender deficit in Irish theatrical traditions, where women are represented rather than representing. Olwen Fouéré, who played the lead parts in the premieres of *The Mai* and *By the Bog of Cats*, describes how Carr, in the former play, seems 'at times, to articulate the female rage of the nation' (ibid.: 169). Here, I wish to suggest that, in her later plays especially, Carr's canvas is larger than Irish women's or Ireland's or even women's concerns and experience. In the context of postmodern playwriting Carr's texts refer playfully and mischievously to the classical Greek and the Irish canons, as well as toy with images from Shakespeare, Rabelais and Irish myth and legend. Anna McMullan's use of the term 'hybrid' in this regard has never been more insightful (Leeney and McMullan 2003): the figures populating Carr's stages are indeed offspring of mixed origins, half gods, half monsters. Yet Carr's work enrages as much as it fascinates and she is no stranger to corrosive critical attack.[1] I will focus here on Carr's play *Ariel* (2002) as the apotheosis of elements manifested in earlier plays, and then offer readings of *On Raftery's Hill* and *By the Bog of Cats* to suggest that these three plays are linked in a dramaturgy concerned with our twenty-first-century world: the anxieties that arise through our love/hate relationship with planet Earth, and how the human family has its feet in the filth and its head in the stars.

Ariel received a very mixed critical response. *Irish Times* critic Fintan O'Toole was perhaps most attuned to the boldness of Carr's enterprise: 'she is laying out the ground that the best dramatists of the young generation must now occupy', he wrote, and despite its 'gaping flaws' found it 'curiously compelling' (Leeney and McMullan 2003: 89–90). Otherwise the majority of critics read Carr's unstable theatrical hybrid of psychotic visions and social realism in the Abbey Theatre production as incoherent; and without doubt the style of the production failed to negotiate the breadth of representational vocabulary deployed in the play.

Ariel represents the negotiations of a relatively new species, the human species, with a very ancient universe. The play is an epic tragedy centred on the Fitzgerald family. The action opens on the sixteenth birthday of the eldest daughter, Ariel, and spans the following 10 years, during which the father (Fermoy) rises to power in politics, the mother (Frances) separates from him, and their younger children (Elaine and Stephen) grow up to become cold and unhappy adults. The family unit is extended to include two observer characters: Fermoy's elder brother Boniface, a monk, and Aunt Sarah, the sister of Fermoy's and Boniface's dead mother. Sarah has taken the maternal role in the Fitzgerald home after the violent death of the boys' mother. The 10-years-on scenes of searing recrimination and repressed grief dominate Acts II and III and arise from Fermoy's secret off-stage murder of Ariel on her sixteenth birthday (a decade earlier in Act I); the father destroys the future of his own beautiful flesh and blood not because he hates his eldest child, but apparently because he loves power more, and believes he will gain it through this Abrahamic sacrifice. Fermoy's rhetoric of the will-to-power is an image of the inflation of greed beyond reason. In reality, his motives are inaccessible and beyond the frame of representation, expressed only in his raving visions. Ariel's body is never found. In true Greek tragic fashion Fermoy's fate is spiritually pre-ordained from the time when, as a 7-year-old, he witnessed and helped in his own father's murder of Fermoy's mother, by drowning her in the Cuura Lake. Fermoy's overweening ambition dooms him in turn.

Act II opens on the tenth anniversary of Ariel's death, when the family stumble back to the commemorative mass marking the girl's disappearance. By now Fermoy is Taoiseach (prime minister) in waiting, and we learn of his power-fuelled aim to 'cahapult the whole nation ouha sleaze and sentimentalihy and gombeenism'; to 'take this country to the moon' (Carr 2002: 63). This image of abandonment of the earth will recur. Fermoy wants the Irish to reinvent themselves without pretence to civilization, and without reference to a gentle Christ-figure who accepts pain and champions the underdog: rather, Fermoy invokes Caesar and Napoleon, for whom 'the world was one big battlefield' (ibid.: 42). He idealizes the thrust of tyranny and overweening ambition expressed in a ruthless will-to-power that sweeps away mercy and justice. He invokes Piero della Francesca's representation of a vengeful Christ, in *Resurrection* (painted in 1463), in which Christ confronts the viewer full-face, his expression promising not salvation but retaliation. His disciple daughter Elaine adores her father and shares the knowledge of his savage deed. When she tells her mother that Ariel will never be coming home, she confirms what Frances has known in her heart: that Fermoy killed Ariel on the night of her birthday.

Frances confronts him, listening disbelievingly as he blames God for his action. She is 'weeping like we've never seen' (57). Fermoy tries to implicate her through her attraction to him as a man who would do anything, who offered her escape from her 'little bungalow life' and gave her 'graveyard excitement and the promise of funerals to come' (59); instead she stabs him repeatedly in a scene so excessively violent that, theatrically, it beggars belief. We may look back to the sacrifice of Iphigenia, to Clytemnestra's murder of Agamemnon in Aeschylus' *Oresteia*, or to Medea's murder of her children in Euripides' play, but these deaths take place off-stage. It is widely believed that death in classical Greek tragedy happened out of sight. Athenian audiences may have seen the bodies of the victims displayed on the mobile platform called the *eccyclema*; but did not, most probably, have to confront the hideous act itself.

Carr first brings unpalatable violence onto the stage in *Portia Coughlan*, when Portia brutally assaults her mother. At the end of *By the Bog of Cats*, Hester kills her daughter before us, and then dances her own death with the Ghost Fancier. At the end of Act I in *On Raftery's Hill*, the audience is saved from witnessing Red's rape of his daughter Sorrell by a merciful blackout. In *Ariel* audiences are not spared: we are faced with what we (hopefully) have never seen, or will see, in our lives; we are also faced with what we rarely have to encounter in the theatre. And it is not yet over. Ariel's decayed corpse, hauled out of Cuura Lake and placed in an open coffin, is at the centre of Act III. Frances is on temporary release from prison to attend the belated funeral rite. Elaine, who guards her father's grave 'like an alsation' (Carr 2002: 62), is poised in fury since she has found out that Frances plans to disturb Fermoy's plot and to bury Ariel with her father. The defeated Stephen has lost even his loyalty to his mother; he rejects her outright and walks out on her, cheered on by Boniface. Indeed, every allegiance within the family structure has been blown asunder – except allegiances with the dead. In an image recalling Hamlet, Elaine takes her long-drowned sister's skull from the coffin and considers her bond with, and her jealousy of, Ariel. Suddenly, the ghost of Fermoy appears, blood-spattered and desolate. Unlike the ghost in *Hamlet*, though, Fermoy does not even recognize his own offspring: as a ghost he is himself haunted – by his murdered daughter, and by his destiny in her destruction.

The theme of betrayal of the younger generation by the older one has been at the heart of Carr's work ever since Millie served as the powerless witness of her parents' tragedy in *The Mai*. Eilis Ní Dhuibhne recognizes this theme as that of the 'wronged child' (Leeney and McMullan 2003: 68) which commonly occurs, across cultures, in fairy tales. It is most acutely present in *On Raftery's Hill*, where the expectation of parental protection is most deeply betrayed. Although this has a literal meaning in the context of the family situations of each drama, it is also metonymic of the betrayal by older generations in their failure to husband the resources of the natural world for those coming after.

When Fermoy's ghost leaves the stage it leaves Elaine defeated by its failure to acknowledge her. She turns on her mother in the final moments. We witness the last ghastly assault, the death of the middle generation, the obliteration of the flawed mother-figure, the meaningless and inarticulate survival of vengeance for its own sake. As Elaine knifes Frances in the throat she claims the identity of all the dead who have gone before. The audience is left with nothing to cling to: no hero or heroine, no sense of right against wrong; only a future formed by bitter recrimination, loss, jealousy and dumb revenge. The extraordinary rhetorical power of the language up to this endgame is silenced. Elaine says nothing. There is nothing left to say.

Ariel is excessive and epic in its passions. Its scope reaches beyond life into the world of hauntings, beyond good and evil into the seductiveness of power for its own sake, and beyond past and future into a terrifying eternity, past imagination, yet echoing the darkest conceivable imaginings of chaos and savagery. Yet, on the surface, it is a play about an Irish family: birthday cakes are baked; the cement business pays the bills; and the world of politics and media as we recognize it is reflected and sent up in the television-interview scene between Fermoy and a slick current-affairs presenter (Carr 2002: 38–46).

Besides the ways in which they echo the tragic families of Euripides and Aeschylus, how do these forgings together of the domestic and the epic work in the play? Two aspects of *Ariel* prompt a reading with a wider meaning than the bloody tale of a doomed family, and a wider meaning even than the Fitzgerald family as a parallel for the state of Ireland under the Celtic Tiger, prey to corruption, private ambition and the ruthless self-interest of those in power. The first aspect centres on the presence in the play of the monk Boniface, and how he enables discussion of God, spirituality, morality and the divine. The second aspect is the shadow-text of the play, concerned with the question of what it is to be human.

Fermoy's elder brother Boniface is a figure of wry humour as he describes his chores as the youngest in his religious community, caring and peace-making amongst his failing and dwindling brethren. He is the Last of the Mohicans, but his faith has deserted him. He believes, residually, in gardening and in cornflowers. He can find no moral ground on which to challenge the megalomaniac rantings of Fermoy. Because of his time away in the novitiate, Boniface has a distance from the traumatic history of his mother's death, yet the moral chaos in Fermoy's soul plays out in Boniface's depression and alcoholism.[2] What emerges in the brothers' discussions is the idea of God as a nexus of ferocity and blind cosmic energy (Carr 2002: 12–21). This God is not merely an Old Testament one, for Fermoy recreates the New Testament with a re-visioning of Christ as a 'big, cranky, vengeful son of God' (ibid.: 44) – as he appears in della Francesca's *Resurrection*, or in Pier Paulo Pasolini's imagining of Christ in *The Gospel According to St Matthew*: an unforgettable embodiment of angry, impatient and unforgiving rigidity. In *Ariel* the construct of God engulfs and sweeps away individuality, and floods over into chemistry, the god that is hydrogen, the power of the split atom, and the primal big bang. In this cosmic scheme, the span of individual experience is torn open by the life of the cosmos beyond human death, and by our utter inconsequence in the face of the seismic workings of the universe and the havoc wreaked on the blue and green vulnerability of the planet that we share. In a moment that makes the hair stand on end, Fermoy describes how 'the earth's over [. . .] ozone layer in tahhers, oceans gone to sewer [. . .] We're goin to lave this place in ashes' (ibid.: 18). Frank Conway's design for the Abbey Theatre production of *Ariel* in 2002 demonstrated this sense of uncontrolled crisis: he made the floor of the stage a botched map of the world, one corner of which jutted perilously into the auditorium and fell away like a cliff collapsing into the ocean.

When Fermoy describes Napoleon's view of the world as one big battlefield, the conflict goes beyond man-made armies and allegiances to evoke images of biological life in man-made jeopardy. Carr is not the only playwright to conjure up visions of the war between the human family on one side, and nature and chemistry on the other. Caryl Churchill's eponymous character in *The Skriker* (1994) is a shape-changer, a demon of multiple identity who mischievously revels in human dislocation and human failure to live in harmony with the natural world. S/he (for the figure is all genders and none) vengefully opens the portals to the underworld, where madness measures the folly of human greed and hubris. Churchill's scene in Hades mirrors the world of ashes evoked by Fermoy in Carr's play. Churchill uses figures and stories from English folk tradition to create representations of the relentless damage done to the earth (embodied by the Skriker), and the cumulative debt amassed by systematic exploitation and despoliation. Elves and goblins embodying ideas of biological and divine order must be appeased; if they are not, the consequences are beyond calculation. Carr uses religious and environmental imagery as a focus to create an associated sense of inevitable catastrophe. In *Ariel* religious imagination becomes a site harbouring our deepest fears.

In both *The Skriker* and *Ariel* individuals are overwhelmed by forces which can be observed but not controlled. Carr dramatizes this idea in her two on-stage observers, Boniface and Aunt Sarah. They are spectators within the drama and they comment on the moral situation of the onlooker: as Sarah says, 'To watch a thing is only to half wish ud' (Carr 2002: 72). This paradox invades life in a media-saturated culture; if our witnessing is mediated by technology, does this absolve us from witness as testimony, from our indifference to horror, despoliation or injustice? In *Ariel* Carr develops this theme of a voyeuristic negotiation with reality in the repeated image of characters pausing in the doorway before they enter a scene and silently observing the action. To be only a watcher, then, is not to be free of responsibility; the watcher is implicated but powerless to take control.

The role of the individual protagonist as the centre of the drama is usurped in *Ariel* by the overpowering sense of persons in the grip of larger forces, whether they are spiritual, chemical, genetic or historical. In theatre the family arguably provides an image of how humans live not only for themselves but for the continuance, or otherwise, of the race. Privileging human concerns over those of other species relies upon a clear definition of the category 'human'. This brings me to the second aspect of *Ariel* that invites us to read the play as concerned with the human condition beyond domesticity or nationality. Carr, in her use of imagery, consistently poses the question: what is it to be human? The notion, of course, is planted even as early as the title,

Ariel. In Shakespeare's *The Tempest* Ariel is the spirit who can fly, swim or 'dive into the fire' (Act 1, Sc. II) to serve Prospero and win liberty. Ariel Fitzgerald is a teenager on the cusp of liberty, brimming with youthful promise and beauty, but she is also more. Later in the play, her father, haunted by the guilt of her murder, has fevered memories of the child as a half-angel, with wings budding from her shoulder blades. He has a dream in which God says of the girl, 'she's not earth flavour' (Carr 2002: 57), indicating that she does not belong in mortal life, but with God. *Ariel* creates a world where flashes of the eternal and the divine co-exist with the bestial and barbaric. Fermoy dreams of dining with Alexander the Great, Napoleon and Caesar, where they 'all had tiger's feeh under the whihe linen tablecloth' (ibid.: 14). Carr demonstrates that civilization has failed to civilize, failed to separate human beings not only from their savage ancestors in the caves, but from amoral beasts: as Plautus phrased it, 'Homo homini lupus' or 'Man is to other men a wolf.'

At the end of *Ariel*, as mother and daughter face each other down, Frances spits out a repellent image of bestial progeniture: 'some zebra stallion grafted you onta me' (ibid.: 74). This disturbing image connects with our current anxieties about genetic engineering, cloning and artificial intelligence. In our time representations of the human family have become a confused patchwork made up from the Garden of Eden, Darwinian models of species change and interconnection, and the porous boundaries between persons and the technologies they invent. In Carr's play the Fitzgerald family is the human family destroying itself, haunted by the costs of power and ambition, yet powerless to control its future.

Carr's use of space and language in *By the Bog of Cats* and *On Raftery's Hill* very much foreshadows the epic scale and themes found in *Ariel*. Carr is intent on interrogating language as a measure of experience, as it relates both to life, and to the conventions of representation in the theatre. Carr uses language to place her audience in thrall, while she consistently casts into doubt its reliability, its stability and its limits. Her dramatic language on-stage points to what is beyond the representational limits of theatre; it both makes those limits visible and breaches them. The language operates closely in relation to space in the plays. There is a spiralling movement from the open skies of the bog in *By the Bog of Cats* to the abruptly claustrophobic interior of *On Raftery's Hill*, and then to the shattered, brutally exposed home of the Fitzgeralds in *Ariel*. With this arc Carr creates a dialectical struggle between landscape or home as vulnerable sanctuary and the bitter, wounding exposure that is negotiated by dramatic language: and all the while stage images and actions force us to doubt the ideological machinery of representation itself. In *On Raftery's Hill* the Raftery family home occupies the stage; its surroundings dominate the language in sickening descriptions of the polluted natural world that is Red Raftery's farm. The title of the play echoes, with deep irony, the name of Raftery or Antoine O Reachtabhra (1784–1835), the blind poet and musician who wandered through Mayo and Galway and is identified by his colloquial lyricism.[3] The notion of an off-stage world beyond the farm, by which the abusiveness on-stage may be measured, is represented by Dara Mood, Sorrell's fiancé: she forces him out of her life (and the play). The audience watches the appropriation of theatrical representation to normalize savage abuse, rape and incest. Dinah makes jeering reference to social workers and 'the guards [Irish police]' (Carr 2000: 38), reminding spectators that the dramatic world on-stage is cut off from the institutions of civilized society. When Ded asks, 'Whah planeh am I on?', his sister replies 'You're on Raftery's planeh' (ibid.: 49).

But this planet is not as foreign as we might wish. *On Raftery's Hill* reveals a patriarchal family structure which recalls Claude Lévi-Strauss's naturalization of the exchange of women as objects or 'gifts' (Lévi-Strauss 1949). Based on Marcel Mauss's idea that exchange is an organizing principle of society, Lévi-Strauss theorizes systems of kinship which consign women to being 'a conduit of a relationship rather than a partner to it' (Rubin 1975: 174). The incest taboo exists to regulate the traffic in women *between* families or groups (not within them), but it does not challenge, per se, the exchange of women between men. Carr confronts the audience with the roots of patriarchal family structure in this exchange, and with the ambivalence of European high culture in relation to its slippage into incest: 'The Grakes [. . .] Zeus and the missus [. . .] sure they were brother and sister [. . .] sure the whole loh a them was ah ud morning, noon and nigh' (Carr 2000: 43).

In *On Raftery's Hill* dramatic language works in a complex dialectic with visual representation, sometimes taking over from action – as when Red prefaces his attack on his daughter with his statement: 'this is how you gut a hare' (Carr 2000: 36); at other times language is in deeply ironic relationship to action – as when Dinah protests: 'We're a respectable family' (ibid.: 56). The relationship between language, action and coherence is radically destabilized. This chaotic interaction symbolizes a chaos larger than the personal worlds that Carr uses to draw us in.

In *Ariel* power and stage space are detached from one another; there is no sense of the space of the performance belonging to anyone occupying it. The characters are dislocated from landscape. Elaine's image of abandonment of the earth is the ultimate hubristic disdain for the natural world. In *By the Bog of Cats* we are presented with an almost pre-lapsarian vision of the bonds between the human figure and her landscape. Hester's identity is deeply rooted in her surroundings; the Bog of Cats is linked in her mind with her longed-for mother. It is a site of survival certainly, of pain too, but also of beauty and of potential harmony. Hester's life is symbiotic with the bog; it contains her life and death; it is the landscape of her emotions, reflecting her states of mind and confirming her power theatrically. By contrast, the off-stage landscape in *On Raftery's Hill* is despoiled and corrupted by Red Raftery; it reflects the patriarch's destruction of his own family. The claustrophobic move indoors is amplified by Carr in Shalome's repeated failure to leave the farm. She spends the entire play marking the limits of Red's control, within which all the Rafterys are trapped. The nightmarish accounts of Red's brutal treatment of farm animals, of his cruelty and destructiveness, strain credibility and caused great controversy – from both actors and audiences (see Leeney and McMullan 2003: 226). Indeed, the play's savagery proved too much for Americans when it was premiered in the US at the John F. Kennedy Centre in Washington, DC (2000). But the extremity of Red's actions is more than mere grotesquery, and perhaps raises questions 'about the probability of any widespread understanding of Carr's particular dramatic "conversations" ' (ibid.). Red's actions feed into the human/ animal category confusion that is articulated at every level in the play, and create a representation of the ruinous consequence of human interaction with nature based on the exercise of power to pollute and exploit.

In the midst of all the darkness that is undoubtedly central to *By the Bog of Cats, On Raftery's Hill* and *Ariel*, it may be hard to believe that Marina Carr can make us laugh at our folly, as we place our toes over the edge of the abyss. However, her wit and playfulness entertain and disturb in equal measure. As in a number of her earlier plays (such as *The Mai, Portia Coughlan*, and *By the Bog of Cats*), Carr fashions, in *Ariel*, images of water as the element that carries human longing, that calls up life beyond mortality. Landscapes, especially lakes and rivers, are a repository for loss, pain and guilt in *The Mai* and *Portia Coughlan*. In *By the Bog of Cats* the bog itself becomes the site of passion. *On Raftery's Hill* marks a move away from the pastoral towards a Hades. At a further extreme in *Ariel*, the bodies of Fermoy's mother and daughter lie at the bottom of Cuura Lake, amongst numerous corpses of the unwanted and despised. Ariel rises twice from her watery grave; first she haunts her father with her account of the great pike that will not rest until he has caught her; then her remains are hauled up and placed at the centre of Act III. Both these images are of a damaged past, of unavoidable pain and the need for retribution. Cuura Lake contains the shameful secrets of the Fitzgerald family and, it is implied, of the wider human community amongst whom they live. It is a reservoir of crimes past, welling up into the present. In *Ariel*, vengeance belongs to Cuura Lake, to the planet and not to a Christian god.

Marina Carr is a writer alert to the currencies of the world around her, and is inspired in her imaginings of its shadows, its burdens, its passions and its possibilities. In her most recent plays Carr has created stage worlds metonymic of aspects of the twenty-first-century world, where nature and culture have collapsed into one another, where technology devalues biological life and blurs the borders between the animal, the human and the machine. In *Ariel* she writes a fearful and bloody tragedy to rival the excesses of the Greeks and the Jacobeans, while also capturing contemporary anxieties about our status and tenure here on earth.

ACKNOWLEDGEMENT

A section of this chapter was published under the title 'Marina Carr' in Anthony Roche (ed.) (2005). *The UCD Aesthetic: Celebrating 150 Years of UCD Writers*. Dublin: New Island Books, 265–73.

NOTES

1 Victor Merriman, for example, is damning of Carr's work and politics, asserting that: 'It is necessary to question the meaning of these representations as constitutive events in the evolution of civil society' (Leeney and McMullan 2003: 152).

2 Elsewhere, in earlier plays, Carr introduces such passive sufferers of grief. Perhaps Portia in *Portia Coughlan* is the most remark-able example, as she fails to throw off the crippling emotional bonds with her dead twin. In Carr's plays, identity overwhelms borders, and individuals struggle and fail to isolate themselves from connections they cannot control, and which may destroy them.

3 Raftery is the blind poet of Yeats's poem 'The Tower'.

PRIMARY READING

Carr, Marina (1998). 'Dealing with the Dead', *Irish University Review* 28:1, 190–6.

Carr, Marina (1999). *Plays 1*. London: Faber.

Carr, Marina (2000). *On Raftery's Hill*. Oldcastle: Gallery Press.

Carr, Marina (2002). *Ariel*. Oldcastle: Gallery Press.

Churchill, Caryl (1994). *The Skriker*. London: Nick Hern.

FURTHER READING

Boland, Eavan (1989). *A Kind of Scar: The Woman Poet in a National Tradition*. Dublin: Attic Press.

Jordan, Eamonn (2000). *Theatre Stuff: Critical Essays on Contemporary Irish Theatre*. Dublin: Carysfort Press.

Leeney, Cathy and McMullan, Anna (eds.) (2003). *The Theatre of Marina Carr: 'Before Rules Was Made'*. Dublin: Carysfort Press.

Lévi-Strauss, Claude (1949). *The Elementary Structures of Kinship*. Boston: Beacon Press.

Read, Alan (2003). 'Enfance, Animaux et Automates' in *Societas Raffaello Sanzio Romeo Castellucci: Epitaph*. Milan: Ubulibri, 28–31.

Rubin, Gayle (1975). 'The Traffic in Women: Notes on the "Political Economy" of Sex' in Rayna Reiter (ed.). *Toward an Anthropology of Women*. New York: Monthly Review Press, 157–210.

Wallace, Clare (2001). 'Tragic Destiny and Abjection in Marina Carr's *The Mai, Portia Coughlan* and *By the Bog of Cats*', *Irish University Review* 31:2, 431–49.

43

Scrubbing up Nice? Tony Harrison's Stagings of the Past

Richard Rowland

Tony Harrison (b. 1937) is the most significant dramatic poet England has produced since John Dryden, and yet in the standard surveys of modern British drama he is scarcely mentioned. The reception of Harrison's theatrical work is not, however, always confined to mere neglect. When the eagerly awaited Royal Shakespeare Company production of the *Hecuba* of Euripides opened in London in the spring of 2005, in a new translation by Harrison, it received a critical mauling remarkable for both its ferocity and its unanimity. The conjunction of Harrison and controversy was hardly anything new, but this particular chorus of disapproval had little in common with the howls of outrage that emanated from the sanctimonious tabloids (or the right-wing broadsheets that were aping their size and style) when Harrison's bruising poem *v.* was aired on television in 1987. On that occasion the *Daily Mail*, having announced (incorrectly) that the published poem's dedicatee was miners' leader Arthur Scargill, quoted approvingly a Tory MP's declaration that Harrison was a 'Bolshie poet seeking to impose his frustrations on the rest of us'(*Daily Mail* 12 October 1987), but in 2005 the same newspaper merely observed that the poet's translation of the *Hecuba* was at times 'over-colloquial'.

It is clear that modern reinventions of ancient drama have not lost the capacity to run into fruitful collision with the reactionary press. In the Wilson & Wilson company's *Mapping the Edge*, a site-specific version of the *Medea* performed in Sheffield in 2001, Maddie/Medea has the enviable ability to make the *Mail* spontaneously combust just by looking at it; in a venomously ironic scene in Martin Crimp's *Cruel and Tender* (2004), a brilliant reworking of the *Trachiniae* of Sophocles, an African refugee from the 'War on Terror' learns English from a sex-advice section of *Cosmopolitan*; the heroine of Caridad Svich's *Iphigenia Crash Land Falls on the Neon Shell That Was Once Her Heart* (2005) has constantly to confront the fetishistic media image of her sacrifice. As the *Guardian*'s republication of his devastating poem 'A Cold Coming' on the eve of the massive 2003 marches against the Iraq war shows, Harrison himself remains our most potent poet of political protest (Whitehead 2005; Chillington-Rutter 1996). How then, when his *Hecuba* began under such impeccably radical auspices – Hecuba played by Vanessa Redgrave, veteran of anti-war demos stretching back to Grosvenor Square in 1968, the published text adorned with a recent photograph of a prisoner in Abu Ghraib prison, and prefaced by the poet's denunciation of the Bush administration and its butchery in and of the Middle East – can this project have made so little impact, theatrical or political? By examining the strengths and weaknesses of Harrison's most recent dramatic work, this chapter will attempt both to answer that question, and to uncover the mainsprings of the talent that prompted Dominic Dromgoole to call Harrison, rightly, the 'vernacular virtuoso behind three of the greatest theatrical events of the last thirty years' (cover for *Hecuba*, 2005).

One of those events was Harrison's version of the *Oresteia* of Aeschylus, produced, under the direction of Peter Hall and with music by Harrison Birtwistle, at the National Theatre in 1981. At first sight, many of the trademarks of Harrison's (largely) acclaimed translation are also present in his *Hecuba*. From the outset we find a preponderance of the compound words – 'blood-grace' (Harrison 2005: 2), 'blood-gift' (12) – with which the poet, seeking to invest the Greek trilogy with the ritualistic and archaic qualities of Anglo-Saxon verse, anchored the lines of his *Oresteia*. Here too we find obsessive alliteration, a technique used only sparingly by the Greeks themselves. Sometimes this works well: when Hecuba taunts Polymestor, the murderer of her child, for boasting of his privileged access to the divine insights of Dionysus, her sardonic 'Pity your prophet didn't prophesy your pain' (48) captures both the violence and the cool irony of Euripides' writing here, and the half-smile with which Redgrave delivered the line clinched the unnerving effect. But when Harrison's Polyxena imagines her 'girl's gullet gashed open' (9) – Euripides' sacrificial victim talks simply of her throat being cut – the idiosyncrasy of the translation registers more powerfully than the young woman's anguish.

Such explosions of hard consonants are a pervasive feature in Harrison's *Oresteia* too, but his decision to deploy this strategy for the Aeschylean trilogy arose, after extensive consultation with the director, from engagement with a specific theatrical problem: preserving the clarity of a *masked* actor's diction (Astley 1991: 279). Indeed, throughout Harrison's correspondence with Peter Hall we find the poet wrestling with details of stagecraft, the difficulties or opportunities that his verse might offer the players. But in the *Hecuba*, although the makeup of the Chorus's faces suggested the mask convention, no masks were used. Moreover, some lines in the recent work seem to have been composed without thought for the challenge they pose for the actor delivering (or the spectator hearing) them: if it's not easy for a reader to comprehend the sentence Polyxena addresses to Odysseus – 'The suppliants' Zeus won't put you on the spot' (Harrison 2005: 13) – for an audience without access to the apostrophe, it's quite impossible.

Similarly, it would take a nimble tongue to wrap itself around the line 'bridal gold not bloodfleck beads should deck' (6), but in this instance the problem is compounded by the fact that not only is the line to be *sung*, but sung in unison by a Chorus comprised of 12 (female) actors. The choruses in the Theatre of Dionysus did of course sing (and dance), and Harrison's attempt to resurrect that convention was a bold one: it certainly avoided the awkwardness that marred the version that opened at the Donmar (trans. Frank McGuinness, dir. Jonathan Kent) six months before Harrison's, an unrelentingly naturalistic production in which the Chorus was played by a single actor, thus undermining Euripides' repeated insistence on the collectivity of the play's women. But if Harrison's decision to use a sung Chorus was justifiable on scholarly, ideological and (in theory) dramatic grounds, all this counted for little when the music itself – variously compared by reviewers to *Godspell, Evita, Les Misérables*, and Gilbert and Sullivan – was so inappropriate. The role of music in Harrison's theatre-work is important and it's a tale of peaks and troughs to which we will return.

When Harrison's Clytemnestra, gloating over the murdered bodies of her husband and his captive concubine, called him 'Shaggermemnon' and Cassandra 'his bash back on shipboard' (88–9), it was one of the most controversial moments in his *Oresteia*. Subsequent research into both the sexual explicitness and the comic properties of Aeschylus' tragic language has proved Harrison triumphantly accurate as well as theatrically sure-footed (see Sommerstein 2002). Such originality can still be found in Harrison's most recent work. In the great Third Stasimon of the *Hecuba*, the Chorus reflect achingly on the pleasures of home and civic life, now lost for ever in the aftermath of a bloody war. Although Euripides actually has the captive Trojan women express here a kind of fellow-feeling with the Greeks – both long for an end to the fighting and a return to domesticity – it is surely as legitimate for Harrison to imagine the occupying forces as 'slaughter-glutted' and 'sex-starved troops' who shout 'Let's finish it off and fuck off home' as it is for him to invent a lament for Troy's streets, imagined as 'blackened rubble, craters, weeds' (35). But more often, despite the polemical agenda within which Harrison sets his translation, we see the poet neutralizing the explosiveness of his source. When Hecuba calls Cassandra 'my little prophetess', and then launches the wild monody of grief over her dead son with the words 'Doomed child of a doomed mama' (24–5), the frenzied (and explicitly Bacchic) properties with which Euripides has characterized both daughter and lament are replaced with sentimentality (see Mossman 1999: 167–8). Likewise, when the Chorus talk of the occupying 'coalition' refusing to set 'Cassandra's cuddles / above the claims of Achilles / with all his kudos from combat' (5), Harrison's compulsive alliteration produces a cosiness quite at odds with the erotic intensity Euripides (surprisingly) attributes to the union between invading general and his new slave/mistress (see Foley 2001: 94). This is a long way from 'Shaggermemnon' indeed.

Harrison is of course not the first to have readdressed the words of ancient dramatists to contemporary crises. When Martin Luther King was assassinated in 1968, Bobby Kennedy sought to calm the black ghetto in Indianapolis by quoting from the chorus of Aeschylus' *Agamemnon*: 'In our sleep pain which cannot forget falls drop by drop upon the heart until, in our despair, against our will, comes wisdom through the awful grace of God' (ll. 179–81). He did so with a translation which infers a reassuringly causal relationship between God, suffering and understanding. We might call it cowardice or wisdom, but Harrison is a proficient enough Greek scholar to know that, typically, Aeschylus withheld any preposition here with which to establish such a comforting connection, and at an early stage Harrison opted to omit these lines from his *Oresteia* altogether. Similarly audacious decisions were made when he approached the masterpieces of English medieval drama.

When Harrison began work on the Mystery Plays, the clashes that would result in the annihilation of the industrial working class in Britain were just around the corner. It was only four years after the miners' strikes had toppled a Conservative government, and with unemployment increasing at the fastest rate since the 1930s, levels of militancy in the trade union movement were high. Although many politically engaged dramatists in the 1970s and 1980s had shown themselves intrigued by the theatrical spaces and non-naturalistic strategies of medieval theatre – *Red Noses* by Peter Barnes, Edward Bond's *The Fool*, and David Edgar's *O Fair Jerusalem* all nod in this direction – no professional playwright had attempted the wholesale reinvention of the entire biblical sequence. For *The Passion*, first performed outside the National Theatre at Easter 1977, Harrison relied exclusively for his raw materials on the York cycle of plays. He cut and redistributed lines, preserved (or in some cases intensified) the northern dialect forms of the original texts, and, above all, orchestrated the sequence visually in order that the 'product placement' practised by the medieval trade guilds that sponsored the city pageants – the Smiths of Coventry, for instance, ghoulishly advertised their wares by providing the spears carried at the crucifixion and 'a new hoke to hange Judas' (see Davidson 1997; Harris 2002) – was reimagined as a demonstration of solidarity by the rank and file of the urban trade unions: the opening ensemble featured appropriately uniformed firemen and bus conductors, shopworkers and building workers, and Jesus as a carpenter in overalls, and the final image of Christ on the cross was illuminated by a single light from a miner's helmet.

By 1981, when Harrison tackled *The Nativity* (which would become the opening of the *Mysteries* when the *Doomsday* play completed the sequence in 1984), the political situation had altered irrevocably, and the poet's methodology shifted with it. He now began to draw on the resources of all four of the major cycles, sometimes juxtaposing scenes from the 'Towneley' plays with scenes from York, and on other occasions fusing material from two (or more) cycles into a single episode, as with the agonizing Abraham and Isaac exchange, which begins as a redaction of the Coventry version but modulates seamlessly into the version from Chester. This eclecticism has several important consequences. First, tonal diversity is considerably expanded. In an overt challenge to the academization and gentrification of recent performances of (especially the York) plays, Harrison's God descends from a fork-lift truck, picks up a fag-end and pops it behind his ear for later, and addresses his creation in an impeccable Barnsley accent; but the broad comedy with which Harrison invests these opening

Creation and Fall scenes from the York plays is then sharply contrasted with the more brutal Towneley version of the Cain and Abel episode.

Harrison's decision to look beyond the York plays for the components with which to assemble the whole trilogy brought problems, however, as well as advantages. Scholars disagree about the political agenda of the York cycle: for some the plays express the ideals of the city's mercantile governors, for some they contain the seeds of an emergent artisanal voice (see Beckwith 2001: 42–55), and for others their displays of the broken – and thus economically unproductive – bodies of Christ and the slaughtered innocents interrogate the valorization of urban labour (Sponsler 1997: 136–60). But, just as Harrison's rendition of the *Mysteries* has been seen as a challenge to a tradition in which the plays have been interpreted (and translated) by a cultural elite 'invested in maintaining lines of authority' (Huk 1993: 217), so too the Towneley plays – probably performed in an area around Wakefield where the population was insufficiently concentrated to sustain guild organization at all (Palmer 1988) – themselves constituted a radical critique of the civic cycles. In contrast to the York plays, in which the scriptures are explained and enacted in order to foster an acknowledgement of and obedience to the urban political structures of the guilds, the Towneley Shepherds' plays demand of their spectators an identification with a trio of empty-handed rural beggars as the precondition for spiritual understanding (see Nisse 2005: 75–98). It is perhaps inevitable, then, particularly for a poet who regards Christianity as a 'catastrophe' (interview, *The South Bank Show*, March 1998), that Harrison's strategies of selection and omission created difficulties, theatrical and political.

Harrison's shepherds, for instance, are drawn largely from those he found in Wakefield's *Second Shepherds' Play*. When they entered in the National Theatre performance (and the subsequent televised broadcast of that show), they did so accompanied by music reminiscent of BBC TV's programme about sheepdog training, *One Man and his Dog*; in other words they were rustics there to entertain an urban audience. Harrison retains some of the lines in which the shepherds lament their poverty, but does not include those in which they voice their resistance to the dominant order – the liveried 'peacocks' of the city – who expropriate both the fruits of their labour and the tools (wagons, ploughs etc.) they need to execute it. More important still, Harrison omits the lines near the end of the Towneley play in which the shepherds *celebrate* their impoverished condition, on the grounds that their acceptance of Christ-like destitution has granted them access – an access denied to 'Patryarkes' and 'prophetys' (Stevens and Cawley 1994: volume 1, ll. 998–9) – to both the vision of Jesus's birth and the truth of scriptural interpretation. What this small example demonstrates is a process of secularization; the importance of religious conviction to this little fraternity of shepherds is diminished, but the polemical edge of their radicalism, to which their newly confirmed faith gives rise, is blunted too.

This process continues throughout, as Harrison's profound knowledge of the original texts enables him to switch from one 'source' to another with increasing confidence as the cycle progresses. Thus, when the Angel appears to the shepherds,

Harrison momentarily abandons the *Second Shepherds' Play*, and adapts the text of the *First*. This decision makes good dramatic sense: the initial reaction of the *First* Wakefield shepherds to divine visitation is fearful wonder, and this enables Harrison to get his shepherds quickly on the road to Bethlehem, whereas the shepherds of the second play launch into a bizarrely recondite discussion of the technical properties of angelic song. Fascinating as their analysis of breves and crotchets is, it would scarcely work in *The Mysteries* because Harrison's Angel doesn't actually sing at all. The production did offer angelic sounds at this point – the exquisitely vulnerable voice of Linda Thompson, a figure of near-cult status on the electric folk scene, soared above the National's Cottesloe theatre – but she sang not the 'Gloria' specified in the Towneley text, but words ('Shay fan yan lay') which evoked the Sufi brand of Islam embraced by Ms Thompson and her former husband Richard, the iconic guitarist and songwriter whose own work features at pivotal moments in Harrison's text.

Music is not incidental to Harrison's theatre-work but absolutely central to its momentum and meaning. When, as with the *Oresteia*, this involves a genuine collaboration between playwright and composer, the result can be one of the most significant triumphs of the production. But, as the actor Jack Shepherd (Satan and Death in *The Mysteries* and a lead in *The Trackers* of 1988) reminds us, the poet was instinctively more at home working with Birtwistle – whose music is unremittingly and unapologetically marked by fierce harmonic and rhythmic complexity – than he was with the folk group, The Home Service, who arranged and performed the music for *The Mysteries* (Astley 1991: 424). Here, as in the *Hecuba*, there is a collision between Harrison's ideological and aesthetic agendas, only this time theology is thrown into the mix too.

The deployment of Richard Thompson's own music in *The Mysteries* encapsulates the problem. At the close of the Abraham and Isaac interlude, the band sing the chorus (only) from Thompson's 'Calvary Cross': 'Everything you do / You do for me / Everything you do you do for me' (48). It is not surprising that a modern sensibility should find this story disturbing: the second of Benjamin Britten's *Canticles*, similarly based on the Chester text, only reaches an uneasy resolution when the voices of father and child combine to produce the voice of the 'merciful' God. But Thompson's song is a terrifying if brilliant dirge concerned with spiritual annihilation, one which specifically denies the consolations offered by myth, and a song so dark that Thompson himself later remarked that he wouldn't want to live in it. If this fragment sits oddly alongside the new lines Harrison writes to illustrate the rationale for God's behaviour here, there is an ideological and philosophical (if not a theological) coherence about concluding *The Passion* with Thompson's 'We Sing Allelujah'. After a strangely muted 'buffeting' – the tormentors '*freeze*' in an emblematic '*tableau*' (*The Mysteries* in Harrison 1999: s.d., 118), Harrison eschewing the extravagant quantities of gore the original cycles deployed to convey both the savagery of Christ's treatment and the salvific properties of the blood he shed (Travis 1985) – Jesus's suffering is summarized by a solitary miner who leaves the playing space, elucidating the significance of the crucifixion in absolute certainty that his message will go unheeded; and the band then plays Thompson's mordantly carnivalesque ballad in its entirety. As the song celebrates people's ability to laugh at their own poverty and mortality, its refrain – 'And we work all day in the old fashioned way' (156–67) – also boasts, ironically, of continuity. Harrison's cycle refuses the transcendent comforts of epiphany, but when *The Passion* took its central place in the trilogy in 1984–5, the 'old-fashioned ways' of both labour itself and the trade union solidarity designed to protect the labourers were in terminal collapse. The miner's departing words, 'ye set nought by my saw' (156), are grimly and doubly prophetic. First, they anticipate the annihilation of the pit communities, a catastrophe movingly charted in Harrison's 1998 *Prometheus* (and we should note that this remarkable fusion of poetry and film is only one of Harrison's contributions to a genre he virtually invented and of which he remains by far the most innovative practitioner – on which see the fine analysis in Hall 2004). Secondly, the phrase articulates the poet's recurring fear that artistic attempts to expose and eradicate injustice will go unheard: when in 1995 Harrison himself took the role of the banned ancient tragedian Phrynichos in *The Labourers of Herakles*, his anxiety that 'art cannot redeem / the cry from Krajina or the Srbrenica scream' was greeted only by the third Labourer's incredulous 'Who the fuck was that?' (Harrison 1996: 143–5).

The Mysteries were commercially successful, but many of Harrison's most ambitious projects have been anything but. Although he has written with eloquence and enthusiasm about the ephemeral nature of theatrical performance, his candour on the subject is understandably tinged with regret, since few contemporary dramatists can have produced so many major works which have failed altogether to achieve realization on the professional stage. So, while Harrison accepts unflinchingly the fact that his first rewriting of the *Lysistrata* of Aristophanes, a 1960s piece written (with the Irish poet James Simmons) for Nigerian student actors and village musicians, is unplayable outside its specific geographical and political context, he acknowledges more ruefully that his second version of the play, published as the first part of *The Common Chorus*, has also been 'marooned in its moment' (Harrison 2002b: 197). This play turned the iconoclastic vitriol of Old Comedy against the machismo which, with alarmingly conflated interventions into issues of gender, sexuality and politics, underpinned US foreign policy in the 1980s. Harrison set both his Aristophanic adaptation, and the version of the *Trojan Women* of Euripides which forms the second part of *The Common Chorus*, at the US air-base at Greenham Common, against which a women's peace camp around the perimeter fence offered an incessant protest for several years.

Harrison's strategies of omission from and embellishment of his sources are again significant. The beginning of the *Trojan Women* is odd even by Euripides' genre-bending standards. Its prologue sounds like an epilogue and it announces a plot which the play itself will not deliver. It also includes an invitation to the audience to watch the pain of Hecuba, 'if anyone wishes to look' (Euripides 1986: l. 36) – a phrase which even the scholiast (the earliest commentator of antiquity) called a cold invitation indeed, and which suggests that in 415 BC Euripides was becoming increasingly uncertain about the moral efficacy of tragedy. Harrison, on the other hand, still believes that to engage with the victims of past atrocities is to 'guarantee that the suffering was not in vain, and that the chain of commemorative empathy is unbroken' (Harrison 2002b: 192). So, it is in keeping with this conviction that Poseidon's laconic challenge is left out, and it is this same conviction that also prompts Harrison's most telling additions, such as the potent blend of scorn and compassion in Cassandra's observation that the dead of the occupying forces will end up as a 'few white dusty ounces / left in a place the newscaster mispronounces' (301).

If this valuable reworking of Euripides proved abortive in terms of performance – and the same was true of the even more radical *Medea: A Sex-War Opera* (1985) – Harrison's encounter with Aristophanes has experienced an even more deplorable fate. It might have been worse – the radical theatre company 7:84 virtually imploded during its attempt to update the *Thesmophoriazusae* of Aristophanes a year earlier (MacLennan 1990: 139–43) – but not much. It is one thing to observe that Aristophanes seems to have found the notion of people *reading* rather than watching plays absurdly funny (e.g. Aristophanes 1996: ll. 52–4, 1407–10), and we might also note the frequency with which Harrison envisages the physical destruction of his own texts – the closing stage direction of *The Kaisers of Carnuntum* has the poet '*scattering the pages of the play's script to the four winds*' (Harrison 1996: 109) – but it is quite another for Faber to have reprinted some copies of *1 Common Chorus* in 2002 with 50 pages of Harrison's adaptation of the *Lysistrata* of Aristophanes replaced by 50 pages of someone else's novel.

It is ironic that the play of Harrison's which has attracted almost unqualified acclaim, and which now seems likely to secure a theatrical legacy of revivals and reinventions, was originally conceived as an ephemeral work (and another in which the poet finally imagines his play text as only bits of urban litter). *The Trackers of Oxyrhynchus* was written, designed and cast for a one-off performance in the Stadium at Delphi in July 1988, but both the success of the premiere, and the increasing severity with which the social and cultural divisions the play addresses were being experienced in Thatcher's Britain, provoked Harrison to undertake a wholesale revision of the text for performances at the National in 1990 (and subsequent shows in Vienna and elsewhere).

Harrison's starting point (in both versions) is the discovery in 1907 of a substantial fragment of the *Ichneutae* of Sophocles, the only sustained example of the tragic poet's work in the genre of the satyr play. Rather like the jigs with which early modern amphitheatre plays (including tragedies) concluded, satyr plays provided the coda to the performance of tragic trilogies in the Theatre of Dionysus. As this fragment shows, these dramas were of considerable length and were scripted as carefully as the tragedies that preceded them, but the irreverence of their content and the obscenity of their lexical registers have combined to ensure both the extinction of almost all the texts themselves and the embarrassment or neglect of modern scholarship in the face of such textual evidence as has survived.

Harrison's response to the fragment itself is rich and complex. He is not, as some critics imply, just delighted to discover that Sophocles could write dirty too; although he translates most of the *Ichneutae* in the course of his own play, he does not, surprisingly, include the aloof nymph Cyllene's extraordinary injunction that the satyr leader should 'Cease to expand your smooth phallus with delight' (Sophocles 1996: 173). But Harrison does wreak creative havoc with both the genre and the plot of the original Greek text. The Sophoclean play is incomplete, and scholars disagree about the direction its narrative might have taken, but Harrison has supplied his own conclusion: the satyrs recover not Apollo's stolen cattle, but the lyre made from their skins, a wondrous instrument which the god then appropriates for his exclusive use, palming his cloven-hoofed assistants off with ghetto-blasters wrapped in gold paper. It is clear, moreover, that the satyr plays were conceived, linguistically and dramatically, within comic rather than tragic conventions (Zagagi 1999), but *Trackers* ends, in the final published text, with the '*silent scream*' of the satyr Silenus, as he confronts the terrible consequences of his complicity with an elitist and exclusionist culture (Harrison 2004: s.d., 148).

The National Theatre version of *Trackers* is a leaner and tougher play than its Delphic predecessor. The part of Hunt, one of the academics who discovered the Sophoclean fragment, is completely reconceived: the amiable pedant of the first version speaks in the second with the urgently admonitory tones of Harrison himself, thus lending his later mutation into the articulate but hapless Silenus a thematic cogency. Ideological inconsistencies are ironed out in the rewrite too. When Silenus mused in Delphi that 'Disco descends directly from the lyre / and global holocaust from cosy fire' (Harrison 2004: 75), Harrison was in danger of validating the very cultural snobbery his play was designed to attack, and the removal of these lines is consistent with the National version's clearer focus on the ways in which 'high' culture – literary, musical, theatrical – has always marginalized (or worse) the voices of the dispossessed. Harrison's most concise assaults on artistic indifference to 'the losers and the tortured' – 'The kithara cadenza, the Muse's mezzo trill / cover the skinning and the screaming still' (Harrison 2004: 80, 138) – are present in both versions, but acquire renewed intensity in the rewrite when the satyrs become the destitute inhabitants of the cardboard city that spectators have to pick their way through on their way to the National Theatre.

This takes us to the heart of the difficult territory Harrison has chosen to occupy within British cultural life. Politically, with his roots in the northern industrial working class, his sympathies lie with the marginalized and dispossessed, and the organizations founded to defend them. Accordingly, he has attempted to incorporate and privilege within his work the forms – linguistic idiom, accent, traditional song, music-hall, even seaside-postcard humour – which that class has developed to express its aspirations, disappointments and playfulness. Intellectually, however, Harrison has consistently immersed himself in the most arcane of studies, counting amongst his closest associates men such as the uncompromising Birtwistle and the classicist Oliver Taplin, whose *The Stagecraft of Aeschylus* was one of the most challenging contributions to Greek scholarship of the twentieth century. It is not simply that Harrison has had to stand astride these two very different worlds; he has attempted, with a combination of formidable erudition and the scholarly equivalent of revolutionary violence, to obliterate the distinctions between high and low culture altogether. In the process, he has also placed on actors and directors demands – of precision, of energy, and of the ability to adapt to unusual performance venues – which very few have either the training or the inclination to meet; Barrie Rutter's magnificent Northern Broadsides company is perhaps the only outfit which has proven itself consistently able to meet them.

In the late summer of 2005 Harrison, stung by the disappointment of the performances of *Hecuba* in the UK, threw himself into overseeing wholesale changes of direction and design for the play's appearance in the USA, and the reception of the work there has been much more favourable. It's typical of this poet, now nearly 70, to display such vigour. Rather like Mak, the sheep-stealer of the *Mysteries*, Harrison has found himself in the pillory – for his iconoclasm, his political commitment and his ambition – but in his case he has willingly placed himself in this vulnerable position. In 1707 Daniel Defoe, another radical dissenter whose literary strategies often earned him opprobrium from his natural allies as well as from the church and Tory establishment, found himself in the pillory too. On that occasion thousands flocked to the scene, and they threw neither wet sponges nor bricks, but flowers, to celebrate – despite the errors of judgement – the writer's intentions and courage. At a time when many theatre practitioners think that adorning productions of Shakespeare or Verdi with actors in orange suits is a sufficiently serious response to the nightmare of Guantanamo, we should, for Harrison, follow the lead of those eighteenth-century Londoners.

PRIMARY READING

Harrison, Tony (1996). *Plays 3*. London: Faber and Faber.

Harrison, Tony (1999). *Plays 1*. London: Faber and Faber.

Harrison, Tony (2002a). *Plays 2*. London: Faber and Faber.

Harrison, Tony (2002b). *Plays 4*. London: Faber and Faber.

Harrison, Tony (2004). *Plays 5*. London: Faber and Faber.

Harrison, Tony (trans.) (2005). *Hecuba by Euripides*. London: Faber and Faber.

FURTHER READING

Aeschylus (1979). *Agamemnon*, trans. Hugh Lloyd-Jones. London: Duckworth.

Aristophanes (1996). *The Frogs*, ed. and trans. Alan H. Sommerstein. Oxford: Aris and Phillips.

Astley, Neil (ed.) (1991). *Tony Harrison*. Newcastle: Bloodaxe.

Beckwith, Sarah (2001). *Signifying God: Social Relations and Symbolic Act in the York Corpus Christi Plays*. Chicago: University of Chicago Press.

Chillington-Rutter, Carol (1996). 'The Poet and the Geldshark: War and the Theatre of Tony Harrison' in Tony Howard and John Stokes (eds.). *Acts of War: the Representation of Military Conflict on the British Stage and Television since 1945*. Aldershot: Scolar Press, 145–63.

Davidson, Clifford (1997). *Technology, Guilds, and Early English Drama*. Kalamazoo: Medieval Institute Publications.

Euripides (1986). *Trojan Women*, ed. Shirley A. Barlow. Warminster: Aris and Phillips.

Euripides (1991). *Hecuba*, ed. C. Collard. Warminster: Aris and Phillips.

Foley, Helene (2001). *Female Acts in Greek Tragedy*. Princeton: Princeton University Press.

Hall, Edith (2004). 'Aeschylus, Race, Class, and War in the 1990s' in Edith Hall, Fiona Macintosh and Amanda Wrigley (eds.). *Dionysus since 69: Greek Tragedy at the Dawn of the Third Millennium*. Oxford: Oxford University Press, 169–97.

Harris, Jonathan Gil (2002). 'Properties of Skill: Product Placement in Early English Artisanal Drama' in Jonathan Gil Harris and Natasha Korda (eds.). *Staged Properties in Early Modern English Drama*. Cambridge: Cambridge University Press, 35–66.

Huk, Romana (1993). 'Postmodern Classics: The Verse Drama of Tony Harrison' in James Acheson (ed.). *British and Irish Drama since 1960*. London: Macmillan, 202–26.

MacLennan, Elizabeth (1990). *The Moon Belongs to Everyone: Making Theatre with 7:84*. London: Methuen.

Mossman, Judith (1999). *Wild Justice: A Study of Euripides' 'Hecuba'*. London: Bristol Classical Press.

Nisse, Ruth (2005). *Defining Acts: Drama and the Politics of Interpretation in Late Medieval England*. Notre Dame, IN: University of Notre Dame Press.

Palmer, Barbara (1988). ' "Towneley Plays" or "Wakefield Cycle" Revisited', *Comparative Drama* 22, 318–48.

Sommerstein, Alan (2002). 'Comic Elements in Tragic Language: The Case of Aeschylus' *Oresteia*' in Andreas Willi (ed.). *The Language of Greek Comedy*. Oxford: Oxford University Press, 151–68.

Sophocles (1996). *Ichneutae* in Hugh Lloyd-Jones (ed.). *Sophocles III*. Cambridge, MA: Harvard University Press.

Sponsler, Claire (1997). *Drama and Resistance: Bodies, Goods, and Theatricality in Late Medieval England*. Minneapolis: University of Minnesota Press.

Stevens, M. and Cawley, A. C. (eds.). (1994). *The Towneley Plays*, 2 vols. Oxford: Early English Text Society.

Travis, Peter (1985). 'The Social Body of the Dramatic Christ in Medieval England', *Early English Drama, Acta* 13, 17–36.

Whitehead, Anne (2005). 'Tony Harrison, the Gulf War and the Poetry of Protest', *Textual Practice* 19:2, 349–72.

Zagagi, Netta (1999). 'Comic Patterns in Sophocles' *Ichneutae*' in Jasper Griffin (ed.). *Sophocles Revisited*. Oxford: Oxford University Press, 177–218.

44

The Question of Multiculturalism: The Plays of Roy Williams

D. Keith Peacock

Since 1996 Roy Williams has been a prolific writer. His plays have been performed in small-scale venues, regional theatres, the Royal Court and the National Theatre. He was born in London in 1968 of Afro-Caribbean parentage and acknowledges that his work inevitably reflects his racial background: 'the fact that I'm black myself, will naturally come through. I have no problem with that. I just write what I want to write about' (Cobham 2004: n.p.). He resists, however, the circumscribing description 'black playwright': 'there are many times when I've been told, "Is he a black playwright, coloured playwright?" I just say, "look you worry about that and I'll do my work. Thank you very much"' (ibid.). He has explored the effect of the West Indian diaspora on first-generation immigrants, and his work (with the exception of *Sing Yer Heart Out for the Lads* in 2002) centres on characters like himself, of Afro-Caribbean descent. His perspective is racially inclusive. This inclusiveness appears to have resulted from 'growing up with white kids at school. When I finished school, I go [*sic*] home with them, have dinner at their houses' (Animashawun 2004: n.p.). Reference in his plays to this interracial experience, not simply in regard to racism, has taken their subject matter into new areas. Although most of his plays are set in London, they do not exhibit a narrow metropolitanism. As John Mcleod has written: 'London's transcultural facticity has made possible new communities and forms of culture indebted to its history of "peopling" which, in turn, come to pose a considerable challenge to the pastoral articulation of English national culture as representative' (McLeod 2004: 18). He adds that 'living in and writing about London affords an opportunity to intervene in, critique and contest the received notions of culture and identity that impact nationally *as well as* locally even though national and local culture is not coincident' (ibid.: 18). Intervening in, critiquing and contesting received notions of culture and identity are fundamental to Williams's project. This begins with the interrogation of what it means to be black, a topic central to his play *Clubland* (2001). In his article 'New Ethnicities' Stuart Hall identifies 'a significant shift that has been going on (and is still going on) in black cultural politics' since

World War II (Hall 1988: 252). Broadly, this has involved a redefinition of the term 'black', which was coined 'as a way of referencing the common experience of racism and marginalization in Britain' and provided an 'organizing category of a new politics of resistance, amongst groups and communities with, in fact, very different histories, traditions and ethnic identities' (ibid.: 252). The aim of this category was for dominant white culture to position blacks as 'other'. Hall suggests that, from the late 1980s, this categorization began to be displaced, in the face of the hegemonic Thatcherite concept of 'Englishness', by a politics of ethnicity predicated on difference and diversity, at the centre of which was the question of 'what it means to be British'. In this politics the races, including, in Williams's plays, the white English, are viewed as different, their identities, both cultural and individual, affected by 'a particular place', a 'particular history', a 'particular experience', a 'particular culture' (ibid.: 258). These factors, as Williams illustrates in his plays, show that what it means to be black and British is different for Africans, Afro-Caribbeans, first-generation immigrants, those born in Britain and those whose British genealogy can be traced back to the eighteenth century. Williams's descriptions of 'black' and 'white' against the dramatis personae in published plays such as *Sing Yer Heart Out* and *Fallout* (2003) should, therefore, not be read simplistically.

In the light of this argument the term 'British' becomes problematic and contested. As Paul Gilroy points out, 'to be British is [...] to contract into a category of administrative convenience rather than an ethnic identity' (Gilroy 1993: 75. 'British' comfortably subsumes the identities of four nations but is, in reality, marshalled around the concept of 'Englishness'. This, suggests Gilroy, makes difficult the 'tasks of creating a more pluralistic sense of national identity and a new conception of national culture' (ibid.: 75). Racial and cultural alignment is a perpetually shifting process and in Williams's plays black *and* white English cultures, in reacting and adjusting to each other, challenge the concept of what it means to be black or white and English. In *Sing Yer Heart Out for the Lads* Williams also sets the examination of English nationalism in the wider context of what it means to be British. In Williams's plays the individual's perception of self owes less to racial background than to environment. He explores how the young, in particular – in the process of discovering their identity in a multiracial society – are affected by that environment. In doing so he interrogates the meaning of 'multicultural' and asks: 'Are we really as multicultural as we say we are?' (Cavendish 2004: 17). The term 'multicultural' has idealistic and, Williams implies, somewhat complacent implications. It refers to immigrants and the indigenous population preserving their cultures and interacting peacefully within one nation. 'Multiracial', on the other hand, is simply descriptive and suggests a mixture of races who may or may not accept each other's cultural values. In Williams's plays, English society is not multicultural: the various races are, on the one hand, in continuous conflict – as represented by the racist nationalist parties; and on the other hand, young and old, male and female, black and white adapt to and even adopt each other's cultural values and lifestyles, establishing their identities in relation to racial stereotyping.

Williams has written about the disappointments of the Jamaican diaspora experienced by his parents' generation in *The No Boys Cricket Club* (1996), set in 1950s Jamaica and present-day London; *Starstruck* (1998), set in 1970s Kingston; and *The Gift* (2000), set in Clarendon, Jamaica. The plays were for him 'a vital means of finding out who I was and where I came from. I just couldn't have written about my take on Britain without first looking at my parents' experience' (Cavendish 2004: 17). Members of Williams's generation, born in Britain, are, however, faced with other challenges, and it is in exploring these that Williams has established his distinctive voice as a dramatist. Although his plays usually centre on characters of Afro-Caribbean descent, they have since *Lift Off* (1999) also exhibited a concern with the individual, both black and white, within a multiracial urban culture. Williams portrays a range of points of view, rather than presenting polemic based on a simplistic social analysis. The selection of the range of viewpoints, the complexity of the dramatic structuring of the interaction between them, and the nature of their resolution can reveal implications beyond the social stereotypes held of 'others' by every social and racial group. Consequently his plays are character- rather than plot-driven. Nevertheless, Williams's characters are not simply one-sided representatives of contemporary multiracial urban culture but are often psychologically contradictory and vulnerable to external influences, and share the fundamental question: who am I? This comprehensiveness is Williams's strength as a writer. As he remarked in an interview, between persecutor and persecuted, between good and bad, 'there's a big grey area we need to look at, rather than going from one extreme to another' (Cavendish 2004: 17). He challenges not only racial, but also xenophobic, sexual and gender-based stereotypes, and often two or more simultaneously. The representative characters include young black men who want to assume Afro-Caribbean male stereotypes of the 'bad bwai' or sexually voracious stud; white men and boys who adopt black talk based on Jamaican patois in order to appear 'cool'; second- and third-generation Afro-Caribbean males who want to be accepted by whites and those who cannot, or do not want to, conform to the stereotypical Caribbean-inspired behaviour of their race and gender; male and female racists, black and white characters who try to be racially liberal but under severe provocation are shocked to discover themselves uttering racist insults; and black girls who aggressively resist sexual exploitation by black men and are jealous of the latter's attraction to white women.

In *Lift Off* Williams explores the effect of Afro-Caribbean stereotypes on the lives of three young men, two black and one white, who in the first act are trying to establish their place within society at their moment of 'lift off' from child to adult. As a black child, Mal creates an inauthentic self by adopting the stereotypical male persona of 'bad bwai' speaking black urban street talk. In the 10 years that elapse between the first and second acts, he has become part of the black drug culture, has had transient sexual relationships, and is perceived by many black and white men and white women as 'cool' and sexy. A male participant in a study of black masculinity by Claire Alexander describes white women's stereotyping of black male sexuality: 'We're well-toned, we're physical, we're funny, we're rhythmic [. . .] We have nice bodies, we look good. Just look at a white man – look at a twenty-five-year-old white man to a twenty-five-year-old black man' (Alexander 2000: 381). Black men, as another participant points out, are also perceived to be 'well-endowed' (ibid.).

Having established Mal's stereotypical black masculinity, Williams explores the realities and moral implications behind the external superficialities of speech, dress and behaviour by depriving the characters of their self-delusions. Racial stereotypes are interrogated, and as in many of Williams's plays, the mood gets progressively darker. Mal's blackness will lead to his death from leukaemia: a bone-marrow transplant could cure him, but the marrow can only be taken from a black man, and black men do not register as potential donors. His own race will let him die. When he takes his white friend Tone to visit a West End club, Mal reveals himself to be violent and racist when he draws a Stanley knife on the black Africans serving in the Kentucky Fried Chicken takeaway. Racism, the exercise of power – in this case, violence – associated with prejudice, is shown not to be confined to the white population (Williams 2002: 208). It also becomes apparent that Mal is not perceived by all white women as 'cool' and, as the white girl Hannah whom they meet in the club points out, he is a hindrance rather than an aid to Tone's attempts to attract women.

Mal's stereotypical black male sexuality is also revealed to be destructive in that it is completely self-centred. Tone's schoolgirl sister thinks that Mal will be exciting to seduce and becomes pregnant. Mal, despite his friendship with Tone, reacts according to what he believes to be the macho stereotype and dismisses her as 'still pussy' (Williams 2002: 230) and 'nuttin but a fuckin little whore' (ibid.: 225). His ultimate self-awareness, revealed by his recognition of the damage caused by his inauthentic self and his admission that he has received his just deserts in the form of his illness, do, however, offer the possibility of change.

The sexually voracious black stereotype is again interrogated in *Clubland*. Ade is a black African immigrant who is considered to be racially different by those of West Indian origin born in Britain, who consider themselves British. One of the latter, Kenny, exhibits racial prejudice, describing Ade as 'so black, he's blue' and calling him 'sooty' (Williams 2004: 61). Ade is, however, like Mal, physically attractive to women, and uses this as a weapon in the struggle he has been waging since his childhood to establish his cultural status as equal and acceptable to the white majority. He represents black male reaction to the wider power structures in society and, as Alexander suggests, 'the powerlessness of black men in white society [is] rearticulated and contested at a street level to empower black men through the use of white women' (Alexander 2000: 379). He wants to have sex with as many white women as possible to prove that he is superior both to the black boys, including Kenny, who did not defend him at school, and to the white boys who beat him up. Again, however, the creation of an inauthentic self, inspired by the racial stereotype of black stud, endears him neither to blacks nor to whites and even debars him from a serious relationship with his black girlfriend, Sandra.

In contrast to the inauthentic, stereotypical, macho black youths Mal and Ade, Rich in *Lift Off* is a black, psychologically authentic schoolboy who acts his age, is gentle, is shy with girls and does not talk black, and his paper aeroplanes symbolically 'lift off' from their urban environment. Because he does not conform to the 'bad bwai' stereotype he is bullied and treated as a misfit, a homosexual, and made to perform like an animal by Mal and Tone, who cannot understand his rejection of the black urban culture they so admire. His presence in the play challenges the stereotype of what it means to be black. In a surrealistic confrontation between the adult Mal and the dead child Rich, who has since escaped the existence into which he was born by 'flying' from a tower-block, Mal admits his culpability for Rich's suicide. The young Mal and Tone exploited, bullied and humiliated Rich because he did not fit a stereotype, but worst of all, they robbed him of his identity. 'U ain't nuttin' man' says Young Mal and 'he ain't black. Fuck know what he is' (Williams 2002: 234–5). Mal also tears up Rich's paper aeroplane, his means of escaping the culture he hates. As the dead Rich tells the guilt-ridden Mal: 'if I ain't better than a white kid, then I'm nuttin. It's what you said' (236). Nevertheless, although their different perceptions of being black kept them apart in life, Mal realizes that he and Rich now have something in common – their mortality. Each is a victim of black urban culture.

The dangers of emulating the black macho stereotype of 'bad bwai' for both black and white children are illustrated in *Sing Yer Heart Out*. Bad T. and Duane, two black teenagers, attempt to impersonate tough gangsta rappers and bully both Asian and white boys such as Glen, who himself tries to emulate them by talking black and being aggressive. When they rob him and he is thwarted from taking revenge on them with a kitchen knife, he attacks the nearest black man who stands in his way, Mark. 'You lot, you think yer so fuckin bad, I'll show you who's bad', cries Glen before he stabs him (Williams 2004: 232). The culture of violence is the reality behind the 'bad bwai' image.

Williams deploys three female characters, the white girls Hannah and Carol in *Lift Off* and the black girl Sandra in *Clubland*, to reveal and interrogate the effects of stereotypical black male sexuality. Carol, Tone's schoolgirl sister in *Lift Off*, emulates black street-talk and tries to appear sexually experienced and liberated. When she enters Tone's bedroom to find him watching a pornographic video she shocks him with her outspokenness: 'Fuck! Is that real?.... Size of his dick man' (Williams 2002: 180). Having borrowed a sexy dress from a friend, she seduces Mal because she is excited by his black sexual persona. The result of the seduction is Carol's pregnancy. Unfortunately for her, in the black macho male culture men treat women merely as sexual trophies who, once won, are callously abandoned. Again Williams reveals both the unpleasant reality behind the stereotype and the dangers of naïvely adopting an inauthentic persona simply because it is superficially exciting.

While in *Lift Off* Hannah questions the truth and attraction of black male sexuality – 'his lot ain't all that you know' (Williams 2002: 209) – in *Clubland* Ade's black girlfriend, Sandra, whom he describes as a 'feisty nigger woman wid attitude' (Williams 2004: 119), disapproves of black male promiscuity with white women.

Her attitude to black men is established forcefully by her telephone conversation with a girlfriend. She is so foul-mouthed that she shocks the listening Ade – 'I told the girl I say "Nicole, Nicole, darlin that Brendan of yours ain't nuttin, he ain't worth shit, he's a fuckin crackhead, drop him" ' (ibid.: 66). This aggressive attitude is primarily defensive, and although she does not appear to have respect for black men, she is jealous of their attraction to white women and wants them to stay with their own race. To achieve this she attempts to succumb to Ade's sexual demands involving handcuffs, but is unable to do so. It is evident that her problem with black men arises from her unwillingness to lose control, evidenced by outspoken lack of respect and unwillingness to be subservient. In Sandra's opinion black men are 'sorry-arsed niggers' whose 'brains are in your dicks' (ibid.: 97). Although she likes to be in control, during her short affair with Kenny she finds his passivity too boring and returns to Ade, who is willing to abandon the black male stereotype and to give up seducing white women. He now acknowledges the sense of security and completeness offered by a close relationship – 'we stay in and watch telly all day like we used to yeah? When we first went out. I go out for KFC. Then we stay in bed all evening and watch *Blind Date*, Sandra?' (ibid.: 120).

In *Lift Off* the consequences and individual implications for males of the adoption of black male stereotypes is examined in terms not only of black males but also of white. The white schoolboy, Tone, has only one friend, a black boy, Mal. Tone seeks to establish a personal and cultural identity by emulating Mal's 'cool' persona, by using black urban talk, wearing black urban-style clothes and being involved in the gang fights led by a black boy, Delroy, who is considered to be 'bad'. As an adult Tone is concerned that he is not 'black' enough and that the reason why he does not attract girls is because his white penis is smaller than a black man's. He becomes aware of the personal inadequacy inherent in this contrivance when the white girl, Hannah, whom he and Mal have met in a West End night club confronts him with the pitifulness of trying to be something he is not: 'There must be something missing in your life if you think acting like them is going to fill it for you' (Williams 2002: 209). This is the first stage in his progression to self-awareness. His fantasy of the black male stereotype on which his persona is constructed is further eroded by Mal's news that their 'bad bwai' icon, Delroy, has now been released from prison and has become a Muslim. Finally, encouraged by Hannah, in angry response to Mal's insults concerning his sister, Carol, Tone recognizes the destructive nature of the black macho stereotype and rejects it in an outburst of racial abuse, calling Mal a 'black bastard' and a 'nigger' (ibid.: 232). Once he has acknowledged the reality behind the racial stereotypes upon which he has based his inauthentic self and realized that he was not being true to himself, he is able to relate to and sympathize with Mal as a fellow human being.

The psychological and social inadequacy represented by the construction of an inauthentic racial self, seen in *Lift Off*, is further illustrated in *Clubland*, where the white male, Ben, asserts his identity in a multiracial society by talking black. He is married, but tries to impress his friends by also adopting a black macho treatment of women, claiming that he dreams of smashing his elbow into his wife's over-large front teeth (Williams 2004: 80). Like Tone he is represented as a sad, self-deluding loser. His inadequacy in establishing interpersonal relationships is indicated by the fact that he collects prostitutes' cards from telephone boxes and occasionally visits them, but only for 'a blow-job' (ibid.: 101). He stays with the wife he loathes because, after four years, her father has recently promoted him to a management post, but the fact that nepotism has taken so long suggests other inadequacies. Ben finally does hit his wife, but his macho image is shattered when she throws him out of their house.

Like other characters, Ben exhibits contradictions. Although his best friend, Kenny, is black, he makes racist jokes based on black stereotypes. He tells Kenny that he has an Alsatian guard dog called Adolf that he has been training 'to attack blacks. Nuff burglaries round here committed by you lot' (ibid.: 75). Although he subsequently admits that the dog's name is Prince, it is not clear whether he really feels threatened by his black neighbours or whether he is making fun of his friend's gullibility. Even more forcibly than Tone, Ben is made to face up to the fact that he is not a macho black stud and has lost his job by acting like one with his wife. He renews his friendship with the white, Nathan, whom he shunned after his marriage when Nathan abandoned laddish pursuits. At the end of the play Ben achieves the self-awareness that may lead to the attainment of a psychologically and racially authentic self. The implication of these examples of self-awareness is that the first stage in multiculturalism is acceptance of one's racial and cultural background and that of others.

In *Clubland* Ben attempts to emulate a black male stereotype while Kenny rejects this and aligns himself with white culture. Kenny is 29, an assistant bank-manager and, in his culture, rather too old to be visiting clubs and not to have a girlfriend or wife. Like Rich in *Lift Off*, he does not fit the stereotype of the young black male. He lacks aggression and is unable to hold his own in a fight. Despite the jibes of friends such as Nathan, he seeks white approval and would like to be a white man. He is happy to be deferential to his white friend Ben, but in doing so he demeans himself by allowing Ben to exercise superiority. In relation to women, Kenny also does not conform to the black macho stereotype and is too shy to approach girls. He is also racist towards Ade. At the close of the play, having been refused marriage by Ade's black ex-girlfriend Sandra, Kenny has acknowledged his difference from the black stereotypical male but has found the courage to approach women without Ben's help and is no longer too eager.

The character who most desires to be accepted by white society is Barry in *Sing Yer Heart Out*, who is used by Williams to explore what it means to be English/British and, as discussed earlier, the relationship between the two. Williams describes his aims in writing the play: 'I very much wanted to write a bigger play, not simply about race, but about British Nationalism: what does it mean to be British in the twenty-first century, who's more British now, the blacks or the whites' (Williams 2004: x). Symbolically, the action occurs during England's World Cup qualifying match with Germany in 2000, in the King George pub in south–west London, with flags showing the cross of St George draped over the bar. It is an English multiracial area which Gina, the pub's landlady, says is 'going nowhere' (ibid.: 137).

Barry is an amateur football player of Afro-Caribbean descent. He has broken away from his own race and does not visit his father or socialize with other members of the Afro-Caribbean community. Like Kenny in *Clubland*, he wants to be accepted by whites and has inscribed his body with the trappings of English nationalism, his face painted with the red cross of St George and a British bulldog tattooed on his lower back. The irony of the red cross of St George is that Barry intends it to signal him as an English supporter, but it has been appropriated by extreme right-wing factions in a negative racist manner that excludes black men from Englishness. To assert his nationalistic credentials Barry has also become a racist, an English football hooligan, and has attacked a Romanian fan with a beer-glass during an earlier football match in 1998 at Charleroi in France against the Germans. Despite the fact that his goal won that day's game the white men's acceptance of him is tenuous. They rub or kiss his bald head in celebration but as Mark later tells him, 'They only pretend to be your friends', and when England is losing, the apparent racial tolerance begins to fracture: Jason's response to Barry's question, 'I'm not white enuff for England?', is that black people always claim victimization, 'going off on one all the time. Whenever someone says the slightest thing' (Williams 2004: 194). It appears that attempting to adopt another race's culture simply demeans one's own. After his brother is stabbed by the white boy Glen, Barry is the only black man left in the bar and in anger threatens to kill his white team-mates and 'friends', symbolically wiping the cross of St George from his face. It would seem that multiculturalism is a distant ideal.

Gina and her father Jimmy occupy a site between races, towards whom they are expected to be racially unbiased. They are involved in business in the mixed-race community and convey the impression of racial impartiality. Nevertheless, when provoked, both reveal latent racism. Gina also illustrates the tensions caused by mixed-race relationships. Her relationship with the black ex-soldier Mark, and then with his friend, a white policeman, Lee, ends the men's friendship and leads to an accusation of racial prejudice. Gina's affair with Lee has terminated because he is getting married, and when Mark accuses her of finishing with him because he is black, she retorts that she finished with him because he was boring: 'if you woke up tomorrow as white as I am, you'll still be boring' (Williams 2004: 208). Her racial equilibrium is tested, however, when the black kids, led by Bad T, steal her son's jacket and mobile phone. Her anger plays into the hands of the skinhead racist Lawrie, who sets off to find her son's possessions and returns with the black boy Duane, a friend of Bad T. Lawrie hits Duane, who earlier had supported Glen against Bad T, and throws him out of the pub. This is a cue for the articulate racist nationalist leader Alan, whose views represent those of the British National Party (BNP), to employ the party's technique of utilizing people's discontents to provoke racism.

I've got nothing against the black myself, but even you have to admit we've got a problem here. There are too many different races all trying to fit into the same box, how is that supposed to work? Now they've got our kids, talking like them. It's no wonder you feel the same. (ibid.: 186)

To which Gina responds firmly that she does not share his views. However, her father, Jimmy, is an easier target.

I can handle the older blacks, Marks dad used to drink in here, blindin fella. But these young ones really know how to push it, mouthin off all the time, for no good reason, carryin like the world owes them a favour. (ibid.: 187)

Again Alan fuels the discontents.

Lee is a policeman who, as his skinhead brother Lawrie puts it, was stabbed by 'some coon' at a rave (Williams 2004: 163). As a policeman he ought to be racially unbiased. His experience of being stabbed by a black assailant, however, makes it difficult for him to remain even-handed and he is guiltily aware of his consequent prejudice. 'That fuckin black bastard stabbed me. I ain't racist, Gina, but it's how I felt, it's how I still feel, is that so wrong?' (ibid.: 201). Gina advises him to try to remain detached and not lose himself in anger, a view he later passes on to Barry. In the face of violent provocation this sounds like an improbable achievement, and it is evident from the ending of the play, in which the pub is besieged by stone-throwing black youngsters, that a violent police response may suppress but will not eradicate racial conflict.

Self-proclaimed racists and their followers are represented in *Sing Yer Heart Out* by Alan and Lawrie. Williams uses Alan, the BNP-style leader, to show (in the discussions with Gina, Jimmy, Barry, Lawrie and Mark) his technique of persuading others to share his opinions concerning race by pointing to multiracialism as the cause of all social problems. Lawrie, the xenophobic skinhead hooligan who uses international football as a pretext for violence and acts as a strong-arm man at racist meetings, recalls the Charleroi match against the Germans. Ironically, he provoked 'a couple of Krauts' with racist references to Nazis and Jews and, when they responded aggressively, beat one of them up. His excuse is nationalism. Later, when England are losing, he tells his brother that 'If those cunts can't do it on the pitch, we can, we will! We're England!' (Williams 2004: 180). For him racism is primarily an excuse to express his innate violence, exploited by others such as Alan as a tool to incite interracial conflict. Lawrie explains to his brother, Lee: 'I woulda killed someone by now if it weren't for Alan. I really would, I can feel myself wantin to do it sometimes. Every morning when I wake up. I wanna make a bomb or summin, go down Brixton and blow everyone of them up' (ibid.: 222).

Although prepared to use Lawrie's violence for his own purposes, Alan disapproves of football hooliganism abroad. When Lawrie responds that 'it's about being English', Alan insults him by associating him with those he despises. 'That wasn't been [*sic*] English, you were acting like a bunch of savages. You were no better than the coons.'

Alan then attempts to engage him by saying that he understands his frustrations about a British society 'that speaks up for Blacks, queers and Pakis' (Williams 2004: 197–8), but that violence alienates the population and marginalizes the racist message.

After revealing the various faces of English racism in *Sing Yer Heart Out*, Williams uses the character Mark to explore the possibility of multiculturalism. Mark has left the army after hitting his commanding officer in response to his racist insults. He feels that he is not valued but merely tolerated by white society as long as he is useful in supporting an agency of white power. He is also shocked that the police force are not, as the Stephen Lawrence inquiry revealed, aware of their institutional racism, represented in the play by the unnecessarily rough treatment meted out by the police to Bad T's mother, Sharon.

The debate between Mark and Alan towards the end of the play summarizes and completes the various exchanges concerning racism already presented, and illustrates Williams's view that racists must be confronted. Mark is challenged by Alan, who claims that the black community is a useful scapegoat for the ruling group as the cause of working-class social problems. Alan's aim is to cause dissension and to encourage immigrants who feel exploited, and disappointed that their dreams have not come true, to return to their homelands. Multiculturalism can never succeed, he claims, because for it to do so whites would have to view black people differently, something that they are innately unable to do. Mark is, however, more intelligent and better read than Alan's other targets, Barry and Lawrie, and is able to respond in kind:

> MARK: How English are you? Where do you draw the line as to who's English. I was born in this country. And my brother. You're white, your culture comes from northern Europe, Scandinavia, Denmark. Your people moved from there thousands of years ago, long before the Celtic people and the Beeker [sic] people, what? You think cos I'm black, I don't read books. Where do you draw the line?
>
> (Williams 2004: 218)

Alan's answer reveals the insubstantiality of his apparently intellectual arguments. 'That's exactly the kind of ridiculous question we have to deal with' (ibid.: 218). Williams provides no solution and the play ends with Mark, the voice of reason, dead, and the wail of approaching police sirens. The only hope lies in Lee's ambiguous advice to Barry: 'Don't lose yerself' (ibid.: 235). This is an echo of Gina's advice to him: 'Don't lose yerself in anger' (ibid.: 201), but may also be a call to Barry not to deny his race and culture.

The accuracy of Williams's reproduction of London's black urban idiom places the action firmly within a contemporary social reality, creates empathy and offers accessibility for an audience. By means of a range of character interactions, Williams analyses, with forensic thoroughness, the concerns facing multiracial Britain. He confronts both black and white communities with issues of individual and cultural identity, demolishes stereotypes and challenges racism and prejudice within and between communities. In doing so he illustrates the antagonism and complexity of inter- and intra-racial relations. Nevertheless, his plays imply that awareness of the cultural, social and political forces underlying those relationships may be a first step in transforming Britain from a multiracial to a multicultural society.

PRIMARY READING

Williams, Roy (2002). *Plays 1* (*No Boys Cricket Club, Starstruck, Lift Off*). London: Methuen.

Williams, Roy (2004). *Plays 2* (*The Gift, Clubland, Sing Yer Heart Out for the Lads*). London: Methuen.

FURTHER READING

Alexander, Claire (2000). 'Black Masculinity' in Kwesi Owusu (ed.). *Black British Culture and Society: A Text Reader*. London: Routledge, 373–84.

Animashawun, Ola (chair) (2004). *Critical Mass. A Panel Discussion*. Royal Court, 13 October, www.royalcourttheatre.com/productions_play_detail_past.asp?PlayID=378.

Cavendish, Dominic (2004). 'Man of the Match', *Daily Telegraph* 19 April, 17.

Cobham, P. J. (2004). 'Roy Williams', *Precious Magazine*, www.preciousonline.co.uk/features/may04/roy.htm.

Dyer, Richard (1997). *White*. New York and London: Routledge.

Gilroy, Paul (1987). *There Ain't No Black in the Union Jack*. London: Unwin Hyman.

Gilroy, Paul (1993). *Small Acts*. London: Serpent's Tail.

Gilroy, Paul (2004). *After Empire: Melancholia and Convivial Culture*. London: Routledge.

Hall, Stuart (1988). 'New Ethnicities' in James Donald and Ali Rattansi (eds.) (1992). *'Race', Culture and Difference*. London: Sage, 252–9.

McLeod, John (2004). *Postcolonial London*. Abingdon: Routledge.

45

Ed Thomas: Jazz Pictures in the Gaps of Language

David Ian Rabey

The Attack of the Welsh Russian Dolls

Ed Thomas's plays suggest, to quote the shape-shifting narrator of Lloyd Jones's novel *Mr Vogel*, that 'Wales, in short, is a bag of tricks – a Russian doll, for as soon as you open one Wales there is another inside waiting to be opened' (Jones 2004: 99). Dominated by British rule, Wales is now slowly emerging as a distinct power and has its own Welsh Assembly. But what is Wales and what is its geography? Jan Morris has provided a memorable description:

> On the Western perimeter of Europe lies the damp, demanding and obsessively interesting country called by its own people Cymru, and known to the rest of the world, if it is known at all, as Wales [. . .] You must look hard to find Wales in an atlas, for it is a peninsula not much larger than Swaziland, rather smaller than Massachussetts, inhabited by a mere 2.9 million people [. . .] Its image is habitually blurred; partly by this geographical unfamiliarity, partly by the opaque and moody climate, partly by its own somewhat obfuscatory character, which is entramelled in a dizzy repertoire of folklore, but most of all by historical circumstance.
>
> For although Wales is a country, it is not a State. It has a capital city, but not a Government; its own postage stamps, but not its own currency; a flag, but no embassies; an indigenous language, but not indigenous laws. All this is because, though it is surrounded on three sides by sea, on the fourth its border marches with the powerful kingdom of England, and for some 700 years it has been absorbed into the political entity of Great Britain, with its seat of power in London. (Morris 1998: 1)

If the Welsh have been dominated by Britain and forced to speak English, then Welsh performance traditions have suffered from a history of invisibility because it has been assumed that Welsh theatre must be like English theatre. In his essay on Welsh theatres, Ioan Williams dispels this myth, arguing that Wales has 'produced an indigenous theatre which demonstrates that it can flourish without the advantages of wealth and cultural continuity' (Williams 2004: 242). Questions of national identity have obsessed many recent playwrights and performers, and a generation of practitioners who emerged in the 1970s have created new forms of Welsh theatre and performance (Adams 1996: *passim*). The plays of Wales's major contemporary dramatists compulsively testify to the rage, pain and humour of the search for meaning – in defiance of the restrictions imposed by colonizing systems of control. Dic Edwards's plays, for example, explore political bewilderment; Greg Cullen's human complexity and Lucy Gough's texts are subversive instruments of performance. Both before and after some degree of devolution, Ed Thomas (b. 1961) has been the most artfully conscious that the obscured profile of Wales is both a curse and an opportunity, just like the image of the Russian dolls as either a confounding or a strategic image of Welsh identity and existence. Is this a land benighted by its postcolonial heritage of historical circumstance, dispossession and collusion, whose inhabitants can never fully be its masters? Or is it an enclave of artful freedom, where the propensity for (self-) mythologizing might be a means of forging new identities?

Thomas's performance texts demonstrate an extraordinary awareness of dramatic possibility, providing open forms for individual actors' improvisation and experimentation. Their challenge and allure are felicitously crystallized in an exchange between the characters Ace and Bron in Thomas's *Gas Station Angel* (1998):

ACE: I like Welsh.
BRON: Why?
ACE: Because it's got gaps.
BRON: What kind of gaps?
ACE: Like it's not all hard and fast; like there are rules but there are still gaps . . . like to fill in, the meaning . . . you got to work the meaning out for yourself . . . You make the pictures up in the gaps.
BRON: Like Jazz.

(Thomas 2002: 368–9)

One of Thomas's main strengths as a dramatist is his ability to create unusual and enticing linguistic structures which test performers to the full. His demand for self-conscious performances of concealment and disclosure, his exploration of formative (if self-deluding) structures of memory, and his preoccupation with the possibility of self-reinvention are central to his theatre aesthetic. In these and other respects, his most kindred theatrical spirits are Samuel Beckett, Howard Barker and Sarah Kane. His plays often bemuse metropolitan directors and critics, even as they engage and move the spectators who attend Thomas's bold and distinctive productions of his own work. In the words of Richard Taylor:

The experience of the plays, rather than being one of intellectual satisfaction, is one of denial. The spectator is denied easy meanings and structures and is instead confronted by the plays, whilst simultaneously being moved by the subtly affecting nature of the language, through which the characters have assonance and resonance with one another... In Thomas's theatre the performer is unusually reliant on the spectator's response to create the performance, and the spectator's only point of contact is with the humanity of the actors, and their act of giving. The experience is not detached nor empathetic as with television or film, but electric, tenuous and potent. (Davies 1998: 177)

Screaming Soul Syndrome

Thomas's career as a director/dramatist began in 1988, with the foundation of his theatre company Y Cwmni, 'The Company' (a name as variably humble and arrogant as the band name, The Band), and the production of his play *House of America* (1988).[1] By forming their own company Thomas and his closest collaborators controlled the means of production of their work from the beginning (in terms comparable only to Barker's theatre company, The Wrestling School). Two core performers were Richard Lynch and Russell Gomer, long-term collaborators in the incarnations of Thomas's 'screaming souls', the stranded voices which echo through the plays frantically asking 'What's real?' and 'What could we make that's *better* than what we're told is real?' These voices express both a despair of life and a desire for reinvention; their sentiments are diagnosed and articulated by Carlyle, the protagonist of *Song from a Forgotten City* (1995):

Do you know what it's like to feel cheated, man... like on a permanent basis?... Convention started life as a good idea... such a good idea that everybody loved it... loved it so much they all took it up. Took it up for so long they forgot what a good idea it used to be. They got stuck in a groove and however much they tried to break free of it, man, convention kept holding on. It held on so tight that it got right into their souls. Even made them forget convention altogether. They imagined themselves to be free. Thought of themselves as individuals living the way they wanted to live, only thing that bothered them was why from time to time did their souls scream. They just put it down to the old screaming soul. They called it the old screaming soul syndrome and their souls screamed as they said it. (Thomas 2002: 44)

House of America demonstrated how members of a family could find fantasy more alluring than reality, but with tragic consequences. Their fantasies are one-way projections onto facades and figures who never reciprocate: Clem names his cat after Marlon Brando; Mam retreats into 'Mr Snow's' world of television interference; and Sid and Gwenny concoct a joint fantasy based on Jack Kerouac's 1957 novel *On the Road* which proves addictive and leads to incest, fratricide, delusion and suicide — memorably staged in the scenes when one brother strangles another, then stands by helplessly as his sister proves fatally unreachable in her rejection of life. Here the fragmentation of the self in response to the impositions of social circumstance and cultural politics condemns these hapless and bewildered 'Russian dolls' to states of abjection, and ultimately death.

Flowers of the Dead Red Sea (1991) strips everything down to a duel fought over the terms of memory. The whole world seems to be shrinking around two slaughter-men, one of whom nevertheless tries to reverse the tide of shame by asking 'WHAT THE FUCK HAS GONE WRONG WITH THE WORLD?' (Thomas 1994: 116, 155). *Flowers* is part of what came to be known as the 'New Wales Trilogy', also including the currently unpublished *Adar heb Adenydd*, or *Birds Without Wings* (1989), and *The Myth of Michael Roderick* (1990): all three plays are linguistically and dramatically differing versions of quests for a ritual to regenerate a nation. In *Flowers*, the characters fight out different interpretations of their world: Mock holds on to a sense of 'mystery' in craft and in death, out of respect for the passive beasts with whom he engages (and whom the theatre audience represent at the opening). He believes metaphor provides a 'start' to counter the otherwise ubiquitous and encroaching 'message' of shame instilled into them by received wisdom: 'YOU ARE THE SAME AS EVERYONE ELSE' – that is, insignificant (Thomas 1994: 165). Mock's workmate Joe dismisses metaphor as 'AVOIDANCE, EVASION, SHEER ORNAMENTATION' (ibid.: 164) and condemns Mock's intimations of dignity and honour as lost causes. The humour and anguish of their exchanges derive from their inability to recall the nature of their surroundings or familial bonds with any conviction (they might be brothers). Joe may be the victor but he is also ingratiatingly subservient to their boss, and Mock refutes Joe's creed of shameful unison, insisting 'I'm still here' (ibid.: 166) – a phrase which, for Welsh-speaking audience members, carries echoes of the political song 'Ni Yma o Hyd', which asserts the persistence of the Welsh language and the political independence of the imagination.

This collective amnesia extends into the more redemptive play *East from the Gantry* (1992), in which the central married couple, Ronnie and Bella, cannot recall their history and are lost in a blur of alcohol and overfamiliarity. The inability to remember is also a defining feature of Thomas's 1993 purgatorial dialogue, *Hiraeth*, in which the characters face exactly the opposite dilemma to the incessantly recollecting damned souls in Beckett's *Play*. *Gantry* continues another of Thomas's leitmotifs – the literally or potentially fatal mistake: Ron shoots his cat, mistaking it for Bella's ex-lover, and Bella burns down their first house out of neglect, careless frustration, or possibly both. Other examples of inadvertent homicides mixed with oppressive family secrets occur in the tale of Uncle Eu in *Gantry*; Thomas's 30-minute television film *Fallen Sons* (1994); and later in *Gas Station Angel* and *Stone City Blue* (2004), where secrets fester, trap, destroy and madden. *Gantry* ultimately demonstrates a communal drive towards 'something good'. The mysterious stranger, Trampas, turns out not to be a harbinger of destruction either to Ronnie and Bella's house or to their marriage, but just a self-conscious drifter. *Gantry* is a heartening, profoundly comic testimony to the potentially benign and resourceful aspect of the Russian doll image: whatever our prehistory and our social conditions, we can still reveal and remake ourselves anew.

Thomas and Richard Lynch, the lead performer in premieres of all of Thomas's plays until *Stone City Blue*, have made the following observations:

ET: The characters' lack of memory in the plays is not a device but a structural necessity. It is both dark and comic if – as in *Flowers* – all that links brothers and sons is an attempt to make up and contest memory in ways which have a rhythm and a musicality.

RL: You have to treat the plays as scores to inform the development of a physical choreography. You have to find out where the cadences and crescendos are going to be, and what gives you a right to silence. We never worried about inventing a history for the characters.

ET: I don't think I've ever 'written a character' in the standard way. *Adar* was a play completely about form; in *Michael Roderick*, the tale was a washing line from which I hung the characters.

RL: The characters are constantly peeling away layers to 'out' themselves. In the process actors are not just playing characters but playing themselves. Actors who approached Ed's work in terms of trying to 'interpret the work, play a character' were actually scared off.

DIR: So the work gave you structures and chords on which to improvise?

RL: Yes. It involved mining facets of our selves for unfamiliar, sometimes painful images, which became surprising to both the individual and the collective. Only by working with people in such a naked way can you build a sense of absolute play, which in itself can become a defining factor.

ET: You have to play your own strings. I would love to do *Flowers* again with Lynch and Gomer when they are old, say in their seventies or eighties. If you have an interest in memory, you can cut in a *design* based on *process* and juxtapose the live performances with the documentary footage and radio recordings of them doing the play in the 1990s, suggesting that they may have been stuck in the same loop of recurrent actions for thirty years. It would be an experiment with the way light controls time in different ways – splitting time to construct something unpredictably poignant.

(interview with Thomas and Lynch 2005)

The Bad Trip/Dancing with the Otherworld

In *Song from a Forgotten City* (1995) Thomas continues his quest for meaning in more drastic, anguished terms. At this time his recurrent phrase 'Take me somewhere good' was used by the Welsh Arts Council to market Cardiff as a 'City of Culture'. The irony was that *Song* is not utopian: it shows how the drive for 'something good' into 'the heart of Saturday night' can take and transform the individual into a raindog (a poetic image drawn from Tom Waits's lyrics) – a stray mongrel that has lost track of the traces which can lead it home again. In *Song* traditional melodies have been forgotten and given way to silence. The writer, Carlyle, is partly an unsettling mock-heroic self-parody of the playwright and his grandiose but desperate rhetorical invocations: 'my job is to give a voice to the voiceless, the dispossessed . . . I'm a writer trying to escape from the corridors of the invisible' (Thomas 2002: 42–3). Carlyle's visions are shown to be the delusions of a manic depressive, trying to mythologize his way out of a dead end. *Song* operates like a hall of cruelly distorting mirrors on personal and national hopes. It is a dream sequence which turns into an uncontrollable nightmare, or a brief incandescent high which collapses into anxious paranoia. Carlyle's former friends Benny and Jojo have turned into bickering addicts and hangers-on: they cling on to his dreams of plays, films and poems which could make them money, even though they know that 'his head chemicals are mixed up' and accuse each other of having 'no soul' (ibid.: 76, 80). *Song* casts a shadow over Thomas's more optimistic dramatic statements by demonstrating that change cannot be brought about by imagination alone. Carlyle and Jojo attempt a verbal jam with optimistic riffs about 'A Welsh metropolis with attitude', but it collapses under a sense of its own effort, tenuousness and marginalization (ibid.: 96–7). As Carlyle admits: 'I've told so many stories Jojo, my memory gets so blurred I don't know where my life ends and my blur begins . . . The blur is all I got' (ibid.: 98–9). Jojo may suggest that he should 'imagine each shiver of cold is like a breeze on a hot summer's day' (ibid.: 104–5), but even the power of imagination has its limits, and can degenerate into unreal dreams pitched haplessly against the brutal facts of economic and social deprivation.[2] *Song*'s menagerie of creative masculinity in crisis ends with the ambivalent sexual image of a furtive transvestite discovered, undressed and bedded by his wife (ibid.: 122). And Carlyle's imagined or enacted suicide provides no grounds for optimism.

Thomas strikes back from the bleakness of *Song* with one of his best plays, *Gas Station Angel* (1998), the story of two families long connected without their knowing it – a device which allows further exploration of how the secrets of the past can shape the present. Bron makes a plea for personal (and by implication political) honesty: 'Secrets and lies. A fucked up past. Maybe if we faced up to the past then maybe we wouldn't find the world so confusing' (Thomas 2002: 315). Bron is watched by the son of a rival family, Ace, who is a believer in stories, mystery and magic, and he behaves in ways that are characteristic of Thomas's most seductive theatricality. Characters often self-consciously describe, explain, interpret and reassess events rather than, or as well as, enacting them. The many plot strands and narrative disclosures of *Angel* have both Dickensian intricacy and qualities of magic realism. *Angel* is poetically very challenging and can demand a second viewing or reading to savour fully. Figures and events are redefined in the loop of time, and characters both living and unquietly dead stalk the stage, observing each other's actions. One of the issues at stake in the play is the simultaneously limiting yet potentially transformative power of language: Ace, for example, exhorts the farm boy Dyfrig into a state of linguistic *hwyl* (inspiration, transportation and ecstasy) which convinces him of his own potential connection to sexual and supernatural forces. Bron states: 'I like things I don't understand. Only things I don't understand interest me. Why celebrate what you already know?' (Thomas 2002: 370). However, *Angel* is not romantically utopian: the characters may believe in and enact the proximity and significance of an angelic/ demonic underworld, but this is their response to 'Growing up in a shrinking land next to a tantrum sea' (ibid.: 337) – a sea which eventually claims the house of Ace's parents. As Ace acknowledges, 'Life in storyland I could control, the ongoing war against the sea and real life I couldn't' (ibid.: 338). Importantly, the version of the script published by Parthian (Thomas 2002) updates the Methuen 1998 (rehearsal) text by retaining but recharacterizing the supernatural: Ace does not disabuse his mother of the possibility of the fairy underworld, but he redefines it in a less fearful, regressive manner (so it is part of the 'mystery' whose 'gaps' you have to complete through imagination); and Ace reveals to Bron that his mother shot her brother, in the hope that by confronting the truth the youngest representatives of both families can begin to heal (Thomas's stage directions specify the enactment of a ghost being laid). *Angel* is Thomas's most artful and atmospheric combination of the magical and the realistic, showing a strong faith in the transformative power of the erotic as a way of revivifying the present and anticipating the future.

Time is Just Memory Mixed with Desire

In the late 1990s Thomas was looking for new ventures: 'By 1998 I'd written a new play every year since 1988, directed them all, toured all over the place, set up a production company, written a screenplay, and produced and directed three series for TV'; then 'people had gone movie crazy – including me' (Thomas 2002: 126). His screen play for *House of America* encountered numerous problems and his foray into directing the film of a James Hawes novel was ill-fated (an experience educatively reassessed in Hawes's 2002 novel, *White Powder, Green Light*, which features an affectionate caricature of Thomas). Thomas then regathered his forces (and his actors) by directing episodes of the increasingly surreal Welsh-language television series *Ffondue, Rhyw a Deinosors* (*Fondue, Sex and Dinosaurs*) written by Delyth Jones. *Ffondue* depicted middle-class media types who were satirically deconstructed, but who nevertheless retained their humanity under Thomas's direction. Ed Thomas's experimentation with theatre, film and television as media which inform one another and meld together continues with his work as artistic director of Fiction Factory, one of Wales's most progressive arts companies.

His confidence and desire for experiment were also renewed by an artistic alliance with Mike Pearson, formerly the artistic director of another major Welsh theatre company, Brith Gof (and now half of the performance team Pearson/Brookes). Y Cwmni and Brith Gof had viewed each other with a mixture of mutual respect and suspicion, until they both found themselves representing Wales at Neil Wallace's 1991 Glasgow Tramway season and forum of 'national theatres'. In 2001 both theatre companies decided to hire a room for seven years, in which they were committed to meeting weekly, making plans and determining a future in what was often a barren climate. This led to an idea of creating an 'anti-epic', a video diary of the dreams of the people of Cardiff. Pearson/Brookes's 2001 work had incorporated footage of orches-trated performance activities in Cardiff city, as filmed by South Wales police surveil-lance cameras and the BBC. Whereas 'digital material seemed to compress time', Pearson was interested in the idea of 'holding it open', and developing with Mike Brookes ways of bringing the filmic and televisual into performance work (interview with Pearson 2005). Their ideas explored how the city, rather than more conventional aesthetic ideas, might drive a performance. The first public presentation by the occasional team which came to be known as Pearson, Brookes and Thomas was *Rain Dogs* in 2002, and it involved a combination of mute movements, film footage, spoken texts and music. The piece was essentially a mosaic of city wanderers, Pearson's fragments often dealing with travelling, Thomas's with 'doing nothing' in a context where loitering is suspicious. A second presentation, *Who Are You Looking At?* (2004), pushed the principles further with the live presences of Pearson, Brookes and Thomas offset by footage of five young Welsh women re-enacting events and being inter-viewed about their own (utopian and dystopian) experiences of the city. Further events are planned, on varying scales, up to 2008.

Thomas re-entered the arena and infrastructure of theatre with *Stone City Blue* (2004), which was importantly informed by interim experiences of *Ffondue* (the cast included several actors from the series) and the Pearson–Brookes collaborations (some of the more autobiographical fragments of *Rain Dogs* are redeveloped in *Stone City Blue*). A third major influence on *Stone City Blue* was Sarah Kane, whose plays *Crave* (1998) and *4:48 Psychosis* (2000) made a particular impression. Thomas has always written by generating pages of written material, often based on experiences and anecdotes, existential howls and linguistic humour, which he subsequently shapes and assigns to different characters. More open forms of collaboration, and Kane's *Crave* in particular, licensed Thomas to present his emotional explorations with a startling directness and depth, simply dividing the text into four voices which partly express the warring but interdependent facets of a single turbulent sensibility in personal and political breakdown. The physical choreography was devised between director and performers. Thomas reflected that:

> Directing *Ffondue* reminded me that precision is arrived at by design, not by accident, and restored my confidence by showing how I could *use* my own fluctuations in confidence to make something emotionally muscular. The Pearson–Brookes collabor-ations started with an appeal to my sense of grandeur of commitment with no concession to any apparent career structure. 'Good afternoon, we'd like to hire a room for seven years' may prove a good way to start a play in the future. My contribution was often adding the pronouns, the personal emotional investments to Mike's concepts. Perhaps *Who Are You Looking at?* wasn't stylized enough, and so contained an unresolved voyeurism in the performers' relationship with the camera, unlike the more stylized *Rain Dogs* which nevertheless retained a sense of the 'I', offering signifiers about the ruination of a life, about the inability of art to control chaos. (interview with Thomas and Lynch 2005)

Stone City Blue explores the themes of memory, personal and national identity, belonging and love. It starts in the anonymity of a hotel room, where

> I'm alone
> With my demons
> My angels
> My naked succubae
> Waiting
> For a stranger
> A perfect stranger
> To knock on my door,

where home is 'just a memory' for the disconnected (Thomas 2004a: 3, 20). The voices testify to the demands of inertia and rage, until 'the glue that's kept us together can't hold', until 'I've been possessed . . . Dehumanized by my own self', 'killing love' which is nevertheless the 'only drug' to 'make life bearable' (ibid.: 34, 36-7, 64). Thomas characteristically asks through these voices if humans amount to no more than their parents' children:

> at the edge of someone else's story
> Whose story?
> What are the possibilities?
> (ibid.: 72)

Even at the bleakest points in Thomas's oeuvre there is a self-undercutting bathos:

> God . . .
> Put someone else in my body instead of me
> Took me off
> Like in soccer
> I got substituted in the first half.
> (ibid.: 90)

The final section suggests that time's river (a recurrent image of both death and vitality for Thomas) may have 'fallen silent', and that things are irrevocably 'lost' in it, even as the directed on-stage action suggests a continual search. The play-poem concludes poised between the despair of the utterance 'That it would come to this' and the hope of a remaining opportunity to say 'I love you'. *Stone City Blue* is, as the title suggests, a *blues* – a partly formalized plaintive and self-accusatory cry of existential nausea, which is nevertheless open in ways which permit startling moments of expressive identification between writer, performer and spectator, and is written in the hope that its *form* might permit a partial transcendence of the dislocation and isolation that are its *matter*. The piece is both unbearably ferocious and forensic in its emotional explorations:

ET: As a younger man, I wrote about the discovery of shameful secrets. In *Stone City Blue*, my secret's out – it's the play of a forty-three-year-old man who has outed his own secrets, both personally and politically.

RL: It's now a theatre of the un-secret.

ET: And can an un-secret be dramatic? I play with all the things you're supposed to eradicate – shame, wanting more, wanting meaning, sexual appetite, forgiveness, what makes a man good or bad – but in a way which always reminds me of a palimpsest crumbled by the sun: the reader has to fill it in, complete it morally. (interview with Thomas and Lynch 2005)

NOTES

1 Y Cwmni are now known as Fiction Factory.
2 This is particularly true of the British political climate of the early 1990s, when Thatcherite policies were negatively affecting the lives of the most vulnerable.

PRIMARY READING

Thomas, Ed (1994). *Three Plays: House of America, Flowers of the Dead Red Sea, East from the Gantry*. Bridgend: Seren.

Thomas, Ed (2002). *{Selected} Work 1995–1998: Song from a Forgotten City, House of America Film Screenplay, Gas Station Angel*. Cardigan: Parthian.

Thomas, Ed (2004a). *Stone City Blue*. London: Methuen.

Thomas, Ed (2004b). 'Corsica, Cardiff', *New Welsh Review* 65, 93–7.

Fiction Factory website at www.btinternet.com/-fictionfactoryltd

Interviews with author: Mike Pearson, 9 and 24 February 2005; Ed Thomas and Richard Lynch, 16 March 2005.

FURTHER READING

Adams, David (1996). *Welsh Nation, Nationalism and Theatre: The Search for Cultural Identity*. Landysul: Gomer.

Davies, H. W. (ed.) (1998). *State of Play: Four Playwrights of Wales*. Llandysul: Gomer.

Jones, Lloyd (2004). *Mr Vogel*. Bridgend: Seren.

Morris, Jan (1998). *Wales: Epic Views of a Small Country*. London: Penguin.

Rabey, David Ian (2003). *English Drama since 1940*. London: Longman.

Savill, C. C. (1991). 'Wales is Dead!', *Planet* 85, 86–97.

Taylor, Anne-Marie (1997). *Welsh Theatre 1979–1997*. Cardiff: University of Wales.

Williams, Ioan (2004). 'Towards National Identities: Welsh Theatres' in Baz Kershaw (ed.). *The Cambridge History of British Theatre. Vol. 3*. Cambridge: Cambridge University Press, 242–72.

46
Theatre and Technology
Andy Lavender

Techne

Let's agree that technology – in the theatre or anywhere else – is never just a matter of hardware. It also involves a 'techne' – the hands-on human processes that shape its use. In the classical Greek sense, 'techne' denotes the *application* of craft skill for particular purposes. Aristotle makes it sound like an attitude, a mix of know-how and can-do (Aristotle 2002: 179). Techne implies not just a kit of parts but a practice – and practices, as we know, are shaped by the press of the historical moment. In other words, the technologies that define theatre at any given moment are not simply the shell that holds the organism or, to use another analogy, the wiring inside the machine. They are expressive of the way a culture thinks, shares its desires, organizes its pleasures.

My argument in this chapter is that theatre is defined by technes in ways that reach beyond the straightforward effects of the technologies in play. Arnold Aronson proposes that 'Theatre [. . .] is shaped not by specific technological developments, but through transformations in consciousness and modes of perception which may, however, be significantly affected by technology. This is the key to understanding the relationship between theatre and technology' (Aronson 1999: 192). I'm not sure that I agree with the first part of this quotation. But I will argue in the following pages that there is a pervasive relationship between the principles of a particular techne and the more widespread practices of theatre-makers.

There are points where changes to technology, and hence to techne, do not merely update the way that theatre is made. They make for an alteration to the modes of representation – how we show things and how we see things. Aronson points to the transition between medieval wagon stages and the 'rooming' of such stages in purpose-built theatres. The audience came inside to see a show (even if there was not necessarily a roof over their heads), rather than the theatre coming to the audience in a temporarily claimed location. The dividends in terms of audience focus and commitment to the event, along with the expanded possibilities in terms of staging arrangements (from simple exits and entrances to more elaborate flying and sub-stage devices), helped to shape a seemingly richer texture to the occasion. It provided theatre-makers with an array of possibilities for new theatrical story-telling – but also demanded a *process* for their work that had a bearing on what they subsequently staged.

Consider, too, the difference made to theatre buildings, backstage areas, production practices and the very appearance of the drama once electric lighting had replaced gaslight as the major mode of illumination. On the face of it, this is simply a *technical* reconfiguration rather than anything more profound (light is produced by electricity rather than gas but, broadly speaking, we are still in the realm of a 'lighted' theatre). Even here, however, this simple shift has implications for the way that people work and the way they watch. Henry Irving famously employed ranks of gasmen and limelight operators at the Lyceum Theatre to enable spectacular yet controlled lighting effects. Meanwhile, Irving declined to play in the 'new' drama of Shaw and Ibsen. That drama, in its newly naturalist colouring, was being written amidst experiments with electric lighting that enabled Thomas Edison's completion of the first incandescent light bulb for public use in 1882. In the theatre, the introduction of electric light eventually allowed clearer illumination of details of the set, graduated changes to lighting states, a closer control of directional light and the prospect of differentiated ambient states. The dramatic texture was different as a consequence – in a way that was captured in the warp and weft of the new playwriting.

Which came first, the techne or the text? Did Ibsen write his plays – with their ambient moodscapes and dynamic lighting effects – in the knowledge of what theatre technologies would eventually provide? Did he happen to write scenarios that needed new staging solutions, some of which may have been unachievable in his time? Or did he write in a modern shape, reconfiguring the older playwriting in accordance with the most modern resources for staging? I don't think there is a single answer, but I prefer the last. Creative practitioners are caught up in the march of culture. They produce altered dramaturgies that chime with the techne of the moment, which itself is always evolving.

My interest for the rest of this chapter, then, is in how technes at the beginning of the twenty-first century produce us as theatre-makers and consumers; and how our expressive needs and desires lead us to (re)figure the technological practices at our disposal. I will say something about what seem to me to be key developments in cultural technologies; examine briefly how these relate to new theatre production; and close with an account of telematic performance, an area of practice whose time is yet to come.

Hypershift

The rapid growth of computer usage provides the most significant shift in our techne over the last twenty or so years. Computers began to be ubiquitous in the 1980s.

Mainframe technology was refined to allow larger sets of data to be processed by smaller machines that became increasingly affordable. The information revolution was given added impetus with the widespread availability of hypertext protocols from 1991, allowing swift and easy interchange of information, and the introduction of Microsoft's Internet Explorer in 1995, which quickly became the standard web browser.

The ensuing protocols of computer-based work have had a profound effect not just on theatre but on cultural production more generally. This does indeed look to be a culture-shift comparable to that of the Industrial Revolution of the eighteenth and nineteenth centuries. As Martin Lister and his colleagues put it: 'In truth, the growth of the Internet since the invention of World Wide Web software ranks as a truly remarkable cultural achievement. The quantity of human labour and ingenuity that has gone into building net-based communications systems in a very short space of time is unprecedented' (Lister et al. 2003: 164). After so much spadework, the playing field looks entirely different. Randall Packer and Ken Jordan suggest that 'Multimedia is emerging as the defining medium of the twenty-first century' (Packer and Jordan 2002: xv). They propose five key characteristics of this suggested new medium: integration, interactivity, hypermedia, immersion and narrativity (ibid.: xxxv). Lister and his co-writers suggest their own list: digitality, interactivity, hypertextuality, dispersal, virtuality (Lister et al. 2003: 13). Janet Murray discusses three 'characteristic pleasures' of digital environments: immersion, agency and trans-formation (Murray 1997: 97–182). Gabriella Gianacchi suggests that virtuality has reshaped the terrain of contemporary performance practice, whilst simultaneity emerges as a defining theme of her book (Gianacchi 2004). Among these writers and others there is broad agreement as to the buzzwords of contemporary culture and what they mean for us as users and consumers of technologies.

You can delve into these at your leisure, although I'd like to gloss three terms here – *hypertext*, *interactivity* and *digitization* – that help us understand a techne that catches theatre in its embrace. Hypertext refers to a network of links between separate data resources. A hypertextual system is non-linear – that is, it does not depend upon inevitable connections between one thing and the next in a chain that will be the same for every user. Its connections can be interrupted, remade or continually added to in a never-ending sequence. What's more, every element in the chain can generate other connections. Non-linearity, then, becomes a key feature of digital culture, along with its shadow twins, simultaneity and multiplicity.

In surfing, navigating, trawling or whatever else we might do in the oceans of data, we are creating paths and products that can be shared with others. There is something profoundly democratic about this, at least on the surface. We interact more routinely with others across larger distances. Interactivity more properly describes our ability also to work with elements (game devices, for instance) in the digital domain, in ways that refigure the thing that we are interacting with. The new media landscape is not simply travelled through – it is *shaped* by its user-inhabitants. This suggests another feature of digital culture: it takes us from a model where people are passive observers to one where they become active participants. Of course such agency is often very limited and sometimes disputable, but broadly it is fair to say that new technologies involve us in *doing* things. If it didn't sound so unsnappy, we might reformulate Marshall McLuhan's celebrated axiom, 'the medium is the message', to suggest that the medium is a continuum for experience – or, in Jeffrey Shaw's nice phrase, 'a latent space of sensual information' (Shaw 2002: 137).

Computer technology is, of course, digital, and is part of a broader turn to digitization that embraces telephone systems, photography, film-making, music production, text production and information storage – the panoply of communications within and across cultures and countries. It is worth a pause for technical thought, since the *effect* of digitality helps explain its prevailing techne, and since I want to come back to binaries of a different kind a little later. Peter Lunenfeld offers a neat summary:

> Digital systems [. . .] translate all input into binary structures of 0s and 1s, which can then be stored, transferred or manipulated at the level of numbers, or 'digits' [. . .] It is the capacity of the computer to encode a vast variety of information digitally that has given it such a central place within contemporary culture. [. . .] The computer, when linked to a network, is unique in the history of technological media: it is the first widely disseminated system that offers the user the opportunity to create, distribute, receive, and consume audiovisual content with the same box. (Lunenfeld 2000: xv, xvi, xix)

As Lunenfeld suggests, digital processes in some respects simply replace analogue ones (such as film-based photography or type-based printing presses) to achieve the same ends (photographs; newspapers) – just as the shift from gaslight to electric light in the theatre maintained the basic function of illuminating what was on the stage. There is a major difference, however, in user protocols – the speed, ubiquity and accessibility of the means by which (re)presentations are made. Digital technology allows for the greater availability of resources (images, sounds, film clips, written texts and so forth); easier interface between these resources; and a far speedier means of getting from raw idea to finished product. The multimedia age, then, arises from the liberating effects of digital technologies. And these technologies have in turn enabled a techne that is processual, interconnective and non-linear.

Theatre and the Digital Domain

How does this bear upon theatre- and performance-making? First and most obvious is the digitization of sound, lighting, video-imaging (hence elements of scenography) and show-control systems. Clearly speed is of the essence. In a digital domain it is much easier to alter design and technical elements without wasting huge amounts of time, tape or trips to the effects library. Fast reworking of materials – often within the rehearsal room itself – is now available to theatre-makers. Across the board, practitioners can more easily propose and achieve alterations to their creations from the middle of their process. We observe the rise of two rather different people. One is the micro-disciplinary expert – the video specialist, say, who understands live media playback protocols like nobody else in the company. The other is the multi-tasking, multimedia technician who is able to fulfil the roles that would previously have been held in a more demarcated way by, say, the stage manager, deputy stage manager and sound operator.

Digitization means that theatre-making is enabled to become more process-centred and less delivery-based. That's to say, different 'departments' – sound, set, costume, lighting, script – do not necessarily have to work up finished products that get bolted together in order to make the final piece. Theatre becomes more open to systems of modelling. Virtual designs, structures and storyboards allow for a series of samples, sometimes made out of elements that will actually appear in the show, that can be changed quickly in relation to the evolving creative process. This is rather different from a 'template' system of production, which depended on the model box and indeed the play text – analogue technologies in their own right.

This is a hybrid theatre-making economy. It depends upon flattened structures of creativity and systems of collaborative authorship that are capable of producing many intertexts. It is no accident that the position of the playwright has been eroded in digital environments, since sound, lighting and visual media designers can interface more easily with the process of content-creation. In which case we are not necessarily talking about authorship in the established sense, but 'agency', to use a term much favoured in discussions of new media.

The thing that is being co-authored is up for grabs. Digitization has contributed to a peculiarly double-edged revision of what we understand theatre to be. It has coincided with a proliferation of more varied sorts of production (in unusual sites, of unorthodox durations and of contested dramatic status). 'Theatre' is destabilized. Meanwhile it is intrinsic to new scenographies that might be described as part of a 'theatrical' theatre, founded on visual and scenic transformations in three-dimensional space and the live moment. 'Theatre' is reaffirmed.

Such a shift in working practices and infrastructures has aesthetic implications. R. L. Rutsky suggests that 'Like technology, [the aesthetic] too comes to be seen as an unsettling, generative process, which continually breaks elements free of their previous context and recombines them in different ways' (Rutsky 1999: 8). Theatre- and performance-makers more routinely draw upon grammars of television, cinema, music, club scene, fine art, video games – a mixed economy that suggests the return of the *Gesamtkunstwerk*, to cite Wagner's resonant formulation of 1849. Wagner envisaged a totalizing artistic practice that fused different elements (we might say different media). The difference in the digital era is that any single finished product isn't as definitely finished as one might have assumed in the middle of the nineteenth century. Instead it constitutes one fusion out of many, since it is made within an environment that is inherently plural and interconnected rather than totalizing and all-consuming. There are aesthetic implications in the very fabric of the pieces that we see. Let's take three examples. Two of them are neither British nor Irish, but allow us to expand our frame of reference given the internationalism of much digital arts practice and the fact that digital culture has spun its web across a wide geographical reach.

In 2004 the London-based theatre company Complicite, under director Simon McBurney, presented a production of Shakespeare's *Measure for Measure* at the National Theatre, London. McBurney began rehearsals with an exercise whereby the cast would line up across the stage. Those in any particular scene would step forward and deliver the words out front, speaking directly to the audience rather than their colleagues on-stage. The exercise reveals structures and patterns in the play and establishes the basis for a more direct contact with the audience. It also treats the play in terms of its various 'bytes' of information, a series of components rather than an organic whole.

The play is set in Vienna. The metropolis of Complicite's production was a city-state subject to modern surveillance technologies. A cameraman wandered around the stage, filming the action for a live feed to on-stage TV monitors. This suggested both the apparatus of contemporary news media and a more insidious surveillance function, policing the play's various suspects and criminals. Prisoners wore orange jumpsuits that directly evoked the political prisoners held by the US in Guantanamo Bay, a contemporary reference underscored when the image of George Bush popped up on the TV screens. This might be thought an obvious and easy cultural reference, but I think the effect is more deeply embedded. The stage is nicely intertextual, combining old and new modes of theatre and resonant icons of modern culture. Its linkages produce a *feel* for the production, to do with the sense of arbitrariness that hangs over the operations of justice (an evident theme of the play) and the reach of the state into personal lives.

Meanwhile the stage remediates its own performance, playing back through TV monitors and projections onto the floor parts of the speeches and movements of characters. The audience gets a different viewing-angle on parts of the action, but also the sense that this is a world of fractured and multiple perspectives where no single position holds (unless through the diktat of those in power). The production, then, is prism-like, refracting its characters and their statements through a hypermediated *mise en scène*.

In *Vivisector* (2004), conceived and co-directed by Klaus Obermaier and choreographed by Chris Haring, four bare-backed individuals with cropped blond hair dance (or not) in a space illuminated by light from a video projector. The bodies of the quartet provide human screens for video images that map exactly onto them. In one sequence, a dancer appears to face the audience, crossing and uncrossing his arms. Another gawps his mouth wider and wider. In both instances this is a digital double playing on the still body of the on-stage performer. The dancers gradually dissolve into a stream of atoms. They sometimes appear as body-parts only, and it is difficult to tell which bits are theirs 'for real' and which are projections. One sequence riffs between the performer himself turning to look over his shoulder at the audience and his digital image likewise peeping round, a doubled body that is simultaneously here and not-here. Throughout, the show playfully confuses the boundaries between live and recorded presence, actual and virtual flesh.

Meredith MacNeill and Paul Rhys in Theatre de Complicite's *Measure for Measure*, National Theatre, London, 2004. Photo: Neil Libbert.

Olaf Reinelke, Tom Hanslmaier and Konstantin Mishin in *Vivisector*, directed by Klaus Obermaier, Royal Festival Hall, London, 2004. Photo: Gabi Hauser.

On one level *Vivisector* is a virtuoso feat of video production, requiring witty editing and pathological control over playback. On another, however, it is suffused with multimedia principles beyond simply the functions of its technologies. This is a hybrid piece that weaves video art, dance, theatre and installation. An often ghoulish video light replaces theatre lighting. The dancers must at times stand still so that virtual bodies can dance on their skin. The images oscillate between the abstract effects of electronic arts and motion-captures of the human body, implicating the two in a permanent stream of data. The show is precise but constantly shifting, media-specific and rampantly intermedial.

Vivisector was a pan-European production, in that it featured Austrian, Russian and German artists and played in various European cities. A very different piece – an American play written in 1993 – can also be seen as a product of the multimedia age that was taking shape around it. Arnold Aronson suggests that Tony Kushner's hit *Angels in America* (1993) bears the press of contemporary cultural process without specifically referencing a world of gadgets and cybergeeks. Given its tapestry-like structure and its combination of actual and imagined locations, the play, in Aronson's description: 'reflects the prevailing non-linear, juxtapositional, hypertextual world of cyberculture [. . .] It has abandoned neoclassicism, Romanticism, naturalism, for a flow of images and ideas that replicates the perceptual processes of contemporary audiences who are shaped by the hypertextual work of electronic media' (Aronson 1999: 196, 197). All three pieces – and we could think of many more – bear witness in their warp and weft to technes of contemporary performance.

Telematic Performance

Let's conclude with a discussion of telematics, since this area of practice throws the comments above into sharper relief and raises provocations for the future. We can define telematic performance as an event involving two or more geographically distinct sites, linked by telecommunications technology so that the event takes place in mutual interaction between the different locations. It is also available to a virtual audience on the internet. The performance is only complete by way of the interaction in real time between the participants, so that a single hyper-event ensues. In some ways it is a post-virtual form of internet chat, relying as much on (doubled) physical presence and fixed geographical location as on mediation and remoteness.

My own interest in telematic performance lies in its dramaturgical possibilities. According to Roy Ascott, a pioneer of telematics in the 1980s, 'the question in human terms, from the point of view of culture and creativity, is: What is the content?' (Ascott 2002: 335). The question hangs unanswered. Issues of narrative and drama-turgy are relatively far down the list of priorities of many telematic exponents, who are understandably more concerned to explore the interface protocols of the commu-nications technology and the corporeal consequences of telematic collaboration. Much of the work to date has been dance-based and improvisational. It is clear, in any event, that in the moment of telematic performance, space, time and embodiment cannot be conceived quite as securely as in the moment of more customary theatrical exchange, where everyone is in the same room at the same time.

Ascott writes, optimistically perhaps, of 'a telematic politic, embodying the features of feedback, self-determination, interaction, and collaborative creativity' (Ascott 2002: 342). A drive to connectedness characterizes the work facilitated by another telematic explorer, Johannes Birringer, who writes in neo-liberal terms of an implied *grand projet* to dissolve cultural as much as geographical boundaries. In 2005 Birringer collaborated with fashion designer Michèle Danjoux on a 'telematic dress' project. Developed at the DAP Lab (Design and Performing Laboratory) in Nottingham (Birringer and Danjoux are the lab's co-directors), the project pursued 'transdisciplinary intersections between fashion and live performance, interactive system architecture, electronic textiles, wearable technologies, choreography and anthropology' (Birringer and Danjoux 2005: 1). It featured performance partners in Europe, the US, Brazil and Japan – dancers who interacted with their costumes, their telematic partners in other locations, and the somatic suggestiveness of their partners' attire. The project pursues a sort of globalized synergy, explained as a deliberate engagement with 'distributed real-time interaction strategies and fluid negotiations for data sharing and processing as a paradigm for contemporary social networks of collaboration and synchronous co-creation' (ibid.: 2). Certainly there are costumes, there are dance interactions that are digitally recorded. But the creation appears, in the co-directors' terms, to centre on a straightforward electronic embrace rather than an exploration of cultural specificities or discrete choreographic procedures. As the authors themselves acknowledge, the concern is not so much 'with semiotic and informatic [*sic*] levels of interactivity but with affective and erotic qualities or freedoms that arise from [costume-based] restriction' (ibid.: 2).

Is it possible to generate another form of telematics – semiotic and affective, yes, but also dramaturgically driven? *Live from Paradise*, presented by the London-based performance company Station House Opera, promised a move in this direction. The project was first presented in Amsterdam in 2004, in a co-production with De Daders, Amsterdam, using three separate locations across the city. It was produced in England the following year, located in an empty, white-walled shop in Birmingham, a disused church in Colchester and a warehouse in London. A different audience in each space witnessed live theatrical action under their noses and watched two screens showing interrelated action at the other sites. The company's website notes the intention 'to create a simultaneous combined performance, telling a story that uses cinematic language to create a fourth imaginary space. The resulting single narrative is like a report transmitted from somewhere metaphysical – live from paradise' (Station House Opera 2005). Blogs and web-based reviews relating to the 2005 production, co-hosted by the *Fierce!* performance arts festival in Birmingham, suggest that the single narrative proved elusive to watchers. Craig Johnson found that 'the characters interacted in abstract and entropic scenes [. . .] as I searched for a thread of narrative that would make some sort of semi-coherency [*sic*]' (Johnson 2005). Ruthc found that she 'couldn't say if there was a story' (Ruthc 2005). Wajid Yaseen suggests that 'trying to draw some sort of narrative from these sorts of performances I find almost impossible though [. . .] the dialogue is usually pretty fractured so no matter what the intended story is, I can usually only draw an abstracted feeling and this performance was no exception' (Yaseen 2005).

Critics are critics, whatever their format, and their testimonies are of course subjective. However, the consistency of the bloggers' responses suggests that narrative, at least, was a slippery commodity in *Live from Paradise*. This may well be a consequence of the technical frameworks for telematic interconnection. The protocols of internet-based information exchange across geographically distant sites mean that there is an inevitable time delay between transmission and reception. The delay might vary depending on the amount of traffic on the net at any one time, so that a performance event that strove for precise synchronicity would struggle in the face of current technological constraints. Better, then, to generate events that allow for a measure of slip and slide, where performers can respond with a degree of spontaneity to the unfolding collaboration, or where mismatch (perhaps, rather, a structure that is 'pretty fractured') is built into the dramaturgy.

From these and other explorations we can draw some initial conclusions. Telematic performance entails a set of binaries, most of which are closely related:

absence/presence
distance/proximity
corporeality/disembodiment
immediacy/hypermediacy
flesh/image (or to put it another way, *corpus/spiritus*)
actual/virtual
here/there
three-dimensional/two-dimensional
locational time/hypermedial time (the inconsistent time of its exchange)

It is not possible for telematic performance to dispense with any part of these binaries. Its effect – its ontology, indeed – lies in the mutual interplay of both elements. Simultaneity is the event-cement, the continuum within which the activities and mediations take shape and effect. Of course you could watch a recording of a telematic performance or access it on the web after its initial presentation. However, if the event is to work in the first place it must involve its participants in the single shared moment. How theatrical, you might say.

Let's briefly address other implications by way of three cornerstones of performance and representation: modes of being, showing and seeing.

1 For the performer, telematic performance involves a 'way of being' that is different from that of theatre or screen drama, where normally one is interacting with fellow performers in the same space. In this instance, the interaction is with co-present colleagues in the same space and the virtual bodies of colleagues in different locations. The ineffable uncertainties of time delay mean that the performers are not only working with virtual partners but must adapt their performance with respect to any glitches in smooth transmission.

2 Telematic performance entails a (re)presentational mode – a 'way of showing' – that is distinct from either screen media or theatre. There is no single, central place of performance that governs the staging of screened images. Instead the live site is multiplied and the screen presences are therefore different in some respects in each site of performance.

3 Telematic performance involves an altered 'way of seeing' on the part of the spectator, in that the screen can only be understood in relation to the live event, and the live event in relation to simultaneous actions in other places. The notion of an originary site of performance is profoundly fractured, in that there are simultaneous quasi-originary sites, each of which is meaningful only in relation to the others. The spectators are in the presence of their own absence, witnesses to a theatrical event that refuses to be whole, and watchers of a set of screens that likewise refuse to be complete. As the Station House Opera website has it, 'the audience is confronted with a global event of a different order – one which makes a performance while questioning their own understanding of film, video and live broadcasting' (Station House Opera 2005).

New forms both demand and impel new dramaturgies. Telematic performance will evolve dramaturgies specific to the possibilities enabled by its (re)presentational technologies. It already operates by way of a techne that deals with process, synthesis and multiplicity. Such a techne will increasingly colour theatre-making. Ironically, given its dependence on the bytes and chips of computer functioning, this is not just a techne for technocrats but one that promises to be both socializing and sensualizing. As ever, it rather depends upon the hand that moves the device, and the mind that guides the hand.

Further reading

Aristotle (2002). *Nicomachean Ethics*, trans. Christopher Rowe. Oxford: Oxford University Press.

Aronson, Arnold (1999). 'Technology and Dramaturgical Development: Five Observations', *Theatre Research International* 24: 2, 188–97.

Ascott, Roy (2002). 'Is There Love in the Telematic Embrace?' in Randall Packer and Ken Jordan (eds.). *Multimedia: From Wagner to Virtual Reality*. London: Norton, 333–44. (Original work published 1990.)

Birringer, Johannes and Danjoux, Michèle (2005). 'The Telematic Dress: Evolving Garments and Distributed Proprioception in Streaming Media and Fashion Performance', art.ntu.ac.uk/performance_research/ birringer/tedress.htm (accessed 2005).

Bolter, Jay David and Grusin, Richard (1999). *Remediation: Understanding New Media*. Cambridge, MA, and London: MIT Press.

Brown, Ross (forthcoming). 'The Theatre Soundscape and the End of Noise', *Performance Research*.

Butler, Jeremy G. (2002). 'The Internet and the World Wide Web' in Dan Harries (ed.). *The New Media Book*. London: BFI Publishing, 40–51.

Giannachi, Gabriella (2004). *Virtual Theatres: An Introduction*. London and New York: Routledge.

Johnson, Craig (2005). 'Pressure to Perform', www.spike magazine.com/0705-fierce-festival.php (accessed 2005).

Lister, Martin, Dovey, John, Giddings, Seth, Grant, Iain and Kelly, Kieran (2003). *New Media: A Critical Introduction*. London and New York: Routledge.

Lunenfeld, Peter (2000). 'Introduction: Screen Grabs: The Digital Dialectic and New Media Theory' in Peter Lunenfeld (ed.). *The Digital Dialectic: New Essays on New Media*. Cambridge, MA, and London: MIT Press, 14–21.

Manovich, Lev (2000). *The Language of New Media*. Cambridge, MA, and London: MIT Press.

Murray, Janet H. (1997). *Hamlet on the Holodeck: The Future of Narrative in Cyberspace*. Cambridge, MA: MIT Press.

Packer, Randall and Jordan, Ken (2002). 'Overture' in Randall Packer and Ken Jordan (eds.). *Multimedia: From Wagner to Virtual Reality*. London: Norton, xv–xxxviii.

Ruthc (2005). 'Live from Paradise', www.mazine.ws/LiveFromParadise (accessed 2005).

Rutsky, R. L. (1999). *High Techne: Art and Technology from the Machine Aesthetic to the Posthuman*. Minneapolis and London: University of Minnesota Press.

Shaw, Jeffrey (2002). 'Modalities of Interactivity and Virtuality' in Randall Packer and Ken Jordan (eds.). *Multimedia: From Wagner to Virtual Reality*. London: Norton, 132–7. (Original work published in 1992.)

Station House Opera (2005). www.stationhouseopera.com/Introduction/index.html (accessed 2005).

Yaseen, Wajid (2005). 'The Fierce Festival: A Weekend of Performance Art', www.lazarus corporation.co.uk/v4/ articles/fiercefestival.php (accessed 2005).

Index

1798 Rebellion 294–5
1800 Act of Union 88
1845–7 Great Hunger 16
1857 Indian Mutiny 350–1, 354
1907 riots 96, 110
1911 linen-mill strike 332
1916 Rebellion 8, 23, 112, 125, 158, 335, 337
1949 Geneva Convention 358
1958 Report on Economic Development *see* Whitaker, T. K.
1967 Sexual Offences Act 226, 262, 401
1968 Paris riots 402
1968 Theatres Act 398–9, 491, 413
1974 Ulster Workers' Strike 297, 337
1979 Winter of Discontent 354, 386
1984–5 Miners' Strike 447, 522
1991 War Crimes Act 323
1993 Downing Street Declaration 335, 449
7:84 Theatre Company 387, 419–26, 444
9/11 291, 247, 368, 373, 395

A. N. *Mr Peppercorn's Awakening* 102, 104
Abbey Theatre 2, 16, 30, 87, 93–7, 110–15, 120–1, 131, 133–4, 248, 295–6, 305, 308–9, 312, 511, 514
Abu Ghraib prison 358, 520
Achurch, Janet 38, 41–2, 44, 48, 52–3, 56, 59
  Mrs Daintree's Daughter 48, 52–5
Ackerley, J. R.
  Prisoners of War 134, 306–7
Ackland, Rodney 164–74
  Absolute Hell (The Pink Room) 171–3
Actors' Orphanage 225
Actresses' Franchise League (AFL) 100

Adelphi Theatre 177
Adorno, Theodor 316–18, 321, 325
Adventures in Motion Pictures 406
Aeschylus
  Agamemnon 521
  Oresteia 512, 520
African National Congress (ANC) 444
Agate, James 354
Agincourt, battle of 351
Ainsley, Henry 103
Albert Hall 101, 234
Albery Theatre 241
Aldwych Theatre 259, 347, 445
Alexander, George 57, 214–15, 221
Allen, Inglis
  Suffragettes' Redemption, The 107
Allen, Jim
  Perdition 322–3
Allen, John
  Other Man, The 319
Allgood, Sarah 92
Almeida Theatre 354, 366
Almost Free Theatre 401, 403
Al-Quaeda 373
Ambassadors Theatre 177
Ambiance Theatre 188
American Academy of Arts and Letters 179–80
American Conservatory Theatre 184
Amnesty International 358, 363–4
Anderson, Maxwell 179
Angry Young Men 30, 153, 165, 175–6
Anski, Solomon 324
anti-suffrage plays 107
Antoine, André 89, 110

Apollo Theatre 307
Arab–Israeli War 319
Archer, William 37–40, 48–51, 78–9
    Old Drama and the New, The 49
    Quicksands 38
    Theatrical 'World' 49
Arden, John 153–63, 280, 385, 387, 411, 420
    All That Fall 155
    Armstrong's Last Goodnight 154
    Awkward Corners 156–7
    Ballygombeen Bequest, The 154, 157
    Happy Haven, The 154, 160
    Island of the Mighty, The 154
    Little Grey Home in the West, The 154
    Live Like Pigs 153
    Non-Stop Connolly Show 154, 158–60
    Sergeant Musgrave's Dance 153, 160–2
    Soldier, Soldier 153
    To Present the Pretence 156
    Vandaleur's Folly 155
    Waters of Babylon, The 153
    Workhouse Donkey, The 154
Arendt, Hannah 316, 318
    Eichmann in Jerusalem 316
Aristophanes 258, 525
    Lysistrata 525
    Thesmophoriazusae 526
Aristotle 242, 551
Armagh prison 156
Armistice Day 301
Arts Council of England 489
Arts Council of Great Britain 425
Arts Theatre (Cambridge) 260, 358
Arts Theatre (London) 177, 263, 344, 359
Asche, Oscar
    Chu Chin Chow 303
Ashcroft, Peggy 180, 183–4
Ashwell, Lena 103, 106
Asmus, Walter 239
'at-homes' 101
Atkinson, Bruce 179
Auden, W. H. 138–49, 214, 311, 329
    Ascent of F6, The 143–4
    Dance of Death 141, 144
    Dog Beneath the Skin, The 141–4
    Enemies of a Bishop 141
    In Memory of W. B. Yeats 329
    On the Frontier 144
    Paid on Both Sides 138–40, 148
Auschwitz 316, 321, 323

Aveling, Edward 37
Avenue Theatre 90
Avignon festival 320
Award of Merit Medal for Drama 179–80
Ayckbourn, Alan 269–78, 387, 390
    Absent Friends 270
    Absurd Person Singular 270, 387
    Body Language 276
    Comic Potential 275
    Communicating Doors 273
    Drowning on Dry Land 275–6
    FlatSpin 270
    Henceforward 274–5
    House & Garden 271–2, 274
    How the Other Half Loves 269, 271–2
    Intimate Exchanges 274
    Invisible Friends 270
    Living Together 271
    Man of the Moment 275–6
    Mr. A's Amazing Maze Plays 273
    My Sister Sadie 275
    Norman Conquests, The 271–2, 274
    Private Fears in Public Places 275–6
    Relatively Speaking 269
    Revenger's Comedies, The 269–70
    Round and Round the Garden 271
    Sisterly Feelings 270, 273
    Small Family Business, A 270
    Sugar Daddies 276
    Table Manners 271
    Taking Steps 270
    Things We Do for Love 272
    Time of My Life 272
    Way Upstream 269–70
    Whenever 273, 276
    Woman in Mind 270

BAFTA (awards and nominations) 354
Bagnold, Enid
    Chalk Garden, The 177–85
    Matter of Gravity, A 185
    National Velvet 177–8
Baker, Edith M.
    Our Happy Home 102, 104
Baker, Elizabeth 79
Baker, Roger
    Mister X 402
Balaclava 343, 350
Balkan Wars 198, 373, 376, 379–80, 449–50
Ballymurphy massacre 333

Barbican 445, 450
Barbusse, Henri
  Under Fire 302
Barker, H. Granville 35, 75–86, 134, 103–4
  characterization 77–8
  Farewell to Theatre 84
  His Majesty 75, 84
  Prefaces to Shakespeare 84
  Prunella 77, 79
  Madras House, The 75–6, 81, 83–4
  Marrying of Anne Leete, The 75, 78, 81–3
  Secret Life, The 75, 82
  Voysey Inheritance, The 75, 81–3
  Waste 75, 77, 82–3
Barker, Howard 374, 390–1, 429, 438, 488–98,
  542–3
  All He Fears 496
  Arguments for a Theatre 488, 493
  Birth on a Hard Shoulder 492
  Castle, The 495
  Claw 490–1
  Crimes in Hot Countries 492
  Death, the One and the Art of Theatre 496–7
  Downchild 491–2
  Ecstatic Bible, The 496
  Edward, the Final Days 490
  Europeans, The 495
  Gertrude 496
  Good Between Us, The 491
  Hang of the Gaol, The 491–2
  Judith 494–5
  Loud Boy's Life, The 492
  Love of a Good Man, The 491
  Passion in Six Days, A 491
  Possibilities, The 495
  Power of the Dog, The 495
  Swing at Night, The 496
  (Uncle) Vanya 496
  Und 496
  Victory 374, 495
Barker, Pat
  Regeneration 302, 312
Barnes, Ben 120–1
Barnes, Peter
  Bewitched, The 387
  Laughter! (including *Auschwitz*) 320
  Red Noses 522
  Ruling Class, The 387
Barrie, J. M.
  Peter Pan 229

Barry, Sebastian 394
Barthes, Roland
  Lover's Discourse, A 379, 494
Bartlett, Neil 213, 406
Barton, John 77
Basho, Matsuo 413
Bayliss, Lilian 103
BBC 53, 170–1, 243, 258, 323, 354, 368, 420,
  445, 548
Beaumont, Hugh 'Binkie' 178–80
Beckett, Samuel 13, 96, 126, 130, 176,
  237–46, 250, 261, 293, 320, 348–9,
  362, 385, 394, 412, 542, 544
  All That Fall 237–8
  Cascando 243
  Catastrophe 243
  Come and Go 238
  Eh Joe 238, 243
  Endgame 238, 240–1, 349
  Footfalls 245
  Happy Days 237, 241–3
  Krapp's Last Tape 243
  Not I 244–5
  Ohio Impromptu 245
  Piece of Monologue, A 245
  Play 237, 243–4, 544
  Quad 243
  Rockaby 245
  Waiting for Godot 13–15, 237–9, 250, 293,
  348–9, 362
  What Where 237
  Words and Music 243
Beerbohm, Max 69
Beerbohm Tree, Herbert 49, 57, 216
Beere, Mrs 216
Begnini, Roberto
  Life is Beautiful 323
Behan, Brendan 27, 164, 247–57
  Big House, The 255
  Brendan Behan's Island 248
  Garden Party, A 255
  Hostage, The (An Giall) 27, 164, 247–50,
  252–6, 295
  Landlady, The 255
  Moving Out 255
  Quare Fellow, The 247–56, 295
  Richard's Cork Leg 255
Belfast Agreement 27
Belgrade Theatre, Coventry 169
Bell, Florence 48–52

Bell, Florence (*cont'd*)
  Alan's Wife 48–51
  At the Works: A Study of a Manufacturing Town 50
Bell, Tom 320
Belsen 317, 320
Benn, Tony 24, 27
Bennett, Alan 390, 393
Bennett, Arnold 79
Benson, Frank 92
Bensusan, Inez 100
Berkshire Theatre Festival 184
Berlin Wall 192–3, 448
Berman, Ed 188, 401
Bhatti, Gurpreet Kaur
  Behzti 2, 395
Bible 200, 238, 251, 293, 513
Billington, Michael 359, 361, 364, 368, 372, 420
Birkenau 319–20
Birmingham Feminist History Group 182
Birmingham Repertory Theatre 2, 201, 295, 303, 394–5, 441–2, 445, 450–1
Birtwhistle, Harrison 520, 524, 527
Bjornsson, Oddur 78
Black Panthers 156
Black Power 188, 190
Black Theatre Co-operative 388
Blair, Tony 26–7, 368, 431–2, 436, 438
Blake, William 24, 26
Blast Theory 392
Blavatsky, Madame 89
Block, Simon 377
Bloody Sunday 330–1, 338, 500, 503–4
Bloolips 406
Blunt, Wilfred Scawen 24, 89
Blyton, Enid
  Famous Five 177
Boer War 159, 228
Boland, Eavan 509
Bond, Edward 322–3, 385, 387, 398, 409–18, 522
  Bingo 387, 415
  Bundle, The 416
  Early Morning 398, 400, 413
  Fool, The 387, 415, 522
  Jackets 416–17
  Lear 412–14, 416
  Man's a Man 413
  Narrow Road to the Deep North 413, 416

Pope's Wedding, The 412, 415
  'Rational Theatre' 410–11, 417
  Restoration 416
  Saved 379, 385, 398, 412–13, 415
  Sea, The 414–15
  Summer 322
  Woman, The 387, 415–16
Borderline 391
Bosquet, Marechal 343
Boucicault, Dion 13–14, 43, 248, 295–6
  Colleen Bawn, The 13
Bourke, Paddy J. 248
Bourne, Bette 406
Bourne, Matthew 406
Bournemouth Repertory Theatre 421
Bowie, David 226
Box, Muriel
  Angels of War 310–11
  Seventh Veil, The 310–11
Boyd, John
  Flats, The 331
Braddon, Mary 43
Brahms, Otto 110
Brando, Marlon 543
Brandt, Willy 318
Brecht, Bertolt 37, 313, 319, 323, 385, 412–13, 417, 434, 441
  Good Soldier Schweyk 313
  Lehrstück 97
  Life of Galileo, The 17, 434, 451
  Mother Courage 434
  Resistible Rise of Arturo Ui, The 319, 441
Brenton, Howard 30–2, 296, 323, 386, 390–2, 399, 430, 446–7, 490–1
  Berlin Bertie 392
  Brassneck 430, 446
  Churchill Play, The 386, 446
  Genius, The 447
  Greenland 390
  H.I.D. (Hess Is Dead) 323
  Magnificence 386
  Pravda 390, 431
  Romans in Britain, The 30–1
  Weapons of Happiness 386
Breton, André 373
Brighton, Pam 333
Bristol New Vic 442
Bristow, Joseph 203
Brit-Art 206, 377
Brith Gof 391, 547

British Council 378
British Library 53, 59
British Museum 232
British National Party 537–8
Britpop 377
Brittain, Vera
  Testament of Youth 302
Britten, Benjamin 524
Broadhurst Theatre 185
Broadway 177, 179, 185, 280, 320, 322, 431–2, 501
Brook, Peter 130–1, 350
  U/S 350
Brookes, Mike 547–8
Brooks, Mel
  Producers, The 319
Brown, John 398
Brown, Pamela 183–4
Bryden, Ronald 155, 280–1, 353, 413
Bryks, Rachmil
  Cat in the Ghetto, A 318
Büchner, Georg
  Woyzeck 380
Buckstone, John Baldwin 43
Buffini, Moira
  Gabriel 324
Burke, Edmund 26
Burke, Gregory 394
Burnett, Ivy Compton 100
Burton, Richard 167, 176
Bury, John 343
Bush, George W. 368, 432, 520, 556
Bush Theatre 374, 377, 393, 442
Butterworth, Jez 377, 393
Byatt, A. S. 25, 33

Cable Street, battle of 169
Campaign for Homosexual Equality (CHE) 402
Campaign for Nuclear Disarmament (CND) 156, 364, 446
Campbell, Mrs Patrick 215
Čapek, Karel *R.U.R.* 275
Cardiff Laboratory Theatre 391
Carfax Gallery 69
Carmichael, Stokely 190
Carpenter, Edward 67, 403
Carr, Henry 282–3
Carr, Marina 2, 119, 333, 394, 509–18
  Ariel 505–17
  By the Bog of Cats 509–10, 512, 515–17

Dazzling Dark, The 510
Low in the Dark 509
Mai, The 509–10, 512, 517
On 'Raftery's Hill 509–10, 512, 515–17
Ullaloo 509
Carrington, Charles 38, 41, 44, 48
Carville, Daragh
  Convictions 339
Casson, Lewis 184
Castro, Fidel 190
Catastrophism *see* Theatre of Catastrophe
Ceasescu, Nicolae 482
Celan, Paul 318–19, 321
  Todesfuge 321
censorship 304, 323, 333, 385–6, 398, 413
  see also lord chamberlain
Channel Four 364
Chaplin, Alice
  At the Gates 102
Charabanc Theatre Company 332–6, 338–9, 391
  Lay Up Your Ends 332
  Now You're Talking 332–3
  Somewhere Over the Balcony 332
Charge of the Light Brigade 343, 350
Charter 88 364
Chayevsky, Paddy 343–4
Chechnyan invasion 373
Chekhov, Anton 37, 77–8, 171, 228, 496
  Cherry Orchard, The 171, 451
Chester Mystery Plays 522
Childress, Alice
  Wine in the Wilderness 206
Christie, Agatha
  Mousetrap, The 177
Christina, Queen 388
Church of England 76, 431
Churchill, Caryl 76, 296, 354, 388, 390–3, 395, 399, 429, 438, 476–87, 514
  Cloud Nine 76, 354, 388, 390–3, 476–7
  Far Away 476, 485, 486
  Fen 476–7, 479–81
  Light Shining in Buckinghamshire 388
  Mad Forest 392
  Mouthful of Birds, A 392, 482
  Owners 388
  Serious Money 390, 476–9, 481, 485
  Skriker, The 476, 481–5, 514
  Top Girls 455, 477
  Traps 477
  Vinegar Tom 388, 476–7

Churchill, Winston 259, 266, 346, 348–9
Circle in the Square 184
Citizens Theatre, Glasgow 391, 456
Clare, John 415, 417
Clarke, James 368
Clash 393
Clean Break Theatre Company 205
Clydebuilt season 424–5
Cockpit Theatre 323
Cold War 166, 342, 393–4, 414
Coleridge, Samuel Taylor 116
Collins, Michael 23
Collins, Wilkie 43
Colum, Patrick 92
Colway Theatre Trust, Devon 391
Comédie Française 78
commedia dell'arte 296
Communicado 391
Congreve, William 217
Connolly, Cyril 226–7
Connolly, James 158–9
'conversion' play 102
Conway, Frank 514
Cooper, Gladys 183–4
Corkery, Daniel 111
Corrie, Joe
    In Time of Strife 424
Costello, General Michael 502
Cottesloe Theatre 524
Coulter, Phil 291
Court Theatre *see* Royal Court Theatre
Coventry Mystery Plays 522
Coward, Noël 25, 180, 225–37, 309–11
    Bitter Sweet 226
    Blithe Spirit 227, 235
    Cavalcade 321
    Dance Little Lady 232
    Design for Living 227, 230, 233
    Easy Virtue 226, 233
    Fallen Angels 226
    Hay Fever 226–7, 230, 232
    Home Chat 227
    In Which We Serve 225
    Mad Dogs and Englishmen 225
    Peace in Our Time 231
    Poor Little Rich Girl 225
    Post Mortem 231, 309–10
    Present Laughter 227, 230, 233–5
    Private Lives 227, 229–31, 233
    Red Peppers 230

Scoundrel, The 225
Shadow Play 234
Sirocco 227
Song at Twilight, A 225–6, 235
South Sea Bubble 226
Star Quality 227
This Time Tomorrow 228
This Year of Grace! 227, 232
Twentieth Century Blues 225, 231
Vortex, The 225–6, 228, 232, 235
Waiting in the Wings 225
Young Idea, The 226, 230
Craig, Edward Gordon 42, 95
Craig, Edy 101, 103–6
Crawford, Michael 350
Creative Evolution 64–5
Creole *see* Trinidadian Creole
Crimean War 350
Crimp, Martin 376, 393
    Attempts on her Life 393
Cross, Victoria 51
Crumlin Road Courthouse and Jail 339
Cukor, George 179
Cullen, Greg 542
Curran Theatre 235
Curteis, Ian
    Falklands Play, The 354
Curtis, Richard
    Blackadder Goes Forth 313
Cyprus emergency 343

Dachau 320–1, 404
Dada 139
Daldry, Stephen 372, 347
Dance, Charles 322
Dance, George
    Suffragettes, The 107
Daniels, Sarah
    Devil's Gateway, The 391
    Masterpieces 391
    Neaptide 391
D'Annunzio, Gabriele 78
Dante Alighieri
    Divine Comedy, The 237–8
D'Arcy, Margaretta 153–63
    Awkward Corners 156–7
    Happy Haven, The 154, 160
    Island of the Mighty, The 154
    Tell Them Everything 156
    Vandaleur's Folly 155

Darlington, W. A. 302–3, 307
Daughters of Erin (*Inghinidhe na hEireann*) 93
Davison, Emily Wilding 102
Davitt, Michael 24
Davy, Shaun 291
de Angelis, April 380
De Daders 559
Deane, Seamus 335
Defoe, Daniel 528
dehiscence 130, 135–6
Delaney, Shelagh 2, 164, 176, 267
   Taste of Honey, A 164, 176, 263
Dench, Judy 431
Devine, George 153
Devlin, Anne 331, 334–5, 339
   After Easter 335, 337
   Ourselves Alone 334
Devlin, Bernadette 504
devolution 394
Dhringa, Dolly 199–200
Dickens, Charles 269, 313, 445
Die Freie Bühne 110
Dietrich, Marlene 388
Digges, Dudley 92
Dimbleby, Richard 317
Divis Flats 332, 334
Dolan, Jill 403
Donmar Warehouse 312, 322, 444, 521
Donnelly, Neil 333
Doone, Rupert 140
Dorfman, Ariel
   Death and the Maiden 366
Dossor, Alan 421
Douglas, Alfred 'Bosie' 213–14, 431
Douglas, Lord 213
Dowie, Claire
   Why is John Lennon Wearing a Skirt? 406
Drahos, Mary
   Eternal Sabbath 319
dramaturgy 11, 35–7, 321, 350, 431–2
   see also Barker, H. Granville
Drill Hall 406
Drinkwater, John
   X = 0 304
Dromgoole, Dominic 374
Druid Theatre Company 16, 112–14, 117–21, 391
DruidSynge 112, 115, 119–21
Dryden, John 519
Du Maurier, Gerald 229, 233–4
DubblJoint

Binlids 333
Forced Upon Us 333
Dublin Theatre Festival 290, 500–1
Dubrovka Theatre siege 375
Duke of York's Theatre 79, 302, 374
DV8 Physical Theatre 392

Eagleton, Terry 213
   Saint Oscar 213
Easter Rising (Easter Rebellion) *see* 1916
   Rebellion
Eatough, Graham 395
Ebb, Fred
   Cabaret 317, 319–20
Edgar, David 164–5, 319, 323–4, 374, 380–1,
   386–7, 390–2, 399–400, 406, 410, 420,
   426, 436, 441–52, 491, 522
   Albert Speer 323–4, 450–1
   Ball Boys 442–3
   Blood Sports 442
   Case of the Workers' Plane, The 442
   Continental Divide 451
   Daughters of the Revolution 451
   Destiny 319, 386, 443–6, 452
   Dick Deterred 442
   Dunkirk Spirit, The 442
   England's Ireland 442
   Entertaining Strangers: A Play for Dorchester 447
   Events Following the Closure of a Motorcycle
     Factory 442
   Fart for Europe, A 442
   Jail Diary of Albie Sachs, The 444–5
   Mary Barnes 445
   Maydays 390, 445
   Mothers Against 451
   National Interest, The 441
   Nicholas Nickleby 445
   O Fair Jerusalem 522
   Our Own People 443
   Playing With Fire 451
   Prisoner's Dilemma, The 449–50
   Rent, or Caught in the Act 442
   Shape of the Table, The 392, 447
   Strange Case of Dr Jekyll and Mr Hyde, The 450
   Tedderella 441
   Teendreams 444
   That Summer 447
   Wreckers 444
Edinburgh Festival (and Fringe) 120, 280,
   311–12, 441

Edison, Thomas 552
Edwardian Golden Age *see* Golden Age
Edwards, Dic 542
Egerton, George 51
Eichmann, Adolf 318, 320
Eldridge, David 377
Eliot, T. S. 138–49, 228, 248–9
    Family Reunion, The 144–6
    Murder in the Cathedral 145–6
    Rock, The 146
    Sweeney Agonistes 138, 141, 146, 148
    Use of Poetry and the Use of Criticism, The 149
    Waste Land, The 146
Elizabeth II, Queen 192, 226
Elliott, Gertrude 143
Ellis, Havelock 37, 40–1
Elton, Ben
    Blackadder Goes Forth 313
Elyot, Kevin 405–6
    My Night With Reg 405
Emin, Tracey 206
enfants terribles 377, 413
English Stage Company 164
Etchells, Tim 392
Ethel Barrymore Theatre 179
Eugene O'Neill Theater Center 320
Euripides 79, 258–9, 266, 412, 415, 512, 519–21, 525–6
    Bacchae, The 259, 482
    Hecuba 415–16, 519
    Trojan Women 525
European Union 9, 22–3
Eurovision Song Contest 291
Evans, Edith 180, 183–4
Evans, Lee 241
Evelyn, Stanley
    Strange Case of Martin Richter, The 319
Eyre, Richard 341, 345, 430–1

Fabian Society 64, 79
Falklands War 311, 341, 354, 389, 479
Farquhar, George 217, 294
Farrell, J. G.
    Siege of Krishnapur, The 354
    Singapore Grip, The 354
Fay, Frank 93
Fay, William G. 92–4
Feydeau, Georges 260
Ffrangcon-Davies, Gwen 183–4
Fianna Fáil 500

Fiction Factory 547
    see also Y Cwmni
Field Day Theatre Company 296, 335–7, 339, 391, 505–6
Fierce! performance arts festival 559
fin de siècle 35, 37, 41, 48–50, 53, 57, 66, 82
Firbank, Ronald 258
Flannery, Peter
    Singer 323–4
Fletcher, Constance ('George Fleming') 53–5, 59
    Mrs Lessingham 53–5, 57
Fontanne, Lynne 230
Forbes-Robertson, Johnston 103
Force Ten Gaels Dance Band 423
Forced Entertainment 392
Ford, Ford Madox
    Good Soldier, The 302
Forster, E. M. 29, 33, 352
    Passage to India, A 352
Fosse, Bob 317
Foucault, Michel
    Discipline and Punish 380, 479
Fouere, Olwen 510
Franco, General Francisco 169–70
Frank, Anne 318
Fraser, Antonia 364
Fraser, Hugh 488
Frayn, Michael 295–6, 390, 393, 410
    Copenhagen 393
    Noises Off 295–6
Freedman, Harold 178
Freire, Paulo 156
French, Samuel 178
Freud, Sigmund 266
Friel, Brian 15, 293, 296, 330–1, 335–7, 339, 387, 391, 466, 499–508
    Communication Cord, The 336, 449
    Dancing at Lughnasa 499–500, 506
    Enemy Within, The 499
    Faith Healer 505
    Freedom of the City, The 330–1, 335, 387, 499–500, 503–5
    Living Quarters 499
    Loves of Cass McGuire, The 502
    Making History 336, 505
    Mundy Scheme, The 503
    Philadelphia, Here I Come! 499–504, 506
    Translations 15, 336–8, 391, 499–500, 505–6
    Volunteers 499, 505
    Wonderful Tennessee 499

Frisch, Max
  Andorra 318
Frohman, Charles 79
Fry, Christopher 176, 179
Fugard, Athol
  Island, The 320
Fukuyama, Francis 376
Furtwangler, Wilhelm 323

Gaelic Athletic Association 88
Gaelic League 88, 92, 110, 114
Gaiety Theatre (Dublin) 92–3
Gaiety Theatre (London) 103
Gaiety Theatre (Manchester) 103
Gallipoli 313
Galsworthy, John 79–82, 126, 138
  Justice 79–81
  Silver Box, The 79–80
  Strife 79–81, 126
Gambon, Michael 241, 431
Gardner, Lyn 372
Garrick Theatre 53
Gate Theatre 380
Gay, John
  Beggar's Opera, The 116
Gay Liberation Front (GLF) 401–2
Gay Sweatshop Theatre Company 320, 388,
  401–3, 405
  Care and Control 402
Gelder, Ian 322
Gellert, Roger
  Quaint Honour 263
Gems, Pam 155, 388
  Dusa, Fish, Stas and Vi 388
General Will Theatre Company 442
George VI, King 348
Gere, Richard 320
Gesamtkunstwerk 555
Ghandi, Mahatma 325
Gibbon, Edward 26
Gibbs, A. M. 68
Gielgud, John 180, 345, 350, 353
Gilbert and Sullivan 25, 142, 303, 521
Gilder, Rosamund 353
Gilman, Charlotte
  Three Women 103
Gilroy, Paul 201, 203
Giradoux, Jean
  Tiger at the Gates 179
Gish, Dorothy 184

Gish, Lilian 184
Gissing, George 50
Glendinning, Robin
  Mumbo Jumbo 338
Globe Theatre 310
Gloria 406
Glover, Evelyn
  Chat with Mrs Chicky, A 101, 104
  Miss Appleyard's Awakening 104
Godfrey, Paul 376
Golden Age 166–8, 172–3
Goldhagen, Daniel 316
Goldsmith, Oliver 296
Gomer, Russell 543
Gonne, Maud 94, 118
Good Friday Agreement 9
Good, Maurice
  John Synge Comes Next 111
Goodrich, Frances
  Diary of Anne Frank, The 179, 317–18
Gorky, Maxim 78
Gorman, Damien
  Loved Ones 339
Gosse, Edmund 37–8
Gough, Lucy 542
GPO 114
Grand Guignol 346
Grand, Sarah 51, 100
Graves, Robert
  Goodbye to All That 302
Great War *see* World War I
Green Room 201
Greer, Herb 431
Gregory, Lady Augusta Persse 9–10, 87–98,
  112–13, 127
  Cathleen ni Houlihan 9–10, 93–4, 472–3
  Gaol Gate, The 96
  Grania 96
  Rising of the Moon, The 96
Gregory, Lord William 89
Greig, David 374, 394–5
  Cosmonaut's Last Message 395
  Europe 395
  Outlying Islands 395
  Victoria 395
Greig, Noel
  As Time Goes By 403
  Dear Love of Comrades, The 403
Grein, J. T. 42, 49–50, 110
Griffith, Arthur 94, 118

Griffiths, Drew
  As Time Goes By 403
  Mister X 402
Griffiths, Richard 313
Griffiths, Trevor 170, 386, 388, 391, 491
  Comedians 386
  Country 170
  Party, The 386
Group Theatre 140–1, 144
Grundy, Sidney
  New Woman, The 56
Grünwald, Malkiel 322
Guantanamo Bay 358, 528, 556
Gulbenkian Studio Theatre 323
Gulf War 311

Hackett, Albert
  Diary of Anne Frank, The 179, 317–18
Haigh, Kenneth 167
Hall, Peter 421, 520
Hall, Stuart 389, 530
Hall, Willis
  Long the Short and the Tall, The 170
Halliwell, Kenneth 258, 262
Hamilton, Cicely 100–1, 103–6
  Diane of Dobson's 103, 106
  How the Vote was Won 101, 104
  Pageant of Great Women, A 101, 105
  Pot and the Kettle, The 101
Hammond, David 335, 505
Hampstead Theatre 359, 377, 447
Hampton, Christopher
  Portage to San Cristobel of A. H., The 322
Hankin, St John 79–81
  Cassilis Engagement, The 80
  Charity that Began At Home, The 80
  Return of the Prodigal 80
Hannan, Chris 394
Hansberry, Lorraine
  Raisin in the Sun, A 177
Hardie, Keir 159
Hardy, Thomas 79, 81
Hare, David 170, 386, 388, 390–2, 395, 399,
    410, 420, 429–40
  Absence of War, The 392, 431, 436
  Amy's View 431, 433, 435, 437
  Bay at Nice, The 430
  Blue Room, The 431
  Brassneck 430, 446
  Breath of Life, The 432

Fanshen 433–4
Great Exhibition, The 430
Judas Kiss, The 431, 435, 437
Knuckle 429
Map of the World, A 430
Murmuring Judges 392, 431, 436
My Zinc Bed 432
Permanent Way, The 395, 429, 432, 435, 437
Plenty 170, 386, 430, 433–5, 466
Pravda 390, 431–3
Racing Demon 392, 431, 436
Secret Rapture, The 390, 431, 435
Skylight 431, 433, 435, 437
Slag 430
Stuff Happens 395, 429, 432–3, 437–8
Teeth 'n Smiles 386, 430
Via Dolorosa 431, 436–7
Hare, John 53
Haring, Chris 556
Harradan, Beatrice 100
Harrison, Tony 519–29
  Agamemnon 376
  Hecuba 519–21, 528
  Kaisers of Carnuntum, The 526
  Labourers of Herakles, The 525
  Lysistrata 525–6
  Medea: A Sex-War Opera 526
  Mystery Plays 522–5
  Oresteia 520, 522, 524
  Prometheus 525
  Thesmophoriazusae 526
  Trackers of Oxyrhynchus, The 524, 526–7
  Trojan Women 525
  v. 519
Harrower, David 394
Harvey, Jonathan 393, 405–6
  Beautiful Thing 405
Harwood, Ronald
  Handyman, The 323
  Taking Sides 323
Hastings, Michael 171
Hauptmann, Gerhart 37, 78, 93, 126
  Weavers, The 126, 133
Havelock, General Henry 346, 351–3
Hawes, James
  White Powder, Green Light 547
Hawtrey, Charles 229, 233
Haymarket Theatre 49, 53, 126, 178, 180, 183
Hazlewood, C. H. 43
Heaney, Seamus 120, 329, 335, 337

Heath, Edward 441, 490
Hegel, G. W. F. 156
Hellman, Lillian
  Children's Hour, The 177
Hemingway, Ernest 233
Herbert, Jocelyn 245
Herman, Henry
  Breaking a Butterfly 38
Hersey, John 318
Hickox, Douglas 260
Hill, Christopher 33
Hippodrome 177
His Majesty's Theatre 303
Hitchcock, Alfred 125
Hitler, Adolf 140, 316, 322, 324, 345, 361, 450
Hobsbawm, Eric 88
Hobson, Harold 280, 351, 413
Hochhuth, Rolf
  Representative, The (*The Deputy*) 318–19
Holborn Centre for Performing Arts 323
Holloway Prison 106
Holocaust 3, 316–28, 359, 365, 451
Home Rule 9–10, 91
Home Service 524
Homosexual Law Reform Society 401
Honderich, Ted 376
Hopkins, Anthony 390
Horniman, Annie 94–5, 103, 113
Hornung, E. W. 354
Houseman, A. E. 286
Houseman, Laurence 77, 79, 100, 103
Howard, Alan 322
Howard, Trevor 350
Hughes, Margaret 105–6
Hugo, Victor 27
Hunt, Hugh 112–13, 121
Hurston, Zora Neale 481
Hurt, John 313
Hussein, Saddam 432, 438
Hutchinson, Ernest
  Votes for Children 107
Hutchinson, Ron 332, 335
  Rat in the Skull 332
Hyde, Douglas 88
Hyde Park 100, 182
Hyde-White, Wilfred 214
Hynes, Garry 16, 114–15, 118–21

Ibsen, Henrik 2, 35–50, 55–8, 65, 78, 93,
  128–9, 228–9, 552

Clever Alice 41
Doll's House, A 38, 40–2, 44, 48, 57
Emperor and Galilean 38
Enemy of the People, An 41
Ghosts 36, 41–3, 50
Hedda Gabler 42, 44, 48–9
John Gabriel Borkmann 40
Lady from the Sea, The 42
Little Eyolf 42
Master Builder, The 48
Peer Gynt 37, 40–1, 44
Pillars of Society, The 38
Rosmersholm 42
Wild Duck, The 129
Independent Theatre 42, 49, 90, 110
Industrial Revolution 553
Inge, William
  Bus Stop 179
International Brigades 169–70
in-yer-face theatre 377–8, 394, 406
Ionesco, Eugène 261
IRA 155, 247, 253–5, 291, 332, 334–5, 338,
  385, 505–6
Ireland, Kenny 488
Irish Free State 95–6, 473
Irish Literary Theatre 90–2
Irish National Dramatic Company 93–4
Irish National Literary Society 89
Irish National Theatre Society *see* Abbey Theatre
Irish Transport and General Workers Union 158
Iron Curtain 22
Irving, David 323
Irving, Henry 41, 552
Isherwood, Christopher 141, 143–4, 311,
  317–18
  Ascent of F6, The 143–4
  Dog Beneath the Skin, The (*Dogskin*) 141–4
  I am a Camera 317
ITV 344, 347
Ivan the Terrible 320

James, Henry 49, 104
Jeanetta Cochrane Theatre 265
Jellicoe, Ann 176, 391, 447
  Sport of My Mad Mother, The 176
Jerrold, Douglas 43
John F. Kennedy Centre 516
John Hewitt Award 333
Johnson, Terry 374
Johnston, Denis 111

Johnston, Jennifer
  Three Monologues 334
Joint Stock Theatre Company 388, 429–30, 432
Jones, Claudia 206
Jones, David 154–5
Jones, Delyth
  Ffondue, Rhyw a Deinosors 547–8
Jones, Henry Arthur 38, 64
  Breaking a Butterfly 38
Jones, Lloyd
  Mr Vogel 541
Jones, Marie 333–5, 339, 391
  Night in November, A 333
  Wedding Community Play, the 339
Jones, Roderick 185
Jonson, Ben 132, 354
  Alchemist, The 132
  Volpone 132
Joseph, Stephen 269
Joyce, James 48, 115, 228, 282–3
  Ulysses 282–3

Kafka, Franz 359
Kander, John
  Cabaret 317, 319–20
Kane, Sarah 2, 371–82, 393–5, 430, 448–9, 542,
  548
  4:48 Psychosis 393
  Blasted 371–81
  Cleansed 371–81
  Crave 548
  Phaedra's Love 372
Kani, John
  Island, The 320
Kassovitz, Peter
  Jakob the Liar 323
Kasztner, Rudolf 322
Keane, John B.
  Many Young Men of Twenty 501
Keefe, Barry
  Gotcha 386
Kennedy, Bobby 521
Kennedy, Jimmy 290
Kennedy, John F. 470
Kent, Jonathan 521
Kenyon, Mel 374
Kerouac, Jack
  On the Road 543
Kidderminster Playhouse 342
Kidman, Nicole 431

Kilroy, Thomas
  Double Cross 337
  Madame MacAdam Travelling Theatre, The 337
King, Dr Martin Luther 521
King's Head 292, 322
Kingston, Gertrude 103
Kingsway Theatre 79, 106
Kinnock, Neil 436
Kinsella, Thomas
  Tain 120
Kipling, Rudyard 345, 347
Kop, Bernard
  Dreams of Anne Frank 323
Korean War 311
Kramer, Larry
  Normal Heart, The 405
Kushner, Tony
  Angels in America 405, 558
Kwei-Armah, Kwame 395

Lally, Mick 114, 118–19
Lampell, Millard
  Wall, The 318–19
Lan, David 392, 482
Land League 24
Lanzmann, Claude 316
Lavery, Bryony 388, 403–4, 406
  Her Aching Heart 403–4, 406
Lawrence, D. H. 28
Lawrence, Gertrude 227, 232
Lawrence, Robert 354–5
Lawrence, Stephen 198, 539
Lawrence, T. E. 232
Lea, Marion 42
Leavis, F. R. 143
Lecompte, Elizabeth 392
Lecoq, Jacques 392
Leger, Fernand 306
Leicester Haymarket 201
Leighton, Dorothy 53, 56–7, 599
  Thyrza Fleming 56–7
Leivick, Harold
  Sage of Rottenberg, The 319
Lemass, Sean 500
Lenin (Vladimir Illych Ulyanov) 282
Lennon, John 350
Lester, Richard 350
Levi, Primo 324–5
  If This is a Man 324
  Truce, The 324

Liberty Hall 158
Liebeskind, Daniel 316
Lind, Jakov
  Ergo 319
Lipstadt, Deborah 323
Little, A. L.
  Shadow of the Sofa, The 102, 104
Littlewood, Joan 164, 177, 252, 302, 319, 343, 347, 385, 420–1, 423
  Oh What a Lovely War 302, 312, 319, 347, 422–3
Liverpool Everyman 394, 421–2
Lochhead, Liz 394, 425, 454–65
  Bagpipe Muzak 456, 461
  Blood and Ice 458–64
  Dracula 458–60, 462–3
  Mary Queen of Scots Got her Head Chopped Off (*MQS*) 454–5, 461–4
  Perfect Days 456, 461–2, 464
  Quelques Fleurs 456, 461, 464
  True Confessions and New Clichés 456
Lockwood, Margaret 214
Łodz 318
lord chamberlain 53, 59, 183, 233, 262–3, 341, 348, 398
Lord, Henrietta Frances 37–40, 42
  Nora 38
Low, David 305
Loyalist Military Command 338
Lucie, Doug
  Doing the Business 390
  Fashion 390
Luckham, Clare 388
Luckhurst, Mary 486
Lunt, Alfred 230
Lyceum Theatre 552
Lynch, Alfred 344
Lynch, Martin 331–2, 335, 339
  Interrogation of Ambrose Fogarty, The 331–2
  Wedding Community Play, The 339
Lynch, Richard 543, 545
Lyric Hammersmith 301
Lyric Theatre (Belfast) 292, 294, 331
Lyric Theatre Studio (London) 359

MacDonagh, Thomas 113–14
MacDonald, James 371–2, 379
MacDonald, Stephen
  Not About Heroes 312
MacIntyre, Clare

Low Level Panic 381
Mackinnon, Gillies 312
MacLennan, Elizabeth 424
Macon Little Theatre 484
Madonna 226
Mahon, Derek 337
Major, John 27
Mamet, David 377–8
Manchester Library 452
Mandela, Nelson 325
Mangan, H. C. 248
Marber, Patrick 377, 393
Marker, Frederick 42
Marker, Lise-Lone 42
Marre, Albert 179
Martyn, Edward 90–2
  Heather Field, The 91
Marx, Eleanor 37–8, 40–2
Marx, Karl 24, 37, 481
Masefield, John 80–1
  Campden Wonder, The 81
  Tragedy of Nan, The 81
Masteroff, Joe 317, 319
Matura, Mustapha 188–97
  As Time Goes By 188–90
  Black Pieces 188
  Coup, The 195–6
  Independence 192–4
  Meetings 194–5
  Party 188
  Play Mas 188, 190–2
Maudsley Hospital, London 379
Maugham, Somerset 229, 232, 234, 310–11
  For Services Rendered 310
McBride, Ray 114
McBurney, Simon 556
McCafferty, Owen 339, 395
McCann, Eamonn 505
McCarthy, Lillah 103
McCartney, Nicola 339
McCracken, Henry Joy 294–5
McDonagh, Martin 114, 119, 378, 394
McDonald, Nicola 394
McDyer, Fr. James 501–3
McEnery, Peter 444
McGahern, John 331
McGinley, Seán 114
McGrath, John 333, 387–8, 391, 419–28
  Albannach, The 423
  Billion Dollar Brain 421

McGrath, John (*cont'd*)
  Blood Red Roses 423
  Bofors Gun, The 421
  Bone Won't Break, The 424–5
  Boom 423
  Border Warfare 423, 426
  Catch, The 423
  Cheviot, the Stag and the Black, Black Oil,
    The 423–4
  Clydebuilt series *see* Clydebuilt season
  Fish in the Sea 421
  Game's a Bogey, The 423
  Good Night Out, A 420, 424–5
  Joe's Drum 423
  Little Red Hen 423
  Mairi Mhor, the Woman of Skye 423
  Out of Our Heads 423
  Reckoning, The 421
  Soft or a Girl? 421
  There is a Happy Land 423
  Unruly Elements 421
  Z-Cars 421
McGuinness, Frank 33, 312, 331, 333, 338–9,
    387, 509, 521
  Carthaginians 338
  Mutabilitie 33
  Observe the Sons of Ulster Marching Towards the
    Somme 312, 338–9
McKellen, Ian 320, 405
McKenzie, Julia 270
McNeil, Ian 437
McPherson, Conor 374, 394
  Weir, The 374
Medley, Robert 140
Melia, Joe 322
Mendes, Sam 312
Mendl, Gladys
  Su'L'Pavé 102
Meredith, George 79
Meyerhold, Vsevolod 42
Mickery Theatre 442
Middleton, Thomas
  Changeling, The 412
  Women Beware Women 496
Mihaileanu, Radu
  Train of Life 323
Mill, John Stuart 99
Miller, Arthur
  After the Fall 319
  Incident at Vichy 319

Milligan, Alice
  Last Feast of the Fianna, The 92
Mills, Hayley 184
Mills, John 184, 353
Mills, Juliet 184
Milton, John *Paradise Lost* 242
Minerva Theatre 323
Minto, Dorothy 103
Mitchell, Gary 339, 395
  In a Little World of Our Own 339
Moffat, Graham
  Maid and the Magistrate, The 101
Molière (Jean Baptiste Poquelin) 117, 119, 134
Monstrous Regiment 338, 444
Monty Python 293
Moonstone 424
Moore, George 90, 92
  Diarmuid and Grania 92
Morris, May 41
Morris, William 24, 69, 73
Morrisey, Eamon 117
Morrison, Danny 333
Morrison, G. E. 303
Moscow Art Theatre 78
Mosley, Oswald 169
Motton, Gregory 376
Mount, Ferdinand 26–7
Moving Being 391
Mrs Worthington's Daughters 310
Mullen, Marie 114, 116–17
Muller, Robert 233
Murphy, Tom 387, 466–75
  Bailegangaire 466, 472–3
  Blue Macushla, The 469–70
  Conversations on a Homecoming 466, 470
  Crucial Week, A 467–9
  Famine 15–18, 468
  Gigli Concert, The 466, 469–72
  House, The 474
  On the Inside 466–7
  On the Outside 466–7
  Sanctuary Lamp, The 471
  Too Late for Logic 473
  Wake, The 473–4
  Whistle in the Dark, A 467–8, 470–1, 473–4
Murray, Gilbert 79

Nagy, Phyllis 393
Nairn, Tom 22–3
Nancy Festival 320

National Front 443
National Institute of Arts and Letters 179
National Service 171, 342–3, 347
National Theatre (concept) 78
National Theatre (NT) 1–2, 30, 170–1, 195,
    226, 280, 318–19, 321–3, 325, 341, 347,
    350–4, 364, 399, 421, 429–32, 447, 451,
    489, 520, 522–4, 526–7, 530, 556
National Union of Women's Suffrage Societies
    (NUWSS) 100
Neeson, Liam 431
Neilson, Anthony 378, 393
   Normal 393
   Penetrator 393
Nevinson, Margaret Wynne
   In the Workhouse 106
New British Artists *see* Brit-Art
'New Drama' 35, 40, 43, 79, 81
New End Theatre 324
'New Wave' 169–70
'New Woman' 2, 38, 41, 46–60, 82
Newman, Valerie 343
Nightingale, Benedict 381
Nightingale, Florence 350, 398, 493
Nixon, Richard M. 442
Nobel Prize 358
Noh theatre 95–6
Nordau, Max 65
Northern Broadsides 528
Northern Irish Arts Council 333
Norton, Fred 303
Norton-Taylor, Richard 318, 395
   Colour of Justice, The 452
   Nuremburg 318
Nottinghill Carnival (including 1976 riots) 206
Novello, Ivor 133, 227
Novelty Theatre 41, 48
Ntshona, Winston
   Island, The 320
Nunn, Trevor 324, 354
Nuremburg Trials 317, 324
Nussbaum, Martha 249

Oakes, Meredith 376
Obermaier, Klaus
   Vivisector 556–8
O'Casey, Sean 96, 125–37, 250, 295, 308–9, 334,
   339
   Autobiographies 126
   Bishop's Bonfire, The 126, 135

Cock-A-Doodle Dandy 135
Drums of Father Ned, The 126, 135
Juno and the Paycock 125–9, 131–3, 339
Plough and the Stars, The 96, 125–9, 133, 135,
   295
Red Roses for Me 132, 135
Shadow of a Gunman, The 125–9, 231–3,
   334
Silver Tassie, The 125–6, 128, 130–1, 133–5,
   308–9
Star Turns Red, The 135
Within the Gates 135
O'Connor, Francis 115
O'Donnell, Paeder
   There Will Be Another Day 501–2
Old Comedy 525
Olivier, Laurence 307
Olivier Theatre 450
O'Malley, Mary 388
O'Neil, Eugene 134, 230
   Strange Interlude 230
O'Neill, Hugh 336
Orange Tree Theatre 171
Orangemen 295
Oregon Shakespeare Festival 451
Organization of African States 22
Ormonde Dramatic Society 93
Orton, Joe 258–68, 349, 385
   Entertaining Mr Sloane 258–61
   Erpingham Camp, The 259, 265–6
   Funeral Games 259–66
   Good and Faithful Servant, The 265
   Loot 258–61, 263–6
   Ruffian on the Stair, The (The Boy
     Hairdresser) 258–60
   What the Butler Saw 258–61, 264, 266, 349
Orwell, George 24, 27
Osborne, John 2, 27–30, 164–74, 175–6,
   178, 184, 226, 341, 385, 411, 430,
   436, 491, 501
   Better Class of Person, A 29
   Entertainer, The 165–8
   Look Back in Anger 27–8, 30, 164–8, 175–8,
     184–5, 430, 501
Oscar (awards and nominations) 311
Oslo Accords 373
Osterneier, Thomas 372–3
Other Place 449
O'Toole, Fintan 121, 510–11
Out of Joint 394

Oval House, London 406
Owen, Wilfred 312

Page, Anthony 171
Page, Louise 388
Paines Plough 394
Parker, Lynne 295–6
Parker, Stuart 7–8, 289–98, 337–9, 387
    Catchpenny Twist 291–2, 337
    Heavenly Bodies 289, 295–6, 337
    Kingdom Come 292
    Nightshade 289, 292–3
    Northern Star 289, 294–5, 327
    Pentecost 290, 296–8, 337, 391–2, 449–50
    Pratt's Fall 293–4
    Shaughraun, The 296
    Spokesong 290–1, 297, 337
Pascal, Julia 323
    Dead Woman on Holiday, A 323
    Dybbuk, The 324
    Holocaust Trilogy 323
    J'accuse 323
    Theresa 323–4
Passchendaele 306
Paulin, Tom 335
Peacock Theatre 121, 291–2, 295
Pearse, Patrick (Padraic) 113, 127
Pearson, Mike 547–8
PEN 364
Penhall, Joe 377–8, 393–4
    Blue/Orange 393
    Some Voices 393
Petit Theatre du Vieux Carre, Le 184
Piaf, Edith 388
Pike Theatre 249–50
Pinero, Arthur Wing 49, 52–4, 233, 235
    Second Mrs Tanqueray, The 52, 54, 57, 233, 235
Pinnock, Winsome 1, 198–209
    Hero's Welcome, A 200, 202
    Leave Taking 202–3, 207
    Mules 200, 205, 207
    One Under 200, 207
    Rock in Water, A 200, 206
    Talking in Tongues 203–5, 207
    Water 200, 206–7
Pinter, Harold 259, 267, 280, 358–70, 377, 385,
        387, 390, 395, 410
    Betrayal 387
    Birthday Party, The 280, 358–63
    Caretaker, The 359, 362–3

Dumb Waiter, The 359, 362
Hothouse, The 359, 363, 365
Mountain Language 364, 366
New World Order, The 364, 366
No Man's Land 387
Old Times 387
One for the Road 359, 364–7, 390
Party Time 366–8
political theatre 369
Press Conference 364, 368
Room, The 358
Various Voices 358, 368
War 358
Pioneer Players 106
Pip Simmons Group
    An Die Musik 319, 324
Pirate Jenny Theatre Company 443
Piscator, Erwin 318
Pit 77
Plato 64
Playfair, Nigel 103
Playgoers' Club 57
Poel, William 78
Poliakoff, Stephen
    City Sugar 386
    Hitting Town 386
    Shout across the River 386
Polka Theatre 323
Pollock, Eileen 297
Pool Theatre 441
Poppy Pierrots 229
Portable Theatre 429
Posener, Jill 338, 402
    Any Woman Can 402
Posner, Ruth 323
potato famine *see* 1845–7 Great Hunger
Pound, Ezra 43, 95
Powell, Enoch 24
'Prague Spring' 402
Preece, Tim 344
Priestley, J. B. 234
Princes Theatre 177
Pritchard, Rebecca 394
Provincetown Players 134

Queen's Royal Theatre 88, 248, 349
Queen's University Belfast 289

Rabelais, François 510
'race riots' 168

Radio Telefis Éireann (RTE) 111, 114
RAF 306
Raffles, Stamford 354
Ramsay, Peggy 154
Randall, Paulette 201
Rattigan, Terence 175–6
Ravenhill, Mark 372, 374, 378, 393–4, 406, 430
  Shopping and Fucking 378, 394, 406
  Some Explicit Polaroids 393
Ray, Catherine 37–8, 42
Rea, Stephen 294, 296–7, 335, 337, 391
Reagan, Ronald 389
Red Hand Commandos 338
Redgrave, Vanessa 350, 520
Redmond, Siobhan 457, 462
Reid, Christina 334–5, 339, 394
  Belle of Belfast City, The 334
  Did You Hear the One About the
    Irishman . . . 334, 337
  Joyriders 334
  Tea in a China Cup 334
Reid, Graham 331, 339
  Billy 331
  Death of Humpty Dumpty, The 331
  Dorothy 331
  Hidden Curriculum 331
  Ties of Blood 331
Reinhardt, Max 42
Remarque, Erich Maria
  All Quiet on the Western Front 302
Renoir, Jean 374–5
  La Règle du Jeu 375
Repatriation Board 306
Resnais, Alain
  Nacht und Nebel 319
Reuters News Agency 185
Richardson, Tony 167–8, 350
Ridley, Philip 378
Robben Island 320
Robertson, T. W.
  Caste 80
Robins, Elizabeth 2, 42, 48–53, 58, 79, 100,
    103–4, 176
  Alan's Wife 48–51
  Votes For Women! 51, 81, 103–4, 176
Robinson, Lennox 249
Roosevelt, Theodore 96
Rossington, Norman 344
Rotten, Johnny 320
Rough Magic 290, 296

Roundabout Theatre 184
Rous, Helena 215
Rowley, George
  Changeling, The 412
Royal Court Theatre (RCT) 2, 69, 75–6, 78–9,
    81, 103, 134, 153, 157, 164–5, 169–70,
    175, 201, 260, 305, 317, 320, 322–3,
    348–9, 364, 371–2, 374, 377, 380–1,
    385, 393, 398–9, 403–5, 411, 413, 421,
    430, 432, 493, 530
Royal Exchange Theatre 44
Royal Festival Hall 557
Royal Shakespeare Company (RSC) 2, 77, 154–5,
    312, 317, 322–3, 353–4, 395, 399, 421,
    443, 445, 449–50, 519
Royal Ulster Constabulary (RUC) 333
Royalty Theatre 42
Rudkin, David
  Ashes 387
  Saxon Shore, The 336–7
Rushdie, Salman
  Satanic Verses, The 23
Russell, George
  Deirdre 93
Rutherford, John
  Forever England 22
Rutter, Barrie 528
Rwandan genocide 373, 376

Sachs, Albie 445
Samuels, Diane
  Kindertransport 323
Sands, Bobby 331
Sardou, Étienne 43
Sassoon, Siegfried 312
Savoy Theatre 79, 307
Scala Theatre 105
Scanlan, Carol 332–3
Scargill, Arthur 519
Schaubühne 373
Schiller-Theater 239
Schneider, Alan 260
Schnitzler, Artur
  Ronde, La 431
Schreider, Olive 100
Scott, Allan 312
Scott, Clement 58
Scott, Paul
  Jewel in the Crown, The 352
  Raj Quartet 312

Scottish Arts Council 45
Scribe, Eugène 43
Selznick, Irene Mayer 178
September 11th *see* 9/11
Sereny, Gitta 316
Sex Pistols 320
Shadwell, Thomas
   Stockjobbers, The 478
Shaffer, Anthony
   This Savage Parade 322–3
Shakespeare, William 1, 22, 24–5, 84, 129, 131,
   134, 239, 269, 303, 342, 351, 411–15, 417,
   442, 449, 510, 515, 528, 556
   Hamlet 283, 496, 512
   Henry IV 448
   Henry V 351
   King Lear 413–15, 448
   Macbeth 411
   Measure for Measure 556
   Richard II 448
   Richard III 442
   Tempest, The 239, 515
   Titus Andronicus 412
   Winter's Tale, The 449–50
Shakespearean Company 92
Shan Van Vocht 92
Shaw, George Bernard 7, 9–11, 24–5, 27, 33, 37–8,
   40–2, 44, 49, 51–3, 59, 63–74, 77–8, 80–1,
   96–7, 100, 103, 118, 129, 131, 133–4, 136,
   138, 217, 219, 229, 302, 304–6, 410, 445, 552
   Androcles and the Lion 305
   Annajanska 305
   Augustus Does His Bit 305
   Back to Methuselah 63–5, 67, 69
   Bolshevik Express, The 305
   Caesar and Cleopatra 63, 69, 71
   Candida 63, 66, 69–70, 72
   Doctor's Dilemma, The 63, 66–70
   Heartbreak House 304–6
   Inca of Perusalem, The 305
   John Bull's Other Island 10–13, 15–18
   Man and Superman 63–4, 66–70, 72
   Mrs Warren's Profession 52, 63–4, 66, 71, 78
   O'Flaherty V.C. 304–5
   Press Cuttings 103
   Pygmalion 63, 67, 69, 72–3, 305
   Saint Joan 126
   Sanity of Art, The 68
   Shewing-Up of Blanco Posnet, The 96
   Widowers' Houses 64

Shaw, Robert 318–19
   Man in the Glass Booth, The 318
Shelley, Mary 458–9
   Frankenstein 458, 463
Shepherd, Jack 524
Sher, Anthony 318, 324–5
   Primo 318, 324
   Primo Time 324
Sheridan, Richard 217, 296
Sherman, Martin 320–1, 323, 403–4
   Bent 320–1, 404–5
   Rose 323
Sherriff, R. C.
   Journey's End 134, 302, 307–8
Shiubhliagh, Maire Nic 92
Sho'ah *see* Holocaust
Shulman, Milton 253
Sibleyras, Gérald
   Heroes 313
Sierz, Aleks 377, 393
   In-Yer-Face Theatre 377
Simmons, James 525
Sinfield, Alan 213
Sinn Féin 25, 27, 32, 118, 334, 506
Situationists 373
Sobol, Joshua
   Ghetto 321, 323
Soho Theatre 324
Solzhenitsyn, Alexander 364
Somme, battle of the 306, 312, 338
Sophocles 519
   Ichneutae 526
   Trachiniae 519
Spa Summer Theatre 184
Spanish Civil War 169–70
Speer, Albert 321, 324, 450–1
Spender, Stephen 311
Spiegelman, Art 316, 323
   Maus 323
Split Britches 406
Springhill massacre 333
Square Chapel 201
St Clair, Winifred
   Science of Forgiveness, The 102, 107
St James's Theatre 57–8, 79, 214
St John, Christopher
   First Actress, The 105–6
   Her Will 106
   How the Vote was Won 101, 104
   Pot and the Kettle, The 101

St Martin's Theatre 177
Stafford, Maeliosa 114
Stafford-Clark, Max 374, 380–1, 430, 432
Stage Society 78
Stalin, Josef 414
Stanislavsky, Constantin 77
Station House Opera
    Live From Paradise 559–60
Steiner, George 322–3, 411
    Death of Tragedy 411
Steiner, Theresa 323
Stephen Joseph Theatre 269
    see also Joseph, Stephen
Stewart, Ena Lamont
    Men Should Weep 424
Stewart, Patrick 354
Stockhausen, Karl Heinz 373
Stoker, Bram
    Dracula 458–9
Stonewall riots 403
Stopes, Marie 229
Stoppard, Tom 280–8, 313, 342, 386, 390, 393
    After Magritte 283
    Arcadia 285–6, 393
    Coast of Utopia, The 284, 286
    Every Good Boy Deserves Favour 283–4
    Hapgood 285
    In the Native State 285
    Indian Ink 285
    Invention of Love, The 286
    Jumpers 281–3, 386
    Night and Day 284
    Professional Foul 284–5
    Real Inspector Hound, The 283, 294
    Real Thing, The 284–5
    Rosencrantz and Guildenstern Are Dead 280–1,
        286, 290, 294
    Travesties 282–3
Stott, Ken 313
Strindberg, August 37, 371
Süddeutscher Rundfunk 243
Suez crisis 160, 165, 168, 175
suffrage theatre 2, 99–109
Surrealist movement 373
Suspect Culture 395
Svich, Caridad
    *Iphigenia Crash Land Falls on the Neon Shell That
        Was Once Her Heart* 519
'Swinging London' 258
Symons, Arthur 89

Synge, John Millington 81, 95–6, 110–24, 129,
        132, 308
    Aran Islands 111, 115
    Deirdre of the Sorrows 111, 115, 119, 121
    In Wicklow and West Kerry 115
    pastoral 116–120
    Playboy of the Western World, The 96, 110–11,
        113–16, 118–21, 129, 132, 295
    Riders to the Sea 111, 115–16
    Shadow of the Glen, The 110–11, 115, 118–19
    Tinker's Wedding, The 111, 115–17
    Well of Saints, The 111–15, 117–18
    When the Moon Has Set 114
Synge Summer School 112
Syrett, Netta 51, 57–9
    Finding of Nancy, The 57–8
    Nobody's Fault 57
Szábo, István
    Mephisto 318, 321

Tabori, George
    Cannibals, The 319–20
    *I Would my Daughter were Dead at my Feet and the
        Jewels in her Ear* 319
    Shylock Variation 319
Taibhdhearc 114
Taplin, Oliver
    Stagecraft of Aeschylus, The 527
Tara Arts 338
Tarantino, Quentin 378, 394
    Kill Bill 394
    Reservoir Dogs 394
Taylor, C. P. 318, 320–3
    Good 318, 320–1, 324
Taylor, Charles 436
Taylor, Elizabeth 177
Temba 388
Tennent, H. M. 178, 180
Tennyson, Alfred, Lord 89
Terry, Ellen 72, 103
Terry, J. E. Harold
    General Post 302
    Man Who Stayed at Home, The 302–3
Terry, Marion 221
Terry's Theatre, London 42, 49
Thatcher, Margaret 30, 354, 364, 381, 389–93,
        404, 445, 478–9, 526
Theatre de Complicite 392, 556, 557
Théâtre Libre 90, 110
Theatre of Catastrophe 488–98

Theatre of Ireland (*Cluithcheoiri na hEireann*) 95
'Theatre of the Absurd' 261
Theatre Royal (Stratford East) 201, 312, 319
Theatre Royal Haymarket 184
Theatre Royal, Newcastle 312
Theatre Upstairs 371–2, 442
Theatre Workshop 164, 177, 252, 343, 347–8,
    421
Thomas, Berte 78
Thomas, Ed 541–50
    Adar heb Adenydd (*Birds Without Wings*) 544–5
    East from the Gantry 544–5
    Fallen Sons 544
    Flowers of the Dead Red Sea 544–5
    Gas Station Angel 542, 544, 546–7
    Hiraeth 544
    House of America 543–4, 547
    Myth of Michael Roderick, The 544–5
    Rain Dogs 548
    Song from a Forgotten City 543, 545–6
    Stone City Blue 544–5, 548–61
    Who Are You Looking At? 548
Thompson, E. P. 33
Thompson, Linda 524
Thompson, Richard 524
Thorndike, Sybil 184
Tinderbox 290
Todd, Susan
    Teendreams 444
Tolstoy, Leo 78
Tomer, Ben-Zion
    Children of the Shadows 319
TONY (awards and nominations) 179, 183
torture 358–70
Towneley Mystery Plays 522–3
Tramway Theatre 423–4, 547
Travers, Ben 259
Traverse Theatre 391, 403
Trewin, J. C. 92
Tricycle Theatre 200–1, 206, 395, 452
Trinidadian Creole 188
Trinity College Dublin 111, 126
Trojan War 304
'Troubles' 329–40, 387
Tynan, Kenneth 168, 176, 180, 229, 280–1, 348–9
Tzara, Tristan 282–3

Ulster Defence Association 338
Ulster Volunteer Force 338
United Irishmen 294

United Nations 22, 358
University College Dublin 126
Upton, Judy 394

Van Druten, John 397
Vaudeville Theatre 42
Vedrenne, J. E. 81
Verdi, Guiseppe 269, 528
Verdun, battle of 306
Vicious, Sid 320
Victoria, Queen 42, 89, 219, 398, 413
Vietnam war 311, 319, 350, 373, 385,
    402, 446
Vilna ghetto theatre 321
Viscount Montgomery 348

Wagner, Richard 555
Waits, Tom 545
Wakefield Mystery Plays *see* Towneley
    Mystery Plays
Wałęsa, Lech 447
Wallace, Neil 547
Waller, Lewis 53
Walsh, Catherine 118
Wandor, Michelene 388, 402
Warsaw ghetto 318
Watergate 442
Waters, Steve 447
Waugh, Evelyn
    Sword of Honour 312
Webb, Beatrice 79
Webb, Sidney 79
Webster, Ben 103
Webster, John
    Duchess of Malfi, The 376
Wedekind, Frank 37
Weiss, Peter
    Investigation, The 318–19
Welch, Robert W. 64
'well-made play' 36, 40, 42
Wells, H. G. 24
Welsh Arts Council 545
Welsh Assembly 541
'Welthorpe, Edna' 265
Wertenbaker, Timberlake 380
Wesker, Arnold 164–74, 267, 385, 411, 442
    Chicken Soup with Barley 169–70
    I'm Talking About Jerusalem 169
    Merchant, The 319
    Roots 169–70

West End 99–100, 175–7, 180, 183, 185, 226, 232, 302–3, 307, 312, 320, 374, 389, 395, 405–7, 429, 431–2, 437, 493
West Yorkshire Playhouse 44, 201, 394
Whelan, Peter
  Accrington Pals 312
Whitaker, T. K. 466, 500, 502
  Report on Economic Development 466, 500
Whitbread, J. W. 248
Whitby, Nick
  To the Green Fields Beyond 312
Whitehouse, Mary 31
Whitelaw, Billie 245
Whitty, May 103
Widgery Inquiry 503–4
Wilcox, Michael 403
Wildcat Stage Productions 391, 423
Wilde, Oscar 24–5, 27, 33, 67, 97, 213–24, 229, 232, 237, 259, 290, 295, 431
  De Profundis 213
  Ideal Husband, An 213, 220, 222–3
  Importance of Being Earnest, The 214–15, 218–19, 282–3
  Lady Windermere's Fan 219–22
  Woman of No Importance, A 215–18
Williams, Harcourt 103
Williams, Heathcote
  AC/DC 387
Williams, Raymond 424
Williams, Roy 395, 530–40
  Clubland 533–7
  Fallout 531
  Gift, The 532
  Lift Off 532–6
  No Boys Cricket Club, The 532
  Sing Yer Heart Out for the Lads 530–1, 534, 536–8
  Starstruck 532
Williams, Tennessee
  Cat on a Hot Tin Roof 179
Wilson & Wilson
  Mapping the Edge 519
Wilson, John
  Hamp 312
Wilson, Richard 324
Wilton, Helen 106
Wincelberg, Shimon
  Windows of Heaven, The 318
Winterland Ballroom 320
Wolfe Tone Memorial Committee 89
Wolfit, Donald 411

Wollstonecroft, Mary 99, 360
Women Writers' Suffrage League 100
Women's Freedom League (WFL) 100–2
Women's Social and Political Union (WSPU) 99–100
Women's Theatre Group 402, 404
  Double Vision 402
Wood, Charles 3, 317, 341–57
  Charge of the Light Brigade, The 350, 353–4
  Cockade Trilogy 344–7
  Dingo 317, 341, 344–52, 354
  Don't Make Me Laugh 347
  H: or Monologues at Front of Burning Cities 345–6, 350–2, 354–5
  Has Washington Legs? 353
  Help! 350
  How I Won the War 350
  Jingo 317, 345, 353–4
  John Thomas 344, 346
  Knack, The 350
  Prisoner and Escort 344, 346–7
  Spare 344, 346–7
  Tumbledown 354–5
  Veterans 345, 352–3
Wood, Mrs Henry 43
Wood, Peter 260, 359
Woods, Vincent
  At the Black Pig's Dyke 338
  Cry From Heaven, A 120
Woolf, Stuart 324
Woolf, Virginia 227–8
Wooster Group 392
Wordsworth, William 116
World War I 28, 64, 78–9, 107, 127, 133, 167, 232, 301–15, 338, 341, 347
World War II 22, 29, 126, 134–5, 144, 170–1, 173, 200, 202, 225, 290, 301, 311–13, 337, 347, 349–50, 358, 361, 395, 435, 446, 495, 531
Worrall, Lechmere
  General Post 302
  Man Who Stayed at Home, The 302–3
Wrestling School 488–9, 496, 543
Writers' Group 411
Wyndham's Theatre 312

X, Malcolm 190

Y Cwmni 543, 547
  see also Fiction Factory

Yalta Conference 447
Yeats, William Butler 7–10, 25–7, 81,
        87–98, 110–13, 118–19, 125, 129,
        133, 307
    At the Hawk's Well 95
    Baile's Strand 93, 95
    Cathleen ni Houlihan 9–10, 93–4, 472–3
    Countess Cathleen, The 91
    Diarmuid and Grania 92
    Four Plays for Dancers 95

Green Helmet, The 95
Herne's Egg, The 96
Land of Heart's Desire, The 90
Only Jealousy of Emer, The 90
Purgatory 96
Words Upon the Window Pane, The 96
York Mystery Plays 522–3
York Theatre Royal 486

Zola, Émile 50